CITIZENS OF LONDON

"Ingenious . . . Olson, an insightful historian, contrasts the idealism of Winant and Murrow with the pragmatism of Harriman. But all three men were colorful, larger-than-life figures, and Olson's absorbing narrative does them justice."

—*Publishers Weekly* (starred review)

"An excellent and revealing chronicle." —*Booklist*

"A nuanced history that captures the intensity of life in a period when victory was not a foregone conclusion."

—*Kirkus Reviews*

"Olson sifts through the immense amount of material on the period and crafts a cracking good read."

—*New York Post*

"Three fascinating Americans living in London helped cement the World War II alliance between Roosevelt and Churchill. Lynne Olson brings us the wonderful saga of Harriman, Murrow, and Winant. Her book is a triumph of research and storytelling. It's history on an intimate level."

—WALTER ISAACSON, author of *Einstein*

England in its finest
inspiring chronicle of the
most. She's turned out a truly
Meacham's majestic *Franklin and Winston*."
—CHRIS MATTHEWS, anchor, MSNBC's *Hardball*

"It doesn't seem possible that support for Britain against the Nazis
was so unpopular in America before December of 1941. In *Citizens
of London*, Lynne Olson tells the stories of Britain's few American
champions—men who ended up on the right side of history. Her book
brings alive this crucial time of our country's recent past, and shows
us how a few leaders can make such a big difference."
—BOB EDWARDS, radio commentator and author of
Edward R. Murrow and the Birth of Broadcast Journalism

"If you don't think there's any more to learn about the power struggles,
rivalries and dramas—both personal and political—about the U.S.–
British alliance in the World War II years, this book will change your
mind, and keep you turning the pages as well."
—JEFF GREENFIELD, senior political correspondent, CBS News

"This is history at its most personal and compelling, a group portrait
of three fascinating individuals—Winant, Harriman, and Murrow—
whose lives intersected at a pivotal moment in the twentieth century.
The result is what the English call 'a rollicking read.'"
—STROBE TALBOTT, author of *The Great Experiment:
Ancient Empires, Modern States, and the Search for a Global Nation*

"Brilliantly bursting with beautiful prose, *Citizens of London* flutters our hearts by capturing the essence of the public and private lives of those who faced death, touched the precipice, hung on by their eyelids, and saved the free world from destruction by the forces of evil."

—BILL GARDNER, secretary of state, New Hampshire

"*Citizens of London* is a great read about a small band of Americans and their courageous role in helping Britain through the darkest days of early World War II. I thought I knew a lot about that dangerous period, but Lynne Olson has taught me so much more."

—TOM BROKAW, author of *The Greatest Generation*

CITIZENS OF
LONDON

RANDOM HOUSE
TRADE PAPERBACKS
NEW YORK

CITIZENS

OF

LONDON

THE AMERICANS WHO STOOD WITH BRITAIN IN ITS DARKEST, FINEST HOUR

LYNNE OLSON

2011 Random House Trade Paperback Edition

Copyright © 2010 by Lynne Olson

Published in the United States by
Random House Trade Paperbacks,
an imprint of The Random House Publishing Group,
a division of Random House, Inc., New York.

RANDOM HOUSE TRADE PAPERBACKS and colophon
are trademarks of Random House, Inc.

This work was originally published in
the United States by Random House,
an imprint of The Random House Publishing Group,
a division of Random House, Inc., in 2010.

ISBN 978-0-8129-7935-0

Printed in the United States of America

www.atrandom.com

12 14 16 18 20 19 17 15 13 11

Book design by Barbara M. Bachman

TO STAN AND CARLY

WITH LOVE

In years to come, men will speak of this war and say,
"I was a soldier," "I was a sailor," or "I was a pilot."
Others will say with equal pride, "I was a citizen of London."
—ERIC SEVAREID, OCTOBER 1940

There's no place I'd rather be than in England.
—JOHN GILBERT WINANT, MARCH 1941

If we are together, nothing is impossible.
If we are divided, all will fail.
—WINSTON CHURCHILL, SEPTEMBER 1943

It was a terrible war, but if you were the right age . . .
and in the right place, it was spectacular.
—PAMELA CHURCHILL HARRIMAN

CONTENTS

INTRODUCTION

On a chilly night in early 1947, a tall, lanky American with tousled dark hair emerged from a theater in London's West End. Other playgoers, pouring into the street from nearby theaters, stopped and stared. They had seen the man's angular face and slightly stooped frame in wartime newsreels and newspaper photographs, and most knew immediately who he was. As he and two companions headed down Shaftesbury Avenue, they were surrounded by a throng of people. "Good evening, Mr. Winant," several in the crowd said. A couple of men doffed their hats. One woman reached out and shyly touched his coat.

For those gathered around him, the sight of John Gilbert Winant conjured up memories of smoke-filled nights in early 1941 when Winant, the American ambassador to Britain, walked the streets of London during the heaviest raids of the Blitz, Germany's nine-month terror bombing of British cities. He asked everyone he met—firemen, dazed victims, air wardens pulling bodies out of the rubble—what he could do to help. In those perilous times, one Londoner remembered, Winant "convinced us that he was a link between ourselves and millions of his countrymen, who, by reason of his inspiration, spoke to our very hearts."

Yet, while he was instantly recognizable in Britain, few Americans had ever heard of Winant. Even fewer were aware of the key role he had played in shaping and maintaining the alliance between the United States and Britain in World War II. In future decades, that extraordinary partnership—the closest and most successful wartime alliance in history—would come to be known as the "special relationship" that helped win the conflict, preserve democracy, and save the world. As the years passed and the legend surrounding the alliance took shape, the manner of its creation seemed almost preordained: first, Winston Churchill rousing his nation to stand alone against

Hitler; then Franklin D. Roosevelt and America coming to the rescue of Churchill and the British.

But in March 1941, when Winant arrived in London to take up his post, such a happy ending was far from certain. In the previous six months, the Luftwaffe had killed tens of thousands of Britons in its attacks on London and other British cities. British armed forces, which lacked adequate arms and ammunition, were on the defensive everywhere. German submarines were operating at will in the Atlantic, sinking vast amounts of merchant shipping and slowly strangling British supply lines. Starvation for the civilian population loomed as a distinct possibility, as did a cross-Channel invasion by Germany. "We were hanging on by our eyelids," recalled Field Marshal Lord Alanbrooke, Britain's top military leader during the war. Winant himself would later write: "There were many times when one felt the sands would run out and it all would be over."

As the British well knew, their only hope for salvation lay in American help. Yet that aid had been miserly thus far, even as Britain's future grew increasingly bleak. Many in Washington had already written the country off. How could this little island, no matter how glorious its military past, resist an invader that had toppled every country in its path like so many duckpins? Among those who believed in Britain's inevitable defeat was Joseph P. Kennedy, Winant's predecessor as U.S. ambassador, who, along with several thousand other American residents of Britain, returned to the United States at the height of the Blitz.

Winant, by contrast, made it clear from the beginning that he was in the country to stay. "There was one man who was with us, who never believed we would surrender, and that was John Gilbert Winant," noted Ernest Bevin, a leading figure in Churchill's government. Within days of the new ambassador's arrival, an embassy subordinate remarked, he had "conveyed to the entire British nation the sure feeling that here was a friend."

Winant, however, was not the only American in London to take a critical role in encouraging the British and pressing for an Anglo-American partnership. Two others—W. Averell Harriman and Edward R. Murrow—were prominent actors in the drama as well. Harriman, the aggressive, ambitious chairman of the Union Pacific Railroad, arrived in the British capital soon after Winant to become administrator of U.S. Lend-Lease aid to Britain. Murrow, the head of

CBS News in Europe, had been stationed in the British capital since 1937.

As the most important Americans in London during the war's early years, Winant, Harriman, and Murrow were key participants in America's debate over whether Britain, the last European country holding out against Hitler, should be saved. While Murrow championed the British cause in his broadcasts to the American people, Harriman and Winant mediated between a desperate prime minister and a cautious president, who was as wary of his isolationist opponents at home as he was initially skeptical of Britain's chances. The famous friendship that developed between these dominating, egocentric leaders—"two prima donnas," Harry Hopkins, Roosevelt's chief aide, called them—was nowhere on the horizon at that point.

In the years since the war, most of the attention and much of the credit for the triumph of the Anglo-American alliance has been given to the intimate collaboration of Roosevelt and Churchill. Much less carefully examined has been the vital part played by men like Winant, Harriman, and Murrow in laying the groundwork for the two leaders' partnership, at a time when Roosevelt and Churchill not only were strangers but were suspicious and even hostile toward each other.

Sent to London as Roosevelt's eyes and ears, Winant and Harriman were to evaluate Britain's capacity for resistance and survival. Both swiftly came to the conclusion that Britain would hold out, and they made clear to Washington they stood with her. The two envoys lobbied Roosevelt and his men to provide as much aid as possible and even to go to war. In more veiled language, Murrow did the same in his broadcasts.

Knowing how important the three men were to his country's survival, Churchill courted them as relentlessly as he would later woo Roosevelt. The prime minister had an open-door policy where Murrow was concerned. Winant and Harriman became part of Churchill's inner circle, with unprecedented access to the prime minister and members of his government. Rarely—before or since—has diplomacy been so personal. That intimacy also extended to the Americans' relationship with members of the prime minister's family. Indeed, so intense were their bonds with the Churchills that Harriman, Winant, and Murrow all engaged in wartime love affairs with Churchill family members.

When the Japanese bombed Pearl Harbor and the United States finally entered the war, the three Americans' resolute support of an alliance between their homeland and Britain finally came to fruition. Their importance in the forging of that union can best be illustrated by their whereabouts on December 7, 1941. While Winant and Harriman were having dinner with Churchill at Chequers, Murrow was at the White House with Roosevelt.

BY ALL ACCOUNTS, the scene that wintry night at the prime minister's country retreat was jubilant. As soon as they heard the news about Pearl Harbor, all those present knew that their long fight was over: America was now in the war. According to one observer, Churchill and Winant did a little dance together around the room. But the complex saga of the Anglo-American alliance had only just begun.

Despite the veneer of collegiality painted by Churchill in his memoirs, the partnership was fragile and fractious from the moment of its birth. The two countries may have shared a common language and heritage, but their political and military leaders, from Churchill and Roosevelt on down, possessed remarkably little understanding and knowledge of each other. Ignorant of the other's history and culture, both allies tended to think of their cousins across the sea in stereotypes, with scant appreciation for their respective political and military difficulties.

Suspicions, strains, prejudices, and rivalries threatened to derail this new and unparalleled confederation before it took hold. Such problems were exacerbated by British condescension toward the Americans and U.S. resentment toward the British. As Sir Michael Howard, a British military historian, has noted, "The British approached the alliance from the point of view that the Americans had everything to learn and the British were there to teach them. The Americans took the approach that if anyone had anything to teach them, it was not the British who had been beaten over and over again and were not a very good army."

In this fraught environment, the role of mediator took on new importance. While Roosevelt and Churchill took justifiable pride in their close and direct communication with each other, both Winant and Harriman continued to act as interpreters and peacemakers between the leaders, explaining the thoughts and actions of one to the other. In addition, Winant worked to alleviate tensions and promote cooperation among the two countries' other top military and government figures. According to the *Times* of London, the American ambassador was the "adhesive" that helped to hold the wartime alliance together. "It was not Mr. Winant who turned the cooperation of the English-speaking peoples into the most intimate alliance recorded in history," the newspaper remarked after the war. "But it was Mr. Winant who established and sustained the mutual understanding in the present—and identity of aim for the future—which made such intimacy possible."

Joining forces with Murrow and General Dwight D. Eisenhower, the first commander of American forces in Britain, Winant also sought to educate the citizens of the two countries about each other, to smooth away the misunderstandings and stresses that increasingly cropped up as the war approached its climax. Those strains were especially felt in war-straitened Britain, as Americans began arriving in massive numbers to prepare for the invasion of Europe. By mid-1943, the American presence in London—and the rest of Britain—was overwhelming. Everywhere one looked, it seemed, a new American Air Force base or Army training camp was being built in a country the size of Georgia or Michigan. The streets and pubs of the British capital, meanwhile, were choked with thousands of brash, boisterous GIs on leave.

As the nerve center of Allied planning for the war in Europe, London was *the* place to be in the early 1940s. "Blacked out, bombed out, expensive and hard to get around in, it was still magnificent—the Paris of World War II," observed one historian. Wealthy, well-connected American civilians, from New York investment bankers to Hollywood directors, vied to be assigned there on temporary government duty, rightly considering it the most exciting, vibrant city in the world during that tumultuous time.

Whether military or civilian, the Americans in London and the rest of the country were paid far more and lived considerably better than the great majority of the British, who struggled daily with scarcity. The vast difference in living standards reflected the profoundly different way in which the two allies experienced the war: one country on the front line, suffering deprivation and hardship; the other thousands of miles away from the battle, its citizens more prosperous than ever before.

Such disparities caused mounting tension, as did America's flexing of its muscle as the larger and stronger partner of the alliance. Late in

World War II, the United States came of age as the greatest economic, military, and political power in the world—and in so doing, revealed an array of complexities and contradictions. On the one hand, Roosevelt and his administration championed freedom, justice, and equality for all nations. On the other hand, the U.S. government left no doubt in the minds of the British—and the smaller European countries in the larger Western alliance—that America was now in charge of running the war and that it would dominate in the postwar world. "This is an American-made victory," the *Chicago Tribune* editorialized in 1944, "and the peace must be an American peace."

While keenly aware that American intervention was rescuing them from Hitler, the British and other Europeans viewed their saviors as throwing their weight around without regard for the long-term international consequences of their actions. They saw an arrogance there, a misguided sense of destiny on the part of the Americans, who, having little knowledge of the globe beyond their borders and scant prior experience in dealing with it, nonetheless planned to take it over and singlehandedly set it to rights. A British woman who worked at U.S. naval headquarters in wartime London used to tell her American coworkers that "they needed to know more about the world before they could lead it."

THROUGHOUT THE WAR, Gil Winant and Ed Murrow, close friends who championed postwar economic and social reform as well as international cooperation, reflected America's idealistic side. Averell Harriman, a tough-minded pragmatist intent on broadening his own power and influence, as well as that of his country, became an exemplar of U.S. exceptionalism. In the postwar era, it was the worldview of Harriman and others like him that dominated American foreign policy. Along with such longtime friends and associates as Dean Acheson, Robert Lovett, and John McCloy (collectively known as the Wise Men), Harriman worked to create a Pax Americana throughout the globe.

In the decades that followed the war, Winant's approach to international relations—"to concentrate on the things that unite humanity rather than on the things that divide it"—was regarded as simplistic and naive. Toughness was now the mantra, as America, brandishing its military and economic might, set out to impose its own ideology and ways of doing things on the rest of the world.

It didn't take long, however, for the world to rebel. Tired of being ordered about, other countries increasingly rejected American leadership and, by the dawn of the twenty-first century, many of them insisted on playing by their own rules. Facing a rapid decline in the influence and power to which it had laid claim only sixty-odd years before, the United States, with the advent of the administration of Barack Obama, began to acknowledge the need to promote global cooperation rather than solely American interests and to build true partnerships with other nations.

As it reaches out more to the world, America might do well to look back at the success of the U.S.-British alliance in World War II—and the yeoman work of Winant, Murrow, Eisenhower, and others in holding it together when nationalism and other forces threatened to tear it apart. Shortly after the United States dropped the atomic bombs on Hiroshima and Nagasaki in 1945, Winant spoke at dedication ceremonies for a monument in southeast England to honor the American forces who landed in France on D-Day. In remarks broadcast by the BBC, the ambassador declared that if man was to survive in this perilous new period, he "must learn to live together in friendship," to act "as if the welfare of a neighboring nation was almost as important as the welfare of your own." Winant acknowledged that the accomplishment of such goals would be a supremely difficult task. "But," he added, "so was D-Day. If that could be done, anything can be done—if we really care to do it."

CITIZENS OF
LONDON

I.

"THERE'S NO PLACE
I'D RATHER BE
THAN IN ENGLAND"

A T THE RAILWAY STATION IN WINDSOR, A SLIGHT, SLENDER MAN in the khaki uniform of a British field marshal waited patiently as a train pulled in and, with a screech of its brakes, shuddered to a stop. A moment later, the lacquered door of one of the coaches swung open, and the new American ambassador to Britain stepped out. With a broad smile, George VI extended his hand to John Gilbert Winant. "I am glad to welcome you here," he said.

With that simple gesture, the forty-five-year-old king made history. Never before had a British monarch abandoned royal protocol and ventured outside his palace to greet a newly arrived foreign envoy. Until the meeting at Windsor station, a new ambassador to Britain was expected to follow a minutely detailed ritual in presenting his credentials to the Court of St. James. Attired in elaborate court dress, he was taken in an ornate carriage, complete with coachman, footmen, and outriders, to Buckingham Palace in London. There he was received by the king in a private ceremony, usually held weeks after his arrival in the country.

But, on this blustery afternoon in March 1941, there was to be no such pomp or pageantry. As a throng of British and American reporters looked on, the king engaged the bareheaded Winant, wearing a rumpled navy blue overcoat and clutching a gray felt hat, in a brief, animated conversation. Then George VI led the ambassador to a waiting car for the drive to Windsor Castle and tea with the queen, followed by a ninety-minute meeting between the two men.

With the survival of Britain dangling by a thread, the king's unprecedented gesture made clear that traditional court niceties were to be set aside, at least for the duration of the war. But more significantly, he was underscoring his country's desperate need for U.S. assistance, along with its hope that Winant, unlike his defeatist-minded predecessor, Joseph P. Kennedy, would persuade his government that such aid was vital *now*.

Kennedy, a former Wall Street speculator and ex-chairman of the Securities and Exchange Commission, had closely aligned himself with the appeasement policies of the previous prime minister, Neville Chamberlain. During his three years in London, he had made no secret of his belief that "wars were bad for business, and what was worse, for *his* business," as journalist James "Scotty" Reston put it. The U.S. ambassador believed this so firmly that he even used his official position to commandeer scarce cargo space on transatlantic ships for his own liquor export business. After Chamberlain and the French prime minister handed over much of Czechoslovakia to Adolf Hitler at Munich in September 1938, Kennedy remarked happily to Jan Masaryk, the Czechoslovak minister to Britain: "Isn't it wonderful [that the crisis is over]? Now I can get to Palm Beach after all!"

In October 1940, at the height of German bombing raids on London and other parts of Britain, he returned home for good, declaring that "England is gone" and "I'm for appeasement one thousand per cent." After meeting with President Roosevelt at the White House, he told reporters that he would "devote my efforts to what seems to me to be the greatest cause in the world today . . . to help the president keep the United States out of war."

Kennedy's outspoken desire to come to terms with Hitler had made his successor's task all the more ticklish. Winant's mission was, according to the *New York Times,* "one of the toughest and biggest jobs the President can give. He has to explain to a country that is daily being bombed why a country, safely 3,000 miles away . . . wants to help but will not fight. That is a difficult thing to tell a person whose home has just been wrecked by a bomb."

On the morning of March 1, shortly after the Senate approved his nomination, the fifty-one-year-old Winant arrived at an airfield near the southern port of Bristol, which had suffered a severe battering by the Luftwaffe just a few weeks earlier. Before being whisked off to a special royal train for his journey to Windsor, the new ambassador wasted no time in demonstrating that he was not Joe Kennedy. Asked by a BBC reporter to say a few words to the British people, he paused a moment, then said quietly into the microphone, "I'm very glad to be here. There is no place I'd rather be at this time than in England."

The following day, his remark was on the front pages of most British newspapers. The *Times* of London, evidently considering the remark a good omen, waxed uncharacteristically poetic when it reported that a "significant incident" had occurred just before the ambassador's arrival. "As his aeroplane was circling to land," the *Times* told its readers, "the sky was overcast and there came a sudden torrential downpour of rain. But as the aircraft came gently to earth, the storm ceased as suddenly as it had begun and the sun burst through the clouds, accompanied by a brilliant rainbow."

Unfortunately for Britain, there were precious few rainbows on the horizon in early 1941. After nine months of standing alone against the mightiest military power in the world, the country—financially, emotionally, and physically exhausted—faced a predicament that was "not only extreme," in the words of historian John Keegan, "but unprecedented in its extremity."

Although Germany had failed to subdue the Royal Air Force during the Battle of Britain in the summer and autumn of 1940, the Luftwaffe continued to ravage London, Bristol, and other British cities. An invasion by sea was a possibility in the near future. The greatest immediate peril, however, was the U-boat threat to British supply lines. German submarines in the Atlantic were sinking hundreds of thousands of tons of merchant shipping each month, with losses that more than doubled in less than four months.

At the end of one of the coldest winters in recorded history, the British were barely hanging on, with little food, scarce heat, and dwindling hope. Imports of food and raw materials had fallen to just over half their prewar levels, prices were skyrocketing, and there were severe shortages of everything from meat to timber.

The week before Winant's arrival in Britain, one of Winston Churchill's private secretaries passed on to the prime minister the latest in a series of reports of merchant ship sinkings. When the secretary remarked how "very distressing" the news was, Churchill glared at him. "Distressing?" he exclaimed. "It is terrifying! If it goes on, it will be the end of us." Top German officials agreed. That same month, Foreign Minister Joachim Ribbentrop told the Japanese ambassador in

Berlin that "even now England was experiencing serious trouble in keeping up her food supply. . . . The important thing now [is] to sink enough ships to reduce England's imports to below the absolute minimum necessary for existence."

SURROUNDED BY A gauntlet of enemy submarines, warships, and aircraft, Britain could survive, Churchill believed, only if a very reluctant America could somehow be persuaded to enter the war. He continued to nurture that hope, even as President Roosevelt said repeatedly that the United States was, and would remain, neutral. "The expert politician in the President is always trying to find a way of winning the war for the Allies—and, if he fails to do that, of ensuring the security of the United States—without the U.S. itself having to take the plunge into the war," the British ambassador to Washington confided to the Foreign Office, which, like the U.S. State Department, was responsible for promoting its country's interests abroad.

Yet it was hard to blame Roosevelt for his caution. After all, the British themselves had done their best to stay out of war in the 1930s, standing quietly by as Hitler rose to power and began his conquest of Europe. For the sake of peace—Britain's peace—the Chamberlain government had done little or nothing in the late 1930s to prevent country after country from being swallowed up by Germany. In the case of Czechoslovakia's Sudetenland, Britain, at the Munich conference, had been complicit in its seizure. Then, in the chaos-filled days of June 1940, the British, to their shock, found themselves facing Germany alone. With their future bordering on the calamitous, they hoped the United States would pay more attention to them than they had paid to Europe.

Churchill, the country's combative new prime minister, was relentless in wheedling, pleading, and coaxing Roosevelt for more support. In his speeches, FDR responded magnificently. He promised all aid short of war, and, after Germany conquered France and launched the Battle of Britain, he declared: "If Britain is to survive, we must act." But, as the British saw it, America's actions did not match its president's words: the help it sent was invariably too little and too late. Even more disturbing, it always came with a cat's cradle of strings attached.

In exchange for the fifty aging U.S. destroyers that Churchill sought in the summer of 1940, the Roosevelt administration demanded that it be awarded ninety-nine-year leases for the use of military bases in Newfoundland, Bermuda, and six British possessions in the Caribbean. The deal was, as everyone knew, far more advantageous for the United States than for Britain, and it was deeply resented by the British government. Nonetheless, the British had little choice but to accept what they considered grossly unfair terms. "This rather smacks of Russia's demands on Finland," John Colville, a private secretary to Churchill, wrote sourly in his diary.

The British felt even more aggrieved when the World War I–era destroyers finally arrived. Dilapidated and obsolete, they could not be used without expensive alteration. "I thought they were the worst destroyers I had ever seen," fumed one British admiral. "Poor seaboats with appalling armament and accommodation." Equally irritated, Churchill was nonetheless persuaded by his advisers to couch his concerns in more diplomatic language. In a cable sent to Roosevelt in late 1940, the prime minister said: "We have so far only been able to bring a very few of your fifty destroyers into action on account of the many defects which they naturally develop when exposed to Atlantic weather after having been laid up so long."

As Britain's situation grew ever more dire, the price of American aid grew ever more onerous. Since November 1939, when Roosevelt persuaded a reluctant Congress to amend the Neutrality Act banning U.S. arms sales to countries at war, Britain had been permitted to purchase American weapons and equipment. But, according to the amendment's terms, the matériel had to be paid for with dollars at the time of purchase, and buyers had to transport the supplies in their own ships.

In the year that followed, heavy armament purchases had drained Britain of most of its dollar and gold reserves. To continue arms shipments, the British Treasury was forced to borrow from the gold reserves of the Belgian government-in-exile in London. So serious was the gold situation that the chancellor of the exchequer advised the cabinet to consider requisitioning from the British people their wedding rings and other gold jewelry. Churchill counseled delay. Such a radical idea, he said, should be adopted only "if we wished to make some striking gesture for the purpose of shaming the Americans."

The prime minister and other British officials repeatedly warned the Roosevelt administration that they were running out of dollars, but the U.S. government refused to believe them. The president, Treasury

Secretary Henry Morgenthau, and Secretary of State Cordell Hull were convinced that the riches of the British empire were virtually limitless. If the British needed more cash, they could simply liquidate some of their investments in North and South America. Morgenthau, in particular, pressed the British to sell to American investors such blue-chip companies as Shell Oil, American Viscose, Lever Brothers, and Dunlop Tires. When the British government protested that such sales (presumably at fire-sale prices) would be a serious blow to the country's postwar economy, Morgenthau snapped that this was no time to be concerned about such matters.

Having had many allies in its long and colorful history, Britain was skilled at using them to further its own goals and interests. Now, however, this proud imperial power was forced to grovel before a former colony that had become its most formidable trade rival. The humiliation was made worse by what the British saw as America's determination to take economic advantage of their misfortune.

The U.S. government offered no apologies. For the British to receive any aid at all, Roosevelt and his men believed, the American people must be persuaded that their own country was getting the better of the deal. "We seek to avoid all risks, all danger, but we make certain to get the profit," said the isolationist senator William Borah.

The administration felt obliged to assure the American public that the scheming, tricky British would not be allowed to lure the United States into another European war. Indeed, Roosevelt shared that common view of the British, once declaring to an aide, "When you sit around a table with a Britisher, he usually gets 80 per cent out of the deal and you get what is left." The government's image of itself as a shrewd Yankee trader did succeed in striking a chord with a large segment of the population. When Herbert Agar, the Pulitzer Prize–winning editor of the *Louisville Courier-Journal* and a staunch interventionist, told fellow newspaper editors that America was getting from England "far more than we deserved," he was dismayed to find his colleagues "happy rather than thoughtful."

THUS, AS THE WORLD faced the greatest crisis in its history, its two most powerful democracies, bound by a common heritage, language, and allegiance to personal liberty, were divided by a prejudice and lack of understanding that had widened into a chasm since their World

War I quasi-alliance. Their famously egocentric leaders, meanwhile, were suspicious of each other to the point of antagonism.

Winston Churchill and Franklin Roosevelt had first met at an official dinner in London during the waning days of the Great War. Then an assistant secretary of the navy, the thirty-six-year-old Roosevelt had come to the British capital as part of a European fact-finding tour. Although charming and good-humored, he did not cut a particularly impressive figure at this early stage of his government career. To one of his colleagues in Washington, he was "likable and attractive but not a heavyweight." According to former secretary of war Henry Stimson (who more than thirty years later would be appointed to the same post in Roosevelt's cabinet), he was "an untried, rather flippant young man." Unabashed by such criticism, Roosevelt always sought to be "the life of the party" and "never happily surrendered the limelight to anyone."

But on the evening of July 29, 1918, the limelight at the dinner at Gray's Inn had been commandeered by a man who was also accustomed to being the center of attention and whose ego was, if anything, even larger than Roosevelt's. At the age of forty-three, Winston Churchill had already held five top positions in the British cabinet in the course of his tumultuous eighteen-year parliamentary career. Now minister of munitions, he was preoccupied that night by a series of arms factory strikes that threatened to disrupt Britain's war effort. He had no interest in, or time for, a cocky young American official named Franklin Roosevelt—and apparently made that fact abundantly clear.

More than twenty years after the evening, FDR still seethed over what he viewed as Churchill's discourtesy. "I have always disliked him since the time I went to England in 1918," the president told Joseph Kennedy in 1939. "He acted like a stinker at a dinner I attended, lording it over all of us." In later years, Churchill could not remember meeting Roosevelt at the dinner, which irritated Roosevelt all the more.

When Churchill tried to arrange a meeting with FDR during a trip to America in 1929, the newly elected governor of New York snubbed him. Throughout the 1930s, Roosevelt, like many in Churchill's homeland, considered him an elderly Victorian has-been. When World War II broke out and the president began a correspondence with Churchill, who had risen from the political dead as first lord of the admiralty, FDR told Kennedy he had done it only because "there is a strong possibility that he will become prime minister, and I want to get my hand in now."

Once Churchill assumed the premiership, Kennedy, who detested him, reinforced Roosevelt's already unfavorable impression with repeated assertions that Churchill was anti-American and anti-FDR. Another of Kennedy's claims—that the prime minister was trying to lure the United States into the war solely to preserve the British empire—reinforced the president's long-held suspicions of British imperialism. To Roosevelt, the ambassador characterized Churchill as a man "always sucking on a whisky bottle," a view also held by undersecretary of state Sumner Welles, who called Churchill "a drunken sot" and a "third or fourth-rate man." Roosevelt apparently accepted the view of Churchill as a serious tippler; when informed of his accession to 10 Downing Street, the president quipped that he "supposed Churchill was the best man that England had, even if he was drunk half of the time."

For his part, Churchill had run out of patience over what he viewed as repeated attempts by Roosevelt and America to take advantage of Britain's dire plight by appropriating its financial and military resources. "We have not had anything from the United States we have not paid for," he indignantly told his foreign secretary, Lord Halifax, in December 1940, "and what we have had has not played an essential part in our resistance."

He was still smarting from an earlier suggestion by FDR that Britain should agree to send its navy to Canada in the event of a German invasion of Britain. Shortly after the prime minister received this proposition, an aide found him "hunched in an attitude of tense anger, like a wild beast ready to spring." In his response to "those bloody Yankees," Churchill insisted that "we could never agree to the slightest compromising of our liberty of action nor tolerate any such defeatist announcement."

As he had done many times before and would do frequently in the future, Lord Halifax persuaded Churchill to soften the cable's language. According to Halifax and the Foreign Office, Britain had no other recourse but to be generous to America in the ongoing negotiations for aid. Churchill, who strongly disagreed, favored hard bargaining. He wanted to pare down the number of British bases exchanged for U.S. destroyers, and he opposed a proposal to share advanced military and industrial technology with America, declaring: "I am not in a hurry to give our secrets until the U.S. is much nearer to the war than she is now." In both cases, however, he capitulated. In addition to the bases, Britain handed over to the U.S. military its blueprints for rockets, gun sights, and new Merlin engines; early-stage plans for the jet engine and atomic bomb; and prototypes for a radar system small enough to use in aircraft. Several of these advances would play a key role in the Allied effort to come.

In late December 1940, Roosevelt, with considerable fanfare, announced a new plan to aid Britain. Caught up in fears for his country's survival, Churchill had no way of knowing the enormous impact that the proposal would ultimately have on Britain and the war. All he knew was that the president had made vast, vague promises before and that nothing much had resulted from them.

He was correct in thinking that, until then, FDR's approach to Britain's plight had been cautious and vacillating. But by the end of December, the president had come to realize that Britain was indeed running out of money and that America must do considerably more to prevent the defeat of the last country still holding out against Hitler. In response to a long, eloquent, and desperate letter from Churchill, he unveiled a groundbreaking new plan that would allow the government to lend or lease war matériel to any nation the president considered vital to the defense of the United States. The Lend-Lease program, he declared, would transform America into the "arsenal of democracy."

In the House of Commons, Churchill called Lend-Lease "the most unsordid action in the history of any nation," but, privately, he was not that impressed. Instead of expressing his appreciation to Roosevelt, he wrote a sharp note, questioning details of the plan and noting that it would not go into effect for several months, even if passed by Congress. In the meantime, how could his financially pressed country pay for the weapons it urgently needed now? Appalled by the hostility of Churchill's draft, the British embassy in Washington urged him to tone it down and to offer unequivocal thanks to Roosevelt for the new offer of aid. The prime minister reluctantly agreed to an expression of gratitude but retained his skepticism and anxiety. "Remember, Mr. President," he wrote, "we do not know what you have in mind, or exactly what the United States is going to do, and we are fighting for our lives."

As 1941 dawned, Churchill's apprehension over his country's precarious future and his resentment at the United States for not doing more to help were shared by a growing number of his countrymen. When Britons were asked in a public opinion poll which non-Axis countries they rated most highly, the United States came in last. "The percentage of unfavorable criticism of America—our friend—equals that of Italy—our enemy," noted the poll takers.

It was during this increasingly poisonous period that Joseph Kennedy finally submitted his resignation as U.S. ambassador to Britain. Kennedy had contributed greatly to the widening gulf between the two countries and their leaders. His successor would now have the monumentally difficult task of trying to heal the breach.

To take on that problematic assignment, the president turned to a shy, tongue-tied former New England governor, a man once touted as a likely successor to Roosevelt himself.

IN THE 1920S and early 1930s, John Gilbert Winant had won national attention as the youngest and most progressive governor in the country. But in 1936, this rising Republican star with presidential dreams forfeited his political future by attacking the GOP for its slashing assaults on the New Deal. Bemused by Winant's self-sacrificing idealism, Roosevelt, whose own devotion to ideals never got the better of his instincts for political survival, dubbed him "Utopian John."

Like the president, Winant came from an old, well-connected New York family with Dutch antecedents. The son of a real estate broker, he grew up on Manhattan's Upper East Side, a poor student but avid reader who lost himself in the novels of Charles Dickens and biographies of his lifelong hero, Abraham Lincoln. His parents, who had an "extremely unhappy" marriage and were later divorced, were miserly in showing any love or affection to him and his three brothers, he once told his secretary. Winant's father, a friend reported, "always told him to be seen and not heard."

At the age of twelve, the bookish, sensitive boy was sent to St. Paul's, the exclusive prep school nestled below the foothills of New Hampshire's White Mountains, on the outskirts of the state capital of Concord. It was the defining moment of Winant's life. He loved the school, but even more, he loved the woods and rolling hills of New Hampshire; as a student, he would walk for hours in the Bow Hills overlooking St. Paul's. Many years later he would tell a reporter that they "came to mean more to him than any other place on earth. He felt at home there."

Modeled after English public schools like Eton, St. Paul's tried to impress upon its pupils, most of whom came from affluent New York, Boston, and Philadelphia families, the importance of public service. "Our function is not to conform to the rich and prosperous world which surrounds us but rather, through its children, to convert it," Dr. Samuel Drury, St. Paul's rector, declared. While most St. Paul's students had no intention of turning their backs on that "rich and prosperous world," Winant developed an enthusiasm for social reform that would last the rest of his life.

During his years at St. Paul's, he became one of its top student leaders, demonstrating a newfound talent to persuade and galvanize others. A few years later, after withdrawing from Princeton because of poor grades, he returned to the school to teach American history. Determined to instill a social conscience in his students, Winant was, in the words of Tom Matthews, one of his pupils, "an incredibly inspiring teacher, conveying the burning conviction that the United States was a wonderful country, the most gloriously hopeful experiment man had ever made." In the evenings, his students would cram into his small, book-filled room to continue the discussions begun in the classroom about Lincoln, Jefferson, and others in Winant's pantheon of heroes. "Like most of the St. Paul's boys of my generation, I admired John Gilbert Winant to the point of idolatry," said Matthews, who thirty years later would become managing editor of *Time* magazine.

The day after the United States entered World War I, Winant quit his teaching job and paid his way to France, where he became a pilot in the fledgling U.S. flying corps. His aviation skills were somewhat shaky, as he later acknowledged to his friends Ed and Janet Murrow; while he was "all right" in the air, he needed "the greatest luck" to take off and land. "He appears to have cracked up innumerable planes," Janet Murrow wrote to her parents. "It's really a wonder he's still alive."

It *was* a wonder, since Winant also possessed a reckless courage that prompted him to volunteer for observation missions over enemy lines that others considered suicidal. When he landed after one such mission, one of his plane's wings had been ripped by a piece of shrapnel, the engine cowling was pierced, and part of the propeller was missing. Having enlisted as a private, he ended the war as a captain, in charge of an observation squadron near Verdun.

Shortly after returning home, Winant married Constance Russell, a wealthy young socialite whose grandfather had been president of the National City Bank of New York (now Citibank). Many of the couple's friends and acquaintances considered it a misguided match: she had no interest in politics, history, or social reform—the main preoccupations of her husband—and much preferred shopping, party giving, theater going, and spending time in places like Southampton and Bar Harbor. "It was one of those high-society marriages where I don't think they were together very much," recalled Abbie Rollins Caverly, whose father had been one of Winant's closest friends and political associates. "They had very little in common. He would sit up all night, brooding over how to make things better. She loved to throw parties."

Following the war, Winant made some money of his own from investments in Texas oil wells. He and Constance settled down to a life of affluence, with an apartment on Park Avenue, chauffeur-driven limousine, butler and maids, yacht, and a stable of Arabian horses. At the same time, however, he had not given up his love for New Hampshire or his burgeoning interest in public service, which had led to a brief stint in the New Hampshire House of Representatives before he went off to France.

In 1919, the Winants bought a house, a roomy white colonial, in Concord, about a quarter of a mile from St. Paul's. From his book-lined library, with its Gilbert Stuart portrait of Thomas Jefferson and first editions of Dickens and John Ruskin, Winant could gaze out on his favorite spot in the world, the pine-covered Bow Hills. While his wife continued to spend most of her time in New York, he made the Concord house his base and in 1920 was elected to the New Hampshire Senate.

The gradual transformation of this diffident, stammering young idealist into a successful politician was surprising in itself. The fact that the transformation took place in a rural, highly conservative state like New Hampshire was nothing short of remarkable. In the Senate, Winant became leader of the minuscule liberal wing of the GOP, introducing legislation to limit the workweek for women and children to forty-eight hours, regulate wage standards, and abolish capital punishment. Most of his fellow legislators came from farming areas, with little understanding of, or interest in, the lamentable living and working conditions of the laborers in New Hampshire's textile mills and other factories. Although they rejected Winant's legislative agenda, he refused to give up what most people considered his quixotic quest for reform.

In 1924, at the age of thirty-five, Winant announced his decision to run for governor, dropping off a copy of his announcement at the office of the state's leading newspaper, the *Manchester Union-Leader*. Frank Knox, who owned the *Union-Leader* and was widely regarded as a shoe-in for the Republican gubernatorial nomination, buried the story deep in the paper, giving it only four lines. Winant's candidacy, in the view of the Republican old guard, was laughable. Who did this liberal New Yorker think he was? New Hampshire voters would never accept him—a rich outsider, an intellectual, and a terrible speaker to boot.

They were certainly right about his speaking ability. Tall and brooding, his profile suggesting a refined Abraham Lincoln, he stood tensely before campaign audiences, his lean face set, his hair as rumpled as his Brooks Brothers suit, his shaggy eyebrows arched over deep-set, piercing gray eyes. His hands clenching and unclenching, he groped for the right word or phrase to express what he wanted to say. Sometimes it would take him minutes to find it, resulting in pauses as agonizing for the people straining to hear him as for Winant himself. "People in the audience wanted to help him, to shout out the word he was searching for," said one New Hampshire resident. After one of Winant's speeches, a woman murmured to an acquaintance: "It's too bad. Such a nice boy—and so badly shell-shocked during the war."

Curiously enough, however, his halting way of speaking helped win him support in his travels throughout the state. Reserved and taciturn themselves, New Hampshire voters found him a welcome contrast to the glib politicians they usually encountered. As awkward as his speeches were, they conveyed warmth and sincerity—and gave his listeners the sense of being taken into his confidence. His audiences "begin by feeling sorry for him," the *New York Times* reported. "They end by standing in the aisle and cheering him."

In the primary, he was opposed by the state's GOP machine, as well as by most of New Hampshire's newspapers and business interests. Nonetheless, he handily defeated Knox and then trounced the Democratic incumbent in the general election.*

As New Hampshire's chief executive, Winant was a man well ahead of his time, showing a zeal for economic justice and social change that equaled or bettered the reforming instincts of New York's

---

* After losing to Winant, Frank Knox went on to become owner and publisher of the *Chicago Daily News* and secretary of the navy under Franklin Roosevelt.

Franklin Roosevelt and far surpassed those of most of his other gubernatorial colleagues around the country. He liked to say that he learned his Republicanism from his hero, Abraham Lincoln, who, Winant declared, valued human rights over property rights. During the Depression, the governor pressed successfully for the creation of radical new state welfare programs that prefigured the New Deal, including an expansion of public works, aid for the elderly, emergency help for dependent mothers and children, and a minimum wage act. He smuggled a young reporter from the *Concord Daily Monitor* into a meeting of the Executive Council, a powerful state government body that acted as a check on the governor and whose meetings had always been closed. The next day, the reporter wrote a front-page story on the council's deliberations, and, from then on, its meetings have been open to the public.

Winant also reorganized and modernized his state's administrative machinery and won passage of laws to reform banking, restrain the influence of the railroads, and expand the power of the state's Public Service Commission to regulate utility companies. "Railroads and power combinations alike must be subservient to the public interest," he told the state legislature. The *New York Herald Tribune* would later write that Winant "put through more progressive legislation than New Hampshire had ever known."

Not surprisingly, the railroads, utilities, textile mills, and other special interests in the state were hostile to virtually everything Winant did. So, too, were the conservative diehards in his own party. But he was enormously popular with the voters, who elected him to an unprecedented three terms as governor. "I don't understand Winant and never did," one New Hampshire politician remarked. "But I take my hat off to him. He knows how to win." (Ironically, Winant's landslide reelection in 1932 provided Herbert Hoover, his ideological opposite, a coattail long enough to hand the president a narrow victory in New Hampshire, one of only five states not carried by Hoover's Democratic challenger, Franklin Roosevelt.)

It was clear that much of Winant's popularity as governor stemmed from his deep empathy and compassion for others. Years later, Dean Dexter, a former New Hampshire state legislator, would compare him to the idealistic characters that actor James Stewart played in *Mr. Smith Goes to Washington* and other movies. For Winant, "every public policy was personal," observed one historian. "It was about people, sometimes specific individuals, and the effect of the policy on them." The door to his capitol office was open to anybody who wanted to see him; on most days, the corridors of the statehouse were crowded with people waiting for a few minutes of the governor's time. Not infrequently, Winant would use his own money to pay a medical bill, cover an educational expense, or help start a business for an impoverished state resident or fellow World War I veteran who had asked for his help. During the Depression, he instructed the Concord police to allow transients to spend the night in the city jail, then feed them in the morning and send the bill to him. Walking to work, he would hand out all the money in his wallet to jobless men sunning themselves against the granite walls of the state capitol. Winant, said one friend, "carried the Christian injunction, 'Give all thy goods to feed the poor,' further than any person I have ever known."

When he left office in January 1935, Winant's ideals and principles had won the endorsement of most of the state's legislators, regardless of party. Some three decades later, Robert Bingham, Winant's legislative counsel in Concord, would remark: "Whenever people want to measure the effectiveness of a governorship, they compare it with Winant's three terms." In 2008, William Gardner, New Hampshire's longtime secretary of state, recalled how impressed he had been, after taking office, by how much state residents "revered and loved" Winant. "People still talked about him when I got here. He was special. Of all the governors we've had, he actually meant something to the people in a very personal way."

FROM WASHINGTON, President Roosevelt monitored Winant's success in New Hampshire with considerable interest. Strikingly similar in their devotion to social reform, the two men had worked closely together as governors. Winant strongly supported FDR's New Deal from the beginning, and New Hampshire was usually the first state to enroll in the many new relief programs that Roosevelt introduced in the first years of his administration. By autumn 1933, Winant had used New Deal funds to launch twelve major public-work projects and distribute tons of food to New Hampshire's needy.

The president, who "loved to pick off bright and promising young Republicans and make them his," had already enlisted Winant's help as an unofficial adviser on labor and other issues. In 1934 he had appointed the governor to head a special board of inquiry that helped end a crippling strike by the United Textile Workers union.

As Roosevelt well knew, Winant increasingly was being touted as the man who might head the 1936 Republican ticket. After the GOP debacle in 1932, it was clear the Republicans needed a "transfusion of new and youthful blood"; as one of the party's few shining stars, Winant was seen by many as a possible presidential nominee.

One of his boosters was the famed Kansas newspaper editor William Allen White, who praised him as the leading Republican on the horizon. The radio commentator Walter Winchell declared in a broadcast that Winant was being groomed by the *New York Herald Tribune,* an influential pro-Republican newspaper, as the next GOP candidate. *Time* and *Collier's* reported that he had a good shot at the nomination, and the *Boston Evening Transcript* ran a headline declaring: "Winant Moves Higher on List for Presidency." According to *American* magazine, the New Hampshire governor "has caught the imagination of the country. . . . He's rich. He can't make a speech. But he wants to do something for the people. And he does it." Letters poured in to Concord from all over the country, urging Winant to run. "You personally carry the esteem and appreciation of this department to a greater degree than any other public official, either in the Democratic party or out of it," wrote an employee of the Federal Emergency Relief Administration in Washington. Even Raymond Moley, a key member of Roosevelt's New Deal brain trust, jumped on the Winant bandwagon, observing that he "would trade fifty Representatives, twenty Senators, six ambassadors and a couple of cabinet members for one Governor Winant."

The Winant boomlet, however, was bound to collapse. Even if he had made a bid in 1936, it's probable that his speech-making problems would have greatly hindered his candidacy. But the point was moot because Winant, as a New Deal supporter, would never have challenged Roosevelt. He decided to put his presidential ambitions on hold, at least until the current incumbent left office.

Roosevelt, apparently, was not entirely sure of that. In late 1934, he nominated Winant as the first American representative to the International Labor Organization, an agency sponsored by the League of Nations and based in Geneva. Some saw the nomination as a Machiavellian ploy to get Winant off the political stage. Among them was Frances Perkins, the president's plainspoken labor secretary, who was a Winant admirer. One day in the Oval Office, Perkins asked FDR point-blank if that was what he had in mind. "No, no, that is not my intent," he protested. "Winant is a good man for the part." As Perkins remembered it, Roosevelt then lowered his eyes and stared down at his desk.

Whatever the president's rationale for offering him the post, Winant, who believed that the United States must break out of its isolationist shell, had no misgivings about taking it. Despite its emergence as the world's leading economic power after World War I, America had been unwilling to accept any of the inherent responsibilities that came with its newly dominant international position. "Most Americans," *Time* magazine remarked, "still thought of international diplomacy with all the repugnance of a Victorian lady contemplating sex." The country refused to join the League of Nations and, when the world depression struck in the early 1930s, insisted that its wartime allies must repay their debts to the United States in full. At the same time it raised its tariffs, making repayment of the debts impossible and helping to push Europe into an even greater economic decline. "Since the war, our attitude is that we do not need friends, and that the public opinion of the world is of no importance," Franklin Roosevelt, soon to be elected governor of New York, wrote in a 1928 issue of *Foreign Affairs* magazine. According to historian Warren Kimball, "Americans dipped in and out of the European scene seemingly at whim," wanting "to lead by distant example instead of active commitment."

In America, the belief took hold that the country had been tricked into World War I by British propaganda and by U.S. bankers and arms buyers who had acted on Britain's behalf. As another war loomed in Europe, an increasingly isolationist Congress, in an attempt to protect the United States from future conflicts, passed the Neutrality Acts and prohibited loans and investments to countries at war. Giving voice to the national mood, Ernest Hemingway wrote in 1935: "Of the hell broth that is brewing in Europe we have no need to drink. . . . We were fools to be sucked in once in a European war, and we shall never be sucked in again."

The International Labor Organization was the only offshoot of the League of Nations that the United States would join. A longtime supporter of the agency's mission to improve the pay and working conditions of laborers throughout the world, Winant moved to Geneva to take up his job. His stay at ILO headquarters, however, was brief. After only five months, on the recommendation of Frances Perkins, Roosevelt summoned him back to Washington to assume one of the most important posts in the government: chairman of the new Social Security Board.

IN AUGUST 1935, despite bitter Republican opposition, Congress passed the Social Security Act, the most sweeping piece of social legislation ever enacted in the United States and the New Deal's most striking achievement. In making unemployment compensation and old-age benefits available to all qualified Americans, it redefined and broadly expanded the government's responsibility to its citizens. It was so revolutionary that the administration feared it would be sabotaged by its many critics before it could take effect. Because of the ferocity of the GOP opposition, Roosevelt insisted that a prominent liberal Republican—Winant—head the three-man Social Security board that would administer the new law.

For the next year and a half, Winant and his fellow board members worked tirelessly to set up and promote the unprecedented new program. With a Senate filibuster holding up their funds, they functioned on a minimal budget for the first several months, borrowing offices in the new Labor Department building and operating with a skeleton staff, much of it lent by other government agencies. During the New Deal, many government agencies were hotbeds of energy and experimentation, but none hovered on the brink of bedlam as much as the makeshift Social Security offices, where "men rush in and out and fume at the slowness of the elevators."

In the middle of the frenzy was Winant, who drove himself as relentlessly in Washington as he had in Concord, snatching only a few hours of sleep each night in his rented Georgetown mansion. "He had no sense of time, or meals, or sleep, or anything to do with the conservation of his own strength," recalled one associate. "He would work right through the meal hour and not know he had missed a meal."

By all accounts, he was a terrible administrator, the despair of his staff and the other board members for his inefficiency and lateness. His desk was piled high with letters awaiting his signature, the room outside his office crammed with people waiting to see him; his filing system consisted of stuffing important papers in his pockets. But even

Winant's severest critics acknowledged that he was an extraordinary leader, a visionary with the ability to inspire. "He was, beyond any shadow of a doubt, one of the great characters in American public life during the past twenty years," Frank Bane, Social Security's first executive director, declared. "Few people have made as significant an impression upon government as it should be, as did Governor Winant."

As the public face of Social Security, Winant became a familiar figure on Capitol Hill and throughout the country, making repeated trips to the hinterlands to educate his fellow Americans about the new program. Under his leadership, the Social Security board, despite its lack of funds and minuscule staff, created in little more than a year a far-flung national organization, with 12 regional offices and 108 field offices, and, during that period, disbursed more than $215 million in old-age benefits to thirty-six states. All the important work of creating the Social Security program as it exists today was carried out under Winant's chairmanship.

Nonetheless, the GOP and much of the nation's business community were intent on killing Social Security. Hoping to convince Alf Landon, the progressive governor of Kansas and the Republicans' 1936 presidential nominee, to support it, Winant provided him with confidential information about the program. But Landon had lost control of his campaign to the party's conservative diehards, and in late September 1936, he made a slashing attack on Social Security, promising to repeal it if elected.

Feeling betrayed, Winant decided he could not remain silent; he would resign from the Social Security board and speak out against Landon. His colleagues on the board and other close advisers did their best to talk him out of committing what they saw as political suicide. Repudiating the GOP, they argued, would mean the end of his political career and any hope of his winning higher office. Even the president tried to dissuade him. But Winant was adamant. After submitting his resignation, he crisscrossed the country giving speeches and making broadcasts in support of Social Security.

In the final week of the campaign, the Republican National Committee supplied employers with millions of flyers, designed to look like official government notices, to stuff into workers' pay envelopes. The flyers warned that a future Congress would divert Social Security funds to other purposes and intimated that workers could look forward to a one percent reduction in pay—the cost of their Social Security contribution—unless they took action against Roosevelt on election day. Winant was so offended by the last-ditch smear that he made a nationwide radio address two days before the election, attacking the Republican move as "shoddy politics" and endorsing Roosevelt for reelection.

His support of the president was the last straw for the GOP and did indeed end any chance of his running for president as a Republican. But it also proved, according to one friend who wrote to him, that "at least one man in high office possesses genuine convictions and the courage to stand by them come what might. . . . I realize that many will call what you did a hopelessly idealistic move, and call it that with a sneer. But idealism is one quality this disordered world needs desperately."

The president apparently agreed. After his landslide victory, he sent Winant back to the ILO in Geneva; in 1939, the former New Hampshire governor became the organization's director. With war looming, Winant also served as an emissary for FDR on the Continent, dispatching frequent reports to the White House about his travels and meetings with European leaders. "More than any other American in public life whom I know, he understands the social forces and changes that have been at work in the last decade, both at home and in Europe," William Shirer, CBS's Berlin correspondent, wrote in his diary after a lunch with Winant. Shirer added: "I think he would make a good president to succeed Roosevelt in 1944 if the latter gets his third term."

When the Nazis occupied all of Czechoslovakia in March 1939, Winant went to Prague as a gesture of solidarity and sympathy with the Czechs. He was in France during Hitler's 1940 blitzkrieg, leaving Paris just a few hours before the Germans marched in. After France's fall, Roosevelt asked him to test the mood of England, the one country still standing against Germany. After a quick tour during the Battle of Britain, he replied that public morale was unbroken: "They will take all the bombing that comes." Ernest Bevin, the British labor minister, would later say that Winant was the only American he met during that period who "gave me the feeling that some people in the world still had faith in Great Britain." Noting Britain's critical shortage of arms and supplies, Winant urged the president to send help as soon as possible: Britain's war, he said, was America's war. It was advice that directly contradicted the cables and letters that Roosevelt had received from Joseph Kennedy.

Following Kennedy's resignation as ambassador, Roosevelt took his time (too much time, in the opinion of many of his associates) to appoint his successor. He wanted someone who was sympathetic to Britain, who could win the trust of Churchill and other government figures and persuade them to be patient while the president did what he could to further their cause. At the same time, FDR, with an eye to the future, wanted the new envoy to establish strong ties with the Labour Party, which he believed would take over leadership of the country during or after the war. Felix Frankfurter, Frances Perkins, and other prominent New Dealers told Roosevelt there was only one man with the necessary qualifications for such a varied, complex portfolio: John Gilbert Winant.

In late January 1941, a few days after his third inaugural, Roosevelt brought Winant to Washington. During their meeting in the Oval Office, the president questioned the ILO director about the European leaders he had met and conditions in Britain and the Nazi-occupied countries. But there was no mention of the ambassadorship. With Winant, as with other officials, Roosevelt's boyish love of secrecy and prankish sense of fun prompted him to withhold news of the appointment. He would let Winant learn about his new job, as others had learned about theirs, from the press.

A few days later, the nation's leading newspapers reported that FDR was sending Winant's name to the Senate for confirmation as ambassador to the Court of Saint James. Within three weeks, he was on his way to London.

IN BRITAIN, NEWS of Winant's appointment was greeted with elation. Anyone who was not Joseph Kennedy undoubtedly would have received an enthusiastic reception, but the reaction to Winant was particularly jubilant. "There is no name that could have been more welcome," wrote the *News Chronicle*. The *Manchester Guardian* declared: "He is an American for whom an Englishman feels an immediate liking, and few Americans have a warmer admiration and regard than he for this country and its people." The *Times* of London noted:

"There is something of the knight errant about him. He believes in his principles with almost romantic passion."

As a result of Winant's ILO work, British newspapers pointed out, he was already well acquainted with several leading members of Churchill's government, including Bevin and the new foreign secretary, Anthony Eden. The papers went on to underline the dramatic differences between Winant and Kennedy in personality and outlook. "One has often felt in the past that . . . American Ambassadors, while enjoying the freedom of the best country houses, have seen too little of the real Britain," the *Star* pointedly noted. "But the sterling metal of John Winant's character will make him reach out to wider fields. . . . Today he will see plain people on the march, and his heart will be with them."

When Winant's train pulled into London's Paddington station after his visit with George VI, he could take satisfaction in the warm welcome he had received both from the king and the British press. But his first encounter with Britain's most daunting figure was yet to come. How would Winston Churchill, still upset over America's foot-dragging, respond to the new U.S. envoy?

Two days later, when Churchill invited him for dinner at his reinforced war rooms in Whitehall, Winant had his answer. Showing no trace of the bulldog belligerence for which he was famed, the prime minister was obviously in a conciliatory mood. Throughout the dinner, he and Winant discussed the latest problem bedeviling Anglo-American relations: Britain's reluctance to complete its part of the destroyers-for-bases deal, announced almost six months before. Although Britain had received the destroyers, its government had not yet formally agreed to one provision of the quid pro quo—the lease of bases in British colonies in the Caribbean. Resentment of the deal in Whitehall, the House of Commons, and the colonies themselves had been too overwhelming.

Churchill assured Winant he would resolve the impasse. The following day, he called a meeting of several cabinet ministers at Downing Street, with Winant present as an observer. As the others debated the issue, Winant watched Churchill—"this stocky figure with a slight stoop"—pace up and down the room, "completely unconscious of any presence beyond his own thoughts." Suddenly, just minutes into the discussion, the prime minister swept aside all objections as immaterial and overruled the concerns voiced by his military advisers. In Churchill's view, it was far more important to stretch America's neutrality policy to the breaking point than to "maintain our pride and to preserve the dignity of a few small islands." Not long afterward, a British-U.S. negotiating commission gave final approval to the deal.

TWO WEEKS AFTER his arrival in Britain, Winant, his head slightly bowed, threaded his way through the packed ballroom of London's Savoy Hotel, following Churchill and the Earl of Derby to the head table. The occasion was a gala luncheon in Winant's honor, sponsored by the Pilgrim Society, an organization aimed at promoting closer Anglo-American relations. Seated before the ambassador, Churchill, and Lord Derby, who was president of the group, was the elite of the British government and business worlds—virtually all the cabinet, as well as the country's leading military figures, industrialists, and newspaper editors and publishers.

Near the end of the luncheon, Churchill rose to his feet and, turning to the ambassador, left no doubt in anyone's mind that he meant to make Winant an ally in his wooing of America. "Mr. Winant," he rumbled, his words carried to the nation over the BBC, "you come to us at a grand turning point in the world's history. We rejoice to have you with us in these days of storm and trial because, in you, we have a friend and a faithful comrade who 'will report us and our cause aright.' "

At the conclusion of his speech, the prime minister declared: "You, Mr. Ambassador, share our purpose. You'll share our dangers. You'll share our interests. You shall share our secrets. And the day will come when the British Empire and the United States will share together . . . the crown of victory." The audience erupted in cheers, and as he sat down, the "lord of language," as one newspaper called Churchill, knew he had done it again. "Every word was alive with meaning, every phrase was an expression of faith and courage," the *Sunday Times* wrote. "On this occasion, he could not have been better."

Now it was time for Winant to respond. He rose, tightly clutching the pages of his speech, and looked out over the audience, moving his weight from foot to foot, "rather like a small boy saying a piece at his first party," according to one onlooker. There was a long pause. Then, quietly, hesitantly, he began to speak. Unlike Churchill, he was "not an orator," the *Daily Herald* noted the following day. "He read, and not too well, every word, looking down at his script. But his words were more than oratory. They were a declaration of faith."

America, Winant said, had finally shaken off its lethargy and "gone into action. With its labor and resources, it will provide the tools—the ships, the planes, the guns, the ammunition and the food—for all those here and everywhere who defend with their lives freedom's frontiers." Yet, although he pledged America's support to Britain, he made clear he had not come to praise his own country for its laggard help. He was there to pay tribute to the resoluteness and courage of Britain and its citizens. "Today it is the honor and destiny of the British people to man the bridgehead of humanity's hopes. It is your privilege to stand against ruthless and powerful dictators who would destroy the lessons of two thousand years of history. It is your destiny to say to them: 'Here you shall not pass.'"

At that point, Winant paused, his eyes sweeping the room. His voice growing stronger, he declared: "The lost years are gone. The road ahead is hard. A new spirit is abroad. Free peoples are again cooperating to win a free world, and no tyranny can frustrate their hopes." The Allies, he said, "with the help of God shall build a citadel of freedom so strong that force may never again seek its destruction."

The audience's reaction to the ambassador's halting yet passionate address mirrored that of the crowds in New Hampshire during his first campaign for governor: they began by feeling sorry for him and ended by giving him a standing ovation. Like the citizens of his state, the Britons attending the luncheon seemed to find in the reserved, awkward Winant a kindred spirit, and they demonstrated that sense of kinship with loud cheers and applause.

The following day, British newspapers were equally outspoken in their enthusiasm. Using "language of simple grandeur," the *Evening Standard* wrote, Winant had "achieved a feat which few orators can equal. He spoke after Mr. Churchill with complete success." In a large front-page headline, the *Daily Mirror* exclaimed: "U.S. ENVOY SPEAKS TO YOU—THE BRITISH PEOPLE!" A columnist for the *Star* wrote: "Nearly everyone I spoke to this morning was asking, 'Did you listen to the Winant broadcast?' I did—and was moved."

It was, proclaimed the *Sunday Times,* "an extraordinary triumph."

2.

"YOU ARE THE
BEST REPORTER IN
ALL OF EUROPE"

WHEN GIL WINANT ARRIVED AT THE U.S. EMBASSY IN LONDON, he was intrigued to discover that the house once occupied by John Adams, America's first envoy to Britain, was just steps away from his office. Both the embassy and the Adams house were on Grosvenor Square, one of the capital's most fashionable addresses since Sir Richard Grosvenor laid it out in the early eighteenth century. From the time of its creation, one contemporary writer remarked, the spacious, tree-lined acreage was "the most magnificent square in the whole Town."

The house leased by John and Abigail Adams from 1785 to 1788 was among several dozen Georgian residences lining the square, which had in its center a gilded statue of George I, surrounded by formal gardens and gravel paths. It was a lovely, gracious place in which to live—if one didn't happen to be the first U.S. emissary to an England still smarting from the loss of its rebellious American colonies.

Like many of their countrymen, the Adamses' aristocratic neighbors (one of whom was Lord North, England's prime minister during the Revolutionary War) treated the American couple with haughty disdain. "An ambassador from America!" sniffed the *Public Advertiser,* a London newspaper. "Good heavens, what a sound!" Few in English official circles expected the upstart nation to survive, but, for as long as it did, they would do their best to ignore its representative. Of the English, Adams wrote to a friend back home: "They hate us." Abigail, meanwhile, complained about the Britons' "studied civility and disguised coldness," which, she said, "cover malignant hearts." She wrote to her sister in 1785: "I shall never have much society with this kind of people, for they would not like me any more than I do them." Three years later, when Congress approved Adams's request to leave London, Abigail was overjoyed. "Some years hence," she wrote, "it may be pleasing to reside here in the character of the American Minister, but with the . . . present temper of the English no one need envy the Embassy."

As later U.S. representatives would find, Britons' patronizing attitude toward their American cousins showed little sign of abating. Nathaniel Hawthorne, who served as U.S. consul in Liverpool in the mid-1850s, wrote: "These people think so loftily of themselves, and so contemptuously of everybody else, that it requires more generosity than I possess to keep always in perfectly good humor with them." Some thirty years later, the noted editor James Russell Lowell, the latest of Adams's successors at the Court of St. James, was similarly exasperated: "The only sure way of bringing about a healthy relation between the two countries is for Englishmen to clear their minds of the notion that we are always to be treated as a kind of inferior and deported Englishman."

By 1941, however, the situation was far different. The British now needed America too much to indulge in public displays of condescension. If Abigail Adams could have made a ghostly visit to Grosvenor Square, she likely would have been as astonished by the U.S. ambassador's new status as by alterations in the square itself.

Although Grosvenor Square was still a sought-after address, many of its stately old houses had been torn down and replaced in the 1930s by blocks of luxury neo-Georgian apartment and office buildings, one of which was now occupied by the U.S. embassy. No. 9 Grosvenor Square, where the Adamses had lived, was among the few eighteenth-century houses still standing. The war had brought still more changes. German bombs had obliterated several of the buildings on the square; in its dusty center, service vehicles and low wooden huts had taken the place of lawns and a tennis court. The huts were occupied by members of the Women's Auxiliary Air Force (WAAF), whose job was to tend a barrage balloon, fondly nicknamed "Romeo," that floated overhead.

The contrast between the British treatment of John Adams and that of Gil Winant was equally dramatic. No longer a scorned parvenu, the United States was now crucial to Britain's continued existence as a free country, and its envoy was not only welcomed but actively wooed by the British monarch, government leaders, and the press. When Winant held his first news conference at the embassy shortly after his arrival, so many journalists clamored to attend that he was forced to hold two separate sessions—one for British and European reporters, the other for American correspondents.

Although the new ambassador received considerably better treatment from the British than John Adams, he was reminiscent of the first U.S. envoy in other ways. A description of Adams by his friend Jonathan Sewell could easily have applied to Winant as well: "He cannot dance, drink, game, flatter, promise, dress, swear with the gentlemen, and small talk and flirt with the ladies; in short, he has none of the essential arts or ornaments which constitute a courtier."

Winant was his usual shy self at both meetings with the press, his hands fidgeting, his voice soft and hesitant, his words "coming so slowly," in the words of one British reporter, "that shorthand is unnecessary." With dozens of flashbulbs exploding in his face, he paced restlessly around his office as journalists fired their questions. He told them he had little to say, but that after he had settled in, he would meet them again and have a further talk. Such taciturnity normally would have raised the hackles of the hard-boiled scribblers of Fleet Street. Yet, once again, Winant was a hit. "EXCELLENT IMPRESSION MADE BY WINANT IN LONDON," read a headline in the *Washington Evening Star* the following day. "In the first five minutes of the conference," noted the *News Chronicle,* "it was obvious that he had won the sympathy of correspondents from all over Britain and the Empire by his charm and diffidence and obvious sincerity and honesty."

Reporters also emphasized the differences between Winant and his gregarious, outspoken predecessor, Joseph Kennedy, who had hired a former *New York Times* correspondent to handle public relations for him in London and who had assiduously courted the American and British press corps. "His political views aside, Mr. Kennedy was a favorite among newspapermen," Bill Stoneman of the *Chicago Daily News* wrote after Winant's session with American reporters. "But it was generally agreed, by those who had not met Mr. Winant before, that his very soft spokenness would be an asset here."

No one was more convinced of that than a tall, lean broadcast correspondent sitting in the back of Winant's office during the press conference. Joseph Kennedy, to put it mildly, had never been a favorite of Edward R. Murrow's. For the past several months, the head of CBS's European operations had lobbied Washington to replace Kennedy, whom he loathed, with Winant, a man he greatly admired.

BY 1941, ED MURROW had become the best-known American in London, the journalist who, according to *Scribner's* magazine, "has more influence upon America's reaction to foreign news than a shipful of newspapermen." He and the men he had hired as CBS correspondents were now the chief sources of European news for many if not most of their countrymen.

Yet four years earlier, when Murrow had tried to join the American Foreign Correspondents' Association in the British capital, that august organization had turned down his application. The reason for the rejection was unassailable: Murrow had not one day of journalistic experience to his credit when he first arrived in London in 1937. As CBS's European director of talks, he had been sent over as a sort of booking agent, a functionary whose job was to arrange broadcasts of various kinds, from debates at the League of Nations to concerts by boys' choirs in Vienna and Prague. At that point, neither CBS nor NBC, the other major U.S. radio network, had any reporters of their own to crisscross the globe and broadcast to listeners back home.

Murrow, however, set out to change that. As the threat of war increased, he convinced William Paley, the chairman of CBS, to let him hire his own band of correspondents, who came to be known in later years as the Murrow Boys. When Germany began its relentless aerial assault on London in September 1940, it was the event Murrow had been preparing for since he arrived in Europe. The Blitz was perfect for radio: it had immediacy, human drama, and, above all, sound—the wail of sirens, the scream of bombs, the crash and thunder of antiaircraft guns. No other news medium could bring home to Americans the reality of the attack in such a powerful way.

Listening to Murrow's broadcasts, with their famed "This is London" opening, became a national habit in the United States. Working eighteen hours a day, subsisting largely on coffee and cigarettes, Murrow emerged as the Boswell of wartime London, describing in little gems of detail how people struggled to live their lives, even as their city and world threatened to shatter around them. "You are the best reporter in all of Europe," Nelson Poynter, the editor and publisher of the *St. Petersburg Times,* wrote to Murrow. "I say this because you do as comprehensive a job as the best of them, and in addition have given to listeners the homey little facts that make this God-awful nightmare real."

In his reporting, Murrow also earned his listeners' trust. If he implied, as he did more and more often, that England couldn't go it alone, that America would have to join the fight, well, maybe he was right, many in his audience thought. Hundreds of Americans wrote him to say his broadcasts had taken them from neutral detachment to support for the British. In September 1940, a Gallup poll reported that 39 percent of Americans favored providing more U.S. aid to Britain. One month later, as bombs fell on London, and Murrow brought the reality of it into American living rooms, 54 percent thought more aid should be sent.

In 1941, the Overseas Press Club in New York named Murrow the best broadcast journalist of the previous year. At the age of thirty-two, he had become a bona fide celebrity. Newspaper and magazine stories were written about him, and his broadcasts were printed as newspaper columns in the United States. "You are the No. 1 man on the air," his CBS colleague William Shirer wrote him from New York. "No one here touches you or has your following."

Murrow now was the man to see in London, the person whom official visitors from Washington sought out for information and guidance about the British government and people. Among those who called on him was Harry Hopkins, the president's closest adviser, who invited Murrow to dinner a few hours after arriving on a special mission for Roosevelt in January 1941. Hopkins had come to London, he told Murrow, to serve as "a catalytic agent between two prima donnas. I want to try to get an understanding of Churchill and of the men he sees after midnight."

Murrow could tell Hopkins what he needed to know because of his intimate access to Churchill and other top officials in the British government. Well aware of the importance of the CBS broadcaster and other influential American journalists to the British cause, the prime minister had been diligent in cultivating them since his accession to power. The Americans, one British reporter said with a tinge of envy, were "treated as tin gods because they were so useful." When British officials turned down Murrow's request to broadcast live during the

Blitz, the matter was referred to Churchill, who immediately approved the idea. Anything that might help persuade America to come to the aid of Britain had the prime minister's blessing.

In late 1940, Murrow and Churchill began to see each other on a more personal level after their wives became friends while working on Bundles for Britain, an American-sponsored program to collect clothing and other supplies for British citizens bombed out of their homes. Ed and Janet Murrow were frequent guests at 10 Downing Street; once, when Murrow dropped by to pick up his wife after a luncheon with Clementine Churchill, the prime minister emerged from his study and waved him inside. "Good to see you," Churchill boomed. "Have you time for several whiskies?"

Like many of his American colleagues in London, Murrow's sympathies were entirely with the British. His country's neutrality, which his CBS bosses supported, was an unworkable policy, he felt, one that failed to take into account the astounding moral inequality between Nazi Germany and the Allies. While covering the German takeover of Austria in 1938, Murrow had observed Nazi thugs burning down Jewish-owned shops, forcing rabbis to their knees to scrub sidewalks, and kicking Jews unconscious. One night, as he was having a drink in a Vienna bar, a man with Semitic features standing near him suddenly pulled a razor from his pocket and slashed his throat. When Murrow returned to London, he found himself unable to rid his mind of the brutalities he had seen. He asked a friend from the BBC if she would let him talk to her about what had happened. Years later, she said: "I still have a picture in my mind of the horror of the scene—and the agony with which he told it." According to economist John Kenneth Galbraith, a friend of Murrow's, "Ed seemed devastated by the Anschluss experience."

Obsessed by the danger that Germany posed to the world and convinced of the importance of Britain's survival, Murrow did little to disguise his disdain for Joseph Kennedy and his pro-appeasement stand. While he never directly criticized Kennedy in his reports, he once broadcast, with great gusto, excerpts from a magazine column by Harold Nicolson, an anti-appeasement member of Parliament, that savaged the ambassador. So strongly did Murrow feel about Kennedy that shortly after the war, he chastised a friend for visiting the Kennedy estate in Palm Beach. Staying with the former ambassador, he said, was like paying a visit to Hermann Göring, Hitler's deputy. Murrow was convinced that "the British somehow would come through this," recalled Eric Sevareid, one of the Murrow Boys. "And he was furious with people who took the defeatist line, even in private conversations."

When Murrow discovered in late 1940 that Kennedy was returning to the United States, he immediately began pressing his acquaintances in the Roosevelt administration to intercede on behalf of Gil Winant as Kennedy's successor. Despite a twenty-year age difference, Murrow and Winant had been friends since the early 1930s, during the former governor's ILO tenure in Geneva. "Ed had enormous regard for [Winant]," recalled a friend of both. The two men, said another mutual acquaintance, had much in common—"both rather inward-looking, both absolutely dedicated, very much on the same wave length." With a strong social conscience of his own, Murrow, like Winant, "expected individuals and their government to live up to high moral standards," Sevareid said in the 1960s. "He believed in a foreign policy based on moral principles, which few people really believe in anymore."

Although he greatly admired Roosevelt, Murrow was increasingly impatient with America's hesitancy in coming to the aid of Britain. In Winant he saw mirrored his own sense of urgency and passionate commitment to ideals—qualities that he longed to see in the president and other U.S. political leaders. "I hope that life goes well for you in America, and that your nostrils are not assailed by the odor of death . . . that permeates the atmosphere over here," he wrote to one friend back home. To another, he remarked: "If the light of the world is to come from the West, somebody had better start lighting some bonfires."

Of Murrow, a British friend recalled: "He was concerned, very concerned, that his own country wasn't aware of the facts of life. And that if Hitler & Co. were not stopped here, the next stop was Manhattan."

WHILE ED MURROW and Gil Winant were alike in many ways, their backgrounds were vastly different. Murrow's father had been an impoverished dirt farmer in Polecat Creek, North Carolina, who moved his wife and four sons to Washington State when Ed was five, to find work in logging camps. The family did not have indoor plumbing until Murrow was fourteen and didn't have a phone during the entire time he lived at home.

Idealistic and at the same time intensely ambitious, Murrow was a critic of unearned privilege who strongly believed that journalists should be champions of the underdog. Yet he also yearned for admission to the clubs and salons of upper-class America and England. In London, he took to wearing Savile Row pinstripes, one of the methods he used to erase the vestiges of his hardscrabble origins. Eric Sevareid never forgot his first glimpse of Murrow—"a young American in a beautifully fitting suit and hard collar chatting easily on the phone with Lady so-and-so. His ease, the cultivation in his voice . . . was difficult for me to believe."

But the farther Murrow traveled from his impoverished, rural roots, the more guilt he seemed to feel for doing so. He told friends in London that he sometimes wished he had stayed home in Washington State and continued working as a lumberjack, his summer job while in high school and college. Murrow used to say that "there was a satisfaction about that life" and that "he had never known that kind of satisfaction since," one friend remembered.

A voracious reader, Murrow attended Washington State College, where he majored in speech, joined the most prestigious fraternity on campus, and was elected president of the student government. After his graduation in 1930, he served as president of the National Student Federation of America, a group representing the student governments of some four hundred American colleges and universities. He later worked for the Institute of International Education, primarily as an organizer of student exchanges and conferences in the United States and Europe. In his frequent overseas travels, Murrow made a number of important new friends and contacts, including the prominent English socialist Harold Laski, who was also a close friend of Gil Winant's. In 1933, through his work at the institute, Murrow became involved in helping eminent German scholars and scientists, among them Paul Tillich, Martin Buber, and Hans J. Morgenthau, emigrate to America from Nazi Germany. That experience, he later said, was "the most richly rewarding of anything I have ever undertaken."

The following year, at the age of twenty-six, he married Janet Brewster, a pretty, dark-haired Mount Holyoke graduate from Connecticut, whose family roots could be traced back to the *Mayflower*.

Quiet and reserved on the surface, Janet had a love of adventure, a wry sense of humor, and a mind of her own; in college, she rejected the conservative Republicanism of her parents and became a committed New Deal Democrat. Before she met Murrow, her ambition had been to move to New York and become a social worker.

In 1935, CBS hired Murrow as its director of talks. Two years later, he was dispatched to London, to oversee CBS cultural, news, and educational programs from England and the Continent. As Europe lurched toward war, Murrow operated a frantic one-man show, traveling to European capitals to arrange debates, talks by international figures, and commentaries by well-known foreign correspondents, as well as coverage of events ranging from concerts to dog shows.

With Hitler about to pounce on Austria, New York agreed in early 1938 to expand the network's European operation. Murrow hired William Shirer, a veteran foreign correspondent based in Berlin. When the Nazis marched into Vienna in March, Murrow and Shirer saw their chance to establish themselves as radio reporters and to make broadcasting history. Several nights after the Anschluss, the two organized the first news roundup ever broadcast to America, with Murrow reporting from Vienna, Shirer and Labour MP Ellen Wilkinson from London, and various American newspaper correspondents from Paris, Berlin, and Rome. The last report came from Washington, where Senator Lewis Schwellenbach, an isolationist on the Senate Foreign Relations Committee, declared: "If the rest of the world wants to involve itself in a brawl, that is its business."

The roundup was a major success for CBS. Murrow and Shirer had proved that radio was not only able to report news as it occurred but also to put it in context, to link it with news from elsewhere—and to do all that with unprecedented speed and immediacy. They also set in motion a chain of events that would lead, in only one year, to radio's emergence as America's chief news medium and to the beginning of CBS's decades-long dominance of broadcast journalism.

DURING NEVILLE CHAMBERLAIN's tenure as British prime minister and head of the Conservative Party, Murrow, although never openly critical of the government's conciliation of Hitler in his broadcasts, frequently reported what Chamberlain's anti-appeasement opponents were saying about the policy. In turn, Downing Street and much of

Whitehall were highly critical of *him*. "They have made it quite clear that they don't like some of the things I've said lately," he wrote to his parents in early 1939. "It may be that I shall be thrown out of this country before the war starts. Several people in high places have been giving me fatherly advice about it being in my own interests to do talks favorable to this country."

Officials counseled him to take his cue from the British Broadcasting Corporation, the sole source of broadcast news for most of Britain. Although the BBC received government funding and was ultimately answerable to Parliament, it was supposed to have editorial independence. Sir John Reith, its director general, viewed his charter differently, however. "Assuming that the BBC is for the people, and the Government is for the people, it follows that the BBC must be for the government," Reith declared. Under Reith, the BBC squelched news that Chamberlain found unpalatable and relied almost entirely on official sources for its news broadcasts; it provided no analysis, no context for what was happening, and no alternative points of view. In the aftermath of the Munich crisis, a high-level BBC official wrote a confidential memo to his superiors accusing them of embarking on a "conspiracy of silence." The public, he charged, had been kept "in ignorance" and denied "essential knowledge" of what was really going on.

Murrow had no intention of following the BBC's example. In addition to his own tough reports on Chamberlain's policies, he invited Winston Churchill and other members of a small band of anti-appeasement Conservative MPs to broadcast to America via CBS. It was the only radio outlet for most of the parliamentary rebels, who had been barred from BBC broadcasts because of their views.

Most of Chamberlain's critics in the Conservative Party were members of the public school old-boy network that dominated British society and government, and they welcomed Murrow and his wife into their upper-class circle. Throughout the Murrows' stay in England, they were frequent guests at elegant Mayfair dinner parties, lunches at exclusive private clubs, and weekend get-togethers at grand country houses. A crack shot, Murrow hunted grouse and pheasant with Lord Cranborne, the future Marquess of Salisbury and scion of one of the most noted aristocratic families in England, at Cranborne's family estate in Hertfordshire. The boy from Polecat Creek was one of the few non-Britons to call Cranborne, a former undersecretary of foreign affairs who was among the most outspoken opponents of Chamberlain, by his childhood nickname of "Bobbety."

He was also included in weekend shooting parties at Ditchley, an eighteenth-century mansion in Oxfordshire and one of England's most opulent country houses, owned by another of the rebels, Ronald Tree. The grandson of the Chicago department-store magnate Marshall Field, the fantastically wealthy Tree had grown up in England and was elected to Parliament in 1933. His wife, Nancy, was the niece of Nancy Astor, the former Virginia belle who became the first woman to win a seat in the House of Commons.

Appalled in the abstract by Britain's rigid class system, Murrow was unapologetic (though sometimes defensive) about his hobnobbing with those in its upper strata. He didn't judge his friends by their class, he declared; in any event, "these people are valuable to me." Janet Murrow had a more jaundiced response. The women in those rarefied circles often ignored her, preferring to focus on her handsome, influential husband. "They had a quick way," she recalled, "of letting you feel that you weren't particularly useful to them." A Connecticut Yankee to her core, she also was not fond of what she viewed as the superficiality of the British upper-class lifestyle. After a stay at Ditchley, she wrote in her diary: "It's a beautiful house—palace—country club—or what have you. But what a lot of trouble people take in their living! Too many people around; too much talk; too much fuss. Why do they do that?"

IN SEPTEMBER 1939, Britain's reluctant declaration of war against Germany put an end to much of the frivolity that Janet Murrow found so distasteful. It also turned her life, and the lives of virtually everyone else in the country, topsy-turvy. More than a million people, rich and poor alike, were evacuated from their homes or left voluntarily, marking the largest migration in Britain since the Great Plague of 1665. Houses were shut up, families separated, careers abandoned, schools and businesses closed.

Ambassador Kennedy advised all Americans in England to leave the country as soon as possible. More than ten thousand U.S. citizens, including his own wife and children, took his advice, departing as fast as ships could carry them—half of them within forty-eight hours of the declaration of war. Long lines of Americans (and more than a few Britons) snaked into the U.S. embassy, seeking help to get out of the country.

In London the trappings of war were everywhere. Sandbags and barbed wire barricades shielded Parliament, 10 Downing Street, and other government buildings, while barrage balloons, tethered on cables, bobbed high above the city. Soldiers and policemen stood guard at bridges and tunnels, keeping a sharp eye out for saboteurs. Store windows were boarded up or taped with strips of brown paper to prevent shattering after bomb blasts. The garish electric signs of Piccadilly Circus and the lighted marquees of West End theaters were doused by the blackout, and the fountains no longer danced in Trafalgar Square.

Looming high above posh Portland Place, Broadcasting House, where Murrow made his broadcasts to America, had been particularly well fortified. The BBC headquarters, a giant white wedge of a building a few blocks from Regent's Park, was considered a prime target for saboteurs and German bombs. Sandbags were piled high around the entrances, and rifle-toting sentries manned the massive bronze front doors, with orders to shoot to kill if necessary. The building's graceful Art Deco interiors were divided by steel partitions and gas-tight doors, its trompe l'oeil murals covered by heavy soundproofing. The seats of the BBC's concert hall were ripped out to create a giant employee dormitory, with mattresses lined up on the stage and floor.

The news division was the only major BBC department to remain at Broadcasting House during the war; the others, including the entertainment division, had been evacuated to buildings in other parts of London and the country. The heart of BBC news—the central control room, studios, and news room—was relocated to the building's sub-basement, three stories below the street. Burrowed deep underground, with drainpipes clanking overhead and the smell of cabbage wafting in from the canteen, editors, announcers, writers, and other staffers worked around the clock to produce the latest news reports.

Murrow and the other American radio journalists broadcast from Studio B-4, a tiny subterranean closet of a room formerly used by the canteen to store its goods. The "studio" was divided by a makeshift curtain. On one side was the broadcasting booth, consisting of a table, microphone, and two chairs; on the other were filing cabinets, clothes tree, desk, and cot, usually occupied by a sleeping reporter, engineer, or censor.

AS DRAMATIC AS the physical changes of the BBC were, the shifts in its philosophy and style were even more startling. Before September 1939, it was, as one employee remembered, "an agreeable, comfortable, cultured, leisured place, remote from the world of business and struggle." The man responsible for setting that high-brow, haughty, slightly puritanical tone was Sir John Reith, who, from the network's inception in 1922, directed its announcers to wear dinner jackets while at the microphone. After delivering a talk over the BBC in 1937, Virginia Woolf described its milieu as "sad and discreet" and "oh so proper, oh so kindly."

When he first arrived in London, Murrow, in a meeting with Reith, made clear that he and CBS had no intention of adopting the BBC's nose-in-the-air attitude. "I want our programs to be anything but intellectual," he said. "I want them to be down to earth and comprehensible to the man in the street." With a dismissive wave of his hand, Reith replied: "Then you will drag radio down to the level of the Hyde Park Speakers' Corner." Murrow nodded. "Exactly."

In early 1940, Reith was named head of the new Ministry of Information; even before his departure, the BBC began a metamorphosis that would make it the most trusted news source in the world by the end of the war. It would also become, as one BBC staffer put it, "Ed's true spiritual home."

A throng of new producers and editors, many of them former print reporters, were hired, bringing a burst of energy and journalistic experience to the newsroom. R. T. Clark, a classics scholar and former editorial writer for the *Manchester Guardian,* was put in charge of the domestic news service. On the day Britain declared war, Clark, a cigarette dangling from his lips, signaled a seismic shift in the BBC's news policy when he announced to his staff: "Well, brothers, now that war's come, your job is to tell the truth. And if you aren't sure it is the truth, don't use it." His statement was cheered not only by the new hires but also by a group of longtime staffers who had been openly critical of the BBC's manipulation of the news and its refusal to allow critics of the Chamberlain government to broadcast. Many of them were friends of

Murrow's, who stood at the back of the newsroom during Clark's announcement and added his own applause to the call for truth.

Like the American radio networks, the prewar BBC had no foreign or domestic correspondents of its own and got most of its news from newspaper and wire service stories. That changed under Clark: on-the-spot reports by BBC journalists became a major feature, along with more interpretation of events and greater liveliness and vigor in its news bulletins. Throughout the war, Clark and other BBC officials fought to maintain the network's independence, resisting repeated attempts by the government under both Chamberlain and Churchill to use the BBC for propaganda purposes. Early in his premiership, a grumbling Churchill referred to the BBC as "one of the major neutrals"; in response, the BBC declared that the maintenance of national morale, laudable though it was, was no excuse for a "deliberate perversion of the truth." For the most part, it succeeded in keeping the government at arm's length. In 1944, the usually cynical George Orwell noted: "The BBC, as far as its news goes, has gained immense prestige. . . . 'I heard it on the wireless' is now almost equivalent to 'I know it must be true.' "

The BBC's wartime evolution had a major impact on Murrow, whose own philosophy and style of reporting the news were still evolving. "We were giving in full the bad news, the hellish communiqués," said one BBC editor, "and this meshed with Ed's desire to tell the truth even if it was a hard and nasty truth. There was a complete meeting of minds on that." Even though Murrow was employed by CBS, the BBC was the first real news organization with which he was closely associated. He and his British colleagues were both creating something new; they had the same ideas about truth and independence; as the war progressed, they learned and grew together.

A key influence on Murrow was Clark, who became a kind of mentor and counselor. After the American's nightly broadcasts, the two would chat for hours in Clark's cramped, book-filled underground office, the smoke from their omnipresent cigarettes spiraling to the ceiling. Not infrequently, Murrow would invite Clark and other BBC staffers back to his flat in nearby Hallam Street to continue their discussions over tumblers of American bourbon. In the words of one participant in those early morning bull sessions, "Everyone regarded [Ed] as part of the outfit here, not simply because the BBC gave him the facilities, but because he fitted in. . . . He was immediately accepted and acceptable. We were very British; he was very American. . . . But we were traveling the same road. In the halls of Broadcasting House, the name of Ed Murrow is there in gold. He was one of us."

NEITHER MURROW NOR the BBC had much major news to report in the first eight months of what at first was a sham conflict, known as the "Bore War" by the British and the "Drôle de Guerre" by their allies, the French. (The neutral Americans called it "Phony.") Britain and France did little but drop millions of propaganda leaflets on enemy territory, impose a naval blockade against Germany, and send a few token patrols across the Maginot Line, France's vaunted chain of fortifications on the French-German border. This somnolent period abruptly ended in April 1940, when Hitler invaded Norway and Denmark and then, a month later, sent his panzers hurtling through the Low Countries and into France. In June, the French capitulated, and Britain, with barely a tenth of the forces fielded by Germany, was left to face the führer's juggernaut on its own.

The soaring, combative rhetoric of Britain's new prime minister, Winston Churchill, inspired his countrymen, but inspiration by itself could hardly ward off a German invasion. "As far as I can see, we are, after years of leisurely preparation, completely unprepared," Sir Alexander Cadogan, the permanent undersecretary of the Foreign Office, wrote in his diary. A government report observed: "Everyone is going around looking as if they want to put their heads into a gas oven."

Once again, Ambassador Kennedy advised the Americans who remained in Britain to flee the country, and several thousand more, including a number of journalists, complied. When Janet Murrow's parents urged her to do the same, she replied with a firm no. "We decided a year ago that the only thing to do was to live dangerously and not run away from things," she wrote. Later, she added: "It just isn't possible for me to go off and enjoy myself when the world I have known over here is about to enter upon the darkest period of its history. I hope you understand."

Yet, while many Americans departed, others arrived, notably a score or more of U.S. correspondents who had covered the Allied debacle in France and Belgium. Among them were several of America's most prominent journalistic heavyweights, whose datelines had ranged from Addis Ababa to Prague to Madrid. There was the handsome, hard-drinking Vincent Sheean, whose memoir, *Personal History*, had been the inspiration for Alfred Hitchcock's movie *Foreign Correspondent*, as well as a major influence on a generation of American reporters. Equally colorful (and bibulous) was Quentin Reynolds, the star war correspondent for *Collier's* magazine. A genial bear of a man, the 220-pound Reynolds was, in the words of the *New York Times*, "a man of facile enthusiasms," whose personality sketches and other feature stories were enormously popular back home.

The newcomers joined Murrow and several dozen other Americans who remained in London after the fall of France to report for U.S. broadcast networks, newspapers, wire services, and news magazines. "Never before, I'm sure, has there been such a concentration of journalists in such a small area," Janet Murrow wrote to her parents. "Already they're ready to tear each other's eyes out!"

The newly arrived Americans were regarded with a certain distrust and hostility by some of their British counterparts. Harry Watt, a news documentary filmmaker, viewed them as "vultures and jackals of the war, who admitted they were there to report on the fall of Britain. They had been on the spot to see all Europe conquered, so now they had their new headlines ready." Not even the air battles between the RAF and Luftwaffe, which began in the summer of 1940, satisfied the Americans' appetite for disaster. Midway through the Battle of Britain, Eric Sevareid of CBS, one of those who had covered the fall of France, joined two colleagues in creating a fake war monument out of a concrete slab, a tomato can, and some wilted poppies. The sign on the slab read: "Here lie three pressmen who died of boredom waiting for the invasion, 1940."

Boredom, however, would soon be the least of their problems.

ON A WARM, drowsy afternoon in early September, Ed Murrow, Vincent Sheean, and Ben Robertson, a correspondent for the New York newspaper *PM*, stopped at the edge of a field several miles south of London. The three had spent the day driving down the Thames estuary in Murrow's Talbot Sunbeam roadster, enjoying the sun and looking for dogfights beween Spitfires and Messerschmitts. Their search had been fruitless, and they stopped to buy apples from a farmer. Stretching out on the field to eat them, they drowsily listened to the chirp of crickets and buzzing of bees. The war seemed very far away. Within minutes, however, it returned with a vengeance. Hearing the harsh throb of aircraft engines, the Americans looked up at a sky filled with wave after wave of swastika-emblazoned bombers that clearly were not heading for their targets of previous days—the coastal defenses and RAF bases of southern England. Following the curve of the Thames, they were aimed straight at London.

In minutes the sky over the capital was suffused with a fiery red glow; black smoke billowed up into a vast cloud that blanketed much of the horizon. When shrapnel from antiaircraft guns rained down around the American reporters, they dived into a nearby ditch, where, stunned, they watched the seemingly endless procession of enemy aircraft flying north. "London is burning. London is burning," Robertson kept repeating. Returning to the city, they found flames sweeping through the East End, consuming dockyards, oil tanks, factories, overcrowded tenements, and everything else in their path. Hundreds of people had been killed, thousands injured or driven from their homes. Under a blood-red moon, women pushed prams piled high with their salvaged belongings.

That horrific evening marked the beginning of the Blitz: from September 7 on, London would endure fifty-seven straight nights of relentless bombing. Until then, no other city in history had ever been subjected to such an onslaught. Warsaw and Rotterdam had been heavily bombed by the Germans early in the war, but not for the length of time of the assault on London.

Although the working-class East End suffered frequent batterings that autumn and winter, no London neighborhood was immune. The fashionable shopping areas of Bond Street and Regent Street were blasted to pieces, the pavements covered with so much shattered glass from department store windows that the scene looked like the aftermath of an unseasonable snowstorm. On Oxford Street, the John Lewis department store was a burned-out ruin. Ten Downing Street suffered bomb damage, as did the Colonial Office, Treasury, and Horse Guards building. Hardly a pane of glass was left in the War Office after one raid, and Buckingham Palace was hit several times. As the Canadian diplomat Charles Ritchie wrote in his diary, every resident of London, regardless of where he or she lived, was "as continually alive to danger as animals in the jungle."

That included the American war correspondents, who no longer were impartial observers with the ability to witness frontline action and then withdraw to the safety of the rear to file their stories. Coming from a country that prided itself on being immune to attack by a foreign power, some had trouble accepting the fact that safety wasn't an option anymore. "You can't do this to me. I'm an American," Eric Sevareid remembered thinking on the first night of the Blitz. "Luckily," he added, "that moment was brief."

The reporters' personal experience in the Blitz became a key element in their coverage. Their empathy with Londoners was strengthened by the fact that they, too, were London residents under fire. They felt the same paralyzing fear when listening to the high-pitched whistle of a falling bomb, the same overwhelming sense of relief when it exploded some distance away. "Like everyone else, I too got to understand the sensation of the frailty of human existence," Ben Robertson wrote. "You were never free from the feeling that death was close— there was always the tension."

Yet, for a number of the American reporters, life was not nearly as dangerous as it was for many citizens of the capital. With their lavish expense accounts, they could afford to live in the city's modern luxury hotels and apartment buildings, whose steel frames were thought to offer considerably more protection than most of London's structures. Ben Robertson stayed at Claridge's, Vincent Sheean at the Dorchester. Quentin Reynolds had a flat at Lansdowne House in Berkeley Square, where he kept three goldfish in the bidet and shared a valet with another American reporter.

In November 1940, correspondents for the *New York Times* and *New York Herald Tribune* moved into the Savoy, where they set up offices. Other reporters followed. The Savoy not only boasted one of the deepest, most luxurious shelters in town but also one of the best restaurants, located in the underground River Room, whose heavy curtains and dance floor orchestra helped shut out the crash of gun barrages outside. Just by walking through the Savoy's revolving door, one was transported from the havoc of war to "the same luxury and brightness and crowds of people that you can find in any good New York hotel," wrote the columnist Ernie Pyle. "The reception clerks were all in tuxedos. The bellboys were in gray uniforms. The elevator operators wore wing collars." Said one wartime resident: "Once inside the Savoy, you'd hardly know there was a war within a thousand miles." The hotel's American Bar became the favored hangout for U.S. journalists—

so much so that Douglas Williams, a Ministry of Information official, moved his nightly briefings for the Americans to the bar, where he held forth, cocktail in hand.

ALTHOUGH ED MURROW came to the Savoy for an occasional drink or dinner, he did not follow his colleagues' example and take up residence there. He and Janet stayed in their apartment block on Hallam Street, which was now deserted except for them and another tenant. Their neighborhood of elegant Regency townhouses and small apartment buildings near Broadcasting House, a prime German bombing target, had become a perilous place in which to live. Although the Murrows' building was never hit, many of the houses and shops around them were demolished. The CBS office, also near the BBC, was bombed in the early days of the Blitz; once relocated, it was hit twice more.

Having lived in London longer than most of his American counterparts, Murrow knew the city better and arguably loved it more. As the bombs rained down, he much preferred roaming its neighborhoods to sitting in hotel bars or interviewing MPs and Whitehall officials. He did cover the government's activities, of course, but more often he yielded to his compulsion to be out on the street, often during the heaviest raids, to find out how the people of London were faring. His BBC friends called him their "messenger from hell," who, disheveled, dusty, and "shaken to the core," would return to Broadcasting House every night to tell them what he had seen outside and then do the same for his listeners at home.

"Words are such puny things," he said once. "There are no words to describe the things that are happening." In his broadcasts, though, he always managed to find them. He was a virtuoso of words, a master at painting verbal portraits of a drama that still seemed distant and incomprehensible to many Americans. Only by putting his listeners in other people's minds and hearts, he believed, would the war begin to have real meaning for them. "He made everything concrete and specific," Eric Sevareid recalled. "He got down to the bare bones of things." Through the "spoken word," added the BBC's Godfrey Talbot, Murrow was able to "give you a picture of what things felt like, smelt like, burned like. . . . So you, the listener, felt yourself standing beside him on the streets of London."

In one broadcast, he described rescue workers tunneling through the wreckage of a bombed-out house, gently lifting out limp figures "looking like broken, castaway, dust-covered dolls." After visiting a makeshift shelter in one of London's Underground stations, he talked of the "cold, choking fog" that had seeped into the shelter and noted how, after his visit, he climbed the stairs "into the damp darkness of the night, pursued by the sound of coughing." In yet another report, he gave his listeners a look at a London antiaircraft battery in action: "They're working in their shirtsleeves, laughing and cursing as they shove the shells into their guns. The spotters and detectors swing slowly around in their reclining carriage. The lens of the night glasses look like the eyes of an overgrown owl in the orange-blue light that belches from the muzzle of the gun."

The Londoners he mentioned in his broadcasts were those for whom Murrow had the greatest admiration. For all the satisfaction he took in associating with Britain's rich and powerful, he felt a much stronger kinship with the middle- and working-class people who bore the brunt of the Blitz—"the little people who live in those little houses, who have no uniforms, who get no decorations for bravery" but who were "exceedingly brave, tough, and prudent." In the Battle of London, the frontline troops were not the toffs of the West End, but the firemen, wardens, doctors, nurses, clergymen, telephone repairmen, and other workers who nightly risked their lives to aid the wounded, retrieve the dead, and bring their battered city back to life. In his broadcasts, Murrow repeatedly focused on these "unsung heroes" who went about their work with bombs falling around them—"those black-faced men with bloodshot eyes fighting fires, the girls who cradle the steering wheel of a heavy ambulance in their arms, the policeman who stands guard over that unexploded bomb."

Like other American reporters, Murrow was struck by the calmness, fortitude, and ironic humor exhibited by Londoners during these days and nights of terror. He enjoyed repeating to his friends the question that one city resident put to him at the height of the Luftwaffe assault: "Do you think we're really brave—or just lacking in imagination?" As Eric Sevareid observed, "This is what he loved about the British. They were steady. They didn't panic, didn't get emotional."

In mid-October, a bomb crashed into the BBC, destroying the music library and several studios and killing seven staffers, several of them friends of Murrow's. The explosion occurred while the announcer Bruce Belfrage was reading the nine o'clock news. Listeners heard a thud, a short pause, and a whispered "Are you all right?" Then, after blowing plaster dust off his script, Belfrage continued with the news. Murrow, who was at the BBC at the time of the blast, told his listeners: "I've seen some horrible sights in this city . . . but not once have I heard man, woman, or child suggest that Britain should throw in her hand."

Indeed, in the midst of the devastation, most Londoners demonstrated a dogged determination to live as normal a life as possible: it was their way of thumbing their nose at Hitler. Each morning, millions of people left their shelters or basements and, despite the constant disruption of the train and Underground systems, went to work as usual, many hitchhiking or walking ten or more miles a day. Their commutes, which frequently involved long detours around collapsed buildings, impassable streets, and unexploded bombs, could take hours. Of the staff at Claridge's, Ben Robertson noted after a particularly violent raid: "Everyone was red-eyed and tired, but they were all there." The head waiter's house had been demolished during the night, but he had shown up, as had the woman who cleaned Robertson's room. "She was buried three hours in the basement of her house," another maid told Robertson. "Three hours! And she got to work this morning as usual."

FOR ALL THE FEAR, pain, and destruction of the Blitz, there was an excitement, a sense of energy about living in London during that period that, in the view of many who were there, was never to be equaled. The threat of death seemed only to heighten the exhilaration and elation of survival. "You walk through the streets . . . and everyone you pass seems to be pulsating with life," Quentin Reynolds wrote in his diary. Ben Robertson later observed: "The city in this crisis had rediscovered itself; it was living as it never had lived. . . . You came out on the street at daybreak now with the feeling that you personally had been helping to save the world."

American correspondents who left London for brief respites in the United States or other neutral countries initially looked forward to getting away from the relentless dread and terror. But, having arrived in their boltholes, many felt a sense of alienation from the people living there, who had no idea of what it was like to live on a battlefield, and they yearned to be back in London. The experience of Robertson, who spent a few days in neutral Ireland, was typical: "It was like reaching heaven to arrive in Dublin from the battleground of London. All the burden of war was lifted from you, and there were lights on and a feeling of airiness, and suddenly you were free." At the same time, he noted, it was "a profoundly disturbing" experience. "All the good life made you very restless. You found when you were away from London . . . you could not keep from worrying. You worried about London and about everyone you knew in London."

For the reporters who left the British capital for good, there was often a deep sense of loss. In mid-October, Eric Sevareid, ill and exhausted, was transferred to Washington by CBS. Four months earlier, after the fall of France, the twenty-seven-year-old Minnesota native had arrived in England with a chip on his shoulder. Like many Americans, he had a deep streak of Anglophobia, disliking, among other things, the way that certain Britons—"stiff dowagers, professional army officers, high-ranking civil servants" among them—made him feel uncomfortable and inadequate by what he perceived as their haughty, patronizing manner. Having seen the collapse of the vaunted French army, he also doubted the ability of the smug, insular British, as he viewed them, to stand up to Hitler.

By October, his doubts and antagonisms had vanished. Once an "American stranger" in London, he now felt himself to be part of that embattled community. Britain and its capital, he wrote years later, "showed the world a face it had not seen before in this war. During those bright days and livid nights of 1940, the spirit of the British called up from despair the spirit of other men. . . . It was this spirit and example which overbore the defeatists in the United States. . . . Americans thought they were saving Britain—and they were. But the spirit and example of Britain also were saving America."

When Sevareid returned home, he emphasized to anyone who would listen the importance of helping the British. A number of the American correspondents who remained in London had their own roles to play in the pro-British propaganda effort. Well aware of the influence of Murrow and the others with the U.S. public, officials in Whitehall sought to capitalize on the reporters' sympathy and identification with Britain and its people. "They are extremely friendly to us, and they can be relied upon to see that our side of the case is put forward, always providing that it is given accurately and quickly to them," wrote Ronald Tree, who joined the Ministry of Information in May 1940.

Some American journalists, including Murrow himself, agreed to narrate British news documentaries aimed at their countrymen, showing Britons' resolve in standing up to the German onslaught. The most famous of the films was *London Can Take It!*, a ten-minute short about Londoners' response to the Blitz, narrated by Quentin Reynolds. The Ministry of Information had originally suggested that Mary Welsh, a reporter for *Time* and *Life* in London (and the future wife of Ernest Hemingway), do the commentary, but the film's director, Harry Watt, hated the idea of a female narrator and chose Reynolds instead.

The filmmakers, however, had a difficult time with the *Collier's* star. Having previously proven his courage in war zones all over the world, he refused to leave the underground American Bar at the Savoy to cover the nightly German raids, admitting later how much he "hated and dreaded" the attacks. Reynolds also had no broadcasting experience, and he initially "bellowed out" the commentary, which he had written, "like a barker in a fairground." Watt and his team finally recorded Reynolds's voice-over in the Savoy bar, "sticking the microphone nearly down his throat" to produce a whispered growl that captured the fancy of America. "I am a neutral reporter," his narration began. "I have watched the people of London live and die . . . I can assure you there is no panic, no fear, no despair in London town."

Warner Brothers, which distributed *London Can Take It!* in the United States, rushed out six hundred prints in early November 1940; the film was featured by eight theaters in downtown New York City alone. An enormous success, it eventually was shown at more than twelve thousand theaters throughout the country. Only Reynolds's name appeared in the film's credits, leading his fellow Americans to believe that it was the unbiased personal report of a U.S. reporter— "a belief that Quent did not battle to belie," Watt recalled.

Reynolds, who had gone to the United States to promote the short, returned to London "an international figure," Watt added, "and amused us by growling sotto voce all the time." But what really tickled the British film team and Reynolds's American compatriots in London was a poster for the film that he brought back, depicting him wearing a tin hat, gazing defiantly at the sky, and warding off a five-hundred-pound bomb with his right arm. "It must have been a lot tougher in the Savoy than we thought," Watt observed.

While Reynolds was working on *London Can Take It!*, Murrow wrote and recorded the commentary for *This Is England*, a full-length feature that also documented British resistance to the Blitz but in much greater detail than the Reynolds short. Churchill reportedly cried when he saw the Murrow film, and President Roosevelt screened it at the White House. It, too, was a major hit.

IN THEIR ADVOCACY of the British cause, there was no question that Murrow and the other American reporters in London were blurring the line between journalism and propaganda. At the very least, they were violating journalistic standards of objectivity—reporting news without personal prejudice, opinion, or point of view. Objectivity is a criterion that has been debated for as long as journalism has existed; in the view of many if not most journalists, it's an impossible standard to meet, since reporters are not robots, with blank slates for minds.

But objectivity and neutrality had been mantras for CBS News from the beginning of the war, ever since the Roosevelt administration, fearing that the broadcast networks would rouse war fever in their audiences, started dropping hints about putting them under federal control. Noting that radio was a "rookie" at handling war stories, White House press secretary Stephen Early warned the networks to behave like "a good child."

At the outset of the conflict, William Paley, the chairman of CBS, decreed that analysis would be allowed on his network, but not opinion. Murrow made mincemeat of that policy from the start. The network, although reproving him occasionally, did little to stop him. "He made no pretense about being neutral or objective," Eric Sevareid observed. "As a reporter, his heart and soul was 'the cause.' . . . He was convinced we'd have to be in the war." Murrow wrote to his brother in early 1941: "I have no desire to use the studio as a privileged pulpit, but I am convinced that some very plain talking is required, even if it be at the price of being labeled a 'warmonger.' . . . I am convinced that the hour is much later than most people at home appreciate."

He subscribed to the view of objectivity set forth years later by a BBC director general, Sir Hugh Carleton Greene, who said that the BBC was objective "except where the fundamental truths of life were concerned. It did not propose ever to be objective about injustice, intolerance, or prejudice." In Europe, Murrow observed to his wife, people were dying and "a thousand years of history and civilization [were] being smashed" while America remained on the sidelines. How could one possibly be objective or neutral about that? "He wanted the Americans to face up to their responsibilities," said BBC correspondent Thomas Barman. "They either had to see the whole Western world go down . . . or stand up and fight."

On September 30, 1940, the second anniversary of the Munich agreement and the end of the Blitz's first month, Murrow tartly told his listeners: "Perhaps you can relax as these people did after Munich. . . . But consider what's happened in the last two years and try to ignore what the next two years will bring—if you can." More often, though, he did not resort to this kind of overt, if craftily worded, advocacy to try to affect American public opinion. He did it through his word pictures of the British at war. "Murrow and his colleagues offered something akin to drama: the vicarious experience of what they were living and observing," noted the broadcast historian Erik Barnouw. "It put the listener in another man's shoes. No better way to influence opinion has ever been found."

Yet, while his broadcasts were generally laudatory of the British, he did not refrain from pointing out what he viewed as the shortcomings of their country and its leaders. He was, for example, one of the most outspoken critics of the British government's penchant for secrecy, which led to extremely tight censorship and withholding of war news. He was also sharply critical of the government's failure to provide decent air raid shelters for the residents of the East End and other working-class areas. "Every shelter is a stinking hole," his wife wrote home.

AS 1940 CAME to its inglorious end, Murrow, like most Londoners, was exhausted. It had been impossible for anybody to get a decent night's sleep during the Blitz; most people were lucky if they snatched three or four hours. As the bombing continued, the novelist Elizabeth Bowen wrote, the city's residents became "disembodied" by tiredness. "The night behind and the night to come met across every noon in an arch of strain. To work or think was to ache."

But even when the Luftwaffe attacks began to lessen in November, Murrow, who had lost thirty pounds in the previous four months, continued living and working like a man possessed. "He looked like a ghost, pale and shaken," a CBS colleague recalled. "I thought he was going to keel over." Increasingly moody and short-tempered, he spent little time with his wife, who later wrote, "Sometimes he seemed not to have any energy for me." Said a friend: "He internalizes world events. They flow right through him like a stream. The fall of Britain would have been as meaningful to him as the loss of a child to one of us."

Taking advantage of a lull in the bombing in late December, Janet Murrow persuaded her husband to spend a relatively relaxed Christmas at home. On December 29, however, the capital's holiday quiet was shattered when German bombers unleashed a ten-hour firestorm on the City, Britain's financial and commercial center and one of London's most historic districts. The most devastating conflagration to sweep through the area since the Great Fire of 1666, it destroyed, among other landmarks, eight churches designed by Christopher Wren and much of the medieval Guildhall, the seat of the city's municipal government since William the Conqueror. Miraculously, St. Paul's Cathedral, looming high in the middle of the inferno, managed to survive. As Murrow walked home early the next morning, he noticed that "the windows in the West End were red with reflected fire, and the raindrops were like blood on the panes."

Two nights later, he spoke with barely suppressed emotion and an edge of anger as he contrasted for his listeners the New Year's Eve celebrations they were enjoying with the bleak experience of most London residents: "You will have no dawn raid, as we shall probably have if the weather is right. You may walk this night in the light. Your families are not scattered by the winds of war. You may drive your high-powered car as far as time and money will permit."

He concluded: "You have not been promised blood and toil and tears and sweat. Yet it is the opinion of nearly every informed observer over here that the decision you take will overshadow all else during this year that opened a few hours ago in London."

A decision, he knew, that could well decide the fate of Britain.

3.

THE OPPORTUNITY
OF A LIFETIME

Six weeks after Ed Murrow's somber New Year's Eve broadcast, Franklin Roosevelt summoned W. Averell Harriman to the Oval Office. Halfway through their rambling discussion, the president offhandedly mentioned he planned to dispatch Harriman to London to oversee the flow of American aid under the Lend-Lease program, which was about to be approved after a bruising fight in Congress.

For the forty-nine-year-old heir to one of America's greatest railroad fortunes, the chat with the president was an oddly unsettling experience. Here FDR was, talking as if it had long been understood that Harriman would get this vital job, when just a few weeks earlier, the White House had brushed him off when he had volunteered his services. In truth, until that moment, Roosevelt had shown little interest in appointing Harriman to anything of substance. In the thirty-five years they had known each other, the president had not been impressed with either the intelligence or personality of the dark-haired, square-jawed man sitting across the desk from him.

The two had numerous social links. Both had grown up on sprawling Hudson River estates; Harriman had been a friend of Eleanor Roosevelt's younger brother, Hall; and Harriman's and FDR's mothers had known each other for years. Moreover, Harriman's older sister, Mary Rumsey, a fervent social reformer and New Dealer, headed the administration's Consumer Advisory Board and was a close colleague of the president's wife.

Yet, despite those connections, the Roosevelts, who were one of the

Hudson Valley's most prominent patrician families, had never quite accepted the nouveau riche Harrimans, whose vast wealth had been derived from means that many people considered ill-gotten. As the man who built the Union Pacific into the most dominant railroad in the country, E. H. Harriman, Averell's father, had won international notoriety as one of America's most powerful robber barons. According to President Theodore Roosevelt, the elder Harriman was among the most egregious "malefactors of great wealth" that the United States had ever seen.

While Franklin Roosevelt had chosen a life in public service, Averell Harriman had followed in his father's footsteps as an aggressive, hard-driving businessman. The emotional opposite of FDR, Harriman had none of the president's charm, gregariousness, interest in people, or sense of fun. He hated gossip and small talk and was renowned for his lack of a sense of humor, especially about himself. Brusque and impatient, he was intensely pragmatic, even in his closest friendships. Harriman "was no good at human relations," said Robert Meiklejohn, his longtime assistant. "God only knows how many thousands of hours I spent in his company, but I do not know one interesting anecdote about his personal life."

Although Harriman had run several businesses by the time of the White House meeting and was currently chairman of Union Pacific, Roosevelt regarded him for the most part as a dilettante sportsman and playboy. He had become a champion polo player in the late 1920s, devoting more than a year to the effort, and in the 1930s had developed Sun Valley, Idaho, as one of the country's preeminent ski resorts. Notwithstanding his dour personality, the twice-married Harriman had also gained a reputation as an inveterate womanizer, with at least one scandalous love affair to his credit. He was catnip to many women—courtly and shy, with a dash of vulnerability, and, despite his legendary stinginess, willing to lavish money on his girlfriends. "He was good-looking, affluent and very aloof back then, which made him quite a lady's man," recalled John McCloy, an assistant secretary of war under FDR, who, as a Wall Street lawyer, had served on the Union Pacific board.

Harriman also had a reputation for spreading money around if it would help him in Washington. "He used to subsidize politicians . . . so that he would have a line into power," McCloy remarked. Like Gil Winant, Harriman had deserted the Republican Party to support

Roosevelt for president. Unlike the new ambassador to Britain, however, Harriman's involvement in the New Deal stemmed not from an interest in helping the common man but in promoting business recovery from the Depression. And also unlike Winant, he believed in covering his bets. After the 1940 election, Roosevelt mentioned to his Republican opponent, Wendell Willkie, that Harriman had contributed $25,000 to his campaign. "Confidentially, Franklin, he contributed $25,000 to mine," Willkie shot back. What's more, Harriman had told a friend before the election that if Willkie won, he'd be happy to join his administration.

On the fringes of the New Deal since 1933, Harriman was desperate for a more important position on Roosevelt's team. And for all his misgivings about Harriman's ambition, loyalty, and sense of purpose, the president was finally persuaded by Harry Hopkins, his closest adviser and another of those whom Harriman had cultivated, to give the wealthy businessman a chance. He would go to London as Roosevelt's Lend-Lease liaison with Churchill and the British government.

It was the job Harriman wanted—indeed, lusted after. Yet, while thrilled with the assignment, he was discomfited by what he perceived as the president's nonchalant attitude toward Lend-Lease. Though he yearned to be at the center of things, he had sought the position because he strongly believed that the United States was obliged to save Britain from defeat. "Are we willing to face a world dominated by Hitler?" he asked in a speech at New York's Yale Club a few days before his meeting with Roosevelt. "If not, we still have time to aid Britain. . . . The most fatal error would be half-hearted and insufficient help."

After the Oval Office session, however, he was unsure whether the president shared his sense of urgency. Throughout the meeting, Roosevelt was vague about the parameters of Lend-Lease and, indeed, about Harriman's post, offering him no guidance and giving him no instructions other than to take a look around Britain and "recommend everything that we can do, short of war, to keep the British Isles afloat." The president "was a bit foggy as to whom I was to work with on this side as he had not yet set up the lend-lease organization," Harriman wrote in a memo to himself shortly after the meeting. "He said I was to communicate with him on any matters that I thought were important enough."

Later that day, when Roosevelt broke the news of Harriman's appointment to White House reporters, he was just as airy and imprecise. Harriman, the president said, would leave for London "as soon as the defense program under the Lend-Spend, Lend-Lease—whatever you call it—bill is perfected. I suppose you will ask about his title, so I thought I would invent one. . . . We decided it was a pretty good idea to call him an 'expediter.' " He laughed. "There's a new one for you."

"Mr. President," one of the journalists called out, "what is Mr. Harriman's relation to our embassy over there? Does he represent you directly?" With a snort, Roosevelt replied, "I don't know, and I don't give a damn!" When another reporter asked whom Harriman would report to in Washington, the president retorted: "I don't know, and I don't care."

Yet, as Harriman thought about it, Roosevelt's haziness, though worrisome in one sense, was the opportunity of a lifetime in another. With few strictures on his actions, he could, with any luck, turn this job into something much more meaningful and important than anyone, including the president, had in mind. And if he accomplished that, he might—finally—emerge from the all-encompassing shadow of E. H. Harriman.

AS A TEENAGER, Averell had grown considerably taller than his diminutive father, yet in other ways, he never felt he measured up. A titan of American business, the elder Harriman had put the fear of God in nearly everyone—from his railroad competitors to the outlaws Butch Cassidy and the Sundance Kid, who regularly robbed his trains until Harriman set a band of relentless Pinkerton detectives on their trail.

Young Averell was under constant pressure to live up to his father's expectations. His relationship with E.H., according to his biographer Rudy Abramson, was "a never-ending lesson in discipline, striving, and self improvement." His stepdaughter noted that Averell "had no fun. He was a child who never learned to express himself." Having received little warmth or outward signs of love and encouragement from his parents, Harriman "needed reinforcement for his self-esteem" throughout his life, said a friend.

He attended Groton, the exclusive prep school in northern Massachusetts, which, like St. Paul's, was modeled after Eton. An undistinguished student, Harriman went on to Yale, where he was tapped for

Skull and Bones, the school's most prestigious secret society, and became coach of Yale's freshman rowing crew. Determined to help Yale regain its former rowing glory over Harvard, he took a six-week leave from classes in his sophomore year for a trip to England to learn from the masters of the sport—the vaunted crews of Oxford. That sort of intensely competitive move was typical of Harriman. "He went into any game lock, stock, and barrel," recalled the former defense secretary Robert Lovett, whose father had been a close associate of E. H. Harriman's and who had known Averell since early childhood. "He would get whatever he needed—the best horses, coaches, equipment, his own bowling alley or croquet lawn—and work like the devil to win."

While his grades were as mediocre at Yale as they had been at Groton, Harriman's education at those two schools gave him a priceless advantage. Like the sons of British industrialists who attended Eton and Oxford, he was given an entrée into his country's elite old-boy network, which presided over the business, social, and government establishments. Among his fellow Yale alumni were Lovett and Dean Acheson, who, like Harriman himself, would go on to play major roles in the emergence of the United States as the leading world power in the 1940s and 1950s.

Four years after Harriman's graduation from Yale, the United States entered World War I, but, unlike most of his college classmates, he chose not to enlist. Instead, with his mother's financial backing, he bought a shipyard in Chester, Pennsylvania, hoping to capitalize on the skyrocketing demand for merchant shipping created by the war. According to his mother, Averell was "trying to match in shipping what his father had achieved as a railroad man." He ended up controlling one of the largest merchant fleets in the world. Once the war was over, however, the enterprise lost considerably more money than it made, and in 1925, he sold out to a German firm.

Harriman spent most of the 1920s chasing business deals all over Europe: a manganese concession in the Soviet Union, coal mines in Silesia, waterworks and streetcar lines in Cologne, steel mills and an electric power plant in Poland. During his travels, he met some of the most important figures in Britain and on the Continent, among them Vladimir Lenin, Benito Mussolini, and Winston Churchill, who was then British chancellor of the exchequer. Throughout his very long life, Harriman relished meeting and befriending powerful people, collecting them, E. J. Kahn Jr. wrote in *The New Yorker*, the way a philatelist collects rare stamps. "Averell's a power snob," said one of his associates. "His attitude always is: 'There's only one guy worth talking to in any situation—the top guy—and I'm the guy who talks to him.'"

The chairman of his family's investment firm, W. A. Harriman and Company, Harriman was far more successful as a deal maker than as a manager. After acquiring a new business, he usually showed little interest in its actual operation, and most of his enterprises failed. His reputation as a playboy was already firmly in place, and, in the view of the other partners at W. A. Harriman, the company would have been far better off if its chairman had spent less time amusing himself and more time running his businesses during his lengthy trips abroad.

His pleasure-seeking image was reinforced in 1928 when he took a sabbatical from the business world and devoted his relentless energy to mastering his new obsession, polo. After becoming one of the top polo players in the country, he returned to his family's business empire and took over the chairmanship of Union Pacific. Seeking to develop new tourist traffic for his railroad, he spent most of the next few years building and promoting Sun Valley, turning it into the most popular ski resort in the nation.

But as successful as Sun Valley was, both it and its founder were regarded as frivolous by much of the country's business and political elite. The fact that Harriman had chosen to profit from World War I, rather than fight in it, was also held against him. Some of his friends from Yale considered his behavior shameful; several would not speak to him for years. "Averell was regarded as something much less than the beau ideal during those days," noted Bob Lovett, who, like Gil Winant, had been a pilot in France during the war. The issue was a sensitive one for Harriman, who, many years later, acknowledged: "Intellectually, I could reason that I had done the right thing because I thought that shipping was the real bottleneck of World War I. But emotionally, I never felt entirely comfortable."

Increasingly restless and eager to embark on new ventures, Harriman turned his attention in the early 1930s to Washington and the New Deal. Thanks to the activist Roosevelt administration, the power in the country had shifted from Wall Street to Pennsylvania Avenue, and Harriman, who had never been involved in politics before, was anxious to become part of the action in the nation's capital.

He was far more interested, however, in reviving American business than in the New Deal's other main focus: promoting economic and social reform. When he finally landed a job, it was as special assistant to Hugh Johnson, head of the National Recovery Administration, who, like Harriman, was focused on business resuscitation. In 1934, Harriman was appointed chief administrative officer of the National Industrial Recovery Board, but he was never given a major New Deal post and, after a year in Washington, returned to Union Pacific. Nonetheless, he remained in close contact with the administration, sending FDR frequent notes and gifts, such as pheasants shot on his estate in upstate New York and bottles of vintage wine. He also wangled an appointment to the president's Business Advisory Council, a group of prominent businessmen (dubbed "Roosevelt's tame millionaires" by New Deal critics) that served as the administration's conduit to big business.

When the administration began a hesitant mobilization for war in the spring of 1940, Roosevelt summoned several business and industrial leaders to Washington to help guide the effort. Harriman was not among them. He was deeply upset by his exclusion, not only because of his desire for power but because he firmly believed that the United States should be more assertive in the fight against Hitler and Mussolini. Like other major Wall Street figures who had invested in the rehabilitation of the Continent after World War I, Harriman was an internationalist who felt that America had a responsibility to the rest of the world and, particularly, to Europe. "Anyone who says we are not affected [by the war in Europe] and its results is not facing reality," he said in early 1940. "America has a destiny at this particular moment in the world's history." As some of his friends saw it, Harriman's commitment to intervention was also a way to atone for his evasion of military service in World War I, which continued to be a major embarrassment.

Whatever the reason, he remained outspoken about the need for America's government and business community to give Britain and France whatever supplies and arms they needed. Wherever he traveled on Union Pacific business, he wrote to a friend, he found that the people he met were not only far more willing to provide aid to Britain and its ally, France, than Roosevelt and his men believed but were desperate for leadership from the White House. "There is a sense of frustration," Harriman added. "People want to know what we are going to do as a nation and what they can do as individuals to help." He clearly counted himself among the frustrated.

In June 1940, Harriman finally was summoned to Washington to advise the government on how best to coordinate the transport of raw materials for the mobilization effort. But he considered it an inconsequential job and, from the day he arrived in the capital, he was determined to find a way to play a more active and substantive part in America's lurch toward war. To help him reach that goal, he turned to a master of Washington intrigue who was said to combine the wiliest qualities of Machiavelli, Svengali, and Rasputin: his friend Harry Hopkins.

WITH HIS UNRIVALED influence and access to the president, the fifty-one-year-old Hopkins was widely regarded as the second most powerful man in Washington. Next to Roosevelt, he was also the most reviled.

The sallow-faced presidential adviser, with his penetrating eyes and sharp features, had been a New Deal lightning rod for nearly a decade, virtually from the day he first came to Washington to direct the administration's massive emergency relief and jobs programs. Hopkins's job had been to spend money, and, as one historian put it, he "spent more of it than any man ever had in the history of the world"—more than $9 billion. On his watch, millions of unemployed persons received emergency aid and then were put back to work, their government-funded jobs ranging from building roads and preventing floods to writing books and painting murals.

A zealot when it came to helping the poor, Hopkins, a former social worker, saw his mission as providing the greatest number of jobs in the shortest amount of time. As long as that goal was achieved, he didn't particularly care how it was done. According to Harold Smith, director of Roosevelt's Bureau of the Budget, Hopkins "was bound by no preconceived notions, no legal inhibitions, and . . . absolutely no respect for tradition." He was accused by his many critics of being slapdash and reckless in administering the programs under his charge, resulting in widespread inefficiency, corruption, and waste of government funds. "Harry never had the faintest conception of the value of money," said the head of a New York charitable organization for which Hopkins had worked in the 1920s.

While conservative opponents of the New Deal were the most vocal in their condemnation of Hopkins and his methods, he also had his share of enemies among the president's supporters. Many administration officials—among them Interior Secretary Harold Ickes, who was regularly outmaneuvered by Hopkins in their frequent bureaucratic duels—resented his intimacy with the president and considered him a malign influence and a political liability for Roosevelt. Hopkins's key role in the attempted 1938 purge of conservative Democrats in Congress and his ruthless tactics, as FDR's chief political operative, in assuring the nominations of Roosevelt and Henry Wallace during the 1940 presidential convention, contributed greatly to that hostility.*

A man of razor-sharp wit, with "a tongue like a skinning knife and a temper like a Tartar," Hopkins responded to his critics by thumbing his nose at them, which only enraged them more. Calling reporters into his shabby, paper-strewn office to answer the latest charges against him, he would slouch in his chair, feet propped up on the desk, and inhale deeply from a cigarette. Then, recalled Marquis Childs of the *St. Louis Post-Dispatch*, "he would snarl back at his prosecutors. . . . He was rarely tactful or tactical. Only half trying, you could get out of him a fine, angry contempt for all [his enemies]."

Hopkins could hurl his insults, secure in the knowledge of the president's appreciation of his tough-mindedness, skill, and all-consuming loyalty to the man he called the Boss. The ultimate White House insider, he had been living since 1939 in the room that once served as Lincoln's study, just down the hall from FDR's bedroom. His was a privileged position, as he well knew, and he was quite sure no one could dislodge him from it.

At one point, he even harbored political ambitions of his own, considering a possible run at the presidency in 1940 if Roosevelt retired after the traditional two terms. The president, of course, did not step down, but even if he had, Hopkins never could have pursued his dream. In 1937, shortly after the death of his second wife, he underwent surgery for stomach cancer. The operation, which removed most of his stomach, was successful, but for the rest of his relatively short life, he suffered from severe nutritional deficiencies and was often so ill he could not function. Nonetheless, in between his bouts of sickness,

* Many in the Democratic Party, even some who were fervent FDR supporters, were uncomfortable about his breaking precedent and seeking a third term. Democrats were also unhappy over Roosevelt's insistence that Wallace, who was the secretary of agriculture and who was unpopular with most of the party faithful, must be selected as his new vice presidential running mate.

Hopkins insisted on returning to work. During the next eight pain-filled years, he would provide his most valuable service for the president, with Averell Harriman acting as one of his chief associates.

HOPKINS'S FRIENDSHIP with Harriman was an outgrowth of his longtime fondness for high living and associating with the rich and famous. From the time he arrived in New York as a young social worker, Hopkins, a native of Grinnell, Iowa, combined a devotion to the poor with a penchant for nightclubs, speakeasies, and racetracks. When he became a key figure in the New Deal two decades later, he cultivated—and was cultivated by—the relatively progressive members of New York's business elite, as well as by its literary and artistic crowd. His weekends were often spent at Harriman's forty-bedroom estate in the Hudson Valley or at the Long Island mansion of the famed newspaper editor Herbert Bayard Swope, where he would play croquet and poker with the likes of Bernard Baruch, William Paley, George S. Kaufman, and John Hay Whitney.

While hardly handsome, Hopkins was witty and charming when he wanted to be—attributes that he used to advantage in his relentless pursuit of beautiful women. "He was pleased and rather proud whenever the hostile press denounced him as a 'playboy,'" the playwright Robert Sherwood wrote. "That made him feel glamorous."

Hopkins and Harriman had been friends since 1933, but their relationship became considerably closer in late 1938, when Roosevelt decided to make Hopkins his secretary of commerce. Knowing that Hopkins was hardly a favorite with many U.S. business leaders, not to mention members of the Senate Commerce Committee, who would have to approve his nomination, Roosevelt asked Harriman to help him in the fight. The Union Pacific chairman persuaded the Business Advisory Council, which he headed at that point, to endorse Hopkins's appointment and then solicited letters of recommendation from other prominent businessmen. The campaign was successful, and after Hopkins was confirmed, Harriman accompanied him to Des Moines, where, in his first major speech as secretary, he played down his record as a social reformer and promised to promote business recovery "with all the vigor and power at [my] command." Harriman, a sour Harold Ickes would later write, "was always willing to scratch Harry Hopkins' back, just as Hopkins was willing to scratch his."

Hopkins's tenure at the Commerce Department was cut short by his recurring illness. After being hospitalized for several months, he returned to Roosevelt's service in November 1940, this time as the president's chief wartime operative and the man in charge of overseeing the country's industrial mobilization and rearmament. Working from a card table in his White House bedroom, Hopkins, who had no official title or job, was relentless in prodding, chastising, and encouraging the captains of business and industry to achieve production goals most believed were impossible.

In January 1941, with the Lend-Lease bill working its way through Congress, FDR gave his top aide a new assignment: to travel to London to determine Britain's defense needs and, even more important, to judge for himself whether the country could hold out against Germany. As he prepared for his mission, Hopkins made clear he planned to resist the famed persuasive talents of Winston Churchill, whose ego, he thought, was considerably greater than his ability. "I suppose Churchill is convinced that he's the greatest man in the world!" he exclaimed to a friend. "Harry," the friend replied, "if you're going to London with that chip on your shoulder, like a damned little small-town chauvinist, you may as well cancel your passage right now."

In London, Churchill responded with a puzzled "Who?" when told that a certain Harry Hopkins was coming to see him on behalf of the president. His advisers soon set him straight, telling him how close Hopkins was to Roosevelt and how important it was to impress him. Hopkins had been informed, they said, that Churchill was anti-Roosevelt. It was vital that the prime minister convince him that this wasn't so and that he held FDR in the highest possible regard.

Churchill did that—and more. He ordered a special train to transport Hopkins to London from the airfield where he landed and then entertained him at Downing Street and Chequers, the prime minister's official country residence in Buckinghamshire. His ministers were told to provide the American with any information he requested. Escorting Hopkins around his battered country, the prime minister introduced him to everyone they met as "the personal representative of the President of the United States."

In the five weeks Hopkins spent in Britain, he and the British leader became close friends. While the relationship between Churchill and Roosevelt has received considerably more attention from historians, the friendship between Hopkins and Churchill was, in fact, much warmer and more personal. Despite their exceedingly different backgrounds, Churchill recognized a kindred spirit in FDR's envoy. Brash and combative himself, he appreciated Hopkins's irreverence, humor-laced cynicism, and straightforward way of speaking. He was also greatly moved by the American's dedication and determination, not to mention his willingness to subject himself to the damp chill of an English winter when he was so obviously ill, keeping himself alive with the personal pharmacy of pills that he carried with him everywhere. In his memoirs, Churchill referred to Hopkins as "that extraordinary man . . . a crumbling lighthouse from which there shone the beams that led great fleets to harbour."

For his part, Hopkins became an unabashed admirer of the prime minister well before his visit was over. Churchill was neither anti-Roosevelt nor anti-America, he wrote FDR. He added: "Churchill is the gov't in every sense of the word. . . . I cannot emphasize too strongly that he is the one and only person over here with whom you need to have a full meeting of minds."

Despite his wisecracking and outward cynicism, Hopkins was somewhat awestruck by his experience in Britain—weekends at Chequers and Ronald Tree's Ditchley, his own valet at Claridge's, luncheon with the king and queen at Buckingham Palace. Here he was, a hick from Iowa, the son of a harness maker no less, now serving as the confidant of a British prime minister and the lunch partner of the queen of England. That same vague feeling of insecurity surfaced again, as he noted to columnist Marquis Childs, when he met Stalin later in the war. "It seemed to me a rather tragic and . . . poignant commentary on the man and . . . on America," Childs recalled. "In a sense it was a commentary on this fantastic role of responsibility and leadership into which we were precipitated, and our unreadiness for it, because at that moment you should not have been thinking about how you were the son of a harness maker."

Hopkins's emotional involvement with Churchill and Britain grew stronger as his visit progressed—an involvement reflected in his impromptu remarks at a dinner in his honor in Scotland in mid-January 1941. "I suppose you wish to know what I am going to say to President Roosevelt on my return," he said to the guests seated before him. Then, turning to Churchill, he quoted a verse from the Bible's Book of Ruth: "Whither thou goest, I will go; and where thou lodgest, I will lodge; thy people shall be my people, and thy God my God." Pausing, he added quietly: "Even to the end." Churchill's eyes welled with tears. Hopkins's heartfelt remarks gave him and his countrymen a new surge of hope that America was on the brink of ending her neutrality—a hope that, unfortunately for them, did not accord with reality.

When he returned to the United States, Hopkins was "a completely changed man," with a "fuller sense of urgency," in the words of the columnists Joseph Alsop and Robert Kintner. Before leaving for home in mid-February, he cabled Roosevelt: "This island needs our help now, Mr. President, with everything we can give them . . . our decisive action now can mean the difference between defeat and victory in this country."

When his flying boat touched down in New York harbor in February 1941, he was met on the dock by Gil Winant, whose appointment as ambassador had just been announced, and also by Averell Harriman. Shortly before Hopkins left for London, Harriman had begged to be allowed to go along. "Let me carry your bag, Harry," he pleaded. "I've met Churchill several times and I know London intimately." Hopkins turned him down but hinted that the president "might have something" for him later. Determined not to let the opportunity escape, Harriman made sure he was in the welcoming committee on Hopkins's arrival.

The day after Hopkins returned to Washington, he convinced Roosevelt that he needed someone in London to coordinate Lend-Lease aid. That person, he said, was Averell Harriman. With some hesitation, the president agreed, and the following day, summoned Harriman to the White House.

WHEN THE SENATE finally (and grudgingly) passed the Lend-Lease bill on March 8, FDR told reporters: "Here in Washington, we are thinking in terms of speed, and speed now. And I hope that that watchword—'speed, and speed now'—will find its way into every home in the nation."

But, as Harriman discovered while preparing for his new assignment, Roosevelt's statement had little basis in truth. Although Washington was struggling hard to come to life in early 1941, it still had not discovered the virtue of speed. For journalists who had been assigned to this languid, slow-paced city after covering Britain's desperate struggle to survive, it seemed complacent and insular—"so orderly and sanitary after the rubble and stench of bombed-out London."

James Reston of the *New York Times,* who, like Eric Sevareid, had been transferred from London to Washington in the fall of 1940, called his new posting "a pleasant place, if you lived in the 'right' part of town and didn't read or think." For his part, Sevareid considered Washington a "leafy, dreaming park" and "clean, well-hedged suburb to the nation," isolated from reality and unable to grasp the significance of the chaos spreading over the globe. David Brinkley, who came to wartime Washington as a young reporter for a North Carolina newspaper, later referred to it as "a town and a government entirely unprepared to take on the global responsibilities suddenly thrust upon it."

Stumbling along, trying to energize itself into becoming a major world capital, Washington was engaged in frantic improvisation. "It is difficult to exaggerate the bewilderment and frenzied uncertainty that prevailed in Washington in those days," noted Robert Sherwood, who had switched from playwriting to writing speeches for Roosevelt in late 1940. Having promised Lend-Lease aid to Britain and now immersed in preparing America for possible war, Washington was grappling with several urgent priorities, including the control of prices, allocation of raw materials, and the refitting of existing factories and construction of new ones for defense work.

In the view of many, the job of defense production and mobilization should have been assigned to a single government agency, headed by an official with the power to coerce obedience from private business and industry. Henry Stimson, Henry Morgenthau, and Bernard Baruch were among those who urged Roosevelt to appoint such a mobilization czar. But the president was having none of it. Loath as always to yield authority and power, he insisted on retaining administrative control. In early January 1941, he set up the Office of Production Management, the first in a series of agencies whose ostensible job it was to manage a wartime economy. But OPM would be given no real power: it could not force industries to convert to war work or ensure that raw materials were used for defense needs rather than the production of civilian goods. And, with a reviving economy, private industry was hardly eager to deny consumers the new cars and other items they were demanding—or to give up the profits that resulted. As a result, OPM limped along, doing the best it could but unable to compel the urgent, all-out industrial effort the president had called for.

"The production program here is not keyed to realities at all," the correspondent Vincent Sheean, who had returned to the United States for a brief visit, wrote to Ed Murrow. "All the big talk about 'defense' and 'aid to Britain' is so much grander than the reality. . . . The people really don't understand . . . anything at all about the seriousness of the moment."

With the authority given him by the Lend-Lease Act, Roosevelt ordered that any new war matériel produced in the United States be split fifty-fifty between the British and American armed services. But, as Harriman found while making his rounds of government offices, the U.S. military chiefs of staff were strongly opposed to giving up scarce weapons and other supplies that were needed so badly by their own services. Both the Army chief, General George Marshall, and the Navy chief, Admiral Harold Stark, were convinced of the need to come to the aid of Britain: indeed, for months, they had urged Roosevelt to provide more help than he was willing to give. But, with the condition of their services so dire and the mobilization of American war production so slow and haphazard, they resisted giving anything to Britain that might be important for America's own defense.

In early 1941, the United States was a fifth-rate military power, its armed forces ranking seventeenth in size compared to other world forces. Long starved of financial support by Congress and the White House, the Army had little more than 300,000 men (most of them just drafted), compared to Germany's 4 million and Britain's 1.6 million. Not a single armored division existed, and draftees were training with broomsticks for rifles and sawhorses for antitank guns. The Army was in such bad shape, according to one military historian, that it would not have been able to "repel raids across the Rio Grande by Mexican bandits." Although the Navy was in better condition, nearly half its vessels dated back to World War I. The Army Air Corps, meanwhile, could boast only about two thousand combat aircraft.

After several rounds of meetings with the chiefs and other key military figures, Harriman noted: "We are so short that everything given up by the Army or Navy comes out of our own blood; there is practically nothing surplus and will not be for many months." The urgent pleas of Harry Hopkins for more help for Britain failed to move the top brass, who thought he had been bewitched by Churchill. "We can't take seriously requests that come late in the evening over a bottle of port," snorted one high-ranking officer, in an obvious reference to the late-night tête-à-têtes between the presidential adviser and prime minister.

The issue of aid was further complicated by the intense Anglophobia of many in the U.S. military, who were convinced that Britain would soon be defeated and that any supplies sent to the British would end up in German hands. In late 1940, Navy Secretary Frank Knox confided to an associate that he "was very much disturbed at finding officers of the United States Navy very defeatist in their point of view." Knox attributed much of that defeatism to "a speech which had been given them by Ambassador Kennedy since his return home."

Within days of his appointment, Harriman realized what a monumental task lay ahead of him. To persuade American military leaders that U.S. munitions and other matériel would be of greater value in British hands than in their own, he would have to convince Churchill and the British to provide compelling evidence that the matériel they wanted was urgently needed and would be put to immediate use. They would have to give up their most sensitive military secrets, including information about their own production and reserves. "Without an understanding and acceptance of [Churchill's] war strategy," Harriman wrote in a memo to himself, "our military men will drag their feet."

Even more important, the president would have to be persuaded to do far more for Britain than send Lend-Lease supplies, which, in any event, would not begin arriving on British shores for several months. Like Stimson, Stark, and several other top administration officials, Harriman believed that the U.S. Navy must begin protecting British merchant ships in their extraordinarily hazardous journey across the Atlantic. Roosevelt, however, strongly resisted any idea of naval convoying. His administration had sold Lend-Lease to the public and Congress as a way of keeping America out of the war, claiming it was the best hope of stopping Germany without having to send American soldiers to fight. (Florida's Claude Pepper, one of the few ardent Lend-Lease supporters in the Senate, put the argument a bit more crassly. He declared that Britain, with American aid, would act "as a sort of mercenary, doing America's fighting for her.") Roosevelt knew that convoying would heighten the chance of U.S. involvement in a shooting war with German naval and air forces—a risk he was not prepared to take, at least not yet.

After a final meeting with FDR before departing for London in early March, Harriman began to wonder just how committed the president was to the survival of Britain. The signs, he thought, were not promising. "I left feeling that the President had not faced what I considered to be the realities of the situation, namely, that there was a good chance Germany . . . could so cripple British shipping as to affect her ability to hold out," Harriman wrote as he headed for Britain. "He seemed unwilling to lead public opinion or to force the issue but hoped, without the background of reasoning, that our material aid would let the British do the job. I am fearful that if things go against England, more specific aid will come too late."

WHEN HARRIMAN ARRIVED in Bristol on March 15, he was met by Churchill's naval aide, who bundled him into a military plane bound for an airfield near Chequers, some fifty miles northwest of London. A few hours later, America's Lend-Lease representative was escorted into the prime minister's bedroom at his country retreat. Although Churchill was in bed with a cold, he immediately got down to business. "He has talked to me personally on all aspects of the war," Harriman later wrote to his wife, Marie, who had stayed behind in New York. "The Battle of the Atlantic and other parts of the naval shipping struggle are uppermost in his mind as the decisive campaign." When Harriman told Churchill that he must be given access to all information about Britain's military resources and needs, no matter how sensitive or top secret, Churchill replied that he would get everything he needed. Echoing his earlier pledge to Winant, he added: "Nothing will be kept from you."

For the most part, Churchill lived up to his word to the two Americans, consulting them both on a wide variety of issues. According to Churchill's secretary John Colville, the American embassy "became little short of an extension to 10 Downing Street. Like others of my colleagues I made frequent journeys to [consult with Winant] at 1 Grosvenor Square." More than once, Churchill sent Colville to the embassy to have Winant vet his speeches. The prime minister's secretary recalled one occasion when the ambassador "made four pertinent observations in respect of the effect on U.S. opinion. I was deeply impressed by his unassertive shrewdness and wisdom. I afterwards explained these points to the PM, who accepted them."

As frequent as his contacts were with 10 Downing Street, Winant formed even closer ties with the Foreign Office and Anthony Eden, who had replaced Lord Halifax as foreign secretary in early 1941. Indeed, the collaboration between the American ambassador and Eden was so easy and intimate that they did not keep records of their official conversations—an unprecedented practice in international diplomacy, as Eden pointed out. "Quite early in our work together," he said, "Mr. Winant and I understood that we could not get through our business if each interview between us—and sometimes there were two or more in a day—was to be the subject of a detailed record." The two usually met in Eden's cavernous office, where Winant would occasionally make a teasing comment about the portrait of George III hanging prominently above the foreign secretary's desk before they launched into discussions about everything from supply problems to their countries' relationship to Vichy France. "We had an odd informal relationship," Winant later wrote, "based not only on personal friendship but also on our regard for each other's country and our own."

A month after he arrived, Harriman wrote to Roosevelt of the "complete confidence and respect that your Ambassador has won from all classes of people in England. He will become, I believe, before he leaves, the most beloved American who has ever been in England. His sympathies are warm, his devotion complete, and his judgment sound."

At the American embassy, Winant proved to be as poor an administrator as he had been as head of the Social Security Board—"one of the world's worst," according to Theodore Achilles, a political attaché at the embassy. He missed appointments and kept British officials and other dignitaries waiting for hours in his outer office. To the despair of the embassy's security officers, he often made his rounds with top secret papers stuffed in his pockets; often, his staff would find confidential cables scattered around the tables and floor of his flat. On one occasion, he forgot to tell his housekeeper that Churchill was coming for dinner. When the prime minister arrived, there was nothing in the flat to eat.

For all his shortcomings, however, Winant was an inspirational leader, just as he had been in Washington. He quickly united a staff that, under his predecessor, had been beset by friction and ill feeling. Under Winant's guidance, the embassy funneled to Washington a stream of information about British war developments that would later aid the American war effort, from the latest advances in surgical treatment of wounds and burns to news of defects in British tank treads, which helped the U.S. military avoid similar problems in its own tanks.

In May 1941, Ed Murrow wrote to a friend in New York: "You might like to know that both Winant and Harriman are doing a first-rate job over here, and this American Embassy functions now with more speed and efficiency than I've ever seen." Yet, as important as Churchill considered Winant, he was focusing for the moment on the Lend-Lease representative, whose influence he considered more crucial at that point for the survival of his country. Its situation was becoming graver by the day: shipping losses continued to escalate, and Hitler was clearly preparing an assault on Greece, which historically had been under British protection. In North Africa, Germany seemed poised to come to the aid of Italy, whose ineffective troops had been trounced by the British. In desperate want of ships, planes, weapons, and equipment, Churchill was determined to woo and seduce the American newcomer, just as he had Hopkins and Winant, to get what he needed.

Within days of Harriman's arrival, he was given an office at the Admiralty and access to secret cables and documents on production and supplies. He attended the meetings of a War Cabinet subcommittee dealing with the Battle of the Atlantic and had regular discussions with the ministers of shipping, supply, aircraft production, food, and economic warfare. "Each of the ministers . . . gave me the most sensitive information," he wrote. "I was somewhat embarrassed that I could not, in response to their questions, tell them exactly what help the United States was prepared to give." Instead of being viewed as a watchdog over American aid, the British treated him, Harriman said, like a "partner in a vast enterprise." In a letter to the president of Union Pacific, he declared, "I am accepted practically as a member of the Cabinet," and to his wife, he proudly noted, "I am with the Prime Minister at least one day a week and usually the weekend as well." Of Harriman's first eight weekends in Britain, seven were spent at Chequers, at the Churchills' invitation. "I was very excited," he recalled years later, "feeling like a country boy popped right into the center of the war."

Flush with a new sense of power, he set about establishing his own empire. His eight-man Lend-Lease mission appropriated twenty-seven rooms at 3 Grosvenor Square, an apartment building next to the embassy; Harriman's own vast office, which, according to his assistant, had "a somewhat Mussolini-like effect," was formerly the living room of a luxurious apartment.

Winant, who had declined to live in the stately official residence of the U.S. ambassador in Kensington, was also a tenant at 3 Grosvenor Square. Anxious to be close to the embassy, he leased a simply furnished three-bedroom flat, where, to the despair of his housekeeper, he subsisted entirely on British civilian rations.

As one of the richest men in the United States, Harriman had no interest in following Winant's example in spartan living. He took up residence in a ground-floor suite at the Dorchester Hotel, built ten years earlier and considered the safest building in London during German air raids. It also boasted exceptional soundproofing: its bedroom floors and ceilings were insulated with compressed seaweed and its outside walls with cork. Located in the heart of Mayfair, the Dorchester housed British cabinet ministers, displaced European royalty and government leaders, generals and admirals from all over the world, and affluent Londoners, among them Somerset Maugham, who had abandoned their less structurally substantial houses for the duration. One London socialite called the Dorchester "that gilded refuge of the rich." Others termed it "a modern wartime Babylon" and "a fortress propped up with moneybags."

While most Londoners coped with increasingly severe shortages of food, patrons of the Dorchester restaurant—which, like other eating establishments in London, was not rationed—dined on strawberries, oysters, and smoked salmon, to the accompaniment of show tunes played by the hotel orchestra. "I've never seen more lavishness, more money spent, or more food consumed than tonight, and the dance floor was packed," noted a Tory member of Parliament after dining at the Dorchester one night during the Blitz. "The contrast between the light and gaiety within, and the blackout and the roaring guns outside was terrific."

Such high living, in the midst of so much death and destruction, was not to everyone's taste. "I never felt easy in the dining rooms of the Savoy and Dorchester and Ritz hotels after the Blitz started," wrote Ben Robertson. "The food and the music got on your conscience when hundreds of thousands were in shelters and when people on every side were dying." Ed Murrow was similarly dismayed by the dramatic contrasts in the living conditions of Londoners under fire. In one broadcast, he pointed up the differences between the squalid, unsafe public shelter across the street from the Dorchester and the hotel's own luxurious bolthole in the basement, complete with eiderdown comforters and fluffy white pillows on the cots.

Harriman, however, expressed no such qualms: he took to the Dorchester—and his new life in London—with great enthusiasm. As the latest American VIP on the scene, he was showered with attention and invitations. "My mail has been staggering," he wrote his wife. "I never knew I had so many friends and acquaintances in England. . . . Invitations—weekends to last till doomsday—dinners—lunches—cocktails, etc., etc." Already heavily engaged in his hobby of people collecting, he told Marie: "I was interrupted by the Prime Minister of Australia who came into my room. He is genial—no airs—I called him 'Bob' the second time I met him."

WHILE ENJOYING HIS busy social schedule, Harriman had to cram it into the nooks and crannies of his hectic workdays. Like Winant, he was thrust into dealing with thorny problems in Anglo-American relations from the day he arrived. Among them was Britain's anger over continued American insistence that it sell off major assets in return for U.S. aid. Roosevelt expected Churchill to help him allay isolationist fears that, with the approval of Lend-Lease, Britain was taking advantage of the United States. In early 1941, the president ordered the dispatch of an American destroyer to South Africa to collect British gold worth £50 million being held there and bring it back to America. His administration also coerced the sale of the American Viscose Corporation, a British-owned textile company, to a group of American bankers, who promptly resold it for a much higher price.

The American actions "wear the aspect of a sheriff collecting the last assets of a helpless debtor," a furious Churchill wrote in a cable to Roosevelt that was never sent. "You will not, I am sure, mind my saying that if you are not able to stand by us in all measures apart from war, we cannot guarantee to beat the Nazi tyranny and gain you the time you require for your rearmament." To one of his cabinet ministers, the prime minister raged: "As far as I can make out, we are not only to be skinned but flayed to the bone." Although Harriman did his best to allay British fury over America's hardheaded business tactics, the feeling of resentment lingered throughout the war. "How the English hate being rescued by the Americans," Canadian diplomat Charles Ritchie wrote in his diary. "They know they must swallow it, but, God, how it sticks in their throats."

While Harriman was coping with the issue of British assets, he and Winant were faced with another difficulty: the growing expectation by Churchill and many of his countrymen that the United States would enter the war by late spring or early summer of 1941. There were several reasons for that misplaced belief, among them Harry Hopkins's "whither thou goest" speech; a comment by Wendell Willkie that if Roosevelt was reelected in 1940, the United States would be in the war by April; and the passage of Lend-Lease itself. Hopkins himself had tried to tamp down such hope, as did Harriman and Winant after him.

Although Lend-Lease was a huge step in the escalation of U.S. involvement, the American envoys warned that it must not be viewed as the decisive one. Again and again, they sought to make clear to officials and the British public the strength of the U.S. isolationist movement and the vagaries of American politics and government, particularly the system of separation of powers. Churchill, who had an American mother, liked to boast that he had a firm understanding of the U.S. political system. In fact, he and those in his government never fully grasped how very different it was from their own parliamentary system, where the executive and legislature were harnessed together and where party divisions were, for the most part, kept under control.

Winant and Harriman kept emphasizing that Roosevelt did not lead Congress the way Churchill led Parliament. According to the U.S. Constitution, it was up to Congress, not the president, to declare war. And, in the spring of 1941, American legislators, many of them isolationists, were nowhere close to doing so.

4.

"HE SEEMS TO
GET CONFIDENCE IN
HAVING US AROUND"

APRIL 16, 1941, WAS A BEAUTIFUL DAY—SUNNY AND WARM—AND
Janet Murrow was determined to take full advantage of it. She coaxed
her husband away from work long enough to take her to dinner at
L'Etoile, a little French bistro in Soho that had become their favorite
restaurant in London.

The streets that evening were crowded with other London residents basking in the glorious weather. The bitter winter was over at
last, and daffodils and hyacinths were blooming everywhere. But the
real tonic for people's spirits was the absence of German bombers:
there had been no major raid on London in more than a month. Londoners had finally begun to lose "that ghastly, tired, haunted look they
had, with red-rimmed eyes that were sunk in their heads . . . caused by
fright and sleepless nights," one woman wrote in her diary. The fear
that invaded most people's minds at dusk was rapidly fading.

Even Ed Murrow had begun to relax. Over dinner, he and Janet
chatted about friends, books, movies—anything but the war. On their
way out, they stopped at nearby tables to say hello to friends from the
BBC, for whom L'Etoile was also a favorite hangout. Enjoying the soft
spring air and the full moon that made navigating the blackout considerably easier, they strolled home, past stately cream-colored houses
with peeling paint and an occasional gap, covered with rubble, where a
house or shop had once stood.

Just before reaching their flat, they heard the familiar banshee cry
of sirens, a distant throb of aircraft engines, and the muffled sound of

explosions to the south. But the lovely night still cast its spell, and Murrow suggested they stop for a pint at the Devonshire Arms, their neighborhood pub and another favorite gathering place for the BBC. Janet, however, felt a prickle of fear. Like every other resident of the city, she knew that a full moon usually meant heavy bombing raids. But this was something more: she had a premonition, she later said, that they shouldn't go to the pub that night. "I'm really scared," she told her husband. "I'd be grateful if you'd walk home with me." Reluctantly he agreed.

Almost as soon as they'd opened the door of their flat, there was the ear-splitting drone of planes overhead—hundreds of them, Janet thought—and a thunderous barrage of antiaircraft guns, followed by rapidly approaching bomb blasts. Climbing the stairs to the roof, the Murrows looked out over a city blazing with light: flares bursting like Roman candles, searchlights crisscrossing the heavens, and fires blossoming everywhere.

Suddenly, they heard a more ominous sound, the freight-train whistle of a bomb that seemed to be aimed straight at them. Running back inside, they crouched in the stairwell, their arms cradling their heads. A deafening explosion rocked the building, throwing them up against the wall. "It's the office," Murrow shouted, and they raced back to the roof. From there, they witnessed a hellish scene: Duchess Street, where the CBS office was located, was ablaze, as were most of the streets nearby. Houses began collapsing with a dull roar, and the harsh, rank smell of plaster dust filled the air. The Devonshire Arms had disappeared. The bomb that narrowly missed the Murrows' building had scored a direct hit on the pub, leaving nothing but a gaping black hole. A towering pillar of dust, debris, smoke, and sparks mushroomed up to the sky.

Grabbing his tin hat, Murrow rushed downstairs and out the door. From her bedroom window, Janet, more terrified than she had ever been in her life, watched the flames, knowing that "many of our friends were gone." The world, she wrote in her diary, "was upside down."

A FEW MILES AWAY, in Grosvenor Square, Gil Winant had been working in his office when the sirens began their howl. Moments later, he heard the scream of a bomb and a massive explosion, followed by the crash of breaking glass: all his office windows had been shattered.

Picking himself up off the floor, the ambassador, accompanied by two aides and his wife, who had just arrived in London for a visit, climbed to the embassy's roof to survey the damage. An incendiary bomb had set ablaze the vacant Italian embassy next door, and U.S. embassy employees were working frantically to put the fire out. Across the street, a lovely Georgian townhouse had been demolished, and all the windows of John Adams's old residence were blasted out. On nearby Oxford Street, flames were devouring one of London's major department stores. Mayfair, like the Murrows' neighborhood near Regent's Park, was now an inferno, as was much of the rest of London.

As the raid continued, Winant and the embassy's political attaché, Theodore Achilles, headed out into the streets to take stock of the damage. Wearing his battered felt hat, the ambassador ignored the crump of bombs in the distance and the shrapnel crackling down around him. He and Achilles walked for miles through dust and smoke so thick it was hard to see more than a couple of feet ahead of them. They passed the smoking ruins of a building just as the bodies of several young nurses were carried out. They visited packed shelters and stopped to watch a fireman atop an extension ladder battling flames on a building's roof, seemingly oblivious to the bombs falling around him. Again and again, the ambassador asked the people he encountered—air raid wardens, firemen, rescue workers, those in the shelters—if there was any help he could give.

It was a typical Winant gesture, Achilles later noted. He recalled that the ambassador's first words to him when he arrived in London were: "Now that I am here, what can I do to help?" Winant's whole approach to his job, Achilles added, was "based in human terms. To those preparing economic reports for him on the situation in Great Britain, he would say time and again, 'Give it to me in the form of shoes, in the form of clothing. . . .' He saw air raids in terms of individuals, of the human tragedy which resulted from the nightly bombings."

Winant and Achilles walked until dawn, a little after the all-clear siren sounded at 5 A.M. following eight hours of continuous bombing. There was now blue sky and sunshine, but only if one looked straight up; at eye level, a pall of gray smoke still cloaked the city. As the weary ambassador and attaché headed back to the embassy, firemen were hosing down the charred remains of buildings while the fortunate Londoners whose homes were still intact—if somewhat battered—

were outside with brooms and shovels, cleaning up the debris and shattered glass.

Back in his office, Winant called friends and acquaintances, both British and American, to make sure they were all right. One of his calls was to the Murrows. They were fine, Janet replied, although Ed had lost his office, his third so far, and more than thirty people had died in the Devonshire Arms, many of whom were friends of theirs. Writing to her mother later that day about the raid's ferocity, she remarked: "I see no reason why anybody should be alive this morning."

A number of people had recognized Winant that night, and the news of his travels around the West End spread quickly throughout Britain, first by word of mouth and then in newspaper stories and on the BBC. Several of the articles underscored the sharp contrast between the new ambassador and his predecessor, who, before he retreated to the United States at the height of the Blitz, escaped every night to a country retreat near Windsor. For many Britons, Winant's presence on the streets of London during the horrific April 16 attack, and in raids to come, was the first tangible evidence that Americans did indeed care what happened to them. "His personality captured the imagination of the entire country as no other ambassador in modern times has been able to do," remarked Virginia Cowles, an American journalist who worked briefly for Winant in London. "He became a symbol to the people of Great Britain . . . and made the office of American ambassador known to virtually every person there."

Sir Arthur Salter, the British undersecretary of shipping and a friend of Winant's, concurred. In Salter's view, the ambassador "typified to the British people the best side of America. . . . He showed that he was deeply and passionately attached to the British and to their fight against Hitler and Nazism. He believed in all that Britain was fighting for." As a result, Salter said, many Britons "developed an unquestioning belief" that Winant was right when he emphasized the importance of close ties between Britain and the United States both during and after the war.

AN ESTIMATED 1,100 Londoners were killed during the April 16 raids—the most devastating night of the Blitz thus far. But it held that distinction for only three days; on April 19, German bombers hit London again, killing more than 1,200 persons. Almost half a million London residents lost their homes in the two attacks.

The capital, however, wasn't the only British city suffering an especially severe pounding that spring. As part of the all-out German attempt to sever Britain's supply lifeline and shut down production of war matériel, the Luftwaffe blasted the country's major industrial and port cities, among them Manchester, Portsmouth, Cardiff, Plymouth, Liverpool, and Bristol. In Liverpool, six consecutive nights of bombing damaged or destroyed almost half the city's docks, reducing the amount of supplies that could be unloaded from incoming ships to just a quarter of the normal tonnage.

Deeply concerned about the spirit of those living outside London, Churchill spent much of his time in morale-building visits to the bombed cities, often taking Harriman and Winant with him. "He seems to get confidence in having us around," Harriman wrote to Roosevelt. But, as Harriman noted, Churchill had another reason for showing off the Americans. Whenever he spoke to those in the hinterlands, he would always introduce the two as Roosevelt's envoys—"his way of letting the crowd know that America stood with them."

Just days before the first April assault on London, Winant and Harriman traveled with the prime minister to several badly damaged port cities in southern England and Wales. As part of the tour, Winant was to receive an honorary doctorate from Churchill at the University of Bristol, which the prime minister served as chancellor.

After a visit to Swansea, Churchill's party arrived in Bristol in the middle of a heavy raid, the sixth experienced by the busy seaport in the past five months. From the prime minister's train, parked under a railway bridge outside the city, he and his entourage watched in dismay as bombs laid waste to a wide swath of Bristol, from the docks to the city center. At first light, they drove into the rubble-covered town, with fires still blazing, streets flooded from broken water mains, and residents searching the ruins of buildings for the dead and wounded. It was, John Colville later wrote in his diary, "devastation such as I had never thought possible."

But when the people on the streets caught a glimpse of the familiar stout figure with his ever-present cigar and walking stick, they put aside all thoughts of their misery, at least for a moment, as they rushed toward him. It was the same everywhere, Winant wrote to Roosevelt.

"The news of his presence spreads rapidly by word of mouth, and before he has gone far, crowds flock about him and people call out to him, 'Hallo, Winnie,' 'Good old Winnie,' 'You will never let us down,' 'That's a man.'"

In notes he took during the Bristol visit, Harriman described Churchill's procession through the city: "He reviews the Home Guard—stiff at attention but a smile on their faces as he goes by. He stops to ask about a decoration—'From the last war, eh?' Next comes the ARP wardens, then the volunteer firemen and finally the women." Yet, as affecting as the prime minister's performance was, Harriman was far more impressed by the people of Bristol. At one point, an elderly woman, who had just been rescued from her badly damaged house, was brought forward to meet the Churchills. She chatted for a moment, then said hurriedly: "I am sorry I can't talk to you any longer. I must go and clean up my house."

Jotting down in his notes the Bristol residents' conversations with Churchill, Harriman—this former businessman who rarely showed emotion—was impassioned, even melodramatic: "They had been in the battle, tasted every fire . . . done their part . . . proud and unafraid. 'See what he did—the Hun,' they said. 'He'll come again but our boys will get him and then the new graves!' 'We'll win in the end, won't we?'"

That same defiance was evident at the University of Bristol, which continued with the ceremony to bestow honorary degrees on Winant and two other dignitaries despite the bombing of its Great Hall, where the event was to have taken place, and several other buildings on the grounds. Virtually all of the university's faculty members and graduates who lined up for the procession had spent the night fighting fires or performing other rescue work. They marched into the small hall where the ceremony was held, their eyes bloodshot, their haggard faces streaked with grime, and the muddy, wet clothing under their academic gowns and richly colored hoods reeking of smoke.

The acrid smell of smoke also drifted in through the shattered windows of the hall, where, just a few hundred yards away, firemen were pouring water on blazes in nearby buildings. Every few minutes, those in attendance could hear the dull explosion of a delayed-action bomb. As Churchill began bestowing the degrees, the wife of Bristol's lord mayor fainted—an incident that "seemed to underline the strain and nightmare of the recent hours," Winant wrote.

When the prime minister left Bristol that afternoon, hundreds of townspeople came to the station to see him off. Watching them wave and cheer as the train pulled away, Churchill shielded his face with a newspaper to hide his tears. "They have such faith," he told Harriman and Winant. "It is a grave responsibility."

For his part, Harriman had been so moved by the courage of the Bristol residents that he sent a substantial cash gift to Clementine Churchill, asking her to forward it to the city's lord mayor to help those who had lost their homes. In her note of thanks, Mrs. Churchill said she hoped that "all this pain and grief . . . may bring our two countries permanently together and that they may grow to understand each other. Anyhow, whatever happens, we do not feel alone any more."

IN MANY OF THEIR letters and cables to Roosevelt and Harry Hopkins, Winant and Harriman emphasized not only the resolution and valor of the British people but also the crucial role that ordinary citizens were playing in the conflict. The expression "people's war" has been greatly overused, but there's no question that the extraordinary volunteer effort in Britain was equaled by few if any other combatant countries in World War II.

Whenever the local or national governments failed to meet a need or solve a problem in Britain during the war, volunteers filled the void. Their response to the dismal conditions in London's Underground stations and other public air raid shelters is a case in point. In most of the shelters, the authorities had made no arrangements for food, heat, beds, bathrooms, or washing facilities. "The stench was frightful—urine and excrement mixed with strong carbolic, sweat, and dirty, unwashed humanity," one witness remarked of the shelters early in the Blitz.

Volunteers soon came to the rescue. Bathrooms were built out of salvaged materials; food was brought in; bunks and coal stoves appeared, as did armchairs and wireless sets in some shelters. London's borough governments, shamed by their initial feeble and shoddy response, made structural and other improvements to the shelters. By the end of the Blitz, the majority of them had been transformed into reasonably comfortable places to spend the long, perilous nights.

The same was true for rest centers, where those who were bombed out of their homes could take temporary refuge. Government authorities had been overwhelmed by the massive homelessness created by German raids; in London alone, 1.4 million people—one in six residents—had lost their homes by the spring of 1941. Again, volunteers came to the fore, providing cots, meals, temporary housing, and other services.

What was particularly striking to American observers like Winant and Harriman was the dominant role that women played in the volunteer effort. "It is the spirit of the British women that is carrying this country through the frightful experience of bombing," Harriman wrote a friend. To his wife, he remarked, "The women are the mainstay of England." After a visit to London later in the war, Treasury Secretary Henry Morgenthau wrote in his diary: "What the women in England were doing was just unbelievable. . . . If it were not for the women, England would cave in today."

Many of the women to whom Harriman and Morgenthau referred were members of an organization called the Women's Voluntary Service, created by the redoubtable widow of the Marquess of Reading, one of the most remarkable women in twentieth-century Britain. Her husband, a former ambassador to the United States who also had served as viceroy to India, believed that the future of democracy depended on a better understanding between the United States and Britain. She agreed. After Lord Reading's death in 1935, she spent several months in America. Traveling throughout the country under the name of Mrs. Read, Lady Reading stayed in dollar-a-night hotel rooms and worked as a dishwasher in order to get to know working-class Americans. Among the people with whom she formed a friendship during her stay was Eleanor Roosevelt. Later, in London, she befriended the Murrows and Winant.

In 1938, the British Home Office asked Lady Reading if she would form an organization to recruit women for civil defense work in the event of war. She accepted the challenge but insisted that the scope of the Women's Voluntary Service be greatly expanded. *Any* job that needed doing, she said, would be a task for her group.

When war was declared in 1939, WVS members, in their signature green tweed suits and red sweaters, helped evacuate children from London and other cities. A few months later, when exhausted British troops were evacuated from the French port of Dunkirk, women from the WVS were waiting for them at docks and railway stations with sandwiches and steaming-hot tea. After Hitler occupied most of the Continent, that "magnificent body of selfless women," as one British mayor called the WVS, helped find housing for the thousands of European refugees who fled to Britain. Its members did the same for the homeless of their own country during the Blitz. They manned hundreds of rest centers, hostels, mobile libraries and canteens, and distributed thousands of tons of clothing and other supplies, collected from America and the Commonwealth, to the needy.

By the end of the war, a majority of British women had been involved in some way in the struggle: most of those who had not been members of the armed and civil defense services, or employees of factories and other war-connected businesses, had worked at least part-time with the Women's Voluntary Service.*

YET, AS VITAL AND valiant as the British civilian effort was, there was only so much it could do. It could not stop the German U-boat depredations on merchant shipping, nor could it stave off the other perils looming in the spring of 1941. Living in Britain during those bleak months—the worst of the war—was like "living in a nightmare, with some calamity hanging constantly over one's head," Harriman wrote Harry Hopkins.

As the days lengthened, the shipping losses in the Atlantic rose to astronomical proportions. The new German battle cruisers *Gneisenau* and *Scharnhorst* joined the U-boat wolf packs in picking off British merchant ships like ducks in a shooting gallery. The amount of matériel sunk in April—nearly 700,000 tons—was more than twice the losses two months earlier. Indeed, the shipping figures were so calamitous that Churchill ordered the Ministry of Information to discontinue their publication, for fear of hurting public morale.

In that period, Britain was as close to extreme hunger as it ever would be during the war. Rationing of many food items was now draconian; individuals were limited, for example, to one ounce of cheese and a minimal amount of meat a week and eight ounces of jam and margarine a month. Some foods, like tomatoes, onions, eggs, and oranges, had disappeared almost completely from store shelves. Clothes

---

* For her immense service to her country's war effort, Lady Reading became the first woman to be elevated to the House of Lords.

rationing had also begun, and most consumer goods, from saucepans to matches, were almost impossible to find. "There is no question that the food situation is very much worse," noted General Raymond Lee, the military attaché at the American embassy, who returned to London in April after three months of temporary duty in Washington. "The people strike me also as being much more solemn than they were in January."

Correspondent Vincent Sheean, who came back to London from the United States at about the same time, was shocked not only at the increased severity of life in the capital but at the toll it had taken on his American reporting colleagues. Ed Murrow, Ben Robertson, and Bill Stoneman, with whom he had drinks one night, were gaunt and hollow-eyed; Murrow, in particular, looked far older than his thirty-three years. "You won't find any of the high-spirited, we-can-take-it stuff of the last year," the CBS newsman told Sheean. "People . . . are getting a little grim. All the novelty is gone. The epic period is over. Food has something to do with it—everyone is probably a little under-nourished."

The vaunted bravery and resolution of the British people were still in evidence, but both were beginning to show deep cracks after eight months of bombing and deepening privation. Courageous the British might be, but they weren't supermen. The question of how long their determination would last, particularly in the cities outside London, was one that haunted Churchill and the country's other decision makers.

The home secretary, Herbert Morrison, "is worried about the effect of the provincial raids on morale," Harold Nicolson, the undersecretary of information, wrote in his diary in early May. "He keeps on underlining the fact that people cannot stand this intensive bombing indefinitely and that sooner or later the morale of towns will go." Although smaller cities like Portsmouth, Plymouth, and Bristol did not experience the nightly pounding that London received, the damage they suffered in raids was far more widespread and devastating than that in the sprawling capital, where there still were vast areas untouched by bombs. The provincial cities also lacked the much greater resources of London: they did not have miles of Underground to serve as makeshift air-raid shelters, nor did they have access to the numbers of rescue and fire personnel or the emergency food, clothing, and other supplies available in the capital.

In Gil Winant's view, however, the gradual erosion of morale in the country had as much to do with the misery of everyday life as it did with the renewed air raids. "The fatigue and the monotony . . . the interrupted transportation . . . the dust . . . the shabby and worn out clothes . . . the drabness that comes from want of things . . . no glass for the replacement of windows . . . stumbling home in the blackout . . . the shortage of light and fuel—all made a dreary picture for even the brave-hearted."

After more than twenty months of war, the struggle seemed unending, with relief nowhere in sight. "All that the country really wants is some assurance of how victory is to be achieved," wrote Harold Nicolson. "They are bored by talks about the righteousness of our cause and our eventual triumph. What they want are facts indicating how we are to beat the Germans. I have no idea at all how we are to give them those facts."

Neither did Churchill or anyone else in the government. The only facts they had at their disposal were ones of unmitigated disaster for the British Army—a series of sieges, evacuations, and defeats. In April, Germany swept through the Balkans, overpowering Greece and, after inflicting heavy casualties, routing British forces there. The British retreated to the island of Crete, where in May they again were driven out by the Germans. It was the fourth evacuation of the war for British forces—and the most humiliating by far. "Serious injury was done to British morale in general," noted Robert Sherwood, "and, in particular, disagreeable disputes were provoked between the three British services." A sour joke made the rounds in Britain that BEF (British Expeditionary Force) really stood for "Back Every Friday."

Meanwhile, a string of early British triumphs over the Italians in Libya turned to dust when General Erwin Rommel and his Afrika Korps rushed to the Italians' rescue. In only ten days the Germans regained almost all the ground that the British had captured in three months, and in doing so, threw the Tommies back to Egypt. Rommel's victory, which Churchill termed "a disaster of the first magnitude," was a strategic calamity for Britain, threatening its access to Middle East oil as well as its control of the Suez Canal, a vital conduit to India and the Far East.

At home, there was increasing doubt about the fighting ability and mettle of British troops, misgivings expressed privately by Churchill and members of his government. "Evacuation going fairly well—that's all we're really good at!" Alexander Cadogan wrote in his diary during the British withdrawal in Greece. "Our soldiers are the most pathetic amateurs, pitted against professionals. . . . Tired, depressed, and defeatist!"

During this bitter time, Churchill himself came under strong parliamentary attack for his conduct of the war, particularly for his order transferring troops from the Middle East in April to shore up British forces in Greece—a move that worked to Rommel's advantage. In a House of Commons debate in May, a number of MPs lacerated the prime minister's leadership and what they saw as his faulty decision making. Angered by the criticism, Churchill nonetheless acknowledged a sense of "discouragement and disheartenment" in the country. He told the House: "I feel that we are fighting for life and survival from day to day and hour to hour."

Painfully aware that his country's only hope was U.S. intervention, Churchill lobbied Winant and Harriman for more aid with an intensity bordering on obsession. Winant began to dread his weekend visits to Chequers, where Churchill would harangue him nonstop and then go off for a nap, leaving a cabinet member or some other top official to continue the argument. After an hour or so, the prime minister would return, refreshed and ready for another go at the weary ambassador. What good were Lend-Lease goods, Churchill repeatedly demanded, if they never made it to Britain? He wanted the U.S. Navy to protect merchant ship convoys, but more than that, he was desperate for America to enter the war.

In late March, British and American military leaders had met in Washington to discuss possible joint action when and if the United States ever joined the fight. They agreed that the main effort against Germany would take place in the Atlantic and Europe. According to the planners, a large detachment of the American Navy would be deployed to guard British merchant ships, while up to thirty U.S. submarines would operate against enemy naval vessels. The British were pleased with the plans, but they never went further since Roosevelt showed no interest in implementing them.

On May 3, a dispirited Churchill dropped all pretense about what Britain really needed from the United States: not destroyers or planes or naval protection of convoys. For the first time since June 1940, he begged Roosevelt to declare war against Germany. "Mr. President, I am sure you will not misunderstand me if I speak to you exactly what is on my mind," Churchill cabled the White House. "The one decisive

counterweight I can see . . . would be if the United States were immediately to range herself with us as a belligerent power."

Would the president heed the prime minister's plea? Or would it
end up like so many of Churchill's messages, swallowed up in the inertia of Washington like a note in a bottle that's been cast into the
ocean? Such questions were pondered not only by anxious British
leaders but by America's representatives in London. "The whole thing
is going to be a race against time," the U.S. military attaché, General
Lee, wrote in his journal. "It is a question whether our support will arrive soon enough to bolster up what is a gradually failing cause."

Roosevelt waited a week to respond. When his reply finally arrived
at Downing Street, it made clear that the president still did not share
the sense of urgency felt in Britain—or, for that matter, by many key
officials in his own administration. At the very least, in the view of the
U.S. chiefs of staff and most of the cabinet, U.S. protection must be
given to British convoys to stanch the hemorrhaging shipping losses.
"The situation is obviously critical in the Atlantic," Admiral Stark
wrote to a colleague. "In my opinion, it is hopeless [unless] we take
strong measures to save it." In a speech, Navy Secretary Frank Knox
declared: "We cannot allow our goods to be sunk in the Atlantic."
Knox, Henry Stimson, Henry Morgenthau, and Harry Hopkins were
among those who urged Roosevelt to act decisively. But the president
disregarded their counsel, just as he rejected Churchill's plea for U.S.
belligerency. Instead he assured the prime minister, as he had done so
often before, that American help soon would arrive.

There was no question that FDR was deeply concerned about the
dire position of the British that spring, yet he was willing only to take
small, incremental steps to come to their aid. He issued an order, urged
on him by Harriman, that would allow American supplies to go directly
to British troops in the Middle East, rather than be unloaded in Britain
for reshipment. He also permitted the repair of damaged British warships in American shipyards—another Harriman recommendation—
and the training of British pilots on American airfields.

In addition, the president enlarged his country's self-proclaimed
security zone in the Atlantic, authorizing U.S. ships and planes to patrol more than two thirds of the watery expanse between America and
Britain. When war broke out in 1939, America had decreed a nonbel-
ligerency area that extended three hundred miles from both coasts and
was monitored by American forces. Roosevelt's decision to widen the

Atlantic zone in April 1941 made it possible for American ships and planes to patrol the ocean as far as Greenland and to warn the British if they spotted German U-boats or surface raiders. But the president also made clear that there was to be no shooting by U.S. forces unless they were fired upon first.

The increased American surveillance was certainly useful to the British, but it did little to stop the U-boat rampage. Since U.S. patrols were prohibited from attacking German vessels, the British remained solely responsible for protecting their convoys, and the losses continued to mount. In the first three weeks of May, German submarines sank twenty British merchant ships in the extended U.S. security zone.

The men closest to the president were baffled, exasperated, and increasingly alarmed by what they saw as his passivity and reluctance to take bolder action. Former ambassador William Bullitt wrote Harriman: "The President is waiting for public opinion to lead and public opinion is waiting for a lead from the President." Most members of the cabinet and many of Roosevelt's other close associates, among them Bullitt and Supreme Court justice Felix Frankfurter, were now convinced that the strategy of "all aid short of war" was no longer enough to rescue Britain. "I told Hopkins that . . . if we were going to save England we would have to get into this war," Henry Morgenthau wrote in his diary, "and that we needed England, if for no other reason, than as a stepping stone to bomb Germany." The treasury secretary added: "I think that both the President and Hopkins are groping as to what to do. . . . [Hopkins] thinks the President is loath to get into this war, and he would rather follow public opinion than lead it." Morgenthau, like others in FDR's circle, sensed that Roosevelt was waiting for a provocative incident that would take the onus of responsibility from his shoulders and give him the excuse to protect British convoys or even to declare war.

In April, Stimson, Knox, Interior Secretary Harold Ickes, and Attorney General Robert Jackson held a secret meeting to discuss how they could put pressure on the president to stop dithering and take more control. "I do know that in every direction I find a growing discontent with the President's lack of leadership," Ickes wrote in his diary. "He still has the country if he will take it and lead it. But he won't have it very much longer unless he does something."

The seventy-three-year-old Stimson, who had served twice as secretary of war and once as secretary of state, decided to assume the initiative himself. One of the most respected men in Washington, Stimson was the only cabinet member with the moral and political stature to get away with telling the president to his face that he was failing in his responsibility to lead. Instead of relying on public opinion to decide what to do, Stimson told FDR, he must guide that opinion. "I cautioned him," the war secretary wrote, ". . . that without a lead on his part, it was useless to expect that people would voluntarily take the initiative in letting him know whether or not they would follow him."

The president, however, paid little or no heed to Stimson's advice. Determined to preserve national unity, he would take no step opposed by the majority of the country unless compelled by Hitler to do so. "How much a part of our democratic way of life will be handled by Mr. Gallup is a pure guess," Admiral Stark grumbled to a colleague.

It was hard, however, to determine exactly *what* it was that Americans wanted in the spring of 1941. Gallup polls showed overwhelming support for aid to Britain, but, when asked whether the Navy should protect British ships, the polls were almost evenly divided on the issue. More than 80 percent of Americans opposed U.S. entry into the war to rescue Britain, although roughly the same percentage believed that the United States would have to defend itself against Germany sooner or later. "The truth was that there was still quite a lot of apathy," said Frances Perkins. The war "was an awful long ways off. It was very hard for most people to visualize it. They didn't feel hot and bothered about the principles at stake. They didn't really care."

In the view of interventionists, the results of the polls showed the failure of Roosevelt to educate the American public about a crucial fact of life: that the danger posed to the United States by Germany was an immediate one, not a peril to be worried about sometime in the gauzy future. "The people as a whole simply do not understand that a Hitler control of Europe, Asia, Africa and the high seas would put us at the mercy of the Nazis for about 25 essential resources," Chet Williams, a federal government official and friend of Murrow's, wrote to the broadcaster. "Facts like that have not been explained."

Belle Roosevelt, the wife of Eleanor Roosevelt's cousin Kermit, and a close friend of the president and his wife, confronted FDR about his reluctance to educate the public. "Why don't you tell the American people the facts, no matter how grim they are?" she demanded. "Can't we take facts, and if we can't, isn't it all the more essential that we, as a nation, should learn to face the actuality? Isn't it part of your job to teach us to face the truth?"

As Roosevelt saw it, however, she and his other interventionist critics failed to understand the complexity of the situation he faced. While public opinion might be blurred and confused, congressional opinion apparently was not: according to one poll, for example, some 80 percent of members of Congress opposed naval convoying, even if "necessary to prevent a British defeat by Hitler." And while most of the major figures in FDR's administration were urging him to be more militant, others, whose doubts about Britain's capacity to wage war and its ability to survive were strengthened by its recent defeats, believed the president had already gone too far in helping the British.

Among those counseling caution were Secretary of State Cordell Hull and several of his assistant secretaries, including Adolf Berle and Breckinridge Long. "World opinion is that [the British] are licked," Long wrote in his diary. "We hear it from South America, from the Far East, from West Africa."

The War Department, too, had its share of naysayers. Although the civilian defense chiefs—Stimson and Knox—and the military chiefs—Marshall and Stark—favored a more aggressive approach to helping Britain, many high-ranking officers opposed such measures. To Stimson, Knox complained about "how he had to fight against the timidity of his own admirals on any aggressive movement, how all their estimates and advice were predicated on the failure of the British."

The war secretary, meanwhile, had his own troubles with the Army. General Marshall might have been in favor of U.S. naval convoys, but he and his top strategists, several of whom were anti-British themselves, resisted the idea of America getting involved in the war until the Army, still badly equipped and undermanned, was ready. When an Army colleague of Raymond Lee's returned to London after a few weeks in Washington, he told Lee that it was "shocking to see how many ranking officers there have adopted a defeatist attitude and are not at all enthusiastic about forwarding the American support of Britain in any way."

FOR THE AMERICANS in London, the spring and summer of 1941 was an agonizing, frustrating period. Washington, with its unwillingness to come to grips with the possible defeat of Britain, seemed like another planet to them. "There is still too much wishful thinking, too much idiotic optimism, too much being left to chance, too much of the democratic 'too little and too late,'" fumed Raymond Lee, one of the most stalwart proponents of the British cause in the American embassy. "It is only by being here that one realizes the actuality and pressure of the emergency."

Averell Harriman was even more irate. "It is impossible for me to understand the ostrich-like attitude of America," he wrote to a friend. "Either we have an interest in the outcome of this war or we have not. . . . If we have, why do we not realize that every day we delay direct participation . . . we are taking an extreme risk that either the war will be lost or the difficulty of winning will be multiplied for each week we delay?" To his wife, Harriman disparaged Roosevelt's expansion of American patrols in the Atlantic, which he described as "using warships as spies instead of to shoot. Hasn't the country any pride? Are we to continue to hide behind the skirts of these poor British women who are holding up the civil defense here? . . . Don't think I am depressed. I am only angry."

Again and again, he and Winant pressed the president and his men for more vigorous action and more direct involvement. "England's strength is bleeding," Harriman cabled Roosevelt in April. "In our own interest, I trust that our Navy can be directly employed before our partner is too weak." As Lend-Lease representative, he did what he could to speed up the flow of aid to Britain, such as persuading American shippers to stow their cargoes in a way that allowed British longshoremen to unload them faster. Yet he also suggested initiatives, like the repair of British vessels in American shipyards, that brought America one step, albeit a small one, closer to belligerency.

At Downing Street and in government offices in Whitehall, there was no doubt that Harriman and Winant wanted their country in the war. Churchill, who was in contact with both Americans virtually every day, told his cabinet that he had been "greatly encouraged" by their attitude. "These two gentlemen," he said, "[are] apparently longing for Germany to commit some overt act that would relieve the president of his . . . declaration regarding keeping out of the war."

For both, it was a difficult balancing act. They were, in effect, serving two governments: they were their country's top representatives in Britain while acting as Churchill's agents for conveying Britain's needs to the United States. But, as they made clear to British officials, their primary duty was to their own chief executive and country. They were, said John Colville, "two men who not only represented their country with exemplary skill but contrived to become close personal friends of Churchill, his family and his entourage without for one moment losing their independence of thought and action."

Both Americans did their best to aid Churchill in selling his views to the president and others in the administration. With their intimate knowledge of the personalities and politics of Washington, they helped the prime minister and his government interpret responses from Roosevelt and his men and took part in the crafting of Churchill's proposals and other messages to the White House. In addition, they pushed the prime minister to tone down his increasingly insistent, splenetic cables to FDR. Once, when Harriman made such a suggestion, Churchill irritatedly rejected it out of hand. Harriman, however, stood firm, and Churchill grudgingly said he'd think about it. The next morning, he handed Harriman a new draft of the cable that incorporated the recommendation.

When Churchill began withholding figures showing the full extent of Britain's shipping losses in the spring, Harriman and Winant urged him to rethink his decision, declaring that he should release more information rather than less. To convince the American public and government of the need for more active involvement, they said, it was essential that the full gravity of the crisis facing Britain be revealed, both on the shipping and military fronts. "What America requires is not propaganda but the facts," Winant declared in a speech. This was one issue, however, on which Churchill would not yield.

At the same time, in an effort to help smooth things over for Churchill on the political front, Winant tried to explain the prime minister to his critics, both at home and abroad. When some disgruntled MPs put pressure on the British leader to give up his position as defense minister (an unprecedented assumption of power by a prime minister), Winant told them that, in taking on both jobs, Churchill was able to deal on a more equal basis with Roosevelt regarding war matters than if his military responsibility was assigned to someone else. And when newly arrived American correspondents complained about Churchill's refusal to hold press conferences like the president, Winant explained that, in a parliamentary system, the prime minister kept the people informed through his weekly question sessions in the

House of Commons. He added that MPs would deeply resent Churchill's bypassing them to report through the press to the public.

ON MAY 10, THE day that Roosevelt issued his nonresponse to Churchill's plea for U.S. belligerency, German bombers returned to London. As devastating as the previous raids had been, none came close to the savagery and destructiveness of this new firestorm. By the next morning, more than two thousand fires were raging out of control across the city, from Hammersmith in the west to Romford in the east, some twenty miles away.

The damage to London's landmarks was catastrophic. Queen's Hall, the city's premier concert venue, lay in ruins, while more than a quarter of a million books were incinerated and a number of galleries destroyed at the British Museum. Bombs smashed into St. James's Palace, Westminster Abbey, Big Ben, and Parliament. The medieval Westminster Hall, though badly damaged, was saved, but not so the House of Commons chamber, the scene of some of the most dramatic events in modern British history. Completely gutted by fire, the little hall, with its vaulted, timbered ceiling, was nothing but a mound of debris, gaping open to the sky.

Every major railroad station but one was put out of action for weeks, as were many Underground stations and lines. A third of the streets in greater London were impassable, and almost a million people were without gas, water, and electricity.

The death toll was even more calamitous: never in London's history had so many of its residents—1,436—died in a single night. Among the dead were Alan Wells, the foreign editor of the BBC's Home Service, and his wife, Claire, who were neighbors and close friends of Ed and Janet Murrow. The Wellses, both volunteer fire wardens, had been trying to extinguish an incendiary bomb near their home when a high-explosive bomb detonated nearby.

Since the Blitz began, some 43,000 British civilians had been killed by bombs, about half of them in London. As of the spring of 1941, far more British women and children had died in the war than had members of the country's armed forces. More than two million houses were damaged or destroyed; in the central London area, only one house in ten had escaped completely unscathed.

A few days after the raid, in a small neighborhood church, the

Murrows attended the last rites for the Wellses, the latest of several funerals to which they had gone in the last few months. At about the same time, Winston Churchill paid a melancholy visit to the ruins of the House of Commons chamber. More than virtually any other MP, he could lay claim to this place as his. Here, he had come as a new member more than forty years before. Here, in the 1930s, he had warned Parliament and the country of the dangers of appeasement. Here, the climactic debate over Neville Chamberlain's conduct of the war occurred in May 1940, leading to Churchill's accession to power. And here, as Britain fought on alone, he delivered his soaring speeches of defiance to the German threat. As the prime minister took a last look around at the wreckage of the chamber, tears streamed down his face.

ON MAY 15, in a speech to the English-Speaking Union in London, Gil Winant noted that, across the street from Parliament and Westminster Abbey, a statue of his hero, Abraham Lincoln, still stood. "As an American," Winant said, "I am proud that Lincoln was there in all that wreckage as a friend and sentinel . . . and a reminder that in [his own] great battle for freedom, he waited quietly for support for those things for which he lived and died."

That veiled comparison of Lincoln to the British people was followed by a somewhat less subtle declaration by the ambassador that he stood firmly with the British—and thought it was time his own country did so, too. "We have all slept while wicked, evil men plotted destruction," he remarked. "We have all tried to make ourselves believe we are not our brother's keeper. But we are now beginning to realize we need our brothers as much as our brothers need us."

As both the *Times* of London and the *New York Times* pointed out, Winant's use of "we" in his speech, one of the most powerful he ever delivered, was aimed as much at the United States as at Britain. "We have made our tasks infinitely more difficult because we failed to do yesterday what we are glad to do today," he declared. "To delay longer will make the war more protracted and increase the sacrifices for victory. Let us stop asking ourselves if it is necessary to do more now. Let us ask ourselves what more we can do today, so we have less to sacrifice tomorrow."

MEMBERS OF THE FAMILY

DURING THE WEEKEND OF THE MASSIVE MAY 10 ATTACK ON LON-
don, Winston and Clementine Churchill were staying at Ditchley,
Ronald and Nancy Tree's country estate near Oxford. Seven months
earlier, the Trees had proposed that, whenever there was a full moon
on weekends, Churchill come to Ditchley instead of Chequers, since
the prime minister's official country residence—a chilly, drafty Eliza-
bethan mansion—was considered a prime target in the event of an enemy raid. The prime minister, who loved the opulence of Ditchley,
took full advantage of the offer, bringing his retinue to the Tree estate
thirteen times over the next two years.

Members of Churchill's entourage spent the weekend enjoying the
Trees' lavish hospitality. Among them was Averell Harriman, who was
approached by Clementine Churchill with an unsettling favor to ask.
The Churchills' eighteen-year-old daughter, Mary, had recently
shocked her parents with the news of her engagement to the twenty-
eight-year-old son and heir of the Earl of Bessborough, whom she had
met just a short time before. Clementine had nothing against the
young man, she told Harriman, but she was convinced that Mary was
not in love with him, that she was too young to know what she was
doing and had "simply been swept off her feet with excitement."

Mary had refused her mother's pleas to reconsider the engagement.
When Clementine asked Winston to talk to their daughter, he had
agreed, but, preoccupied as he was with running the war, he never
found the time. In desperation, Clementine turned to Harriman. He

had two daughters, she said. He knew what young women were like. Would he please try to reason with Mary?

It was, on several levels, an extraordinary request. Above all, it revealed how, in a few short weeks, Harriman, along with Winant, had become not only a key figure in the prime minister's government circle but a de facto member of the Churchill family as well. Since their arrival in Britain, one or both of the Americans had spent every weekend with the prime minister and his family at Chequers or Ditchley.

To Clementine's dismay, Churchill had resisted her view that weekends in the country should be quiet respites from the wartime madness of London. He had never seen the virtue of separating work from family life and, in the interwar years, had entertained a steady stream of political and military visitors during weekends at Chartwell, the Churchills' country house in Kent. During the war, his weekend retreats overflowed with generals, admirals, air marshals, cabinet ministers, foreign government leaders, and a sprinkling of Churchill family members. Sometimes there would be as many as three shifts of guests: some summoned just for luncheon, others for dinner, still others spending the entire weekend.

With Churchill in residence, life at Chequers and Ditchley always seemed poised on the edge of chaos. According to his bodyguard, life with the prime minister "had less schedule than a forest fire and less peace than a hurricane." Secretaries scurried around; telephones shrilled; government cars, challenged by military sentries, came and went; dispatch riders bustled in and out with official pouches. When not involved in top secret conferences, guests played tennis or croquet, or as Sir Charles Portal, chief of the air staff, did, relaxed by chopping weeds in Ditchley's gardens. At the center of the action was the cigar-puffing prime minister, who, when he was not dominating the meetings, was holding court during lunch and dinner. Churchill "loved an audience at meals," his biographer Roy Jenkins wrote. "He was not . . . good at bilateral conversation, but with a table he could often be brilliant. And his brilliance not only amused and inspired his guests . . . but also provided an essential boost to his own zest and morale."

Harriman and Winant, while part of the official retinue, were pulled into the life of the Churchills and their children in ways that other visitors were not. Both became close personal friends of Churchill and his family, invited, as John Colville noted, "as much for the pleasure of their company as for the business to be done."

Still, the idea of counseling Mary Churchill about her love life must have seemed, at least initially, a somewhat daunting challenge to Harriman. His own two daughters had been raised by their mother, who divorced him when they were young; he had spent little time with them while they were growing up. Most of his recent experiences with young women had been as a lover, not as an avuncular adviser. Nonetheless, he gamely agreed to do as Clementine asked. Taking Mary aside for a heart-to-heart chat, he listened quietly as she poured out her side of the story and then talked to her about the uncertainties of war and the perils of making a hasty decision about such a vital, life-changing event as marriage. Mary herself had begun to have misgivings about her engagement, and, after her talk with Harriman, she decided to postpone it; soon afterward, she ended the relationship entirely. "I want to thank you very sincerely for your sympathy and helpfulness," she wrote Harriman a few days later. "I thought it was most sweet of you—when you are so busy and have so many important claims on your time—to listen so patiently to a recital of my stupidities and heart-aches! You helped me such a lot—and made me take myself less seriously—which was an excellent thing!"

For Harriman, the fact that Clementine Churchill had singled him out to play father confessor to Mary, no matter how uncomfortable it might have been at the time, was a source of tremendous gratification. His close access to the Churchills had taken away some of the sting of his exclusion from Roosevelt's New Deal team for so many years. Even though the inner circle to which he had been admitted was that of the British prime minister, not the American president, he was now in the center of the action, just as he had always longed to be.

In his courtship of Churchill and his family, Harriman employed the same energy and determination he previously had devoted to polo and his other enthusiasms. When he first arrived in London, he presented Clementine with a small bag of tangerines he had picked up in Lisbon. Her expression of delight made him realize how severely the sharp reduction in British food imports had affected even the prime minister's household. From then on, Harriman, a man usually known for his parsimony, played Santa Claus to the Churchills, plying them with goods that had long since disappeared from British stores—smoked Virginia hams, fresh fruit, handkerchiefs, silk stockings, Havana cigars.

Besides playing to Churchill's penchant for rich friends and luxury,

Harriman made himself available whenever the prime minister wanted to chat, no matter the hour or place. Often it would be close to midnight when he received a call from 10 Downing Street or from Churchill's study at Chequers, requesting his presence for a few hands of bezique, a complicated card game that was one of Churchill's favorite ways of relaxing. As they played until two or three in the morning, Churchill, who was fascinated by the making and unmaking of great fortunes, would regale his wealthy companion with stories of how he himself lost a great deal of money in the 1929 Wall Street crash. Notwithstanding that disaster, he would fantasize to Harriman about "what a wonderful life it would be to be a speculator." The prime minister would also use Harriman as a sounding board for his thoughts on the latest developments in the war and Anglo-American relations. It was a useful exercise for both men, with Harriman gaining an insight into Churchill's mind and Churchill getting Harriman's views on the actions and reactions of Roosevelt and his government.

Intriguingly, however, Harriman, as single-minded and ambitious as he was, chose to put his privileged position with Churchill and his family in jeopardy almost as soon as he had achieved it, by beginning an affair with Pamela Churchill, the prime minister's twenty-one-year-old daughter-in-law.

THE TWO HAD MET over lunch at Chequers in late March 1941, less than two weeks after the Lend-Lease representative had arrived in Britain. Like Harriman, the auburn-haired, blue-eyed Pamela had a fondness for cultivating important men and a fascination for political power. By all accounts, she was immediately captivated by this businessman almost thirty years her senior, who was, she was informed by a friend, "the most important American in London." At lunch, he had pumped her for information about Churchill and the press baron Lord Beaverbrook, an old friend and adviser of Churchill's and one of the most powerful and controversial men in Britain. Harriman, she later said, "was a hick from America. He knew nothing" about the current British political scene. But she also recalled how "absolutely marvelous looking" he seemed to her—"very athletic, very tan, very healthy." Focusing on Harriman with laser-beam intensity, she launched into what friends called her "mating dance," asking him questions, listening raptly to his comments, and laughing when he attempted a witticism.

She had charmed her father-in-law with the same warmly flirtatious manner and, in doing so, had become one of his favorite companions. With her husband, Randolph, in the Middle East, and her six-month-old son, Winston, tended by a nanny in the country, she spent much of her free time at Downing Street and Chequers, playing cards with Churchill, listening to his stories, and comforting him whenever he was worried or depressed.

Indeed, virtually from the beginning of her marriage, Pamela had a far better relationship with Winston and Clementine than with her twenty-seven-year-old husband. The daughter of Lord Digby, an impoverished Dorset aristocrat, she had met Randolph Churchill a few days after the war began. Afraid that "I would get trapped in Dorset for the rest of my life," she was desperate, she later said, for "new horizons and challenges. . . . I wanted to experience whatever there was to experience." Randolph proposed to her the night after they met, and the marriage took place two weeks later. For both, the union was "as cold and calculated as a business deal," Sally Bedell Smith, one of Pamela's biographers, wrote. "He wanted an heir and she wanted a name and position." They each got what they were after, but, not surprisingly, the relationship was an emotional disaster from the start.

Spoiled and indulged by his father, Randolph was a lively speaker and gifted writer who could be charming and witty when in the mood. More often, however, he was a blustering bully whose drinking, gambling, and womanizing were a constant source of embarrassment for his parents. Randolph, said Mary Churchill, "could be quite alarming—very noisy and quarrelsome. If he was in the right mood, he'd pick a quarrel with a chair." Considerably more scalding in his assessment of Randolph, John Colville wrote in his diary: "One of the most objectionable people I had ever met; noisy, self-assertive, whining and frankly unpleasant. . . . At dinner he was anything but kind to Winston, who adores him." In February 1941, to Pamela's great relief, Randolph's regiment was packed off to Egypt, and she was finally free to enjoy the erotic frenzy of wartime London.

The saying "Live today, for tomorrow we die" might be a war movie cliché, but it resonated all the same throughout the British capital in 1941—in hotels and nightclubs, pubs and palaces, situation rooms and bedrooms. "There was a diffused gallantry in the air, an unmarriedness," observed one British writer. "It came to be rumoured about the country that everybody in London was in love." Such romantic fatalism and hedonism was intoxicating to a good many Americans who encountered it during the war. For them, as for numerous Britons and exiled Europeans who spent time in the capital, conventional morality was laid to rest for the duration. "The normal barriers to having an affair with somebody were thrown to the winds," recalled CBS head William Paley, who was in London for several months during the war. "If it looked pretty good, you felt good, well, what in hell was the difference?"

Adding to this uninhibited atmosphere was the heady new sense of freedom and independence experienced by young British women. Having grown up in a society in which few women worked outside the home or went to college, they had been expected to remain primly in life's background and to demand little more than the satisfaction of having served their husbands and raised their children. That staid and predictable existence was shattered, however, when Britain declared war on Germany. Hundreds of thousands of women, even debutantes like Pamela who had never so much as boiled an egg, signed up for jobs in defense industries or enlisted in the Women's Auxiliary Air Force and other military units. As one former deb recalled, "It was a liberation, it set me free." Women began wearing slacks. They appeared in public without stockings. They smoked, they drank, and they had sex outside marriage—more often and with fewer qualms and less guilt than their mothers and grandmothers. The few American women in the capital were infected with a similar sense of freedom. "London was a Garden of Eden for women in those years," recalled *Time-Life* correspondent Mary Welsh, "a serpent dangling from every tree and street lamp, offering tempting gifts, companionship, warm if temporary affections."

Pamela Churchill was in the vanguard of this early women's liberation movement, securing a job at the Ministry of Supply and a room at the Dorchester Hotel. Years later, she remembered walking down a Dorchester corridor, thinking, "Here I am, 20 years old, totally free [and] wondering who will walk into my life." When she met Averell Harriman, she immediately set her sights for him. It was a spectacularly easy conquest. Harriman had been a hedonist long before coming to London, and he didn't need the city's carpe diem mentality to convince him he ought to be enjoying himself. In the 1920s, he had carried on a long liaison with Teddy Gerard, an actress and nightclub singer who had appeared in the *Ziegfeld Follies*. There were a number of other women over the years; shortly before leaving for London, he had indulged in a fling with the ballerina Vera Zorina, then married to George Balanchine.

His affair with Pamela likely began in the midst of the devastating April 16 Luftwaffe raid on London, little more than two weeks after they met. They both had been guests at a dinner party at the Dorchester in honor of Adele Astaire Cavendish, the sister of Fred Astaire and wife of Lord Charles Cavendish, son of the 9th Duke of Devonshire. While Gil Winant walked the streets of west London and Ed Murrow witnessed the destruction of his office and favorite pub that night, Harriman and his fellow dinner guests watched the fireworks from an eighth-floor room at the Dorchester, then retreated to the comparative safety of Harriman's suite on the ground floor.

When the others left, Pamela apparently remained behind. Early the next morning, John Colville saw Harriman and his boss's daughter-in-law walking arm in arm through the Horse Guards Parade, examining the devastation from the night before. Later that day, Harriman wrote his wife: "Last night was a real 'Blitz'—perhaps the most widespread bombing of the war. . . . Bombs dropped all around. Needless to say, my sleep was intermittent." He included chatty details about the dinner party and listed the names of those who had been there, with one prominent exception—Pamela Churchill.

Initially, at least, the pair tried to keep their relationship as quiet as possible. They were circumspect toward each other and "acted like friends" when with other people, said an acquaintance. Nonetheless, people began to notice—and talk. Duncan Sandys, the husband of the Churchills' eldest daughter, Diana, "intercepted glances and felt vibrations" between the two, and there was gossip that Harriman had been spotted tiptoeing down a hall at Chequers late at night.

Among those who deduced the truth was Lord Beaverbrook, who encouraged the liaison from the start. The owner of three major daily newspapers, Max Beaverbrook had been an outspoken appeaser of Hitler until May 1940. Once Britain was directly threatened by Germany, however, he threw himself into the war effort with the same energy with which he had opposed it before.

Clementine Churchill detested Beaverbrook, calling him a "microbe" and a "bottle imp" and begging her husband not to see so much of him. "Some thought him evil," recalled Drew Middleton, then a London correspondent for the Associated Press. "I found him amoral

[and] coldly calculating. He was a man of great energy, callous mental brutality, a passion for intrigue (sometimes, it seemed, for intrigue's sake) and a vast generosity." Once, when Bill Paley was invited to Beaverbrook's house for dinner, Ed Murrow warned him that the press magnate "took particular pleasure in extracting indiscreet information from his guests by getting them as drunk as possible."

Beaverbrook—who, as Churchill's minister of supply, was in charge of most of Britain's war production—was particularly well known for his munificence to a wide circle of women friends, including Pamela, to whom he became a patron of sorts. He gave her advice, lent her money to pay off Randolph's gambling debts, and housed her baby son and his nanny at Cherkley, his country estate in Surrey. Knowing only too well how much Britain needed American aid and how important Harriman was in getting it, he championed her affair with the American. Like Churchill, the newspaper mogul was determined to drag the United States into the war, and he strongly believed that the liaison between Harriman and Pamela could be used as a tool in that effort. A man who equated information with power, he was desperate to find out more about what the Americans were thinking and planning— something he could do, he thought, with Pamela's help. Soon the lovers were frequent guests at Cherkley, and Churchill's daughter-in-law became a back channel to Beaverbrook for news of the goings-on at Grosvenor Square. "She passed everything she knew about anybody to Beaverbrook," said the American journalist Tex McCrary. The affair was professionally beneficial to Harriman as well. "It was very helpful to him . . . to have an in like that," Pamela later said. "It made an enormous difference."

In the attempt to keep their relationship under wraps, Harriman and Pamela were aided by the arrival in June of Harriman's twenty-three-year-old daughter, Kathleen, who had come to keep her father company for a few months. A recent graduate of Bennington College, she had landed a temporary job, with Harriman's help, as a reporter in the London bureau of William Randolph Hearst's International News Service. Unaware of the affair at first, she formed a close friendship with Pamela, and when the Harrimans moved into a larger suite at the Dorchester, Pamela moved in with them. Later that summer, the two young women, with Harriman's money, rented a cottage together in Surrey for use on the weekends. Harriman often joined them there.

Kathleen was a perceptive young woman, and it didn't take her long to figure out what was going on between her father and new best friend. Having been raised in a worldly, sophisticated milieu where such extramarital trysts were common, she kept the secret to herself. She was not close to her stepmother and seemed to regard Harriman more as a generous friend than a father. Having discovered the affair, she decided to stay in London indefinitely, to keep an eye on her father and to act as camouflage.

Nonetheless, despite everyone's best efforts, the relationship eventually became common knowledge in both London and Washington. Harry Hopkins passed on the news to President Roosevelt, who, according to Hopkins, "got a big kick out of it." Hopkins himself was disturbed, "fearing stories to the effect that the President's envoy was breaking up the Prime Minister's son's marriage," Pamela later told historian Arthur Schlesinger Jr.

Both Pamela and Harriman knew they were playing with fire. The affair, she noted, "could have gone the other way," igniting a public scandal that would have caused great damage to all concerned. It still remains unclear whether either Winston or Clementine Churchill knew what was occurring under their roof at Chequers in the weeks and months after the relationship began. According to their middle daughter, Sarah, the Churchills and their children placed a high premium on personal privacy. "We do not ask questions of each other or pry into each other's affairs," Sarah Churchill said. "We believe passionately in the privacy of our lives and other people's."

At the same time, it's hard to believe that neither of the Churchills had an inkling early on of what was happening. For Clementine, who had a tortured relationship with her wayward son, the knowledge might not have been that difficult to accept. But Churchill doted on Randolph despite his boorishness, and the news of his son's cuckoldry would certainly have come as a rude shock. Yet, whatever his feelings, he needed Harriman and the Americans, and he had no intention of letting personal matters interfere with the national interest. Besides, Pamela had proved to be a useful conduit for him and Harriman, passing on to each man information and insights she had gleaned from the other.

Pamela, for her part, believed that the Churchills were well aware of what was going on. She noted, however, that neither directly confronted her. At one point in the war, Churchill casually commented to her: "You know, they're saying a lot of things about Averell in relation to you." She replied: "Well, a lot of people have nothing else to do in wartime but indulge in gossip." "I quite agree," Churchill said—and never raised the subject again.

WHILE HARRIMAN WAS becoming involved with Pamela, Gil Winant was developing close personal relationships of his own with several members of the Churchill family. The ambassador had the ability, as his friend Felix Frankfurter put it, to make everyone he met "feel as if they were the most important individuals on earth"—a quality that endeared him to the Churchills. "A man of quiet, intensely concentrated charm, Gil had very quickly become a dear friend of us all," Mary Churchill Soames later wrote, "entering into our joys and sorrows, jokes and rows (in these last always as a peacemaker)."

For all his shyness and occasional awkwardness, Winant had that same effect on others who met him on his official rounds. John Colville described him as a "gentle, dreamy idealist, whom most men and all women loved"—a characterization supported by comments about the ambassador in the diaries and letters of many prominent Britons of the time. "When Winant enters the room," remarked one woman who knew him, "everyone somehow feels better." Another acquaintance said: "There was something . . . magnetic about him." Tory MP Chips Channon noted how the young and beautiful Duchess of Kent, seated next to Winant at a luncheon at Chequers, "quite lost her heart" to him. Harold Nicolson called Winant "one of the most charming men I have ever met," adding that "the superb character of the man pierces through." Lord Moran, Churchill's doctor, mused in his diary: "Other men have to win the confidence of those they meet; Winant is allowed to skip that stage. Before he utters a syllable, people want to see more of him."

Even General Alan Brooke, the tart-tongued, irascible chief of the Imperial General Staff, who had nothing good to say about most Americans, fell under Winant's spell. At an official gathering one night, Lord Moran watched in amazement as Brooke, a passionate birder, chatted animatedly with Winant about the value of seeking solace in nature, especially during wartime. "There was Winant talking eagerly . . . and Brooke—a new Brooke to me—hardly able to wait his turn," Moran wrote in his diary. "When Winant had done, how his words cascaded." The two men became good friends, and years after the war, Brooke, now Field Marshal Lord Alanbrooke, said he considered his association with Winant to be "one of those great blessings which the war occasionally provided as an antidote to all its horrors."

But there was one important figure who remained somewhat impervious to Winant's diffident charm: Winston Churchill himself. Churchill was fond of the ambassador. He admired and respected him, declaring on more than one occasion, "Winant gives me fresh strength whenever I see him." Yet the prime minister felt uncomfortable around Winant and much preferred the company of Harriman and Harry Hopkins. "The P.M. is attracted by Winant's optimism, but . . . he prefers the tart cleverness of Hopkins, for the same reason that he is drawn to Max Beaverbrook," wrote Moran. Like Beaverbrook, Churchill's closest friends tended to be flamboyant, quick-witted men with a "touch of loucheness," who liked to gamble, drink, and talk late into the night. As Roy Jenkins has so aptly noted, the prime minister "liked bounders." And if there was one thing that John Gilbert Winant most emphatically was not, it was a bounder.

Clementine Churchill, on the other hand, much preferred Winant to Harriman. While she was grateful for Harriman's intercession with her daughter and enjoyed playing croquet with him (both were expert at the game), she generally thought of him, in the words of writer Christopher Ogden, as "one more rich businessman and icily ambitious maneuverer," who, like many of Churchill's rich, ambitious friends, "would isolate her more from her husband." Winant, she felt, was actually interested in and sympathetic to *her.* According to Mary Soames, Winant "understood intuitively" her mother's complicated nature and the strains and stresses of her life, and, as a result, she often confided in him—something she rarely did with anyone.

TO THE GUESTS invited to Downing Street, Chequers, or Ditchley, Clementine Churchill was an elegant, intelligent, caring hostess who did everything in her power to make them feel at home. Many used the word "charming" to describe her: Harry Hopkins called her the "most charming and entertaining" of all the people he met in Britain; Janet Murrow said she was "charming, vivacious, and attractive"; and Eleanor Roosevelt used practically the same words—"very attractive, young-looking and charming."

Yet Mrs. Roosevelt suspected that another Clementine Churchill lay hidden beneath that calm, self-controlled exterior: "One feels that, being in public life, she has had to assume a role and that the role is now a part of her, but one wonders what she is like underneath." As the wife of the president of the United States, Eleanor Roosevelt knew a great deal about public roles versus reality, and her shrewd guess about her British counterpart was in fact correct. Behind the serene, poised facade that Clementine Churchill presented to the world was a passionate, emotionally fragile, lonely, and often deeply unhappy woman.

For more than thirty years, Clementine had made her husband her life's work, giving short shrift to everything and everyone else—her children and friends as well as her own needs and desires. She once told Pamela Churchill that "when she married Winston, she had decided to give her life totally to him. . . . She lived for Winston." He, however, did not return the favor. Although he undoubtedly loved her and was heavily dependent on her, as his hundreds of tender, solicitous letters to her make clear, Churchill was, in the words of John Pearson, a Churchill family biographer, a "total egotist" who never made much time for his wife. His pursuit of political power and his own personal interests almost always took precedence over her and their children. "In his heart, he adored her, but I don't think it ever occurred to him that she might need a little more," Pamela noted. She added: "Churchills expect their women to understand them totally [but] they don't spend much time trying to understand their women."

Throughout their marriage, Clementine was plagued by financial worries, thanks to Churchill's insistence on leading a luxurious, extravagant lifestyle that most of the time they could not afford. "I am easily satisfied," he liked to say, then after a pause would add impishly, "with the very best." The Churchills' money troubles were exacerbated by his occasional penchant for gambling and stock market speculation and by his 1922 purchase of Chartwell, a ramshackle redbrick Victorian mansion with overgrown grounds and spectacular views of the countryside in Kent. The house, about twenty miles south of London, was meant to be a country retreat for the Churchills and their children. Furious that he had bought the house without consulting her, Clementine believed it would be a money pit for as long as they owned it, as indeed it was. Her mother, recalled Mary Churchill Soames, would reprimand her children "for not turning the lights off. The house was a great burden to her."

Although both Churchill and his wife came from aristocratic back-

John Gilbert Winant.
LIBRARY OF CONGRESS

Gil Winant, caught in the middle of shaving, in a lighthearted moment with two fellow American pilots in France during World War I.
FRANKLIN D. ROOSEVELT PRESIDENTIAL LIBRARY

John Gilbert Winant, first chairman of the Social Security Board, meets with his two fellow commissioners, Arthur J. Altmeyer (left) and Vincent M. Miles (right) in 1935.

Edward R. Murrow, in the uniform of a U.S. war correspondent, shortly after the United States entered World War II.

A young Ed Murrow, dressed in the tattered shirt and jeans he wore as a lumberjack, his summer job during high school and college. Years later, in London, Murrow would tell friends that "there was a satisfaction about that life" and that "he had never known that kind of satisfaction since."

Ed Murrow with his wife, Janet, soon after their marriage in 1934.

Ed Murrow in central London in 1941.

Averell Harriman, the new Lend-Lease administrator for Britain, at his office in London in mid-1941.

GETTY IMAGES

Averell Harriman learned to ride at a very young age at his father's sprawling estate in New York. He went on to become a world-class polo player.

HARRIMAN COLLECTION,
LIBRARY OF CONGRESS

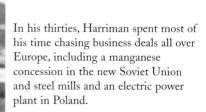

In his thirties, Harriman spent most of his time chasing business deals all over Europe, including a manganese concession in the new Soviet Union and steel mills and an electric power plant in Poland.

LIBRARY OF CONGRESS

Harriman and
his wife, Marie,
enjoying a night out
at the Stork Club
in New York.

Harriman on the slopes
at Sun Valley, Idaho,
which he transformed
into the country's
premier ski resort in
the late 1930s.

George VI greets John Gilbert Winant, the new U.S. ambassador to Britain, at the Windsor train station in March 1941. The king's unprecedented gesture—venturing outside his palace to welcome a newly arrived foreign envoy—underscored the importance that Britain attached to U.S. help in fighting off Hitler and the Germans. BRITISH PATHE/WPA FILM LIBRARY

Members of the Auxiliary Territorial Service, the women's branch of the British army, manning an antiaircraft gun in London during the war.

LIBRARY OF CONGRESS

Firemen work to put out a blaze caused by a massive German bombing attack on central London during the Blitz in late 1940.

LIBRARY OF CONGRESS

Pamela Churchill takes a stroll with her toddler son, Winston, on a London street in 1942. The year before, Churchill's daughter-in-law embarked on an affair with Averell Harriman, and when Harriman was named U.S. ambassador to the Soviet Union in 1943, she became involved with Ed Murrow. Some thirty years later, she married Harriman. LIBRARY OF CONGRESS

Sarah Churchill, the prime minister's favorite daughter, was the peacemaker of her family. She and John Gilbert Winant had an intense wartime relationship. LIBRARY OF CONGRESS

Members of the Eagle Squadron, an all-American unit who defied their country's neutrality laws to fight with the Royal Air Force before the United States entered the war. LIBRARY OF CONGRESS

Looking very pleased at being at the center of the action, Averell Harriman sits between Winston Churchill and Russian leader Joseph Stalin in Moscow in August 1942. Harriman wangled an invitation to the Churchill-Stalin session, one of many such summit meetings he would attend during the war.

Two young British servicewomen unload Winchester rifles just arrived from the United States, as part of the U.S. Lend-Lease agreement with Britain.

John Gilbert Winant and his wife, Constance (next to Winant), welcome General Dwight D. Eisenhower and Admiral Harold Stark, the two highest-ranking U.S. military leaders in London, at a July 4, 1942, reception at the ambassador's offical residence.

John Gilbert Winant with Winston Churchill and Joseph Davies, former U.S. ambassador to the Soviet Union, at Chequers, the prime minister's official country home. Winant and Harriman spent many weekends with the Churchills at Chequers. LIBRARY OF CONGRESS

U.S. servicemen buy goods not available for sale to the British at a U.S. military post exchange in London. American forces in Britain had a much higher standard of living than did most British citizens. LIBRARY OF CONGRESS

Eighteen-year-old Tommy Hitchcock in his French aviator's uniform. Hitchcock, who flew with the Lafayette Escadrille during World War I and was the youngest American to win a pilot's wings in the conflict, shot down two German planes before being shot down himself.

LIBRARY OF CONGRESS

Widely regarded as the best polo player in the world, Hitchcock helped make polo one of the most popular spectator sports in America in the 1920s and '30s.

LIBRARY OF CONGRESS

Thanks to Gil Winant, Hitchcock became assistant military attaché in the American embassy in London, where he played a key role in the U.S. adoption of the P-51B Mustang, the fighter plane that helped make D-Day possible.

LIBRARY OF CONGRESS

A Mustang undergoes a test flight in California. After the war, a top
U.S. Air Force official acknowledged that the plane appeared in the fight
against Germany "at just the saving moment, in the very nick of time."

In a tender wartime moment, an American soldier buys a corsage from a flower seller in London's Piccadilly Circus and pins it on his girlfriend's jacket.

GETTY IMAGES

Ed Murrow, with his ever-present cigarette, prepares a newscast at the CBS bureau in London.

LIBRARY OF CONGRESS

President Roosevelt and Prime Minister Churchill meet with Chinese leader Chiang Kai-shek at the Cairo Conference in November 1943. Also attending were Gil Winant (behind Roosevelt) and Averell Harriman (behind Madame Chiang Kai-shek). Presidential aide Harry Hopkins is at the extreme right.

Housewives in suburban London hand out tea and food in June 1944 to American troops on their way to the southern coast of England—and Normandy.

General Dwight D. Eisenhower stands between his two principal British bête noires—General Alan Brooke, chief of the Imperial General Staff, on the left, and General Bernard Montgomery, on the right. Scornful of Eisenhower's military ability, both British generals were constantly second-guessing him.

Stalin, Roosevelt, and Churchill at the Yalta Conference in February 1945. Harriman is behind Stalin and Roosevelt. Standing on the right is Sarah Churchill, acting as aide-de-camp to her father, and British foreign secretary Anthony Eden.

General Eisenhower receives the Freedom of the City of London, an honor dating back to medieval days, in an elaborate ceremony in late June 1945, shortly after the Allies' victory in Europe.

Jubilant young American servicemen celebrate V-E Day—May 8, 1945— with London residents in Piccadilly Circus.

Ed and Janet Murrow with their son, Casey, a couple of years after the war.

grounds, neither had family money, and Churchill's parliamentary salary was relatively meager. In order to pay for their lavish way of life, he was dependent on his writing of books and articles, which, although prolific, did not always supply the vast amounts of money needed. At one point, to cover their monthly bills, Clementine sold a ruby and diamond necklace that Winston had given her as a wedding present. When someone asked her many years later how Winston was able so effortlessly to combine writing, painting, and involvement in politics and government, she replied acerbically that he "never did anything he didn't want to do, and left someone else to clear up the mess afterwards."

During the war, Churchill was more the center of attention than ever; at Chequers and Ditchley, the world revolved around him. While Clementine made sure that all the Churchills' official guests were well taken care of, not many of them paid much attention to her or, for that matter, to any of the few other women included in the weekend house parties. "A weekend here is very different from anywhere else," Kathleen Harriman wrote to her sister after a stay at Chequers in the summer of 1941. "Never for a moment is the war forgotten. . . . Women are rather in the way. They leave [the dining room] right after dinner and then aren't expected to stay for too long when the men come out, which sometimes isn't until way after midnight."

In Kathleen's view, Clementine was very gracious in "taking a back seat" to her husband. She told her sister: "Everyone in the family looks upon him as God and she's rather left out, and when anyone pays any attention to her she's overjoyed. . . . But don't get the idea she's mousy, not at all. She's got a mind of her own, only she's a big enough person not to use it unless he wants her to."

Although Clementine had a keen wit and strong, well-thought-out views on most issues, she rarely tried to inject her thoughts into the torrent of arguments and opinions voiced by her husband and his guests during meals. On the infrequent occasions when she tried to start a conversation about some other topic, the attempts usually were squelched. As the war continued, she began retreating more and more to her bedroom during the dinner hour, asking Pamela, one of the few regular female guests, to substitute as hostess in the dining room. In Pamela's view, Clementine ate more meals on a tray in her room than with Churchill and his company and, indeed, spent as much as 80 percent of her life alone.

It's not surprising, then, that she warmed so quickly to the new American ambassador, who made clear he enjoyed *her* company and conversation. Shortly after Winant arrived in London, Clementine invited him to lunch at Downing Street but noted that Churchill probably would not be there. "This sounds as though I was trying to prevent you and Winston from getting together!" she wrote. "This is not really my wicked intention but it *did* occur to me that if he were not here to engross your attention, I would enjoy your company even more."

The ambassador and prime minister's wife were kindred spirits in a number of ways. Both were shy and reserved by nature, allowing few people to see below the surface. They also shared a sense of idealism, a dedication to the concept that government had a responsibility to help the underclass. Like Winant, Clementine Churchill had been somewhat of a radical since her youth. As a girl, she had loved school and wanted to go to college, a rare path for an upper-class young woman of her generation to follow; her mother, aghast at the idea, refused to allow it. Throughout her life, Clementine was in favor of financial independence for women (although she never experienced such freedom herself) and, long before women's suffrage became a reality, strongly backed the right of women to vote.

As an ardent member of the Liberal Party, she was discomfited when Churchill left the Liberals to rejoin the Conservative Party in 1924. Although she loyally switched her official party allegiance as well, she never lost her interest in bettering the lives of Britain's poor or her hostility to her husband's Tory colleagues who opposed such reforms. She loathed Lord Beaverbrook and most of Churchill's other wealthy friends, not only because of what she saw as their empty, dissolute lifestyle but also because of their indifference to the nation's less privileged citizens. "Do not let the glamour of elegance & refinement . . . blind you," she once wrote to her husband. "The charming people you are meeting today . . . are ignorant, vulgar, prejudiced. They can't bear the idea of the lower classes being independent & free."

Clementine was never shy about letting those who angered her know exactly how she felt. During a weekend at Blenheim Palace, the Duke of Marlborough, who owned Blenheim and was Churchill's first cousin, told her she must not write to the Tories' archenemy—the former Liberal prime minister David Lloyd George—on Blenheim stationery. Hearing that, she put down her pen, went to her room, packed her things, and, ignoring the duke's pleas to stay, returned to London.

After another occasion when Clementine turned on one of her husband's associates, Churchill noted with some pride and even awe: "She dropped on him like a jaguar out of a tree!"

During both world wars, Clementine translated her interest in reform into an active involvement in efforts to improve the living conditions of the country's working class. In the Great War, she ran nine canteens for munitions workers in north London, feeding up to five thousand men and women a day. During the Blitz, she lobbied for government payments for volunteer civil defense workers and played an important role in the improvement of London's air raid shelters. After receiving a flood of letters from people about the shelters' abysmal conditions, she made a series of unannounced visits to several in different parts of the city to see for herself how bad the situation was. Her subsequent reports to her husband about the appalling lack of hygiene and basic comforts were, to a large degree, responsible for bringing about government improvements in the shelters. As word of her involvement spread, other examples of government inertia or inefficiency in helping the public were brought to her attention by, among others, MPs, clergymen, social workers, and doctors. She spent considerable time trying to help resolve these problems as well, often after discussing them with Winant.

FOR THE AMERICAN AMBASSADOR, inclusion in the Churchill family circle brought an occasional respite from his crushing workload but, more important, it gave him a sense of belonging. A workaholic all his adult life, he had spent little time with his own family while serving as governor and as head of Social Security and the ILO. His daughter, Constance, was now married; his elder son, John Jr., was a student at Princeton, and his younger son, Rivington, attended Deerfield Academy, a prep school in western Massachusetts. Although Winant's wife came to London periodically, the couple had a distant relationship. Abbie Rollins Caverly, an old family friend of the Winants, said the ambassador was "one of the loneliest men I've ever known. I think he sometimes desperately needed someone to talk to, and at home, there was no one to listen to him."

While he enjoyed being around Clementine and the other Churchills at Chequers, Winant found himself gravitating more and more to the company of twenty-seven-year-old Sarah, the prime minister's favorite daughter. Independent and strong-willed like her father, the red-haired, green-eyed Sarah was known as "the Mule" by her family. Like both her sisters, she considered herself a daddy's girl, yet she was the only one with enough mettle to stand up to him.

As was true of her siblings, Sarah was the product of an emotionally difficult childhood. In Britain, it was not uncommon for British upper-class children to see little of their parents, but the Churchill household carried that practice to extremes. "As children, we soon became aware that our parents' main interest and time were consumed by immensely important tasks, besides which our own demands and concerns were trivial," Mary recalled. "We never expected either of them to attend our school plays, prize givings or sports days. . . . When our mother did manage to grace any of these important occasions, we were ecstatically grateful."

Churchill had delegated the raising of their children to Clementine; absorbed in his career and other interests, he was often absent from the family circle during school holidays and other important occasions. Left to handle their growing brood on her own, Clementine often opted out herself. She loved her children but, by all accounts, including her own, was never good at mothering. "A wife first and mother very distant second" was how one friend described her. She once told Mary that "it took me all my time and strength just to keep up with [Winston]. I never had anything left over." Her pregnancies and the births of her children left her physically and emotionally exhausted—so much so that in 1918, expecting her fourth child and beset by money worries, she offered to give the new baby to a friend who was childless. The amazed woman accepted, but Clementine obviously thought better of her bizarre, spur-of-the-moment suggestion, and nothing more was said about the matter.

Two and a half years later, in August 1921, the Churchills left their four children, including Marigold, the baby whom Clementine had impetuously offered to give away, with a nursemaid in the south of England while Clementine took part in a tennis tournament and Winston tended to business in London. Two-year-old Marigold, who had been suffering from a throat infection since the beginning of the summer holiday, suddenly developed septicemia. Rushing to her bedside, her parents were with her when she died a week later. According to Sarah, her mother never fully recovered from her grief over Marigold's death or her guilt at being absent during the child's illness.

Nonetheless, Clementine continued her practice, established early in her marriage, of taking long sabbaticals from her family, often at health spas on the Continent. There, she recuperated from the frenzy of her life with her children and demanding husband, and regathered her strength to face them all again. When she was home, she was, in Mary's words, "a mixture of tenderness and severity," while Sarah called her "an authoritarian figure with whom you could not argue." While both Sarah and Mary drew close to Clementine as young adults, Diana, the oldest child, had a problematic relationship with her mother that lasted for the rest of her life. Mary, who later wrote a sympathetic biography of Clementine, noted: "Although her children loved and revered her, they did not find in her a fun maker or a companion."

Winston, on the other hand, was both. During the rare occasions when he spent concentrated amounts of time with his children, he was relaxed, warm, and fun-loving, much like a child himself. He played with them and recruited them for various expeditions and projects, including laying bricks for a wall at Chartwell. His daughters adored him, and he returned their love. But the real apple of his eye was Randolph, whom he outrageously spoiled and always forgave, no matter how egregious his behavior. Churchill and his son, whom he viewed as his political heir, would often engage in hectoring, high-volume arguments over dinner, with other guests chiming in, as Sarah and Diana looked on silently. Of the dinner conversations, Churchill's nephew, Peregrine Churchill, said: "All those overpowering egos! All that endless talk on politics! After a certain age, I felt the need to get away from all those Churchills. Otherwise they would have squashed me." Years later, Diana would tell her daughter that she married her first husband to "escape from all the endless talk around the Chartwell dinner table."

AS A CHILD, Sarah Churchill had been sickly, solitary, and dreamy. She doted on her father but was intimidated by his quick wit and his single-minded focus on work. "If I really wanted to say or ask anything important, I could not trust my tongue to get it right, and I would scribble him a note," she later wrote. "It became the best way of communicating, and the least tiring and time-absorbing for him." Yet underneath her sweet, shy, quiet facade was a streak of toughness and rebellion that neither Diana nor Mary shared.

When she made her debut at the age of eighteen, she became known as the "Bolshie deb" because of her outspoken dislike for what she saw as the luxurious but shallow lifestyle of Churchill's rich friends—the same view held by her mother and one that greatly annoyed her father. She irritated him even further by getting a job as a dancer in a major London theatrical review when she was twenty. From childhood, Sarah had been far more interested in artistic endeavors than in the political milieu in which she had been raised. In her early teens, she began writing poetry, an avocation she continued for much of her life. Anxious to make her mark in the creative world, she persuaded her parents to let her take dancing lessons. She loved the experience, and when she was hired for the chorus of the review *Follow the Sun,* she recalled, "I walked out of that theatre feeling an inch taller. Suddenly life had a meaning. . . . The adventure had started at last."

Winston and Clementine, however, were never reconciled to the idea of a daughter of theirs on the stage. When others, including her sister Mary, maintained that Sarah had real acting and dancing talent, they insisted otherwise. Having been influenced by his boss's opinion of Sarah's ability, John Colville, who went to see her act in a play in the London's West End during the war, was amazed to find that she in fact "gave a good performance."

Sarah upset her parents even more when, at twenty-one, she announced plans to marry thirty-eight-year-old Vic Oliver, a twice-divorced Jewish comedian from Austria and the star of *Follow the Sun.* Exploding in anger, Churchill refused to shake hands with Oliver when they met and pronounced him "common as dirt." In his attempt to persuade Sarah to change her mind, her father, she later said, "addressed me like a public meeting" on the dangers posed by "this itinerant vagabond."

Sarah, however, held firm. She followed Oliver to New York, where he was starring in a new review, and Churchill promptly sent Randolph in hot pursuit on the next transatlantic liner. Dubbing Sarah "the runaway debutante," London and New York newspapers, not surprisingly, had a field day with the story, running such banner headlines as "DASH ACROSS ATLANTIC" and "BROTHER CHASES CUPID." Her father hired private detectives and lawyers to try to stop the marriage but failed in his attempts. Sarah wed Oliver in late 1936 and brought him back to England, where they acted, first together, then separately, in repertory companies throughout the country and in the West End.

Notwithstanding the past rows with her parents, Sarah was regarded as the peacemaker in her family, the empathetic one who tried to mediate family quarrels and bring everyone together. She was close to both her sisters, and Diana's young daughters, Edwina and Celia Sandys, adored her. She was, Edwina Sandys remarked, "a magical creature for me as a child. She flitted in and out of our prosaic lives like a colourful imp. She was beautiful and utterly charming." Known for her "raucous, irreverent giggle," Sarah was blessed with a highly developed sense of humor. "Some of the funniest moments of my life were shared with her," Edwina added. "We laughed until we cried." Of Sarah, a newspaper journalist would later observe: "More than anybody I have ever interviewed, she was a life enhancer, who made everything seem rosier, more entertaining, more glamorous. At the same time, she was vulnerable. She wanted you to like her and was touched if you did."

As Sarah won better and more varied theater roles in the late 1930s, her confidence grew and her dependence on her charming but controlling husband lessened. At about the same time, she discovered that Oliver was having affairs with other young women. By the time Sarah met Winant in the spring of 1941, her marriage was all but over. In a letter to her sister, Kathleen Harriman wrote that "Sarah is a terribly nice girl, but I don't think much of her husband Vic." Harriman's daughter added: "She seems desperately unhappy, but she's got guts enough to stick with Vic on account of her father. Going on the stage is the one way she can keep from going mad."

Unknown to Kathleen, however, Sarah had another solace: her growing friendship with Winant, with whom she was spending considerable time at Chequers and in London. As their relationship deepened over the next few months, she revealed her troubles to him, as well as her dreams and hopes for the future. Attracted by her warmth, wit, and sense of caring, Winant, in turn, lowered what Alan Brooke called "the iron curtain of his reserve" and confided in her in a way he had rarely done with anyone else.

In the midst of Britain's greatest crisis in history, the American ambassador found himself falling in love with the prime minister's daughter.

6.

"MR. HARRIMAN
ENJOYS MY COMPLETE
CONFIDENCE"

ON MAY 30, 1941, HUNDREDS OF PEOPLE LINED THE OBSERVA-
tion deck at New York's La Guardia Airport to welcome Gil Winant
back home. They were there in response to a front-page story in that
morning's *New York Times,* reporting the ambassador's unexpected, un-
explained return for talks with the president and other leading administration figures. Discomfited by the crowd's cheering and applause,
Winant diffidently raised his hat as he strode from his plane to the
terminal. Outside, he faced a battery of newsreel cameras. "This is
worse than a bombing," he muttered before politely but firmly refusing
to comment on why he had returned to the United States.

American and British newspapers showed no such hesitation in
speculating about the reason for his sudden visit. "There is no doubt
that Mr. Winant hurried back to tell what England needs most, and to
make clear that the need is urgent . . . that the war has reached a crisis," the columnist Anne O'Hare McCormick wrote in the *New York
Times.* A correspondent for London's *Daily Mail* reported he had been
told by "a high Washington authority" that the "meeting between
Winant and Roosevelt is as important as a meeting between the President and Mr. Churchill himself. It is a strategy conference."

In London, both Winant and Averell Harriman had felt increasingly cut off from what was happening in Washington and the rest of
the United States. Cable traffic from Roosevelt, Hopkins, and other
officials was spotty, and letters often took more than a month to arrive
from America, if they ever came at all. (Much of the mail between the

United States and Britain during this period was lost in merchant ship sinkings.) Harriman complained to FDR that there was "almost a Chinese wall" of silence between London and the American capital. "My source of information is entirely from British ministries," he wrote the president. "My usefulness will be in direct proportion to the extent to which I am kept informed of developments in fact and thought in Washington."

What little he and Winant knew about the situation in America spelled disaster for Britain. According to the latest polls, the percentage of Americans willing to risk war by aiding the British was declining. The first Lend-Lease shipments of food—dried eggs, evaporated milk, bacon, beans, and canned meat—had arrived in Britain in late May, providing some relief. But there was little of anything else. Weapons, planes, tanks, and other matériel still were not being produced in large numbers in the United States, and there were not enough ships to carry to Britain the trickle of armaments that had come off the assembly line. Despite the administration's urging, American industries continued to resist a large-scale conversion to war production. What's more, several industrial tycoons, like car manufacturer Henry Ford, were rabid isolationists and refused to fill orders for the British. A Senate investigation revealed that government production targets had not been met and that a sizable number of the companies that did accept government contracts were guilty of corruption and waste. "We are advertising to the world . . . that we are in a mess," one Democratic senator said in disgust. Unless the United States intensified its mobilization, a government report warned, its war production would be outstripped by Britain and Canada within the year.

Indeed, the Lend-Lease situation was so dismal in the summer of 1941 that William Whitney, one of Harriman's top aides in London, quit in protest over America's failure to do more. "We are deceiving the people on both sides of the Atlantic by allowing them to think that there is today a stream of lease-lend war materiels crossing the Atlantic, when in fact there is little or none," Whitney wrote in his letter of resignation. "My view is that the Administration . . . should show Congress and the people, that while we are boasting that we are at enmity with Hitler alongside Britain, we are doing a disgracefully small share of the job."

Three days before Winant returned to America, the president had appeared to signal a profound shift in course. Pledging to prevent

Germany from controlling the Atlantic, Roosevelt declared an unlimited national emergency and seemed to imply that the United States would soon begin convoying: "The delivery of needed supplies to Britain is imperative. I say this can be done; it must be done; it will be done." To many in America and Britain, FDR's declaration sounded "almost like a call to arms." His speech, noted Robert Sherwood, was "taken as a solemn commitment; the entry of the United States in the war against Germany was now considered inevitable and even imminent." But at a press conference the following day, Roosevelt, as he had done so often before, backed away from all notions of belligerency: there would be no convoying, at least for the present, and no fighting. In the view of Dean Acheson, then an assistant secretary of state, the president, along with much of his administration and most of the country, seemed "paralyzed between apprehension and action."

Armed with firsthand knowledge of Britain's perilous position, Winant, who, in the words of General Raymond Lee, was "straining every nerve and resorting to every expediency" to bring the United States into the conflict, was determined to press Roosevelt and his administration as hard as he could. In a memo to Foreign Office subordinates, Anthony Eden wrote: "Winant asked me today to consider what, short of war, the USA could do to help us. . . . I had the impression he would not at all mind if the proposals entailed risks of war."

In Washington, Winant, at Roosevelt's invitation, stayed at the White House. In his meetings with the president and other administration officials, he forcefully emphasized the desperate future facing Britain and its people. They urgently needed military aid, particularly planes and tanks, as well as U.S. naval protection for convoys. There was no truth to current rumors that Britain was on the verge of seeking a negotiated peace, the ambassador said. But if the United States failed to provide enough aid, he warned, the British will to resist, resolute as it was, might begin to weaken. "We must not wait too long."

FDR responded—up to a point. He authorized the dispatch of four thousand marines to Iceland to take over its defense from the British, a step that placed American troops nearer Britain in case of invasion. He also authorized naval protection of U.S. merchant vessels and troopships as far as Iceland, with instructions to shoot on sight if necessary; British convoys remained unprotected. In public, Roosevelt downplayed the urgency of the ambassador's visit.

On Winant's return to Britain, Churchill ordered a plane to pick him up at the base in Scotland where he landed and bring him immediately to Chequers. When the ambassador told the prime minister about the new American actions, Churchill, while somewhat heartened, knew they were far from enough to stave off disaster. "If Munich had been Great Britain's least glorious hour, mid-1941 was surely America's," a British historian later wrote.

BACK AT WORK IN LONDON, Winant was forced to come to grips with another intractable problem: his increasingly problematic relationship with Averell Harriman. Taking advantage of his nebulous job description—an "excellent mandate, in no way tying my hands"—the ambitious Harriman was involving himself more and more in matters that had nothing to do with Lend-Lease. As a businessman and sportsman, he had long been known for his sharp-edged, elbows-out tactics. In a practice match preceding a 1920s championship polo contest, he had, for example, urged Manuel Andrada, a member of the opposing team, to harass Laddie Sanford, one of Harriman's own team members, who was vying with him for a place on the championship squad. "Laddie was not the most courageous man in the world and Andrada was one of the toughest," Harriman said years later. "The upshot was that he knocked Sanford to hell and gone. I don't know if Laddie was a better player than I was, but he was no good that day, I can tell you. It's an amusing incident, but I was determined to get back. I just could not believe I couldn't beat Laddie. Because, you know, he was soft."

Years later, when Harriman came to Washington to advise the Roosevelt administration on the transport of raw materials, he set out to appropriate the duties of the businessman advising the government on railroads and the rest of the transportation industry—the job he had wanted. In London, he encroached on Winant's turf in much the same way. Although Harriman assured Roosevelt in a memo that "we are working together as one team" and added that "I have never worked in a more congenial atmosphere, largely due to Gil's generous personality," he operated with little regard for the ambassador. In his diary, Raymond Lee complained that Harriman was using his position to "interfere in anything and everything," adding that Winant "has been entirely too patient." Harriman controlled his own payroll and communications, reporting directly to Roosevelt and Hopkins, and invited official visitors from Washington who had nothing to do with his mission to use the Lend-Lease offices as their London base and to consult with him about their dealings with British officials.

But it was his diligent cultivation of Churchill that produced the richest dividends in expanding the scope and influence of his job. In June, while Winant was in Washington consulting with Roosevelt, the prime minister, in the wake of his country's recent military disasters, asked Harriman to go to the Middle East and Africa to assess the state of British forces and facilities there and determine what America could do to help. For a man who had no official diplomatic accreditation to Britain and whose own country wasn't even in the war, it was an extraordinary assignment by any standard. To his military commanders in the region, the prime minister made clear that Harriman should be treated as his own personal representative and given the same opportunities for inspection as if he had been a member of Britain's War Cabinet: "Mr. Harriman enjoys my complete confidence and is in the most intimate relations with the President and Mr. Harry Hopkins. No one can do more for you. . . . I commend Mr. Harriman to your most attentive consideration." Harriman, not surprisingly, was jubilant about the assignment. "I don't think I've ever seen him so excited about anything," Kathleen Harriman wrote to her sister.

During his five-week expedition, Harriman traveled sixteen thousand miles, crisscrossing the Middle East and much of Africa. He inspected ports, harbors, aircraft assembly facilities, and ship repair docks, and talked to dozens of British troops, pilots, civil servants, mechanics, and others involved in the fight against the Germans. Intriguingly, his military escort in Cairo turned out to be none other than the man he was cuckolding in London. Randolph Churchill, now working as a public information officer at British headquarters, had been detailed by his father to act as Harriman's aide while the American toured military installations and conferred with the brass in the Egyptian capital. Of Harriman, Churchill wrote to his son: "I have made great friends with him and have the highest regard for him. He does all he can to help us."

Harriman, who never let his heart rule his head, apparently was unperturbed at finding himself in this ticklish situation, and he and Churchill's son chatted amiably about Pamela and what was going on in London. A few days later, Randolph, who at that point clearly did not know about his wife's affair, wrote to Pamela about how much he liked Harriman: "I found him absolutely charming, & it was lovely to be able to hear so much news of you & all my friends. . . . He spoke delightfully about you & I fear that I have a serious rival!" To his father, Randolph wrote even more glowingly of Harriman: "He has definitely become my favorite American. . . . He clearly regards himself more as your servant than Roosevelt's. I think he is the most objective and shrewd of all those who are around you."

From Cairo, Harriman sent Churchill an unsparing, toughly worded report about the many shortcomings he had found in Britain's Middle East operations, including a waste of equipment; poorly trained tank crewmen; inadequate intelligence; lack of coordination between the RAF, army, and navy; and "a sense of complacency and absence of urgency" at the Cairo headquarters. Above all, he focused on the shortage of vital armaments and supplies—tanks, ships, fuel, transport vehicles, even spare parts. While the other difficulties were clearly part of Churchill's bailiwick, the shortages were a problem that only American aid could rectify.

The U.S. envoy's diligence, unrelenting hard work, and persistent questioning during the grueling inspection tour won the respect, albeit much of it grudging, of many of those whose work he scrutinized. A British friend passed on to Harriman a conversation he had overheard between two Whitehall officials: " 'Mr. Harriman is a go-getter, isn't he?' Reply: 'I expect he is.' 'He asks very potent and embarrassing questions.' Reply: 'Oh, does he?' 'Yes, insists on an answer and gets it.' "

Churchill, too, was much impressed by Harriman's efforts, but, as the Lend-Lease representative discovered when he returned to London in early July, the prime minister was now preoccupied by more pressing matters than the Middle East snafus. On June 22, Hitler had broken his 1939 nonaggression treaty with Joseph Stalin and invaded the Soviet Union with more than two million troops. Late that night, Churchill made a broadcast to his countrymen pledging Britain's full support to the Soviet Union, despite his long-held view of its government leaders as "the mortal foes of civilized freedom." As much as the prime minister despised Stalin's "wicked regime," he needed the Russians to bear the brunt of a new German onslaught, to lift some of the burden of fighting from British shoulders so that he and his severely weakened country could regroup.

Then, a few days after the German invasion, Harry Hopkins arrived in London with an invitation to Churchill to meet Roosevelt the following month off the coast of Newfoundland—their first encounter since the infamous Gray's Inn dinner in 1918. As soon as he heard of the gathering, Harriman was determined to be a participant. Churchill, who was anxious to make a good impression on the president, was not averse to having the sympathetic Harriman by his side to give him counsel and reassurance. As a result, the American had no trouble convincing the prime minister he should be included in the entourage. But when Harriman returned to Washington in late July to deliver a first-hand report of his Middle East trip, he learned to his chagrin that Roosevelt had no intention of inviting him along.

FDR had wanted a small, intimate meeting with Churchill, with only a few close advisers in attendance. When Churchill urged that the senior military staffs of both countries be included, the president reluctantly agreed. But he refused to add Harriman to the party, despite the intercession of Harry Hopkins and appeals from Harriman himself, who told the president that Churchill expected to see him there. At the last moment, however, Churchill added Sir Alexander Cadogan of the Foreign Office to the conference's mushrooming list of participants, and Roosevelt finally relented, extending an invitation to Harriman and undersecretary of state Sumner Welles to join the presidential entourage.

EARLY ON THE MORNING of August 9, the British battleship *Prince of Wales,* showing the scars of its recent clash with Germany's naval behemoth the *Bismarck,* glided into Newfoundland's Placentia Bay. On the admiral's bridge, a tense Winston Churchill peered out at the mist-shrouded horizon, searching for the American ships carrying Roosevelt and his party.

The prime minister regarded the upcoming meeting with the president as one of the most fateful encounters of his life. During the five-day voyage from Britain, he had been nervous yet buoyant; his bodyguard remarked that Churchill "probably never had shown so much exuberance and excitement" since his school days at Harrow. Said another of Churchill's aides: "He had firmly determined from 1940 onwards that nothing must stand in the way of his friendship for the President on which so much depended."

Harry Hopkins, who accompanied Churchill on the *Prince of Wales,* was equally anxious. As he had told Ed Murrow earlier, both the prime minister and president were prima donnas, accustomed to being the center of attention and getting their own way. It was his job, Hopkins said, "to keep those two in close and friendly relations."

As the camouflaged *Prince of Wales*, flanked by her destroyer escorts, edged into the bay, Churchill spotted the looming shapes of the American flotilla—five destroyers and the heavy cruiser *Augusta*, the flagship of the U.S. Atlantic Fleet. Clambering aboard the *Augusta*, as the U.S. Marine Band played "God Save the King," he was greeted by a beaming Franklin Roosevelt, holding tight to the arm of his son Elliott. "At last we've gotten together," the president declared. Churchill, smiling just as broadly, nodded: "Yes, we have."

Throughout the four-day conference, Averell Harriman hovered in the background, acting as an adviser to Churchill and having little to do with Roosevelt or the other Americans. Unsure of the impression he was making on the president, Churchill repeatedly asked him: "Does he like me, Averell? Do you think he likes me?" The answer was yes, although Churchill initially annoyed Roosevelt by telling him how happy he was that they were finally meeting face-to-face after so many months of cables and phone calls. His face darkening, FDR reminded him of the Gray's Inn dinner thirty-three years earlier. "Papa completely forgot they had met before," Mary Soames remarked years later. "He hadn't been warned or reminded, and it had just slipped his mind." Although Roosevelt reportedly never quite got over his annoyance at Churchill for what he viewed as a slight, he was as determined as the prime minister to make the conference a success and laughed off Churchill's lapse in memory.

Indeed, by most accounts, both leaders kept their formidable egos under tight control during the conference. Thirty-year-old Elliott Roosevelt, who was accustomed to seeing his father "dominating every gathering he was part of," was amazed that, during the sessions with Churchill, he actually listened. Churchill, for his part, was assiduous in deferring to FDR and repeatedly described himself as "the president's lieutenant." By the end of lunch on the first day, they were calling each other "Franklin" and "Winston."

While their friendship was never as close as Churchill later made it out to be, the American and British leaders, as Robert Sherwood put it, established an "easy intimacy, a joking informality . . . a degree of frankness" at the meeting that continued throughout their four-year relationship. After their last shipboard session, Roosevelt urged Churchill's bodyguard to "take care of him. He's about the greatest man in the world. In fact he may very likely *be* the greatest." The president would later tell his wife that the Newfoundland conference "had broken the ice," adding that he "knew now that Churchill, who he thought was typical of John Bull, was a man with whom he could really work." About Roosevelt, Churchill wrote years later: "I formed a very strong affection which grew with our years of comradeship."

Yet for all the bonhomie of that initial wartime encounter and Churchill's outward display of satisfaction at its conclusion, its outcome was a crushing disappointment for the British. Before crossing the Atlantic, Churchill had told a group of Dominion prime ministers that he did not think Roosevelt would have called the conference unless he was prepared to enter the war. "I would rather have a declaration of war now and no supplies for six months than double the supplies and no declaration," he had declared to his associates. At Churchill's first meeting with the president, Elliott Roosevelt quoted him as saying: "You've got to come in beside us! If you don't declare war without waiting for them to strike the first blow, they'll strike it after we've gone under, and their first blow will be their last as well! . . . You must come in, if you are to survive!"

The president, however, rejected Churchill's appeal, explaining that Congress and the American public were in no mood to enter the conflict. Indeed, during the week of the Placentia Bay meeting, legislation mandating a one-year extension for a limited military draft, instituted in 1940, came perilously close to defeat in the House of Representatives, surviving by only one vote.

To lessen the sting of his rebuff, Roosevelt promised Churchill that the United States would become more "provocative" in the Atlantic by providing armed escorts for British as well as American merchant ships as far as Iceland. He also made clear that "he would look for an 'incident' which would justify him in opening hostilities." In addition, the president promised to ask for another $5 billion for Lend-Lease from Congress and to expedite the shipment of planes and tanks to Britain. In return, he persuaded the prime minister to join him in proclaiming the goals and principles that should govern a postwar world, including the right of all nations to self-determination. Dubbed the Atlantic Charter, this declaration of war aims was the only publicly announced result of the conference.

After returning home, Churchill glumly wrote to his son: "The

President, for all his warm heart and good intentions, is thought by many of his admirers to move with public opinion rather than to lead and form it." The prime minister's chagrin over the collapse of his hopes was shared by many of his countrymen. "The flood is raging . . . and all America will do is give us dry clothes if we reach the shore," the *Times* remarked. "We understand her attitude . . . but we think it would be no strain on her resources to wade in, at least up to her waist. We say this because we are frankly disappointed with the American contribution to the rescue."

When Roosevelt held a press conference to assure the American people that the Newfoundland meeting had brought the United States no closer to war, Churchill dashed off a telegram to Hopkins about the disheartening effect of the president's statement on Parliament and the British public. "I don't know what will happen if England is fighting alone when 1942 comes," the prime minister's cable concluded.

BUT WHILE THE meeting might have ended in frustration for Churchill, it had a handsome payoff for Harriman. Thanks to Hopkins's intercession, he managed to get himself appointed chief U.S. delegate of a high-level Anglo-American mission to Britain's new and very reluctant ally, the Soviet Union.

Immediately after the German invasion of Russia, Roosevelt had been somewhat cautious about supporting Churchill's promise of all-out aid to Stalin. He had no doubt that the Soviets were in great need of such help: in the first few weeks of the onslaught, the Wehrmacht overran Soviet territory as swiftly as it had done in Poland and Western Europe. By August, the Russian army was close to collapse, its troops lacking everything from tanks and planes to rifles and boots. But there was considerable opposition in the United States, particularly among Catholics, to any idea of aid for the Communist dictatorship; many Americans believed that the Nazis and Communists should be left to destroy each other. George Marshall and other military leaders warned the president that help for the Russians would result in a significant cutback in military resources for both the United States and Britain.

Nonetheless, as long as the Russians held out—and they were holding out much longer than anyone in the West believed was possible—they provided Britain with a respite from German bombing and a possible invasion. The calamitous May 10 raid on London was the last major enemy attack on Britain in 1941, thanks to the Luftwaffe's new mission to fight the Soviets. In London's East End, windows in shops and flats were adorned with pro-Russian signs, one of which read: "They Gave Us Quiet Nights." For his part, Roosevelt believed that, in addition to helping Britain, continued Russian resistance might also take some of the pressure off the United States to enter the war. By the time he met Churchill in August, the president had already decided to send Stalin all the help he needed.

When the two leaders agreed at Placentia Bay to dispatch a joint delegation to Moscow to work out an aid agreement with the Russians, Hopkins, at the behest of Harriman, nominated the Lend-Lease expediter as chief American representative. In making the pitch for his friend, Hopkins noted that Harriman had negotiated with the Soviets some twenty years earlier over manganese concessions. But Hopkins's depiction of the former New York businessman as a skilled, seasoned negotiator was far from accurate: he had gone into those talks with little knowledge of Russia and its people and had been outsmarted by the fledgling Soviet government, which had withheld the richest manganese deposits for itself and later forced Harriman to sell out. He also failed to mention to Hopkins or anyone else that he still had more than $1 million in Russian investments, including over $500,000 worth of Soviet government notes from the liquidation of his manganese contract. Obviously, Harriman had his own personal reasons for making sure that the Western Allies did everything in their power to help the Russians ward off defeat.

His British counterpart for the Moscow mission was Lord Beaverbrook, who, like Harriman, had no experience in diplomatic negotiations. Yet, when they arrived in the Soviet capital, Harriman and Beaverbrook excluded their countries' ambassadors and other Soviet experts from the talks with Stalin, himself a tough-minded and wily bargainer. The two ambassadors—Laurence Steinhardt of the United States and Sir Stafford Cripps of Britain—had considerable experience in dealing with the Soviets and few illusions about the government's willingness to cooperate with Britain and America. Both envoys urged Harriman and Beaverbrook to demand, at the very least, a quid pro quo from Stalin—detailed information about Soviet production, resources, and defense plans (all of which Britain had been forced to provide to the United States before it received its aid) in exchange for weapons and supplies.

The delegation heads, however, rejected the recommendations out of hand. Their objective, Harriman told Steinhardt, was to "give and give and give, with no expectation of any return." Not surprisingly, Stalin, who delivered scornful lectures to Harriman and Beaverbrook about the paucity of Western help thus far, was in full agreement with that aim. The Russian leader was given virtually everything he asked for—a cornucopia of weapons, trucks, planes, supplies, and raw materials—with no strings attached.

As he left Moscow, an exultant Harriman was sure that the joint mission had helped eradicate any "suspicion that has existed between the Soviet government and our two governments." Others in the delegation were not so sure. Among them was General Hastings "Pug" Ismay, military secretary to the British War Cabinet and Churchill's liaison with his chiefs of staff, who later wrote: "No one will deny that it was in our own interests to give the Russians the wherewithal. . . . But it was surely unnecessary and even unwise to allow them to bully us in the way that they did."

Yet, despite the severe sacrifices that would result from transferring so much aid to the Soviets, especially for Britain, Churchill and Roosevelt approved the deal. From the first weeks of the invasion, Stalin had made demands on the British that were impossible to meet at the time—a new front in northern France, for example, and the dispatch of twenty-five to thirty British divisions to Russia. Both Western leaders were afraid that if a massive amount of weapons and supplies was not sent immediately, Stalin might make a separate peace with Hitler— a view that the Russian leader did nothing to discourage.

In his report to the president on the Moscow meeting, Harriman declared that Ambassador Steinhardt was no longer effective in the Soviet capital because of his skepticism of the Russians and recommended that he be replaced. Roosevelt followed his suggestion. Having helped get rid of Steinhardt, Harriman then maneuvered himself into the role of unofficial liaison between the White House, Downing Street, and the Kremlin. It was the defining role of his life, one on which he would capitalize for the next four years and beyond.

7.

"I WANT TO BE IN IT WITH YOU— FROM THE START"

AT A TIME WHEN THE U.S. GOVERNMENT WAS STILL RELUCTANT to put its servicemen in harm's way, a memorial service was held at St. Paul's Cathedral in London to honor one young American who already had lost his life in the fight against Germany. In the crypt of the bomb-scarred cathedral, several hundred people, among them Gil Winant, gathered on July 4, 1941, for the unveiling of a plaque in memory of William Fiske III, who, in the words engraved on the plaque, "died that England might live."

The first U.S. citizen to join the Royal Air Force and the first American pilot killed in action during the war in Europe, Billy Fiske had been born in New York but spent his adolescence and young adulthood in Europe. Addicted to speed and adventure, Fiske, the son of a wealthy stockbroker, drove a supercharged Bentley and, in his teens and early twenties, had twice won Olympic gold medals in the daredevil sport of bobsledding. He was, said one friend, "very much the golden boy—good looks, wealth, charm, intelligence—he had it all." A Cambridge graduate, he told his British friends in the 1930s that, if war came, "I want to be in it with you—from the start."

But when the conflict did break out in September 1939, the twenty-eight-year-old Fiske found that if he honored his pledge, he would be considered an outlaw in his own country. In its desperate attempt to keep the United States out of war, the American government had enacted a series of regulations that, among other things, made it illegal to join a warring power's military service, travel on a belligerent ship, or use a U.S. passport to go to a foreign country to enlist. Those who were caught were subject to a $10,000 fine, several years' imprisonment, and loss of their American citizenship.

Bypassing the regulations by falsely claiming Canadian citizenship, Fiske joined the RAF less than three weeks after Britain's declaration of war against Germany. He was posted to 601 Squadron, known as the "Millionaires' Squadron" because of all the affluent young men, several of whom were prewar friends of Fiske's, in its ranks. The squadron's pilots lined their uniform jackets with red silk and their overcoats with mink, and won and lost hundreds of pounds in poker games while waiting to fly and fight. "They were arrogant and looked terrific, and probably the other squadrons hated their guts," Fiske's wife, Rose, remarked. But they also were expert pilots, and even though Fiske only had ninety hours of solo flying time to his credit when he joined the RAF, he soon matched them in skill. "It was unbelievable how good he was," Sir Archibald Hope, 601's commanding officer, later noted. "He picked it up so fast. . . . He was a natural as a fighter pilot."

On August 16, 1940, during one of the Luftwaffe's heaviest attacks on RAF airfields in the Battle of Britain, Fiske's Hurricane was hit; despite severe burns, he managed to nurse his badly damaged plane back to his base. Two days later, he died of his injuries. "He had no obligation to fight for this country," declared Britain's air minister, Sir Archibald Sinclair, at the St. Paul's ceremony. "He was not an Englishman. . . . He gave his life for his friends and for the common cause of free men everywhere, the cause of liberty." Sitting in the audience that day, dressed in RAF blue, were several of the other Americans who took part in the Battle of Britain. In all, seven U.S. citizens flew in the battle, joining more than five hundred other non-British pilots, including Poles, Czechs, Belgians, French, New Zealanders, and South Africans. Of all the members of this polyglot air force, only the Americans were breaking the laws of their country by flying.

By the time of the ceremony honoring Fiske, thousands of Americans had disregarded their country's prohibitions and enlisted on Britain's side. About three hundred were flying in the RAF, dozens more had joined the British Army, and well over five thousand were in the Canadian forces in Britain. While most were young and adventure-loving, several dozen were paunchy, gray-haired, and affluent, with professions ranging from investment banking to the law to architecture. Longtime residents of London, they were members of the only American unit in Britain's Home Guard, the civilian volunteers who were to protect Britain in case of German invasion.

The Home Guard was created in June 1940 after the British retreat from Dunkirk and the fall of France. More than a million men answered the call, including some seventy American businessmen and professionals living in the capital. "Our homes are here, and we wanted to show in some practical way that we were ready, with the British, to share the responsibility of defending their soil," said Wade Hayes, an investment banker and commander of the group. "Also, we wanted to give a lead to the people back home."

Initially, however, the Americans faced stiff opposition from both the British and their own government. British regulations barred foreigners from joining the Home Guard, and Joseph Kennedy was livid that these pillars of the American expatriate community not only refused to return home but planned to fight on behalf of the British. The ambassador warned Hayes, who had served on General John Pershing's staff in World War I, that creation of the unit "might lead to all United States citizens being shot as franc-tireurs [guerrilla fighters] when the Germans occupied London." Neither Kennedy's admonition nor his threat to see that Hayes's U.S. citizenship was revoked had any effect. In the end, George VI came to the Americans' rescue, issuing a special order making them eligible for membership in the Guard.

Like other Home Guardsmen throughout the country, the Americans drilled several times a week—after work and on the weekends. But in sharp contrast to their British counterparts, who trained with pitchforks and kitchen knives tied to broomsticks, the U.S. expatriates, using their own money, armed themselves with Winchester automatic rifles, grenades, and Thompson submachine guns, which they obtained from the United States. The envy of British units for their sophisticated weaponry and their eighteen camouflaged armored cars, the Americans, thanks to their Tommy guns, were known as "the gangsters."

In the British military, there was considerable skepticism, to put it mildly, about the effectiveness of the skimpily trained Home Guard in helping to stop a German invasion. But in July 1940, the Americans proved to the military brass that their unit, at least, shouldn't be taken lightly. During training maneuvers, the U.S. businessmen captured the headquarters of an army brigade protecting a key airbase outside London, guarded by some five hundred regular troops wielding Bren guns and heavy machine guns. Rushing and overpowering a sentry, the Americans tossed tear gas bombs through the windows of the head-quarters, knocked down the door, dismantled the switchboard, trussed up several British officers, and seized secret maps and other docu-ments. The British protested that the assault came too early. The Americans replied that they had attacked at the first moment permis-sible under the maneuvers' guidelines. "The Germans," they added, "will not wait either."

THE CAPITULATION OF France also brought the first influx of Ameri-can pilots to Britain. Not yet aware of how serious their offense was regarded by the U.S. powers-that-be, three of the earliest volunteers checked in at the American embassy in London in June 1940, only to be attacked by Kennedy for "jeopardizing U.S. neutrality" and ordered back to the United States on the next ship. Instead, they headed straight for the British Air Ministry, enlisting in time to fly in the Bat-tle of Britain.

The Americans who joined the RAF had grown up in the age of Charles Lindbergh, when the mere idea of aviation captivated young people all over the world. Most of them already were experienced fliers. Some had dusted crops for a living; some were barnstormers and stunt pilots; one was a pilot for the Metro-Goldwyn-Mayer studio in Los Angeles, whose job had been to ferry movie stars and other Holly-wood VIPs around California. They had come to England for a variety of reasons, but most had one trait in common: an addiction to excite-ment, danger, and speed. A sizable number had tried to enlist in the U.S. Army Air Corps but could not meet the strict physical qualifica-tions; the RAF, about to face the Luftwaffe onslaught, could not af-ford to be so discriminating. Virtually all of them were anxious to fly the hot new high-performance British fighters—the Hurricanes and Spitfires—they had heard and read so much about.

A desire for romance and adventure also played its part. Some Americans wanted to follow in the footsteps of the Lafayette Es-cadrille, the dashing band of U.S. aviators who signed up to fight with the French in World War I. Others had seen the Howard Hughes movie *Hell's Angels,* depicting Americans in the British air force during the 1914–18 war, and they visualized themselves taking the same role in this conflict. Here was their chance "to play opposite alluring platinum blondes like Jean Harlow that they had seen in the picture," noted James Childers, a U.S. colonel who wrote a book during the war about Americans in the RAF. This was the next "Big Show . . . and they, like all normal boys, wanted to see it, to be a part of it. They didn't want to miss anything."

A few, however, volunteered for more idealistic reasons. A number of them recalled after the war that Ed Murrow's broadcasts had inspired them to volunteer. "I felt that this was America's war as much as England's and France's," said one Battle of Britain veteran. Another young American had been aboard the *Athenia*, the British passenger liner torpedoed by a German submarine in September 1939 while en route to New York. Feeling "an overwhelming fury" toward Germany over the loss of more than one hundred of his fellow passengers, he returned to Britain and joined the RAF. Still another U.S. citizen enlisted after his grandmother and grandfather were killed in the German invasion of Holland.

Whatever the reason for their decision to fight, all of them knew they were breaking the laws of their country by doing so. Although FBI agents were posted at a number of Canadian border crossings to prevent U.S. citizens from leaving to enlist in British and Canadian forces, most of the fliers managed to slip across to Canada, where they boarded ships to Britain. Those who were stopped and sent home usually tried again; most made it the second time.

Once they'd crossed the Atlantic, the Americans were given three weeks of flight training and then assigned to various RAF squadrons. They generally were given warm if bemused receptions by their British counterparts, who found the newcomers to be flippant, cocky, brash, and, for the most part, immensely likable. A British pilot described two U.S. fliers who reported for duty to his squadron as "typical Americans . . . always ready with some devastating wisecrack (frequently at the expense of authority)." He later wrote of the amazing "colour, variety and vocabulary" that they had contributed to the squadron.

By the end of the Battle of Britain, so many Americans had enlisted in the RAF that they were given their own unit, known as the Eagle Squadron. The idea for the all-American squadron came from Charles Sweeny, a wealthy twenty-eight-year-old American businessman in London who was the chief organizer and a leading member of the U.S. Home Guard unit. Having grown up in England and returning there after graduating from Yale, Sweeny felt a strong allegiance both to his native country and adopted homeland and was convinced that "the war could not be won without the assistance of the U.S." With the British seemingly on the ropes and Germany about to launch a massive aerial assault, Sweeny believed that Americans must come to the aid of Britain in the air. Along with his uncle, brother, and other affluent U.S. expatriates in London, he set up a recruiting network for fliers in the United States and provided funds to bring them to Britain.

In June 1940, Sweeny approached Lord Beaverbrook and Brendan Bracken, Churchill's closest aide, with the idea of an RAF squadron modeled after the Lafayette Escadrille. Bracken forwarded the proposal to Churchill, who instantly saw what a powerful propaganda tool an American squadron could be and enthusiastically endorsed the idea. Young Americans flying and dying for Britain while their country remained aloof would, in his view, go far to undermine American neutrality. In October 1940, the RAF welcomed 71 Squadron to its ranks, with two more American squadrons created the following year. In all, 244 Americans flew in the three squadrons during the next two years of the war.

THANKS TO THEIR heroics in turning back the Luftwaffe in the Battle of Britain, all RAF fighter pilots were heroes in the country from the summer of 1940 on. The American fliers received the same unambiguous affection from the people as did their British counterparts. Bus conductors refused to let them pay their fares, and waiters and pub owners gave them free meals and drinks. One pilot wrote to his parents in Minnesota: "These people almost worship the Royal Air Force pilots. . . . I've had just ordinary people say to me, 'Words can't express how we feel toward you boys!' 'You're wonderful,' 'You're the greatest heroes we've ever had.'"

But there did seem to be an extra measure of enthusiasm for the Yanks. "They were always telling us, 'Thank God you're here and thank God you're helping,'" said one Eagle Squadron pilot. Another remarked: "It just seemed like they couldn't do enough for you. They gave you the best they had, the best food, the best of everything."

The American fliers became the darlings of London, invited to the theater, to society tea dances, to weekends at elegant country homes.

The king's brother, the Duke of Gloucester, extended an invitation to several young Americans to sit in his box at the Royal Albert Hall for a concert of the London Philharmonic Orchestra. Treated as celebrities, too, by their fellow Americans in the British capital, the pilots had a standing invitation from the U.S. correspondents at the Savoy to eat and drink there whenever they were on leave. They were frequent overnight guests at Quentin Reynolds's luxurious Berkeley Square flat.

Unlike the hordes of Yanks who descended on Britain prior to D-Day, the early U.S. volunteers became an integral part of the British military and society. The phrase "overpaid, oversexed, and over here" was as yet uncoined. British pilots generally accepted their American counterparts with alacrity, although a good-natured Anglo-American rivalry surfaced on occasion. At a particularly memorable, champagne-fueled party, an American squadron faced off against a British unit in a reenactment of General Cornwallis's defeat at the Battle of Yorktown in 1781, with the Americans using fire extinguishers and the British fighting back with soda siphons. Afterward, a British pilot ruefully noted: "Once again . . . the Americans had the upper hand."

The U.S. pilots' exuberant, often rowdy behavior—a "mad bunch of Wild Westerners," one man called them—was greeted with tolerance by the British public, who, for the most part, had never met an American before. Of the members of one U.S. squadron, a British magazine wrote: "Their exploits . . . are still spoken of in awe in the town near their aerodrome." When an American veteran of the Battle of Britain married a wealthy young British heiress, his fellow Eagle Squadron members buzzed the garden wedding reception as well as the nearby town of Epping. Responding to complaints from a scattering of townspeople, the mayor of Epping declared: "Look, these people are risking their lives for us. If they want to celebrate a comrade's wedding, then so they should."

The fondness of Britons for the uninhibited pilots was reciprocated by most of the Americans. Even those who had no real interest in aiding the British cause when they first enlisted in the RAF found themselves admiring the bravery and determination of the public in standing up to Hitler. "They were, without a shadow of a doubt, the most courageous people that I have ever known," said one American. "Although their cities were in shambles, I never heard one Briton lose faith." Another U.S. pilot declared: "To fight side by side with these people was the greatest of privileges."

After the war, Bill Geiger, who'd been a student at California's Pasadena City College before he came to Britain, recalled the exact moment when he knew that the British cause was his as well. Leaving a London tailor's shop, where he had just been measured for his RAF uniform, he noticed a man working at the bottom of a deep hole in the street, surrounded by barricades. "What's he doing?" Geiger asked a policeman. "Sir," the bobby replied, "he's defusing a bomb." Everyone standing there—the bobby, pedestrians, the man in the hole—was "so cool and calm and collected," Geiger remembered. He added: "You get caught up in that kind of courage, and then pretty soon you say, 'Now I want to be a part of this. I want to be part of these people. I want to be a part of what I see here and what I feel here.' "

AS WINSTON CHURCHILL had hoped, the announcement of the Eagle Squadron's formation in October 1940 set off a media frenzy. British and U.S. journalists swarmed to the squadron's base in Kirton Lindsey to learn more about these young men who had defied their country's laws to fight for Britain, and glowing articles and broadcasts soon followed. The Americans were inundated with official visitors, among them Archibald Sinclair; Prince Bernhard of the Netherlands; the playwright Noël Coward; and Air Marshal Sholto Douglas, commander of the RAF's Fighter Command. Each week, the BBC broadcast a program to the United States featuring one or more of the Eagles, and Ed Murrow interviewed several of them for CBS.

While heady stuff, the attention was distracting and somewhat embarrassing for a unit that was nowhere close to being operational. The squadron had not yet received its Spitfires, but even if it had, its pilots were far from ready to fly them. Before joining the RAF, most of the Americans had had no military training, and few showed much tolerance for military regulations. Indeed, as one Eagle Squadron leader, an Englishman, recalled of his American charges: "They were saboteurs of military tradition." At the same time, he added, "not one of them lacked the moral fiber to get the job done."

It took more than three months to weld these unruly young individualists into a cohesive, well-trained unit. Finally, in January 1941, 71 Squadron was made operational, followed soon afterward by 121 and 133 Squadrons. A few months later, as all three American units were finally showing their mettle, Hollywood came calling.

Producer Walter Wanger, whose films included *Stagecoach* and *Foreign Correspondent,* approached Harry Watt, the British documentary director who made *London Can Take It!,* with the idea of directing a film about 71 Squadron, using the real fliers as characters. Watt's most recent film, *Target for Tonight,* skillfully employed both documentary footage and dramatic reconstruction to tell the story of a British bomber crew on a mission to Germany. *Target for Tonight* was a critical and popular success, and Wanger wanted Watt to use the same techniques in *Eagle Squadron.*

Although he'd never directed a full-length feature film before, Watt was seduced by Wanger's offer of $100 a week—a huge salary in war-straitened Britain—and free bed and board at the Savoy. However, disillusion, in the form of an associate producer sent by Wanger to oversee the production, swiftly set in. At that point, 71 Squadron was participating in low-level bombing attacks on France and the Low Countries, and casualties were mounting. Watt explained to the man from Hollywood that the high casualty rate precluded focusing on individual pilots for the film, since they might be killed or wounded before production had ended. In response, the producer asked the British Air Ministry to withdraw the squadron from action while the movie was being made. The ministry's reply was predictable: according to Watt, it "politely told him where he could go."

Then followed "four weeks of the most utter chaos I have ever been involved in," said Watt, who spent most of his time quarreling with the producer about the script and virtually every other aspect of the production. The conflict between the two was resolved by tragedy. On a mission to France one Sunday afternoon, 71 Squadron was hit hard: three of the nine planes that set out from Kirton Lindsey were shot down. One of the pilots lost that day was the fun-loving, immensely popular Eugene "Red" Tobin, who had flown in the Battle of Britain and was a good friend of Watt, Quentin Reynolds, and many other Americans in London. After Tobin's death, Watt pulled out of the making of *Eagle Squadron.*

The movie was finally finished in Hollywood and released in July 1942, to almost universal critical censure. "Far from the genuine drama about American fliers with the R.A.F. that it should be," wrote the *New York Times* film critic Bosley Crowther, *Eagle Squadron* "is rather a highfalutin war adventure film which waxes embarrassingly mawkish about English courage and American spunk." Starring a young Robert

Stack, the movie focused on a moody American pilot in Britain who, at the end, proves himself by hijacking a deadly new German warplane and single-handedly completing a commando mission botched by the British. The best thing about the film, according to Crowther, was its preface—footage of the real Eagle Squadron fliers shot by Watt and narrated by Quentin Reynolds.

When *Eagle Squadron* opened in London, several squadron members went to the premiere. Their response to the melodramatic heroics on the screen was a chorus of subdued boos and groans. "You know, they're going to keep on flinging that bull at us until some of it sticks," one of the pilots told a friend. "They're going to keep on telling us that hero rot until we believe it ourselves." Most of the American pilots walked out of the movie before its end.

By the time of the premiere, the United States was in the war, and a few months later, virtually all the Americans serving in the RAF transferred to the U.S. Army Air Forces.* Only 4 of the original 34 Eagle Squadron members were still on active duty: most of the others had been killed or taken prisoner. Of the 244 Americans who flew with the Eagles, more than 40 percent did not survive the conflict. In their nineteen months of service, the three Eagle Squadrons were credited with shooting down more than seventy German planes. Two Americans won the Distinguished Flying Cross, the RAF's top decoration for achievement and valor, and one, Newton Anderson of New Orleans, received an even more coveted RAF accolade. He was named commander of 222 Squadron, an all-British unit—the first American to be given such an honor.

SHORTLY BEFORE GIL WINANT arrived in England, the U.S. government announced it would not prosecute Americans who enlisted in British and Canadian forces, even though doing so remained an illegal act. But the ambassador was determined to do more than look the other way. From his first days in London, he showed active support of the volunteers. He reviewed the American unit of the Home Guard, visited Eagle Squadron bases, was the guest of honor at a Thanksgiving dinner thrown by one of the American units, and pointedly attended the memorial service for Billy Fiske. At one Eagle Squadron

---

* The U.S. Army Air Corps changed its name to the U.S. Army Air Forces in June 1941.

luncheon, Sholto Douglas recalled how, during the Great War, "a rather scruffy-looking officer turned up at my airdrome and asked if I would lend him a fighter plane. I said, 'You can have it but don't break it.' He came back and landed it all right." Turning to Winant, the head of RAF's Fighter Command added with a smile: "That was the last I saw of the American ambassador until I met him again about six months ago."

While Winant's own background as a combat pilot gave him a keen interest in the U.S. fliers, he also paid considerable attention to the young Americans who had enlisted in the far less glamorous military service—the armies of Britain and Canada. These expatriates were not wined and dined by socialites and American correspondents in London, nor were movies made about them. Occasionally, a reporter might write a story about them before they disappeared into their new, tough, and demanding life, as *PM* correspondent Ben Robertson did with 150 Americans who had just arrived in Britain with a Canadian regiment. Among them, wrote Robertson, were "truck drivers, coal miners, a former member of the Lincoln Brigade in Spain, a member of the Michigan legislature, butcher boys, and soda jerkers." Lugging baseball bats and banjos in their belongings, they were "irrepressible, light-hearted, colorful, rich in variety and personality." When Robertson asked the recruits why they had come to Britain, they "laughed and joked about their reasons but turned serious when Francis Myers, a Texan, said to me, 'We also got a sneaking feeling we'd like to help.'"

In his five years in London, Winant befriended hundreds of U.S. soldiers, but he was particularly attached to five young Americans who enlisted in the British Army in July 1941. Graduates of Dartmouth and Harvard, they had joined the 60th Regiment of the King's Royal Rifle Corps, a British infantry unit formed in colonial America during the French and Indian War and originally called the 62nd Royal Americans. Winant had met the five in London during their first leave from officer's training. When they ran out of money, he invited them to camp out at his flat. He later attended the commissioning ceremony of their class, as did Anthony Eden, who had been in the 60th Regiment in the Great War. Shortly before the ceremony began, the Americans learned that, in order to become officers in the British Army, they would have to take an oath of allegiance to the king, which meant an automatic revocation of their U.S. citizenship. In the anxious debate that followed, Winant came up with a solution, as he would do in a number of later Anglo-American crises. Learning that the king was also the honorary colonel of the regiment, he suggested that the five take their oath to the regimental colonel, not the king. The Americans and the British authorities agreed to the idea, and a minor international incident was averted.

In the months to come, Winant would become somewhat of a surrogate father to the five Ivy Leaguers. They regularly wrote to him and stayed at his flat when they came to London on leave. In the fall of 1942, all of them participated in the Battle of El Alamein, in northern Egypt, which resulted in Britain's first major victory over German forces. Three of the Americans were seriously wounded and one was killed. When Winant was informed of the young lieutenant's death, he wrote to the man's father that his son and the others had been Winant's "contact with life. . . . Knowing them helped me keep faith with America—and faith in its ultimate willingness to sacrifice and fight." They were, he later said, "as gallant a group as I have ever seen. They made you very proud to be an American."

8.

"PEARL HARBOR ATTACKED?"

IN EARLY NOVEMBER 1941, ED MURROW DASHED OFF A QUICK NOTE to Gil Winant from a hotel room in Bristol, just before boarding a plane for America. "Leaving this country at this time is not easy," Murrow wrote. "It is, in fact, more difficult than I had expected." As he headed home for a three-month lecture tour, he felt as if he were abandoning England at an especially fateful time. "I am convinced that the hour is much later," he told another friend, "than most people at home appreciate."

The Germans had advanced to the outskirts of Moscow and seemed poised to crush the Soviets in weeks, if not days. The British, in urgent need of the military aid they were providing to the Red Army, were stalled in the Middle East. And now the Japanese seemed about to make *their* move. Three months before, Japan had overrun all of Indochina and demanded army bases from Thailand. There was no doubt in anyone's mind that the British and Dutch possessions in the Far East—Malaya, Burma, Singapore, Hong Kong, and the Dutch East Indies—were all under direct threat.

In Washington, the president, whose attention was focused on the Battle of the Atlantic and the war in Russia, had tried his best for more than a year to avert a showdown with Japan. His plan was to "baby the Japs along," he told advisers. As he saw it, a fight with Japan would be "the wrong war in the wrong ocean at the wrong time." That view was reinforced by General George Marshall and Admiral Harold

Stark, who repeatedly warned Roosevelt that America was not ready to fight and that a two-front war would be disastrous.

When Japan occupied Indochina, the president retaliated economically, hoping that the restrictions imposed by the United States would restrain Japan without forcing it into war. But America's actions—the freezing of Japanese assets in the United States and an embargo on the shipment of oil, as well as iron and steel products—served only to infuriate the Japanese. The crisis continued to escalate.

At their meeting in Newfoundland, Churchill, at Winant's suggestion, had appealed to Roosevelt to join him in warning the Japanese that any future incursions in Asia would be met with British *and* American force. It was impossible for Britain to respond on its own: its military cupboard was virtually bare, with no troops to send to Singapore or Malaya, no spare ships to patrol the waters off those colonies. Field Marshal Sir John Dill, Alan Brooke's predecessor as chief of the Imperial General Staff, told Brooke that the country "had done practically nothing to meet the threat . . . that we were already so weak on all fronts that it was impossible to denude them any further." But Roosevelt declined to issue a blunt ultimatum. As the situation in the Far East grew more perilous, Churchill feared that Britain might soon face a war with Germany and Japan—all without American assistance.

What would it take, the prime minister wondered, to propel Roosevelt and his country into this conflict? Again and again, the president had tiptoed to the edge of confrontation, only to pull back at the last minute. In September, he had seemed on the verge of entering the fray in the Battle of the Atlantic. After the American destroyer *Greer* exchanged torpedoes with a German submarine in the middle of the Atlantic (resulting in no damage or casualties), Roosevelt announced that, from then on, American vessels would "shoot on sight" any German U-boats or warships they encountered. At the same time, he ordered a Navy escort for all merchant shipping—not just U.S. ships—as far as Iceland. In effect, he had embarked on a naval war against Germany.

His decision won widespread support from the American people. Yet there still was no popular sentiment for taking the final, irrevocable step of an official declaration of war, not even when two more American naval vessels were fired upon by German submarines. On October 16, the destroyer *Kearny* was badly damaged by German torpedoes when it raced to the rescue of a convoy under attack. Two weeks later, another destroyer, the *Reuben James,* was sunk near Iceland, killing 115 members of its crew. But, instead of a popular outcry in the United States, demanding that Roosevelt avenge "our boys," the predominant reaction seemed to be one of apathy.

"In this looming crisis, the United States seemed deadlocked—its President handcuffed, its Congress irresolute, its people divided and confused," wrote James MacGregor Burns, a Roosevelt biographer. "Now—by early November 1941—there seemed to be nothing more [FDR] could say. There seemed to be little more he could do. He had called his people to their battle stations—but there was no battle."

Near the end of his emotional tether, Churchill railed to his subordinates about America's paralysis and Roosevelt's unwillingness to do anything about it. In a speech to the House of Commons, he declared: "Nothing is more dangerous in wartime than to live in the temperamental atmosphere of Gallup polls or of feeling one's pulse or taking one's temperature. . . . There is only one duty, only one safe course, and that is to be right and not to fear to do or say what you believe to be right."

Ed Murrow agreed. The continuing reluctance of the United States to enter the conflict had so infuriated him that he briefly considered leaving CBS to become a full-time activist for American intervention. He also flirted with the idea of pushing Winant to run for president in the next election. "If some time in the unpredictable future, you decide to go home and seek political power," he told the ambassador in his letter, "I may be one of the 'goodly company' to travel with you."

MURROW HAD NOT been back to the United States since 1938—a time that seemed almost unimaginable now, a time when the world was not at war. Over and over, he had been told he'd become a celebrity at home, that everyone was listening to his broadcasts, that he had greatly influenced public opinion. From New York, Bill Shirer had written to Murrow: "Everywhere I go, old dowagers and young things ask if I know you and whether you really are as handsome as your photographs and what you eat for breakfast and when you are coming home."

But when he sat in that stuffy, closet-sized BBC studio every night, inhaling the rank odor of cabbage, it was difficult to grasp that millions of people thousands of miles away had clicked on their radios just to hear him. There was a remoteness to the process of broadcasting, a sense that his words were absorbed by the ether like tiny paper boats swallowed up by the sea.

It wasn't until the thirty-three-year-old broadcaster stepped off the Pan Am Clipper in New York that the reality of his fame finally set in. As Bill Paley put it, "Edward R. Murrow had become a national hero." Waiting for him was a flock of print reporters and newsreel journalists, all of them acting as if he were Greta Garbo or Clark Gable. Everywhere he went in New York over the next few weeks, he was followed by autograph seekers, photographers, and newspaper and magazine writers begging for interviews. As unsettling as this celebrity was for Murrow, he had even more difficulty coming to grips with America's continued refusal to commit itself to war.

When he arrived, he found the isolationists in full cry—an "America First" rally at Madison Square Garden, Senator Burton Wheeler and Charles Lindbergh escalating their demands that Roosevelt keep the country at peace. Although isolationist leaders were gradually losing support in the country, they had become considerably more strident and aggressive in their attacks on the president and his administration. The interventionist movement was equally outspoken in firing back. It was, said one historian, "a period of loud noise in the nation."

Like his fellow London-based correspondents who had returned home, Murrow had trouble coping with the sheer *normality* of America, the seeming lack of concern about the fighting and dying on the other side of the ocean, the apparent refusal to acknowledge that Americans had any stake in the outcome of this cataclysm. "He walked along Fifth Avenue and Madison and saw the stores stocked with beautiful things, and it positively made him angry," said a friend. "He'd see all the food in the restaurants and say 'I don't think I can eat, when I think of what's going on back there.'" In a letter to a friend, the English socialist Harold Laski, Murrow said he was "spending most of my time trying to keep my temper in check," seeing "so many well-dressed, well-fed, complacent-looking people" and hearing "wealthy friends moaning about ruinous taxation." He added: "Words mean something entirely different over here. . . . Maybe it was a mistake to come."

Had all his broadcasts about the horror and heroism of the Blitz gone for naught? Had he failed in his effort to put Americans in the shoes of those caught up in war? Years later, he would remark during a BBC broadcast: "It is difficult to explain the meaning of cold to people who are warm, the meaning of privation to people who have wanted only for luxuries. . . . It is almost impossible to substitute intelligence for experience." Perhaps. But as speaker after speaker noted at a gala banquet in Murrow's honor at the Waldorf-Astoria, he had done more to bridge that gap of understanding than anyone had previously thought possible.

The December 2 banquet was Bill Paley's idea. "Almost every eminent American," he said, "pressed us for an invitation," and more than one thousand dignitaries attended. When Murrow was introduced, the black-tie audience rose to its feet in a crescendo of cheers and applause. To Janet Murrow, sitting at a front-row table, her husband seemed "stunned by the whole thing—it was so out of our experience." Murrow did not mince words that night: if Britain was to survive and Hitler to be stopped, America had to enter the war. The conflict, he said, would be decided "along the banks of the Potomac. General headquarters for the forces of decency is now on Pennsylvania Avenue."

Those who spoke in his honor, however, maintained that, despite the doubts Murrow expressed about America's resoluteness, the country *had* drawn closer to war, even if it was not yet fully committed. One of the key reasons for that shift, they said, was his reporting from London. "You burned the city of London in our houses and we felt the flames that burned it," the poet Archibald MacLeish observed. "You laid the dead of London at our door and we knew that the dead were our dead . . . were mankind's dead." In a telegram read to the guests, President Roosevelt declared: "You . . . who gather tonight to honor Ed Murrow repay but a tiny fraction of the debt owed him by millions of Americans." To underline their appreciation for what Murrow had done, Roosevelt and his wife invited the Murrows to dine with them at the White House. The date was fixed for Sunday, December 7.

IN ENGLAND, GIL WINANT and Averell Harriman had been invited to spend December 7 with the Churchills at Chequers. As he drove to the prime minister's country house, Winant knew that the day would be anything but relaxing. The Japanese were on the move, and an attack was expected at any moment. The day before, Roosevelt had been handed a belligerent message from the Japanese government to their embassy in Washington. After reading the dispatch, which had been cracked by U.S. Army code breakers, the president declared, "This means war." Two large convoys of Japanese warships had been sighted steaming south, but no one knew their exact destination. All the intelligence pointed, however, to Malaya, Singapore, or the Dutch East Indies.

When Winant arrived at Chequers in early afternoon, he found Churchill waiting for him outside. The ambassador had scarcely emerged from his car when Churchill exclaimed: "Do you think there will be war with Japan?" When Winant said, "Yes," the British leader declared: "If they declare war on you, we shall declare war on them within the hour."

"I understand, Prime Minister," Winant said. "You have stated this publicly."

"If they declare war on us, will you declare war on them?"

"I can't answer that, Prime Minister. Only the Congress has the right to declare war under the United States Constitution."

Churchill was silent for a moment, and Winant knew what he was thinking: a Japanese attack on British territory in Asia would force his country into a two-front war, with no lifeline from the United States. Then he roused himself and, turning to Winant "with the charm of manner that I saw so often in difficult moments," said to the American: "We're late, you know. You get washed, and we will go in to lunch together."

A large house party that included Kathleen Harriman and Pamela Churchill had gathered at Chequers that weekend. But the weather was cloudy and cold, and Churchill—tired, moody, and obviously depressed—uncharacteristically had little to say to anyone. Most of the guests had already gone home Sunday when dinner was served a little before nine o'clock. Exhausted by family and war worries, Clementine Churchill stayed in her room. At the table that night were the Harrimans, Pamela, Winant, a couple of Churchill's staffers, and the prime minister himself, who spent much of the dinner with his head in his hands, absorbed in his thoughts. It was Churchill's habit to listen to the nine o'clock BBC news and, rousing himself from his gloom, he asked Sawyers, his valet, to bring in his flip-top portable radio, a gift from Harry Hopkins a few months before.

It seemed a routine broadcast at first: war communiqués at the beginning, followed by a few tidbits of domestic news. Then, at the end, one brief, unemotional sentence: "The news has just been given that Japanese aircraft have raided Pearl Harbor, the American naval base in Hawaii." There was silence around the table until Churchill, sitting bolt upright, shouted, "What did he say? Pearl Harbor attacked?" Stunned, Harriman repeated, "The Japanese have raided Pearl Harbor." Commander C. R. Thompson, Churchill's naval aide, interrupted the American: "No, no, he said Pearl River." As Harriman and Thompson argued, Sawyers entered the dining room. "It's quite true," the valet told Churchill. "We heard it ourselves outside. The Japanese have attacked the Americans."

With that, Churchill was on his feet and heading toward the door, exclaiming, "We shall declare war on Japan!" Throwing his napkin on the table, Winant jumped up and ran after him. "Good God," he said, "you can't declare war on a radio announcement!" Churchill stopped and, looking at him quizzically, asked, "What shall I do?" When Winant said he would call Roosevelt at once, Churchill replied, "And I shall talk to him too."

A few minutes later, FDR was on the phone. "Mr. President, what's this about Japan?" Churchill asked. Roosevelt replied: "They've attacked us at Pearl Harbor. We are all in the same boat now." The prime minister was euphoric, and so were his two American guests. In an early draft of his memoirs, Churchill recalled that Winant and Harriman received the news about Pearl Harbor with "exaltation—in fact they nearly danced with joy." (Indeed, according to John Colville, Winant and Churchill "sort of danced around the room together" that night.) In his final draft, Churchill replaced his description of unrestrained jubilation with a toned-down version: "They did not wail or lament that their country was at war. . . . In fact, one might almost have thought that they had been delivered from a long pain." He shared that exuberant sense of release. That night, he wrote, he "slept the sleep of the saved and thankful," quite convinced now that "we had won the war. England would live."

DECEMBER 7 HAD dawned unseasonably warm in Washington. Taking advantage of the balminess, Ed Murrow was playing golf at the Burning Tree course in nearby Bethesda when he heard the news of Pearl Harbor. Returning to town, he drove past the Japanese embassy, where diplomats, their arms loaded with papers, scurried back and forth between the embassy and a bonfire in the garden. From their hotel, Janet called Eleanor Roosevelt, expecting to hear that their dinner invitation had been canceled. Absolutely not, replied Mrs. Roosevelt. "We still have to eat. We want you to come."

That evening, the Murrows threaded their way through throngs of people gathered outside the brightly lit White House, some in Lafayette Park across the street, others pressing against the tall iron fence in front. Inside the presidential mansion, there was an atmosphere of barely controlled chaos, with phones jangling and officials rushing from one office to another. After greeting Murrow and his wife, Eleanor Roosevelt explained that her husband was too busy to join them for dinner; he had been closeted in conferences since early afternoon.

Those who saw the president that day testified to his extreme difficulty in coming to grips with the magnitude of the attack. When cabinet members entered his study for a meeting that evening, he didn't look up. In fact, he acted at first as if they weren't even there. "He was living off in another area," noted Frances Perkins. "He wasn't noticing what went on the other side of the desk. . . . His face and lips were pulled down, looking quite gray. . . . It was obvious to me that Roosevelt was having a dreadful time just accepting the idea that the Navy could be caught off guard."

After Mrs. Roosevelt and her guests finished a light supper of scrambled eggs and pudding, the president's wife told Murrow that FDR wanted to see him. Could he stay a little longer? Janet went back to the hotel, while the broadcaster waited on a bench outside Roosevelt's study, smoking cigarette after cigarette, as he watched cabinet members and congressional and military leaders hurry in and out. The tension in the air was palpable: striding down the corridor, a senator turned to the admiral beside him and shouted: "You're not fit to command a rowboat!" Spotting Murrow, several officials, including Hopkins, Knox, Cordell Hull, and Henry Stimson, stopped to exchange gloomy comments on what was shaping up to be the most devastating military disaster in American history.

Finally, near midnight, FDR called Murrow into his study. Here they were, arguably the two best communicators in the country, certainly the two best-known voices on American radio. But there was no time for reflections on that score or, for that matter, for any pleasantries at all. The president asked Murrow about the British public's morale and then, over beer and sandwiches, told him of the staggering losses at Pearl Harbor—the eight battleships sunk or badly damaged, the hundreds of planes destroyed, the thousands of men dead, wounded, and missing. Roosevelt kept his rage under control until he started talking about the aircraft. "Destroyed on the ground, by God!" he exclaimed, pounding his fist on the table. "On the ground!" As Murrow later recalled, "the idea seemed to hurt him."

When he finally left the White House early the next morning, Murrow joined Eric Sevareid at CBS's Washington bureau, a few blocks away. "What did you think when you saw that crowd of people tonight staring through the White House fence?" Murrow asked. Sevareid replied: "They reminded me of the crowds around the Quai d'Orsay a couple of years ago." Nodding, Murrow said: "That's what I was thinking. The same look on their faces that they had in Downing Street."

It was an expression both men knew well—the look of a people steeling themselves for war.

9.

CREATING THE ALLIANCE

THE MORNING AFTER PEARL HARBOR, CHURCHILL AWOKE FROM A sound sleep and announced he planned to leave at once for Washington. A dubious Anthony Eden told him he didn't think the Americans would want to see him so soon. Eden was right. When Roosevelt heard about the prime minister's proposed trip, he advised Lord Halifax, now the British ambassador in Washington, that it might be better to wait. But Churchill would brook no delay. "He was like a child in his impatience to meet the President," recalled Lord Moran. "He spoke as if every minute counted." Four days after the United States entered the war, Churchill and his military advisers were on their way to the American capital to set up the alliance he had pursued for so long.

Aboard the battleship *Duke of York,* the British leader appeared, in the view of his doctor, to be decades younger than he had looked just days before. "The Winston I knew in London frightened me," Moran wrote in his diary. "And now, in a night it seems—a younger man has taken his place. . . . The tired, dull look has gone from his eye. He is gay and voluble, sometimes even playful."

After docking at Hampton Roads, Virginia, on December 22, Churchill and his subordinates flew to Washington. The United States had been at war for two weeks. Congress, at Roosevelt's request, had declared war against Japan on December 8; three days later, Germany and the United States declared war against each other. But, if the blazing lights of the capital that night were any indication, the conflict clearly was still remote to most Americans, psychologically as well as geographically. Pressing their faces against the plane's windows like schoolboys, the members of Churchill's party, accustomed to London's Stygian nighttime darkness, marveled at the brilliant glow beneath them. To John Martin, Churchill's principal private secretary, it was "one of the most beautiful sights I have ever seen." To another Churchill staffer, Washington, "with its myriad dancing neon signs, looked like a fairy city."

That same warmth and sparkle were apparent in the greeting given Churchill by Roosevelt, who, having surrendered to the prime minister's sense of urgency, met him at National Airport. The president drove him back to the White House and installed him in an upstairs suite down the hall from FDR's own bedroom. "We're here as a big family, in the greatest intimacy and informality," Churchill wrote delightedly to Clement Attlee, his deputy prime minister.

Roosevelt's White House was noted for what Churchill called its "Olympian calm," but with the prime minister in temporary residence, it seemed caught up in a whirlwind. Just as at Chequers and Ditchley, secretaries rushed around, and messengers, carrying red leather dispatch boxes, bustled to and fro. Churchill and Roosevelt wandered in and out of each other's rooms at will and studied the war maps that the prime minister tacked up in the Monroe Room. Churchill celebrated Christmas with the Roosevelts, took part in FDR's preprandial cocktail hours, shared most meals with the president, and, to Eleanor Roosevelt's great dismay, kept her husband up until the early hours each morning, drinking brandy, puffing cigars, and talking endlessly about everything.

But, in at least one regard, the British leader did not follow his usual routine: he did not dominate the conversations or hold court at meals as he usually did at home. In some of their meetings to come, the two leaders would resemble "a pair of master showmen who were determined that no scenes would be stolen by the other," as Secret Service agent Mike Reilly put it. "Being with them was like sitting between two lions roaring at the same time," remarked Mary Churchill Soames. Yet in Washington, as during the Placentia Bay meeting, the prime minister played up to Roosevelt. Churchill "was always full of stories," a friend of Mrs. Roosevelt's noted, "but at meals, no matter how far apart the two were sitting or who was next to him, he tried to talk with FDR. The whole flow of Churchill's conversation was directed at the President." Lord Moran observed in his diary: "You could almost feel the importance he attaches to bringing the President along with him, and in that good cause he has become a very model of restraint and self-discipline." At night, Churchill, thinking of himself as "Sir Walter Raleigh spreading his cloak before Queen Elizabeth," insisted on pushing FDR in his wheelchair from the sitting room to the elevator as "a mark of respect."

In their discussions, Churchill, to his great relief, found no trace of Roosevelt's pre–Pearl Harbor caution and indecision. FDR's resolution and determination to fight the war "with everything we've got" was echoed by that of the American people, who, in the words of Robert Sherwood, "cast off isolationism readily, rapidly, even gratefully— though perhaps not permanently." Even more important in the prime minister's eyes, the president declared that the defeat of Germany should be the Allies' first objective. The two leaders agreed that a vanguard of American forces should be dispatched immediately to Britain—two Army units to defend Northern Ireland and several bomber squadrons to begin raids against Germany from British bases.

Roosevelt and Churchill also made an unprecedented decision: to bring their forces together under a unified command. In each theater of operations, a single commander would have authority over all British and American soldiers, sailors, and airmen, while a Combined Chiefs of Staff Committee would base itself in Washington to coordinate Anglo-American strategy. In addition, U.S.-British agencies would be created to control munitions, shipping, raw materials, food, and production. It was, George Marshall declared later, "the most complete unification of military effort ever achieved by two allied nations."

True enough. But achieving that "complete unification of military effort" was an enormous, friction-filled struggle that would last until the end of the war. In its relatively short history, the United States, strictly speaking, had never been a true ally of any country. During World War I, President Wilson had declared his country "an Associated Power" rather than an Ally; in the field, General John Pershing, the head of the American Expeditionary Force, kept his troops as a separate entity under his command. The British, on the other hand, had had a wide variety of alliances over the centuries, many if not most conducted with mutual frustration and antipathy.

To some Americans, it seemed that the British, with their superior attitude, still looked on them as misbehaving colonists rather than as an independent, equal people. It was maddening to be treated like ignorant adolescents, who needed to be taken in tow by a wise, all-knowing mentor, who would educate them in the ways of the world. Sir Ronald Lindsay, the British ambassador to the United States in the mid-1930s, displayed such condescension when he wrote to the Foreign Office in 1937: "The United States is still extraordinarily young and sensitive. She resembles a young lady just launched into society and highly susceptible to a little deference from an older man"—meaning Britain, of course. Churchill used similar analogies himself, often comparing the United States to a skittish young woman who could be brought around to the right way of thinking by wooing and seduction.

THE DIVISIONS BETWEEN the two countries surfaced almost immediately during military staff talks in Washington. Their prime minister might have agreed to the American proposals for a unified command and a Washington-based committee to plan strategy, but the British brass were appalled by both ideas. What did the Americans, unready for war as they were, know about commanding allied forces? For that matter, what did they know about waging war?

"I have never seen so many motor cars, but I have not seen a military vehicle," Field Marshal Sir John Dill, after his first few days in Washington, wrote to Alan Brooke, who had just taken over from Dill as chief of the Imperial General Staff. "And yet amid all this unpreparedness, the ordinary American firmly believes that they can finish off the war quite quickly—and without too much disturbance. . . . This country has not—repeat not—the slightest conception of what the war means, and their armed forces are more unready for war than it is possible to imagine." (Dill would have been even more shocked if he had been in Washington on December 8, when all U.S. military officers were ordered to report to work in full uniform. Since most had worn mufti on duty in the pre–Pearl Harbor days, the corridors of the Army and Navy Building that Monday morning "were filled with officers [wearing] uniforms and parts of uniforms dating back to 1918. . . . Majors were in outfits they had bought when second lieutenants. . . . It was a rummage sale called to war.")

Ironically, considering Dill's initial skepticism about his country's new ally, he would emerge as one of the key figures in preserving the unity of this fragile new union. At Brooke's suggestion, Dill was named senior British member of the Combined Chiefs of Staff in Washington; his tact, charm, courtesy, and persuasiveness quickly won over American military leaders, particularly George Marshall, with whom he formed a close friendship. Time and again, the diplomatic Dill would help find solutions to the constant disputes between British and American military leaders. When Dill died of aplastic anemia in 1944, Marshall insisted that he be buried in Arlington National Cemetery, as he had wished. Although the burial of foreigners was banned at Arlington, Congress passed a joint resolution making an exception for the popular British field marshal. The route of his cortege was lined with thousands of U.S. troops, and a witness at the graveside reported: "I have never seen so many men so visibly shaken by sadness. Marshall's face was truly stricken."

In the four years of the alliance, the U.S. Army chief of staff would develop no such rapport, however, with the acidic Brooke, his British counterpart. When Brooke, who stayed behind in London during the Washington meetings, learned that Churchill had agreed to a joint command headquarters in the U.S. capital, he was furious. "I could see no reason why, at this stage, with American forces totally unprepared to play a major part, we should agree to a central control in Washington," he wrote in his diary.

But the conflict over unified command paled in comparison to the Anglo-American division over where to hit the Germans first—a fight that would rage for the next seven months. Marshall and his subordinates wanted to go straight for the German jugular—an invasion of France across the English Channel. They envisioned a massive buildup of American troops in Britain, followed by an assault on the Continent in the summer of 1943. If a collapse of Russia seemed imminent in 1942, then a less ambitious attack on France could be carried out to secure a beachhead.

"As is usual with the Americans, once having decided to go to war, they determined to fight a bigger and better war than ever was fought before," Lieutenant General Sir Frederick Morgan, the British chief planner of D-Day, sardonically noted years afterward. The American strategy was based on a fundamental principle of the U.S. military dating back to the Civil War, the longest and most costly conflict in which the country had engaged to date. That principle—to destroy the enemy with overwhelming force as quickly as possible—was the strategy used by Union general Ulysses S. Grant in his drive against the Confederate army of Robert E. Lee.

Churchill, Brooke, and the rest of the British military were dumb-founded by what they regarded as the recklessness and amateurishness of the proposal. Didn't the Americans realize that an invasion as early as 1942 would be sheer madness? How could the Allies return to West-ern Europe, with its twenty-seven German divisions, when American forces were still so paltry, both Allies were woefully ill-equipped and armed, not enough shipping existed to bring the huge numbers of men and supplies needed across the Atlantic, and amphibious landing craft were in such short supply? "One might think we are going across the Channel to play baccarat at Le Touquet or to bathe at Paris Plage!" Brooke snorted.

Churchill and his army chief believed that the first Allied strikes against Germany should take place in North Africa and other targets on the perimeter of Europe, to greatly weaken the Germans before go-ing in for the kill. That kind of peripheral strategy was one to which the British, with its superior naval power and lack of large land forces, had subscribed for centuries. The murderous trench warfare of World War I was an exception for Britain; having lost more than 750,000 men in that four-year bloodbath, the country was determined that such a catastrophe would never be repeated. If a cross-Channel land-ing was to be carried out in the near future, the bulk of the troops would be British, as Churchill and Brooke well knew. "We had sus-tained disaster after disaster, and the skin of our teeth was wearing a bit thin," observed Frederick Morgan. "Small wonder if those who bore the full responsibility were not overenthusiastic about sticking their necks out farther than they had ever stuck them out before."

Marshall and the rest of the American military were unconvinced by the British arguments. They were sure that their ally's plan for North Africa was simply a scheme to protect the British empire—to keep the Suez Canal safe and to safeguard Britain's oil and other interests in the Middle East. "For Marshall, suspicion of British imperial designs under Churchill underlay every wartime scheme," historian Stanley Weintraub has written. Marshall himself acknowledged after the war that "too much anti-British feeling [existed] on our side, more than we should have had. Our people were always ready to find Albion perfidious."

ALTHOUGH MARSHALL AND Brooke remained unimpressed with each other for the duration of the war, they nonetheless had a good deal in common. They both were considered the preeminent figures in their country's high commands and were the closest and most trusted military advisers to their heads of government. Each was a superb leader who made a vital contribution to ultimate victory. They shared many of the same personality traits—they were brusque, stern, obstinate, intensely private, impatient, and distinctly formidable.

But there was one key difference between them, of which both generals were acutely aware. Unlike Brooke, Marshall had never led troops in battle, despite his keen desire to do so. During World War I, he had been chief of operations for the 1st Infantry Division in France and later served on General Pershing's staff. After holding virtually every important staff job in the Army, he became chief of staff on September 1, 1939, the day Hitler invaded Poland. Over the next two years, Marshall embarked on a complete overhaul of the Army. With single-minded determination, he rooted out hundreds of senior officers he considered deadweight, handpicked the most promising new commanders, stepped up training, ordered massive maneuvers, created an armored division, and oversaw the introduction of a multitude of new weapons. Called "the epitome of the modern military manager," he did all this in the face of stiff resistance from an isolationist Congress, as well as from some New Dealers within the Roosevelt administration. "Not even the president could intimidate Marshall, who never hesitated to disagree with Roosevelt when he thought his commander in chief was mistaken," noted one historian.

Brooke conceded that Marshall was "a big man and a very great gentleman." He saw "a great charm and dignity" in his American counterpart "which could not fail to appeal to me." But, in the British chief's mind, those favorable qualities were overshadowed by Marshall's lack of battlefield experience and what Brooke viewed as the American's ineptitude as a strategist.

By 1941, Brooke's own experiences on the battlefield had made the very thought of war repugnant to him. In 1916, as a young lieutenant, he had fought in the horrific Battle of the Somme, which claimed a total of 420,000 British casualties, nearly 70,000 of them on the battle's first day alone. After Britain declared war on Germany in 1939, Brooke commanded a corps of the British Expeditionary Force in France and was given most of the credit for the successful evacuation of some 200,000 British troops from Dunkirk in June 1940. "By almost universal testimony, it was due largely to his skill and resolution that not only his own Corps but the whole BEF escaped destruction" in its retreat from the German blitzkrieg, wrote Sir James Grigg, the permanent head of the War Office. Shortly thereafter, Churchill sent Brooke back to France to take command of the remaining British forces in the western part of the country; he was forced to organize yet another evacuation when the situation became untenable and the French government capitulated to Germany. In July 1940, he was put in charge of British forces in England and oversaw the reorganization of Britain's defenses, in anticipation of a German invasion of the island.

Having experienced the enemy blitzkrieg firsthand, Brooke was stunned when he discovered, during his first meeting with Marshall in the spring of 1942, that the Americans had no idea of the German fury lying in wait for Allied troops if they somehow managed an early landing in France. "I found [Marshall] had not begun to consider any form of plan of action and had not even begun to visualize the problems that would face an army after landing," Brooke later wrote. "I saw a great deal of him throughout the rest of the war, and the more I saw of him, the more clearly I appreciated that his strategic ability was of the poorest."

That was hardly the sharpest comment that Brooke, who concealed a seething, sensitive nature under a cloak of imperturbability, would make about Marshall. "Rather over-filled with his own importance," read one of his many astringent diary entries about his American counterpart. Another was: "In many respects he is a very dangerous man." (Although Marshall didn't think much of Brooke either, he apparently was not as outspoken in his disdain. In one of the few recorded instances where he revealed his feelings about Brooke, Marshall told Harry Hopkins that "although he may be a good fighting man, he hasn't got Dill's brains.")

WHILE ALLIED COMMANDERS were debating the course of future operations in early 1942, a multitude of military disasters faced them in the present. America's entry into the war was accompanied by one crushing Allied defeat after another. For Americans, the shock of losing much of the U.S. fleet at Pearl Harbor was followed by Japanese conquests of Guam, Wake Island, and the Philippines. For the British, the situation was far worse. Vanquished earlier by the Germans in

France, Greece, and Crete, they now lost their empire in the Far East and the Pacific to the Japanese, suffering, as they did so, some of their most humiliating military defeats in history.

On December 9, two of Britain's biggest and best fighting ships—the battleship *Prince of Wales,* on which Churchill had traveled to his Placentia Bay meeting with Roosevelt, and the battle cruiser *Repulse*—were sunk by Japanese warplanes in the South China Sea, off the coast of Malaya. More than 650 men lost their lives. "In my whole experience," Churchill said, "I do not remember any naval blow so heavy or so painful."

On Christmas Day, Hong Kong fell, followed by Singapore, Burma, and Malaya. "We seem to lose a new bit of the Empire almost every day," Brooke wrote glumly to a friend, "and are faced with one nightmare situation after another." The surrender of Singapore, previously regarded as an invincible British bulwark in the Far East, was a particular shock to the country, which couldn't understand how Singapore's 85,000-man garrison could give up so readily. Speaking in the House of Commons, Churchill called it "the greatest disaster in British arms which our history records." Malaya also was lost without the waging of a single major battle.

Yet this *annus horribilis* was far from over. In North Africa, Rommel bottled up a new British offensive in Libya, pushing the Tommies back and recapturing Benghazi and Gazala. In June, after holding out against a long siege, Tobruk, a key British bastion on the coast in eastern Libya, capitulated, with more than thirty thousand troops surrendering to a considerably smaller German force. A far greater strategic disaster than the loss of Singapore, the capture of Tobruk cleared the way for a German advance toward Cairo and the Suez Canal, threatening the entire British presence in the Middle East. Of Tobruk's fall, Churchill declared: "Defeat is one thing; disgrace is another."*

As one calamity followed another in 1942, the mood in Britain

---

* The only bright note for Churchill, who was in Washington at the time of Tobruk's capitulation, was the sympathy and concern displayed by Roosevelt and Marshall. At Churchill's request, they immediately authorized the dispatch of three hundred American tanks to the Middle East to help the British defense. Abandoning his usual testiness, Brooke acknowledged that American generosity during this dark period "did a great deal towards laying the foundations of friendship and understanding" between Britain and the United States during the war (Danchev and Todman, *War Diaries,* p. 269).

grew progressively fractious and sour. Among the public and in Parliament, there was widespread criticism of the government's handling of the war and renewed suggestions that the prime minister give up his other role as minister of defense. No amount of Churchillian eloquence could stem the discontent. "You . . . hear people say that they've had enough of fine oratory," correspondent Mollie Panter-Downes wrote in *The New Yorker*. "What they would like is action and a sign from Mr. Churchill that he understands the profoundly worried temper of the country."

In January and again in July, Churchill faced votes of censure in the House of Commons over his direction of the war. Although he won both handily, the drumbeat of attacks on his leadership—and the defeats that prompted them—took a severe toll on the usually ebullient prime minister. "During my period of guarding him—beginning in 1921—I have never seen him so disheartened," observed Walter Thompson, Churchill's bodyguard. "He could take the worst sort of knock, but this seemed one that was beyond his control. . . . These were bitter days. He could not sleep or eat." Mary Churchill noted in her diary that her father was "at a very low ebb. He is not too well physically, and he is worn down by the continuous crushing pressure of events."

While coping with this seemingly endless string of military catastrophes, Churchill also had to deal with a deepening crisis in the Battle of the Atlantic, with German submarines now preying on merchant ships off the East Coast of the United States. Silhouetted against the bright lights on shore, the ships made spectacularly easy targets. According to a U.S. Navy report, "the massacre enjoyed by the U-boats along our Atlantic Coast in 1942 was as much a national disaster as if saboteurs had destroyed half a dozen of our biggest war plants." Marshall agreed, writing: "The losses by submarines off our Atlantic seaboard and in the Caribbean now threaten our entire war effort." In the first six months of 1942, largely because of U-boat successes in American waters, Allied shipping losses were more than a million tons greater than they had been in the first half of the previous year.

At 10 Downing Street one day, Lord Moran found Churchill in his Map Room, staring fixedly at a huge chart of the Atlantic dotted with large black pins representing German submarines. "Terrible," the prime minister muttered, then turned on his heel and brushed abruptly past his doctor, head down, without saying another word. "He knows that we may lose the war at sea in a few months and that he can do nothing about it," Moran wrote in his diary. "I wish to God I could put out the fires that seem to be consuming him."

The rising shipping losses, meanwhile, meant a continued drop in the British standard of living, with food imports plummeting to less than half of what they had been before the war. Japanese victories in the Far East exacerbated the problem, cutting off Britain's usual sources for tea, rice, sugar, and other commodities. Everything seemed to be in increasingly short supply, including coal, which hit the British people especially hard during one of the coldest winters in memory.

With all the crises facing them, it's not surprising that most Britons' reaction to America's entry into the war, an event they had long awaited, was hardly one of unrestrained joy. "We simply can't be beaten with America in," Harold Nicolson wrote his wife. "But how strange it is that this great event should be recorded and welcomed here without any jubilation. . . . Not an American flag flying in the whole of London."

Among some Britons, according to a public opinion survey, there was a sense of "malicious delight that at long last the Americans would have a taste of war." Many British citizens felt that "Americans ought really to have been helping us right through the early part of the war, just like the Canadians and Australians," added a government report.

Canadian diplomat Charles Ritchie observed that the attack on Pearl Harbor "has caused very human sardonic satisfaction to everyone I have happened to see today. . . . The note of outraged American indignation at the treachery of which the U.S.A. has been a victim meets with no real echo here. It is like a hardened old tart who hears a girl crying because a man has deceived her for the first time. We have become very much accustomed to treachery—now let the Americans learn the facts of life and see how they like them."

SUCH SCHADENFREUDE ON the part of the British reflected the deep chasm in knowledge and understanding that existed between their country and America at the start of the wartime alliance. "Broadly speaking, there is a lack of positive admiration for either American achievements or American institutions," the Ministry of Information concluded.

Unquestionably, the citizens of both nations had severely warped ideas of each other. According to one U.S. historian, the primary image of the British that Americans had taken away from their history lessons was one of murderous redcoats who tried to destroy the infant United States during the Revolutionary War. General Dwight D. Eisenhower, who would lead Allied forces in North Africa and Europe later in the war, concurred in that analysis. "The seeds of discord between ourselves and our British allies were sown, on our side, as far back as when we read our little red school history books," Eisenhower wrote Marshall in 1943.

Yet, as distorted as the teaching of British history might have been in the United States, at least it was taught in American schools, as was British literature. By contrast, most Britons had learned virtually nothing about American history or literature during their school days. "Probably not one Englishman in twenty could have explained the meaning of the Boston Tea Party," wrote a British historian. "Not one in fifty could have named any American president before Franklin Delano Roosevelt, except Lincoln." After the Ministry of Information conducted a series of interviews with Britons to see how much they knew about the United States, one interviewer remarked: "I met so many 'Don't knows' that even I began to feel embarrassed."

Few Britons had ever met an American, and fewer yet had crossed the Atlantic. Any ideas they had about the United States and its people usually came from Hollywood movies. To a young Whitehall official, America was a "mixture of slaves in the South, gangsters in Chicago, and musicals with Fred Astaire." When Sergeant Robert Arbib, a former New York advertising executive, arrived in Britain with the first American forces in 1942, he was peppered with such questions as "Are you from Texas?" "Have you seen a gangster?" and "Do you live in a penthouse?"

Acutely aware of the misunderstandings, lack of knowledge, and tensions between his countrymen and the British, Gil Winant made it his mission during the war to ease such difficulties. As a former history teacher, he believed that education was the key to creating the understanding that was needed. Whenever he could grab a day or two away from the increasing frenzy of Grosvenor Square, the ambassador traveled throughout England to talk about the history and culture of the United States, with special emphasis on its ties to Britain. "I hope you will help your country understand my country," he told one group of teachers. "My time in England has taught me that in all the fundamental things, we work from a common denominator." He recruited Janet Murrow and other Americans in Britain to lead similar discussions and persuaded the noted American historian Allan Nevins, then a visiting professor at Oxford, to write a short history of the United States. The Nevins book became a required textbook in British schools both during and after the war.

Winant "wanted the people of Britain to know the American people as he knew them," said Wallace Carroll, the former chief of the United Press news service in London. "He wanted them to know the . . . farmers around Concord, New Hampshire. He wanted them to know the workers of the steel mills and textile mills, the coal mines, the railroads and the shipyards, to whose welfare he had dedicated a great part of his life. He wanted them to know not the America of the films but the America which had created the Tennessee Valley Authority and the Social Security Board."

Carroll, who had been a correspondent in London during the Blitz, was recruited by Winant to head an American information service in Britain, under the auspices of the Office of War Information, a new U.S. agency whose mission was to support the American war effort with news and propaganda for foreign and domestic consumption. With Carroll as director, the London operation focused on providing objective information, not propaganda, to the British. It transmitted news reports and other material about America to newspapers, Whitehall officials, MPs, and average citizens. "We set out to use every legitimate means of informing [the British] about America without trying to sell them any neatly wrapped ideas," recalled Carroll, "and we all agreed that we should make no effort to cover up disagreeable truths." By the end of 1942, thanks in part to the information service, "British newspapers [were] printing more serious American news than at any time since the war began," according to Raymond Daniell, London bureau chief of the *New York Times*.

With popular demand growing in Britain for information about the country's new ally, Winant also established a library on the ground floor of the U.S. embassy in London, aimed at MPs, writers, educators, editors, students, and other members of the British public who wanted access to American books, magazines, and newspapers. An enormous success, the library spurred the postwar creation of a network of similar reading rooms at U.S. embassies throughout the world. Janet Murrow—whose husband, as director of the U.S. Information Agency, would be in charge of overseeing those facilities twenty years later—noted to her parents in 1942 that the library also helped sate the hunger of American expatriates in London for news of their homeland. "I would like to spend all my time there," she wrote.

Such efforts by Winant and others to promote an understanding of the United States and its people in Britain bore considerable fruit. In Washington, an acquaintance of Felix Frankfurter's who had just returned from England told the Supreme Court justice of "a surprising new and deep interest in America there . . . to a degree for which there is no comparable interest or understanding of things British on this side." Frankfurter believed that the British government needed to make a comparable educational effort in the United States, to combat the popular American view of Britain as "an oppressor people, itself under the rule of a foxhunting, old-school-tie, Buckingham Palace, George the Third society."

AS FRANKFURTER INDICATED, the American people were as little enamored of their new allies across the Atlantic as the British public, at least initially, were of them. When Americans were asked by pollsters in 1942 if Britain was doing all it could to win the war, only about 50 percent replied in the affirmative. Many Americans shared the skepticism of their political and military leaders toward British motives in fighting the war; in the same poll, more than half condemned Britain's colonial policy, although, according to the pollsters, "their factual knowledge about the British Empire was vague and distorted."

When Ed Murrow returned to London in March 1942 after his four-month sojourn in the United States, he told Harold Nicolson he had found an "intense" anti-British feeling in his homeland. It stemmed, Nicolson wrote in his diary, "partly from the hard core of anglophobes, partly from the frustration produced by war without early victory, partly from our bad behaviour at Singapore, and partly from the tendency common to all countries at war to blame their allies for doing nothing."

Before Murrow left the United States, Harry Hopkins and Robert Sherwood, who had been put in charge of the Office of War Information's foreign operations, had tried to convince him to stay in Washington and become the U.S. government's "voice of America"—its chief broadcaster for English-language news reports beamed by the

OWI to Europe. After much soul-searching, Murrow declined. Having played a major role in bringing America into the war on the side of the British, he chose to spend the duration in England, doing his best to stimulate a mutual understanding between his own country and the land that had been his home for the past five years. "It would be personally more pleasant to remain here," he wired Hopkins, "but, foreseeing troublous times ahead for the Anglo-American alliance, I am convinced it is my duty to go back."

Over the next three years, in his CBS broadcasts and in frequent appearances on the BBC, Murrow tried to explain the politics, personality traits, and peculiarities of each ally to the other. "We might understand each other better if we had more frank conversations between Britons and Americans," he observed during one BBC broadcast. "You must bear in mind that we are, on the whole, more emotional, vociferous and intolerant than you. We'll go to a baseball game or a football match and shout for the blood of the referee, and on occasion, fling beer bottles at him. Our domestic controversies are conducted in strong language, with much name-calling—in short, we're inclined to say what we think, even when we have not thought very much." At the same time, he pointed out similarities between the two nations: "We, like you, are testy and headstrong, with a certain range and variety of character, wishing neither to command or obey, but to be kings in our own houses."

As part of his education campaign, Murrow participated in a number of special series on CBS and the BBC designed to make the Anglo-American alliance more meaningful to both U.S. and British radio audiences. Among them was a joint CBS-BBC effort, with broadcasts originating one week from America and the next from Britain, but aired simultaneously in both countries. Another was an eight-part series, called *An American in England*, produced by Murrow and the BBC, and broadcast by CBS.

Murrow also created a new series for the BBC called *Meet Uncle Sam*, which one historian called "a cram course on the American experience for British listeners," featuring, in addition to Murrow himself, such guests as Allan Nevins and Alistair Cooke, a U.S.-based BBC correspondent. The show, Murrow made clear, would contain no whitewashing of his country. "Later on in this series," he said during its first broadcast, "you will hear all about the New Deal, our racial problems, and how we came to be a nation of which one third is ill-clothed, ill-housed and ill-fed. You will also hear something of our achievements." Startled by his candid comments, a BBC announcer, at the end of the program, noted Murrow's "vigorous criticisms of some things American, which would come ill from an Englishman."

Such directness, however, had always been at the heart of his broadcasting philosophy. "Frankness and honesty *may* divide America and Britain," Murrow once said, "but polite fiction *certainly* will."

10.

"AN ENGLISHMAN SPOKE IN GROSVENOR SQUARE"

THE EFFORTS OF GIL WINANT AND ED MURROW TO PROMOTE UNderstanding between Britons and Americans were put to their first real test in the spring of 1942. That's when the initial contingent of American troops arrived in Northern Ireland, and the first planes and crews of the Eighth Air Force settled in eastern England, along with service troops to build bases, depots, and fields. Britain was now the Allies' nerve center and front line in Europe. From there, they would bomb—and eventually invade—the Continent.

By the summer of 1942, London was awash with American soldiers and airmen on leave. Most of the buildings in and around Grosvenor Square had been appropriated by U.S. military and other government agencies. The number of Americans in the neighborhood mushroomed so quickly that one wit wrote a parody of the lyrics to the popular song "A Nightingale Sang in Berkeley Square," changing the title to "An Englishman Spoke in Grosvenor Square."

With the Americans' arrival, central London took on "an air of near-frantic urgency," noted one city resident. Olive green cars shuttled high-ranking U.S. military officers back and forth between Grosvenor Square and the British War Office, a couple of miles away, while dispatch riders on motorcycles zigzagged through traffic that seemed as heavy as in prewar days. Flats and hotel rooms became increasingly difficult to find (during one visit, the U.S. chiefs of staff took over no fewer than sixteen rooms at Claridge's), and at some restaurants it was almost impossible to get a reservation.

American military policemen, known as "snowdrops" because of their white helmets and gaiters, now patrolled Piccadilly and other major thoroughfares; they became so familiar with the city's layout that, in time, they were asked for directions not only by visiting GIs but by Britons as well. On summer afternoons, the MPs played base-ball in Green Park, attracting a large crowd of spectators, who brought blankets and deck chairs to watch what was, for most of them, a game as foreign as cricket was for the Americans.

Indeed, so Americanized had Grosvenor Square and surrounding neighborhoods become that, in the words of an American journalist, "the sight of the Union Jack flying from a nearby building seems an anomaly." South Audley Street was turned into "a miniature Fifth Avenue," while a mansion facing Stanhope Gate became a club for high-ranking U.S. officers. The bomb-damaged Washington Hotel in Curzon Street was renovated into a social and residential club for en-listed men, with posters of the American West and South on the walls and doughnuts covered with powdered sugar always available. To a *Daily Telegraph* reporter, the Washington Club, with its shoeshine par-lor, barber shop, and vases filled with flowers, resembled "a million-aires' club" far more than it did "a centre for doughboys," the World War I term for U.S. soldiers.

The American invasion, meanwhile, proved to be a gold mine for the shopkeepers and other small businessmen near the square. "There was not a tailor, a shoemaker, a laundry or a cleaner in our neighbor-hood that did not start working overtime to cope with this influx," a Londoner remarked. "Whereas eighteen months earlier, during the night raids, these little tradesmen had carried on stoically with an or-der here and there, prosperity now burst upon them. They hammered and sewed, they ironed and they washed, all day and far into the night."

KNOWN AS "LITTLE AMERICA," Grosvenor Square acquired another nickname—"Eisenhowerplatz"—when General Dwight Eisenhower arrived in June to assume command of American forces in the Euro-pean theater. The selection of the fifty-one-year-old Eisenhower to take charge of American troops was, at first glance, an odd one. An obscure general with an infectious grin and affable manner, he had never commanded an Army unit larger than a battalion and had never fought in a war. Much to his dismay, he, like George Marshall, had been a staff officer for most of his career; he'd come to England from Washington, where he had headed the War Plans Division and had been the chief architect of the American plan to invade the Continent.

Beneath Eisenhower's gregarious, easygoing persona, however, was a keen mind, fierce ambition and resolve, and explosive temper. A Marshall protégé, he was a master organizer and prodigiously hard worker. Above all, he was one of America's few generals who was not an Anglophobe. From the start, he was determined to forge a close working relationship with his country's new allies; indeed, he described himself as a "fanatic" on the subject. "Gentlemen," he told his staff shortly after arriving in London, "we have one chance and only one of winning this war, and that is in complete and unqualified partnership with the British. . . . I shall govern myself accordingly and expect you to do likewise."

Nonetheless, his introduction into the sniffy upper-class world in which his British counterparts operated was a rocky one. A country boy from Abilene, Kansas, Eisenhower had grown up in a house on the wrong side of the tracks, with no running water or indoor plumbing. "There is no question," wrote one of his biographers, "that poverty steeled young Dwight's ambition and his determination to excel [and to] succeed." Yet, although he concealed it well, his humble roots also left him with a deep sense of insecurity, a fear of being perceived as a country bumpkin—a not uncommon unease felt by other Americans when mingling with upper-crust Britons. "He feared nothing so much as exposure," said an associate.

When Eisenhower visited the country estate of Lord Mountbatten, the commander of British combined operations, the evident disdain of the elderly manservant who unpacked the meager contents of his suitcase so embarrassed him that he left the man an especially large tip. He was made equally self-conscious by the haughty butler assigned to him at Claridge's, who made no secret of his scorn for the general's unassuming ways. Eisenhower detested everything about Claridge's, including his suite, with its black-and-gold sitting room—"Makes me feel as if I'm living in sin"—and its "whorehouse pink" bedroom. (He later moved to the Dorchester but felt no more comfortable there.)

He also hated the social whirl of wartime London. "Despite the fact that he was tremendously sought after by London hostesses, he became almost as much of a recluse as Greta Garbo," recalled Kay

Summersby, the young Irishwoman who became his driver in the capital. "He was impatient with anything that took his time or energy away from the war." After one society reception, he stormed to Summersby, "I don't think my blood pressure can take it if one more silly woman calls me 'My deeaah general.' I'm nobody's goddamned 'deeah general,' and I'm not fighting this war over tea cups." Shortly after he arrived in London, Eisenhower instituted a seven-day workweek in his command. "After all, it is a war," he said. "We're here to fight and not to be wined and dined."

In his rejection of a high-profile social presence in London, as in much else, Eisenhower resembled Gil Winant, with whom, he said later, he formed a close working relationship and intimate friendship. Both were unpretentious, modest men who hated the floodlight of publicity and who put all their energy into work. Although not frequent churchgoers, they both were deeply religious. Above all, both were determined to do everything in their power to make the U.S.-British alliance a success. "From the outset he regarded Anglo-American friendship almost as a religion," General Pug Ismay, Churchill's liaison with the British chiefs of staff, said of Eisenhower. Throughout the war, he remained the voice of reason and conciliation, even in the midst of the most bitter disputes. His emphasis on teamwork went unappreciated by many of his own American generals, who later would accuse him of favoring the British over his countrymen.

When Eisenhower first arrived in the British capital, both Murrow and Winant helped guide him through its social and political minefields. Harry Butcher, Eisenhower's personal aide, noted in his diary that the general "was having difficulty in determining who was important and who was not, who should be seen and who could be put off. . . . I got Ed Murrow to help us on this."

Winant, meanwhile, came to the general's rescue in a thorny situation related to his heavy smoking. For much of his life, Eisenhower had been a chain-smoker, a habit that intensified as the pressures on him grew more intense. The ambassador repeatedly reminded him that, at official British dinners, there was to be no smoking until near the end of the dinner and the offering of toasts, a ban that Eisenhower repeatedly forgot. Finally, to make it easier on him and to avoid a minor strain in Anglo-American relations, Winant arranged that, at dinners where Eisenhower was present, the toasts would be offered immediately following the serving of the first course.

After establishing his headquarters at 20 Grosvenor Square, diagonally opposite the embassy, the general frequently crossed the square to consult Winant on various issues, and Winant did the same. The two "see eye to eye" on almost everything, Butcher observed. Noting the similarity between his and Eisenhower's outlook and attitudes, the ambassador, who referred to himself as "another of Ike's lieutenants," sometimes asked his advice on such things as the wording of a cable to Washington. In turn, Eisenhower sought Winant's help on a number of questions, including the relationship between the British public and American troops in the country.

In London, Winant was the civilian counterpart to Eisenhower, directing the embassy staff as well as overseeing the London outposts of a rapidly growing number of American wartime civilian agencies. The military and civilian operations were enormous: in 1942, more than three thousand people worked for the U.S government in London, a figure that would skyrocket over the next two years.

The embassy itself was now the diplomatic nerve center for the war in Europe and a focal point for coordination of the Allied war effort. With 675 staffers, it was also the largest U.S. mission in the world, requiring twenty-four telephone operators to handle the more than six thousand calls that flooded in each day. The post of ambassador "was a big job when [Winant] came to it; it has developed into a gigantic one now," the *New York Herald Tribune* wrote. "His functions, methods, and surroundings are more like those of a president of a big corporation." Winant's burden was "extremely heavy," noted one British official. "Everything, inevitably, found its way to the Ambassador's desk."

Among the new agencies whose work Winant oversaw were the London branches of the Office of War Information, Board of Economic Warfare, and Office of Strategic Services, America's first official intelligence agency. The equivalent of Britain's Secret Intelligence Service (MI6) and Special Operations Executive, the OSS had two principal functions: to obtain information about the enemy and to promote the sabotage of enemy armaments, facilities, and morale. From the heavily guarded OSS headquarters at 70 Grosvenor Street, agents would later be sent to France and other occupied countries, as well as into Germany itself.

Winant was as bad an administrator as ever, missing appointments, keeping people waiting, sometimes forgetting the names of his own personal staff. Once, in a fit of absentmindedness, he asked Herschel

Johnson, his minister-counselor, to take a letter as he paced back and forth in his office. As the number two man at the embassy, Johnson, not surprisingly, was annoyed at being asked to perform a stenographer's job; nonetheless, he pulled out a pen and jotted down Winant's dictation. Entering the ambassador's office a few days later, Johnson again found Winant dictating a letter, oblivious to everything but the ideas he was trying to frame into words. This time, it was Admiral Harold Stark, the former chief of naval operations and now the chief of American naval forces in the European theater, who was sitting in a chair and frantically scribbling down what the ambassador said.

Yet, for all his eccentric administrative habits, Winant continued to be an inspirational leader who, in the words of Wallace Carroll, "exerted an uncanny magnetism." Echoing Eisenhower's orders to his staff, the ambassador insisted that all agency officials and embassy employees in his domain must work together as a team. For the most part, they complied; by virtually all accounts, a close and harmonious collaboration existed among the many American government departments in London. "Every informant . . . agrees that Ambassador Winant is largely responsible for the high degree of cooperation that exists here among representatives of the Army, Navy, State Department, Board of Economic Warfare, OWI, OSS, and others," reported Bert Andrews, the *New York Herald Tribune*'s chief Washington correspondent.

As wartime Washington mushroomed, Andrews had devoted much of his time to reporting on the bitter feuds and conflicts that had erupted within and among government agencies, all of them vying for more power and influence. "Many of us," recalled assistant secretary of state Dean Acheson, "spent an inordinate amount of time in bureaucratic warfare for survival" in what was called "the Battle of Pennsylvania Avenue."

Andrews decided to travel to London to "to see whether the representatives of American agencies in England were getting along any better" than their counterparts back home. He was pleased, he told his readers, to discover that they were. "The Winant system seems to work admirably," Andrews concluded, "and the scene is, oh, so peaceful, compared with the feuding grounds in Washington."

ONE IMPORTANT FIGURE, however, was, most emphatically, not a player on the Winant team. Averell Harriman continued to undermine the ambassador, communicating directly with Hopkins and Roosevelt and in general involving himself in Anglo-American issues that were Winant's province. Even worse, according to the journalist Harrison Salisbury, "Averell substantively undercut Winant's relationship" with Churchill.

When Churchill visited Washington after Pearl Harbor, Harriman wangled an invitation from the prime minister to accompany him. But when he arrived, American officials, who had ignored him at the Placentia Bay conference, once again paid him little heed. In the view of Secretary of State Cordell Hull and others, Harriman was vastly exceeding his brief as Lend-Lease expediter. Nonetheless, when Churchill made a second visit to Roosevelt in June 1942, Harriman was again at the prime minister's side. Two months later, when Churchill decided he must travel to Moscow to explain to Stalin why there would be no second front that year, Harriman persuaded Churchill and Anthony Eden that an American official—namely, he—should be present at the meetings. Roosevelt initially refused to give permission for Harriman's trip, but, when Churchill, at Harriman's request, cabled the president urging his attendance, FDR gave in.

Just as he had excluded Laurence Steinhardt from his Lend-Lease talks with Stalin the year before, Harriman now persuaded Churchill to bar Steinhardt's successor as ambassador, Admiral William Standley, from the latest discussions. A former chief of U.S. naval operations, Standley was furious at Harriman's highhandedness and considered him a dilettante, "a moth fluttering around the sparks and the flame." Archibald Clark Kerr, the new British ambassador to Moscow, had a similarly jaundiced view of Harriman; he believed that Churchill's fondness for the American stemmed from Harriman's obsequiousness to the prime minister. "Every now and then [Churchill] would take Harriman by the hand, making remarks like 'I am so glad, Averell, that you're here with me. You are a tower of strength,' " Clark Kerr wrote sourly in his diary. "I think Harriman's presence is bad for him. . . . [He's] no more than a champion bum sucker."

After returning to London, Harriman kept in frequent communication with Churchill but failed to keep Winant informed of his dealings with the British leader. For all his public protestations of support for the ambassador, Harriman privately disparaged Winant as a dreamer—too idealistic, too concerned about helping his fellow man, not pragmatic or tough enough to operate in the cutthroat world of wartime politics. To Harriman, it was incomprehensible that Winant would occasionally keep British officials and other VIPs waiting in his outer office while he talked to GIs or other nondignitaries. It was equally unfathomable to the Lend-Lease representative that, when Winant hosted one of his rare receptions at the U.S. ambassador's official residence in Kensington, he often paid more attention to the embassy's janitors, charwomen, and other employees, whom he had invited, than to his official guests. Years later, Harriman indicated to journalist Elie Abel, who collaborated with him on his autobiography, that Roosevelt should have chosen *him* as ambassador: "I think I could have done as well if I had been ambassador and had this [Lend-Lease] job, too."

Harriman's disdain for Winant rubbed off on his daughter and Pamela Churchill. "He's not a good speaker or writer," Kathleen Harriman wrote to her sister about the ambassador, "but despite that, everyone over here is still convinced he's a great man, with capital letters. Anthony Eden spoke of him yesterday as being 'one of the men who can influence the tide of world affairs.' God help world affairs!"

IN THE SUMMER OF 1942, Winant appealed to Roosevelt and Harry Hopkins to clarify his authority. He may have been, as the *Times* of London later said, the "adhesive" of the Anglo-American alliance, but he found himself increasingly shut out of the two governments' high-level deliberations and decision making. "Winant was very unhappy with the fact that I was the major personality in our relations with Churchill," Harriman observed to Elie Abel. Deriding what he called the ambassador's "stupid jealousy," Harriman told Abel, "I utterly disregarded it."

While Harriman certainly had a role to play in Winant's exclusion, it was also due to Churchill's and Roosevelt's habit of communicating directly with each other, bypassing the State Department, Foreign Office, and their countries' embassies. It stemmed, too, from the president's long-standing habit of sending his own personal representatives and delegations to consult with foreign leaders without informing others in the administration who were working on the same issues. In a telegram to Hopkins, Winant reported that, when he contacted British ministries about a particular problem or concern, he was repeatedly told that a special U.S. mission had taken charge of the matter.

The ambassador was hardly the only major figure in the Roosevelt administration to find himself bypassed by the White House. Many cabinet secretaries and agency heads—among them, the highly respected war secretary, Henry Stimson—were also shut out of decision making directly related to their departments. That was the president's style: to keep the reins of power and authority in his own hands and to control the programs and policies he considered most important to himself and the country. "Roosevelt always saw to it that he himself was last judge and arbiter," one historian wrote.

No government official, however, felt the sting of exclusion more than did Cordell Hull. Throughout his eleven-year tenure as secretary of state, the courtly, white-haired Tennessean, who looked as if he'd just stepped out of a Victorian daguerreotype, was given virtually no role in the making of U.S. foreign policy. Winant told a British official that if Hull and Roosevelt "saw each other once a month, their relations could be considered very close." Hull, a former senator and head of the Democratic National Committee, had been chosen for his cabinet post not because of his experience in foreign affairs, which was nil, but because of his extensive political power and influence on Capitol Hill. In the years just before World War II and during the war itself, Roosevelt acted as his own secretary of state, ignoring not only Hull but the State Department as a whole. Winant, like other U.S. ambassadors, felt the brunt of that exclusionary policy.

In the view of James Reston, who took a short wartime sabbatical from the *New York Times* to serve in the U.S. embassy in London, the White House's cavalier treatment of Winant and the Foreign Service officers who worked under him was nothing short of "a political disgrace." In his memoirs, Reston declared: "I can think of nothing that has contributed more to the misconduct of American foreign affairs than the tendency to appoint inexperienced secretaries of state, bypass the Foreign Service, and try to operate foreign policy out of the White House."

Although Roosevelt had no intention of curtailing his direct dealings with Churchill and the British government, he did have a high regard for Winant and the job he was doing in London; he once told his friend Belle Roosevelt that "there were very few people who were presidential timber, and one of the very few was Winant." Learning of the ambassador's unhappiness, the president tried to make amends. To Winant, he wrote in a somewhat incoherent letter: "You are doing a magnificent job—and I say that not only for myself but as an expression of what everybody over here is unanimous on. In fact, hardly a new job turns up in Washington that somebody does not suggest that I bring you back to handle it. . . . I tell them that there is no one over here that I or anybody else can think of who could fill your place in London."

What's more, he ordered Harry Hopkins, during one of his trips to London, to inform Churchill and Harriman that Harriman's job was to implement Lend-Lease, not to make policy or meddle in political matters. Hopkins told the embassy's military attaché, General Raymond Lee: "I have given Harriman the most strict and explicit instructions not to touch anything which is in any way political. That is the ambassador's business and his alone. I also told Churchill that we had at that moment in England the best, the finest and most highly qualified ambassador . . . and that he must deal with Winant direct and fully in all matters which had any political aspect whatever."

Those instructions, however, were delivered with a wink and a nudge. Hopkins, who took Harriman with him to all his meetings with Churchill and British military leaders, had no intention of cutting his friend out of the political loop. He was overheard telling Harriman to "be careful" because Winant "was after all, the ambassador." Taking their cue from the president's right-hand man, Churchill and Harriman paid little attention to the president's admonition.

When Eleanor Roosevelt paid an official visit to England in the fall of 1942, Hopkins, making clear that he considered Harriman to be the key American in London, urged her not to bother with Winant but to deal directly with the Lend-Lease administrator during her stay. The president's wife was furious. "I had known Mr. Winant for a long time, and I had great respect and admiration for him, as did my husband," she later wrote. "I made no answer to Harry's suggestion except to say that I had known Averell Harriman since he was a small boy." (She left unmentioned the fact that she had never thought much of him.) "Harry always tended to lean primarily on his own friends . . . I think he never really knew or understood Mr. Winant."

In London, Mrs. Roosevelt would have nothing to do with Harriman. Instead, she relied on Winant for advice about virtually every aspect of her visit, including her short stay with the king and queen at Buckingham Palace. Like Eisenhower, she felt trepidation and "a feeling of inadequacy" at the thought of socializing with British aristocracy, and particularly with the monarch himself. She was so nervous, in fact, that she began to wonder "why on earth I had ever let myself be inveigled into coming on this trip." Although Winant helped relieve some of her worries, she, again like Eisenhower, was embarrassed by the paltriness of her wardrobe and wondered what the maid at Buckingham Palace thought when she unpacked the few items of clothing in her suitcase. Years afterward, Mrs. Roosevelt would wryly note that in America, "a country where people had shed their blood to be independent of a king, there is still an awe of royalty and the panoply which surrounds it."

When she wrote about her trip in her memoirs, Mrs. Roosevelt observed that the time she spent with Winant helped deepen their friendship and increased her admiration for this shy man who "gave little thought to his own comfort but much thought to helping his friends. . . . I prized highly what he gave me, and I had a feeling that he shed light in many dark places."

ANGRY AND DISCOURAGED by the bureaucratic end runs around him ("He took it as a personal affront," said one of his aides), Winant was also bone-tired. As he always had done—in New Hampshire, Washington, and Geneva—he worked nonstop, driving himself to the point of exhaustion. "He carried the troubles of the world on his shoulders," noted political attaché Theodore Achilles. "He found it extremely hard to relax." The ambassador's only exercise was an occasional walk through London's parks.

Secretary of Labor Frances Perkins and David Gray, the U.S. ambassador to Ireland and Eleanor Roosevelt's uncle, were among Winant's many friends who worried about what they considered his excessive devotion to work. Perkins sent Winant some vitamin pills to give him more energy. Gray admonished his colleague: "If you break down, what does any of it amount to? Your personality and sense of values are the important thing, and, if necessary, you should be kept in a glass case or, better yet, spend two or three days a week in the country, walking yourself tired." Sharing Gray's and Perkins's concerns was Anthony Eden, who later described Winant as "caring much for his work, little for party politics, and not at all for himself."

In fact, Eden and Winant were quite alike—in their workaholic tendencies as in much else. The forty-three-year-old foreign secretary usually was at his desk in the Foreign Office from early morning to late in the evening, snatching a few hours of sleep at night in a small flat he kept in the same building. A skilled negotiator and master diplomat ("one of the best I have ever met," Winant said), Eden, like his American friend, also found himself overshadowed and bypassed by his boss—in his case, the prime minister, who continually poached on Eden's turf of foreign affairs.

In the 1930s, Eden had been the golden boy of British politics—a handsome, glamorous war hero and a figure of international stature before he turned thirty-five. He was so popular in the country that when he resigned as Neville Chamberlain's foreign secretary in 1938 over the prime minister's appeasement of Mussolini, he might well have successfully challenged Chamberlain for the premiership. But, as Eden himself said, "I lack the spunk," and the leadership baton eventually went to Churchill. Although Eden complained throughout the war of Churchill's interference with the Foreign Office, he nonetheless managed to carve out for himself a highly influential role in foreign affairs.

Winant's friendship with the foreign secretary was, with the exception of his involvement with Sarah Churchill, the relationship most important to him in London. The two were in close contact virtually every day, either on the phone or in person; Winant was one of the few people given the key to a private elevator that went directly to Eden's office. On weekends, Eden often took Winant with him to his country house in Sussex, where the two worked on their official papers in the garden. Eden was an avid gardener: "I have never known anyone," Winant recalled, "who cared more about flowers or vegetables or fruit trees, or the wind blowing across wheat fields, or the green pastures which marked out the Sussex Downs." When they wanted a break from work, Winant and Eden would lay their papers aside and root out weeds in the garden. "We would put our dispatch boxes at either end," Winant said, "and when we had completed a row, we would do penance by reading messages and writing the necessary replies. Then we would start again on [weeding]."

As close as he was to Eden, however, Winant found his greatest comfort in his deepening relationship with Sarah Churchill. She had separated from Vic Oliver in late 1941, and sometime later, she and Winant embarked on an affair. After leaving Oliver, Sarah had given up her acting career and joined the Women's Auxiliary Air Force. Independent as ever, she rejected her father's offer of a job in the operations room at RAF Fighter Command and instead became an analyst of reconnaissance photos at an RAF base in Berkshire. It was a demanding, high-pressure, top secret post, and she found, to her great surprise and satisfaction, that she was very good at it. Among other things, she and the other analysts examined aerial photographs of German shipping facilities, trying to determine and predict movements of the enemy's naval forces.

In late 1942, on the day before the Allied invasion of North Africa, her father told her with barely suppressed excitement: "At this very moment, sliding stealthily through the Straits of Gibraltar under cover of darkness, go 542 ships for the landings in North Africa."

Not exactly, said Sarah. "It's 543."

Churchill stared stonily at his daughter. "How do you know?"

"I've only been working on it for three months."

"Why didn't you tell me?"

"I believe there is such a thing as security."

Churchill's face clouded over, and Sarah feared he would scold her for her impudence. Instead, he chuckled, and at dinner that night at Chequers, told the story of her one-upsmanship with great relish.

For the rest of the war, Sarah led two separate lives: weekdays of intense, all-consuming work in Berkshire and weekends at Chequers or her small flat in Park Lane, a five-minute walk from the American embassy. Winant spent as much time with her as he could. Unlike Harriman and Pamela Churchill, whose affair had now become common knowledge in London, Sarah and Winant were exceptionally discreet about their involvement. Her separation from her husband had been kept secret from everybody but her family and friends; to keep up appearances, she still occasionally appeared in public with Oliver. Since both she and Winant were still married, albeit unhappily, Sarah was determined to avoid a scandal that, in her view, would cause great damage both to Winant and to her adored father.

As careful as they were, however, it was impossible to keep the relationship a total secret. Several people close to Churchill, including John Colville, learned about it, as did Churchill himself, Sarah believed. Years later she would wistfully write about this "love affair which my father suspected but about which we did not speak."

"HE'LL NEVER
LET US DOWN"

IN THE MIDST OF JUGGLING THE MYRIAD PROBLEMS, BOTH PRO-
fessional and personal, that confronted him in the spring and summer
of 1942, Winant received a call from Clement Attlee, leader of the
Labour Party and deputy prime minister. Attlee told the ambassador
he needed his help to resolve an urgent domestic crisis that had little
to do with the Anglo-American alliance.

Early in June, coal miners in northern England had gone out on
strike, posing a grave threat to the country's war production and perilously fragile economy at a time when the Allies' military outlook was
at its bleakest. With the Germans close to capturing the Suez Canal
and seemingly on the verge of victory in the Soviet Union, it was the
worst possible moment for a coal strike—a point that Attlee, Ernest
Bevin, and other Labour members of the coalition government made
when trying to persuade the miners to end the walkout. The strikers,
however, were obdurate. It was then that Attlee turned to Winant.
Would he travel to Durham to help settle the strike?

Involving the ambassador of the United States in a British labor
dispute was, by any standard, an exotic, even revolutionary, idea. But
Attlee, who had been a friend of Winant's since the mid-1930s, knew
how popular the American was with British workingmen. In his ILO
days, Winant had toured Britain's depressed areas at the Labour
Party's request and made recommendations for easing the regions'
widespread unemployment. As ambassador, he had made several trips
outside London to visit miners and other industrial workers. "He had

an unusual understanding of working men," noted an ILO colleague. "He was born of rich parents but was able to speak the same language as Bevin, who was born and bred a worker."

On one trip to South Wales, Winant was introduced to two retired miners standing by the roadside, whom he engaged in a spirited conversation. "He understood them, and they understood him," observed the Labour MP Arthur Jenkins, who made the introductions. "Many times since that day I have met those men, and they always ask about the ambassador. Those few minutes together made them friends of John Winant." Jenkins added: "Most people in this country feel that well nigh any problem could be satisfactorily settled if we could assemble in the conference room men with his qualities."

When the Office of War Information's Wallace Carroll traveled throughout Britain during the war, he, too, was asked about Winant wherever he traveled. "If you went among the miners of Wales, they would tell you, 'Your man Winant, he's all right.' And if you talked to the textile workers of Lancashire or the shipyard workers along the Clyde, they would say, 'We know Winant—he'll never let us down.'"

WINANT DIDN'T NEED Attlee to tell him how perilous a prolonged coal strike would be for Britain. Coal was the life's blood of British industry, and its production, in the words of one historian, "was every bit as essential to Britain's victory as going on the battlefield." Yet mining that coal was, as it always had been, dangerous, miserable, poorly rewarded work. Miners descended half a mile underground into the blackness of a coal pit; worked in a crouched position in a cramped tunnel for seven hours or more a shift; inhaled toxic fumes and coal dust; risked injury and death every day; and, for that, were paid wages that barely kept them and their families from starvation.

Interested primarily in quick profits, most British mine owners had done little or nothing to modernize their operations and improve their employees' working conditions, which reminded one observer "more of work in the [slave] galleys which are portrayed in the films than modern conditions of industrial Labour." In the previous twenty years, the number of coal miners had fallen dramatically. Young men from coal regions had increasingly looked elsewhere for jobs; when the war began, they flocked to enlist in the military. Meanwhile, the productivity of those still in the pits had plummeted, leading to a serious shortfall of coal that spelled trouble not only for war production but also for the heating of British homes.

When war broke out, stringent government controls, including wage controls and a ban on strikes, were imposed on miners. In return, they were promised an improvement in working conditions and an increase in wages. Those pledges, however, were not always kept. In 1941, for example, the management of a Northumberland mine asked its workers to increase their output; when they complied, they then were asked to accept a cut in pay.

Aggrieved by what they considered exploitation by both their employers and the government, the miners who went out on strike in the summer of 1942 thought it was time that someone started thinking about *them*. Like other Britons, they had accepted the rigorous wartime regimentation and controls imposed by the state on its citizens, as well as the forfeiture of most of their personal rights. Early in the conflict, the government had been given a blank check to do virtually anything it wanted to ensure public safety and wage war. Precious British liberties like habeas corpus were swept away. Government officials were given the authority to jail indefinitely without trial any person judged to be a danger to the public interest. They also could prevent the holding of demonstrations; requisition without payment any building or other property, from a horse to a railway; tell farmers what to plant and what to do with their crops; and enter anyone's home without warning or a warrant.

At the same time, the government mobilized the vast majority of adults in the nation to participate directly in the war effort; in late 1941, Britain became the first major industrial country to draft its female citizens for war work. As Ed Murrow told his listeners, "Everything save conscience can now be conscripted in this country." By 1943, the level of government control over its people had "drawn so tight," wrote historian Angus Calder, "that one could say, with only a little exaggeration, that every seamstress, every railway guard . . . was as crucial a part of the national effort as aircraft fitters on assembly work or soldiers."

Although most Britons "hated, with the free Englishman's sense of injured personal dignity, this maze of complexities called 'government controls,' " most acknowledged their necessity for the duration. British civilians, like soldiers on far-off battlefields, had been on the front lines since the summer of 1940. Like British troops, they had sacrificed and suffered for their country; many had died. Now, they felt, the government owed them something in return—the promise of major reforms after the conflict that would put an end to the rigid, class-bound British society of prewar days and create social justice and economic opportunity for all. During the war, recalled the writer C. P. Snow, Britons had two major concerns: "what they were going to eat today and what was going to happen in Britain tomorrow. It's important to remember how idealistic everyone was in those days, despite the rigours and pressure of war."

That same hope and idealism infected a good many Americans who spent time in Britain during the war. Among them were Winant, Murrow, and Eleanor Roosevelt, who, during her visit to the country in 1942, was delighted to see that British women from widely varied economic backgrounds were working so closely together in the war effort. "These British Isles," she later wrote, "which we always regarded as class conscious, as a place where people were so nearly frozen in their classes that they rarely moved from one to another, became welded together by the war into a closely knit community in which many of the old distinctions lost their point."

For his part, Murrow had predicted the melting down of the old Britain and the forging of a new nation as early as the fiery hell of the Blitz. If this war was about anything, he thought, it was about the well-being and future of ordinary people. War had a purpose beyond the defeat of Germany and certainly beyond the restoration of the status quo ante. The postwar world had to commit itself to the eradication of poverty, inequality, and injustice.

In 1940, as Britain fought for its survival, Murrow was already raising questions about its postwar future. "What are the war aims of this country?" he asked in one broadcast. "What shall we do with victory when it's won? What sort of Europe will be built when and if this stress has passed?" He told his American listeners: "There must be equality under the bombs." The British working man "must be convinced that, after all he has suffered, a better world will emerge."

Murrow's vision of a brave new world was shared by a number of other American correspondents in London. "We would talk about this, Ed and I, Scotty Reston, and the others," recalled Eric Sevareid. "We thought that perhaps a wonderful thing was happening to the British people. Some kind of moral revolution was underway, and out of it would come the regeneration of a great people. . . . For the first time, the war seemed to have taken on a positive meaning."

FOR WINSTON CHURCHILL, however, such discussions were nothing but pie-in-the-sky blather. His only goal in 1942 was victory over the Axis, and he resented the raising of issues that he considered irrelevant, distracting, and likely to cause friction within his coalition government. "With Winston, war is an end in itself rather than a means to an end," Lord Moran noted in his diary. "It fascinates him, he loves it . . . he neither believes in nor is interested in what comes after the war."

At the age of sixty-seven, Churchill was far removed from his youthful days as a Liberal cabinet minister, when he had emerged briefly as something of a social reformer himself. Together with David Lloyd George, he had been the driving force behind the introduction of major welfare reforms in Britain shortly after the turn of the century, including measures to reduce poverty and unemployment. Unlike Lloyd George, however, Churchill was not—and never would be—a social radical. His view of society tended to be extremely paternalistic, rather like an "old, benevolent Tory squire," said the Labour Party's Herbert Morrison, "who does all he can for the people—provided always that they are good obedient people and loyally recognize his position, and theirs."

As Clementine Churchill once confided to Lord Moran, the prime minister knew virtually nothing about how ordinary Britons lived— and had no real interest in correcting that deficiency. "He's never been in a bus," Clementine said, "and only once on the Underground. That was during the [1926] General Strike, when I deposited him at South Kensington [station]. He went round and round, not knowing where to get out, and had to be rescued eventually." With some vehemence, she added: "Winston is selfish. . . . You see, he has always had the ability and force to live his life exactly as he wanted."

Yet, despite the great social chasm between him and most of his countrymen, Churchill had managed to forge an almost mystical connection with them in regard to fighting the war. Even before he became prime minister, he had inspired the British people with his resolve to battle the enemy until the end, no matter what the cost. As first lord of the Admiralty from September 1939 to May 1940, he had emerged as the most popular public figure in the nation. "In Mr.

Churchill," wrote the editor Kingsley Martin, "we have seen a man of action, who . . . reminds us that, whatever else we are or think we are, we were born and bred British, and British we must now live or die."

As Martin suggested, Churchill and the British people shared many of the same qualities—dogged resolution, courage, energy, and combativeness. When they traveled with the prime minister during the Blitz, Winant and Averell Harriman witnessed the close affinity he had with his compatriots, who mobbed him wherever he went. Three years later, on V-E Day, Churchill would stand on a Whitehall balcony and declare to the vast, delirious crowds standing before him: "This is *your* victory." As one, they would roar back: "No, it's *yours*."

When it came to social policy, however, there was almost no con-nection between Churchill and the people—a fact that was underscored by the reaction of the prime minister and his government to the release of the Beveridge Report in late 1942. Named for Sir William Beveridge, its chief author, the report proposed the creation of a social safety net to ensure a minimum standard of living for all Britons that included fam-ily allowances, a national health service, and a full employment policy.

The public went wild over the report, which was portrayed as a so-cial Magna Carta and became an immediate bestseller. Londoners stood in line for hours "to buy this heavy two-shilling slab of involved economics as though it were unrationed manna dropped from some heaven," Mollie Panter-Downes reported in *The New Yorker*. Throughout the rest of the war, the reforms proposed by the Beveridge Report dominated the political debate in Britain. While many in the Labour Party demanded that the government begin immediate discus-sions on how to implement this blueprint for the future, Churchill and most of his fellow Tories resisted such ideas. The prime minister viewed the report as an unwelcome distraction from the war effort and its proposals as far too costly for an economically straitened Britain to undertake after the conflict was over. As he saw it, the document's au-thor, a former head of the London School of Economics, was little more than "an awful windbag and dreamer." Other government offi-cials did their best to ignore the report, refusing to discuss it or give it any official publicity.

AN ARDENT ADVOCATE of the aims of the Beveridge plan, Gil Winant was dismayed by Churchill's hostile reaction to the idea of postwar social reforms. Like Murrow, Winant had close ties to Beveridge and many other prominent left-wing intellectuals and writers in Britain, including Harold Laski, H. G. Wells, R. H. Tawney, and John Maynard Keynes. The ambassador spent many evenings in the basement kitchen of Keynes's home in Bloomsbury; in turn, he hosted small dinners for Keynes, Laski, and others in his Grosvenor Square flat, where far-ranging discussions about planning for the postwar world continued far into the night.

For decades, Winant's main focus had been on social justice and the creation of a better life for workingmen and -women throughout the world. "When the war has been won by democracy, we must be prepared to conquer the peace," he said on the day he was named ambassador to Britain. A few months earlier, he had talked to William Shirer about his ideas for the postwar reconstruction of Europe and the creation of a peace economy "without the maladjustment, the great unemployment and deflation and depression that followed the last war." In a BBC broadcast, he declared: "There is a deep consciousness that peace and social justice must come hand in hand." Ever since he arrived in Britain, Winant's speeches and private conversations had centered on the need to persuade the nations of the world "to concentrate on the things that unite humanity rather than on the things that divide it."

Roosevelt had sent him to Britain precisely because of his intimate ties with left-wing intellectuals and politicians, who the president believed would take over leadership of the country during or immediately after the war. But, in his tenure as ambassador, Winant had become personally close to Churchill as well. Refusing to give up on the prime minister where social reforms were concerned, he occasionally tried to nudge him in the right direction. When Churchill, at a meeting of employers and workers' representatives, praised British trade union members for giving up certain rights for the duration, Winant, speaking at the same meeting, gently encouraged the British leader to give more consideration to the workers' needs. Fighting the enemy, he said, "requires not only skill and hard work and materials, but an understanding that is sensitive to the devoted loyalty of the people."

ON JUNE 6, 1942, the U.S. ambassador gazed out from a train window at the bleak, hardscrabble landscape of northeast England's coal country. He had acceded to Clem Attlee's plea for help in ending the coal strike, and now the two of them were on their way to Durham, where union leaders and more than four hundred delegates, representing thousands of striking miners, were waiting.

When he and Attlee arrived at the grimy union hall, Winant was given an enthusiastic welcome by the miners. He immediately launched into his speech, which, without mentioning the strikes, equated the battle against fascism with the fight for social democracy. The miners and other workers, he said, were on the front lines just as much as soldiers in the field, with the same responsibility to continue the fight. "You who suffered so deeply in the long Depression years know we must move on a great social offensive if we are to win the war completely. It is not a short-term military job. We must solemnly resolve that in our future order we will not tolerate the economic evils which breed poverty and war." Then, in an exquisitely subtle admonition directed at the British government, Winant added: "This is not something that we shelve for the duration. It is part of the war."

It was one of Winant's finest speeches. His usual hesitancy at the beginning, the long pauses and the stumbling over words, dropped away as he offered with passionate intensity his vision for a new postwar world. Leaning forward in their seats, the miners focused intently on every word.

"What we want is not complicated," the ambassador declared. "We have enough technical knowledge and organizing ability. . . . We have enough courage. We must put it to use. When war is done, the drive for tanks must become a drive for houses. The drive for food to prevent the enemy from starving us must become a drive for food to satisfy the needs of all people in all countries. The drive for manpower in war must become a drive for employment to make freedom from want a living reality. . . . Just as the peoples of democracy are united in a common objective today, so we are committed to a common objective tomorrow. We are committed to the establishment of the people's democracy."

Winant's eyes swept over his audience. "We must always remember," he said, "that it is the things of the spirit that in the end prevail. That caring counts. That where there is no vision, people perish. That hope and faith count, and that without charity there can be nothing good. That by daring to live dangerously, we are learning to live generously. And that by believing in the inherent goodness of man, we may meet the call of your great Prime Minister and 'stride forward into the unknown with growing confidence.' "

When he finished, there was a long moment of silence, followed by an explosion of applause and thundering shouts of "Hear, hear." For the next hour and a half, the miners peppered Winant with questions about America, the war, and the general state of the world. Afterward, he was swallowed up in a boisterous throng wanting to shake his hand and thank him for coming. "We think, sir," exclaimed the union's treasurer, "that you are a grand guy." A few hours later, the striking miners in Durham voted to return to work, as did miners in Lancashire and Yorkshire.

"WINANT TALKS, STRIKE ENDS" read a banner headline in the following day's *Daily Express*. Lamenting the backwardness of the British government in defining the postwar world, the *Daily Herald* compared Winant's speech to Lincoln's Gettysburg Address in its call for "a new, greater world emancipation." The *Herald* urged that the ambassador's words "be committed to memory, recited in all the schools, preached about in all the churches." The *Manchester Guardian*, meanwhile, hailed Winant's remarks as "one of the great speeches of the war."

Yet, though the ambassador's eloquence helped resolve the coal strike, the larger question of war aims—what were the reasons for fighting this war?—remained a highly contentious issue. A few months after the strike, that issue would be at the heart of an ugly controversy in the midst of Operation Torch, the Anglo-American assault on North Africa. Winant and Murrow would again be involved, but this time on opposite sides. Murrow would openly defy his network and the U.S government, while Winant would be compelled to defend a policy he privately believed to be tragically misguided.

12.

"ARE WE FIGHTING NAZIS OR SLEEPING WITH THEM?"

THE GENERAL CHOSEN TO HEAD THE INVASION OF NORTH AFRICA was appalled by his new assignment. Dwight Eisenhower had been dispatched to England in June 1942 to oversee the buildup of American forces in Britain and, he thought, to prepare for an Allied landing in France. That was the plan he had devised as war plans chief in Washington and the one toward which he and George Marshall had been working for the previous seven months. But to the disgust of both generals, Winston Churchill persuaded Roosevelt in July that the initial Anglo-American assault should take place in North Africa later that year. In Eisenhower's view, the day that Roosevelt agreed with Churchill was the "blackest day in history."

Adamant that the Allies lacked the resources to challenge Hitler on the Continent, the British argued that a landing on the rim of Africa would, in fact, clear the way for an eventual successful attack on Europe. After establishing control in French North Africa, the Allies would sweep east and strike at the rear of Rommel and the Afrika Korps, while the British Eighth Army would hit the Germans from the west. As the British saw it, the ouster of Axis troops from the region would not only save Egypt and the Suez Canal but also reopen the Mediterranean to Allied supply vessels and troopships, now forced to steam thousands of miles out of their way to reach the Middle East and India. In Alan Brooke's estimation, a victory in North Africa would release at least half a million tons of shipping for use in a large-scale offensive operation on the Continent.

Roosevelt, however, was less convinced by the shipping argument than by the fact that American troops finally would see action against the Germans. In response to Stalin's incessant demands for a second front, the president had promised the Soviet foreign minister in May that the Allies expected to open such a front later that year. FDR was also facing pressure from an increasingly restive American public, who, after Pearl Harbor, considered Japan, not Germany, to be the country's primary enemy. Unless U.S. forces were sent to the European theater soon, congressional and public pressure might force a massive shift of American resources to the fight against Japan. "Only by an intellectual effort," Henry Stimson wrote to Churchill, had the American people been "convinced that Germany was their most dangerous enemy and should be disposed of before Japan."

In exchange for his agreement to the North Africa operation, Roosevelt insisted that he be allowed to set most of its ground rules. Above all, he said, it must be a predominantly American operation, with an American commander, to dissuade Vichy French forces in North Africa from resisting. When France capitulated to Germany in June 1940, the French government, under its new president, Marshal Philippe Pétain, was allowed by Hitler to establish itself in Vichy, a town in central France. The French, FDR told Churchill, would be far less likely to oppose U.S. troops than they would the British, who had destroyed much of the French fleet at the Algerian port of Oran two years before and who supported Charles de Gaulle, the rebel general who had escaped to London to rally the French against Vichy and the Reich.

Unlike Britain, the United States had maintained diplomatic relations with the Vichy government, which had been permitted by the Germans to retain control of French North Africa and the country's other colonial possessions, as well as its fleet. The Roosevelt administration had come under severe criticism at home for its ties to Vichy, which had collaborated closely with the Nazis and imposed authoritarian rule in the region it controlled in southern France. Vichy officials had instituted repressive policies against Jews long before receiving German orders to do so, and later assisted the Nazis in rounding up Jews for deportation to concentration and death camps. When they were hired, Vichy police had to take the following oath: "I swear to fight against democracy, against Gaullist insurrection and against Jewish leprosy." Roosevelt, however, believed that, despite all their sins, it was important to stay on good terms with the Vichy leaders, who he hoped would keep French North Africa and the fleet out of Nazi hands and perhaps, at some point, come over to the Allied side.

At the same time, the president had taken a great dislike to the prickly, difficult de Gaulle, even though he had never met him. Another U.S. condition for Torch was exclusion of the general and his Free French forces from the operation. In addition, Roosevelt decreed that de Gaulle must be given no prior information about the landings, "regardless of how irritated and irritating he may become." Having won the battle over North Africa, Churchill was more than willing to agree to Roosevelt's terms. "I consider myself your lieutenant," he cabled the president. "This is an American enterprise in which we are your help mates."

It was, however, an American enterprise that Eisenhower, on every level, considered a nightmare. He and his subordinates had just a few months to plan one of the most audacious amphibious landings in history, bringing two assault forces from the United States and Britain to the shores of a continent "where no major military campaign had been conducted for centuries." As Churchill's military adviser, Pug Ismay, observed in his memoirs, any amphibious operation was an extraordinarily difficult feat to pull off. It required "highly trained personnel, a great variety of equipment, a detailed knowledge of the points at which the landings are to take place, accurate information about the enemy's strength and dispositions, and perhaps above all, meticulous planning and preparation." None of those conditions could be said to apply to Torch.

Eisenhower and his subordinates worried about the battle-readiness of American assault troops, most of whom had been given little or no combat training. Indeed, some did not learn how to load, aim, or fire a rifle until they were on the ships transporting them to North Africa. The American command was also concerned that too few weapons, supplies, and ships were available to support such a massive undertaking. "We were still existing in a state of scarcity," Eisenhower later wrote. "There was no such thing as plenty of everything." And, until just a few weeks before the invasion was launched, arguments still raged about where the landings would take place.

The British wanted to go ashore as far east as possible, so that troops could quickly move into Tunisia, Torch's chief objective, to forestall the landing of additional German troops there and to take control of Tunis and Bizerte, the country's crucial deep-water ports. According to the British scenario, Rommel would then find himself trapped between the Torch forces and the Eighth Army. Eisenhower supported the British plan, only to be overruled by Marshall and his lieutenants, who feared that, by landing so far east, the Allies would be the ones caught in a trap—attacked from the rear by German forces advancing through neutral Spain. The American brass insisted that the assault troops must land at Casablanca, on the Atlantic coast of Morocco, some one thousand miles west of Tunis. Although Churchill felt that Marshall was being overly cautious (as did Eisenhower), the British leader once again acquiesced. The result was a compromise. Allied forces would land at three widely separated sites: Casablanca in Morocco, and Algiers and Oran in Algeria. Algiers, the site closest to Tunis, was still more than five hundred miles away from the operation's main target.

THE ASSIGNMENT HANDED to Eisenhower that summer would have taxed the most superhuman of commanders. In addition to organizing what James MacGregor Burns would later describe as "this bizarre, doubt-ridden and unpredictable" mission, he had to create from whole cloth a unified command for Torch's two national forces. Since no such structure had existed in all of military history, he had no manual to consult or precedent to follow. His Army friends told him it was an impossible task. He and Torch were doomed to failure, they said, and he would be made the scapegoat for the inevitable defeat. "I was regaled," Eisenhower later wrote, "with tales of allied failure, starting with the Greeks, five hundred years before Christ, and coming down through the ages of allied quarrels to the bitter French-British recriminations of 1940."

For their part, the British, who had opposed the concept of a unified command from the start, were far from happy that an unknown American general with no combat experience was about to lead their men into battle. Alan Brooke was as dismissive of Eisenhower as he was of Marshall, and the relationship between the two was frosty until the end of the war. While condescendingly crediting the American with "wonderful charm" and "a greater share of luck than most of us receive in life," Brooke had almost nothing good to say about Eisenhower's prowess as a commander, once remarking that he "had only the vaguest conception of war." A British admiral who served under Eisenhower described him during this period as "completely sincere, straightforward, and very modest," but "not very sure of himself."

Still, while Eisenhower may have been tentative and unsure about many things, he never wavered in his demands for a complete integration of the Anglo-American war effort. According to Mark Perry, a biographer of Eisenhower and Marshall, no other officer of Eisenhower's generation, British or American, had "a comparable understanding of the importance of forging and maintaining such a coalition." When the British argued that their field commanders should have the right to appeal to the War Office if they disagreed with one of his orders, the commander of Torch declared that such a loophole would violate the Anglo-American agreement on unified command. He negotiated a compromise: British commanders who disputed an order must consult him first before any further action could be taken. "This was the Eisenhower formula which was to have far more important consequences than its author could have seen at the start," Wallace Carroll observed. "Everyone who came into his theater, whether military or civilian, American or British, had to forsake old allegiances and submit to the authority of the theater commander."

EISENHOWER'S SEEDBED for Anglo-American unity was Norfolk House, a brick-and-stone neo-Georgian building a few doors down from Nancy Astor's residence in elegant St. James's Square. Designated the Allied Force Headquarters for Torch, Norfolk House was, in the minds of some, a somewhat inauspicious location for the alliance's first joint command. A little more than two hundred years before, George III had been born in the original Norfolk House, a mansion belonging to the Duke of York, on the same site.

Eisenhower couldn't have cared less about George III. He insisted that the Americans and Britons on his staff put aside the generations-old divisions between their two countries and act as if they "belonged to a single nation." It was, he acknowledged, an order that was much easier to deliver than to carry out. Having had very little contact between the two world wars, the U.S. and British military knew almost nothing about the way the other operated. When General Frederick Morgan was assigned to Eisenhower's command in the fall of 1942, he received a document from Allied headquarters that he read in complete bewilderment. Morgan recalled that he "did not understand one single word" of what he was staring at. "Here was a vast assemblage of words which were undoubtedly English but which conveyed to me not one single thing, and I was eventually forced to call for skilled interpretation of American military language."

In the beginning, there also were personality clashes, misunderstandings, and feuds—so many, in fact, that Eisenhower likened the early relationship between the two nationalities on his staff to "the attitude of a bulldog meeting a tomcat." Some American officers disliked the whole idea of Torch, "apparently regarding it," in Eisenhower's words, "as a British plan into which America had been dragged by the heels." Although the commander privately shared their views, he warned his countrymen that, if they didn't put all their energies into the operation and learn to get along with their British counterparts, he would send them home. Over time, his bulldog determination paid off: the Americans on his staff came to acknowledge, as his personal aide, Harry Butcher put it, that "the British are really not red-coated devils" and the British conceded that the Americans might occasionally have a good idea or two.

However, many combat commanders under him, American and British alike, disagreed. Two of Eisenhower's closest friends—Mark Clark, his deputy and the chief planner for Torch, and George Patton, leader of one of the invasion's task forces—were both violently Anglophobic. Patton, who came to London for briefings in the summer of 1942, groused in his diary: "It is very noticeable that most of the American officers here are pro-British, even Ike. . . . I am *not*, repeat *not*, pro-British."

Although Eisenhower maintained his relaxed manner and easy grin in public, those closest to him knew the enormous physical and emotional toll that the Torch preparations were exacting. Was it really possible, he wondered, to "invade a neutral country to create a friend," as Roosevelt had suggested? Smoking up to four packs of Camels a day, he was snappish and depressed—"a three-star bundle of nervous tension," said Kay Summersby. An American on his staff noted: "He had aged ten years." Though exhausted, Eisenhower was often unable to sleep at night. When that happened, he would get out of bed and sit by a window, staring out into the darkness for hours, absorbed in anxieties and fears he revealed to no one.

ON NOVEMBER 4, 1942, the British Eighth Army, commanded by General Bernard Law Montgomery, routed Rommel's forces at El Alamein, clearing them out of Egypt and pushing them westward in headlong retreat. It was Britain's first major victory over the Germans in the war, and it gave new life and vigor to Churchill and his beleaguered government, as well as to the country.

Four days later, some thirty-three thousand American and British troops poured onto the beaches of North Africa. From the first moments of the Torch operation, the inexperience of both planners and troops was glaringly evident. At Casablanca, more than half the landing craft and light tanks sank or foundered in the pounding surf. Many soldiers had no idea what to do when they first got off their ships. General Lucian Truscott, the commander of forces landing at a site north of Casablanca, recalled that "men wandered about aimlessly, hopelessly lost . . . swearing at each other."

Nothing, including the French response to the landings, went as planned. Roosevelt's conviction that French troops would welcome the American invaders had been based in large part on intelligence from a network of amateur U.S. spies installed in North Africa before the United States entered the war. In a secret deal with Vichy in March 1941, Roosevelt had unfrozen French funds in the United States in exchange for stationing twelve American vice consuls—i.e., intelligence agents—throughout the region. The twelve were hardly professional operatives—they included a winemaker and a Coca-Cola salesman—and German military intelligence, which knew all about them, concluded: "We can only congratulate ourselves on the selection of this group of enemy agents who will give us no trouble."

The vice consuls assured the White House that the French army would put up only token resistance against American troops. In turn, the troops were assured that the French would greet the invaders "with brass bands." In fact, the French fought back fiercely at almost every landing site, with the sharpest resistance aimed at the all-American force at Casablanca. An American major later told the War Department that his "officers as well as men were absolutely dumbfounded at their first taste of battle." Lucian Truscott noted: "As far as I could see along the beach, there was chaos." In the view of a disgusted Patton, the Americans would never even have reached the beaches if they had been fighting Germans instead of the French.

Making matters worse, the French military refused to accept the man handpicked by the Roosevelt administration to make peace in North Africa and become the region's new leader. General Henri Giraud, who had been captured by the Germans in 1940 before France capitulated, had recently escaped from a prison fortress in Germany and made his way to Vichy. Viewing Giraud as an alternative to both de Gaulle and Pétain, U.S. officials persuaded him to cooperate with the invasion and smuggled him by submarine from France to Gibraltar. Once there, however, Giraud insisted on taking command of the entire operation. When an astonished Eisenhower rejected his demand, he refused to accompany the first invasion troops. Ever hopeful, the Allies announced in a broadcast to North Africa that Giraud soon would assume leadership of French forces there. The announcement, as Eisenhower remembered, "had no effect whatsoever" on the French; indeed, it was "completely ignored." The French rejection of Giraud, the Torch commander acknowledged, was "a terrible blow to our expectations." In a cable to Roosevelt, he noted that the situation in North Africa did "not even remotely resemble prior calculations."

At that point, Eisenhower's sole aim was to end the bloodshed and put his troops on the road to Tunisia. Anyone who helped him achieve that goal would have his support, even if it turned out—as it did—that his putative savior was one of Vichy's most shameless Nazi collaborators. He was Admiral Jean Darlan, commander of the Vichy armed forces and Pétain's right-hand man, who happened to be in Algiers visiting his desperately sick son at the time of the landings. Next to Pierre Laval, whom he succeeded as Pétain's deputy, Darlan was the most reviled of all Vichy officials. He had handed over Indochina to the Japanese, allowed the persecution of French Jews, ordered the mass arrests of Vichy opponents, and supplied Rommel's troops with food, trucks, and gas. At the time of the landings, Darlan, an ardent Anglophobe, had ordered French forces to fire on Allied troops.

But for the apolitical Eisenhower, who had virtually no knowledge of internal French matters and little understanding of the national trauma afflicting the country, Darlan's reported transgressions were not germane. He offered the admiral a deal: in exchange for his engineering a cease-fire, the Allies would appoint him high commissioner, or governor, of North Africa. At first, Darlan dragged his heels, agreeing to the plan and then reneging on it. It wasn't until he learned that the Germans had occupied Vichy France on November 11 that he ordered an armistice. With that, the fighting in North Africa finally ended.

For much of the rest of the world, however, Darlan's transgressions were very much to the point. Eisenhower's deal, which Roosevelt approved and to which Churchill reluctantly acquiesced, was greeted with a storm of protest around the globe, but particularly in the United States and Britain. "In both our nations, Darlan is a deep-dyed villain," Eisenhower conceded to his staff.

To its critics, the deal betrayed a cynicism that undermined the lofty moral position of Allied leaders, chiefly Roosevelt. "America had spoken such fine words, America had proclaimed such proud principles, and now, at the very first temptation, America had to all appearances cast principle aside and struck a bargain with one of the most despicable of Hitler's foreign lackeys," Wallace Carroll observed. As the military historian Rick Atkinson put it some sixty years later, "a callow, clumsy army had arrived in North Africa with little notion of how to act as a world power."

Darlan's first actions as high commissioner only stoked his critics' anger. He upheld anti-Semitic laws in North Africa; imprisoned de Gaulle supporters and other Vichy opponents, including many who had aided the Allied invasion; reinstated Vichy officials who had been deposed in the assault's initial days; and ordered the jamming of BBC broadcasts. Declaring that "we did not come here to interfere in someone else's business," Eisenhower declined to get involved in what he regarded as domestic concerns. An incensed Charles Collingwood, the CBS correspondent covering Torch from Algiers, wrote to his parents about America's role in Darlan's rise to power: "We have perpetuated and tacitly supported a regime which is a reasonably accurate facsimile of what we are fighting against. Our excuse is that we must not interfere with French politics. I wonder whether we will enter Germany and say that we must not interfere with German politics."

In Algiers, some American critics of Darlan's actions did more than complain. Officers working in the psychological warfare branch of Eisenhower's headquarters found hiding places for de Gaulle supporters on the run from Vichy police and even smuggled a few aboard Allied ships bound for Britain. One or two of the more daring Americans wore the Cross of Lorraine, the Free French flag, in their lapels.

His psychological warfare staff, Eisenhower later said, gave him more trouble than all the Germans in Africa.

In London, an apprehensive Winston Churchill warned Roosevelt that recognition of Darlan had stirred up intense revulsion in Britain and on the Continent. "We must not overlook the serious political injury which may be done to our cause . . . by the feeling that we are ready to make terms with the local Quislings," he said. Mollie Panter-Downes observed in *The New Yorker* than many Londoners equated the Darlan agreement with Neville Chamberlain's conciliation of Hitler. Britons "are convinced," Panter-Downes wrote, "that appeasement of a man of Vichy or a man of Munich smells just about the same, no matter what fancy name you want to call it." From the American embassy in London, Wallace Carroll wrote to Roosevelt and his Office of War Information superiors in Washington that the "honeymoon is over" in Britain. "From now on we shall have to fight hard to retain the respect and confidence of the British people."

Churchill himself was caught on the horns of the morality-versus-expediency dilemma. Even though his government had not been consulted beforehand about the Darlan deal, both he and Roosevelt had given permission to Eisenhower to use any means necessary to win French cooperation in North Africa. The prime minister had often referred to Darlan as a "turncoat" and "traitor," but, shortly before the invasion began, he declared: "Much as I hate him, I would cheerfully crawl on my hands and knees for a mile if, by doing so, I could get him to bring that fleet of his into the circle of Allied forces." But Darlan was never able to claim the fleet—it was scuttled by the French after the Germans occupied Vichy-controlled southern France—and the cease-fire he belatedly ordered did not prevent a tidal wave of German troops from flooding into Tunisia. In short, except for ending the fighting, the deal did not achieve any of the Allies' goals in making it.

The agreement—and Churchill's indirect role in it—were so embarrassing to him that he refused to offer an explanation of the deal to the House of Commons unless it met in secret session. When the session took place, the prime minister played both sides, supporting Roosevelt and Eisenhower in the name of Allied unity but pointing out that the agreement had been brokered solely by the Americans. "Since 1776 we have not been in the position of being able to decide the policy of the United States," he said. "Neither militarily nor politically are we directly controlling the course of events."

In the United States, meanwhile, prominent newspaper columnists and radio commentators condemned the deal, as did members of Roosevelt's own cabinet. Henry Morgenthau, for one, denounced Darlan as a traitor who had sold thousands of his countrymen into slavery and told Roosevelt that the situation in North Africa was "something that afflicts my soul." Together with Felix Frankfurter, Morgenthau urged the president to clarify American policy toward North Africa and Darlan. Stung by the outpouring of criticism, the president, though resentful, did what the treasury secretary asked. In a statement, he declared that the Darlan agreement had been necessary to save lives but also called it "only a temporary expedient, justified solely by the stress of battle."

THE IMPETUS FOR Morgenthau's angst was an incendiary broadcast made by Ed Murrow shortly after the Darlan deal became public. Appalled by his country's leading role in the affair, the most influential broadcast journalist in the United States threw off all pretense of objectivity. "What the hell is this all about?" he stormed to a friend. "Are we fighting Nazis or sleeping with them?" In the broadcast heard by Morgenthau, Murrow ticked off a list of Darlan's sins. When a German officer was killed in Nantes, Darlan turned over thirty Frenchmen as hostages to the Nazis, all of whom were shot. After taking power in North Africa, he sent European political refugees back to their German-occupied countries. Was this, Murrow asked, the kind of ally we wanted in our fight against the Nazis? Whether the deal was done for military expediency or not, "there is nothing in the strategic position of the Allies to indicate that we are either so strong or so weak that we can afford to ignore the principles for which this war is being fought." After listening to Murrow's broadcast, Morgenthau gave transcripts of it to Henry Stimson and Roosevelt himself.

As it turned out, this was far from Murrow's only broadcast on the subject. Of all the journalistic critics of the Darlan deal, he was arguably the most outspoken, overtly challenging the administration's policy again and again. "This is a matter of high principle in which we carry a moral burden we cannot escape," he told his listeners. "Wherever American forces go, they will carry with them food and money and power, and the quislings will rally to our side if we permit it."

The Roosevelt administration was stunned and angered by the

faultfinding of a man whom the president considered an ally, a broad-caster in whom FDR had confided on the night of Pearl Harbor and had once tried to hire. When Murrow returned to America for a short visit a couple of months later, he was summoned to the State Department, where an infuriated Cordell Hull gave him a tongue-lashing for allegedly undermining the war effort. "He never raised his voice . . . made no gesture, but every word cut and stung," a shaken Murrow told an acquaintance.

His vehemence over Darlan brought him more public criticism than he had ever before encountered. CBS sponsors and some in his audience complained, as did Paul White, the network's news editor in New York. "You are endangering your good reputation by seeming to be a constant critic of America," White cabled Murrow. "It is a fairly common thing these days to hear the crack 'Ed Murrow is becoming more British than the British.'" In late November, International Silver, the sponsor of a weekly Murrow analysis program, canceled its contract, cutting his income in half. (The company, however, evidently thought better of jettisoning one of radio's most popular news broadcasts and reinstated its sponsorship a month later.)

Throughout the uproar, Murrow remained unrepentant. To a listener who criticized his Darlan broadcasts as anti-American and "definitely dangerous," he wrote: "I believe that all Governments are capable of making mistakes, just as are all broadcasters." In a letter to a friend at home, he declared: "Developments in North Africa would be heartbreaking for anyone who had any hope of a decent post-war world." To another friend, Murrow remarked: "The British fear that America will do what Britain did in the 19th century. . . . Our policy, as it has been displayed in North Africa, looks like a sort of amateur imperialism." He confessed to feeling increasingly distant from his homeland: "Maybe I have been away from home too long, but I am day by day more convinced that the values here, whatever the motives, are different from the values of home."

Like Murrow, Gil Winant believed that the Roosevelt administration had made a monumental error in appointing Darlan to power. At a cocktail party in his honor one evening, he spent much of the time sequestered in a corner with Murrow and a BBC broadcaster, bemoaning what had happened. He agreed with Churchill and Anthony Eden that the administration must be made to realize just how unpopular the Darlan deal was in Britain.

But as the chief representative of the U.S government there, Winant also felt obliged to defend the American position in public and to seek support for that stand with critical British officials, many of whom were personal friends. For two years, the ambassador had urged the British working class to press the fight against Nazism; now he was forced to back a deal with a leading Nazi collaborator. Profoundly uncomfortable, he nonetheless continued to parrot the administration's line. At one dinner party, Harold Nicolson listened as the ambassador told his skeptical fellow guests that the military advantages of the Darlan deal outweighed its moral drawbacks. "Darlan was there almost by chance . . . and they realized that he could deliver the goods," Nicolson quoted Winant as saying. "It means the saving of infinite time and 50,000 American lives. . . . It was worth it." Musing about the party, Nicolson wrote in his diary: "Winant is such a splendid fellow that one is almost convinced by his advocacy of ill."

THOUGH THE WHITE HOUSE was heavily criticized for supporting the Darlan agreement, it was Eisenhower who received the brunt of the attacks. "No matter what victories he wins, Ike will never live this one down," Harry Hopkins told the writer John Gunther. In Gunther's opinion, the remark was exceedingly unfair. Eisenhower, he later wrote, "was completely unskilled in political affairs, and his only motive was to drive ahead quickly and save American lives." The ultimate responsibility, Gunther believed, belonged to Roosevelt.

The controversy was finally resolved on Christmas Eve 1942 when a twenty-year-old French royalist burst into Darlan's headquarters in Algiers and shot him twice. Darlan died a few hours later, and after being found guilty during a secret military trial, his assassin was executed by firing squad on December 26. (There were—and still are—suspicions that the British and American secret services were involved in the killing, but nothing has ever been definitely proved.) Although Darlan had disappeared from the scene, Eisenhower remained embroiled in French politics and intrigues. Henri Giraud, who was named to replace Darlan, continued his predecessor's persecution of Jews and Vichy opponents in North Africa. "Giraud was of no help," Eisenhower later wrote. "He hated politics, not merely crookedness and chicanery in politics, but every part of the necessary task of developing an orderly, democratic system of government."

Caught up in his problems with the French, Eisenhower was also confronted with a host of new troubles as Allied troops, confident they would mop up North Africa in weeks if not days, headed for Tunisia. They were in for a rude surprise. While the Allies took their time ambling eastward, Hitler, having declared that "North Africa . . . must be held at all costs," had dispatched tens of thousands of troops to Tunisia. Hastily trained and ill equipped, neither the Americans nor British were any match for the veteran forces and superior armor, artillery, and airpower they encountered in their initial skirmishes with the enemy.

In those first months of fighting, disorganized Allied commanders squabbled among themselves and made repeated tactical mistakes. Their forces were spread too thin, with little cohesion between American and British troops or even between the units of each country. Cautious and tentative, officers failed to concentrate their men for massed attacks. "The German army makes war better than we are now making it," concluded a U.S. War Department report. "The enemy is regarded as the visiting team. . . . Both officers and men are psychologically unprepared for war." With their offensive stalled, Allied forces prepared for a long siege.

In February 1943, Rommel's troops, withdrawing to the west after their defeat at El Alamein, went on the attack. They smashed through the Kasserine Pass, a mountain gateway to Tunis, and inflicted heavy casualties on the unseasoned and undisciplined American troops of II Corps who tried to defend it. It was the first major battle in which America had taken part, and it ended in a rout, marked by poor tactics and leadership by the U.S. command. About Kasserine, Harry Butcher wrote glumly in his diary: "The proud and cocky Americans today stand humiliated by one of the greatest defeats in our history."

Although the British Army had hardly covered itself in glory since the war began, its troops and commanders poured scorn on American forces after Kasserine. British troops sang "How Green Was My Ally," and some referred to the Yanks as "our Italians." About the Americans, British general John Crocker wrote his wife: "So far as soldiering is concerned, believe me, the British have nothing at all to learn from them." Saying the same and more to U.S. and British correspondents, Crocker put the blame for a failed battle later that spring squarely on the shoulders of American troops. After Crocker's press briefing, *Time* magazine reported that the battle had been "downright embarrassing" for the Americans and had "afforded a sharp comparison between British and U.S. troops."

Much of the British finger-pointing was directed at Eisenhower, who, distracted by political squabbles, had failed to assert his authority and live up to his responsibilities as field commander. "Eisenhower as a general is hopeless!" Alan Brooke raged in his diary. "He submerges himself in politics and neglects his military duties, partly, I am afraid, because he knows little if anything about military matters." While stung by the criticism, Eisenhower did not disagree with it. "The best way to describe our operations to date," he wrote a friend, "is that they have violated every recognized principle of war, are in conflict with all operational and logistic methods laid down in textbooks, and will be condemned, in their entirety, by all . . . war college classes for the next 25 years."

When British and U.S. military chiefs met with Churchill and Roosevelt in Casablanca in January 1943, Brooke engineered a move to kick Eisenhower upstairs and place a British general, Harold Alexander, in direct command of the Allied campaign's ground forces in Tunisia. Alexander had been Montgomery's superior in the El Alamein battle and had overseen the Eighth Army as it moved west in pursuit of Rommel. With the Eighth preparing to link up with Torch forces, the time was ripe, in Brooke's opinion, to put Alexander in charge. As he later noted, "we were pushing Eisenhower up into the stratosphere and rarefied atmosphere of a Supreme Commander . . . whilst we inserted under him one of our commanders to . . . restore the necessary drive and co-ordination which had been so seriously lacking." Alexander, as it turned out, was as scathing about the Yanks as any of his countrymen. He wrote Brooke that the Americans were "soft, green, and quite untrained" and "lack the will to fight"—an opinion he held for much of the rest of the war, even when later battles proved him wrong.

For their part, American combat commanders, most of whom had been anti-British before Torch began, bitterly resented what they correctly viewed as the patronizing, disdainful attitude of their British counterparts. They pointed out that Montgomery and the suave, unflappable Alexander had allowed much of the Afrika Korps to slip away from them at Alamein; the Eighth Army's failure to pursue Rommel's forces with the utmost vigor gave the Germans the opportunity to hit the Americans at Kasserine.

"How he hates the British," another American general said of

George Patton, who took command of II Corps after the Kasserine debacle. Mark Clark, Eisenhower's imperious, publicity-seeking deputy, meanwhile, had infuriated virtually every British officer at Allied headquarters with his "niggling and insulting" Anglophobic barbs. When Clark, who was fond of quoting the Napoleonic aphorism "It is better to fight an ally than be one," stepped down to become a battlefield general, there was general rejoicing at Allied headquarters.

As a result of the growing Anglo-American hostility, Eisenhower, in addition to coping with his other troubles, was forced to spend considerable time and effort trying to make peace among his commanders. "In his current efforts to improve British and American relations," Harry Butcher wrote, "I see in Ike something akin to a fireman atop an observation tower searching a forest for smoke or flame." Despite repeated provocations from his lieutenants, Eisenhower persisted in his belief that victory could be achieved only if Americans and Britons worked closely together. "One of the constant sources of danger to us in this war," he wrote to a friend, "is the temptation to regard as our first enemy the partner that must work with us in defeating the real enemy." At a meeting with Alexander and Patton, Eisenhower declared that he did not think of himself "as an American but as an ally." He told his subordinates they must follow any order they received "without even pausing to consider whether that order emanated from a British or American source."

His appeals for harmony and cooperation, however, won him no plaudits from the Americans under him. Clark, Patton, and Omar Bradley, the deputy head of II Corps, attacked their chief for what they saw as his favoritism to the British. Grousing that "Ike is more British than the British," Patton accused him of being "damned near a Benedict Arnold" and added that the British "are playing us for suckers." Weary of the unrelieved backbiting, a U.S. officer on Eisenhower's staff wrote in his diary: "God, I wish we could forget our egos for a while!"

Yet, even as the carping continued, the pendulum in the North Africa campaign began to swing in favor of the Allies. Under Patton's tough brand of discipline, the soldiers in II Corps started learning how to fight, as did those in the U.S. First Army. Of the average GI in North Africa, Ernie Pyle observed: "His blood was up. He was fighting for his life, and killing for him was a profession. . . . He was truly at war." At the same time, with U.S. industrial mobilization finally gearing up, American supplies and armaments poured into the region. In one month alone, 24,000 vehicles, a million tons of cargo, and some 84,000 troop reinforcements landed in North Africa. "The American army does not solve its problems," one British general said. "It overwhelms them."

In the early spring of 1943, the German troops in Tunisia found themselves increasingly boxed in between the Torch forces and the Eighth Army. Now, the quarrels between British and American commanders focused on who was going to get the credit for the approaching victory. When an enraged Patton learned that Alexander planned to make the final push largely with his own country's troops, he warned the British general that if the U.S. Army appeared to be "acting in a minor role, the repercussions might be unfortunate." George Marshall himself joined the fray, cautioning Eisenhower about "a marked fall in prestige of American troops" and urging him to make sure U.S. forces had a major role in sealing the victory. As it turned out, they did.

On May 7, Tunis fell to the Allies, and, five days later, fighting ceased throughout the area. Britain and America had captured their first major prize—the Middle East and North Africa—and engineered a crucial turning point in the conflict. The momentum of the seemingly unstoppable Germans had finally been halted: just a few months before their defeat in Tunisia, they had been crushed by the Russians at Stalingrad. Thanks to the Western Allies, "one continent had been redeemed," Churchill wrote in his memoirs. "In London, there was, for the first time in the war, a real lifting of spirits." Hitler had lost the strategic initiative forever.

Although the Russians never acknowledged the fact, the Anglo-American triumph helped make their victory at Stalingrad possible. More than 150,000 German soldiers and hundreds of bombers had been diverted from Russia to fight the Allies in North Africa. It might not have been the second front that Stalin had in mind, but the diversion undoubtedly aided him in his successful effort to gain the offensive against the Reich.

The operation in North Africa also saved the United States and Britain from the disaster that almost certainly would have occurred if they had made an early landing in France, as the Americans had wanted. As historian Eric Larrabee observed, North Africa provided "a place to be lousy in, somewhere to let the gift for combat and command be discovered." It would take several years for Marshall, Eisenhower, and other Americans to admit that British opposition to a quick assault on France had not been misguided. "Alan Brooke, for all his nose-in-the-air dramatics, was essentially right," noted Mark Perry. "This was a cross-Channel suicide operation."

DESPITE HAVING LOST the first round, American military leaders remained committed to their plan for crossing the Channel. Once North Africa was mopped up, they believed, the Western Allies should start preparing for the invasion of France. The British disagreed. At the Casablanca conference, where the next Anglo-American offensive was to be decided, the battle over strategy was joined once more.

Before the conference began, Roosevelt warned his lieutenants that "the British will have a plan and stick to it." He was right. Having worked out their differences in London beforehand, Churchill and Britain's military brass presented a united front at Casablanca, urging a continuation of their peripheral strategy to weaken Germany before delivering the knockout blow. After North Africa, they wanted to strike across the Mediterranean—landing at Sicily, forcing Italy out of the war, and, they hoped, persuading Turkey to enter the conflict on the Allied side.

The fact that the British still were doing most of the fighting helped add force to their argument. Despite the American buildup in early 1943, three times as many British troops had fought in the combined campaigns in Tunisia, and the British suffered far more casualties—38,000 men killed, injured, and missing, compared to 19,000 for the Americans. But what really won the day for Churchill and his men was their superior organization and preparation in pressing their case at Casablanca. Backed by innumerable charts and graphs, they had worked everything out to the last detail. Whenever a statistic was needed, one of the many staffers brought from London would inevitably produce the right leather folder containing it. As Roosevelt had predicted, the British arguments and logic were relentless, much like "the dripping of water on a stone." Afterward, General Tom Handy, Eisenhower's successor as head of war plans in Washington, remarked about the British: "One thing they understood—the Prime Minister above all—was the principle of the objective. You headed them off one way and they'd come at you in another way. . . . Our people . . . were all behind the eight ball."

Prescient as he was about the British preparations, Roosevelt had failed to follow their example. In his only meeting with U.S. military leaders before the conference, he declined to commit himself to a new strategic objective to follow North Africa. With no clear lead from their commander in chief, the U.S. Joint Chiefs of Staff disagreed among themselves about the future course of the war and, indeed, openly vented their differences in front of the British at Casablanca. While George Marshall advocated a cross-Channel landing, Ernest King, the chief of naval operations, wanted more supplies and troops diverted to the Pacific. For his part, General Henry "Hap" Arnold, head of the U.S. Army Air Forces, called for a huge Britain-based bomber offensive against Germany.

In response to Marshall's arguments, the British took out their red leather folders once more, producing facts and figures to demonstrate why the Allies still were not ready to mount an invasion of the Continent. Despite the avowed emphasis on Germany first, more than half the American troops and equipment sent overseas were involved in the fight against Japan. There simply were not enough men, supplies, ships, and landing craft to open a new front in France.

At the conference's end, Roosevelt concurred with the British. The decision was made to attack Sicily, an operation that laid the groundwork for the 1943–44 Allied campaign in Italy. In a nod to the Americans, there was also an agreement to build up U.S. forces in England, in preparation for an eventual assault on the Continent.

As the conference participants headed for home, there was no doubt in anyone's mind that, once again, the Americans had been outmaneuvered by their British cousins. "They swarmed down upon us like locusts," acknowledged General Albert Wedemeyer, a member of the Army's war plans department. "We came, we listened, and we were conquered." Pug Ismay's deputy, General Ian Jacob, boasted: "Our ideas had prevailed almost throughout."

Such gloating, however, would not last for long. With the Americans about to emerge as the dominant power in the alliance, Casablanca would mark the final time in the war that Britain would get its way over strategic objectives—or much of anything else.

IN PREPARING FOR the combat to come, Eisenhower was well aware that Brooke and other British generals were trying to undercut him.

His relationship with them—in particular, Montgomery, the egocentric, vainglorious hero of El Alamein—would grow even more contentious as the war moved to Europe. He would also be subjected to more sniping from Patton, Bradley, Clark, and other American commanders.

Yet, thanks to the lessons he learned in the crucible of North Africa, Eisenhower would remain, despite all the difficulties he would face and the slights he would endure, firmly in command. As Rick Atkinson has pointed out, "no soldier in Africa had changed more—grown more—than Eisenhower." His mistakes had been many, and they might well have toppled him from his post. But, to his own surprise, they did not, and, having shed his naïveté and insecurity, he was determined to see that they did not happen again. "Before he left for Europe in 1942," Eisenhower's son, John, later wrote, "I knew him as an aggressive, intelligent personality." North Africa, John Eisenhower added, transformed his father "from a mere person to a personage . . . full of authority, and truly in command." A British general might well have been talking about Eisenhower when he remarked: "One of the fascinations of the war was to see how Americans developed their great men so quickly."

In the two years of combat that followed the North Africa campaign, Eisenhower never faltered in his conviction that the war could be won only if the Allied coalition remained a close-knit unit. While often angry or hurt by the aspersions cast at him by the British (about Montgomery, he once exploded: "Goddamn it, I can deal with anybody except that son of a bitch!"), he remained adamant about the importance of the British war effort. No other military leader—British or American—worked as hard as he did to make the alliance a success. "Eisenhower was probably the least chauvinistic American and the least chauvinistic military commander in history," observed Don Cook, a war correspondent for the *New York Herald Tribune*. "He never lost his American patriotism or pride; he simply added another patriotism to it."

For all his disparaging remarks about Eisenhower, Brooke acknowledged after the war: "Where he shone was in his ability to handle allied forces, to treat them all with strict impartiality, and to get the very best out of an inter-allied force." That ability, as Eisenhower always believed, was the key to his ultimate success—and to victory.

13.

THE FORGOTTEN ALLIES

For months following the Americans' deal with Darlan, European exiles gathered at the White Tower, York Minster, and other favored restaurants and pubs in London to smoke endless cigarettes and discuss the agreement's implications. The Free French were the ones most directly affected, of course. But the other émigrés—Norwegians, Poles, Czechoslovaks, Belgians, and Dutch—were also worried about what the deal might mean for the future. The Nazis had invaded and occupied their countries, too. When the time came for those nations to be liberated, would the Americans cooperate with traitors like Darlan?

Most of the Europeans meeting over wine-stained tablecloths that winter had escaped to London in the chaos-filled spring of 1940, when German troops conquered Norway and Denmark, then rolled through France and the Low Countries. Every other day, it seemed, George VI and Winston Churchill had been summoned to one of the city's train stations to welcome yet another king, queen, president, or prime minister. As the only country in Europe still holding out against Hitler, Britain was, as Polish troops put it, the "Last Hope Island" for émigrés who wanted to continue the fight. And London, which housed de Gaulle's movement and six governments-in-exile, had become the de facto capital of free Europe.

The exiles were everywhere in the city. De Gaulle and his French staff were ensconced in a stately white mansion in Carlton Gardens, overlooking St. James's Park. Less than a mile away, Queen Wilhelmina of the Netherlands invited escaped Dutch resistance fighters to tea at her bomb-pitted townhouse in Chester Square. Three blocks from the queen, General Wladyslaw Sikorski, the Polish prime minister and commander in chief, conducted business at the Rubens Hotel. The Norwegian, Dutch, and Belgian governments operated from Stratton House, across from the Ritz on Piccadilly. Other foreign offices were scattered throughout Belgravia, Kensington, Mayfair, Knightsbridge, and St. James's.

By 1943, some 100,000 European pilots, soldiers, and sailors had fetched up in Britain, joining not only the fast-growing U.S. forces but also troops from Canada, Australia, New Zealand, South Africa, and India. Unlike the American and Commonwealth military, the Europeans had risked everything to get there. "To cross over to England, you had to sacrifice all you loved, including probably your life, for this one privilege: to fight the Nazis as a free man," said Erik Hazelhoff, a Dutch law student when the war broke out. "Everybody's goal was the same: to get to England and join the Allied forces." In 1940 and early 1941, most of the rest of the world had expected Britain to be defeated within months, if not weeks. But still the Europeans came—"all those insane, unarmed heroes who had defied a triumphant Hitler," said the French journalist Eve Curie, the daughter of the physicists Marie and Pierre Curie and herself an escapee to London.

Thanks to the exiles, London was now a vibrant, cosmopolitan metropolis, humming with gossip, energy, and life. A native Londoner never knew who might sit next to him on the bus or tube, in a restaurant or pub. It might be a Polish pilot just returned from a bombing raid, a Norwegian seaman rescued from his torpedoed ship, a resistance fighter smuggled out of France. Like exotic, brightly plumed birds, European military men crowded London's bomb-blasted streets—French sailors in their striped shirts and berets topped with red pompoms; French army officers wearing white capes and their own distinctive headgear, the flat-topped kepi; Polish soldiers with their four-cornered caps, looking like nineteenth-century dragoons; Dutch policemen in smart black uniforms with gray-silver braid. For the Canadian diplomat Charles Ritchie, walking in Kensington Gardens alongside the European allies was like "swimming in the full tide of history."

While foreigners were visible in many parts of London, the center of wartime émigré life was Soho, a haven for European expatriates since the seventeenth century. Bohemian, noisy, and inexpensive, the neighborhood was filled with French, Italian, Greek, Chinese, and other ethnic restaurants favored by the exiles. The York Minster, on Dean Street, was one of the best known meeting places, attracting the Free French and lower-ranking officials from the Belgian government, among others.

De Gaulle and the heads of the governments-in-exile, by contrast, did most of their socializing at exclusive British watering holes—the Savoy, Ritz, Claridge's, and Connaught—pleading their countries' cause with British and American officials. The exile governments often competed with one another for the favor of the two largest Western Allies; among and within the governments, there were suspicions, factions, feuds, and infighting. In a tongue-in-cheek *New Yorker* article about inter-Allied rivalries, A. J. Liebling noted how "ministers got reports on their opposite numbers in half a dozen other governments, and operatives shadowed each other—to the point that lunch at Claridge's or the Ritz Grill resembled a traffic jam of characters out of an Alfred Hitchcock film."

For foreign troops, however, London was less a hub of intrigue than a place for relaxation, camaraderie, excitement, and romance. Throughout the war, European pilots from nearby airbases and soldiers on leave from more distant posts like Tobruk and Tripoli swarmed into the city to enjoy its pleasures, as did other Allied servicemen. "No matter our varied origins and uncertain futures, we stood shoulder to shoulder, even if only for beer," recalled Erik Hazelhoff. "We drank together, took our girls to the same nightclubs—the Suvi, the Embassy Club, the 400. Norwegians, Hollanders, Poles, French, English, all were there—everyone packed together on those tiny dance floors."

Of all the Europeans, the Poles and Free French had the greatest success in winning the company and affections of British women, who were captivated by their dash, daring, and continental charm. The novelist Nancy Mitford was among those smitten by a Frenchman; in 1942, she began a tempestuous and ultimately ill-fated affair with Gaston Palewski, de Gaulle's charming, womanizing chief of staff. But it was the Poles, with their hand kissing and penchant for sending flowers, who won the greatest reputations as gallants. In contemporary diaries and letters, and in later recollections, Polish fliers, who were described by Quentin Reynolds as "the glamor boys of England," described their wartime romances in Britain with some amazement. "As for the women," one of them wrote in his diary, "one just cannot shake them off."

FOR THOSE LEFT behind in occupied Europe, Britain and its capital were seen very differently. They were not places for fun and romance but beacons of hope and talismans against despair. Shortly after the Germans invaded Holland, Erik Hazelhoff had stood on a beach near The Hague and watched in wonderment as two Spitfires flashed overhead, their RAF markings bright in the sun. "The Occupation had descended on us with such crushing finality," he later wrote, "that England, like freedom, had become a mere concept. To believe in it as something real, a chunk of land where free people bucked the Nazi tide, required a concrete manifestation like a sign from God: England exists!" For him, the Spitfires were that sign. Less than a year later, he pirated a fishing boat, escaped to England, and became an RAF pilot himself.

For many other residents of captive countries, hope came in the form of the BBC. Benumbed by the shock, humiliation, and terror of Nazi occupation, they were encouraged by daily BBC broadcasts to feel that they were not alone. Listening to London radio—an activity punished by imprisonment and, in some countries, death—was, for many Europeans, their first act of standing up to their occupiers. Every day, they retrieved their radio sets from a variety of hiding places— below floorboards, behind canned goods in the kitchen cupboard, secreted in the chimney. In northern Norway, fishermen rowed out to a tiny island several miles offshore, where they'd hidden a radio in a cave. In whatever the setting, the owners of the sets switched them on and tuned to the BBC in time to hear the chiming of Big Ben and the magical words: "This is London calling." They'd listen to the war news of the day in their own language, and often they'd hear the leaders of their countries—King Haakon of Norway; Queen Wilhelmina; General Sikorski; Jan Masaryk, the Czechoslovak foreign minister—call on them to trust in their eventual liberation and, in the meantime, to do everything they could to resist the enemy.

A vast number of Europeans regarded the BBC broadcasts as their only lifeline to freedom. In a letter smuggled out of Czechoslovakia, a man wrote to the BBC: "It would drive me mad to miss a single broadcast from London. It is the only thing to feed the soul." A Frenchman who escaped to London late in the war recalled: "It's impossible to explain how much we depended on the BBC. In the beginning, it was everything."

Only those who had experienced the invasion of their countries, Eve Curie once remarked, could truly understand the reality of war and the preciousness of the freedom that London symbolized. An Englishwoman, walking down Piccadilly with a Belgian journalist friend who'd just escaped from a Nazi prison, was struck by the same thought. Her friend, "almost drunk with happiness," was gazing around, she noted, as if trying to memorize everything he saw. "Do you know I have been dreaming of this moment for months?" he exclaimed. "Isn't it wonderful to be here! Why, millions of people all over the continent are thinking at this very moment of London!" For all their privations and all their sufferings in the Blitz, the Englishwoman mused, "Londoners are apt to forget what privileged folk they are."

WHILE IT WAS TRUE that the European exiles and their compatriots back home had benefited greatly from their English ally, it was also true that Britain, the United States, and even the Soviet Union received much in return. Although the Europeans were now greatly overshadowed by the coalition's Big Three, they provided vital assistance to the Allied cause. In the critical years of 1940 and 1941, they helped save Britain from defeat and, in the latter part of the war, proved to be of immense benefit to the overall Allied effort.

When Germany launched its aerial assault on southern England in July 1940, the Royal Air Force was in a shambles, having lost a third of its most experienced fighter pilots and half its planes in the fighting in France and Belgium. Hundreds of experienced European pilots—Belgian, French, Czech, and, above all, Polish—filled the gap. The Polish fliers, who had already fought the Luftwaffe in their own country and France, were considered the most skilled of all; one of their squadrons was credited with downing more German aircraft during the Battle of Britain than any other unit attached to the RAF. According to top RAF officials, the contributions of the Poles were crucial to the Battle of Britain victory; some believe it was decisive. "If Poland had not stood with us in those days . . . the candle of freedom might have been snuffed out," Queen Elizabeth declared in 1996.

To help the British with their skyrocketing shipping losses, Norway, which boasted the fourth largest merchant marine fleet in the world, leased more than 1,300 ships and crews to Britain. Belgium, meanwhile, loaned the British some of its gold reserves when dollars were needed to pay for U.S. armaments before Roosevelt instituted Lend-Lease. The abundant natural resources of the Belgian Congo, such as rubber and oil, were also used to aid the Allied cause.

But the Europeans' greatest contribution was in the field of intelligence. Just before the Battle of Britain began, British code breakers at Bletchley Park succeeded in cracking the Luftwaffe's version of the cipher produced by Germany's complex Enigma machine. Months later, they broke the Enigma cipher of the German navy and then the army. The information produced by British cryptographers about German military tactics and plans proved critical to the winning of the Battle of the Atlantic and to Allied victory. But Bletchley Park could not have done it without the help of the French and, above all, the Poles. Using documents supplied by French intelligence, Polish cryptographers in the early 1930s were the first to decipher Enigma intercepts. In the summer of 1939, shortly before the war began, Poland's intelligence agency presented British and French cryptographers with exact replicas of the Enigma machine. That device, and information about German codes passed on by the Poles, provided the foundation upon which the British built their own fabled code-breaking system.

A master at taking credit for wartime intelligence successes that did not, in fact, originate in his agency, Stewart Menzies, head of the vaunted Secret Intelligence Service (MI6), had been quick to claim control of Bletchley Park. That gave him the pleasurable job of presenting Churchill with Bletchley's latest "golden eggs" of intelligence. While Menzies "bathed in the reflected glory cast upon him . . . the truth was that SIS could not claim exclusive responsibility for any of the major intelligence coups of the war," declared one British intelligence official. The source for almost all of them was the intelligence services of occupied Europe.

Throughout the globe, Britain's secret service had enjoyed a sterling reputation, thanks largely to the image of a highly skilled, omniscient SIS that had been promulgated by prewar British spy novels. Churchill considered the British intelligence service "the finest in the world," as did SS head Heinrich Himmler and his deputy, Reinhard Heydrich, both addicts of British espionage fiction. The reality, however, was far different. Starved of government funds between the two world wars, MI6 had long been understaffed, underfinanced, and short of talent and technology. Until Germany invaded France and the Low Countries, SIS leaders inclined toward appeasement; lured by a bogus German peace overture to Britain, two SIS agents had been abducted by Heydrich's agents in Holland in late 1939. Compounding SIS's humiliation over this affair was the fact that, when interrogated, the agents readily revealed details of the agency's operations, including names of SIS operatives throughout Western Europe. In the course of the German blitzkrieg, the operatives were arrested and the SIS networks largely destroyed.

For Stewart Menzies and his deputy, Claude Dansey, the arrival of the European secret services in London was a heaven-sent opportunity to save themselves and their agency from disaster. In exchange for providing financial, communications, and transportation support to the exile services, the SIS, under Dansey's direction, assumed control of most of their operations and took credit for their successes. Thanks, for example, to the Czechoslovak secret service, the SIS learned beforehand of German plans to invade France through the Ardennes in 1940 and to conquer Yugoslavia and Greece in the spring of 1941. (The Ardennes intelligence coup—and Britain's and France's failure to do anything about it—prove that, however good information might be, it is of no use unless action is taken as a result.)

In Norway, meanwhile, hundreds of wireless operators monitored and reported the movements of German submarines and warships along the Norwegian coast. One of them informed London in 1941 that he'd spotted four German warships in a fjord in central Norway—information that led to the sinking of the *Bismarck* and the crippling of the *Prinz Eugen*. In addition to reporting on the location of enemy ships, troops, and fortifications, agents from the French resistance stole plans for German coastal defenses along the Normandy coast, which proved invaluable to the Allied staff planning the D-Day invasion.

Of all the European services, however, it was the Poles who provided the lion's share of Allied intelligence during the war. In 2005, the British government acknowledged that nearly 50 percent of the secret information obtained by the Allies from wartime Europe came from Polish sources. "The Poles had the best special services in Europe," said Douglas Dodds-Parker, a British intelligence official who worked with them during the war. "They had needed these . . . during and between the centuries of occupation and partition" by their more power-ful neighbors—Russia, Germany, and Austria. "With generations of clandestine action behind them," Dodds-Parker added, "they had edu-cated the rest of us."

From the day Poland regained its independence in 1918, it had given top priority to intelligence gathering and code breaking, specifi-cally aimed at its two most powerful historical enemies, Germany and Russia. In the words of a former chief of Polish intelligence, "If you live trapped between the two wheels of a grindstone, you have to learn how to keep from being crushed." In 1939, Polish intelligence leaders were unable to prevent that from happening, but, before escaping west, they did leave in place a sophisticated clandestine network within the country that later provided a cornucopia of information to London, including reports of German military movements to the Russian front. In addition, Poland had agents in Scandinavia, the Baltic states, Switzerland, Italy, Belgium, the Balkans, North Africa, and Germany itself. In France, Poles ran several of the largest intelligence networks. By 1944, one of these networks, code-named F-2, had seven hundred full-time and two thousand part-time operatives, most of them French, working in such locales as ports, railway stations, armaments plants, and even German war production offices.

In the early 1940s, thanks to F-2 and a variety of other European in-telligence sources, the Allies learned of trials being carried out on two new secret German weapons—the V-1 flying bomb and V-2 rocket—at Peenemünde, on the Baltic coast of Germany. Armed with that information, more than five hundred RAF bombers pounded Peen-emünde in August 1943, setting back production of the weapons more than six months and preventing their use on the millions of Allied troops gathering in England for the invasion.

WHEN THE OSS SET up operations in London in 1942, it had no idea that the stream of intelligence it received from MI6 was actually pro-duced by the European services. Like virtually everyone else in the in-ternational intelligence community, officials of the fledgling U.S. spy and sabotage agency believed in the invincibility of the SIS. "We ar-rived in London as the new boys in school, untested, unknown, scorned and derided" by the British, recalled William Casey, who served with the OSS in wartime London and later went on to become head of the CIA. Among those who mocked the Americans was the writer Malcolm Muggeridge, an SIS agent during the war, who wrote in his memoirs: "How well I remember them, arriving like *jeunes filles en fleur* straight from a finishing school, all fresh and innocent, to start work in our frowsy old intelligence brothel."

It didn't take long, though, for these innocents to discover what was really going on behind the brothel's tightly closed doors. "The truth is that, on the positive intelligence side, [SIS] is lamentably weak," David Bruce, the head of the London OSS office, observed in his diary. "Most of the reports they send us are duplicates of those already received by us from European secret intelligence services." Despite strenuous opposition from Claude Dansey, the OSS insisted on opening its own channels with the European clandestine services, providing them with financial and other support and, with their help, establishing its own espionage networks on the Continent.

In the area of sabotage, OSS joined forces with a new British government agency called the Special Operations Executive (SOE), which was training Europeans in the fine art of subversion and other forms of active resistance. In stately manor houses throughout the English and Scottish countryside, Norwegians, Dutchmen, Poles, Frenchmen, Czechoslovaks, and Belgians were given new identities and taught how to make parachute drops, operate wireless transmitters, read codes, set off bombs, and kill SS men at close quarters. Then they were sent back to their countries to train others.

In 1943, Norwegian commandos, under orders from Churchill himself, destroyed a heavy-water factory in their country to help prevent Germany from developing an atomic bomb. Before and after D-Day, the sabotage carried out by the French resistance was, in Eisenhower's words, of "inestimable value" to the Allied landings and advance across France. In Belgium, the underground prevented the Germans from blowing up the crucial port at Antwerp. The Polish resistance, the largest and most highly developed underground movement in Europe, was responsible for massive delays and disruptions of German rail transports through Poland to the eastern front, thus contributing to the collapse of the German offensive against the Soviet Union.

In another invaluable service to the Allies, the resistance movements in every captive country helped rescue and spirit back to England thousands of British and American pilots downed behind enemy lines, as well as other Allied servicemen caught in German-held territory. In Belgium, for example, a young woman named Andrée de Jongh set up an escape route called the Comet Line through her native country and France, manned mostly by her friends, to return Britons and Americans to England. De Jongh herself escorted more than one hundred servicemen over the Pyrenees Mountains to safety in neutral Spain.

As de Jongh and her colleagues knew, being active in the resistance, regardless of gender, was far more perilous than fighting on the battle-field or in the air. If captured, uniformed servicemen on the Western front were sent to prisoner of war camps, where Geneva Convention rules usually applied. When resistance members were caught, they faced torture, the horrors of a German concentration camp, and/or ex-ecution. The danger of capture was particularly great for those who sheltered British or American fighting men, most of whom did not speak the language of the country in which they were hiding and who generally stuck out like the proverbial sore thumb. As one British in-telligence officer observed, "It is not an easy matter to hide and feed a foreigner in your midst, especially when it happens to be a red-haired Scotsman of six feet, three inches, or a gum-chewing American from the Middle West."

James Langley, the head of a British agency that aided the Euro-pean escape lines, later estimated that, for every Englishman or Amer-ican rescued, at least one resistance worker lost his or her life. Andrée de Jongh managed to escape that fate. Caught in January 1943 and sent to the Ravensbruck concentration camp in Germany, she survived the war because, although she freely admitted to creating the Comet Line, the Germans could not believe that a young girl had devised such an intricate operation.

IN THE LATE NINETEENTH century, Lord Salisbury, then the prime minister of Britain, declared with a sniff: "Britain does not solicit al-liances. She grants them." Winston Churchill never had that luxury. As Britain faced a possible German invasion in 1940 and 1941, the prime minister had needed all the allies he could get, no matter how insignificant, to help stave off defeat.

Despite opposition from members of his cabinet and much of the rest of Whitehall, he had insisted that all governments-in-exile be welcomed to Britain, along with their armed forces. "We shall conquer together or we shall die together," he told General Sikorski and the Poles in June 1940. When France capitulated to Germany, Charles de Gaulle, a minor figure in the government and the most junior brigadier in the army, was the only French official who dared denounce the armistice and come to London. "You are alone," Churchill told him. "Well, I shall recognize you alone." When other British cabinet members wanted to go slow in withdrawing recognition from the Pétain government, Churchill demanded that Britain acknowledge de Gaulle as "leader of all Frenchmen, wherever they may be, who rally to him in support of the Allied cause."

But the British prime minister's wholehearted support for his European allies lasted only until the Soviet Union and United States were propelled into the war. When those two powerful nations joined the alliance, the early solidarity between England and occupied Europe gave way to the exigencies of realpolitik. Although well aware of the debt he owed the Europeans for their help, Churchill needed the two newcomers considerably more.

As a result, the position of every European government was dramatically diminished, particularly when the United States entered the conflict. Despite his endorsement of freedom and equality for all nations, Roosevelt, supported by Churchill, served notice that the United States would be calling the shots from now on. Reeling from the losses of Singapore, Hong Kong, Malaya, and Burma, the British prime minister was in desperate need of American help and made clear that his main allegiance now lay with the American president.

In January 1942, Roosevelt and Churchill stage-managed the signing in Washington of an agreement by the United Nations, as the president dubbed the twenty-six nations then in the alliance, all of them pledging their full resources to the fight and reiterating their commitment to the principles of the Atlantic Charter. "The United Nations constitute an association of independent peoples of equal dignity and equal importance," Roosevelt declared. Yet only the Soviet Union and China were consulted in advance about the drafting of the document, and only the Soviet and Chinese ambassadors received formal invitations to the White House signing ceremony with Roosevelt and Churchill. The ambassadors of the other Allied countries were merely informed that they could drop by, at their convenience, to sign the declaration.

After the signing, at a dinner at the White House, a guest mentioned King Zog, whose country, Albania, had been invaded by Mussolini in 1939. "Winston, we forgot Zog!" the president exclaimed. "I believe there's an Albanian minister or representative here—we must get him to sign our little document." The other guests laughed, but one of them—a writer of Slovenian descent named Louis Adamic, who had been invited to the dinner by Eleanor Roosevelt—was bothered by what he considered the frivolous, patronizing tone of Roosevelt's and Churchill's conversation about Albania. "A couple of emperors!" Adamic thought to himself. "Says one emperor to the other across the dinner table: 'Oh, say, we forgot Zog.' It's funny as hell. But too damned personal, haphazard, high-handed, casual. What else have they overlooked?"

The president's attitude toward the countries of occupied Europe and the other small allies revealed some of the contradictions in his immensely complex personality. Like Woodrow Wilson, with his notion that World War I would "make the world safe for democracy," Roosevelt believed that America's mission after World War II was to help build a freer and more just world. Yet he also believed—as did Stalin and, to a slightly lesser extent, Churchill—that the Big Three had the right to dictate to the less powerful states, not only during the war but afterward as well. The president, said Arthur Schlesinger Jr., "talked idealism but played the power game."

In the spring of 1942, at a meeting with Soviet foreign minister Vyacheslav Molotov, FDR sketched a picture of a postwar world very different from the one envisioned in the Atlantic Charter. This world would be governed not by the ideals of equality and justice but by Great Power politics. The United States, Soviet Union, Great Britain, and China would make up the world's police force, and smaller countries, having been shorn of all their armaments except rifles, would submit to the police force's will. Roosevelt continued to champion this idea, even as he simultaneously pushed his vision of an international federation of nations.

As the war proceeded, the less powerful allies were excluded from any significant role in war operations and from discussions about the geopolitical shape that the postwar world would take. Foreign visitors to the White House were taken aback by Roosevelt's blithe way of talking about the fates of other nations as if they were his alone to decide. In his meeting with Molotov, for example, the president declared that the Soviet Union needed a northern port that was not icebound in the winter and suggested it take over the Norwegian port of Narvik. The startled Soviets turned down the proposal, noting that they did not "have any territorial or other claims against Norway."

Of Roosevelt, Oliver Lyttelton, the British minister of production, wrote: "He allowed his thoughts and conversations to flit across the tumultuous and troubled [world] scene with a lightness and inconsequence which were truly frightening in one wielding so much power." Lyttelton made the observation after a late night chat with FDR in his White House study in early 1943. In the course of their discussion, the president mentioned the divisions between Belgium's two main ethnic groups—the Dutch-speaking Flemings and the French-speaking Walloons. After declaring that the Flemings and Walloons "can't live together," he proposed that "after the war, we should make two states, one known as Walloonia and one as Flamingia, and we should amalgamate Luxembourg with Flamingia. What do you say to that?" Incredulous at the idea of forcing a European ally to partition itself, Lyttelton could only remark that he thought the idea "required a good deal of study." When he later reported Roosevelt's comments to Anthony Eden, the British foreign secretary said he was sure the president was joking. But when Eden himself visited the White House a few weeks later, Roosevelt reintroduced the proposal. "I poured water, I hope politely, [on the idea]," Eden wrote in his diary, "and the President did not revert to the subject again."

In his memoirs, Eden remarked: "Roosevelt was familiar with the history and geography of Europe . . . but the sweeping opinions which he built upon it were alarming in their cheerful fecklessness. He seemed to see himself disposing of the fate of many lands, allied no less than enemy. He did all this with so much grace that it was not easy to dissent. Yet it was too like a conjuror, skillfully juggling with balls of dynamite, whose nature he failed to understand."

HAVING LITTLE OR no knowledge of Roosevelt's private attitudes toward the future of their countries, the governments and people of occupied Europe regarded him, in the words of the British intellectual Isaiah Berlin, as "a kind of benevolent demigod who alone could and would save them in the end." But some of them began to question that faith after the Darlan deal. A few days after the admiral was assassinated, Ed Murrow wrote an acquaintance: "There is a great fear, not only in this country but amongst the Governments in exile, of the use that America will make of its predominant power once this war is ended."

Wallace Carroll noted that rumors began to swirl in London exile circles as soon as the agreement was announced: "What would the American generals do next? Would they strike a bargain with Petain and Laval in France, with Quisling in Norway, with Degrelle in Belgium, with Mussert in Holland?" Members of European resistance movements, whose lives were in constant danger due in large part to collaborators like Darlan, were the most outspoken in expressing their dismay and anger. According to a report by the Special Operations Executive, the Allies' collusion with Darlan "has produced violent reactions on all our subterranean organizations in enemy-occupied countries, particularly in France, where it has had a blasting and withering effect." The governments-in-exile were also disturbed that, for the sake of military expediency, de Gaulle, whom they all backed as leader of the Free French, was being ignored by the United States and, following in America's wake, by Britain.

In truth, the tall, stork-legged general was not an easy man to support. Even his most loyal followers were exasperated by his arrogance, touchiness, and autocratic style of leadership. Many prominent anti-Vichy Frenchmen, like Jean Monnet, who became an adviser to President Roosevelt in Washington, would have nothing to do with him. De Gaulle, Lord Moran said, "positively goes out of his way to be difficult. . . . An improbable creature, like a human giraffe, sniffing down his nostrils at mortals beneath his gaze."

At the same time, de Gaulle had much to be obstreperous about. He was, as Pug Ismay noted, "in a hideously difficult position." The Vichy government had condemned him to death for treason, few French troops or officials had initially followed him to London, and his beloved France was deeply demoralized and divided. While many Frenchmen opposed Vichy's capitulation to Germany from the beginning, many more had put their faith in Pétain, a deeply revered World War I hero, to bring stability to their humiliated country and to their own lives.

For de Gaulle, the daunting task of inspiring and unifying his faction-riven homeland was complicated by the fact that, unlike the European governments-in-exile, his movement was not recognized by Britain or the United States as the official governing body of his country. To his chagrin, he and his fellow exile leaders did have one thing in common: their governments and his movement were almost completely dependent for their financial support on Britain—and, indirectly, on the United States, through Lend-Lease.* "Coming to [the British] as a beggar, with his country's wretchedness branded on his forehead and in his heart, was unbearable" for him, observed the wife of Edward Spears, Churchill's liaison with the general.

Yet, unlike the other European leaders, de Gaulle refused to acknowledge his inferior position. He insisted that the Free French, by virtue of France's historic preeminence in Europe, must have a major role in fighting the war. "I am no man's subordinate," he once remarked. "I have one mission and one mission only, that of carrying on the struggle for my country's liberation." To Spears, he declared: "You think I am interested in England winning the war? I am not. I am only interested in France's victory." When a shocked Spears replied, "They are all the same," de Gaulle shot back: "Not at all."

Such stiff-necked rebellion drove Churchill wild. The prime minister, who had a deep love for France and had visited it frequently in prewar years, was greatly conflicted about de Gaulle. On the one hand, he had tremendous admiration for the general's refusal to accept defeat and his iron-willed determination to fight on in the face of what appeared to be impossible odds—qualities shared by Churchill himself. At the same time, he was angered and hurt by de Gaulle's seeming lack of appreciation for what Churchill had done for him, as evidenced by his constant complaints and criticisms, many of them made publicly, about what he saw as Britain's neglect and infringement of French interests. The pair's wartime arguments were monumental in their ferocity, and Churchill often declared he would have nothing more to do with the temperamental Frenchman. After listening to one such tirade, Harold Nicolson remarked to Churchill: "You may be right, Prime Minister, but surely all that is irrelevant, since Gen. de Gaulle is a great man." Churchill stared hard at him. "A great man?" he raged. "Why, he's selfish! He's arrogant! He thinks he's the center of the universe! He . . . He . . ." Failing to come up with more epithets, the prime minister paused for a moment. "You're right," he said. "He *is* a great man."

---

* The U.S. provided more than $50 billion in Lend-Lease aid to forty-four countries during the war. Britain and its commonwealth received the largest amount of aid, with the Soviet Union coming in second.

De Gaulle, in turn, occasionally unbent a bit to show *his* appreciation for Churchill. In the middle of the war, he sent a French picture book about the Duke of Marlborough, Churchill's illustrious ancestor, to the prime minister's grandson, also named Winston. In a letter to Pamela Churchill, the child's mother, de Gaulle wrote that the book "is almost the only thing I brought from France. If, later, the young Winston Churchill looks through these drawings, perhaps he will spare a minute's thought for a French General who was, in the greatest war of History, the sincere admirer of his grandfather and the faithful ally of his country."

For his part, Roosevelt never shared Churchill's view of de Gaulle as a great man. Unlike the prime minister, the president felt nothing but disdain for the general and his defeated country. By capitulating to Germany, he believed, France had lost its place among the Western powers. In the president's mind, "France had failed, and failure had to be punished," wrote Ted Morgan, an FDR biographer. Roosevelt had little understanding of the complexity of the situation in France and scant sympathy for its dazed, traumatized citizens. "There is no France," he declared, insisting that the country would not really exist again until after its liberation. As for de Gaulle, Roosevelt considered him insignificant and absurd, a British puppet with grandiose ambitions as a dictator but little support among his own countrymen. "He takes himself for Joan of Arc, for Napoleon, for Clemenceau," the president snorted. Roosevelt was "convinced," Wallace Carroll wrote, "that de Gaulle's ambitions were a threat to Allied harmony and a menace to French democracy. Accordingly, he made up his mind—and once it was made up, it was never changed—that the U.S. would make no concession which would help de Gaulle to achieve his ambitions."

Even when the OSS dispatched a French underground leader to Washington in late 1942 to make clear that France's resistance movements accepted de Gaulle as their leader, Roosevelt refused to budge. The general and his followers, he told Churchill, must be given no role in the liberation and governance of North Africa and France. De Gaulle later remarked: "Roosevelt meant the peace to be an American peace, convinced that he must be the one to dictate its structure and that France in particular should recognize him as its savior and its arbiter. . . . Like any star performer, he was touchy as to the roles that fell to other actors." According to the journalist and author John Gunther, the president "talked about the French empire as if it were his personal possession and would say things like 'I haven't quite decided what to do about Tunis.' "

By the end of the North Africa campaign, however, it was clear that the president was fighting a losing battle where de Gaulle was concerned. Thousands of Vichy French soldiers in North Africa had switched sides, joining the Free French (now called the Fighting French) and making de Gaulle's movement a much more potent military force. In France, opposition to Pétain had mushroomed, as had the size of the resistance movements and their support for de Gaulle. The general was also backed by the European governments-in-exile, as well as by most of the British public, press, and Parliament, and a large segment of American public opinion besides. By contrast, General Giraud, named by the Americans to replace Darlan as the French leader of North Africa, had virtually no support except within the Roosevelt administration. "Between Giraud and de Gaulle, there is no real choice," a French resistance leader told Harold Nicolson. "Giraud is not a name at all in France. De Gaulle is more than a name, he is a legend."

Finally bowing a bit to what most people saw as inevitable, Roosevelt acknowledged that de Gaulle could not be wholly excluded from the North Africa government and authorized his association with Giraud. In June 1943, the French Committee of National Liberation was formed in Algiers, with Giraud and de Gaulle as co-chairmen. Within weeks, however, it became apparent that a struggle for power was taking place within the committee and that de Gaulle was winning it.

Determined to prevent his bête noir from taking control, Roosevelt, who long had chided Churchill for failing to restrain his "problem child," now pressed the prime minister to withdraw all British support from de Gaulle. Passing on documents that portrayed the general as sabotaging his allies, the president declared to Churchill that de Gaulle "has been and is now injuring our war effort and . . . is a very dangerous threat to us."

The prime minister found himself in an exceedingly difficult position. Having pledged to support de Gaulle as the leader of free Frenchmen everywhere, he could hardly go back on his word. If he did what Roosevelt wanted, he would face stiff resistance from the British people and many officials in his own government. While the United States, tucked away on the North American continent, could easily afford to write off France as a postwar power, Britain regarded it as essential that its closest European neighbor be as strong as possible after the war to help balance a renascent Germany and increasingly powerful Soviet Union. Yet there also was no question that, in June 1943, Churchill needed the United States far more than he did France. The prime minister would later declare to de Gaulle: "Every time we must choose between Europe and the open sea, we shall always choose the open sea. Every time I must choose between you and Roosevelt, I shall always choose Roosevelt."

Swayed by Roosevelt's anti–de Gaulle arguments, Churchill, describing the general as "this vain and even malignant man," urged his cabinet to consider "whether we should not now eliminate de Gaulle as a political force." Cabinet members, strongly influenced by Anthony Eden, rejected the idea, declaring that "we would not only make him a national martyr but would find ourselves accused . . . of interfering improperly in French international affairs with a view to treating France as an Anglo-American protectorate." In 1940, the Foreign Office, under Lord Halifax, had taken the lead in opposing Churchill's recognition of de Gaulle; now, it was the Foreign Office, under Eden, that spearheaded the effort to shield the general from the wrath of both Churchill and Roosevelt.

ROOSEVELT'S ADAMANT opposition to de Gaulle and his movement was a source of frustration not only for the British but also for U.S. officials and military leaders in London and Algiers. It certainly made life more difficult for Eisenhower, who, through painful experience, now knew considerably more about the tangled complexity of European and North African politics than did FDR. In his memoirs, Eisenhower noted that Roosevelt referred to French North Africa and its inhabitants "in terms of orders, instructions, and compulsion. . . . He continued, perhaps subconsciously, to discuss local problems from the viewpoint of a conqueror. It would have been so much easier for us if we could have done the same!"

Perhaps the most outspoken American critic of Roosevelt's policy was Wallace Carroll, London's Office of War Information director, who claimed that the president's directives had resulted in a serious propaganda and political defeat for the United States. "It seemed," Carroll observed, "that we were showing a kind of arrogance, an attitude that denied the right of smaller and less fortunate nations to question American actions." David Bruce agreed, telling Gil Winant that preparations for the invasion of France, which were heavily dependent on information from the French underground, might be put in jeopardy if the man regarded by the resistance as its leader was shunned by the Americans and British.

For their part, OSS operatives, who worked closely with resistance members in the captive countries of Europe and knew what risks they were taking to help the Allies, had no patience for what they saw as Machiavellian political power games that "were being played at the expense of smaller nations and powerless people." Like a number of other American officials in London, they felt estranged from their superiors in Washington, who, safe and remote from the war's dangers, moved people around like pawns on a chessboard and issued orders without seeming to understand or care what their effects would be.

Gil Winant shared those concerns. While remaining "at all times the devoted servitor of the President," the ambassador also "saw the cost to the United States of its emotional attitude toward de Gaulle," Wallace Carroll noted. Even though the United States had no official ties with the Fighting French, Winant established a close informal relationship with de Gaulle, who, putting aside his waspishness for a moment, later praised the American as "a diplomat of great intelligence and feeling" and a "splendid ambassador." Winant played peacemaker on several occasions when disputes arose between the general and American officials in London and North Africa. He was well aware that, like it or not, de Gaulle would have a major role to play in liberated France.

In one of his many conversations with Carroll on the subject, Winant asked rhetorically: "Who is it who is saving our flyers when they bail out over France?" As he paced back and forth in his office, he answered his own question: "It's the people who recognize de Gaulle as their leader. Who gives us most of the intelligence we get from France? It's de Gaulle's men, isn't it? When we go into France, we will have to come to terms with de Gaulle. . . . There isn't anybody else who can take over the civil administration."

In midsummer 1943, Winant worked with Eden to try to persuade Churchill and Roosevelt to recognize the French Committee of National Liberation as the main governing body of North Africa and other liberated French colonies, as well as the sole voice of free France. The European governments-in-exile had all granted recognition to the committee, as had Canada, Australia, and South Africa; the Soviet Union was poised to do the same. Eisenhower and most members of Britain's Parliament had also advocated recognition. Winant joined the chorus, sending a note to FDR urging him to take official notice of the committee. Of the ambassador's message, Carroll said: "I do not think it increased his popularity in Washington, and it produced no notable effect." Winant himself told British officials that he "was in the dog kennel" for pushing for recognition. Roosevelt continued to resist all pressure, even when Churchill finally succumbed to it and told the president he might have to break with him over the issue: "I am reaching the point where it may be necessary for me to take this step so far as Great Britain and the Anglo-French interests . . . are concerned."

Finally, faced with the opposition of virtually every other country in the Great Alliance, FDR agreed in late August 1943 to a severely limited U.S. recognition of the French Committee. (On the same day, the British government issued its own, less restrained statement of recognition.) At the same time, however, the president refused to halt his efforts to get rid of de Gaulle, to the general's intense anger and resentment. FDR continued to try to boost the standing of Giraud, inviting him to the United States and receiving him with full honors at the White House. The campaign had no effect. In November, Giraud was forced out as the committee's co-chairman, and de Gaulle took full control.

OVERSHADOWED BY THE Sturm und Drang of the controversy over France, another captive European nation—Poland—also found itself at odds with its larger, more powerful allies. Until the Soviet Union was catapulted into the war in June 1941, Poland had contributed more to Britain's survival than any other declared ally. The two countries also had strong official ties: Britain, committed by treaty to defend Polish sovereignty and independence, had gone to war with Germany after it invaded Poland in September 1939.

But Germany was not the only country to attack the Poles that September. The Soviets, given carte blanche by Hitler under the Ribbentrop-Molotov pact to invade Poland from the east, occupied almost half of its territory and deported over a million Poles to labor and prison camps in Siberia and other remote reaches of the Soviet Union.

From the first days of his abrupt and reluctant alliance with the West, Stalin made clear he planned to retain the Polish territory he had taken in 1939 and hinted of his interest in controlling the rest of the country after the war. For its part, the Polish government-in-exile unsurprisingly opposed any Soviet designs on Poland's territory or independence. Although he sympathized with the Poles, Churchill needed Stalin far more, and he and Eden pressed Sikorski to sign a treaty with the Soviets in the summer of 1941 that left open the question of Poland's postwar borders. Eden, who later would express such deep concern about U.S. and British interference in France's internal affairs, told the Polish prime minister: "Whether you wish it or not, a treaty must be signed."

The reality was that while Britain's own political and military interests were inextricably tied to the future of France and the rest of Western Europe, the British had no such interests in Eastern European countries like Poland. Count Edward Raczynski, the Polish ambassador to Britain, pointed out that de Gaulle "could afford to irritate British . . . statesmen and tell them unpleasant truths to their faces. They might not like it, but they could not afford to abandon either him or France. However they could and did treat the Polish cause and that of the whole of eastern Europe as something secondary, not as a vital interest of their own, but as a debt of honour to be discharged, if possible without excessive risk or effort."

In early 1942, Stalin pressed Britain to sign a secret agreement recognizing Soviet claims to eastern Poland and the Baltic states. At first, Churchill rejected the idea, but under the strains of repeated British military defeats and the Russian leader's intensified demands for a second front, he decided to give in. "The increasing gravity of the war has led me to feel that the principles of the Atlantic Charter ought not to be construed so as to deny Russia the frontiers she occupied when Germany attacked her," the prime minister wrote to Roosevelt.

Although the United States initially opposed such a deal, Roosevelt changed his mind less than a year later. Poland had much less of a claim on U.S. loyalties and interests than on Britain's allegiance: there were no U.S.-Polish treaties to be concerned about, no U.S. debt to Polish pilots or troops for helping the country survive. To Roosevelt, who was intent on keeping Stalin happy, Poland was a peripheral problem. He told Eden in March 1943 that it was up to the Americans, Soviets, and British to decide Poland's borders; he, for one, had no intention of "go[ing] to the peace conference and bargain[ing] with Poland or the other small states." Poland was to be organized "in a way that will maintain the peace of the world." In other words, he would not stand in the way of Soviet demands.

For the two Western leaders, the alliance with Stalin posed a peculiar moral dilemma. Roosevelt and Churchill, the British military historian Max Hastings noted, "found it convenient, perhaps essential, to allow Stalin's citizens to bear a scale of human sacrifice which was necessary to destroy the Nazi armies, but which their own nations' sensibilities rendered them unwilling to accept." As a result, they traded "dependence upon one tyranny"—the Soviet Union—for "the destruction of another"—Nazi Germany.

In doing so, they traded away Poland's future.

14.

"A CAUL OF PRIVILEGE"

ONE DAY IN THE MIDDLE OF THE WAR, *TIME-LIFE* CORRESPON-
dent Mary Welsh strolled down Piccadilly holding an orange, a gift
from American friends who had just arrived in Britain. Her fellow
pedestrians stared at the orange in astonishment, reacting to it, she
later said, as if it were "a human head." More than two years had
passed since most Londoners had seen an orange, or for that matter, a
lemon or banana. By the end of the war, many British children, having
never set eyes on a banana or forgotten what they looked like, had no
idea how to eat one. Onions were another rare commodity, so scarce
they were offered as prizes in raffles.

Although London had taken on a cosmopolitan air, thanks to the
foreign exiles in temporary residence, it also had become increasingly
shabby and bedraggled. For most of its residents, austerity and deprivation were the norm. Severe shortages of food and consumer items
meant long hours of standing in queues for just about anything Londoners wanted to purchase, from drinking glasses to toothbrushes to
sewing needles. Spying a queue of about seventy people lined up outside one store, a man asked another bystander what they were waiting
to buy. "I don't suppose they know what they are queuing for," he was
told. "It is a hysteria with some people—whenever they see a queue,
they just join on the end." A London housewife remarked: "Many a
time we waited over an hour for just one pound of potatoes or half a
pound of liver."

Next to the war and politics, food was the most popular topic of conversation among the Britons Mary Welsh knew. "The whole island sounded like a club of dieting women," she observed, "the emphasis of chat being on the acquisition of nourishment other than that in potatoes and Brussels sprouts and cabbage." After the war, Theodora FitzGibbon, an artist's model living in Chelsea, wrote: "It is difficult to realize now that we were *always* hungry. There simply wasn't enough to eat." The novelist and foreign correspondent Derek Lambert, who was a teenager during the conflict, recalled how, for his mother, "every day was a fight to provide calories, vitamins, carbohydrates and warmth for my father and I. . . . We ate in the kitchen because there was not enough coal to light the fire and shivered in unison. My mother was left to fight and forage, to save and improvise, to cajole the butcher and berate the grocer." Faced with drastic reductions in coal supplies and electrical service, families went to bed early to keep warm; during the day, women pushing prams and carrying market baskets lined up at emergency coal dumps to try to obtain a few precious lumps.

For most Londoners, buying new clothes was just as difficult as obtaining enough food and fuel. Mary Welsh was proud of her foresight in acquiring several dozen pairs of stockings for herself and her English friends during a visit to New York in 1942, but she neglected to stockpile underwear. By 1944, her lack of undergarments had become "a crucial problem"; when her garter belt gave out, she was forced to resort to rubber bands to hold up her prized stockings. In a letter to her parents in May 1943, Janet Murrow described the drab, threadbare clothes worn by the onlookers at a Home Guard parade outside Buckingham Palace. "It's a case of summer wardrobes being almost nonexistent . . . so that old skirts are worn with old jackets that don't belong. It can make a crowd look sad despite smiling faces."

For many GIs just arrived in Britain, the contrast between the conditions at home and those at their new posting came as a severe shock. "I think it would be easier for me to tell you what wasn't rationed over here, except that I can't think of anything that isn't," an American lieutenant wrote to his mother. "For instance, they get two ounces of butter a *week*. Mom, you can put a whole week's ration on two slices of bread. Try it and then you can see what the British are down to. . . . Do you realize, Mom, that many people over here haven't been able to buy any new clothes since 1939? And they are lucky if they see one egg in a fortnight. . . . My impression in the short time that I have been here is that the Americans haven't shown much in the way of sacrifices to further the war effort, in comparison with the English."

As the young lieutenant indicated, the war was experienced in a profoundly different way in Britain than it was in America. While both countries endured rationing and the grief of losing hundreds of thousands of young men, the conflict remained remote for most people in the United States, causing far less deprivation and suffering than in Britain or occupied Europe. There was no bombing of the U.S. mainland, no civilian casualties, no destruction of millions of homes. Indeed, while the standard of living plummeted for the vast majority of Britons during the war, many if not most Americans lived better than ever before. "No war is 'good,'" British historian David Reynolds has remarked, "but America's war was about as good as one could get."

Thanks to the massive mobilization of industry, the American economy was booming, finally putting an end to the privations of the Great Depression. In 1940, more than 14 percent of the country's workforce was still unemployed; three years later, the number of unemployed had dropped to less than 2 percent. The annual income of Americans had risen by more than 50 percent, and many in the country were now earning wages beyond their wildest dreams just a few years earlier. Even with the rationing of certain food and other items, there were plenty of goods on which to spend money. Between 1939 and 1944, U.S. consumer spending on food increased by 8 percent and on clothing and shoes by 23 percent.

"There was money to burn, and it burned in a bright, gay flame," observed Eric Sevareid, who was appalled at what he saw as America's lack of willingness to sacrifice. "Fifth Avenue shops sold handkerchiefs embroidered with patriotic monograms for ten dollars apiece, newsreels pointed out the military motif in the latest fashions, resort hotels ran out of space. . . . The nation was encouraged to believe that it could produce its way to victory or buy its victory by the simple measure of writing a check. Life was easy and getting more prosperous every week, and nobody believed in death."

Rationing was not imposed in the United States until several months after Pearl Harbor. Hoping to avoid mandatory controls altogether, Roosevelt initially tried to persuade the American people to make voluntary cutbacks in their consumption of food and consumer goods on behalf of the war effort. While many Americans did what he asked, most did not. As a result, some goods became scarce, prices skyrocketed, and inflation set in. In April 1942, the president, declaring the need for "an equality of sacrifice," proposed higher taxes, wage and price controls, and comprehensive rationing.

Much less stringent than the controls in Britain, the U.S. rationing system, when finally introduced in the late spring of 1942, resulted in serious inconvenience rather than austerity. Eggs, which were almost nonexistent in Britain, became a meat substitute in America. Margarine took the place of butter, and when sugar was rationed, it was replaced by corn syrup and saccharin. Although severely restricted by gasoline and tire rationing, American motorists never had to give up their cars entirely, as most British car owners were forced to do. In Britain, a man could buy a new suit only once every two years, while in the United States, men could purchase all the suits they wanted, albeit now with cuffless trousers and narrower jacket lapels. Women's dresses were shorter and pleatless. As a result of iron and steel shortages, the production of a wide variety of U.S. consumer goods, from refrigerators to vacuum cleaners to washing machines, was halted for the duration.

While many U.S. citizens found these cutbacks galling, Americans who returned to their homeland after a stint in wartime Britain found it to be a paradise of abundance by comparison. Among the expatriates was Tania Long, a London-based correspondent for the *New York Times,* who came back to New York for a visit in late 1943. "Aside from the general atmosphere of freedom and plenty, the first thing a woman notices upon returning to this city is how dowdy she looks—and how well dressed every other woman is," Long wrote in the *Times.* "To a woman accustomed to shop in stores with half-empty shelves, a coupon book in one hand and a shopping bag in another, an expedition into one of New York's department stores is like a fabulous journey through the pages of 'The Arabian Nights.' There is so much of everything, and everything is so beautiful and enticing."

The same was true for food, she wrote. "Although New Yorkers grumble over the fact that they may no longer get steak and other luxuries in restaurants and at the butcher shops, a person just back from Britain has a hard time deciding what to choose from the many tempting dishes on a menu. . . . Alternating between cabbage, Brussels sprouts and spinach for two years, one forgets the existence of squash, fresh peas, corn, eggplant, and tomatoes." Her trip, Long said, had convinced her that "London and New York truly belong in different worlds. To attempt to draw a comparison between the two is almost as futile as it would be to try and compare the earth with Mars."

In the United States, unlike in Britain, most citizens never felt that their country's survival was at stake during the war and thus were less inclined to make the sacrifices for which the Roosevelt administration was calling. Frances Perkins would later note: "Most parts of the war didn't interest [Americans]. Sure, they wanted the boys to have everything and to win, but they still couldn't see why they couldn't have butter."

When the Roosevelt administration announced that because of the rubber shortage, girdles would no longer be manufactured, there was such a violent outcry from women across the country that the government capitulated, declaring that foundation garments were a vital part of a woman's wardrobe and would continue to be produced. "The American people, who were so willing and proud to give whatever was required of them in blood and sweat, were loudly reluctant to cut down on their normal consumption of red meat and gasoline and their use of such essentials as electric toasters and elastic girdles," Robert Sherwood observed. "More than any other people on earth, Americans were addicted to the principle that you can eat your cake and have it, which was entirely understandable, for Americans have been assured from the cradle that 'there is always more cake from where that came from.'" Exasperated by his countrymen's sense of detachment from the war, Roosevelt told Harold Ickes: "It really would be a good thing for us if a few German bombs could be dropped over here."

In Washington, members of Congress fought Roosevelt's call for higher taxes, tried to eviscerate the Office of Price Control, and insisted they were entitled to unlimited gasoline supplies because, they argued, their driving was essential for the war effort. "The very men to whom the whole country looks to set an example and to encourage the public to accept the personal inconvenience are doing exactly the reverse," Raymond Clapper, a noted Washington newspaper columnist, wrote in disgust. "Instead of trying to cooperate, they are cackling like wet hens to hold their special privileges."

Even with Washington's characteristic Southern lassitude swallowed up in the frantic busyness of a mushrooming bureaucracy, the American capital still seemed curiously untouched by the worldwide conflict. To Eric Sevareid, Washington "seemed to be no part of the war, however vast its work for war." Roosevelt thought that there was "less realization of the actual war effort in Washington D.C. than any-where else." The capital's lights still glowed brightly at night, and its social life was, if anything, considerably more hectic than it had been before December 1941. There were hunt breakfasts, lunches, tea dances, dinners—and, of course, an endless round of cocktail parties and dip-lomatic receptions. The society editor of the *Washington Post* justified such merrymaking by claiming it provided a venue for "influential people . . . to transact business, make contacts and otherwise advance the war effort."

Mary Lee Settle, a twenty-one-year-old former model from West Virginia who worked at the British embassy in Washington, was among those caught up in the capital's feverish social life. Settle, who was married to a British citizen, later remarked that the parties she at-tended in Washington reminded her of the depiction in Tolstoy's *War and Peace* of the socializing in St. Petersburg at the time of Napoleon's invasion of Russia. As was true of the aristocrats in the Russian capi-tal, the denizens of Washington were constantly talking about the war with no real knowledge or experience of what it was about. Both cities, she wrote, were unreal places, "where manners were important and gestures meant more than action, and war was someplace else."

AS THEY OBSERVED the United States trying to come to grips with ra-tioning and other wartime restraints, longtime American residents of London were unimpressed by what they viewed as their countrymen's paltry efforts to give up their comforts for the common good. After reading a self-congratulatory story in her hometown newspaper about townspeople going without meat one day a week, Janet Murrow fired off an irate letter to her parents. The article, she wrote, "makes one want to cry. So little apparently does our country understand the plight in which the rest of the world finds itself. What is one meatless day? . . . I should like to point out that the meat ration here almost never stretches further than two meals a week. Since Christmas, I have had five real eggs—the first in months—people sent them for Christmas presents. . . . Americans will never come to this fare, but they'll have to make an approach far greater than one meatless day a week if the rest of the world is going to regain its health."

In a letter to Harry Hopkins, Averell Harriman echoed Janet Murrow's criticism. "It was all very well when the British were suitors for our favor to expect them to make the biggest sacrifices while we were living off the fat of the land," Harriman wrote. "Now they look on us as partners, and when we ask them to make sacrifices, they expect us to do the same. . . . There are a lot of things on the American end which are hard for the British to understand."

Yet, throughout his stay in London, Harriman made sure that he and his daughter rarely, if ever, had to go without the large and small luxuries to which they had grown accustomed back home. At a time when liquor and wine were virtually unobtainable, for example, Harriman imported cases of Roederer champagne, Château Margaux, gin, and Canadian whiskey from the United States.

Kathleen Harriman, for her part, never had to experience the pinch of clothes rationing. In a February 1942 letter to her stepmother, she noted how she walked into the London showroom of the House of Worth and "bought a beautiful black evening [gown]—the model—because I can't stand having umpteen fittings." Later, she thanked her stepmother for sending a trunkful of new designer clothes from New York, exclaiming: "It's such fun to be in the state of not knowing which of three new dresses to wear in the evening. Even though there's an awful lot of talk about London looking out-of-the-elbows after three years of clothes rationing, I can't say I look forward to me joining that group. As it is, Averell kicks when I wear 'old clothes' in the country."

It was important for Kathleen to look her best because the social whirl in London for her and other well-connected Americans had never been more frenetic. The British capital was now the wartime base for some of the most noted names in American business and cultural life—investment bankers, heirs to great fortunes, company heads, playwrights, actors, movie directors, broadcast executives, newspaper and magazine publishers and editors—who joined the OSS and OWI or were given military desk jobs.

Despite its dilapidation, London was an undeniably exciting place to be during the war. Sergeant Robert Arbib, a New Yorker who first came there in 1942, was among the many American newcomers entranced by its exuberance and zest. "London was one of the most crowded cities in the world and one of the most fascinating," he recalled. "It swarmed with scores of different uniforms and it spoke in a hundred different tongues. On Saturday evenings it was almost bedlam. . . . I always thought of it as the hub of the world in those days. London was the Babel, the Metropolis, the Mecca. London was It."

In the year prior to D-Day, London contained, said Harrison Salisbury, "the fastest company I had ever seen." Many of the newcomers were friends and longtime associates of Harriman's from the East Coast—wealthy businessmen, bankers, and lawyers with Ivy League degrees and, in some cases, impeccable social pedigrees who had lived their lives, according to an observer, "with a feeling that the . . . century was about to be placed in their charge." Most of them were internationalist in outlook, having spent considerable time in England and on the Continent since childhood. Like Harriman, they had been active in urging the Roosevelt administration to aid Britain since before the United States entered the war.

Among the members of this elite was David Bruce, the son-in-law of the financier Andrew Mellon, who had been recruited by General William Donovan, the founder of the OSS, to head the intelligence agency's London headquarters. (For his London office, Donovan also hired, among others, Junius Morgan of the New York banking family; Lester Armour of the Chicago meatpacking Armours; and Raymond Guest, a champion polo player and horse breeder—thus earning OSS the sobriquet "Oh So Social.")

At first glance, the choice of Bruce, a Virginia patrician whose wealth came from his Mellon connections, was an odd one for such an important post: he had no experience in intelligence work or, for that matter, in serious, sustained employment of any kind. Viewed by the press and many of his peers as a charming dilettante, he had dabbled in investment banking, briefly served in the Foreign Service, and was elected to one term each in the Virginia and Maryland state legislatures. But he also had spent considerable time in London, including a stint during the Blitz as a representative of the American Red Cross, and had built up a daunting array of contacts in British society and government. Possessing "an abounding self-esteem and consciousness of superiority," the urbane Bruce was as at ease with British aristocrats and American generals as he was with exiled European leaders. He frequently invited members of all three groups to dinner or cocktails at White's, the most exclusive men's club in London, where no bottle of nonvintage wine was ever served and no woman ever allowed to enter. Like Harriman, Bruce managed to live exceedingly well in the British capital, filling his diary with accounts of the lavish meals he enjoyed, like the dinner at White's that included smoked salmon, lamb, Brussels sprouts, potatoes, prune tart, cocktails, a 1924 Château Margaux, and vintage port.

Another recruit to U.S. government service in London was John Hay "Jock" Whitney, the playboy prince of New York society, whose enormous family fortune had blessed him with an annual income of more than $1 million, as well as six homes, two private planes, a yacht, and a string of twenty polo ponies. Whitney, whose Green Tree Stables had produced some of America's finest racehorses and who had provided much of the financing for the movie *Gone With the Wind,* was now acting as a public information officer at the U.S. Eighth Air Force headquarters. He got the job, according to one source, because he was "one of the few available men who were awed neither by the sight of a newspaper reporter nor by the sound of a British accent." (Whitney's counterpart at U.S. naval headquarters in London was Barry Bingham, owner and publisher of the *Louisville Courier-Journal.*)

The grandson of John Hay, Abraham Lincoln's personal secretary and the secretary of state under Presidents William McKinley and Theodore Roosevelt, Whitney was well acquainted with London. In 1926, to celebrate the victory of one of his horses in a British race, he threw a party that according to the *New York Times* was "the most elaborate and costly party" seen in London in over a decade. During the war, he leased a spacious luxury apartment on Grosvenor Square, where he staged soirees renowned for their fine food and drink and beautiful female guests.

Enjoying the feminine companionship at Whitney's parties was, among others, William Paley, who, like many of his New York counterparts, saw the war as a way not only of serving his country but of exchanging the tedium of family and business obligations for the exhilaration of freewheeling London. After setting up Allied radio stations for the OWI in North Africa and Italy, the CBS chairman was assigned, with the rank of colonel, to Eisenhower's staff in the British capital as chief of psychological warfare broadcasting in Europe. He lived at Claridge's, where he had a personal valet and frequently dined on such delicacies as cold salmon, lobster, and fresh asparagus. Of the war, he would later remark that "life had never been so exciting and immediate and never would be again."

To his subordinates, Paley was noted more for his love of pleasure than for his devotion to hard work. For him, as for others, the romantic fatalism and hedonism of wartime London were particularly appealing. He could eat, drink, and have as many affairs as he liked, with very little chance that tomorrow, or anytime soon, he would die—since, like most of the other New York and Hollywood dignitaries in Britain, he never saw combat. In the eyes of many in the career U.S. military, Paley and the other former civilians were "bourbon whiskey colonels" with "cellophane commissions" ("you could see through them, but they kept the draft off").

There were, however, at least three prominent exceptions to the no-combat rule. James Stewart, who recently had won an Academy Award for his acting in *The Philadelphia Story,* was the commander of a U.S. bomber squadron, based near Norwich, that flew B-24s on missions over Germany. Stewart, who flew twenty missions himself, was awarded the Distinguished Flying Cross for his courage and coolness under fire. Another popular Hollywood star, Clark Gable, accompanied U.S. bomber crews on several raids for a short training film that he produced on aerial gunnery. On one mission, he was nearly killed when a German shell ripped through his plane.

Director William Wyler and his crew, meanwhile, flew five B-17 missions to France and Germany in mid-1943 while filming Wyler's famed documentary on the bomber *Memphis Belle.* "The guy had guts," *Memphis Belle*'s navigator said of the Hollywood director, who, before one mission, persuaded the pilot to break regulations and let him ride in the ball turret under the aircraft's belly during takeoff and landing—an extraordinarily dangerous maneuver—so that he could get film of the wheels and runway.

To Wyler's intense embarrassment, his Oscar-winning film *Mrs. Miniver* premiered in London while he was making *Memphis Belle.* The story of the experiences of an upper-middle-class family in the London suburbs at the time of the British evacuation at Dunkirk and the Blitz, *Mrs. Miniver* was America's top-grossing film in 1942 and a huge success in Britain the following year; Churchill, who loved it, called it "propaganda worth a hundred battleships." Wyler, who was intensely pro-British, had indeed meant the film as propaganda. "I was a warmonger," he said. "I was concerned about Americans being isolationists." But when he arrived in Britain and saw the reality of war—the flattened houses, malnourished people, shabby cities, and the horrific casualties among British and American bomber crews—he came to regard *Mrs. Miniver* as little more than a sugarcoated, idealized portrait of the conflict. It "only scratched the surface of war," he remarked. Years later, Wyler declared that, for him, the war, with all its horror and heroism, had been "an escape *into* reality."

APART FROM WYLER, Stewart, Gable, and a few others, the American notables in Britain lived in a walled-off world of cocktail parties and black-market restaurants, with virtually no idea of what life was like outside their comfortable cocoons. The London of these American newcomers was "unreal, a stage on which a play called 'the war' was running," observed Mary Lee Settle, the young West Virginian who had worked in the British embassy in Washington and who later spent a year as a WAAF on an RAF base in southwest England. "Even the uniforms they wore were like costumes—well-cut, no grease marks, no ground-in dirt, no fading. . . . Most of them had no experience of the strictures we lived by . . . no inkling of what it was like to live on rationing or of scrounging unrationed food, of standing in queues hour after hour, gray-faced with fatigue."

When Britain entered the war, Settle and her husband were living in New York, where she worked as a model and he as an advertising executive. He immediately enlisted in the Canadian forces, and she sought to join the WAAF. "We were young and zealous, and we knew we were right," she later wrote. "For the first time in our lives, we thought about something beyond ourselves and for the common good." After more than a year of fighting red tape, she finally made it to England and became a radio operator at an RAF base in the Cotswolds, transmitting orders and messages between flight controllers and pilots.

As an aircraft woman 2nd class, Settle was part of what the British call the other ranks (enlisted men and women) and, as such, was exposed to the "cold, brutal division" between officers and those subordinate to them, most of whom came from the working class. "It was my first glimpse of the [class] stratification, almost Chinese in its complication and formality, which covered everything from a hairdo to a state of health . . . and by which each Englishman holds himself apart from his fellows," she noted. Like her counterparts, Settle lived a harsh, austere life, sleeping on a straw mattress in a Nissen hut heated by a stove barely warm to the touch, hauling coal, cleaning floors, and subsisting on a spartan diet that left her perpetually hungry and dreaming of food.

After a year of exposure over her headset to a constant buzzing caused by the German jamming of airwaves, Settle developed what doctors called "signals shock" and could no longer function efficiently at her job. Handed a medical discharge, she was hired as an OWI writer in London, where she found herself thrust into an Alice-in-Wonderland world of luxury and comfort, "as heady as champagne," for which she was not prepared. Like most American civilians working in a professional capacity in war zones, she was given a temporary officer's rank (in her case, major) and thus had access to the wondrous U.S. military post exchanges, where one could buy American cigarettes, chocolate, razor blades, fruit juice, soap, toothpaste, shaving cream, handkerchiefs, and dozens of other consumer items that were to be found nowhere else in Britain. She no longer had to endure the harshness of British cigarettes, which in any case were so scarce that when she smoked one and the butt became too short to hold in her fingers, she used a pin to keep it steady while she eked out the last few precious puffs.

During the day, Settle, who was to become a noted novelist after the war, lived and worked in "a caul of privilege" that her OWI co-workers and the other Americans with whom she associated seemed to take for granted. At night, she returned to the room she rented in a threadbare, fifth-floor Kensington walk-up, where her landlady regarded the American candy bars she brought home from the PX as a precious treat and sliced them into tiny pieces, serving them on china plates for afternoon tea.

To her co-workers, the pretty, auburn-haired Settle was as much of an oddity as they were to her. "I had had the experience and directly touched the war they had come to share," she recalled. "What I had learned to take for granted—service in the forces—was, to them, a fascination. It made them seem somehow younger than I was." When she first arrived at OWI, the actors Burgess Meredith and Paul Douglas, who were making U.S. government films in London, decided that, having lived on British rations for so long, she was too thin and in desperate need of a good meal. Treating her "as if I were bone china," they escorted Settle to a black-market restaurant with mahogany paneling, leather banquettes, damask napkins, and the overpowering smell of food. The actors insisted on ordering for her: a two-inch-thick lamb chop, green beans, and a baked potato slathered with a two-week ration of butter. The rich aromas of the meat and butter were too much for Settle. She excused herself and barely made it to the ladies' room before she became violently ill.

THERE WAS ANOTHER young woman in London, however, who had come to accept such luxuries as a matter of course. Thanks to the largesse of Averell Harriman and other wealthy American friends, Pamela Churchill had become one of the capital's leading hostesses, throwing sparkling dinner parties featuring such prized items as oysters, salmon, steaks, and whiskey. "We were really sort of puritanical in England about rationing," recalled John Colville. "But if you dined with Pamela, you would have a five- or six-course dinner . . . and foods you didn't ordinarily see. My guess is that all of us around the table were sort of smirking and saying that Averell was taking good care of his girlfriend." Years later, Pamela would observe: "It was a terrible war, but if you were the right age . . . and in the right place, it was spectacular."

In April 1942, Pamela, Harriman, and his daughter had moved out of the Dorchester Hotel and into a spacious flat in the same Grosvenor Square building where Gil Winant lived. It soon became apparent that the prime minister's daughter-in-law was, in fact, living with Roosevelt's Lend-Lease representative. "They were caught out and people were a bit upset because he had a wife," said an acquaintance of Pamela's. "Living with him took it over the line. It wasn't discreet. . . . We thought she was being very stupid and naughty."

When Randolph Churchill came home on leave and discovered the affair, he exploded with rage. His anger stemmed not so much from jealousy, friends said, but from a sense of having been betrayed by Harriman, whom he had befriended in Cairo at his father's request. Randolph bitterly accused his parents of condoning adultery "beneath their own roof" at Chequers and doing it solely because of the importance of Harriman and the Americans to Britain. "He used terrible language and created a rift that never healed," said Alastair Forbes, a friend of both Randolph and Mary Churchill's. "He said they must have known, and they said they didn't know." According to Pamela, Randolph, from whom she was now estranged, threatened at one point to make her affair with Harriman public, a situation "that might do a lot of harm to people in high places." To mollify him, she agreed "to find a place of my own in the country . . . and not see too much of his parents."*

Another problem for the couple was Marie Harriman's discovery of their relationship. A worldly woman who was involved with the band-leader Eddy Duchin, Marie was less bothered by the affair itself than by the fact that others knew about it. "Keep your affairs clean and out of the papers," she cabled her husband, "or you will be facing the most costly divorce in the history of the republic." Painfully aware that a split from Marie would not only put a serious dent in his net worth but ruin his budding diplomatic career, Harriman agreed to stop see-ing Pamela—a promise on which he promptly reneged. "Ave couldn't marry her," said a friend, "but he didn't want to give her up."

Pamela moved out of the Harrimans' apartment and into a luxury flat at 49 Grosvenor Square, around the corner from the Harrimans' and across the street from the Connaught Hotel. In addition to paying for the apartment, her lover provided her with a car and gasoline ration and gave her a yearly allowance of £3,000, a princely amount at the time. The only British citizen to take up residence in her building, Pamela had become thoroughly Americanized. Most of her friends and acquaintances were now American; on the bookshelf in her draw-ing room were photographs of Harriman, Eisenhower, Harry Hop-kins, and Roosevelt, who had sent the portrait of himself to her. In her letter of thanks, she told FDR: "My son is not yet old enough to dis-tinguish between [the photos of] you and Winston. I am afraid he calls both of you Grandpapa." She spent much of her time entertain-ing newly arrived American journalists, generals, and government officials—hosting dinners for them, taking them around town, and, in general, introducing them to London. Janet Murrow, who attended one of Pamela's dinners, felt very much out of place. "Unless you were important in some way, you weren't very welcome there," she noted.

In the fall of 1943, Pamela volunteered to work at the Churchill Club, an exclusive gathering place for university-educated American

---

* The affair between Pamela and Harriman rankled Randolph Churchill for years. At a Washington dinner party in 1961, he noted: "Averell Harriman is the man who cuck-olded me when I was away in the Army—cuckolded me in the Prime Minister's very house." The hostess of the party asked: "But, Randolph, how many men did you cuckold when you were away in the Army?" Churchill replied: "Perhaps—but never in the house of a Prime Minister" (Schlesinger, p. 139).

and Canadian officers and enlisted men in Ashburnam House, a stately old mansion behind Westminster Abbey. It was a spot, said the art historian Kenneth Clark, where high-profile Americans "could escape from the noisy bonhomie of army life" to learn about English culture. There were, indeed, plenty of concerts, lectures, and dramatic readings, but there also was considerable martini-fueled partying by Americans, many of whom were generals and other high-ranking officers. "The information you could pick up there!" marveled *Time-Life* correspondent Bill Walton. "Rank was abandoned at the door, and the room would be filled with generals, captains and majors, all of whom were mad for Pamela."

Dwight Eisenhower might have sworn off an active social life in London, but most of his subordinates declined to follow his example. Eric Sevareid observed in his journal that many high-ranking American officers "don't want this war to end. They are making more money, living better, more comfortable, more glamorous lives than they ever did at home in peacetime." In the novel *The Americanization of Emily*, whose author served as a U.S. admiral's aide in London during the war, a British female military driver says ruefully: "The war's just a long night out of town to the [Americans] I meet."

According to Kay Summersby, the top brass of the Air Force was particularly partial to having a good time. While Eisenhower relaxed at his modest country cottage outside London by playing bridge or reading Western pulp novels, the staff of General Carl "Tooey" Spaatz, commander of the Eighth Air Force, threw lavish parties in the general's suite at Claridge's. "The Air Force had the reputation of being the glamorous service and [Spaatz's] staff worked hard at maintaining that reputation," Summersby observed. Walking into the Eighth Air Force headquarters at the end of the day, she said, was like "entering a crowded cocktail lounge—lots of people, lots of smoke, lots of chatter, lots of flirtations."

AS ONE U.S. JOURNALIST noted, flirtations and casual affairs (and some that were not so casual) were rife among Americans in wartime London: "It was the mood of the time. . . . Most American men who came were married but had girlfriends, and nobody cared." Eisenhower himself had a close personal relationship with Summersby, although whether it was a full-fledged affair is still murky. When

General James Gavin, commander of the 82nd Airborne, asked an American journalist if the gossip about a liaison between Eisenhower and Summersby was true, the correspondent replied: "Well, I have never before seen a chauffeur get out of a car and kiss the general good morning when he comes from his office." Years afterward, Summersby recalled: "The war was an irresistible catalyst. It overwhelmed everything, forced relationships like a hothouse, so that in a matter of days one would achieve a closeness with someone that would have taken months to develop in peacetime."

Gavin himself had a fling with *Life* photojournalist Margaret Bourke-White. General Robert McClure, the Allied Supreme Headquarters's chief of information and censorship, had an affair with Mary Welsh, who was also juggling her Australian journalist husband, along with the writer Irwin Shaw, in London to work on Army propaganda films, and, starting in 1944, Ernest Hemingway. Eisenhower's personal aide, Harry Butcher, was involved with an English Red Cross worker, whom he married after the war. David Bruce married Evangeline Bell, a twenty-five-year-old Anglo-American who worked for him at the OSS, after divorcing his first wife in 1945. The former newspaper editor Herbert Agar, in London as Winant's assistant, also got a divorce, in order to marry Barbie Wallace, the widowed daughter of the famed British architect Edwin Lutyens. William Paley took up with Edwina Mountbatten, whose husband, Lord Mountbatten, served as supreme Allied commander in Southeast Asia at the time. Beatrice Eden, the wife of the British foreign secretary, embarked on a liaison with C. D. Jackson, a former Time Inc. executive on Eisenhower's staff. After the liberation of Paris in 1944, she left her husband to live with Jackson in the French capital, and when the war ended, moved to New York to be with him, although the two never married.

British commanders, for their part, observed this game of musical beds with considerable bemusement. "We did not have the same primeval need to prove our manhood that the Americans did," sniffed one British officer, although a fair number of his colleagues eventually succumbed to temptation as well.

Pamela Churchill had her own share of flings with well-connected Americans. "In my life," she later observed, "I have always lived with men, for men, through men." Neither she nor Harriman was faithful to each other, and she became involved with, among others, Jock Whitney and General Frederick Anderson, the thirty-seven-year-old head of the Eighth Air Force's Bomber Command. According to Bill Walton, a good friend of Pamela's, the prime minister knew about the affair with Anderson and "would question her on . . . [his] position on certain key bombing strategies." She in turn would pass on to Churchill any information that she gleaned from the general. Lord Beaverbrook invited the couple for weekends at Cherkley, where he pumped Anderson for information.

Another of Pamela's besotted admirers was Air Chief Marshal Sir Charles Portal, the head of the British air staff. He wrote long letters to her late in the war from the conferences at Yalta and Potsdam, addressing her as "DP" ("Darling Pamela") and declaring "I think of you many times a day and wish I could be with you." Notwithstanding the ardor of Portal's letters, the relationship was an innocent one, Pamela later said. "A lot of people were . . . in love with me who I didn't really give the time of day to."

TWO MONTHS AFTER the Churchill Club opened, Harriman dropped out of Pamela's life, reluctantly succumbing to intense pressure from Roosevelt and Hopkins to become U.S. ambassador to the Soviet Union. He did not want the job. Having undermined both Winant and the two previous American ambassadors in Moscow, Harriman knew how precarious and difficult an ambassador's position could be, especially in the Soviet capital.

In his dealings with the Soviet government, Harriman had excluded the retired admiral William Standley, who had replaced Laurence Steinhardt as the American envoy, just as he had shut out Steinhardt. Standley, who strongly believed that America should stand up to Soviet bullying, was irritated that Harriman, like other officials whom Roosevelt sent to Moscow to confer with Stalin, "follow[ed] the Rooseveltian policy: Do not antagonize the Russians [and] give them everything they want." Years later, Harriman acknowledged that Standley, whom he and Roosevelt basically treated as an errand boy, had a point. "A large number of important people in the West, including the Prime Minister and the President, as well as some lesser lights, had the idea that they knew how to get along with Stalin," he wrote. "I confess that I was not entirely immune to that infectious idea."

By mid-1943, Standley had had enough. At a press conference for American correspondents in Moscow, he accused the Soviet government of bad faith, specifically for concealing from its people the fact that virtually all of the Soviets' military resources came from the United States and Britain. After an international furor erupted over his remarks, he resigned his post.

Although Harriman was firmly convinced of his ability to succeed in Moscow where the others had failed, he was hesitant to leave London. His reluctance stemmed not so much from leaving Pamela, although he was fond of her, but from the fact that he no longer would be at the center of Allied action. He would lose the niche he had so painstakingly carved out for himself as conduit and buffer between Roosevelt, Stalin, and Churchill. "I am sure I can be of more use to you and the war in London than to remain in Moscow as glorified communications officer," he wrote the president. When Roosevelt argued that the Moscow assignment was far more important, Harriman gave in, but not before insisting that if he took the job, he must have authority over all American missions and delegations in Moscow—an attempt to prevent others from doing to him what he had done to Winant and to his own predecessors in Moscow. Roosevelt agreed, and in September 1943, Harriman and his daughter left for the Soviet capital.

He did not let Pamela know until the last minute that he was going. "That was a dark day," she recalled. "When he left, it was a big, big blow." Though she was upset by his sudden departure, it did not take her long to recover. Pamela claimed after the war that she had never thought of her relationship with Harriman as anything more than a temporary romance. "All through the war years," she said, "it never occurred to me that Averell and I would ever get married. We never even discussed it. We never thought of it."

The relationship had been fun while it lasted, and it had made her financially secure: while in Moscow, Harriman continued to pay for her apartment and give her an allowance. Just as important, perhaps, his absence cleared the way for her passionate involvement with the man she later would call the love of her life—Edward R. Murrow. When Harriman left, she said, "I cried on Ed's shoulder and ended up in bed with Ed."

TWO YEARS EARLIER, thanks to Kathleen Harriman, Pamela had been introduced to Murrow and other American journalists in London and had become part of their social circle. "I think she decided when Averell disappeared that Ed was the person she wanted," Janet Murrow remarked later. On his part, there apparently was very little hesitation. "Ed was knocked off his feet by this absolutely glorious and desirable young woman," said CBS correspondent Charles Collingwood, who had some trouble keeping his own feet under him in Pamela's presence. "Her connections impressed him. But it wasn't for any of those self-seeking reasons that he was attracted. She just bowled him over."

For both Pamela and the thirty-five-year-old Murrow, it was a startling relationship. Neither wealthy nor a man about town like most of her previous conquests, he was serious, idealistic, often withdrawn, and inclined to frequent bouts of depression. As *Scribner's* magazine put it, Murrow wrapped "his privacy around him like a protective covering." For years, his work had been at the center of his existence. Although the lean, handsome broadcaster had been pursued by more than a few women in the past, he had not previously succumbed. Somewhat naive and shy where women were concerned, he had been a rare phenomenon of virtue in live-and-let-live London.

But his once close marriage to Janet was showing signs of serious fraying; working to the point of exhaustion, he had largely shut her out of his life since before the war began. "Ed very curt and uninterested in seeing me," she wrote in her diary in March 1938. "I must be patient. . . . He has gotten out of the habit of seeing me. But it does hurt so much to call him up and have him say, 'Is it anything important? If not, hang up.' . . . Treats me like a stranger who's bothering him."

At one point early in the Blitz, Murrow encouraged Janet to rent a house in the country, where she could live safely; he and his friends would join her on weekends. She went along with this arrangement for a while, but the men rarely showed up. "They didn't want to leave the excitement of London," she later said. She remarked in her diary: "I hate seeing Ed only at parties and with other people." Later she wrote: "Gloomy, gloomy day by myself in the country. Couldn't feel happy about this life at all. . . . Hate it." She finally gave up the house.

Lonely and depressed, she turned for comfort to Philip Jordan, a well-known correspondent for London's *News Chronicle* and a good friend of the Murrows', who was described by Eric Sevareid as "a lovely, suave, gentlemanly man." Janet and Jordan fell in love, but their affair was short-lived, ending when he was sent by his paper to

Moscow in July 1941. Devastated by his departure, Janet wrote, "I long for him more than I could have believed."

It's not clear whether Murrow ever knew about his wife's liaison with Jordan, but Janet certainly was aware of his affair with Pamela. Much of London, it seemed, knew about it. After evenings out with friends, the couple occasionally spent the night at her apartment or a flat that CBS rented for traveling correspondents. Pamela often accompanied Murrow late at night to Broadcasting House and sat with him in the studio while he delivered his broadcasts. "I know they used to go out into the country for walks," Janet said after the war. "She always left something from those trips—once it was a book of poems which had her name in it. Another time it was one of Pamela's gloves in one of Ed's pockets."

Although infatuated with the prime minister's daughter-in-law, Murrow didn't indulge her the way her other lovers did. Revealing his conflicted feelings about wealth and social status, he seemed attracted by her aristocratic background and luxurious lifestyle while at the same time denigrating them. "Ed was very much full of complexes," Pamela recalled. "He was always happy to remind you that . . . he only had hand-me-down clothes" while growing up. "He had a chip on his shoulder and was conscious that everything he had, and had done, was through his own making and by his own grit."

Murrow spoke disparagingly of the pampered lives led by Pamela and Harriman, whom he regarded as a calculating opportunist. "Averell," said Pamela, "was everything that Ed thought he didn't like—somebody born to wealth." During the previous two years, the two men also had clashed over a number of political issues, including the controversy surrounding France and de Gaulle. Harriman had accused Murrow of being "a stooge for the Free French," while Murrow charged Harriman with being pro-Vichy.

As Pamela later remembered it, Murrow told her: "You're spoiled. Everything is easy for you. You were too much adored at too tender an age, and you don't understand what real life is." Among her faults, he said, was her obliviousness to the hardships afflicting others less fortunate. When he showed up at her apartment one day and discovered an aide to his rival, General Anderson, dropping off a carton of steaks, he was furious. While his anger at her was certainly fueled by jealousy, he explained it away by telling her it was highly inappropriate for her to accept goods paid for by U.S. taxpayers and meant for American troops.

Although annoyed by his criticisms, Pamela loved the fact that Murrow talked to her about weighty political and social issues, argued with her about ideas, and treated her as an intellectual equal rather than just a bedmate. "He was totally different from anybody I'd ever met," she said. "He fascinated me, and I fascinated him, obviously." She began pressing him hard to divorce Janet and marry her. He was tempted, although such a decision would have gone against everything he had been brought up to believe. "He loved Janet very, very much," said a friend. "But he wanted Pam."

For Murrow, as for others in London, it was an exceedingly complicated time.

"A CHASE PILOT—FIRST, LAST, AND ALWAYS"

WHILE MOST OF AMERICA'S GILDED ELITE IN LONDON MERELY played at war, one of the group's best-known members, Tommy Hitchcock, helped determine its outcome. Without Hitchcock, America's bombing campaign against Germany might well have failed, and D-Day might have been postponed or even scrubbed. And without Gil Winant, Tommy Hitchcock probably would never have come to London.

Hitchcock, it seemed, was the kind of man other people wanted to be. Wealthy businessmen like Averell Harriman and Jock Whitney idolized him. David Bruce called him the only perfect man he had ever met. F. Scott Fitzgerald, who modeled characters in his two best-known novels on Hitchcock, wrote that he was high "in my pantheon of heroes."

Before the war, Tommy Hitchcock had been the most renowned polo player in America and, arguably, the world. An international celebrity from young adulthood, he was largely responsible for turning polo into one of America's most popular spectator sports in the 1920s and 1930s. Indeed, Hitchcock was to polo what Babe Ruth was to baseball and Bobby Jones was to golf, bringing energy and excitement to the game and, according to the *New York Times,* "firing the American imagination" like no other polo player in history.

Hitchcock's marriage to a Mellon family heiress in 1928 was covered as if he were royalty. Wherever he went, he was besieged by throngs of admirers. When he arrived at a polo match, a camel's hair coat draped over his shoulders, crowds surged around him and people applauded wildly. "There was a sort of godlike worship for Daddy," his eldest daughter, Louise, remembered. "Mummy said it was kind of un-healthy."

Polo—a difficult, dangerous, and extremely expensive sport that originated in Persia before the birth of Christ—was introduced to the United States from Britain in 1876. It quickly became the favorite pas-time of a number of wealthy horsemen across the country. But it wasn't until Tommy Hitchcock got into the game that newspapers covered it as a sport of mass appeal and tens of thousands of spectators flocked to Long Island, the mecca of American polo, for international championship matches between the United States and its two main competitors—Britain and Argentina.

In 1924, the Prince of Wales, a polo player himself, was among the 45,000 people in the stands at Long Island's Meadow Brook Club to watch Hitchcock and the rest of the American team take on the British. A few years earlier, Hitchcock had played against Britain's team in London, with George V and Winston Churchill, another polo player, in the audience. The Americans won in two straight games, thanks in large part to Hitchcock, who scored five goals in the first game, more than all the members of the British team combined. "Most U.S. citizens never saw a game of polo," *Time* magazine wrote in 1944, "but people who got no closer to one than the [newspaper] rotogravure sections knew that Tommy Hitchcock played it."

Known simply as "Tommy" to his legions of fans, the stocky, sandy-haired Hitchcock was a whirling dervish on the polo field, wielding his mallet with violent force and driving the ball astonishing distances. "Sometimes he did things on the field that simply made you wonder," remarked a fellow player. Soft-spoken and generous to other players away from the game, he was noted for his unrelenting aggressiveness while playing it, often charging straight at an opponent and pulling up just a split second before a collision. "He didn't have a nerve in his body," one player observed. Another said simply: "There was no player like him—ever."

F. Scott Fitzgerald's two Hitchcock-inspired characters were Tom Buchanan in *The Great Gatsby* and Tommy Barban in *Tender Is the Night*. Each reflected different facets of the novelist's love-hate-envy relationship with the rich and powerful. From all accounts, Hitchcock had little in common with the cruel, amoral Buchanan except for physical appearance ("always leaning aggressively forward") and a sense of relentless force. The depiction of Barban more closely resembled the polo star. "Tommy Barban was a ruler," Fitzgerald wrote. "Tommy was a hero. . . . As a rule he drank little; courage was his game and his companions were always afraid of him."

The supremely self-confident Hitchcock was aloof, reserved, and fiercely competitive, with a slight whiff of danger about him. Unlike Harriman, Whitney, and others in the upper-class society circles in which he moved, he was not a "clubbable" man. He did not join private clubs or other organizations for their social advantages nor did he allow many people to get close to him. One prominent exception was Winant, who had known Hitchcock since the younger man's school days at St. Paul's, where Winant had been one of his teachers.

The son of a wealthy New York sportsman who was an avid polo player himself, Hitchcock grew up on his family's estates in Long Island and Aiken, South Carolina. At St. Paul's, he was one of the many students who crowded into the room of their popular history teacher at night to talk about Lincoln, Jefferson, and Winant's other heroes. Hitchcock greatly admired Winant's idealism and passion for social reform, and as president of the school's sixth form (senior class), helped him in his successful effort to disband the school's secret societies, whose members were known for their undisciplined behavior and sometimes cruel treatment of other students.

In early 1917, a few months before the United States entered World War I, Hitchcock, then seventeen, told the twenty-six-year-old Winant of his plans to leave school early and join the Lafayette Escadrille in France. He knew that Winant was planning to enlist as a pilot, too, as soon as America joined the fray, but, impatient to get into the war, Hitchcock was unwilling to wait that long. With the help of former president Theodore Roosevelt, a family friend, who wrote a letter persuading French officials to permit the underage schoolboy to enlist, Hitchcock became the youngest American to win a pilot's commission during the conflict.

As aggressive in the air as he was on the polo field, he shot down two German planes (winning a Croix de Guerre) before being downed himself inside German territory on March 6, 1918. Badly wounded, he spent several months in a prisoner of war camp, where his two main thoughts, he later said, were of food and escape. Late that summer, while being taken by train to another camp, Hitchcock stole a map from a sleeping guard and leaped from the train. Escaping detection, he hiked nearly a hundred miles to neutral Switzerland. He was not yet nineteen.

For Hitchcock, combat flying was the ultimate thrill. "Polo is exciting," he said, "but you can't compare it to flying in wartime. That's the best sport in the world." When the war ended in November 1918, he went to Harvard, playing polo in his spare time. On the field, a friend noted, "he was a chase pilot—first, last, and always." Even at the height of his career (which lasted some twenty years), he never took the pride in his polo prowess that he did in flying and in his later accomplishments as an investment banker. On the morning of one key international match, he spent several hours before the contest calmly discussing the philosopher Nietzsche with a friend, who asked incredulously, "How can you sit there and talk about philosophy on a day like this?" Hitchcock shrugged. "Why not?" he replied. "It's just a game."

In the early 1930s, Hitchcock became a partner in the investment banking firm Lehman Brothers and brokered a number of key deals, including the purchase of one of the country's leading shipping companies. Unlike Winant and many of his Wall Street associates, he was a fervent isolationist as Europe drew closer to war in the late 1930s. Having seen the carnage of the previous world war, he abhorred the thought of another and believed that America should stay as far away from the conflict as possible.

But as soon as the United States entered the war, the forty-one-year-old Hitchcock volunteered his services as a fighter pilot to General Hap Arnold, chief of staff of the U.S. Army Air Forces. Despite his fame and the fact that he "knew more people than God," the Air Force turned him down, telling him that he could have practically any Washington desk job he wanted but that he was too old to fly again in combat.

Angry and frustrated, he was rescued by Gil Winant, who was in Washington for consultations with Roosevelt. If he couldn't fly, Winant said, why didn't he come to London as assistant U.S. military attaché, to act as liaison between the Eighth Air Force and the RAF's Fighter Command? At least, he would be in a place where there was real fighting, instead of being mired in the bureaucratic combat of Washington. And if he could help persuade the two air forces to work together, he would be performing a real service. Without hesitation, Hitchcock accepted the job.

WHEN HE ARRIVED in London in the late spring of 1942, Tommy Hitchcock found that the glory days of fighter planes and pilots were already considered a thing of the past. Two years before, hundreds of doughty little Hurricanes and Spitfires had saved England by winning the Battle of Britain. Now, with the Allies going on the offensive against Germany in the air, the spotlight had switched to the heavy bombers—the U.S. Flying Fortresses (B-17s) and Liberators (B-24s) and the British Wellingtons and Lancasters.

Even before the war began, the chiefs of both countries' air forces were convinced that strategic bombing—destroying an enemy's war-making ability by striking at its industrial base, communications, and civilian morale—could win a conflict virtually by itself, making ground battles unnecessary and saving hundreds of thousands, even millions, of lives. With memories of the World War I bloodbath in France still fresh, such a theory had immense appeal for the government leaders and people of Britain and the United States. "There is one thing that will bring [Hitler] down, and that is an absolutely devastating, exterminating attack by very heavy bombers from this country upon the Nazi homeland," Winston Churchill declared.

In the spring of 1940, RAF bombers began attacking factories and other targets in the Ruhr and Rhineland, Germany's industrial heartland. The results of the daylight raids hardly supported the RAF's grandiose promises: the bombings did little serious damage, and the destruction of aircraft and crews was staggering. To reduce the losses, Bomber Command switched to nighttime raids, which made precision bombing of industrial targets impossible. Conceding defeat in its effort to smash Germany's industrial might, the RAF dramatically shifted its strategy: from then on, it would bomb German cities, with the primary aim of shattering civilian morale. Although Churchill previously had declared that Britain would never deliberately bomb non-combatants, he saw no other way of striking directly at Germany and reluctantly approved the RAF's new and very controversial approach.

Keeping tabs on Britain's ragged bombing effort, Hap Arnold and his associates were convinced that, thanks to superlative American technology and aircraft, they could succeed where the RAF had failed.

In the process, they hoped to prove what they had long believed: that airpower was far superior to any other armed force.

Unlike their Army and Navy counterparts, Arnold and his men were true pioneers in a service barely out of its infancy. Only thirty-eight years had elapsed since Orville and Wilbur Wright first flew over the sandy beaches of Kitty Hawk, North Carolina. Arnold himself had taken flying lessons from the Wright brothers and had gone on to become one of America's first four military pilots. His chief of staff, General Carl "Tooey" Spaatz, had been a combat pilot in France during World War I, the first major conflict that saw the use of aircraft. Attached to the Army, the fledging American air force played a relatively minor role in that war, however, and when Arnold took over as its chief in 1938, it was still under Army control.

Although Arnold was given considerable autonomy by George Marshall and was regarded as a full member of the U.S. Joint Chiefs of Staff and the U.S.-British Combined Chiefs of Staff, he waged a relentless campaign to prove the superior merit of his service and thus win its formal independence, making it equal in status and power to the Army and Navy. A driven, supremely impatient man, he was noted for his violent temper and savage tirades aimed at his subordinates. A colonel subjected to one of Arnold's harangues collapsed and died of a massive heart attack in front of him. Arnold himself would suffer four heart attacks before the war was over.

When the British failed in their effort at pinpoint bombing, Arnold and his men saw a golden opportunity for their own bombers, thanks in large part to a revolutionary technological development called the Norden bombsight. An extremely complex instrument, the bombsight supposedly made it possible for B-17 and B-24 bombardiers to hit industrial targets with surgical precision, even from heights of twenty thousand feet and higher. According to the theory developed by the Air Force brass, the bombers, particularly the rugged, heavily armed Flying Fortresses, would be virtually unstoppable, flying too high and too fast for effective retaliation by enemy fighter aircraft and ground gunners. As a result, there would be no need to develop a long-range fighter escort plane to protect the bombers as they flew to their targets and back. "We just closed our minds to [long-range escorts]," General Laurence S. Kuter, a deputy to Arnold, said after the war. "We couldn't be stopped. The bomber was invincible."

The Air Force higher-ups were so convinced that their theories would work that they failed to subject them to rigorous tests or take into account actual combat conditions before putting them into effect in the skies over Europe. Practice bombing runs, for example, were flown in dry, cloudless weather in Arizona, where bombardiers had perfect visibility, plenty of time for the difficult mathematical calculations required to use the Norden bombsight, and no enemy fire to distract them. No one at Air Force headquarters in Washington showed much awareness of the fact that the weather over Northern Europe bore almost no resemblance to that of Arizona; heavy clouds shrouded the Continent much of the year, making visual bombing, especially from high altitudes, virtually impossible. Nor did there seem to be any real acknowledgment that German technology was also quite sophisticated, allowing the Luftwaffe to detect the approach of enemy bombers well in advance and send up swarms of enemy fighters to meet them.

To America's bomber barons, "the important thing . . . was to establish a presence, to prove a doctrine, to stake out a position in public consciousness," Harrison Salisbury later wrote. "If this cost the lives of many fine young men and inflicted no really serious damage on Germany's fighting capability, that was too bad."

As it turned out, virtually every major theory espoused by Arnold and his subordinates proved to be wrong when put into practice in what became the most protracted campaign of World War II. As Salisbury indicated, tens of thousands of young American crewmen would die as a result, and many others would suffer serious injuries— "pawns," according to an official Air Force historian, "in a great experiment being tried by the Army Air Forces."

ON FEBRUARY 4, 1942, less than two months after Pearl Harbor, seven U.S. Army Air Forces officers left Washington for London to begin the hugely daunting task of building an entire air force from scratch on British soil. Although American industry was finally mobilizing to build bombers and fighter planes en masse, only a trickle had come off the production line thus far, and the number of trained pilots and crew members was just as minimal. It would be more than a year, Hap Arnold had been told by his planners, before the Air Force had enough planes and men to mount an all-out bombing assault on targets in German-occupied Europe. But with Japan on the march in Asia and the Pacific—and Germany seemingly close to victory in the Middle

East and Soviet Union—the United States no longer had the luxury of waiting. "It looked," said Arnold, "as if the Allies were losing the war."

With no possibility of sending U.S. ground forces into action in the immediate future, Roosevelt had agreed to dispatch American bombers to Britain to begin raids against Germany. In Arnold's view, it was essential that the new U.S. air operation in Britain—the Eighth Air Force—make its presence felt as quickly as possible, in large part to prevent Churchill from convincing the president that U.S. bombers should be turned over to the RAF. From the beginning, the British had been opposed to an independent Eighth Air Force: they favored either its absorption by the RAF or a transfer of its heavy bombers to their own nighttime operations. Both ideas were anathema to Arnold and his lieutenants, who argued that if American planes were to be based in Britain, they must be flown by American crews under American command.

To underscore the importance of the American air presence in Britain, Arnold named Tooey Spaatz, his chief of staff and closest friend, as first commander of the Eighth Air Force. Taking over the Eighth's Bomber Command was Brigadier General Ira Eaker, a soft-spoken, ferociously ambitious Texan, who was put in charge of the advance guard sent to Britain in February. To the surprise of many, Eaker formed an immediate, close relationship with his British counterpart—Air Marshal Arthur "Bomber" Harris, the controversial head of the RAF's Bomber Command. Harris warmly welcomed Eaker, sharing intelligence and operations information with him, helping him find a suitable location for his headquarters, even inviting the American to stay with his family when he first arrived in Britain. Beneath the warmth of their camaraderie, however, was a fierce rivalry. While Eaker was firmly convinced that daylight bombing was the answer, Harris was equally persuaded that the Americans would fail in that effort and that they would be forced to join forces with the nighttime British operation.

In a determined campaign to avoid such an outcome, Eaker's boss, Tooey Spaatz, created a highly sophisticated public relations operation to tout the virtues of the Eighth. That operation, according to Harrison Salisbury, quickly emerged as a "high-octane outfit . . . run by ambitious men and backed by an ambitious command in Washington." Manned by former newspaper reporters and editors, publicity agents, and advertising executives, the Eighth's PR office included Tex McCrary, a

Groton and Yale alumnus and former columnist for the *New York Daily Mirror*. Andy Rooney, a reporter for *Stars and Stripes* in London during the war, would later call McCrary "one of the great public relations experts and con artists of all time."

From Spaatz and Eaker on down, the brass of the Eighth Air Force did everything they could to further its cause—wining, dining, and playing poker with important Englishmen and visiting Americans; issuing a prodigious number of press releases touting the Eighth's sometimes spurious successes; even, later in the war, sending albums to Roosevelt and Churchill filled with photographs of the damage done by American bombs. Such efforts, they believed, were necessary to counteract the British air force's increasingly insistent grab for dominance.

On May 30, 1942, the RAF sent one thousand bombers on a raid over Cologne—a move that Arnold and Spaatz saw as a publicity ploy to demonstrate Britain's overwhelming edge in the air and add force to Churchill's appeals to Roosevelt that he be allowed to take control of American aircraft. By late summer, there were fewer than one hundred U.S. bombers in Britain, manned by crews with little experience or training. Nonetheless, under intense pressure from Washington to get American boys into the fight, B-17s began flying short-range assaults against German industrial targets in France and Holland.

Like American troops in North Africa, U.S. airmen had an abundance of confidence on the eve of their first encounters with the enemy. "We thought we were supermen," one of them remembered. That cheerful certainty lasted until swarms of German fighters began darting in and out of their bomber formations, attacking them from every possible angle and direction. To give Americans at home an idea of what it was like to pilot a B-17 in close formation under enemy attack, Tex McCrary came up with this colorful analogy: "You're driving one of 24 fifty-ton trucks down Broadway, fender to fender at 275 miles an hour, while the whole New York police force is blazing away at you with tommy guns."

Those early raids were nothing but "suicide missions," said an American pilot. "No one knew a thing. There had been no time; the war came on the country so quickly." Panicked U.S. gunners fired indiscriminately, hitting more American bombers and fighters than they did the enemy. Navigators had trouble finding their targets; some even had difficulty locating their own bases in Britain after their missions were over. The bombing errors during one U.S. raid over France were "so large and so recurrent," noted an official report, "that unless we can drastically reduce them, we shall derive very little advantage from our excellent Norden sight."

Such failures, however, were kept a closely guarded secret. Informing reporters that the raids had been a success, Eighth Air Force publicists released "grossly exaggerated reports of Nazi fighter losses and the tonnage of our bombs that hit German targets," a veteran American navigator recalled years later. An inflation of bombing results would be a hallmark of both American and British air campaigns throughout the war.

Despite the early missions' disappointing results, which included a sizable loss of aircraft, Arnold demanded more and bigger raids. As U.S. bombers thrust deeper into enemy-occupied territory, finally penetrating Germany without the protection of long-range fighters, their losses mushroomed. The Reich's defenses were far more sophisticated and massive than American planners had envisioned. German antiaircraft flak proved to be extremely accurate, and its fighter strength was overwhelming. In response to the intensifying Allied assault on Germany's key industrial centers, Luftwaffe leaders had shifted hundreds of crack fighter pilots and planes from the Russian front to protect their homeland. The pet theory of Arnold and his men—that enemy aircraft and ground gunners could not stop the high-flying, heavily armed B-17s—turned out to be a supremely costly illusion.

IT DIDN'T TAKE LONG for the Eighth's pilots and crews to realize that, in coming to Britain, they had been handed one of the most dangerous jobs of the war. U.S. Army Air Forces casualties, particularly in the Eighth, were astronomically greater than those in either of the two other military services. According to conventional wisdom, a crew member's chances of completing his normal tour of duty—twenty-five missions—were less than one in four. In its first ten months of operation, the Eighth lost 188 heavy bombers and some 1,900 crewmen; those numbers would skyrocket over the next year and a half. By the end of the conflict, the U.S. air operations in Europe would suffer more fatalities—26,000—than the entire Marine Corps in its protracted bloody campaigns in the Pacific. "To fly in the Eighth Air Force in those days," recalled Harrison Salisbury, "was to hold a ticket to a funeral. Your own."

The savagery of the air war was not due solely to the ferocity of German defenses. Early in the war, when the Air Force brass in Washington were touting the advantages of high-altitude flying, they failed to realize that the extreme atmospheric conditions experienced by the crews could kill as effectively as a Messerschmitt or Focke-Wulf. "There are apparently little things that one doesn't think about prior to getting into operations," commented Dr. Malcolm Grow, the Eighth's chief medical officer. Little things like oxygen deprivation, which could cause unconsciousness and death in a matter of minutes, or extensive frostbite, caused by several hours of exposure to temperatures of 50 to 60 degrees below zero. Until early 1944, more airmen were hospitalized for frostbite than for combat injuries.

As the war progressed, "bomber bases were damn depressing places to visit," recalled Andy Rooney. "Death was always in the air." Struggling with the knowledge that their chances of escaping injury or death were slim, a sizable number of pilots and crewmen suffered physical and mental breakdowns. "With deeper penetration raids into enemy airspace, casualties rose, and with no replacements on the horizon, men began to see the situation as hopeless," historian Donald Miller wrote. "Many airmen began to feel conflicted about their country: willing to fight for it, they also felt abandoned by it."

Yet, as the pressures on Allied crews intensified, so, too, did the bombing campaign. At the Casablanca conference in January 1943, Roosevelt and Churchill authorized Operation Pointblank, an all-out aerial offensive against the German aircraft industry, to take place before the cross-Channel invasion. For an assault on the Continent to have any chance of success, the Allies had to gain unquestioned supremacy in the air. To accomplish that, the leaders believed, Allied planes must not only clear the skies of existing Luftwaffe aircraft but destroy aircraft production facilities in Germany.

It would be another four months before American planes and crews started arriving in Britain in large numbers, yet, thanks to their top commanders, U.S. airmen now were committed to achieving this staggering goal in little more than a year. Acutely aware of Churchill's stepped-up requests to Roosevelt for American participation in night bombing, Eaker, who had replaced Tooey Spaatz as head of the

Eighth, insisted that daylight bombing would have no trouble doing the job. Both Eaker and Harris promised that German planes would be swept from the air by the time of the Allied invasion. "My personal message to you—this is a *must*—is to destroy the enemy air forces wherever you find them, in the air, on the ground, and in the factories," Hap Arnold wrote to Eighth Air Force commanders.

In the view of those flying the bombers, however, there was no chance of winning this fight without long-range escorts for the Eighth's aircraft. Until Arnold and the others understood that fact, the Luftwaffe would continue to rule the skies over Europe, and the carnage of Allied airmen would become exponentially worse. Still, the Air Force chief and his lieutenants resisted. It was then that Tommy Hitchcock entered the fray.

AS AN ASSISTANT military attaché, Hitchcock was assigned to the U.S. embassy rather than to the high-testosterone headquarters of the Eighth Air Force. His modus operandi was vastly different from that of the Eighth's leaders: he thought it far more important to cooperate with—and perhaps learn from—the RAF than to compete with it. Drawing on his own experience as a fighter pilot, Hitchcock concluded that the British were superior to the Americans in fighter combat tactics and training procedures, as well as in many aspects of the design and engineering of fighter planes themselves. "In those days, it would kill any idea if you said to Americans: 'British operational experience has shown . . . ,' " Tex McCrary, a friend of Hitchcock's, wrote late in the war. "Somehow, if a thing was British, two strikes were already chalked up against it in America. Tommy reversed the formula. If an idea had been tested and okayed in Britain's battle lab, then Hitchcock called it right. He knew that the toughest air fighting in the world was over here. Anything that survived had to be good."

Gil Winant, who held the same view, had lobbied U.S. military authorities for many months to take heed of new British developments in aircraft technology and design. "Since I have been here, I have done everything in my power to see that . . . American pilots are provided with every aircraft improvement that the British, through experience, have found essential," Winant wrote to Roosevelt in January 1942. Yet, despite those efforts, "the fact remains that there is still an unnecessary time lag incorporating the latest British design changes in our production lines." Roosevelt passed on Winant's letter to Hap Arnold, who rejected the ambassador's arguments out of hand.

Shortly after he arrived in Britain, Hitchcock paid a visit to the RAF's development facility at Duxford, a few miles outside Cambridge, to observe the performance tests of a promising new fighter, produced in America solely for British use. The brainchild of a German émigré who once designed Messerschmitt fighters, the P-51 Mustang had been built by California's North American Aviation Co. for the RAF, which planned to use it as a low-level tactical fighter-bomber.

Once the test flights began, the RAF knew it had something special. The Mustang, with its streamlined frame, was faster than the Spitfire, had a longer range, and, at medium and low altitudes, was nimbler at diving. It was, said one observer, "the cleanest and sweetest thing in the air." But the Mustang's test pilot and others who saw the plane in action believed that its performance could be enhanced even more if its underpowered American engine was replaced by the high-performance Merlin engine manufactured by Rolls-Royce, a British company.

RAF development officials agreed, and the Mustang airframe was mated with the Merlin. Hitchcock was stunned at the results. Observing the Mustang hybrid in the air and poring over charts and graphs outlining its performance, he realized that it was, in the words of historian Donald Miller, "the plane the Bomber Mafia had claimed was impossible to build, a fighter that could go as fast and as far as the bombers without losing its fighting characteristics." In a memo to Air Force headquarters in Washington, Hitchcock urged that the plane be transformed into a high-altitude fighter, predicting that its cross-breeding with the Merlin engine "would produce the best fighter plane on the Western Front."

His superiors, however, were not impressed. In their eyes, the Mustang belonged to the British; that fact alone made it inferior, despite its American origins. As Hitchcock noted, "Sired by the English out of an American mother, the Mustang has had no parent in the [Air Force] . . . to appreciate and push its good points." Faced with bureaucratic intransigence, he refused to give up. Throughout the summer and fall of 1942, he worked to drum up support for the Mustang hybrid, sending a flood of statistics to Washington demonstrating its sterling test performances and hosting lavish dinner parties at his elegant London flat to lobby RAF and Eighth Air Force higher-ups, as well as visiting dignitaries from the Roosevelt administration. He even took the Mustang up for a test spin himself, much to the chagrin of his nephew, Averell Clark, a USAAF fighter pilot who had flown with the RAF's Eagle Squadron before America's entry into the war. Standing with his uncle on the Duxford airfield, Clark exclaimed: "Look, Uncle Tommy, you'd better not fly that thing. The test pilot is the only guy who's been up in it." Hitchcock stared hard at his nephew. "Oh, the hell with that," he snapped, then strode to the Mustang, climbed in, and took off. "He was right to do it," Clark said years later. After all, "it was mainly his idea."

Winant acted as Hitchcock's partner in his Mustang crusade. Together, the two former World War I pilots peppered Roosevelt, Harry Hopkins, and other administration officials with cables and memos underscoring the plane's potential as a long-range fighter escort. According to political attaché Theodore Achilles, Winant "pushed the very daylights" out of those who might be helpful in clearing the way for the plane's adoption. In addition to his own background as a fighter pilot, there was another reason for Winant's intense interest in Hitchcock's project. The ambassador's elder son, John, had dropped out of Princeton the year before to enlist in the Air Force. Now in training to become a B-17 pilot, the younger Winant would soon head for Britain to join the Eighth Air Force—one of the multitude of young Americans who would face the full fury of German defenses during Operation Pointblank.

IN NOVEMBER 1942, Hitchcock flew to Washington to take the fight for the Mustang to Hap Arnold himself. "The word *channels,* like the word *no,* was an utterance he sometimes could not hear well," observed Nelson W. Aldrich Jr., Hitchcock's biographer. "He planned on going straight to the top." When, despite Hitchcock's best lobbying efforts, Arnold expressed little interest in the Mustang, he turned to one of Arnold's civilian bosses, undersecretary of war Robert Lovett, for help. The two had been friends since the Great War, when Hitchcock had flown for France and Lovett had been a pilot in Britain's Royal Naval Air Service and then in his own country's Air Corps. The undersecretary did not need to be convinced of the quality of Rolls-Royce engines—the British planes he had flown during the war had been equipped with them—and, after considerable investigation on his own, he agreed with Hitchcock that the Air Force must push forward with adoption of the Mustang as a long-distance escort for bombers. He urged Arnold to give the matter his immediate attention.

Pressed hard by Lovett and others in the War Department, Arnold reluctantly gave in, ordering the production of an initial 2,200 P-51Bs, as the hybrid Mustangs were called. But while the order was supposed to have the highest priority, there was a lag in producing the planes, and Arnold did little to speed it up. "His hands were tied by his mouth," Lovett noted. "He said our only need was Flying Fortresses . . . [that] very few fighters could keep up with them." But, as Lovett added, "the Messerschmitts had no difficulty at all."

With Arnold doing little, Hitchcock appointed himself the ramrod of the project, making repeated trips in early 1943 to the plants where the Mustangs were manufactured, to ensure that the planes were coming off the production line as quickly as possible. Despite his intercession, the first large shipment of P-51s did not arrive in Britain until January 1944. They came just in time to help save the D-Day invasion but not soon enough to help John Winant Jr. and thousands of other American crewmen who, during the horrific summer and autumn of 1943, flew straight and unprotected into the German maw.

BY THE TIME Operation Pointblank began in July 1943, the Eighth Air Force could count more than 100,000 airmen and 1,500 bombers on its roster. Yet, while the buildup of men and machines was enormous, so were the number of crewmen and planes lost in this massive, desperate attempt to wipe out Germany's aircraft industry. Officially called the Combined Bomber Offensive, Pointblank was meant to be a joint operation—an around-the-clock battering of key German targets by British and American bombers. In fact, there was little cooperation between the Americans and Arthur Harris, who, while paying lip service to Pointblank, refused to switch from his strategy of smashing German cities to atoms. Harris's operation, in the words of historian Michael Sherry, "took on almost an aimless quality, piling up vast rubble yet too dispersed in time and space to apply a decisive shock to either morale or production."

The American effort was hardly more effective. Both Allied air forces dropped record amounts of explosives on Germany's heartland that summer and fall, with little tangible results to show for it other than the staggering number of casualties on the ground and in the air. In the first week of Pointblank alone, the Eighth lost ninety-seven Flying Fortresses and almost one thousand crewmen—10 percent of the attacking force.

Hap Arnold, under enormous pressure to prove the efficacy of daylight bombing, was beside himself with rage. He accused Eaker and his subordinates of not sending enough bombers on missions because of the fear of large losses. For their part, the Eighth's top command believed that Arnold, in his Washington ivory tower, did not have the remotest idea of the extraordinary physical and emotional costs exacted by all-out aerial war. "It began to look," said an aide to Eaker, "as if generals Arnold and Eaker were devoting more time to fighting each other than to defeating the Germans."

In mid-August, Eaker, pushed hard by Arnold, ordered the largest American raid of the war thus far—a five-hundred-bomber assault on ball bearing factories in Schweinfurt and on a Messerschmitt assembly plant in Regensburg. Both cities were deep inside Germany, which meant that the bombers would have to fly several hours without escorts before they reached their targets, which were safeguarded by some of the most fearsome antiaircraft defenses in the Reich. Yet Arnold and his lieutenants convinced themselves that, despite the formidable odds, this dual mission could deliver a blow hard enough to knock the Luftwaffe out of the conflict. As Curtis LeMay, a major in command of the Eighth's 305th Bomb Group, observed, the honchos in Washington were trying "to find an easy way of winning the war in Europe. That's just about like searching for the Fountain of Youth—there is no such thing; never was."

There certainly would be nothing easy about these two missions. Hundreds of Luftwaffe fighters, the mightiest air defense force the Americans had yet seen, assailed the formations long before they reached their targets. Under their withering fire, bombers tumbled out of the sky by the dozens. More than 475 aircraft started out on the missions. Of the slightly more than 300 that reached their targets, 60 planes were shot down, and nearly six hundred men were killed. Half the planes that managed to limp back to their bases, one of which was piloted by Lieutenant John Winant, were badly damaged. It was, Nelson Aldrich Jr. wrote, "the Eighth Air Force's Verdun. Men were on the verge of mutiny, refusing to fly into Germany without some sort of escort that could protect them . . . over the target."

Though the losses were stunning, the Eighth's commanders comforted themselves with the belief that their bombers had wreaked crippling damage on Germany's aircraft industry. Regensburg, one general exulted, had been "literally wiped off the map." Hardly. While the Messerschmitt assembly plant had indeed been damaged, it was repaired and back in action within weeks. At Schweinfurt, about a third of the explosives missed their target and hit residential neighborhoods instead, killing two hundred civilians. The bombs that did strike the ball bearing factories did little damage, only briefly slowing down production. Writing about the Regensburg-Schweinfurt raids in his memoirs, Albert Speer, Hitler's war production chief, noted that the Reich had escaped "a catastrophic blow."

At the end of Pointblank's summer campaign, the Eighth Air Force struggled to stanch its human and material losses. But despite the terrible costs of the offensive, there would be no letup; with the Germans still masters of the air in Europe, the meat-grinder raids must continue. On September 6, 45 Flying Fortresses were lost over Stuttgart. On October 8 and 9, 58 Forts were shot down in raids over Bremen, Marienburg, and Anklam. The following day, the bombing target was Münster, an old walled city in western Germany. As daunting as the German fighter defense had been during the Regensburg-Schweinfurt mission, the aerial blitzkrieg over Münster was even more ferocious. In wave after wave, some two hundred fighter planes—"the greatest concentration of Nazi fighters ever hurled at an American bomber formation"—attacked the Fortresses head-on, scattering them all over the sky. So many crewmen bailed out, said one pilot, that it looked like an airborne invasion. Of the 275 B-17s that set out from Britain on that crisp fall day, 30 did not return. Among them was the Fortress piloted by John Winant, who was on his thirteenth bombing mission.

That night, Air Force authorities called Gil Winant with the news that his twenty-two-year-old son was missing, shot down while returning from Münster. According to witnesses, John Winant's plane had crashed after being attacked by three German fighters. The pilot of the mission's lead plane was able to offer a slight ray of hope: he told the ambassador he had seen several parachutes blossom under the B-17 shortly before it went down. But the pilot and other witnesses also had seen the German fighters firing at the parachutists. No one knew if any of the crew had survived.

For five agonizing weeks, Winant had no idea whether his son was dead or alive. During that time, he was showered with hundreds of messages of sympathy from all over the United States and Britain. While a good number were from dignitaries—Franklin and Eleanor Roosevelt, Winston and Clementine Churchill, Anthony Eden, Lord Beaverbrook, and Harry Hopkins among them—many more were from ordinary citizens. In a front-page story, the *Daily Express* noted the "deep sense of personal grief" felt by Britons when they heard the news of Winant's missing son. "Ever since his appointment, the British people have had a special regard for Mr. Winant, not only as American Ambassador but as a man," the *Express* added. He "has touched the mainspring of our affection."

On November 11, Winant received the news he had been hoping for: John was alive and now a prisoner of war in Germany. The ambassador's relief, however, soon gave way to deep concern when he learned that his son, along with several other high-profile Allied prisoners, were being held as potential hostages in the event of a German defeat. Dubbed the Prominente by the Germans, the VIP prisoners of war included a nephew of Winston Churchill's and close relatives of both the king and queen. Toward the end of the war, they all would be sequestered at Colditz, a forbidding medieval fortress near Leipzig that had been transformed into a high-security prison. The Germans never made clear what they had in mind for Winant and the other Prominente. But the British War Office feared that, should an Allied victory appear imminent, the hostages would either be used as bargaining counters or face summary execution as a way of exacting revenge.

THREE MONTHS AFTER the Münster debacle, on a dark, rainy day over central Germany, there came the first inkling that the fight for air supremacy was about to take a dramatic turn. Like a cat crouched outside a mouse hole, a pack of enemy fighters pounced on what looked like easy prey—a B-17 formation heading for a Focke-Wulf factory a few dozen miles west of Berlin. But on that icy, wet morning, the mice had a surprise of their own. Suddenly, seemingly out of nowhere, a sleek Allied fighter plane—the Mustang P-51B—streaked through the swarm of Focke-Wulfs and, just like that, shot two of them down. The Focke-Wulf pilots were dumbfounded: never before had an Allied fighter challenged the Luftwaffe so far inside Germany.

For more than half an hour, the single Mustang, piloted by Major James Howard, weaved and bobbed, dived and climbed, in its furious attack on the Focke-Wulfs. Although three of his four machine guns jammed, Howard continued the assault until his fuel ran low and he was forced to return to his base in Britain. He claimed only two kills, but several Fortress crew members who witnessed his extraordinary performance swore they saw him shoot down at least six. Sixty Allied bombers were lost on that January 11 mission, but not one plane went down from the group defended by Howard. He later won the Medal of Honor for his remarkable single-handed fight.

Howard's plane had been part of a small Mustang formation assigned to escort the B-17s over their target—one of the first groups of the new long-range fighter hybrid to go into action. But the other Mustangs had been scattered in heavy clouds, and Howard was the only one to make contact with the enemy. "It was up to me to do it," he later said. "There were 10-man crews in those bombers and no one else to protect them."

For the Eighth Air Force, Howard's performance—and that of his plane—were a small burst of light in a very dark sky. After the war, Hap Arnold acknowledged that the Mustang appeared "over Germany at just the saving moment, in the very nick of time." With the addition of fuselage and drop tanks, the Mustang now had the range of a B-17 or B-24 and could reach speeds of over four hundred miles per hour and altitudes well above thirty thousand feet.

The Regensburg-Schweinfurt raids the previous summer had finally changed Arnold's mind about the necessity of providing long-range fighter escorts for U.S. bombers. Later, Arnold admitted it was "the Air Force's own fault" that the Mustang was not put into service earlier. "The story of the P-51," the official wartime history of the USAAF declared, "came close to representing the costliest mistake made by the Army Air Forces in World War II." Donald Miller, author of a magisterial history of the Eighth Air Force, was even blunter, calling the USAAF's protracted resistance to the Mustang "one of the most egregious errors in the history of American airpower."

Five crucial months would elapse, however, between Arnold's acknowledgment of the need for the Mustangs and their arrival in large numbers in Britain. In the interim, there was no letup in the Eighth's deep-penetration raids into Germany or their hellish casualties. A second trip to Schweinfurt in October, for example, claimed 77 bombers, 17 of them in crash landings on their return to Britain. Of the mission's 229 planes, only 33 landed without damage. With the invasion of France only a few months away, General Frederick Anderson, Pamela Churchill's sometime lover and the hard-edged new chief of the U.S. bombing effort, told Arnold that the Eighth would strike "regardless of cost." When an aide protested the dispatch of B-24s on one raid, noting they could not fly as high as B-17s and that "God, [the crews] will just get killed in them," Anderson gave him an icy look and responded: "Well?"

THE FIRST LARGE-SCALE shipment of Mustangs to Britain in early 1944 coincided with the appointment of General James Doolittle, leader of the famed American air raid on Tokyo in April 1942, to take over the Eighth. For Doolittle, the key weapons in the fight for mastery of the air were not the heavy bombers, which had failed to halt Germany's aircraft production, but the Allied fighters. Instead of flying close to the bombers to protect them from attack, the fighters were ordered to go on the offensive, intercepting Luftwaffe fighters before they reached the bombers and then strafing ground targets on their way home. Each type of fighter would have its own role to play. Spitfires would protect the bombers as they flew over Britain to Europe and back, P-47 Thunderbolts and P-38 Lightnings would escort them to the German border, and the new high flyers—the P-51 Mustangs—would take them to and from their targets, which by March would extend as far as Munich and Berlin.

From February until shortly before D-Day, the bombers would essentially be used as bait, there to lure enemy fighters into battle so the Mustangs could destroy them. In the series of savage air battles that followed, losses of planes and crews soared to record levels. In 1942, Air Force planners in Washington had predicted that no more than 300 heavy bombers would be lost during the entire course of the war. In one week alone in early 1944, 226 bombers, with more than two thousand men on board, were shot down over the Reich. In the five months before D-Day, over 2,600 bombers (and 980 fighters) were downed, and more than ten thousand crewmen were killed.

The morale of bomber crews, already in the depths, plummeted still further. The number of mental breakdowns skyrocketed, as did cases of alcohol and drug abuse. When an inebriated young pilot made a scene one night in the bar of a luxury London hotel, an Air Force staff officer ordered him to leave. "Colonel," the pilot snarled, "yesterday at noon, I was over Berlin. Where in the hell were you?" Said another airman: "Alcohol was the only thing that made our existence bearable."

Yet, as wrenching and costly as it was, Doolittle's strategy did indeed produce the results he was seeking. In March 1944 alone, Allied aircraft—primarily the Mustangs—shot down more than twice as many enemy planes as the number destroyed in the years 1942 and 1943 combined. During a raid over Berlin that month, B-17 crews were astonished to discover that not a single enemy fighter rose to meet them. The Germans still had plenty of fighter planes—they were churning them out in record numbers—but they were not able to replace the hundreds of experienced pilots who had been wounded or killed since the advent of the Mustang. "The war of attrition had reached the mortal phase," noted one German historian, "when neither courage nor skill availed further." Asked by an American interrogator after the war when he realized that Germany would lose the conflict, Luftwaffe chief Hermann Göring replied: "The first time your bombers came over Hanover, escorted by fighters, I began to be worried. When they came with fighter escorts over Berlin, I knew the jig was up."

In the weeks before D-Day, Allied bombers, unhindered by enemy fighters, smashed the railway networks of France and northern Belgium, choking off the main supply and reinforcement routes of the Wehrmacht. After his capture in 1945, Field Marshal Wilhelm Keitel, head of the German high command, told Allied officials that the Normandy landings had been successful only due "to our inability to bring up our reserves at the proper time. . . . Nobody can ever prove to me that we could not have repelled the invasion had not the superiority of the enemy air force in bombers and fighters made it impossible to throw these divisions in the fight."

On the eve of the invasion of Europe, General Eisenhower assured his troops: "If you see fighting aircraft over you, they will be ours."

Thanks in no small part to an ex–polo star and the plane he championed, Eisenhower was absolutely right.

THERE WAS LITTLE DOUBT, in the minds of many people involved in the Mustang effort, that, if it hadn't been for Tommy Hitchcock, the U.S. Army Air Forces would never have adopted the plane that ultimately became the best, most famed American fighter of the war. "Tommy Hitchcock was largely responsible for the P-51B, for pushing on that project until it got through," Robert Lovett observed. "The only person who could have done this was someone who was both knowledgeable as a pilot and who had the qualities of leadership to take a grasp of disparate people and get them moving in a common direction." Shortly after D-Day, Tex McCrary wrote that "the tenacity, the sincerity and the sheer butt-headedness of Hitchcock pushed the plane through the ranks of all its critics until it became the fighter it is today."

But Hitchcock had no intention of resting on his laurels. After spearheading the struggle to accelerate P-51 production in the United States, he returned to London in the spring of 1943 with little enthusiasm for resuming his duties as assistant military attaché at the embassy. "Life in London," he wrote to his wife, Margaret, "is much too easy to make one think that one is actually engaged in waging a war." In his work on the Mustang, Hitchcock had been bitten once more by the combat bug: his dream now was to fly the plane for which he had pushed so hard. "Fighting in a Mustang," he told friends, "ought to be like playing polo—but with pistols."

Shortly after his return, the forty-three-year-old Hitchcock took time off to attend the RAF's central gunnery school, where, in the company of young Britons who were at least twenty years younger, he learned how to fly and fight in a Spitfire. Most of his friends and acquaintances considered his ambition to fly a Mustang in combat, perhaps as the head of his own squadron, to be little more than a pipe dream. But late in 1943, he was assigned to a base in Abilene, Texas, to assume command of the 408th Fighter Group, then in training for combat in Europe. No one knew how he did it, and the taciturn Hitchcock never explained.

However it happened, the assignment gave him more personal satisfaction than anything he had done since his days as a Lafayette Escadrille pilot in the Great War. "The amount of work that must be done is staggering," he wrote his wife. "In 90 days' time the group is supposed to be ready to fight for its life. . . . I do not feel that I know all the answers, not by a long shot. [But] I have got what I wanted and it is up to me to make the very best of it."

Then, almost as suddenly as it materialized, the dream fell apart. Hitchcock's unit was disbanded in early February 1944, and his thirty-six pilots were sent overseas as individual replacements for men lost in action or completing their tours. Hitchcock himself was named deputy chief of staff of the 9th Tactical Air Command in England, whose fighters were to supply direct tactical support for ground forces in the coming invasion. Again, there was no official explanation for the decision.

Devastated by his shift in assignment, Hitchcock spent a few days in New York with his wife and four young children before returning to Britain. On his last day at home, his nine-year-old daughter, Peggy, said goodbye, and then, as she was going to school, went back to say goodbye once more. "I suddenly had the awful premonition that I might never see him again," she said years afterward. "I remember running back for one last glimpse of my father still sitting at the dining room table with my mother and thinking to myself, I must fix his image in my mind so that I will never forget him."

Once back in England, Hitchcock swallowed his disappointment and flung himself into his new duties as head of the 9th's research and development efforts. In addition, he spent considerable time with its pilots, many of whom had just arrived from the United States. "Tommy Hitchcock had a tremendous dynamic and magnetic influence on these young men, and it was not because of athletic prowess or reputation," said Lieutenant General Elwood "Pete" Quesada, the 9th's commander. "Most of the boys in our fighter groups didn't know a thing about polo or give a damn about it. Their admiration for him was deeper. . . . They quickly recognized his basic character, his depth of knowledge and the sympathy that comes with experience. He knew how to talk to them."

Hitchcock took great satisfaction in the sterling performance of the Mustang, which was fast becoming the fighter workhorse of the war. He was particularly delighted when his nephew, now a group leader, reported to him that his men had shot down 160 enemy aircraft in their first month of flying Mustangs, compared to a score of 120 kills in the previous eleven months. Averell Clark's group, Hitchcock wrote his wife, "has been going great guns since switching over to Mustangs. They are now the highest scoring U.S. group in England . . . making deep penetrations into Germany and chasing German planes all around the tree tops."

But in the first few months of 1944, there was a growing worry about the Mustangs: several of them had recently crashed for no apparent reason. They were, according to Quesada, "just diving into the ground. We couldn't understand it, and Tommy couldn't. Obviously, you can't have a useful force that is going to destroy itself." As head of research and development, Hitchcock was the man responsible for finding out what was wrong. He and his technical advisers believed that the addition of a new fuel tank in the fuselage, enabling the Mustang to fly to Berlin and beyond, was destabilizing the plane when it dived in combat. If so, pilots would be instructed to burn as much of the fuel in the new tanks as possible before tangling with the enemy.

Although Hitchcock had test pilots in his command whose job it was to check out such hypotheses in the air, he insisted on doing it himself. On a bright April morning, he drove to his development station's airfield near Salisbury, southwest of London, and climbed into a test Mustang, the fuel tank in place behind his seat in the fuselage. Flying toward a nearby bombing range, he put the plane into a dive from a height of fifteen thousand feet. Suddenly, without warning, it hurtled down, faster and faster, until it smashed into the ground, sending a plume of oily black smoke into the sky. Hitchcock's body was found nearby.

In a front-page story reporting Hitchcock's death, the *New York Times* wrote that the accident "brought to a close one of the most gallant and one of the most spectacular careers in modern American life." Gil Winant, who notified Hitchcock's family of his death, wrote a long letter to his widow eleven days later. Just as he had done in polo, Hitchcock "spent every minute of his time [in war] trying to win," the ambassador told Margaret Hitchcock. The Mustang, Winant wrote, "is tangible evidence of Tommy's contribution to victory. Without it we would not be winning the air war over Germany today."

16.

"CROSSING THE OCEAN DOESN'T AUTOMATICALLY MAKE YOU A HERO"

Dear old England's not the same,
The dread invasion, well it came.
But no, it's not the beastly Hun.
The god-damn Yankee army's come.

IN EARLY 1944, C. D. JACKSON, WHO HAD JUST ARRIVED IN LONDON as head of Eisenhower's psychological warfare staff, wrote to a friend about the extraordinary crush of Americans in the British capital. "There is not a single square inch of London on which an American is not standing," Jackson declared, "and add to that the fact that if he is standing after dark, he is standing unsteadily." Jackson's remark might have been an exaggeration, but in certain parts of the city, it was not much of one.

During the previous summer, Roosevelt and his military leaders had finally prevailed on the British to agree to a firm date—May 1, 1944—for the invasion of Europe. As a result, the British Isles became not only the staging ground for D-Day but, as Eisenhower put it, "the greatest operating military base of all time." At the end of May 1943, U.S. troops in the country numbered 133,000. Six months later, there were half a million, and six months after that, more than 1.65 million. The American invasion was, according to one British historian, the largest influx of foreigners in Britain since the coming of the Normans nine centuries before. "It was as if the Atlantic had ceased to exist," a

Londoner wrote, "and the vast American continent was only at the bottom of the road."

The initial dilemma facing British and American officials was how to shoehorn all those men onto an island the size of Georgia but with more than twenty times the number of that state's residents. East Anglia, a sleepy rural area in eastern England, was the first to feel the brunt. With its flat landscape and close proximity to the Continent, it was the site of the mushrooming Eighth Air Force empire, which by the summer of 1943 had grown to sixty-six airbases and 200,000 men. By D-Day, U.S. airbases in the region, some of them covering as much as five hundred acres and housing up to three thousand servicemen, were separated by an average distance of only eight miles.

Like many parts of Britain, East Anglia had never had much exposure to foreigners. Suddenly, the somnolence of its villages was shattered by hundreds of young U.S. servicemen swarming into shops, careening through narrow streets in jeeps and trucks, making passes at girls, and drinking local pubs dry. For the area's residents, the American invasion was an overwhelming, sometimes traumatic, experience— one that many more Britons would soon share.

The story was somewhat different in the British capital. As the center of the British empire, London had seen more than its share of foreigners over the centuries; now, as the de facto capital of Europe, it housed tens of thousands of Continental exiles. But even Londoners found themselves daunted by the flood of Americans pouring into their city during the last two years of the war.

By 1944, the U.S. military had commandeered thousands of buildings in the London area, from large country estates just outside the capital to apartment and office blocks in its central districts. Three hundred buildings alone were used to house American troops in London, including twenty-four hotels transformed into officers' billets. The two-story ballroom of the fashionable Grosvenor House Hotel became the largest military dining mess in the world, catering to officers from the various U.S. headquarters staffs. Known as Willow Run, after the Ford Company's mile-long aircraft-assembly plant outside Detroit, the one-thousand-seat mess served more than six thousand meals a day.

The hotel was just a few blocks from Grosvenor Square, which, along with the neighborhoods surrounding it, remained the hub of American war activity in Britain. According to one English writer, the area had been "captured—lock, stock, and barrel—by the United States." It was rare to find a house or office near the square that had not been taken over by a U.S. military or civilian agency. On some streets, as the columnist Ernie Pyle noted, "an Englishman stood out as incongruously as he would in North Platte, Nebraska." Watching a seemingly endless flow of uniformed Americans enter and leave their west London offices one day, Pyle concluded that the military bureaucracy was as bloated in London as it was in Washington, perhaps even more so.

Pyle, a native of Indiana who wrote for the Scripps Howard newspaper chain, was bemused by the American military's practice of saluting virtually everything that moved. "Everybody had to salute," Pyle wrote. "Second lieutenants saluted other second lieutenants. Arms flailed up and down by the thousands, as though everybody were crazy. . . . On one short street, much traveled by the Americans, they had to make sidewalk traffic one way, presumably to prevent salute casualties." Ordered by their superiors to "show proper respect" to their British and other Allied counterparts, U.S. servicemen, in the words of one sergeant, simply saluted "everyone in uniform . . . including, I suspect, even hotel doormen."

Just as Grosvenor Square was the epicenter of U.S. forces at work in London, Piccadilly Circus was the favored place for Americans at play. From early morning to late at night, thousands of U.S. servicemen on leave joined throngs of other Allied troops in roaming this "bawdy, rowdy ant hill," as Sergeant Robert Arbib called it, some in search of restaurants and theaters but most looking for liquor and girls.

One of the busiest traffic crossroads in the city, Piccadilly Circus had served as the metaphorical heart of the British empire since its construction in the nineteenth century. Here, colonial officials and traders just back from India or Africa had met their friends for dinner, a drink, or a night on the town after years away from home. Lined with eating places, pubs, music halls, and theaters, the circus was London's Times Square; before the war, giant signs, emblazoned with electric lights, had bathed the area in a dazzling glow. The lights had been doused in 1939, but even with the blackout, Piccadilly Circus remained the liveliest, most crowded spot in London, helping make the city, in the words of Donald Miller, "one of the most sensational places on the planet." After experiencing the nighttime delights of the area, one American colonel wrote home: "The conviviality of London in wartime is unimaginable, unless you have actually experienced it. I have seen people who literally hadn't seen each other five minutes earlier become comrades. Romantic attachments are formed on the spot." The streets around the circus, observed Miller, "were jammed beyond belief. . . . Everywhere there were people in search of food, friends, liquor, and sex."

IN HIS LETTER noting the horde of bibulous Americans in the capital, C. D. Jackson concluded with the comment: "I think that there is plenty of trouble brewing."* Gil Winant, well aware that the massive American buildup was making life considerably more difficult for Britons, agreed. According to Theodore Achilles, the ambassador worried about "the reaction of the GIs toward the British people and the reactions of British soldiers toward the GIs, who had come to Great Britain with more money and nattier-looking uniforms." Days after the United States entered the war, Winant began acting as an intermediary between U.S. military authorities and British officials to try to make the invasion of American troops as peaceful as possible.

When Eisenhower arrived in London in June 1942, he became a fully committed partner in Winant's effort. Like the ambassador, the general was concerned about the material and psychological strains placed on British society by the massive influx of his countrymen. "Every American soldier coming to Britain was almost certain to consider himself a privileged crusader, sent there to help Britain out of a hole. He would expect to be treated as such," Eisenhower later wrote. "On the other hand, the British public looked upon itself as one of the saviors of democracy, particularly because, for an entire year, it had stood alone as the unbreakable opponent of Nazism."

As always for Winant—and for Eisenhower, too—education was the key to creating mutual understanding. Both men were instrumental in launching a U.S.-British program to teach GIs about Britain before they arrived there. A film co-produced by the British Ministry of Information and U.S. Office of War Information, and starring Burgess Meredith in the role of a U.S. soldier, demonstrated how different the two countries were, despite their common language, and gave tips to

---

* Jackson, of course, added to that trouble himself by having an affair with Beatrice Eden.

American troops on how to avoid offending the British. Those en route to Britain also received a handbook written by the British-born novelist Eric Knight, who had become a U.S. citizen. "The British will welcome you as friends and allies," Knight wrote. "But remember that crossing the ocean doesn't automatically make you a hero. . . . You are coming to Britain from a country where your home is still safe, food is still plentiful, and lights are still burning. So stop and think before you sound off about lukewarm beer, or cold boiled potatoes, or the way English cigarettes taste. . . . Don't make fun of British speech or accents. You sound just as funny to them but they will be too polite to show it."

Having built up, in Anthony Eden's words, "a remarkable personal relationship with the people of Great Britain," Winant now drew heavily on that relationship in his parallel effort to prepare the British public for the American troops' arrival. His campaign included participation in a series of BBC broadcasts called *Let's Get Acquainted.*

For the rest of the war, much of Winant's time and effort was spent trying to resolve problems relating to the American incursion and to foster a good relationship between U.S. servicemen and their British hosts. Although he worked closely with Eisenhower, the general was gone from Britain for much of the war—in North Africa from November 1942 to January 1944 and in France after June 1944. When Eisenhower was in London, his attention was necessarily focused on the upcoming military campaigns; as a result, he left many of the details of the American-British relationship to the ambassador and his subordinates. "No one else could possibly have been so effective as yourself in helping me solve many important problems which, without your assistance, might well have had the most serious results," Eisenhower wrote to Winant shortly before leaving for North Africa in late 1942. "I want you to know that any success that may spring from our present military efforts will be, in no small measure, due to you."

When American military men got into trouble, Winant was largely responsible for ensuring they would be judged by their own authorities rather than by British courts. Shortly after the first GIs arrived in the country, he read in a newspaper that an American soldier found guilty of robbing a cab driver at gunpoint had been sentenced to a whipping as well as to a six-month jail term. Winant persuaded the British home secretary, Herbert Morrison, to cancel the whipping. Then he joined forces with Eisenhower and Eden to press for legislation giving U.S. military authorities sole jurisdiction over criminal offenses committed in Britain by American servicemen. The issue, not surprisingly, was highly controversial, but, thanks in no small part to Winant's close relations with the Foreign Office and many MPs, the law, which applied to no other Allied force, was passed by Parliament with little opposition.

THE TROOP-RELATED problems with which Winant and the U.S. military had to cope were many and various, ranging from an epidemic of traffic accidents caused by Americans driving on the wrong side of the road to the destruction of huge swaths of English countryside for the building of U.S. airfields and training grounds. In East Anglia, American crews felled centuries-old hedgerows, trees, and thatched cottages, and plowed up hundreds of thousands of acres of prime farmland to build their mosaic of airbases. Watching a farmer chase a U.S. military surveyor off his beet field one day, Robert Arbib, an Army engineer, felt a pang of sadness and loss. A Yale graduate and amateur conservationist, Arbib knew that, no matter how hard the farmer fought, his "heritage and masterpiece" would soon be buried under eight inches of concrete. "The war," Arbib later wrote, "wrecked this man's monument—his family's monument—just as surely as bombs wrecked the monuments of architects and stonemasons when they exploded beautiful churches in London." But Arbib, who would become a National Audubon Society executive years after the war, acknowledged that most of his engineering and construction colleagues failed to share his sensitivity to despoiling nature: they "saw it as a job to be done and went to work with no remorse."

In Devon, on the southwest coast of England, there was similar angst when the British government in late 1943 ordered the eviction of several seaside villages and towns, together with some five hundred farms, so that American forces could use the area for amphibious training in preparation for D-Day. As one writer noted, "compensation was minimal, complaints unproductive." Without the exercises, the U.S. military argued, the invasion of France would fail; military leaders enlisted Winant's aid to put pressure on Churchill and the cabinet to authorize the evictions. When the plan was announced, the U.S. consul in Plymouth reported considerable criticism of the "autocratic and undemocratic methods" used in banishing some 2,700 people from their homes and livelihoods for the indefinite future.

As they left, Anglican vicars in the area pinned a notice from their bishop to the front doors of their evacuated churches. Addressed to "our United States allies," the notice read in part: "This church has stood for several hundred years. Around it has grown a community which has lived in these houses and tilled these fields ever since there was a church. This church, this churchyard in which their loved ones lie at rest; these homes, these fields are as dear to those who have left them as are the homes and graves which you, our Allies, have left behind you. They hope to return one day, as you hope to return to yours, to find them waiting to welcome them home."

Naturally, these evacuations and the destruction of British property did nothing to endear Americans to the British, nor did they help Winant's and Eisenhower's attempts to promote a greater mutual understanding. Complicating that job even further was the lack of interest on the part of many GIs in getting to know their British hosts. Before being shipped to Britain, a sizable number of American troops had never been outside their home states before, let alone their country. Many came from German and Irish immigrant families that were traditionally hostile to the British. GIs, for the most part, were interested in little but an end to the war and a quick trip home. "They hadn't wanted to come, so it followed—did it not?—that their hearts were not with us in our hour of need," remarked a British woman worker in an American Red Cross club. Pinpointing the difference in thinking between the two countries, Harold Nicolson noted that "for us, Anglo-American cooperation means security, [but] for them it suggests danger."

The problem was exacerbated by the fact that most Britons encountered Americans only when the GIs were off duty. Trying to relieve the regimentation of Army life and the boredom of endless training, they invaded pubs, talked loudly, got drunk, picked up women, and in the words of the anthropologist Margaret Mead, acted "as if they owned the world." As Maurice Gorham, a BBC executive, put it, "We never saw an American soldier *doing* anything." When Gorham traveled to France after D-Day and observed "how the Americans could look when they were on the job, I longed to bring a handful of them back to London and say to the people in Piccadilly, 'Look, these are Americans, too.' "

Gorham believed, as did Winant and Eisenhower, that the GIs in Britain were too isolated from the British people. Their camps and bases were American oases, with their own newspapers, radio programs, and movies—and little communication or interest in the world outside. That mentality was fostered by many American commanders, who had the mind-set that "these men are fighters. They are being conditioned for combat. They don't have to know whether they are in Britain or New Britain; it makes no difference to them." As a result of their exposure to this "scrupulously American environment," said Gorham, GIs "had nothing in common" with the British. "They had not eaten the same food, read the same news or even heard the same radio. They had no common ground."

To a fair number of American troops, brimming over with hustle and pent-up energy, Britain was little more than a small, battered, backward country with primitive living conditions, unfriendly citizens, weak beer, and a sluggish, passive approach to life. "The general reaction of many Americans to the British people was, 'If they'd forget the damn tea and crumpets in the middle of the afternoon, wake up and get moving, we wouldn't have to fight their war for them,' " recalled one GI.

Some American soldiers were not shy about voicing their unfavorable opinions about the country to the British themselves. One day, two military policemen on duty outside U.S. Army headquarters in London were approached by a pretty young woman in the uniform of the Auxiliary Territorial Service (ATS), the women's branch of the British Army. After chatting with the men awhile, she asked them how they liked England. "I like it fine," one MP politely responded, but the other blurted out, "Lady, they should cut all those goddamn [barrage] balloons loose and let this SOB place sink." Giving the MPs "one hell of a look," the young woman turned on her heel and walked away. A civilian guard scurried over. "Do you know who that was?" he asked. "That was Princess Elizabeth. She's doing her time in the Army." Years later, the MP who had answered politely declared: "I was so embarrassed I couldn't think of a thing to say. I shall just never forget that long, hard look" given him and his outspoken compatriot by the future queen of England.

While Princess Elizabeth never made public any disapproval she might have felt about the Americans, many of her countrymen were considerably less restrained. To the British, who had lost so much during the war, their brash, wisecracking U.S. allies seemed like rich, spoiled, arrogant, and boastful children. The American troops, they felt, had no respect or appreciation for their history and institutions and, as Eisenhower noted, no sense of the sacrifices their country had made to stop Hitler and save democracy.

The gulf between the two nationalities was delightfully illustrated in a wartime encounter between Harold Nicolson and a group of GIs touring Parliament. A witty and gregarious habitué of White's and other London clubs, Nicolson was—in addition to being a member of Parliament, novelist, biographer, and former diplomat—the husband of the writer and Bloomsbury denizen Vita Sackville-West. A graduate of Oxford's Balliol College, he had always considered himself superior to most men, but especially to Americans. Not surprisingly, then, he reacted with utter dismay when asked one day to act as a tour guide around Parliament for a group of American soldiers.

"In they slouched," Nicolson wrote that night to his two sons, "chewing gum, conscious of their inferiority in training, equipment, breeding, culture, experience and history, determined in no circumstances to be either interested or impressed." In the House of Lords chamber, Nicolson and his bored Americans ran into another covey of U.S. troops, being shown around by none other than Sir John Simon, the British lord chancellor and former foreign secretary, who had been one of the foremost champions of appeasement in the 1930s. The pompous, self-important Simon proceeded to lecture the two groups— "fifty blank faces, their jaws working at the gum"—about the operations of the House of Commons and House of Lords. "Now," said Simon, "come to my room, boys—or should I call you doughboys?— and I will show you the Great Seal." Nicolson described the scene that followed:

Through the corridors they slouched apathetically, expecting to be shown a large wet animal such as they had seen so often at the aquarium in San Francisco. But not at all. All they were shown were two cylinders of steel with a pattern inside. And then a man fetched the mace for them to see. "I must now ask you, my friends, to leave me to my labours. Even a Lord Chan-

cellor sometimes has work to do. Harold, perhaps you will conduct our friends to the exit?" Harold did. We slouched along to
Central Hall. To my surprise and pleasure, one of the doughboys suddenly ceased chewing, flung his wad of Wrigley into his
cheek with a deft movement of his tongue, and said, "Say, Sur,
who *was* that guy?"

CONVINCED THAT DEEPER personal contact would help lessen the
power of stereotypes and increase rapport between the soldiers and the
British, Winant and Eisenhower, supported by Anthony Eden and
the Foreign Office, strongly promoted a program encouraging GIs to
visit British homes. Eisenhower felt, Harry Butcher wrote, that "if an
American soldier has the opportunity of living, say, for a weekend, in
the home of a British family . . . there could be developed a much
greater degree of friendliness and companionship than if both are
standoffish." The idea had been advanced by Lady Reading's Women's
Voluntary Service, whose members had provided the only hospitality
to newly arrived GIs in the early days of the Anglo-American alliance,
welcoming them at British ports with sandwiches and cups of tea. In
proposing the home visits, Lady Reading told the women of WVS:
"This is a wonderful opportunity to get to know the people with
whom our destiny is now completely bound up." Following Winant's
advice that Americans shouldn't add to British privations, Eisenhower
suggested that, when troops did visit British families, they should take
with them food items that were hard to find in the country, like meat,
fats, and sweets.

The home visit idea, however, ran into immediate roadblocks.
Many U.S. military commanders opposed it, preferring their troops to
have as little contact with local citizens as possible. In a letter to her
parents, Janet Murrow noted that several of her British friends, who
were anxious to entertain GIs, had been rebuffed by American military
authorities and were "bewildered, hurt, and completely baffled." She
added: "Many, many opportunities to make friends are being missed—
and it's *not* the fault of the British."

But the fiercest opponent of closer American-British interaction
was the American Red Cross, which the U.S. Army had placed in
charge of GIs' welfare in Britain when they were away from their
bases. The Red Cross operated dozens of clubs for American troops

throughout the country, including the famed Rainbow Corner in Piccadilly Circus, which boasted snack bars serving hamburgers and Cokes, hot showers, pinball machines, jukeboxes, a shoeshine parlor, and pool tables. The Red Cross clubs were meant to be distinctly American oases, offering homesick GIs a cornucopia of homestyle comforts and amenities that could be found nowhere else in Britain. Indeed, if the American Red Cross had had its way, it and the clubs it ran would have been completely isolated from Britain and its people.

Unfortunately for the organization, the British had a great deal to do with the clubs: the British government had paid for their acquisition, renovation, and equipment, and British women, most of them Women's Voluntary Service members, made up the vast majority of their staffs. Red Cross officials couldn't do much about that—there weren't enough American women in Britain to staff the clubs—but they did insist that the WVS members doff their own distinctive outfits and put on American Red Cross uniforms if they were to continue working in what was meant to be an all-American environment. "The men in these facilities we run have a right to expect to come into contact only with Americans," one Red Cross official declared.

Not surprisingly, Lady Reading and her members were furious. The WVS head protested directly to Eisenhower, who was sympathetic but could not budge the Red Cross from its stand. "The British women . . . rightfully feel they have earned [their uniforms] through their service in the blitzes, and this is certainly true," Harry Butcher mused in his diary. "If the situation was reversed, what would American women do? You know damn well."

The American Red Cross further isolated the GIs to whom it catered by imposing a partial ban on British and other Allied troops from its clubs. (Non-American soldiers were allowed in only if a GI invited them to share a meal. They were not permitted to use any of the clubs' other facilities.) While still a WAAF, Mary Lee Settle was turned away from Rainbow Corner during one of her leaves in London. It made no difference that she was an American, a Red Cross supervisor told Settle. She was in a British uniform, and Rainbow Corner was not a place for Allied troops. Settle stared hard at the woman. "All right," she said. "And if *you* want to join the war sometime, I'll lend you my uniform." She stormed out and never set foot in the place again.

In a letter passed on to George Marshall, Anthony Eden accused the American Red Cross of building barriers rather than bridges between American soldiers and British citizens, adding that the organization "deliberately discourages any intrusion of British friendliness." James Warburg, the head of the Office of War Information's foreign propaganda department, agreed. "The greatest danger to Anglo-American relations resulting from the presence of American troops in Great Britain," Warburg told Eisenhower, "appears to be the [desire] of some of our government and private agencies . . . to build a little America within the British Isles."

Roosevelt and Marshall, however, made no apologies for supplying GIs in privation-plagued Britain with as many of the comforts and conveniences of home as they could. It was important, they believed, to keep the morale of these citizen soldiers, most of them draftees, as high as possible while they prepared for battle. In the last two years of the war, considerable scarce shipping space was used to transport such goods as meat, fresh vegetables and fruits, coffee, eggs, and cigarettes to Britain for GI consumption. When British officials urged him to let their country supply U.S. troops with food, Roosevelt replied bluntly: "American soldiers could not live on British rations." Any attempt to cut back on the GIs' relatively high standard of living, Marshall told one British official, would lead to "thousands of mothers writing to their Congressmen to complain that the American army authorities were not providing properly for their sons."

Though Eisenhower agreed with his superiors about the importance of keeping up the troops' morale, he bemoaned the fact that most of the soldiers under his command, while demanding the rights and privileges of American citizenship, had little knowledge of or interest in living up to the responsibilities that came with that citizenship. "Differences between democracy and totalitarianism were matters of academic rather than personal interest," Eisenhower wrote. "Soldiers saw no apparent reason why the conflict between the two was any concern of America." There was, he added, "a dismaying lack of comprehension on the part of our soldiers as to the fundamental causes of the war."

A young Army sergeant named Forrest Pogue, who years later would write a highly acclaimed biography of Marshall, echoed Eisenhower's concerns. During the war, Pogue observed, he often talked with his buddies about "the listlessness of the American soldier, and the fact that he seldom seemed to know what he was fighting for.

Some of [my friends] argued that there had never been any reason for our coming over, that all the U.S. needed was a strong navy. I doubted if we could ever make people see what they were fighting for, unless we were invaded."

IN THE SUMMER of 1942, Gil Winant wrote a letter to Roosevelt, urging that something be done to minimize the vast difference in pay between British and U.S. troops. Among his suggestions was a campaign to encourage GIs to buy special high-interest Treasury bonds that could be redeemed as soon as they were discharged. FDR rejected the ambassador's ideas, declaring that there was "no simple and wholly satisfactory solution" to the problems created by the Americans' comparatively high pay and living conditions.

Problems there certainly were. As Winant had feared, the GIs' superior rations, smart uniforms, greater pay, and access to a plethora of consumer items caused resentment and hostility among many Britons, particularly among servicemen who envied the popularity of the free-spending Americans with young British women. "They could have looked like Quasimodo," observed one British soldier, "and it would have made no difference, as long as they were American." Another Tommy declared: "The Yanks were the most joyful thing that ever happened to British womanhood. They had everything—money in particular, glamour, boldness, cigarettes, chocolate, nylons, Jeeps. . . ."

When they arrived in Britain, American soldiers were handed a small newspaper with the word WELCOME emblazoned in large capital letters on the front page. Underneath was the message: "Wherever you go in this country, you will be among friends. Our fighting men look upon you as comrades and brothers-in-arms." But, as one former GI remarked, "Some of these brothers finished up in the arms of [British soldiers'] sweethearts and even wives. . . . I think the Tommies had good grounds for resentment."

Frequent barroom brawls between British and American soldiers were among the problems with which Winant and the U.S. military had to deal. Another was a venereal disease epidemic among GIs in late 1943 and 1944. Approximately 30 percent of the VD cases were contracted in London, where armies of prostitutes, armed with flashlights in the blackout, congregated around Piccadilly Circus, Leicester Square, and other popular GI haunts. "In the darkness of London

1944, every doorway was a love nest," recalled an American military policeman.

Many proper young British women were warned by their parents and others that Americans "were wild, promiscuous, and a threat to every female under 70" and that no nice girl would ever consent to be seen with them. Yet, when they actually encountered GIs, they discovered that, while brash and flirtatious, a good number of the Yanks were not the lecherous ogres they had been made out to be. "There was a hard core of drinkers and womanizers," observed one woman who had been a teenager during the war. She added, however, that most Americans she met treated her with courtesy and respect—and at the same time injected gaiety and laughter into an atmosphere notably deficient of both.

She was hardly alone in that view. Although the GIs' swaggering boastfulness and determination to enjoy themselves grated on many Britons' nerves, others found their zest for life to be a welcome antidote to the numbing austerity and gray monotony of wartime life in Britain. "As good as a tonic," one Briton called the Americans. A teenager in Liverpool declared: "The arrival of the GIs was certainly something our drab, dreary old town needed." A woman who worked at an American military club during the war noted that entering the club "was like stepping into another world. The war, rationing, and coupons were all forgotten." When she left each night, "I would step out into the blackout, back to reality, leaving behind the warmth and friendship of America."

WHILE THE QUESTION of GIs and sex proved to be a major headache for U.S. and British authorities, the issue of race was even more explosive. The American military was rigidly segregated, and the more than 100,000 U.S. black soldiers in Britain were kept as separate as possible from their white counterparts, both at work and off duty. Pubs, dance halls, and clubs in some towns were designated for whites or blacks only. In other places, an elaborate system of rotating passes was set up, to allow blacks and whites to go into town on different nights.

Britain, which then had very few blacks within its borders, was not a segregated country, and its citizens, many of whom had never seen a nonwhite person, were shocked by the American policy—and the blatant racism that underlay it. As Eisenhower explained to his bosses in

Washington: "To most English people, including the village girls—even those of perfectly fine character—the Negro soldier is just another man." U.S. military leaders didn't see it that way. Having initially resisted the inclusion of blacks in the Army, they were forced by Roosevelt to accept a 10 percent quota of black soldiers in every theater of war, most of whom were then assigned to menial noncombatant duties, such as peeling potatoes, cleaning latrines, and digging ditches. In the minds of the British, such marginalization and discrimination were particularly unseemly on the part of an ally that claimed to be fighting for freedom and democracy for all men.

Britons were especially appalled by the intense hostility and contempt that some white GIs, many of them from the segregated South, showed to their black colleagues. They refused to enter pubs that served black Americans, tried to evict blacks from pubs and dance halls, declined to dance with British girls who had danced with blacks, and smashed glasses from which blacks had drunk. When a British airman invited a black soldier to sit down in a compartment on a crowded train from Cardiff to York, a white GI shouted, "Get out, you goddamned nigger!" The Tommy later said he told the American "to belt up, and he came for me. My teeth were knocked right through my tongue." An aircraft worker from Blackpool recalled: "I have personally seen the American troops literally kick—and I mean kick—the coloured soldiers off the pavement, yelling 'stinking black pigs' and 'black trash' and 'uppity niggers.'"

The British government, caught in the middle of this burgeoning controversy between its own people and its most vital ally, tried to have it both ways. Officially, government leaders distanced themselves from the U.S. segregation policy, declaring that Britain would not sanction "discrimination as regards the treatment of coloured troops" and that there "must be no restriction of facilities." Unofficially, however, they supported the policy, ordering the British military to instruct their forces, particularly those in the women's branches, not to socialize with black Americans. "It was desirable," the War Cabinet concluded, "that the people of this country should avoid becoming too friendly with coloured American troops." Brendan Bracken, Churchill's minister of information, wrote: "The American policy of segregation is the best practical contribution to the avoidance of trouble. Let us second it in every way."

Black servicemen, however, were very popular among the British public, who viewed them as polite, soft-spoken, and self-effacing—that is, much like the British themselves. "The general consensus of opinion," George Orwell remarked, "seems to be that the only American soldiers with decent manners are the Negroes." Another Englishman commented: "I don't mind the Yanks, but I don't care much for the white fellows they've brought with them." A sizable percentage of Britons, taken aback by their government's complicity in a policy they considered immoral, resisted any official attempt to treat black GIs as inferior human beings. "The opinion has been expressed from many quarters," a Ministry of Information report noted, "that we should not allow American views on this matter to be imposed on this country."

When the order to keep aloof from black Americans was read to one British Army bomb disposal squad, its members responded with scornful hoots and jeers. "It savoured of Hitlerism," remarked one squad member. " 'Just like Hitler and the Jews' was our reaction to the order." Pubs displayed signs on their doors reading: "For British people and coloured Americans only." On some buses, conductors told blacks not to give up their seats to whites because "they were in England now." When a black GI, on the basis of extremely tenuous evidence, was found guilty of rape and sentenced to death, there was a huge public outcry in the country. Deluged with protesting letters and phone calls, Eisenhower ordered an investigation of the case, which found the evidence to be insufficient. The serviceman was cleared of the charge and restored to duty.

The race question became even more sensitive when white GIs humiliated or attacked blacks who were citizens of British Commonwealth countries. In one case, Learie Constantine, a famed cricket player from the West Indies, was asked to leave a hotel after several American officers staying there threatened to cancel their reservations if he was not ejected. In another instance, a West Indian sergeant in the RAF was beaten up by two Americans for dancing with a white girl. "The Negro British nationals are rightly incensed," admitted one U.S. Army commander. "They . . . have been cursed, made to get off the sidewalk, leave eating places, and separated from their white wives by American soldiers."

More enlightened than most American military leaders when it came to race, Eisenhower tried to crack down on such attacks. He also forbade U.S. commanders to restrict black soldiers' association with British civilians and ordered that black GIs be treated no differently than whites. "The colored troops," he told American reporters, "are to have everything as good" as their white counterparts. But, as was true in the United States, equality, when accompanied by segregation and ingrained racism, proved to be impossible to achieve. Despite Eisenhower's directives, many local commanders turned a blind eye to instances of discrimination on and off their bases.

Overall, few Americans in wartime Britain acquitted themselves well in regard to their country's treatment of blacks. Ed Murrow, for example, offered a tortured semi-defense of an indefensible institution—slavery—during a discussion of the book *Uncle Tom's Cabin* on the BBC. An outspoken liberal on most social issues, Murrow had been raised by poor Southern parents whose families had strong ties to the Confederacy; one of his grandfathers had fought in the Confederate army. While acknowledging that the system of slavery had produced "abuses," Murrow insisted that slaves were "well cared for generally" and argued that "American slavery was on the whole a humane and civilized institution compared with the present practices of the Germans"—a breathtakingly lame defense, as the CBS broadcaster assuredly knew.

Clearly conflicted by the racial question, Murrow, at the same time, was not averse to letting his fellow Americans know how black servicemen felt about their mistreatment by fellow soldiers. During the making of the CBS dramatic series *An American in England*, Joseph Julian, one of the actors, recorded an interview with a black Army corporal, who made clear how much he preferred the company of the British to his own countrymen. "Sure, man, they drink with you, they talk with you. There ain't no difference with them. I'd like to stay here after the war except the United States is still your home, and you have a feeling you want to go back to your home, no matter how bad things are."

Julian asked Norman Corwin, the creator, writer, and producer of the series, to include the interview in one of the episodes. Noting that it might stir up trouble at home, Corwin agreed but said the final decision was Murrow's. When he was shown the dialogue, Murrow slammed a fist into the palm of his hand and exclaimed: "Let's do it! Let's raise a little hell back home!" The series' next program contained the corporal's remarks.

For his part, Gil Winant, concerned about the prospect of trouble, expressed some reservations to Roosevelt early in the war about the advisability of sending black GIs to Britain. Once the decision was made, however, the ambassador, by all accounts, worked hard to lessen the resulting strife and tension that cropped up between Americans and Britons and black and white GIs. At the U.S. embassy's initiative, the British-American Liaison Board, a joint Anglo-American committee, was set up to investigate and try to settle problems between the British public and American troops. Winant recruited Janet Murrow as the committee's chief U.S. representative; for several months, she traveled throughout the country, reporting on clashes between white and black American soldiers and other instances of local friction.

Winant also persuaded Roland Hayes, the famed black American tenor, to stay on in Britain after a concert tour and talk to black GIs around the country about their treatment by the Army. Hayes's report, showing widespread discrimination, was sent to Eleanor Roosevelt, who passed it on to the Pentagon. The report, in turn, was transmitted to General Jacob Devers, the head of the Army's European Theater of Operations in 1943, who promptly denied all such charges. After Walter White, the executive secretary of the National Association for the Advancement of Colored People (NAACP), made a trip to Britain in early 1944 to see for himself how black troops were treated, he reported to Mrs. Roosevelt that he had found "great unhappiness" among the men with whom he talked. At the same time, White was full of praise for the efforts of Eisenhower and Winant to alleviate the blacks' situation, inadequate as they turned out to be.

THERE'S NO QUESTION that the mistreatment of black troops was, in British eyes as well as in truth, a blot on the good name of the U.S. military and America itself. As *Time* magazine put it, "America's polite, liquid-voiced, smartly uniformed Negro soldiers were a surprise, a pleasure, and a happy opportunity for [the British] to thumb the nose of moral self-righteousness at the U.S." Yet, for all the problems created by race, and for all the other strains caused by the overwhelming American presence in Britain, it is remarkable that, in the end, this dramatic confrontation between two countries and cultures worked out as smoothly as it did.

In the early spring of 1944, Sir Basil Liddell Hart, a noted British military commentator and strategist, traveled around England to gauge the temperature of American-British relations. While observing a number of instances of abrasive behavior by both U.S. soldiers and Britons, he concluded that he could "not think of any case in history" where relations between friendly occupiers and the country being invaded had been so good. "Still less," he added, "can I recall any case where two great allied armies have got along so well." A Ministry of Information report in mid-1944 noted "an increasingly kindly feeling toward U.S. troops" in the country, which it attributed to the fact that "people are getting to know the Americans better."

The relatively harmonious coexistence of U.S. soldiers and British civilians at a time of great stress and pressure owed much to the work of Eisenhower, Eden, and the other American and British officials who laid the groundwork and smoothed the way. But, in the view of some, the lion's share of the credit belonged to Winant. According to *The Nation*, it was Winant, with his "firmness and good sense," who found the solutions for most of the "problems, some of which assumed the status of substantial crises," caused by the "presence in Britain of our huge army." The GI newspaper *Stars and Stripes* underscored the ambassador's role as an Anglo-American mediator when it published a cartoon showing a tipsy American soldier, surrounded by angry patrons in a pub after creating a disturbance, making a telephone call. The caption read: "Mr. Winant, please! Mr. John G. Winant . . ."

When Bernard Bellush, a GI from New York, visited London on leave in 1944, virtually every British civilian he met told him how much they admired Winant and how "this caring and courageous envoy had strengthened their will and determination to fight Hitler." Thanks to their fondness for Winant, Bellush added, the Britons he met went out of their way to "make American GIs like myself welcome."

Whenever he could break away from his work for an hour or two, Winant liked to go out on the streets of London to talk to GIs and find out how they were coping with their lives in Britain—"no airs, no brass hat–ism, just a swell guy," in the words of one soldier. Sometimes, the ambassador would lend money to his young countrymen or buy them a beer at a nearby pub. Occasionally, as he did with his Ivy League friends early in the war, he would invite a few of them back to his office to continue the conversation, while other visitors with appointments waited impatiently outside. GIs who couldn't find a bed at a hotel or Red Cross club were invited to spend the night on the floor of his flat.

Winant urged the Americans he met to write and let him know how they were doing, and many did just that. Among his correspondents was a young OSS officer named Stewart Alsop, later a noted columnist and author, who told Winant he had fallen in love with an English girl and wanted to marry her. Her parents, however, were skeptical about the match, and Alsop, who was a distant cousin of Eleanor Roosevelt's, asked the ambassador if he would contact them and vouch for his character and family background. Winant, who had met Alsop through Mrs. Roosevelt, complied, permission was given, and the couple soon married.

In his meetings with young Americans, Winant invariably encouraged them to get to know the British. While many GIs left the country without doing so, thousands of others did form close bonds with British civilians. For some, it began with regular outings at the local pub, where they soon got to know all the regulars. Writing about the pub he frequented in Watford, a town in Hertfordshire, Robert Arbib observed: "You hadn't been at the Unicorn very long before you were one of the family, calling the boss Dora and the chief barman Jimmy, and being called 'my Yank' . . . and eventually, 'Bob' or 'dear.' " Befriended by a number of townspeople he met there, Arbib "ate at their tables, slept on couches in their parlours, went to parties and dances with them . . . and made myself completely at home."

Americans stationed for long periods of time in one place, like the airmen of the Eighth Air Force, had a particularly good opportunity to get to know the residents of nearby villages and towns on a more personal basis. A woman who lived in an East Anglia village adjacent to a U.S. Army Air Forces base recalled: "By 1943, the GIs were part of our community. We knew the names of their planes. We knew the crews who flew them and the ground crews who serviced them." When the planes returned from bombing runs in the afternoon, "we'd hear the thunder of their engines and would pause in our games or work," praying that all the Yanks had come back safely.

Other Americans, meanwhile, formed intimate friendships with British families who invited them to their homes for Sunday dinners and holiday celebrations or offered them permanent billets. Among them was Lieutenant Dick Winters, a paratrooper with the 101st Airborne. Shortly after Winters arrived for training near the Wiltshire village of Aldbourne, an elderly couple, whose RAF son had recently been killed in action, invited him to tea. He accepted, and, after a few more visits, the couple asked if he would like to board with them. Given permission by his superiors to do so, he became in effect their surrogate son. "They adopted me and made me part of the family," said Winters, whose later distinguished combat career in Europe was highlighted in the Stephen Ambrose book and HBO miniseries, *Band of Brothers*. "I'd found a home away from home. . . . This helped me prepare mentally for what I was about to face."

That was apparently true for many other GIs as well. When U.S. military authorities examined the mail that American soldiers sent back from Normandy in July 1944, they discovered that more than a quarter of the letters were addressed to British homes.

17.

"YOU WILL FIND
US LINING UP WITH
THE RUSSIANS"

WHILE THE TIES BETWEEN BRITISH CIVILIANS AND AMERICAN GIs may have strengthened as the war advanced, the feeling of kinship between the two countries' leaders ebbed dramatically. In the first two years of the Anglo-American alliance, Franklin Roosevelt and Winston Churchill had conferred seven times. They had celebrated Christmas and other holidays in each other's company. They had joked, fished, sung, and drunk together. As early as mid-1943, however, Roosevelt began to pull back from his comradeship with the British prime minister. Indeed, it sometimes appeared that he wanted as little to do with Churchill as possible. "In the last eighteen months of Roosevelt's life, I thought the openheartedness diminished," recalled John Colville. "The brotherly tone of the President's messages seemed to change."

With the United States now dominant in the number of troops, weapons, and other resources devoted to the war, Churchill, to his considerable pain and alarm, found himself and his country being treated as junior partners in the alliance. "Increasingly, as the war went on, the Americans paid no attention to anything we said, unless it happened to coincide with something that they wanted to do," observed General Ian Jacob, Pug Ismay's deputy. Eric Sevareid noted: "For many years [the British] had urged Americans to accept the facts of life and come into the world—and now the Americans . . . had done so, and in so doing had created a complete new set of life's facts which the British had hardly expected and were beginning now bitterly to resent. . . . Englishmen were not only no longer the unique heroes of the fight, they were of secondary importance."

The fraying of the Roosevelt-Churchill relationship occurred at a critical period. With the tide of the war turning in the Allies' favor, it was becoming obvious that Hitler's defeat was only a matter of time. By the fall of 1943, the Germans were gone from North Africa, and the Battle of the Atlantic finally was won. Sicily had been captured, Mussolini overthrown, and Allied troops had begun to slog their way up the boot of Italy. On the eastern front, the Russians followed their victory at Stalingrad with a major offensive against the Germans, taking back much of the Soviet territory occupied by the Wehrmacht in 1941. Planning for the invasion of Europe intensified, and preliminary discussions began over surrender terms, the occupation of Germany, and Roosevelt's cherished dream—a new world organization of nations to keep the peace. Among the Allies, the main concern was no longer national survival; it now was the protection of each country's postwar interests.

In response to the fast-moving military situation, Roosevelt and Churchill met twice in four months—in Washington in May 1943 and Quebec and Hyde Park in August. The fact that both conferences were again on Roosevelt's home turf—or at least his home continent—was very much a sore point for Churchill, whose attempts to persuade the president to come to Britain for at least one wartime visit had thus far met with failure. According to Harry Hopkins, FDR was wary of traveling to Britain for "political reasons," fearing he might be seen by American voters as too sympathetic to the British empire. In the eyes of the sixty-eight-year-old prime minister, who had endured a succession of long sea voyages and transatlantic flights to meet with Roosevelt, such a response was hardly gracious treatment of a loyal ally.

But in the summer of 1943, Roosevelt and his military advisers were not in a mood to yield much of anything. Having been outmaneuvered by the British at earlier conferences, particularly at Casablanca, the American high command was determined to have its way on strategic operations until the war's end. During the 1943 meetings, the British did win agreement for their proposal to invade Italy in September—a continuation of their Mediterranean strategy. But U.S. officials, increasingly exasperated by Churchill's foot-dragging on a landing in France, insisted that the British must commit themselves to May 1, 1944, as a firm date for D-Day. Even Churchill's old friend Harry

Hopkins had turned against him on the issue. "Harry is sure that Winston's obstinacy, his drawn-out struggle to postpone a second front in France, has in fact prolonged the war," Lord Moran wrote in his diary. "It appears that the President and Hopkins are no longer prepared to acknowledge Winston as an infallible guide in military matters." (In truth, they never did; they simply had become more out-spoken about the fact.) Against Churchill's strenuous opposition, the Americans also pushed through a plan to support the D-Day landings with an invasion of southern France.

Distressed by U.S. resistance to his strategic ideas, the prime minister was wounded on a deeper level by the president's growing coolness. Both politically and personally, he needed FDR far more than Roosevelt needed him. Churchill was warmer and considerably more emotional than Roosevelt, whom Arthur Schlesinger Jr. described as "glittering, impersonal . . . superficially warm, basically cold." Missy LeHand, FDR's private secretary, once told a reporter that her boss, on whom she doted, "was really incapable of a personal friendship with anyone." Churchill, on the other hand, was "a gentleman to whom the personal element means a great deal," as Eleanor Roosevelt noted. Churchill himself observed to Anthony Eden that "my whole system is founded on friendship with Roosevelt." He later added: "Our friendship is the rock on which I build for the future of the world." To Roosevelt, Churchill remarked: "Anything like a serious difference between you and me would break my heart."

In the early period of the pair's relationship, there did seem to be an authentic personal closeness, a "real friendship and understanding" between the two, as Daisy Suckley, a distant cousin and sometime confidante of the president's, put it. After watching Roosevelt and Churchill together in Washington in June 1942, Suckley noted that FDR's "manner was easy and intimate—His face humorous or very serious, according to the subject of conversation, and entirely *natural*. Not a trace of having to guard his words or expression, just the opposite of his manner at a press conference, when he is an actor on a stage." As for Churchill, Suckley took away the impression that he "*adores* the President . . . looks up to him, defers to him."

But even in those halcyon days of the relationship, there was an unspoken rivalry between these two leaders, which only increased as the war approached its climax. "Roosevelt envied Churchill's genius, and Churchill increasingly envied Roosevelt's power," the historian John

Grigg has written. Samuel Rosenman, one of FDR's top speechwriters, observed that the president "was prone to jealousy of competitors in his field. He liked flattery, especially as he grew older, and he seemed frequently to be jealous of compliments paid to others for political sagacity, eloquence, statesmanship or accomplishments in public life."

Many years later, Arthur Schlesinger Jr. asked Pamela Churchill Harriman whether she thought Roosevelt and Churchill would ever have become friends if there had been no war. Her answer was an emphatic no. "They had nothing in common," she said. "They were not each other's type. They were not amused by the same things. They did not like the same sort of people. . . . They had a different attitude toward the past. . . . But they had to get on with each other, and both worked at it."

The truth was that, for all Churchill's romanticizing in his memoirs about his relationship with Roosevelt, neither he nor the president ever allowed their friendship to interfere with what they considered the national interests of their respective countries. In the words of the historian David K. Adams, "Each used the other, each exploited the other and drove hard bargains when interests conflicted. Out of their creative tension, great good came and heroic myths were created."

THE CONFLICTS BETWEEN Roosevelt and Churchill extended far beyond the question of when and where Allied forces should land in Europe. An adamant opponent of Britain's empire, Roosevelt spent much of the war trying to pressure Churchill and his government to begin the process of granting independence to their country's imperial possessions. Even before the United States entered the war, the president made his position clear, telling his son Elliott: "We've got to make clear to the British from the very outset that we don't intend to be simply a good-time Charlie who can be used to help the British empire out of a tight spot. . . . I think I speak as America's President when I say that America won't help England in this war simply so that she will be able to continue to ride roughshod over colonial peoples."

During Churchill's first visit to Washington, Roosevelt raised the issue of self-determination for India, the most precious jewel in the British empire's crown. Churchill reacted so negatively, he later wrote, that the president never brought up the subject again. That was not exactly the case. In future meetings and in his correspondence with the prime minister, FDR repeatedly raised the question of India and of British imperialism in general. Elliott Roosevelt, for example, remembered that at Casablanca, his father "dropped in a remark about the past relationship between French and British financiers, [who] combined into . . . syndicates for the purpose of dredging riches out of colonies."

The president's antipathy toward British colonialism was echoed in an October 12, 1942, *Life* editorial entitled "An Open Letter to the People of England." In it, the magazine's editors declared: "One thing we are sure we are *not* fighting for is to hold the British Empire together. We don't like to put the matter so bluntly, but we don't want you to have any illusions." The editorial urged the British to forgo "your side of the war," which meant colonialism, and join "our side," which translated into "fighting for freedom throughout the world."

For Henry Luce, the publishing mogul who owned *Life, Time,* and *Fortune,* the twentieth century was destined to be the "American Century." Of Luce, a bemused Tom Matthews, who worked for him as *Time's* managing editor, said: "If he had been British, he would certainly have been an extreme Tory, proud of the Empire, protestingly furious at its liquidation. As an American with an imperial sense of America's future, he was glad to see Britain's competition dwindle."

Infuriated by the *Life* editorial, Churchill declared in a London speech that he had "not become the King's First Minister in order to preside over the liquidation of the British Empire." Throughout the war, he manfully did his best to follow Roosevelt's wishes, except when it came to the empire, which was a deeply personal, emotional issue for him. In the 1930s, he had led a lengthy, vitriolic campaign against a British government proposal for limited self-government for India. His attitude was regarded by most MPs as reactionary and unrealistic, and it was responsible in part for his exclusion from any high posts in the governments of Stanley Baldwin and Neville Chamberlain. Churchill's views on India also prevented him from attracting a large following in the House of Commons when he first began warning about the growing menace of a rearmed Germany.

In 1942, many members of Parliament, as well as a large number of British government officials, would have agreed with Roosevelt that India must be given more autonomy and, at some point, its independence. Some also would have agreed that Britain had a great many stains on its colonial record. What they objected to was the American attitude toward British imperialism, which they regarded as smug, self-righteous, and deeply hypocritical.

After all, in the nineteenth and early twentieth centuries, the United States had embarked on its own version of imperialism, seizing half of Mexico, invading Cuba, and annexing Puerto Rico, Hawaii, and the Philippines, among other territories. Oliver Stanley, the British colonial minister, reminded Roosevelt of that fact in 1945 when the president said to him: "I do not want to be unkind or rude to the British, but in 1841, when you acquired Hong Kong, you did not acquire it by purchase." Stanley shot back: "Let me see, Mr. President, that was about the time of the Mexican War."

But Roosevelt, like most of his compatriots, refused to accept the imperialist label. As Americans saw it, the United States had been an expansionist power, not a colonial one: its mission was to civilize and protect, not exploit, the foreign peoples who came under its dominion. According to the historian Justus Doenecke, "Roosevelt's picture of American history was highly chauvinistic. In his view, American action in the world arena reflected sheer altruism." But not all residents of U.S.-controlled territories viewed it that way, nor did the British, who had often used the altruism argument themselves when adding to their empire.

Churchill and others in the British government also suspected that behind the Americans' high-minded sermons about freeing British possessions from colonial rule was a generous dollop of economic self-interest. Their suspicions would certainly have been reinforced if they had overheard a casual comment that Roosevelt made to his son Elliott at Casablanca: "British bankers and German bankers have had world trade pretty well sewn up in their pockets for a long time, despite the fact that Germany lost in the last war. Well, now, that's not so good for American trade, is it?" In the sardonic view of Anthony Eden, "Roosevelt's dislike of colonialism, while it was a principle with him, was none the less cherished for its possible advantages."

Those advantages included British bases in the Pacific, on which the Pentagon had its eye, and oil concessions in the Middle East. Aware that America's oil reserves were insufficient to meet its future needs, U.S. government officials were determined to break Britain's dominance in the region and acquire concessions of their own. American businessmen, meanwhile, were anxious to acquire access to markets protected by Britain's imperial preference system, which bound Britain and its empire together in an economic common market and imposed stiff tariffs on imported goods from nonempire countries. While the military alliance between the two countries was unprecedentedly close, "it is similarly true," as historian Kathleen Burk has noted, "that the United States treated Britain as a rival which had to be cut down."

Even before the United States entered the war, Washington, citing rumors that the British were using Lend-Lease goods for export, pressured London to agree to forgo not only the export of American supplies but also the export of British goods of a similar nature. The reports of British abuse of Lend-Lease for their own economic gain proved to be unsubstantiated, but American policymakers remained adamant that Britain must be prevented from acquiring any commercial edge during the war. Eden and other British officials were infuriated by the U.S. demands, which they viewed as economic blackmail, but in the end, Gil Winant convinced them to sign the agreement, citing the importance of minimizing "friction and misunderstanding on both sides." As it happened, the reduction of British exports during the war helped open many world markets to American penetration. At the end of the conflict, British exports had plummeted 50 percent while American exports had expanded threefold.

At the same time, however, the British strenuously resisted another American effort to use Lend-Lease as a stick. In the summer of 1941, the Roosevelt administration proposed that, as a payback for Lend-Lease, the British agree to end its imperial preference system. Arguing that such trade discrimination greatly inhibited international economic growth, American officials pushed free trade as the path to postwar peace and prosperity. As the British saw it, free trade was particularly good for the United States, which had long sought access to empire trade on equal terms but, at the same time, insisted on keeping its own high tariffs. (The Americans argued that their tariffs were not discriminatory because they applied to all U.S. trading partners.)

Although a staunch imperialist, Churchill did not much like the imperial preference system. But he and his cabinet were vehemently opposed to the idea of being coerced into agreeing to a postwar economic order that favored the United States. Indeed, they wondered, why was there any need for a Lend-Lease payback at all? At the pinnacle of its might as an empire, Britain paid its allies to fight on its behalf and did not expect financial reimbursement afterward. Why shouldn't America follow Britain's example?

In February 1942, Churchill raised that point in an irate cable to Roosevelt that was never sent: "It must be remembered that for a large part of 27 months we carried on the struggle single-handed. . . . Had we failed, the full malice of the Axis Powers . . . would have fallen upon the United States." In a cable that *was* dispatched to the president, Churchill noted that the British cabinet had already decided the issue. It voted against swapping imperial preference for Lend-Lease, feeling that, if Britain did so, "we should have accepted an intervention in the domestic affairs of the British Empire."

In the end, a compromise was worked out. It committed both governments to take postwar action to achieve international economic cooperation but eliminated an explicit British commitment to end imperial preference. The Americans, however, would raise the subject again at the end of the war, and, this time, the British would not escape.

THE UNRAVELING OF Churchill and Roosevelt's relationship in the late stages of the war was exacerbated by the failing health of both leaders. The crushing, constant pressure of the conflict had taken an immensely heavy physical toll on them and on virtually every other major figure in their governments. In wartime diaries and letters, high-level British and American officials, both military and civilian, complained that the war's physical and mental strain had left them perpetually exhausted, chronically ill, and, in many cases, drinking too much. Reading his waspish late 1943 diary entries several years later, Alan Brooke, for example, recalled that he had not been well at the time, adding: "I am inclined to think that I cannot have been very far off from a nervous breakdown."

After the Casablanca conference in early 1943, both Roosevelt and Churchill fell seriously ill—Churchill with pneumonia and Roosevelt with influenza—and, afterward, both seemed to have lost much of the vitality that had been their trademark. When David Brinkley, then a young newspaper reporter, first saw Roosevelt in 1943 at the White House, he was shocked by the president's ravaged face. "In newspaper and magazine and newsreel pictures, it was the face of a handsome man with strong, well-formed features," Brinkley observed. "Here was the reality—a man who looked terribly old and tired. . . . This man's face was more gray than pink, his hands shook, his eyes were hazy and wandering, his neck drooped in stringy, sagging folds." When Brinkley asked FDR's press secretary what was wrong with him, the official shrugged and said: "He's just tired. Running a world war is a hell of a job." Roosevelt, who had been president for eleven years at that point, was more than tired: he was showing the signs of the severe hypertension and heart disease that would kill him less than two years later. His family and aides were increasingly concerned by his growing listlessness and bouts of forgetfulness.

Overstrained and overtired, Churchill seemed to be losing his own legendary powers of concentration. "I began to feel . . . that the stupendous burden that he had been carrying so valiantly throughout the war was gradually crushing him," Alan Brooke remarked. Seven years older than the president, Churchill had been waging war for a considerably longer period than FDR—and under arguably greater pressure. That strain, compounded by the demands of frequent trips to visit Roosevelt, other allies, and British troops, made him gloomy, sick, tired, and even more impulsive than usual. The prime minister's doctor noted that his work had begun to suffer. Brooke and others in the British government worried about Churchill's abrupt change of moods and positions on strategy and tactics, his "inability to finish one subject before taking up another," and an occasional "instability of judgment." In October 1943, Brooke exploded in his diary: "I am slowly becoming convinced that in his old age, he is becoming less and less well balanced! I can control him no more. . . . He refuses to listen to any arguments." In their increasingly frequent verbal battles, both Churchill and Brooke were, as Brooke's biographer Arthur Bryant pointed out, "too exhausted to realize that the other was in the same state."

ON NOVEMBER 12, 1943, Roosevelt boarded the USS *Iowa* in Chesapeake Bay for the first leg of an arduous journey to the Middle East—first, to Cairo, for a session with Churchill and China's Chiang Kai-shek, and then to Tehran, for the Western leaders' first conference with their fretful Soviet ally, Joseph Stalin. Neither Churchill nor Roosevelt wanted the summit to be held in Tehran (Roosevelt, recovering from a new bout with the flu, told Daisy Suckley that the Iranian capital was "full of disease"), and both tried to convince Stalin to meet somewhere else. Stalin refused: if they wanted to see him, they would have to accept the site he designated.

A day after Roosevelt's departure, Churchill, who was suffering from a sore throat and heavy cold, sailed from Plymouth on the HMS *Renown*. Included in his large retinue were his daughter Sarah, acting as his personal aide-de-camp, and Gil Winant, who was making his first appearance at a Roosevelt-Churchill conference. While Averell Harriman, Winant's bête noire, had managed to get himself included in all but one of the Western leaders' wartime meetings, the ambassador had been sidelined from all of them except Cairo and Tehran. Even worse, as he saw it, was the fact that nobody in Washington ever let him know what happened at the sessions; he was forced to rely on Churchill and Eden to fill him in on what was discussed. In a letter to Roosevelt after the 1943 Quebec meeting, Winant noted that, except for briefings from the prime minister and Eden, "I have had no information . . . on any major policy decisions."

With an Allied victory drawing closer and talks beginning on economic and political settlements, Winant was anxious to play a significant role in the construction of the postwar world. His frustration and anger at being bypassed and uninformed by the White House boiled over shortly before the Tehran conference, when British and American newspapers ran stories speculating that he would soon return to Washington as secretary of labor. The articles also referred to rumors that either Hopkins or Harriman would replace him in London. Winant immediately shot off a cable to Hopkins, informing him of the reports and adding that "these things would not be damaging if it were not known that you and Averell have done a considerable part of the exchange that normally falls to the office I hold." Further, he declared, "an ambassador cannot be an effective representative in London unless he is better informed and given more support than I am receiving."

As he had in the past, Hopkins sought to pacify Winant. "I know exactly how you feel," he wrote, "and if I were in your shoes I would feel just the same." The president's chief aide denied the rumors of Winant's being replaced, declaring that Roosevelt "not only has absolute confidence in you but feels you are doing the best job of any Ambassador to England. . . . I know of no one who has made a greater contribution to the war than you have, and that opinion is shared by all of your friends here." This time, Hopkins's soothing words were backed up by action: an invitation to Winant to come to Cairo and Tehran.

IN CAIRO, ROOSEVELT hosted a festive Thanksgiving dinner for Churchill and the other top-level British and American officials attending the conference, among them Winant and Harriman. That evening, the old Churchill-Roosevelt camaraderie was very much on display. The president carved two huge turkeys for those around the table, and, after the convivial meal, Sarah, the only woman there, danced with Winant and many of the other male guests, while her father waltzed happily around the room with General Edwin "Pa" Watson, Roosevelt's chief military aide. In his dinner toast, Roosevelt remarked: "Large families are usually more closely united than small ones . . . and so, this year, with the people of the United Kingdom in our family, we are a large family, and more united than before. I propose a toast to this unity, and may it long continue!"

The unity, however, lasted only until Tehran. Throughout the conference, the president ostentatiously ignored Churchill, making clear he was far more interested in wooing Stalin, whose fury over the lack of a second front in Europe had steadily escalated in the previous few months. There was no doubt that, despite the image of a happy, problem-free alliance promoted by Churchill and Roosevelt in Britain and the United States, the Western allies' relationship with the Soviets was in considerable trouble. At Tehran, Roosevelt's plan, according to Cordell Hull, was to "talk Mr. Stalin out of his shell . . . away from his aloofness, secretiveness and suspiciousness until he broadens his views." The president once told his cabinet he was sure that Stalin's brief training for the Russian Orthodox priesthood had "entered his nature" and that he would behave in "the way in which a Christian gentleman should behave." Said Charles Bohlen, a young American diplomat and Soviet expert who translated for the president at Tehran: "I do not think Roosevelt had any real comprehension of the great gulf that separated the thinking of a Bolshevik from a non-Bolshevik, and particularly from an American. He felt that Stalin viewed the world somewhat in the same light that he did." Bohlen added: "A deeper knowledge of history and certainly a better understanding of foreign peoples would have been useful to the President."

Just before the conference began, Harry Hopkins told Lord Moran: "You will find us lining up with the Russians." The "us" to whom Hopkins referred included Harriman, Churchill's old confidant and bezique partner. The new U.S. ambassador to the Soviet Union, who advised the president to stay with Stalin at the Soviet embassy in Tehran rather than with Churchill at the British legation, no longer functioned as an unofficial adviser to the prime minister, there to soothe and reassure him. Now he was seen by the British as an antagonist, who, in Brooke's words, was "endeavouring to improve the American situation with Stalin at our expense." Alexander Cadogan, the longtime permanent undersecretary of the Foreign Office, was infuriated when Harriman at one point gave him and Anthony Eden pointers on "how to conduct international conferences" when "I've forgotten a great deal more than he ever knew." As the conference opened, Brooke told Lord Moran: "Stalin has got the President in his pocket."

When Churchill invited Roosevelt to lunch, the president declined. Hopkins explained that Roosevelt did not want "the impression to get abroad that he and Winston are putting their heads together in order to plan Stalin's discomfiture." Instead, Roosevelt joined forces with Stalin to discomfit Churchill. At a dinner early in the proceedings, the Soviet leader persisted in needling the prime minister, while FDR, according to Bohlen, "not only backed Stalin but seemed to enjoy the Churchill-Stalin exchanges." Bohlen, who years later would become ambassador to Moscow himself, remarked that the president "should have come to the defense of a close friend and ally, who was really being put upon by Stalin." Roosevelt "always enjoyed other people's discomfort," Harriman later noted. "I think it is fair to say that it never bothered him very much when other people were unhappy."

A couple of days later, the president decided to try another tactic to get Stalin on his side: mocking Churchill as Stalin had done earlier. He began by whispering to Stalin: "Winston is cranky this morning. He got up on the wrong side of the bed." Encouraged by Stalin's slight smile, the president twitted Churchill directly, chaffing him about "his Britishness, about John Bull, about his cigars, about his habits." The more Churchill reddened and scowled, the more the Russian leader smiled, until he finally broke into loud laugh. "For the first time in three days I saw light," Roosevelt later exulted to Frances Perkins. "From that time on, our relations were personal. We talked like men and brothers."

Bohlen disagreed with FDR's analysis. In his view, the president's ganging up on Churchill was "a basic error. . . . Russian leaders always expected and realized that Britain and the United States were bound to be much closer in their thinking and in their opinions than either could conceivably be with the Soviet Union. In his rather transparent attempt to dissociate himself from Churchill, the President was not fooling anybody and in all probability aroused the secret amusement of Stalin."

Churchill, for his part, was greatly hurt by what his eldest grandson, also named Winston Churchill, called Roosevelt's "childish exercise in currying favor." According to the younger Churchill, the prime minister never made public how he felt about the incident, revealing only to his family "his huge disappointment and discomfort at what had happened."

IN THE VIEW of most of those present, Stalin was easily the best negotiator of the three leaders at Tehran. There, and later at Yalta, British and American diplomats and military authorities shared the uneasy feeling, as one British official put it, that the "immediate gains had always gone to Russia; the vague promises about the future to the United States and Britain." Stalin finally received a firm commitment for Operation Overlord, the long awaited invasion of mainland Europe. With Roosevelt's help, the Soviet leader stymied Churchill's proposal for expanded Allied operations in the Mediterranean and the Balkans. Stalin, in turn, promised to go to war against Japan after the defeat of Germany.

In addition, Churchill and Roosevelt secretly agreed to one of Stalin's key demands: postwar Soviet control of eastern Poland. Even though Churchill had repeatedly promised the Polish government-in-exile and armed forces that they would get their homeland back after the war, he abandoned that pledge after Stalin, supported by Roosevelt, demanded that Russia be allowed to keep the large chunk of Poland it occupied in 1939. Later, the president would tell Harriman that he "didn't care whether the countries bordering Russia went Communist or not."

British officials were struck by the fact that Roosevelt, who opposed Britain's imperialism so strongly, refused to view Stalin's obvious determination to control his country's neighboring states in the same light. At Tehran, FDR told Stalin: "The United States and the Soviet Union are not colonial powers, so it is easy for us to discuss" the problems created by colonialist empires like Britain and France. The president, Lord Moran wrote in his diary, "cannot leave the [British] Empire alone. It seems to upset him, though he never turns a hair when a great chunk of Europe falls into the clutches of the Soviet Union."

REPORTERS WERE NOT permitted to cover the Tehran conference. After it ended, there were no communiqués released, no details given, about what had been agreed upon or discussed. When Roosevelt and Churchill returned home, they confined themselves to praising the summit meeting as a triumph in which the Big Three had "become friends in fact, in spirit, and in purpose."

Ed Murrow was one of the few British or American journalists who injected a note of doubt about that rosy statement. From his sources in the European governments-in-exile and elsewhere, he had a fairly good idea what had happened in Tehran, and it wasn't a story of unalloyed friendship. An ardent admirer of the Red Army and its victories on the eastern front, Murrow, nonetheless, had always been wary of Stalin and his intentions toward Eastern Europe. "People who have had much talk with Stalin tell me that he isn't interested in acquiring more territory," the CBS newsman said in a broadcast before Tehran. "But Russia's neighbor nations aren't so sure about that. They would like to learn that Britain and America had come to some agreement with Russia which would ensure them that they could, in fact, count on the blessings promised in the Atlantic Charter."

After Tehran, Murrow reported that there had indeed been dissension at the conference. He criticized what he saw as the draining away of the Western Allies' principles and idealism—statements for which he was heavily criticized by sponsors and listeners. "People seem to want to be misled, want to believe that things are going to be easy, that three leaders can sit down in four days and reach fundamental conclusions," he wrote a friend in New York. "Any slight effort at realism is immediately labeled weariness, cynicism and pessimism. I have been getting a lot of that from home recently."

He added: "There was a time in this war when I was one of the few optimistic Americans in London because then the issues were simple.

The outcome would be decided by the nerves and guts of a people who have a strong sense of history. There wasn't any particular reason to worry at that time. But now it seems to me we are entering the stage where decisions must be made—and those decisions simply are not being made."

FOR ALL HIS idealistic rhetoric about creating a just and conflict-free world after the war, Roosevelt, like Churchill, had little interest in serious long-range planning for translating that world into reality. Indeed, for much of the war, the president staunchly opposed any detailed discussion of how to organize and keep the peace. Both Western leaders focused on the task at hand—winning the war. Stalin, by contrast, made clear at Tehran that his wartime actions were inextricably linked to his postwar strategy of gaining dominance over Poland and other neighboring states.

Roosevelt's vision of postwar friendship with the Soviets was, as the historian Warren Kimball put it, "vague and ill defined," unsupported by any practical plans for how to implement such a relationship. The president certainly seemed unworried about possible perils that might arise from making the Soviet Union one of the world's policemen after the war, as he had proposed. Indeed, some skeptics asked, what was there to prevent any one of the Big Four policemen—the United States, Britain, the Soviet Union, and China—from imposing its will on less powerful states? (After raising that question with her husband, Eleanor Roosevelt told him she thought his policemen idea was "fraught with danger.") And how did the president reconcile his concept of the four all-powerful peacekeepers with his proposal for an international organization of equal and independent nations?

In April 1943, FDR spent one afternoon musing to Daisy Suckley how he envisioned the structure of the new organization. He would like to be its head, he told her, with Gil Winant and Harry Hopkins as his assistants. As he saw it, the organization would hold meetings every year in different countries and would be based at least half the year on an island, with a good airfield nearby. He would have a small personal staff, mainly secretaries and stenographers, but there also would be staff members from other nations.

Obviously, this was just fanciful daydreaming, but, later, as the war drew to a close, FDR still offered few hard specifics about how the or-

ganization would work to keep the peace. As was his habit with difficult domestic subjects, his way of dealing with this and a number of
other postwar issues, including America's relations with the Soviets,
was "to postpone, avoid, evade, and dodge," as Warren Kimball put it.
The president clearly was determined to keep his options open for as
long as possible. When undersecretary of state Sumner Welles suggested creation of a group of Allied representatives to begin planning
peace settlements and postwar international policies, Roosevelt, according to Welles, "summarily turned down" the idea. He was similarly
unenthusiastic about efforts by British government officials, particularly Anthony Eden and his subordinates in the Foreign Office, to undertake their own planning, which included the outlines of a possible
future peace settlement. (While Churchill himself had no interest in
such work, he made no attempt to stop Eden and others in his government from pursuing it.) Harry Hopkins warned the British against
trying to take the lead in drawing up blueprints for the postwar world.
The president, Hopkins said, was "rather touchy on these questions as
he regarded the post-war settlement, so to speak, as being his particular preserve."

A strong proponent of postwar planning himself, Gil Winant was
caught between the president, on one hand, and Eden and the European
governments-in-exile, on the other. By early 1943, the governments-in-
exile were pressing Britain and the United States to begin planning for
the economic reconstruction of Europe after the war. Winant lobbied
Washington hard to take a position on postwar reconstruction, noting
that the British government "is accused of stalling at the time when it
really is anxious to go ahead but is held back by us. . . . It is important
that we do not dally too long and leave our continental European Allies
feeling doubtful whether we will cooperate or draw out as we did after
the last war."

But the U.S. government *did* continue to dally over the reconstruction question, just as it did over the problem of organizing relief operations for European populations once they were liberated from German
occupation. It was not until the British set up an inter-Allied commission to plan for European relief and reconstruction that the United
States finally intervened, creating the United Nations Relief and Rehabilitation Administration to oversee the Allied effort.

The Roosevelt administration was determined to retain control
over all aspects of Anglo-American postwar planning. Neither the

president nor Hull looked favorably on any substantive discussions held outside Washington. As it turned out, such recalcitrance would play a part in the torpedoing of efforts to resolve one of the most vital—and explosive—questions facing the Allies: the postwar future of Germany.

SHORTLY BEFORE THE Tehran conference, Roosevelt, Churchill, and Stalin created an Anglo-American-Soviet commission to draw up plans for the surrender and postwar occupation of Germany, as well as long-term proposals for stimulating the recovery of occupied Europe. Dubbed the European Advisory Commission, the body was the brain-child of Anthony Eden, who viewed all three Allies' participation in such broad-scale planning as essential if postwar conflicts were to be avoided. Hull, however, made clear that the United States was not in favor of such a sweeping mandate for the commission, and in the end, it dealt only with Germany.

At Tehran, the three leaders wrestled briefly with the fate of Germany and reached agreement on only a couple of questions—joint control of Berlin and division of the country into three occupation zones, to be governed by the major allies. The leaders left the details of how that division would be achieved—and all other Reich-related issues, including its possible dismemberment—to the London-based European Advisory Commission, whose members were Winant; Feodor Gusev, the Soviet ambassador to Britain; and Sir William Strang, a top official of the British Foreign Office.

When the commission met for the first time in January 1944, Strang was armed with twenty-nine working papers, including a draft surrender instrument and a proposed agreement on the specifics of the British, Soviet, and American zones of occupation. Gusev, too, had his marching orders. Winant alone had no specific directives or proposals from his government, in large part because of deep divisions between the War Department and State Department over postwar German policy. War Department officials insisted that surrender and occupation terms were purely military matters and had no business being considered by the EAC. In a memo to Harry Hopkins, John McCloy, an assistant secretary of war, claimed that the British were trying to control postwar planning for Germany and that no civilian body, particularly one based in London, should have any role in making major decisions. In vehement opposition to that view, Winant, along with a number of State Department officials, contended that all three Allies must be included in the planning for Germany; otherwise there would be chaos and unilateral occupation decisions at the end of the war.

In the end, the War Department won the bureaucratic battle, blocking any effective U.S. participation in the commission's proceedings. When Winant sent the British working papers to Hull and requested guidance, he received no comment from Washington for almost two months. Again and again, the ambassador, "acutely embarrassed" by his government's intransigence, pleaded with Hull and Roosevelt for guidance and directives, but to no avail. The president, who wanted to keep postwar decision making in the hands of Stalin, Churchill, and himself, had never been enthusiastic about the commission, nor did he like the idea of outlining specific peace terms before the end of the war. "I have been worrying a good deal," he wrote Churchill in February 1944, about the Allies' "tendency to prepare for future events in such detail that we may be letting ourselves in for trouble when the time arrives."

Others, including Winant, worried that the opposite would occur—that the failure to plan for the war's aftermath would spawn trouble far beyond the president's imagining.

18.

"WOULD THE DAMN
THING WORK?"

FOR ANYONE LIVING IN THE SOUTH AND EAST OF ENGLAND IN THE spring of 1944, there was little doubt that the long-awaited invasion of Europe was imminent. The sky over East Anglia was "as full of traffic as Piccadilly Circus," jammed day and night with thundering Fortresses, Liberators, Lancasters, and Wellingtons on their way to bomb railroads and shipping facilities in France. Truck convoys, tanks, and speeding jeeps choked roads and lanes in the south, while camouflaged artillery and weapons, along with millions of crates of supplies, were piled high in woods, fields, playgrounds, village greens, and along roads and other byways. According to *The New Yorker*'s Mollie Panter-Downes, the rustic charm of the English countryside had become "mostly something that you read about in books."

The docks of the country's southern ports, lined with towering cranes, were crowded with seagoing vessels of all descriptions—British and American warships, landing craft, and merchant freighters from around the world. Above all, the island was chock-full of soldiers— more than two million Britons, Americans, Canadians, and other nationalities—who endured rigorous training exercises on the coast and elsewhere during the week, then streamed into villages and towns on Saturday nights to let off steam. Living in England during that period, Panter-Downes noted, was like "living on a vast combination of an aircraft carrier, a floating dock jammed with men, and a warehouse stacked to the ceiling with material labeled 'Europe.'"

It was a beautiful spring that year, but few people in Britain paid attention to its glories—or to much of anything but the invasion. Rumors about its date and destination swept through London like a virus. Everyone simply waited, Robert Arbib recalled, "staying close to the radio, snatching at newspapers, and watching the sky and the weather." People kept watch on the sky, added Mary Lee Settle, "as a farmer watches it, to read the future."

NO ONE WAS MORE watchful or tense than the man chosen to head the operation. General Dwight Eisenhower had returned to London in January 1944 with a weighty new title—commander of Supreme Headquarters Allied Expeditionary Force (SHAEF)—and even weightier responsibilities. Over the next four months, he was to organize and direct the most complex, fateful, and massive military venture in history.

His way had been somewhat eased by Sir Frederick Morgan, the British general who for almost a year had overseen the initial planning for Operation Overlord. Blessed with a lively sense of humor and a liking for Americans, Morgan had won the respect and trust of both Marshall and Eisenhower, who later credited him with "making D-Day possible." Like Eisenhower during the planning of Torch, Morgan was determined to weld the varied nationalities on his staff into a unified team, but, also like Ike, he faced great difficulties in the beginning. There were "incessant clashes of personalities," Morgan remembered, not only between Americans and Britons but also among the representatives of the different military services and within each nationality. "What is remarkable," he added, "is not that discord existed but that it was repressed."

Morgan himself helped contribute to the eventual blossoming of good feeling by developing an extraordinarily tight-knit relationship with his American chief of staff, General Ray W. Baker. At the beginning of their collaboration, each general removed a button from his military blouse and gave it to the other, to be sewn on his uniform as a symbol of fraternity. Morgan also aided the cause by installing a bar at Norfolk House in St. James's Square, where Torch had been planned and where his staff was now based. At the bar, where staffers gathered after work, "there was never a moment's doubt with regard to the completeness of integration," he remarked. The Americans on Morgan's staff might have hated British food, and vice versa, but "when it comes to a matter of liquid refreshment, American and British habits seem remarkably similar." When Morgan and his subordinates completed the first draft of the Overlord plans, they celebrated with an exuberant party on the top floor of Norfolk House, complete with a British dance orchestra and American swing band. "All entered wholeheartedly into the occasion," he remembered.

The planning staff's growing closeness and mutual trust was demonstrated one day during a transatlantic telephone conversation with U.S. military leaders in Washington. As was customary, several people listened in at both ends of the conversation. At its conclusion, the main speaker in Washington—a senior Army general—admonished his listeners in London, "For Christ's sake, don't tell the British" about the subjects under discussion. Hearing howls of laughter at the other end, the general demanded to know what was so funny. He was told that his listeners included, among other Britons, two generals and an admiral.

When Eisenhower took charge of Overlord, he was intent on fostering the same kind of camaraderie within his own staff, just as he had done with Torch. But this time, he was determined to do it outside the confines of Norfolk House. Much to the dismay of many on the SHAEF team, Eisenhower moved his headquarters from the temptations and pleasures of west London to Bushy Park, a suburb close to Henry VIII's palace at Hampton Court and some ten miles from the heart of the capital. "That way, we won't get caught up in all that la-di-da London society stuff," Eisenhower told Kay Summersby, "and the officers will be thrown together so they'll get to know each other and each other's ways fast."

There were considerable "protests and gloomy predictions," as well as numerous inter-Allied disagreements and clashes of personality, the general noted in his memoirs. Nonetheless, he said, those on his team eventually "developed a relationship that far more than made up for minor inconveniences." Such "inconveniences" included unheated administrative buildings with concrete floors, Quonset huts as sleeping quarters for junior officers, and tents for enlisted men. Yet, for all the discomforts, many if not most of those who worked at SHAEF in the months before D-Day remembered the experience as happy and harmonious, thanks in large part to their chief. Eisenhower was "loved and respected by almost everyone," said one U.S. intelligence officer on the SHAEF staff. The British historian John Wheeler-Bennett, who also was a SHAEF staffer during the war, observed that the supreme commander "deliberately thought himself into a state of mind in which he literally did not know the difference between the two major allies under his command." Norman Longmate, another future historian who worked at SHAEF, said that he and his British compatriots "regarded Ike as a hero. He was believed to be genuinely concerned with the welfare of everyone working at HQ," as shown by his insistence that British soldiers be given the same PX privileges as Americans.

OF OPERATION OVERLORD, historian Max Hastings has written: It was "the greatest organizational achievement of the Second World War, a feat of staff work that has dazzled history, a monument to the imagination of British and American planners and logisticians which may never be surpassed in war." That analysis was written, of course, well after the D-Day landings took place. Before they occurred, many of those involved in their planning, including Eisenhower himself, were consumed with worry that the Allies were not ready for the operation and that it would end in utter failure—"a disaster" as Frederick Morgan put it, "of the most crushing dimension."

The sheer magnitude of Overlord made Torch—and virtually every other previous American or British military operation—look like a kindergarten exercise. In all, nearly two million soldiers, sailors, and airmen from half a dozen Allied countries would take part in the landings and subsequent march across Normandy, causing logistical and other problems that staggered the imagination. The Allies would have to accomplish what no one had done since William the Conqueror in 1066—mount a successful assault across the English Channel.

There were doubts and anxieties about virtually every aspect of the operation—from insufficient numbers of landing craft to the famously unpredictable weather over the Channel to a shortage of supplies. For weeks, Eisenhower wrangled with the Allied bomber barons, Tooey Spaatz and Arthur Harris, who continued to believe that their air forces could win the war on their own, all evidence to the contrary, and balked at placing their planes and crews under Ike's direct command. "By God," Eisenhower stormed to a British colleague, "you tell that bunch that if they can't get together and stop quarreling like children, I will tell the Prime Minister to get someone else to run this damn war!" Both Spaatz and Harris eventually capitulated, but as General Omar

Bradley, who was to lead the U.S. First Army in Normandy, later noted, one result of their recalcitrance was that "we went into France almost totally untrained in air-ground cooperation."

As difficult as the Air Force commanders were, they were far from the main concern of Eisenhower and his lieutenants. Above all, the SHAEF brass feared that the Allied ground troops—the linchpins of the operation—would not measure up to the task. Ike, Bradley, and other combat commanders had been unimpressed, to put it mildly, by the troops' performance in amphibious and other exercises they had witnessed on the south coast of England that spring. Bradley called the simulated amphibious landing "more like a peacetime maneuver than a dress rehearsal of an assault against the continent." Harry Butcher wrote in his diary that many young American officers seemed to lack drive and purpose, seeming to "regard the war as one grand maneuver in which they are having a happy time."

Haunted by memories of the calamitous Gallipoli landings and the bloodbath of World War I, Churchill shared Eisenhower's worries. Having resisted Overlord, with its enormous dangers, for so long, both Churchill and Alan Brooke were, in Brooke's words, "torn to shreds with doubts and misgivings" as the operation's launch date grew closer. "I never want to go through a time like the present one," Brooke wrote in his diary on May 27. "The cross-Channel operation is just eating into my heart."

For his part, Eisenhower, who had been one of the foremost champions of that operation since the beginning of the alliance, exuded confidence in public as he always did. Emotionally and physically, however, he was a wreck. He was smoking and drinking too much and suffered from headaches, recurring throat infections, a bad cough, skyrocketing blood pressure, stomach pains, and chronic insomnia. "He was as nervous as I had ever seen him and extremely depressed," Kay Summersby observed.

With Overlord, the SHAEF commander knew, there would be no second roll of the dice. "In this particular venture, we are not merely risking a tactical defeat," he wrote in early April, "we are putting the whole works on one number."

WHILE EISENHOWER and his staff agonized over D-Day at Bushy Park, a frenzied carnival atmosphere took hold in overcrowded, clamorous London. Traffic was gridlocked, restaurants and clubs were packed, and it took days, sometimes weeks, for newcomers to the capital to find a vacant hotel room or flat. Many of the new arrivals were American journalists, flooding in from all over the globe to be on hand for the biggest story of the war. Ernie Pyle, who had come to London from Tunisia, wrote: "I decided that if the Army failed to get ashore on D-Day, there would be enough American correspondents to force through a beachhead on their own."

Like Pyle, many of the five hundred U.S. reporters now in the British capital had arrived from other battlefronts—North Africa, Italy, Asia, the Pacific. Some of the correspondents were grizzled veterans who had covered World War I, while others were wide-eyed journalistic novices, fresh from their newspapers' city, society, and sports desks. A good number represented publications like *Vogue* and *Sporting News,* never previously known for their keen interest in war reporting. Bemused by the eclectic nature of his new, untried colleagues, Pyle quipped that "if *Dog News* didn't get a man over pretty quickly to cover the dog angle of the invasion, I personally would never buy another copy."

While waiting for D-Day, the newcomers found themselves caught up in London's superheated social life; for many, the weeks before the invasion turned into one continuous party. There were lunches, dinners, cocktail parties, dancing cheek to cheek at nightclubs, and all-night poker sessions in hotel rooms reeking of gin and cigarettes. By then, liquor and wine had become almost impossible to find for most London residents, but, with their quasi-officer status and large salaries and expense accounts, U.S. journalists, like their compatriots in the military, had no trouble unearthing large quantities of both.

Years after the war, Bill Paley looked back fondly on those hedonistic preinvasion days and nights. Recalling a riotous, boozy stag party at Charles Collingwood's apartment that spilled out into the street and didn't end till dawn, the head of CBS said: "Everything that happened that night was funny. . . . Everyone loved each other and it was just a brawl, a big lousy brawl, but it was one of those nights in my life that was very outstanding."

Another inveterate partyer during that period was Ernest Hemingway, who had arrived in London in May as a special reporter for *Collier's*. The famed novelist's assignment to cover Overlord stemmed not from a late-blooming passion to become a war correspondent but from a desire to spite his journalist wife, Martha Gellhorn, from whom he had become estranged. A *Collier's* correspondent herself, Gellhorn, who had covered the Italian campaign, wrote to Hemingway in late 1943: "I believe you will feel very deprived, as a writer, if this is all over and you have not had a share in it."

Knowing that if he wrote for *Collier's,* he would overshadow Gellhorn at the magazine, he wangled an assignment to cover the RAF. Once in London (which he insisted on calling "dear old London town"), he took up residence at the Dorchester, intent more on drinking and womanizing than on journalism. John Pudney, a young RAF public relations officer assigned to help Hemingway, found him boorish and offensive. "To me, he was a fellow obsessed with playing the part of Ernest Hemingway," Pudney said, "a sentimental nineteenth-century actor called upon to act the part of a twentieth-century tough guy. Set beside . . . a crowd of young men who walked so modestly and stylishly with Death, he seemed a bizarre cardboard figure."

Within days of his arrival in London, Hemingway had met Mary Welsh and announced he planned to marry her. To Welsh, he complained about being beset by a throng of London socialites and aristocrats, who, enticed by his fame and macho image, came to his hotel room for flirtations and brief sexual encounters. "They want to stay all night," he groused, "and then have [me] take them home just in time to meet His Lordship leaving for the office in the morning."

NOT EVERY AMERICAN journalist, however, participated in the capital's frenetic social whirl. Ed Murrow, like several other longtime London correspondents, was too busy planning the news coverage of Overlord to have time for such frivolity. In a reflection of his status as the preeminent American journalist in the capital, Murrow, now the president of the American Foreign Correspondents Association, was deeply involved in virtually every aspect of the D-Day preparations. Along with three other reporters, he collaborated with SHAEF to work out the myriad logistical problems of press coverage: how many journalists would cover the landings, how they would get there, where they would go, how they would file their stories. Because of the uncertainties of broadcasting from France, the American radio networks had agreed to pool their Overlord reports, and Murrow had been named to direct their combined efforts. He also had been chosen to broadcast Eisenhower's proclamation to Allied troops on D-Day.

All these duties were a signal honor for the CBS broadcaster, but he was happy with none of them. The assignment he coveted was to cover the invasion. For the last four years, he had done little actual war reporting, staying behind in the backwater of London and envying his correspondents who were on the front lines, from Tunisia to the South China Sea. For a man who hated sitting behind a desk, such inaction was torture.

The night before Charles Collingwood left for North Africa in 1942, he and Murrow went out drinking. As they stumbled back to Murrow's apartment in the blackout, both more than a little drunk, Murrow kicked over a garbage can and shouted, "By God, I envy you for going off! I wish I could go along with you!" A few months later, he did spend a few weeks at the front in Tunisia, but his CBS superiors made clear to him that he was too valuable to the network to risk his life like that on a regular basis. Of the twenty-eight U.S. correspondents named to cover D-Day, five would represent CBS—a remarkable achievement for a news organization that didn't even exist seven years before. But as he knew from the beginning, the man who had been most instrumental in creating that organization would not be among the lucky five.

Still, although he was barred from the battlefield, Murrow managed to find a way to court wartime danger. In the previous five months, he had hitched a ride on more than a dozen RAF and Eighth Air Force bombing missions, most of them bound for Germany. Murrow's story about one of his flights, made in December 1943, was among the best-known news broadcasts of World War II. An unvarnished account of the terror of aerial warfare, both on the ground and in the sky, it began with the sentence: "Last night, some of the young gentlemen of the RAF took me to Berlin." An exhausted, shaken, red-eyed Murrow, just back from the mission, talked of the killing that had gone on around and below him—"Men die in the sky while others are roasted in their cellars"—and described how "very frightened" he was when his RAF bomber was trapped in the glare of German searchlights. That night, he said, Berlin was "a kind of orchestrated hell. . . . In about 35 minutes it was hit with about three times the amount of stuff that ever came down on London in a nightlong blitz."

In the days that followed, the CBS newsman was besieged by congratulatory letters and telegrams from around the world. The BBC, calling his story "one of the finest broadcasts ever," transmitted it across the country, and newspapers throughout England and the United States published it on their front pages. Among them was the *Daily Express,* whose editor, Arthur Christensen, termed the piece "magnificent" and "the only good bombing story written." He sent a check to Murrow, which the broadcaster used to buy books and a new radio for the RAF base housing the aircrew that flew him to Berlin. "Ed was cynical about life in general," Pamela Churchill observed, "but the one thing he could absolutely one hundred per cent admire were the young flyers."

At a gala dinner at the Savoy celebrating the BBC's twenty-first birthday, Brendan Bracken, the minister of information, turned the occasion into a paean to Murrow ("the most faithful friend of Britain") and his story ("one of the finest pieces of writing I've seen"). About the same time, Bracken wrote to Murrow: "My dear Ed, Your attempts to corner trouble are altogether deplorable. The value of your war work cannot be over-estimated. And no one can take your place." Bracken, like many of Murrow's other friends, was appalled by his penchant for putting himself in harm's way again and again. One bombing mission to Germany, perhaps. But more than a dozen? Why did he do it?

In the view of BBC executive Dick Marriott, the reason lay in Murrow's sense of guilt for not participating in the fight himself: "I think this was a compensation in a way for not being in the war." Herbert Agar believed it was the lure of danger that drew the newsman to the bombing missions: "It was a drug without which he felt deflated. . . . Ed was always at his best when the bombs were falling or he had broken all the rules to go aloft and have another look at death." Eric Sevareid said his boss had "a thing about speed. . . . He loved speeds, high speeds. It gave him some kind of thrill."

For his part, Murrow had several rationales for why he repeatedly gambled his life in the air. One reason, he acknowledged to *The New Yorker,* was, as Sevareid surmised, his love of speed. Another was vanity: "Three or four times in London, when I'd be sitting in the office, we'd hear the BBC playing back things I'd said, and nothing has ever made me feel as good as that." To a friend, he wrote: "In order to write or talk about danger, you must experience it. The experience teaches you something about what happens to fighting men and, perhaps more important, it teaches you something about yourself." But, as he acknowledged in a letter to his sister-in-law, he also used the missions as an escape from the ceaseless personal and professional pressures to which he subjected himself. He was living, Murrow wrote her, in an almost continuous state of "fatigue and frustration." His stresses at work were multiplying, and his home life was increasingly tense and unhappy, thanks in large part to his affair with Pamela Churchill. "When I fly," he said, the unhappiness "seems to go away. But it always returns."

Whatever the reasons for Murrow's compulsion, Bill Paley wanted it to stop. "I tried to convince him that he was a damn fool to go out on so many missions," Paley recalled. "I thought he had a death wish. I don't know what it was, but danger to him was an exhilarating experience." In 1943, the CBS chairman extracted a promise from Murrow not to go on any more flights, but within days, he had broken his pledge. By the time the war was over, Murrow had flown on twenty-four bombing raids. Just a few days before D-Day, he made the first live radio broadcast from an American bomber, flying on a mission over occupied France.

AT THE END of May 1944, London began to empty out. The throngs of soldiers, sailors, and airmen—who just days before had sauntered down Piccadilly, eyeing the girls on corners and pushing into already packed pubs—were fast disappearing. They were on their way to marshaling camps on the south coast of England, which had been sealed off to visitors. Day after day, seemingly endless lines of camouflaged trucks, some of the convoys stretching for miles, rumbled down country roads, their occupants bound for Channel ports—and ultimately for Normandy.

For many Americans and Britons, it proved to be a wrenching leave-taking. Among those who felt a sense of loss was Robert Arbib, who like a number of other GIs had come to feel at home in England. "No longer a strange, unknown land," Britain and its way of life had become "our way of life, and its people were my friends," Arbib later wrote. "Just as we had been reluctant to leave America, we were reluctant now to say good-bye to England."

In Bristol, a column of U.S. Army trucks braked to a halt outside a house at 4 A.M. so a young American soldier could dash in and say goodbye to a family who had befriended him. "We stood out on the sidewalk, hugged and kissed and had our spell of tears," he recalled years afterward. In a small town in southern England, another convoy of American tanks and trucks came to a brief stop in front of a row of houses, watched by a crowd of townspeople. Suddenly, a woman emerged from a house carrying bowls of strawberries and cream. She handed one to a young lieutenant named Bob Sheehan, kissed his forehead, and whispered, "Good luck. Come back safe." Galvanized by her gesture of kindness, other townspeople disappeared into their houses and moments later brought out tea and lemonade for the hot, thirsty GIs. Still others invited some of the Americans inside for a bath or a shave. For those few minutes, Sheehan remembered, "there was a kind of togetherness that I had never seen before. A sharing of spirit. It was no longer them and us. We were family, and danger was afoot."

Later that day, a young woman in Plymouth watched as hundreds of American troops boarded their assault craft in the harbor. "My heart ached," she recalled. "I could hardly see for tears." Another young Englishwoman noted: "It was so drab when they had gone. The whole world had been opened up to me, and then it was closed down again."

WHEN THEY HEARD the roar of the bombers, the people of England knew that D-Day had finally come. Just after midnight on June 6, hundreds of British and American aircraft filled the air over East Anglia, the loud throb of their engines sounding, in Ed Murrow's words, "like a giant factory in the sky." Throughout the night, the thunder continued, and when day finally broke, Britons rushed out of their houses, waving tablecloths and Union Jacks at the fleet of planes flying wing to wing above them toward France. "In perfect, geometric formation, they roared overhead," one woman remarked. "They kept coming and coming, as if the whole sky belonged to them." An Eighth Air Force crewman recalled: "The sky looked like we were being invaded by locusts. . . . Having been one of the early Americans to cross the Channel when fifty to one hundred planes was an enormous flight, it put a lump in my throat and a tear in my eye. The Luftwaffe had had its day, and now we were having ours."

The official announcement of the invasion came shortly before 9 A.M. "Ladies and gentlemen, we have landed in France," the managing director of a British aircraft factory told his workers. There was stunned silence, then, as one, the people standing before him, many with tears coursing down their cheeks, began singing "Land of Hope and Glory." After that, said a worker, "We went quietly back to work—for victory."

In London, the few American military men still there were stopped on the street by strangers who wanted to shake their hands. In both Britain and the United States, stores and movie theaters shut down for the day and sporting events were canceled, as citizens flocked to churches in record numbers. One of the churchgoers in Britain was Janet Murrow, who wrote to her parents: "The church was fuller than I've ever known it to be—even on Easter and Christmas." From Washington, Franklin Roosevelt led his nation in prayer, asking God to protect "our sons. . . . Lead them straight and true; give strength to their arms, stoutness in their hearts, steadfastness in their faith. . . . Their road will be long and hard."

In Britain, there was little sense of excitement or rejoicing. "Except for the planes overhead, it was all so quiet," Pamela Churchill wrote Averell Harriman. "It was a great day, & none of the people left behind knew what to do with it." On the surface, it seemed like any other day. People went to their offices and factories, shopped for dinner, played with their children, queued up to buy the newspapers' latest editions. "Walking along the streets of London, you almost wanted to shout at them and say, 'Don't you know that history is being made this day?' " Murrow told his American listeners. Of course, they did, as he well knew; they just didn't know how that history would turn out. "There was a kind of holding of the breath," observed the author William Saroyan, an Army private who worked for the Office of War Information in London. "Everybody seemed to be praying. . . . You could see it in their faces and the way every man went about his business. Would the damn thing work? That was the question." Musing about London's "queer hush" that day, Mollie Panter-Downes wrote in *The New Yorker:* "One could sense the strain of a city trying to project itself across the intervening English orchards and cornfields, across the strip of water, to the men already beginning to die in the French orchards and cornfields which once more had become 'over there.' "

AS DAWN BROKE on June 6, Richard C. Hottelet, a CBS newsman flying aboard a B-26, looked down at the English Channel and sharply drew in his breath. There below, knifing ahead in wind-whipped waves, was the mightiest armada in history—rank after rank of ships stretching as far as he could see, all bearing down on the beaches of Normandy. After returning to London, Hottelet told a colleague: "If I had had to parachute out of the plane, I could have walked across the channel on the ships."

In those ships—and the waves of bombers and fighters overhead—one could see the full power and grandeur of the Western alliance. The British, American, and Canadian troops in the first wave of the invasion were ferried to Normandy by U.S., British, Norwegian, Polish, and French ships. They were given air cover by American, British, Dutch, Norwegian, Polish, Belgian, Czech, and French pilots and aircrews. Unchallenged by the Luftwaffe and encountering only light flak, Allied planes roared low over Normandy in heavy gray rain clouds and dropped their bombs. More than fourteen thousand bombing and fighter sorties were made that day, with only a handful of aircraft failing to return to their bases.

Even though Allied air forces controlled the skies, the enemy's heavy guns took a heavy initial toll on the invaders, especially on the Americans landing at Omaha Beach. Nonetheless, by day's end, some 150,000 troops, along with their vehicles, equipment, and munitions, were on French soil and heading inland. Within a week, some half a million men had landed in France.

WHEN WORD FINALLY came of the landings' success, Britons were jubilant, but their happiness was short-lived. Just one week after D-Day, the good news from Normandy was overshadowed by the beginning of a fearsome new German attack on London. Once again, British citizens found themselves experiencing, along with their soldiers on the battlefield, the rigors and terrors of war.

Early in the morning of June 13, a stubby black object the size of a small fighter plane, with the sound of a spluttering motorcycle engine, crashed into a mews in a London suburb, killing six people. For the next three months, thousands of these pilotless missiles—known as V-1s, or buzz bombs—were launched by the Germans from the French and Dutch coasts. They showered down on London and its outskirts, killing and injuring more than 33,000 people, destroying some 25,000 houses, and damaging about 800,000 others.

Since the Blitz, Londoners had endured a number of lesser German bombing assaults, including a series of attacks, known as the "baby Blitz," in the winter of 1944. While noisier and more concentrated than those in 1940 and 1941, the early 1944 raids seldom lasted for more than an hour. The V-1 bombs, on the other hand, plummeted to earth day and night, coming so often that only brief respites separated the scream of alerts. Most people considered the new onslaught to be far worse than the Blitz. "In the old days, dawn would have brought us relief," said one London resident. "This time the start of a new day did not help matters in the slightest." In his memoirs, Churchill recalled the unbearable strain that the V-1s exacted on his fellow citizens: "The man going home in the evening never knew what he would find; his wife, alone all day or with the children could not be certain of his safe return. The blind impersonal nature of the missile made the individual on the ground feel helpless. There was little he could do, no human enemy that he could see shot down."

V-1s slammed into people walking to work, shopping for groceries, typing in their office, or lunching at a restaurant. Five young WAAFs leaning out of an Air Ministry window to follow the progress of a buzz bomb were sucked out of the building by its blast, their bodies crashing to the pavement. The V-1s were "as impersonal as a plague," Evelyn Waugh wrote, "as though the city were infected with enormous, venomous insects." A woman in London noted: "We now live, sleep (when we can), eat and think of nothing but flying bombs. They are always with us."

Residents of the capital found themselves constantly on the alert, listening for the bomb's distinctive sound: a distant whine escalating to a loud roar, followed by a few agonizing moments of silence as the V-1 plunged to earth. For many, the stress of hearing the bomb cut out and then waiting for the explosion came close to being unbearable. In the face of the V-1s, even the most phlegmatic Briton sometimes found it hard to show the "stiff upper lip" characteristic of his countrymen. When the sputter of a bomb halted overhead, conversation would falter, then stop, and eyes would dart around uneasily until the blast was heard. Some people, less inhibited about showing their fear, would fling themselves to the ground or under a table.

For the first time, a large number of Americans got a taste of what it was like to be a Londoner under siege. The strain was particularly acute for Eisenhower and his staff at Bushy Park, which lay directly beneath the bombs' flight path. Hundreds of V-1s fell nearby, shaking the cottage where the supreme commander slept and breaking windows and knocking the plaster off ceilings at headquarter buildings. In one six-hour period alone, Harry Butcher counted twenty-five "violent, earthshaking explosions" in the near distance. Eisenhower, together with Butcher and his other close aides, was repeatedly forced to retreat to shelters at home and work, sometimes several times a day. "Most of the people I know," Butcher wrote, "are semi-dazed from loss of sleep and have the jitters, which they show when a door bangs, or the sounds of motors, from motorcycles to aircraft, are heard."

Indeed, a number of the U.S. military brass believed that living in London was far more dangerous than being at the front in Normandy. When a buzz bomb exploded outside a restaurant where George Patton was lunching, the flamboyant general told a companion that he was going back to the countryside, explaining: "I'm afraid of being killed—that is, except on the battlefield." During one of his visits to Normandy, Eisenhower noted that many American GIs asked him "in worried tones whether I could give them any news about particular towns [near London] where they had been stationed."

In late August, Allied troops overran most of the V-1 launching sites, but stopping the buzz bombs brought no relief to London. On September 8, the Germans unleashed an even more terrifying guided missile—the much larger and deadlier V-2 rocket. The V-2s—which carried a larger explosive charge than their predecessors, traveled faster than sound, and approached their targets in total silence—tormented the capital until just a few months before the end of the war. More than one thousand V-2s exploded in and around London, rocking the city like an earthquake, devastating entire neighborhoods, and killing nearly three thousand people.

The combined V-1 and V-2 attacks damaged British morale far more than any other wartime event, not only because of the assaults' devastating nature, but because, after half a decade of privation and suffering, many residents of Britain had reached their limit in emotional and physical exhaustion. The old camaraderie and exhilaration of the Blitz was nowhere in evidence. "We have had to face up to horrible things for nearly five years," Vivienne Hall, a Londoner, wrote in her diary, "and I suppose we shall continue to do so, but, God, how tired we are of it! Just working and living and sleeping through one mad, noisome form of destruction, week after week, month after month. . . . Are we never to be free of damage and death?"

The diaries and letters of other London residents from the period—whether Britons or Americans, government officials or private citizens—are likewise filled with confessions of a profound weariness that their writers simply could not shed. "The nation's deep fatigue is evident on train journeys," Mollie Panter-Downes wrote, "when civilians, as well as service men and women, fall asleep almost as soon as they sit down." In his memoirs, John Wheeler-Bennett noted: "Like everyone else in England, I was dead tired," adding that by the end of 1944, "Whitehall had lost much of its spring and efficiency and, in many cases, it was barely ticking over." Even the usually ebullient prime minister was affected. Churchill, looking "very old and very tired," told Alan Brooke he had lost his old energy, adding he no longer jumped out of bed the way he used to and felt as if he would be "quite content to spend the whole day" under the covers.

In a letter to her parents, Janet Murrow remarked "how tired" she and Ed were, adding: "I can only hope the war's over soon. There must be a limit to what the human frame can stand." When Murrow was asked by a friend in America why the British people, who had endured so much, were now so disheartened as victory approached, he responded: "Look . . . the first time someone hits you over the head with a hammer, it hurts. The second time, it's worse. The third time, you can't stand it!"

In the last half of 1944, more than a million Londoners packed up and fled the city. Worker productivity declined dramatically, children stopped going to school, and restaurants and theaters, jammed just a few weeks before, were virtually empty. "London is deserted . . . the West End is dead," one woman wrote. "It gives one a queer, lonely feeling."

WHILE LONDONERS endured the misery of buzz bombs that summer, Allied forces, after their initial success in Normandy, found themselves in an intractable battle against a still deadly foe in France. After their breakout from the beachhead, they stumbled into a countryside filled with hedgerows—six-foot-high earthen walls topped with trees and bushes—that made combat not only confusing but extremely brutal and difficult. For the troops, the fighting was a series of quick, heart-stopping rushes across fields, from hedgerow to hedgerow, and sudden, violent clashes with pockets of German soldiers. After six weeks of picking their bloody way across the maze, the Allies were still only some twenty miles from where they started.*

The mounting frustrations on the battlefield were mirrored by sharp differences of opinion between London and Washington about how to deal with military and political operations in France. For more than a year, Churchill had fiercely opposed Operation Anvil, the plan to supplement the Normandy invasion with an assault on southern France. Even though Anvil had been agreed to at the Churchill-Roosevelt meeting in Quebec and at the Big Three summit in Tehran, the prime minister continued to fight it until shortly before it finally was launched in August. Indeed, the Anvil dispute turned out to be Churchill's most acrimonious and passionate quarrel with the Americans during the entire war.

The prime minister argued that by diverting forces from Italy to southern France, the Italian campaign would be weakened at the precise moment when it had begun to succeed. In the late spring of 1944, after months of savage combat, the Allies had finally cracked the fearsome German defenses midway up the Italian boot. Rome had fallen on June 4, two days before D-Day, and the German army in Italy was in full retreat. Churchill and his military chiefs contended that the Italian campaign had already siphoned off several German divisions from France, taking pressure away from Eisenhower's forces and thus making a second invasion in France unnecessary. Now, they argued, was the moment to pursue the Germans north into the Po Valley, destroy them, then head into the Balkans toward Austria.

Knowing that the Russians were now on the offensive, heading west toward Germany and the Balkans, the prime minister was deeply concerned about possible Soviet incursions into countries like Greece and Turkey, where the British had long-term interests. He was determined to keep the threat of Communism as far east as possible. "Win-

---

* After the war, George Marshall told his biographer that he and his planners had no idea before the invasion of the difficulty of the Normandy terrain. Army intelligence, he said, "never told me what I needed to know. They didn't tell me about the hedgerows, and it was not until later, after much bloodshed, that we were able to deal with them" (Andrew Roberts, *Masters and Commanders: How Four Titans Won the War in the West, 1941–1945* [New York: HarperCollins, 2009], p. 490).

ston never talks of Hitler these days; he is always harping on the dangers of Communism," Lord Moran noted that summer. "He dreams of the Red Army spreading like a cancer from one country to another. It has become an obsession, and he seems to think of nothing else."

But Churchill had still another reason for his fervid support of the Italian campaign: Italy was primarily a British show—fought predominantly by British forces under a British commander, General Harold Alexander—while France was an overwhelmingly American operation. By the end of July, nearly one million U.S. troops had poured into France, compared to 660,000 British. That disparity would become even more lopsided as the summer progressed.

Thus, as Churchill knew all too well, Anvil would divert resources from the only front where the British were still the most powerful Allied force. "Winston hated having to give up the position of the predominant partner which we had held at the start," Brooke noted. In a letter to his wife in August 1944, Churchill gloomily wrote that two thirds of British forces in the war were "being mis-employed for American convenience and the other third is under American command."

Roosevelt and his military commanders, however, had little sympathy for the prime minister and his growing sense of impotence. For George Marshall, who had been opposed to the Mediterranean operation from the beginning, Italy and the Balkans were nothing but a dead end—a flawed peripheral strategy that could lead to military disaster and result in possible conflict with the Soviets. Anvil, he believed, was necessary to reinforce Eisenhower's forces in France and open up Marseilles and other badly needed ports. When Eisenhower, who was more sympathetic to the British point of view than his Washington bosses, wavered at one point on the need for Anvil, Marshall told him it *must* go forward. Caught in the middle, the supreme commander was forced to endure a series of painful confrontations with an emotional Churchill, who, during one meeting, charged that the Americans were "bullying" the British.

The British leader made a last-minute appeal to Roosevelt, who firmly turned it down. Worried about possible effects of the growing rift between the two leaders, Gil Winant wrote Roosevelt: "I wanted you to know how deeply the Prime Minister has felt the differences that have ended in his accepting your decisions. I have never seen him as badly shaken."

When Anvil (renamed Dragoon by Churchill, to underscore his feeling of having been dragooned by the Americans into cooperating with the operation), finally was launched on August 15, it easily succeeded in accomplishing its primary goals: opening up the ports, freeing southern France, and linking up with the main American forces. But, as the British feared, it also foreclosed the option of heading east into the Balkans. For decades after the operation, the rights and wrongs of both positions continued to be a subject of intense discussion and controversy.

AS THE ANVIL DRAMA unfolded, Eisenhower and Winant were dealing with yet another Anglo-American soap opera, this one involving Charles de Gaulle and the question of who would govern liberated France. Even as Allied troops stormed the beaches on D-Day, that issue, which had been debated for months, remained unsettled.

To Eisenhower, Winant, and most other American officials in London, as well as to Whitehall, there was no question that de Gaulle and his French Committee of National Liberation, having edged out all possible competitors, should be anointed as the provisional government of France. As British intelligence reports noted, de Gaulle had won the support of the majority of his countrymen: "There is one name and one name only on every lip—de Gaulle. About this there could be no doubt and no two opinions. The testimony was overwhelming and indeed seemingly unanimous." De Gaulle agreed, writing to an aide: "We are the French administration. . . . There is us or chaos."

Roosevelt, however, remained unrelenting in his hostility to de Gaulle and refused to consider giving the Frenchman any role in the administration of his country. According to the president, American military forces should govern France until it could hold postwar elections. Indeed, dozens of Army personnel had already been dispatched to Charlottesville, Virginia, for a two-month crash course in public administration and the French language. Amused skeptics of the plan dubbed them "the sixty-day marvels."

For his part, Churchill was once again trapped between his determination to support Roosevelt on French political issues and growing pressure from British public opinion and his own government to recognize de Gaulle. Voicing strong criticism of the prime minister for his and Roosevelt's treatment of the general, much of the British press and Parliament had already come out in favor of recognizing de Gaulle and his committee. "It seems to me," Harold Nicolson said in a House of Commons debate, "that the United States government, with His Majesty's Government in their train, instead of helping the French and welcoming them, lose no opportunity of administering any snub which ingenuity can devise and ill manners perpetrate." As Churchill explained to Roosevelt, the British people "feel that the French should be with us when we liberate France. . . . No one will understand them being cold-shouldered."

For Eisenhower, there was considerably more at stake here than public opinion: if the Allies failed to reach a modus vivendi with de Gaulle, it might put the liberation of France itself in jeopardy. On D-Day and in the weeks to come, the SHAEF commander was counting on hundreds of thousands of French resistance members, most of whom supported de Gaulle, to come to the aid of his forces. In addition, seven French divisions were training to take part in future battles in their country. "An open clash with de Gaulle would hurt us immeasurably," Eisenhower wrote, "and would result in bitter recrimination and unnecessary loss of life." He also was loath to assume the administrative burden of governing the country; in his opinion, that task was better left to French civil authorities. Although Eisenhower never publicly stated how he felt about Roosevelt's intransigence toward de Gaulle, C. D. Jackson, head of SHAEF's psychological warfare division, undoubtedly had his chief's view in mind when he wrote to a friend: "All circles seem to be agreed that the President's behavior toward the French is pretty outrageous and can only lead to trouble, if not disaster."

At Roosevelt's insistence, de Gaulle, who was still in Algiers, where the Committee of National Liberation was based, was not consulted about the invasion nor was he informed when and where it would take place. Finally, at Eisenhower's and Eden's urging, Churchill told the president in May that the Frenchman could not be left entirely out of Overlord: he must be invited to London, brought up to date on the operation, and be included in discussions about the future administration of France. After FDR reluctantly gave his approval, de Gaulle arrived in England less than forty-eight hours before Overlord was launched.

Not surprisingly, his encounter with Churchill did not go well. The proud, haughty Frenchman bitterly resented being shut out of the invasion of his own country, while the prime minister was, as historians Antony Beevor and Artemis Cooper put it, in "a state of subdued frenzy," fearing that the landings would be a bloody failure. When he and Eisenhower told de Gaulle that the supreme commander would broadcast to the French people on D-Day and asked him to do the same, de Gaulle exploded with rage. Eisenhower's proclamation, which had already been printed, called on the French nation to follow the orders of the Allied invasion force; it contained no mention of de Gaulle or his men. As de Gaulle saw it, his country, rather than being liberated, was going to be occupied like Italy. He refused to follow Eisenhower's broadcast with one of his own, and his talk with Churchill turned into a nasty verbal brawl. When it was over, the prime minister, shaking with rage, accused de Gaulle of "treason at the height of battle" and ordered him sent back to Algiers, "in chains if necessary."

The lieutenants of both leaders could not believe what they were witnessing: de Gaulle and Churchill exchanging insults and epithets at the moment that Allied paratroopers were preparing to drop into Normandy. "It's pandemonium!" a senior French official exclaimed. Alexander Cadogan disgustedly likened the situation to a "girls' school. Roosevelt, the Prime Minister, and—it must be admitted, de Gaulle—all behave like girls approaching the age of puberty." In the hours just before the landings, Eden and French officials did yeoman work in calming down the two men. When de Gaulle complained to Eden about Britain's slavish dependence on the Americans, the foreign secretary responded that "it was a fatal mistake . . . to have too much pride. 'She stoops to conquer' was an action which we could each of us find useful to observe at times." Thanks to his and others' efforts, de Gaulle finally agreed to deliver a broadcast, and Churchill's written order to expel the errant general from the country was rescinded and destroyed.

While Churchill's fury at de Gaulle remained unabated ("The Prime Minister is almost insane at times in his hatred of Gen. de Gaulle," a Foreign Office staffer wrote on June 9), he reluctantly agreed to allow him to return to his homeland for a brief visit the week after D-Day. The prime minister was responding to heavy pressure from the British press and public to do so, as well as to strong urging by Eisenhower. In effect, the Allied commander, who had been given considerable latitude by Roosevelt and Cordell Hull in governing the newly liberated areas of France, was making an end run around Washington. Eisenhower and his staff believed that "in the initial stages of the operation at least, de Gaulle would represent the only authority that could produce any kind of French co-ordination and unification, and that no harm would come from giving him the kind of recognition he sought."

On June 14, de Gaulle's visit to the town of Bayeux, on the Normandy coast, was met with an extraordinary outpouring of emotion. Huge crowds of cheering, sobbing townspeople mobbed him wherever he went. When he returned to England that night, he left behind in Normandy François Coulet, one of his top aides, who had been chosen to act as the French committee's governor of the region. With Ike's tacit support, de Gaulle was undermining Roosevelt's attempts to impose an Allied military administration. When the "60-day marvels" began to arrive a few days later, they found themselves totally ignored by the French—and by SHAEF. "The brigadiers who had assembled at embarkation ports, putative gauleiters . . . briefed in the Code Napoleon and other lore for taking over their allotted districts, stole silently away, unwanted," wrote Malcolm Muggeridge. Whether Washington liked it or not, de Gaulle was now in control of the freed areas of his country.

Having begun to realize that he was "flogging a dead horse," as his biographer Jean Edward Smith put it, Roosevelt finally invited de Gaulle to Washington in July and recognized his committee as the de facto civil authority in France. But the conversations between the two were cool and perfunctory, and the president refused to follow the lead of the European governments-in-exile, as well as a number of other countries around the world, in acknowledging the committee as France's provisional government. "FDR . . . believes that de Gaulle will crumble," Henry Stimson wrote in his diary. "He thinks that other parties will spring up as the liberation goes on and that de Gaulle will become a very little figure." A few days before de Gaulle came to Washington, Roosevelt declared to his aides: "He's a nut."

For three months, Roosevelt refused to budge from his position, even after Paris was liberated and de Gaulle was received as a conquering hero—and after Churchill, Hull, Winant, Eisenhower, and the Joint Chiefs of Staff all banded together to urge recognition. Finding himself completely isolated on the issue and with a presidential election fast approaching, the president finally gave in on October 23, abruptly announcing that the United States recognized de Gaulle's committee as France's provisional government. He made the announcement without first informing Churchill, who, despite growing misgivings, had loyally continued to follow Roosevelt's lead. Caught flat-footed, the British government scrambled to issue its own announcement of recognition. An irate Alexander Cadogan wrote to Eden: "As a cordial relationship with a restored and liberated France is a vital British interest, I should have hoped the President might have allowed our right to a preponderant voice in this matter."

For his part, de Gaulle would never forgive or forget what he considered the president's and prime minister's shabby treatment of him during the war. After returning to power in France in 1958, he vetoed Britain's application to join the European Economic Community, recalling Churchill's words that the British would always choose America over Europe. His government's relationship with the United States was equally thorny. According to Jean Edward Smith, "FDR's pique against de Gaulle poisoned the well of Franco-American relations, the legacy of which continues to this day."

WHEN ALLIED TROOPS liberated Paris on August 25, the reaction of Britons was surprisingly subdued. French exiles celebrated noisily at their Soho haunts, French tricolors fluttered from many windows, but, in general, London had "a sleepy, empty look," giving the impression of a "city only half alive." A profound sense of exhaustion and ennui pervaded the capital, as Eric Sevareid discovered when he returned to the British capital after covering Operation Anvil. "Where every man and woman was a hero, heroism was a bore," he wrote. "Where men of all known tongues had swarmed, the lingering Americans were a bore. . . . War itself was a bore." London, Sevareid observed in a broadcast, was "like a once-smart hotel gone seamy and threadbare after an interminable convention of businessmen. . . . The exaltation of danger is gone."

For much of the war, bomb-battered London had been the most exciting, exhilarating place on earth—"the Paris of World War II," as Donald Miller dubbed it. But now the real Paris, its beauty unmarred by bombs, was again open for business and pleasure, and many in London—Americans, Britons, Commonwealth residents, and Europeans—scrambled to go there. In the vanguard of the new

Allied invasion were OSS chief David Bruce and his new traveling companion, Ernest Hemingway, who raced to the Ritz bar on the day Paris was liberated and ordered fifty martinis for themselves and the group of French partisans accompanying them.

The Allies took over hundreds of hotels in Paris for their own use and, within days, a frenzied round of partying had begun. Most Parisians—and Frenchmen, in general—had very little to eat, but there was a thriving black market in food, liquor, and wine. The city's best restaurants, which had served members of the Wehrmacht and Gestapo just a few days before, were now welcoming the hordes of Allied officers and journalists who flocked to them.

Yet, while enjoying what Paris had to offer, a number of those who left London felt a sense of guilt for doing so. Among them was the future historian John Wheeler-Bennett, who wandered around Paris admiring its hotels' and shops' plate glass windows, gleaming "in guilty splendour," and the gravel paths in the Tuileries gardens, "raked with meticulous perfection." Drab, pockmarked London boasted no such neatness or elegance, Wheeler-Bennett thought, but it still retained a "spirit and pride which was unshakeable and magnificent." Paris, by contrast, had reclaimed "her panache and the arrogance of her egotism," but "she had not, then or at any later date, succeeded in rediscovering her soul."

In his own brief visit to Paris, Ed Murrow remarked on the same contrasts between the two cities. In a broadcast, he noted with an edge of contempt that the French capital and its residents seemed relatively unscathed by the war. Describing what he called the "familiar, well-fed but still empty-looking faces around the fashionable bars," he added that the "last four years seem to have changed them very little." After forty-eight hours in Paris, Murrow could take no more and returned to London. Pamela Churchill, who had followed him to Paris, stayed on, spending time at the Ritz with her other American journalist friends, including Charles Collingwood and Bill Walton. "Perhaps the world looked open to her then," Walton said. "Paris was free."

19.

CRISIS IN THE ALLIANCE

WHILE PARIS WAS REVELING IN ITS LIBERATION, THE RESIDENTS of another occupied European capital were in the midst of their own desperate fight for freedom. Three weeks before Allied troops marched into Paris, some 25,000 members of the Polish underground launched an uprising in Warsaw against their Nazi occupiers. Their rebellion coincided with a vast westward offensive by Soviet troops who, having pushed the Germans out of western Russia, were surging through Poland like a great tidal wave. The Red Army was nearing Warsaw just as the Poles began their uprising; indeed, several days earlier, Soviet radio broadcasts made impassioned appeals to Warsaw residents to join Soviet forces in combat. The Germans fought back hard against the Poles, bringing in massive reinforcements, and shelling and bombing Warsaw twenty-four hours a day. Hopelessly outnumbered, the underground appealed to London and Moscow for help. While Churchill urged British military leaders to aid the Polish insurgents with "maximum effort," Stalin denounced them as adventurers, and no help came from the Red Army, now camped on the outskirts of Warsaw.

In Moscow, Averell Harriman pleaded with the Soviets to reconsider their refusal to provide assistance, declaring it was "in the interests of the [Allied] cause and of humanity to support" the Poles. The ambassador wrote to Harry Hopkins: "The time has come when we must make clear what we expect of them as the price of our goodwill. Unless we take issue, there is every indication the Soviet Union will become a world bully wherever their interests are involved." It was a remarkable turnaround for a man who once advocated unconditional support for the Soviets, said that all problems with them could be solved "with a frank personal relationship," and claimed that "Stalin could be handled."

In a variety of ways, Harriman's eleven-month tenure in the Soviet Union had been an exercise in humiliation. His earlier foreboding about the precarious, difficult nature of the ambassador's job proved to be correct: he was sidelined in Moscow by Roosevelt and Hopkins, just as Gil Winant had been in London. Soon after he arrived in the Soviet capital, Harriman complained to Hopkins that nobody in Washington was telling him anything and he was "put in the humiliating position of depending upon the Russian Foreign Office for news as to the latest decisions made by [my] own government."

Like his predecessors in Moscow, he also was largely ignored by Stalin and the rest of the Soviet government—a mortifying situation for Harriman, who, as Roosevelt's personal emissary to the Soviets early in the war, was accustomed to being given special entrée to the Kremlin and treated with a certain deference and respect. Imperious and aloof, he did not impress—at least initially—the young Soviet specialists in the U.S. embassy, all of whom were students of Russian and Soviet history and ideology. They admired Harriman's dedication to public service and enormous capacity for hard work but decried his lack of interest in the hard slog of diplomacy. "He wanted to operate on a higher plane," said George Kennan, who as minister-counselor was Harriman's right-hand man. "He felt that he could learn more that was important in one interview with Stalin than the rest of us could learn in months of pedestrian study of Soviet publications." Charles Bohlen observed: "I cannot say that I ever felt that he really fully understood the nature of the Soviet system. Reading ideological books was not his forte."

Nonetheless, the longer Harriman lived in Moscow, the more he realized that Roosevelt's vision of a genuine political partnership between the United States and Soviet Union was little more than fantasy. He saw firsthand how suspicious the Russians were of their Western allies, refusing to give them the most elementary information about their war effort. He also discovered that they were using some Lend-Lease equipment for civilian purposes or hiding it away for use after the war was over. The ambassador began to urge Roosevelt and his administration to scrutinize the Russians' Lend-Lease requests more closely and to demand more military cooperation. "They are tough, and they expect us to be tough," he declared. His recommendations, however, were largely ignored.

In his increasingly hard-nosed stance toward the Soviets, Harriman was heavily influenced by Kennan, who, in Harrison Salisbury's view, "knew the Russians as no one else in my generation." After arriving in Moscow in June 1944, Kennan, who first had served there in the early 1930s, emphasized to the ambassador that "my views on policy toward the Soviet Union were not exactly those of the Administration." As it turned out, his views quickly became Harriman's as well. About Kennan, Harriman would later say: "I used him on every occasion that I could, and I consulted him on every subject."

According to Salisbury, who was the *New York Times*'s Moscow correspondent for the last two years of the war, Kennan was a major reason for Harriman's postwar emergence as one of the "Wise Men" of U.S. foreign policy. "A great deal would later be said by Averell and others about his excellent judgement and tactics in dealing with the Russians," Salisbury wrote. "He became known as a man who took their measure at a time when others did not." But it wasn't until Kennan arrived in Moscow, Salisbury observed, that "I noticed any extraordinary perception in Harriman. . . . After Kennan's arrival, Harriman proved himself a good learner. He grew with the years."

Both Harriman and Kennan had come to regard Poland as "the touchstone of Soviet behavior in the postwar world, the first test of Stalin's attitude toward his less powerful neighbors." As they saw it, the Soviets failed the test miserably. In its refusal to help the Poles, Kennan said, Stalin's government was sending this message to the West: "We intend to have Poland, lock, stock and barrel. We don't care a fig for those Polish underground fighters. . . . It is a matter of indifference to us what you think of all this. You are going to have no part in determining the affairs of Poland from here on out, and it is time you realized it."

Harriman, joined by Gil Winant in London, urged Roosevelt to press Stalin, at the very least, to permit the use of Soviet landing bases by Allied bombers flying long-distance relief missions to Poland. Churchill also favored the idea, declaring that if the Soviet leader rejected the request, the bombers should go ahead and land at Soviet airfields without permission. Roosevelt, however, was unwilling to confront Stalin, who, once it was clear the Warsaw uprising was doomed, permitted the use of Soviet airfields for just one U.S. relief mission. After holding off the Germans for sixty days, the Polish underground finally capitulated to the Germans on October 2. Some 250,000 residents of Warsaw—about a quarter of its population—had been killed in the uprising. Those who survived were ordered to leave the city, which then was systematically burned and dynamited to the ground.

The fate of the Poles in Warsaw preyed on Harriman's mind for decades to come. When Churchill's grandson once asked him how the Western Allies could have allowed the destruction of the Polish capital to occur, Harriman's face turned ashen. Saying nothing, he "turned on his heel," the younger Winston Churchill remembered, "and walked away."

WITH CONCERNS MOUNTING in the West about Stalin's postwar ambitions in Europe and with Allied armies closing in on Germany from the east and west, Winant grew increasingly worried about the Allies' failure to make firm decisions about the division and occupation of the Reich. In a letter to Roosevelt, the ambassador observed that he and the other members of the European Advisory Commission had made great strides in hammering out agreements regarding surrender terms and occupation zones. Having noted the rapid eastward progress of Anglo-American forces, even the Russians had reached the conclusion that an overall plan delineating the Allies' occupation policy was a necessity. If such a plan was not finalized before the end of the war, Winant warned, "rivalry for control over Germany . . . would follow."

The question of Germany's fate, however, became even murkier in September 1944, when Roosevelt and Churchill, meeting in Quebec, approved a sweeping plan by Treasury Secretary Henry Morgenthau to destroy German industry and transform the country into an agrarian state. Like Roosevelt, Churchill had given little serious thought to the postwar treatment of Germany; he told Lord Moran at Quebec that "there will be plenty of time to go into that when we have won the war."

Most U.S. and British officials, including the two leaders' closest advisers, were horrified by the Morgenthau idea, declaring that the pastoralization of Germany would greatly harm the postwar economic recovery of Europe and create a power vacuum in the middle of the

Continent. So furious that he could barely speak, Anthony Eden shouted at Churchill: "You can't do this!" Referring to Roosevelt, Cordell Hull exclaimed: "In Christ's name, what has happened to the man?"

Stung by the vehemence of their lieutenants' opposition, both Roosevelt and Churchill backed away from the plan, with the president telling Henry Stimson that he had no recollection of approving it. From that point on, Roosevelt made clear he was not interested in signing off on any long-range occupation policy for Germany before the end of the war. "I dislike making detailed plans for a country which we do not yet occupy," he wrote to Hull. "We must emphasize the fact that the European Advisory Commission is 'Advisory' and that you and I are not bound by its advice."

In response to the administration's delaying tactics, the usually soft-spoken Winant shot off a telegram to Roosevelt and other officials that was striking in its forcefulness and, in the words of one historian, "placed his prestige as ambassador on the line." American interests, Winant declared, had been put at a "decided disadvantage" as the result of the U.S. government's dilatory attitude in approving plans for the postwar treatment of Germany. "I do not think," he added, "that any conference or commission created by governments for a serious purpose has had less support from the governments creating it than the European Advisory Commission." He was speaking, he made clear, primarily about his own government.

THE LACK OF A clear-cut policy toward Germany was just one of the many problems bedeviling the Western alliance as the war entered its final months. With military victory inching closer, relations between American and British field commanders—never good—sank to their lowest point in the conflict. The rivalries, suspicions, and infighting that marked the North Africa campaign grew considerably fiercer on the battlefields of Europe.

When British and Canadian forces under General Montgomery were slow to break out of their sector in Normandy, American military leaders and the press spread the word that Montgomery was leaving all the heavy fighting to U.S. troops. The invidious comparison of the success of the American thrust and the sluggishness of Montgomery's forces was difficult for the British to stomach. "We hear that the

British are doing nothing and suffering no casualties, whilst the Americans are bearing all the brunt of the war!!" Alan Brooke fumed in his diary. "I am tired to death with and by humanity and all its pettiness! Will we ever learn to 'love our allies as ourselves'??? I doubt it!" Churchill, meanwhile, complained to his wife: "The only times I ever quarrel with the Americans are when they fail to give us a fair share of opportunity to win glory."

Beleaguered by U.S. and British commanders demanding priority for their operations, Eisenhower alone seemed uninfected by the fever of nationalism. His continued emphasis on consensus, compromise, and teamwork was derided by generals from both countries, who repeatedly challenged his authority. They had little sympathy, it appeared, for the enormous responsibilities and problems he faced in presiding over a massive military coalition comprising millions of troops, airmen, and sailors from at least eight countries.

Eisenhower's own chief, General Marshall, was not above nationalism himself. Angered by British newspaper stories claiming that Eisenhower was a figurehead leader and that senior British commanders were actually leading the Overlord charge, Marshall ordered Eisenhower to take direct operational command of the campaign's land forces. Until that point, Eisenhower had acted as supreme commander, with separate commanders under him for land, sea, and air operations. Because Britain had more troops in the field on D-Day, Montgomery had been named to head the Allied ground campaign. But by August 1944, well over half of all soldiers fighting in France were American. Most of the Allied armaments and supplies also came from the United States, as did the planes and ships. It was time, Marshall felt, to underscore America's dominance, no matter how much Churchill, Brooke, and the rest of the British might protest.

Protest they certainly did. When the announcement was made that Eisenhower was taking charge of Allied troops and that Montgomery now had the same status as General Omar Bradley, America's highest-ranking field commander, the British press and people greeted the news as "a national slap in the face." Thanks to his victory at El Alamein in late 1942, Montgomery had become Britain's most popular military figure, and his countrymen were incensed by his demotion. In an oblique thumb of his nose at the Americans, Churchill raised Montgomery to the rank of field marshal—equivalent to a five-star general—which meant he outranked Eisenhower and every other senior U.S. commander in the field. Now it was the Americans' turn for outrage. "Montgomery is a third-rate general and he never did anything or won any battle that any other general could not have won as well or better," Bradley exploded.

Shocked at having to give up the top command, Montgomery never fully accepted the move and continued to defy Eisenhower's authority for the rest of the war. In particular, he challenged Ike's strategy calling for an Allied advance into Germany on a broad front, thus giving the various countries' armies a chance to distinguish themselves. Montgomery insisted that a bold thrust to the northeast, carried out by British forces and supported by American troops, would have a much better chance of breaking into Germany and bringing the war to a close. As much as he disliked the prickly, overbearing field marshal, Eisenhower understood and empathized with the injured feelings of the British, the deep distress they felt over their fast-accelerating loss of power and control. It was important, he felt, to placate Montgomery as much as possible.

He agreed to a compromise. Montgomery would head northeast toward Antwerp, a key Belgian port, with the U.S. First Army supporting his advance. Bradley's forces, meanwhile, would continue their push farther south, toward the Siegfried Line, a system of bunkers and tank traps along the German border. Unfortunately for George Patton, the plan meant a temporary halt to his Third Army's headlong race to the east; a large portion of the gasoline and other supplies meant for his army was diverted to help Montgomery's effort. Not surprisingly, Patton was beside himself with rage. More than a year earlier, in Sicily, he had declared: "The U.S. must win, not as an ally but as a conqueror." A Red Cross worker attached to his headquarters later observed: "There was arrogance unspeakable there, authority unrelinquished even to his superior officer, the Supreme Allied Commander." In his diary, Patton wrote with disgust: "Ike is bound hand and foot by the British and does not know it. Poor fool."

At first, Eisenhower's bifurcated strategy seemed to pay off. In early September, the British 11th Armoured Division swept into Belgium and captured Antwerp, with its crucial port facilities intact. Savoring their triumph, Mongomery's forces failed, however, to clear German units from the forty-mile estuary linking Antwerp and the sea. The German troops already there were soon reinforced, and it would take another two months for Allied forces to gain control of the estuary and open the port for the unloading of Allied supplies and troops. One of the most serious blunders of the war in Europe, the fumbled handling of Antwerp played a significant role in the Allies' failure to advance into Germany and end the war in 1944.

At the time, however, few if any in the Allied high command realized the gravity of the situation. The lightning-fast conquest of German forces in France and Belgium had produced an exuberant optimism at SHAEF headquarters, a sense that victory was in tantalizing reach and could be wrapped up by Christmas. With that in mind, Montgomery unveiled a new proposal that he said would enable his forces to cross the Rhine "in a powerful, full-blooded thrust to the heart of Germany." Called Operation Market Garden, it called for U.S., British, and Polish paratroopers to seize a series of bridges and canal crossings in Holland and establish bridgeheads for advancing Allied troops. The last bridge to be captured, by the British 1st Airborne, spanned the Rhine at the Dutch town of Arnhem.

Disregarding warnings from several of his own advisers that he was underestimating the strength of the Germans and that the proposal was severely flawed, Montgomery persuaded Eisenhower to authorize the operation. The assessment of the Market Garden critics proved to be right: the mission was poorly planned and carried out, and German resistance was savage and overwhelming. Despite the extraordinary courage displayed by Allied paratroopers, thousands of whom were killed or captured, the enemy held on to the bridge at Arnhem.

Due in no small part to the twin fiascos of Arnhem and Antwerp, Germany remained unbreached that autumn and winter, and the war on the western front slipped into a stalemate. Reinforcing their defenses, the Germans dug in deep and held the line in the forested hills separating their homeland from Belgium and Luxembourg. "Between our front and the Rhine," Bradley remarked, "a determined enemy held every foot of ground and would not yield. Each day, the weather grew colder, our troops more miserable. We were mired in a ghastly war of attrition."

Among the Allied generals, the war of finger-pointing and name-calling accelerated. The Americans attacked Montgomery and the British for their failures at Arnhem and Antwerp. Montgomery, who insisted he should be allowed to continue his single-thrust campaign, blamed Eisenhower for causing the military stalemate and sent message after message to his superiors in London sniping at the SHAEF commander. Patton and Bradley, meanwhile, criticized Eisenhower for not reining Montgomery in. Even Ike's own chief of staff, General Walter Bedell Smith, participated in the blame game, observing of his boss and friend: "He lacked the firmness of will to deal with Monty as he should."

Caught in the middle, Eisenhower struggled to maintain his authority over his squabbling generals, refusing to agree to any more of Montgomery's gambles and insisting on his own broad-front strategy. Overstressed and physically exhausted, he complained there was not one part of his body that did not cause him pain. The same could be said for his relationship with his prima donna field commanders.

ON DECEMBER 16, 1944, the standoff between the Allies and Germany ended with the outbreak of the largest and most savage battle on the western front. In a last-ditch effort to regain the offensive, German troops burst out of the Ardennes Forest in Belgium and launched a surprise attack against American forces. Undetected ahead of time by Allied intelligence, the massive assault ripped through U.S. defenses, creating a bulge in the overextended Allied line and threatening newly liberated Antwerp. In response, Eisenhower ordered reinforcements to the breakthrough point and dispatched the 101st Airborne to protect the Belgian town of Bastogne, a major road junction and key German objective. When Bastogne was surrounded by German troops, Patton's forces raced to its defense and, with the help of Allied airpower, lifted the siege the day after Christmas. Montgomery, pressed hard by Eisenhower to counterattack in the north with British and American forces, finally did so on January 3. It was clear the Germans had lost their desperate gamble. Four days later, the Battle of the Bulge came to an end.

On the Allied side, American troops had borne the brunt of the fighting (more than ten thousand killed and forty thousand wounded) and had been largely responsible for eking out the victory. Yet on January 7, Montgomery implied at a press conference that it was he who had been "the savior of the Americans," as Eisenhower exasperatedly put it. Despite the fact that only one British division took part in the battle, the British press took up the same theme, claiming that their country's forces, led by Montgomery, had saved the Americans from defeat. "MONTGOMERY STOPS THE ROT!" exclaimed one

British newsreel caption. According to U.S. general Joseph L. Collins, Montgomery's press conference "so irritated Bradley and Patton and many of us who fought on the northern front of the Bulge that it left a sour note to what actually was a great cooperative allied army and air effort." Added Bradley: "It did more to undermine Anglo-American unity than anything I can remember."

Montgomery's superiors in London, meanwhile, insisted that Eisenhower had failed as commander of Allied land forces and that Montgomery's plan for a single thrust to Berlin should now be adopted in lieu of Ike's broad-front strategy. At a rancorous meeting held shortly before the Yalta conference in February 1945, British and American military leaders almost came to blows as they argued about how to wage the final campaign of the war. The session, recalled Marshall, was "terrible." When Marshall declared that Eisenhower would resign if the British plan were approved and Roosevelt sent word he supported the U.S. strategy, the British high command reluctantly conceded defeat.

In years to come, Eisenhower would receive considerable criticism from historians for his failure to keep his generals in line, as well as for numerous tactical and strategic mistakes in the European war. But as Max Hastings pointed out, "it remains impossible to imagine anyone doing Eisenhower's job better than he did it. Instead of focusing upon his limitations, which were real enough, what matters is that he kept the alliance working." In Hastings's view, Eisenhower's "behavior at moments of Anglo-American tension, his extraordinary generosity of spirit to his difficult subordinates, proved his greatness as Supreme Commander."

IN THE WEEKS preceding Yalta, relations between the White House and 10 Downing Street were also greatly strained. "Something very like a crisis exists beneath the surface in the relations between the Allies who are fighting this war," observed the American newspaper columnist Marquis Childs in December 1944.

When Britain balked at a proposal to give U.S. airlines access to all worldwide air routes after the war, Roosevelt sent Winant a cable in November 1944, to be given to Churchill, indicating that the United States might cut off Lend-Lease aid to the British if they did not agree to the plan. The message was, wrote John Colville, "pure blackmail." It was the kind of threat, added one historian, that "one might make to a ward heeler or a recalcitrant union boss." The British, fearing that their own civil aviation program would be crushed by the United States without some kind of protection, had favored an international regulatory agency with power to distribute routes and fix schedules. The president would have none of that. He told Winant: "Please take the following message personally to Winston and convince him that he has got to come through." When he handed the telegram to the prime minister at Chequers, Winant was so shamefaced by its hectoring tone, according to Colville, that he declined Churchill's invitation to stay for lunch. But the prime minister insisted, saying "that even a declaration of war should not prevent them from having a good lunch."

The Roosevelt administration used similar coercive tactics in a controversy involving the rise to power of ultranationalists in Argentina. In an effort to bring pressure on the Argentine government, which Washington said was pro-German, the administration sought to persuade Britain to recall its ambassador and refrain from signing a long-term contract for the purchase of Argentine beef, a commodity sorely needed by the meat-deprived British. Again, Roosevelt used the Lend-Lease club, warning Churchill that failure to follow the U.S. lead would have unfortunate repercussions in Congress. Infuriated by the president's hard-balling, Churchill shot back: "You would not send your soldiers into battle on the British meat service ration, which is far above what is given to workmen. Your people are eating per head more meat and more poultry than before the war, whilst ours are mostly sharply cut."

While these two economic disputes were raging, the United States and Britain were also locked in a fierce verbal battle over Britain's military intervention against Communist guerrillas in recently liberated Greece. Worried about the Soviets' push toward the Balkans and the possibility of a Communist takeover in Greece, Churchill had dispatched British troops to fight the guerrillas, who, having played a key role in resisting the Germans, were now making a bid for power in the country.

The prime minister's move touched off a public outcry in the United States, with much of the press and many members of Congress denouncing the prime minister as a reactionary and the administration itself sharply reprimanding Churchill. Stunned by Washington's response, the British leader made clear to Roosevelt he felt he'd been betrayed. Reminding the president that "I have loyally tried to support any statements to which you were personally committed," he said he was "much hurt" at this attempt "to administer a public rebuke."

As it turned out, many of Churchill's own countrymen were also upset about the prime minister's actions in Greece, which they considered anti-democratic. Indeed, the chief government whip in the House of Commons told John Colville it was the first time he had seen the House "really irritated and impatient" with Churchill. But the British saved most of their indignation for what they considered the sanctimonious moralizing of the United States, which admonished Churchill while showing little interest in getting involved in postwar European affairs itself. In a conversation with Averell Harriman, Roosevelt had underscored that lack of interest when he said that "European questions were so impossible that he wanted to stay out of them as far as practicable."

The Economist, an influential British political and international affairs journal, gave voice to Britons' burgeoning sense of resentment against the United States in a scalding leader (editorial) that sparked a furor at home and across the Atlantic. "What makes the American criticisms so intolerable," the leader declared, "is not merely that they are unjust, but that they come from a source which has done so little to earn the right to postures of superiority. . . . It would be insufferable enough to a people struggling through their sixth winter of blackout and blockade and bombs, of queues and rations and coldness—but when the criticism comes from a nation that was practicing cash and carry during the Battle of Britain, whose consumption has risen through the war years . . . then it is not to be borne." The article—written by Barbara Ward, a young economist who later would win global prominence for her writings on developing nations—argued that Britain must put an end "to the policy of appeasement which, at Mr. Churchill's personal bidding, has been followed with all the humiliations and abasements it has brought in its train."

Ward's editorial was greeted by a chorus of approval throughout Britain. "We do not mind being lectured by Americans within reason," noted the *Yorkshire Post,* "but we want to know how far we can rely on them in the future for the maintenance of peace. . . . They freely tell us what we ought to do. What are they willing to do?" While many in the United States rejected the premise of the *Economist* article, a few prominent Americans said it had merit. Until the United States demonstrated a genuine willingness to share in the responsibility of creating a new world order, said Representative J. William Fulbright, "there is good reason for the skepticism of our allies."

THE COMPOSITION of that postwar world was the main subject under discussion at the second and last Big Three summit of the war, held in the Black Sea resort town of Yalta. Once again, Stalin had successfully resisted efforts by Churchill and Roosevelt to hold the meeting at a place more geographically convenient for them. In considerably worse health than they had been fourteen months earlier at Tehran, the Western leaders found the trip to Yalta to be a heavy strain.

Both had come down with serious illnesses after Tehran. After Roosevelt failed to shake off the effects of what was thought to be a bad case of the flu early in 1944, doctors examined him and discovered he was suffering from several life-threatening diseases, including congestive heart failure and severe hypertension. Afflicted by chronic headaches and fatigue, he seemed increasingly withdrawn, irritable, and uninterested in what was going on around him, including his own successful third reelection bid. "He just doesn't seem to give a damn," said one aide. After a meeting with FDR, Vice President Harry Truman told an assistant, "Physically, he's just going to pieces."

When Roosevelt, Churchill, and their aides met briefly on the island of Malta before proceeding to the Black Sea, British officials were shocked by the president's marked physical deterioriation since they had last seen him. His hands trembled, his eyes were glassy and sunken, his face was gaunt, his body frail. In a draft copy of his memoirs, Churchill wrote that conversing with Roosevelt at Malta and Yalta was like "talking to a friendly but darkening void." In fact, the president had only ten weeks left to live.

According to members of Churchill's entourage, the prime minister's own physical and mental vitality had also ebbed significantly in the previous year. He had barely survived an attack of pneumonia immediately after Tehran, and his health never fully recovered; during the meetings at Malta and Yalta, he ran a fever and spent considerable time in bed. Like Roosevelt, too, Churchill was having more and more trouble concentrating on key wartime and postwar issues. "The P.M.'s box is in a frightful state, with scores of urgent papers demanding a decision," John Colville wrote a few weeks before Yalta. "He has frit-tered away his time in the last week and has seemed unable or unwill-ing or too tired to give his attention to complex matters. . . . Result: chaos." In late January 1945, Alan Brooke fumed: "I don't feel that I can stand another day working with Winston; he is quite hopeless . . . incapable of grasping any military situation and unable to give a deci-sion."

According to their aides, neither Churchill nor Roosevelt was well prepared for the Yalta conference. The prime minister, said a young Foreign Office official, "was tired and below his form. He also suffered from the belief that he knew everything, and need not read briefs. Stalin and foreign minister Vyacheslav Molotov, always very well briefed, would put pointed questions. 'What's the answer to that?' the prime minister would say, turning round with difficulty to his advisers sitting behind him. We could not say, 'If you had read our brief, you would know.'" Sir Alexander Cadogan, meanwhile, wrote in his diary: "I must say I think Uncle Joe much the most impressive of the three men. . . . The President flapped about and the P.M. boomed, but Joe just sat, taking it all in and being rather amused."

Just as at Tehran, Roosevelt resisted all attempts by Churchill to coordinate Anglo-American strategy or even to exchange views before they met with the Soviet leader. He did not want Stalin to think he and Churchill were conspiring against him. After declining the prime minister's invitation to stop in Britain on the way to the Crimea, Roo-sevelt had finally agreed to the brief meeting at Malta, but he avoided any serious conversation about the talks to come.

When the summit finally got under way, Roosevelt agreed with Stalin on most of the major issues under discussion; once again, Churchill felt very much the odd man out. "It was two to one against us" throughout much of the meeting, a senior member of the British government recalled. Another close Churchill associate noted: "That the President should deal with Churchill and Stalin as if they were people of equal standing in American eyes shocked Churchill pro-foundly." At one plenary session, Roosevelt and Stalin began confer-ring before Churchill arrived. When the president was told by an aide that the prime minister was waiting outside, FDR's response was a blunt "Let him wait."

Thanks to the Red Army's successes, there was no question that Stalin held the initiative at Yalta. By the time of the conference, Soviet forces had swept German troops out of most of Poland, Hungary, and Yugoslavia, and were in effective control of Bulgaria and Romania. They had marched into Czechoslovakia and Austria and advanced deep into Germany. Indeed, Russian units were now on the Oder River, just forty-five miles east of Berlin. For Churchill, the rapid advance of the Soviets across Eastern and Central Europe was nothing short of a nightmare. As Cecil King, editor and publisher of the *Daily Mirror*, put it, "We went into the war . . . to check Germany's policy of expansion, which looked as if it might soon absorb the whole of Europe. The actual effect has been a radical shift in political power away from western Europe" toward the Soviet Union. "We have now created a Frankenstein monster that dominates the European-Asiatic land mass from Vladivostok to Vienna and beyond."

Roosevelt, seemingly unconcerned about leaving the Soviet Union as the Continent's dominant military and political power, made matters worse, in Churchill's view, by telling Stalin at Yalta he planned to pull all U.S. troops from Europe, including Germany, after two years. To thwart such Soviet dominance, Churchill "fought like a tiger" at the summit to make sure that France's postwar role in Europe was as strong as possible. By doing that, he thought, both Britain and France could serve—to some extent, at least—as counterweights to Russia. Under heavy pressure from the prime minister, who was supported by Harry Hopkins, Roosevelt and Stalin reluctantly agreed to make France one of the occupying powers in Germany.

However, when the discussion turned to the question of creating an independent government in Poland, Churchill, who repeatedly had promised the Poles in London he would win back their freedom, did not put up the same kind of fight as he had for France. True, his position had been undercut earlier in the conference when Roosevelt declared that "coming from America," he had a "distant view on the Polish question" and made plain that his interest in it was essentially limited to its effect on his own political fortunes.

The question of Poland dominated Yalta, taking up more time and causing more friction than any of the other subjects on the agenda. Nonetheless, the discussions were an exercise in futility. As much as Churchill tried to convince himself otherwise, Poland's fate was already settled. Soviet troops now occupied most of the country, and Stalin made plain that the puppet government he had established in the eastern Polish city of Lublin in 1944 would take control of Poland after the war. A protesting Churchill declared: "We could never accept any settlement which did not leave [Poland] free, independent, and sovereign." Yet, faced with Stalin's obduracy, he and Roosevelt did accept such a plan, albeit one with some democratic window dressing. Under the agreement, the Lublin government would be enlarged to include several leaders from "Polish émigré circles," and free elections would be held as soon as possible to create a permanent government. Stalin, however, refused to allow British and American officials to supervise the elections, and Roosevelt and Churchill didn't argue the point. They decided to take the Soviet leader's word that the voting would be free of coercion, even though the Soviets had never allowed a free election in their own country.

Other key decisions taken at Yalta were the establishment of operating procedures for the new United Nations, as well as Stalin's pledge to enter the war against Japan in exchange for possession of the Japanese-held Kuril Islands and Port Arthur, a seaport on the coast of northeast China. At long last, the Big Three also ratified German surrender documents and a protocol outlining the division of Germany into three occupation zones. (At Yalta, Roosevelt and Churchill agreed that France's zone would be carved out of the German territory that their countries would administer.) Berlin would also be split into Allied zones of occupation.

Approval of those provisions was a close-run thing. Although the British in late 1944 had signed off on the agreements, which were drafted by the European Advisory Commission, the American government had not. Just days before the Yalta conference began, Winant, who had not been invited to Yalta, forcefully pointed out to the president, Hopkins, and Edward Stettinius, who had succeeded Cordell Hull as secretary of state, the growing dangers of procrastination over Germany. Western Allied forces, the ambassador noted, had not yet entered Germany, while Russian troops were nearing the outskirts of Berlin. Unless the Big Three formally adopted the agreements on occupation zones, he declared, the Red Army "might reach the border of its zone and then keep on going." Agreeing with Winant that the matter was "of the greatest urgency," both Hopkins and Stettinius joined the ambassador in urging prompt ratification. Their efforts were successful: on February 1, Stettinius informed Winant and the European Advisory Commission that the United States was finally on board. Russian approval was given five days later. Thanks in large part to pressure from Winant, the Roosevelt administration also agreed to participate in the occupation and control of postwar Austria—a commitment that the president had previously opposed.

At the same time, other thorny issues relating to Germany were left unresolved at Yalta. The three leaders could not agree on whether or how to dismember Germany; as was their wont on difficult questions, they created a new committee to study the idea of partition. There also was no decision on a Soviet demand for $20 billion worth of reparations from Germany. And, although the Big Three approved the placement of Berlin in the Soviet zone of occupation, they failed to settle the question of specific U.S. and British access routes to their zones within the city. Noting that the Soviets had agreed to provide these routes, Winant pressed the president to consent to the proposal. He did not. On this issue, as on the others, "I think our attitude should be one of study and postponement of the final decision," Roosevelt told the ambassador.

Having made clear to the president how unhappy he was at being excluded from Yalta, Winant was invited to join Roosevelt in Egypt after the conference and to accompany him by sea as far as Algiers. During his three days with the presidential party, the ambassador tried to impress upon Roosevelt the urgent need to devise a comprehensive, long-range policy for dealing with the Reich after the war. The president, however, was too exhausted to focus on the subject and changed the discussion to his travels in Germany when he was a boy. It was the last time Winant would see FDR.

LESS THAN TWO WEEKS after the Yalta agreements were signed, Stalin signaled that he had no intention of abiding by them, at least as far as Poland was concerned. The Soviet government rejected virtually every non-Communist Polish leader proposed by Harriman and British ambassador Archibald Clark Kerr to participate in talks on creation of a new Polish government. The Soviets, Churchill remarked, "clearly wanted to make a farce of consulting the 'non-Lublin Poles.' " In notes he made as talking points before a meeting with the Soviets, Harriman wrote: "Looks as if you have taken hold of Poland & excluded all leaders who were not ready to take orders. Why is it necessary to dominate Polish life?" The U.S. ambassador urged the Roosevelt administration to get tough with the Soviets. If it didn't, he warned, "the Soviet Government will become convinced that they can force us to accept any of their decisions on all matters, and it will be increasingly difficult to stop their aggressive policy."

The Soviets also reneged on a pledge they had made at Yalta to allow foreign observers into Poland, including Anglo-American military teams who were to help in the repatriation of American and British prisoners of war held in German camps there. To Churchill, it became increasingly apparent that the Soviet government wanted to delay for as long as possible the circulation of British and American eyewitness accounts of its tightening grip over the country. "There is no doubt in my mind," the prime minister told Roosevelt, "that the Soviets fear very much our seeing what is going on in Poland."

In Churchill's view, Poland was the measure of whether the Big Three's postwar alliance would succeed or fail. For the next month, until Roosevelt's death, the British leader bombarded FDR with urgent cables, proposing that the two of them join forces to intervene forcefully with Stalin over Poland. The president's response was to hold off taking any action that Stalin might interpret as a threat. Under the best of circumstances, Roosevelt's tendency was to delay difficult, controversial decisions. Frail and weak as he was in the early spring of 1945, he was even more inclined toward postponement. He thought it best, he told Churchill, to go slow on personal intervention.

Churchill sharply disagreed. Poland was on the brink of total Soviet domination, and his repeated promises of independence to the Poles were about to turn to ash. There was no time to waste. Pushed hard by the prime minister, Roosevelt, in the last weeks of his life, finally began to express concern about the fate of the Yalta accords. He voiced indignation, too, over the shabby Soviet treatment of American POWs as well as Stalin's sudden announcement that Soviet foreign minister Vyacheslav Molotov would not attend ceremonies in San Francisco marking the birth of FDR's dream, the United Nations. When the Soviet leader accused the Western Allies in early April of colluding with the Germans to arrange a separate peace, Roosevelt dispatched a sharp cable expressing his "feeling of bitter resentment" over the charge. Startled, Stalin backed off, declaring he never doubted Roosevelt's trustworthiness and integrity. His apologetic response put FDR in a much more conciliatory mood. On April 11, the day before he died, he wrote Churchill that he planned to "minimize the general Soviet problem as much as possible, because these problems, in one form or another, seem to arise every day, and most of them straighten out."

IN EARLY MARCH, Eisenhower's forces began crossing the Rhine and pouring into Germany. On his own initiative, the SHAEF commander informed Stalin that his troops would not compete with the Red Army for the trophy of Berlin. Instead, Ike said, he hoped the two Allied forces could meet at the Elbe River, some forty miles west of the German capital. In a cable to the Combined Chiefs of Staff telling them of his decision, Eisenhower declared that "Berlin has lost much of its former military importance." Capturing Berlin, he believed, was not worth the massive troop losses that such a drive would incur; Omar Bradley estimated that SHAEF casualties would exceed 100,000 in an Allied push toward the city.

Stunned by Eisenhower's unilateral move, Churchill fought hard to overturn it, exchanging a series of indignant cables with the American commander and urging Roosevelt to intervene. The ailing president declined to do so, and Marshall endorsed Eisenhower's decision. "Churchill's anger that Berlin was to be forsaken as a prize," Max Hastings wrote, "reflected the deeper grief which haunted the last months of his war, that Hitler's dominance of eastern Europe was now to be supplanted by that of Stalin."

Still, the fact remained that no military action in the spring of 1945, however symbolically important, could have changed in any significant way the postwar settlements to which the prime minister and Roosevelt had agreed at Tehran and Yalta.

20.

"FINIS"

O N THE NIGHT OF APRIL 11, 1945, ED MURROW WAS MORE CHEER-
ful than he'd been in a long time. He had finally escaped the leash of
London and was now with George Patton's forces deep inside Germany. Hitler's Reich was collapsing, and the war was fast drawing to a
close. And Murrow, who loved playing poker but never had much luck
at it, had just won thousands of dollars in an "uproarious" game with
some of the other correspondents covering Patton's Third Army.

The next morning, he stuffed his winnings into a money belt and
set off with U.S. troops toward the city of Weimar. Passing well-fed
farmers plowing their fields, the Americans came to a hill a few miles
outside the city. At the top was a concentration camp, enclosed by
barbed wire, whose German guards had fled three days before. The
camp's name was Buchenwald.

When Murrow and the other Americans stepped through its main
gate, the broadcaster felt as if he'd been sucker-punched. Dozens of
emaciated men, most of them little more than skeletal wraiths, flocked
around him. "Men and boys reached out to touch me," he said in a
broadcast a few days later. "They were in rags and the remnants of uniforms. Death had already marked many of them, but they were smiling
with their eyes." To his shock, he realized he had met several of them
before the war, including a former mayor of Prague, an eminent professor from Poland, a doctor from Vienna. As Murrow stood there, a
man fell dead in front of him. "Two others—they must have been over

sixty—were crawling toward the latrine. I saw it—but will not describe it." Murrow took notes of what the prisoners told him: six thousand men dead in March, two hundred "on the day we got here—& people outside are so well fed."

As several of the inmates escorted him through the camp, he felt, he later said, like vomiting. In a small courtyard, he found "two rows of bodies stacked like cordwood. They were thin and very white. Some of the bodies were terribly bruised. . . . I tried to count them as best I could and arrived at the conclusion that all that was mortal of more than 500 men and boys lay there in two neat piles." More than once during his few hours at Buchenwald, Murrow broke down in tears. He took his winnings of the night before from his money belt and distributed it all to the camp's occupants.

Although Buchenwald technically was not an extermination camp, more than fifty thousand of its inmates died during the war, most of starvation and disease. The true Nazi death camps, most of them in Poland, were liberated by Russian troops at about the same time as Buchenwald. Early in the war, Murrow and his CBS team, along with other American and British news organizations, had brought to public attention several reports about the Nazis' mass slaughter of Jews in those extermination camps. But for the remainder of the conflict, journalists from Allied countries provided little further coverage of the continuing persecution of the Jews and other enemies of the Reich. For Western news organizations, the Holocaust was not a major wartime story; its full extent was not known until after the conflict ended. Absent undeniable proof of such mass killings, it was virtually impossible for those living in democratic countries to comprehend the scale and savagery of the German attempt to wipe out the Jewish population of Europe.

Certainly, the U.S. and British governments, which had access to more information about the Holocaust than their citizens, did little to make the public aware of the atrocities or to take any substantive action to save the Jews. A number of officials in both countries, including Gil Winant and Henry Morgenthau, pushed their leaders to do more, but with sparse results. Insisting that the only way to help the Jews was to win the war, the Roosevelt administration declined to press for a change in America's restrictive immigration laws so that more Jews could be admitted to the country. In 1944, Roosevelt established the War Refugee Board to help facilitate the rescue of Jews from occupied nations, but the last-minute attempt was, as a number of historians have pointed out, much too little, much too late.

After returning to London from Buchenwald, Murrow was determined to open the eyes of his audience to the bestiality he had just witnessed. "What he had seen, he wanted the world to know," said BBC broadcaster Geoffrey Bridson, a friend of Murrow's. He was aiming, Bridson said, at "the starry-eyed listener who thought, 'Oh, well, that's a long way away, doesn't really have anything to do with us.' Well, Ed was just in a mood to kick them right in the teeth."

Three days after leaving Germany, Murrow sat down at the microphone and, in a voice suffused with anger, described what he had seen at the camp—the stacked bodies, the living skeletons, the torture chambers, the piles of shoes, hair, and gold teeth. At the end of his broadcast, he said flatly: "I pray you to believe what I have said about Buchenwald. I have reported what I saw and heard, but only part of it. For most of it I have no words. . . . If I've offended you by this rather mild account of Buchenwald—I'm not in the least sorry." Bridson, who was in the studio during the broadcast, said that Murrow "was shaking with rage by the time he finished."

Many people thought it was the best broadcast he had ever made, but Murrow disagreed. He felt he had not done full justice to the horror he had seen. "One shoe, two shoes, a dozen shoes, yes," he said. "But how can you describe several thousand shoes?"

ON APRIL 12, the day Murrow visited Buchenwald, Franklin D. Roosevelt died of a cerebral hemorrhage in Warm Springs, Georgia. The news of his death sparked an outpouring of shock and grief throughout the world, but few people were more affected than Gil Winant. Barely recovered from a severe bout of the flu, he was shattered by the news, which reached him in the middle of the night and left him literally prostrate for hours.

Despite his frustrations with a number of FDR's policies and the president's occasional offhand treatment of him, Winant never wavered in his support and fondness for the leader who had been his friend and close ally for more than a decade. "I'm Roosevelt's man," he once said. "If Roosevelt wants me to do anything, I'll do it. That's my political future." In a telegram to the president several years before,

Winant said simply: "Thank God for you." In another, he remarked: "I always think of you and miss seeing you very much." Just a few months earlier, he had scoured London antique shops for the perfect Christmas gift to send to Roosevelt, eventually settling on a walking stick that George Washington had presented to Jerome Bonaparte, Napoleon's younger brother.

In turn, Roosevelt had frequently expressed admiration and affection for the shy idealist who had sacrificed his political career for him and the New Deal. On several occasions, he talked about appointing Winant to top cabinet positions, including secretary of state. In 1944, he gave some thought to choosing Winant as his vice presidential running mate, floating the ambassador's name to a number of his closest associates, including Henry Morgenthau and Harold Ickes. Mentioning the possibility of Winant's candidacy at a meeting with his aides, FDR noted that the ambassador "could make the rottenest speech and yet when he finished, give the impression he was Abraham Lincoln." Nobody but Roosevelt was enthusiastic about the idea, however, and the president chose Harry Truman instead.

Like Winant, Winston Churchill was staggered by the report of FDR's death; it struck him, he later said, like a physical blow. At three in the morning on April 13, he summoned Walter Thompson, his principal bodyguard, to his study, where, as Thompson recalled, he talked about Roosevelt—"weeping, reminiscing, smiling, going over the days, the years; recalling conversations; wishing he had done this . . . agreeing, disagreeing, reliving." To Thompson, Churchill declared: "He was a great friend to us all. He gave us immeasurable help. . . . Without him and the Americans behind him, surely we would have been smothered."

The British people shared their prime minister's grief. Most of them knew little about the conflicts roiling the Anglo-American alliance; to them, Roosevelt was simply the savior of their nation. "This country," said the *Daily Telegraph*, "owes him a debt which can never be repaid for his understanding, help and confidence in its darkest hours." The day after FDR died, flags in London fluttered at half-staff, the king and his court declared seven days of mourning, and the usually bustling area around Piccadilly Circus was as "quiet as a small back street." Londoners "stood in the streets staring blankly at the first incredible newspaper headlines [and] queued up patiently for succeeding editions," Mollie Panter-Downes noted in *The New Yorker*. A U.S.

Army clerk recalled "being stopped on the street by at least a dozen people who expressed sympathy to me as if [the president] had been one of my own family." The writer C. P. Snow observed: "I don't think I have ever seen London quite so devastated by an event. Even my old landlady was crying. The Underground was full of tearful faces—far more than if Winston had died, I'm sure."

On April 18, more than three thousand people, including the British king and queen and several exiled European monarchs, jammed St. Paul's Cathedral for a memorial service for Roosevelt, while thousands more listened to the service outside. Winant, who escorted a weeping Churchill, read the lesson, taken from the Book of Revelation. Later that day, Churchill would declare to the House of Commons that Roosevelt "was the greatest American friend we have ever known and the greatest champion of freedom who has ever brought help and comfort from the new world to the old."

Churchill's reaction to the president's death was far more complex, however, than his eloquent eulogy revealed. There was no doubt he was deeply saddened, but the sadness warred with the anger and hurt he still felt over what he regarded as FDR's slighting treatment of him and Britain in the previous year and a half. The day after FDR's death, he dithered over the question of whether to fly to Washington for the president's funeral. Lord Halifax cabled him that Harry Hopkins thought he should come, that his visit would have "an immense effect for good." Roosevelt's successor, Harry Truman, also urged the trip, telling the prime minister "how greatly he would personally value the opportunity" of meeting him.

Nonetheless, in the end, Churchill chose not to go, claiming he had too much work to do in London. His decision puzzled many of his associates, who noted that he never before had hesitated to travel to Washington when he felt the need. As Max Hastings has written, "It is difficult not to regard the prime minister's absence from Roosevelt's funeral as a reflection of the alienation between himself and the president, which grew grave indeed in the last months of Roosevelt's life." Churchill's decision could also be explained by the fact that Roosevelt had never visited him in London, despite repeated invitations. Further, he always had been the suitor, the one to press for the Anglo-American meetings. Now, Churchill apparently felt, the shoe should be on the other foot. "I think that it would be a good thing that President Truman should come over here," he wrote to the king.

Truman, however, never visited London while Churchill was prime minister.

THE SPRING OF 1945 spawned a whirlwind of events: the discovery of the true extent of the Holocaust, Roosevelt's death, and the fall of German cities and towns, one after the other, like plums into the Allies' lap. In late April, Allied armies hurtled across the Reich, the Americans and British from the west, the Russians from the east. On April 25, U.S. and Soviet advance units met at the Elbe River, as Eisenhower had planned. On April 30, Hitler committed suicide, with Soviet troops less than a mile away from his bunker. On May 7, the war in Europe was over. At 2:41 that morning, General Alfred Jodl, the chief of operations of the German armed forces, signed his country's formal declaration of surrender at SHAEF headquarters, a drab red-brick schoolhouse in the French city of Reims. "With this signing," Jodl told General Walter Bedell Smith, "the German people and the German forces are, for better or worse, delivered into the victor's hands."

The following day in London, hundreds of thousands of people jammed Piccadilly Circus, Trafalgar Square, the streets surrounding Parliament and Whitehall, and the parks around Buckingham Palace, awaiting the official announcement of the war's end. It was a glorious spring day, and the joyful, exuberant crowds reveled in the warm sun. It seemed, one Londoner observed, as if the city had been "taken over by an enormous family picnic." Mothers adorned their babies' hair with red, white, and blue ribbons, and dogs sported red, white, and blue bows. Soldiers kissed laughing young women as they strolled by. One GI, his face covered with lipstick smudges, called out to the women who passed him: "Won't you join my collection?" In Piccadilly, American sailors formed a conga line, with everyone around them joining in. Church bells pealed. From tugboats on the Thames horns blared in celebration.

Broadcasting live from a van in the center of London, Ed Murrow described for his listeners the sight of thousands of people streaming out of flats and offices to join the merrymaking. He was one of the few Americans in the city who had been there from the beginning of the war and had seen it through to the end. To a certain extent, he must have been talking about himself when he noted in his broadcast that, notwithstanding the jubilation, many Londoners were not inclined to do much celebrating that day. "Their minds," he said, "must be filled with memories of friends who've died in the streets or on the battle-fields. Six years is a long time. I've observed today that people have very little to say. There are no words."

That evening, Murrow returned to his Regent's Park neighborhood to summon up his own memories of the war. On one corner, he remarked, his best friend, BBC editor Alan Wells, had been killed. Passing a water tank, he recalled "almost with a start, that there used to be a pub there, hit with a two-thousand pounder one night, thirty people killed." He admitted he was having trouble coming to grips with the idea of peace: "Trying to realize what has happened, one's mind takes refuge in the past. The war that was seems more real than the peace that has come."

FOR GIL WINANT, the war was not yet over. He spent a quiet V-E Day with friends, reminiscing about Roosevelt and what the day would have meant to him—but, most of all, caught up in worry over the fate of his elder son. A month before the war ended, the ambassador received word that John Winant and the other VIP prisoners of war held by the Germans as hostages had been removed from Colditz by the Gestapo just hours before American troops liberated the prison. What Winant did *not* know was that, with Germany plummeting into chaos, SS head Heinrich Himmler had ordered the Allied hostages to be taken to the Black Forest and shot. "When the whole German people are weeping," Himmler declared, "the English royal family should not be laughing."

But the general assigned to oversee the executions played for time, knowing full well what the victorious Allies would do to him if he carried out the order. When the high command in Berlin entrusted the assignment to another officer, the general contacted Swiss officials, who arranged for the POWs' transfer to an American command post in Austria. Two days after V-E Day, Gil Winant got the call he had hoped for but feared he would never receive: John was safe and on his way back to London. After hearing the news, Lord Beaverbrook wrote the ambassador: "That your anxiety for him should have been removed in the hour of triumph to which you have so greatly contributed, will be cause for rejoicing among all your friends in this country. And that means the whole British people."

FOR WINSTON CHURCHILL, meanwhile, V-E Day was a bittersweet moment. Vast crowds cheered him as he drove to Buckingham Palace, then to Parliament, to announce the German surrender. He rejoiced in the victory, but later that night, in a speech broadcast throughout Britain, he alluded to the fate of Poland and other Soviet-dominated countries when he said: "On the continent of Europe, we have yet to make sure that the simple and honorable purposes for which we entered the war are not brushed aside . . . and that the words 'freedom,' 'democracy' and 'liberation' are not distorted from their true meaning."

Four days earlier, in a telegram to his wife, Churchill admitted to a profound discouragement in the face of the "poisonous politics and deadly international rivalries" underlying the Allied triumph. The idealism of the conflict's early years, with its hopes and dreams of greater freedom, justice, and equality in the world, had dissolved in a welter of wartime deals and misunderstandings. Immediately ahead lay the nuclear infernos at Hiroshima and Nagasaki, the surrender of Japan, and the beginning of the Cold War.

AT REIMS, Dwight D. Eisenhower celebrated V-E Day by hosting a luncheon for twenty-five top British and American officers on his SHAEF staff, most of whom had formed close bonds with one another over the previous year and a half. It was a joyful, high-spirited occasion—at least until the end. "By the time [it] was over and everybody began to tell everybody goodbye, all of a sudden this group of generals recognized they no longer had a job," one of the participants recalled. "The companionship of months and days was gone. And it was almost like having attended your own funeral. . . . By the time we left everybody was sad, and General Eisenhower was saying goodbye with tears in his eyes."

A month later, the citizens of London paid tribute to Eisenhower for his inestimable role in guiding Allied forces to victory. In an elaborate ceremony at the bomb-damaged Guildhall, the American general was presented with the Honorary Freedom of the City of London, an·

honor dating back to medieval days and the highest the city can bestow. Virtually everyone of note in London was there—leaders of Parliament, top figures in business and the law, the British military brass,
members of the cabinet, and Winston Churchill. One by one, they pa-
raded up the aisle of the Guildhall's Great Hall to be received by the
lord mayor and sheriffs in their ceremonial robes. Near the end of the
procession came Gil Winant. "There had been applause in various degrees for the others," noted an American official, but when Winant's
name was announced, "there was a storm surpassed only by the greet-
ings to the Prime Minister and [Eisenhower] himself."

In the glow of victory, the earlier animus of the British military
toward Eisenhower seemed to have drained away. Even Alan Brooke
became an admirer—at least for the day. "Ike made a *wonderful* speech
and impressed all hearers in the Guildhall," Brooke noted in his diary.
"He then made an equally good speech of a different kind outside the
Mansion House, and a first-class speech at the Mansion House lunch.
I had never realized that Ike was as big a man until I heard his performance today!"

IN BRITAIN, HOWEVER, victory's glow faded quickly. Shortly after
V-E Day, the Labour Party announced it was leaving Churchill's coalition government, prompting the prime minister to call for the country's first general election since 1935. Most people expected Churchill
and the Conservative Party to triumph, but Winant was not among
them. Months before the election, the ambassador told Churchill's
doctor that he "was worried about Winston, who had become so en-
grossed in the war that he had lost touch with the feeling in the country." When the votes were tallied on July 26, he was proved to be right.
The leader who had been so inspirational in wartime was turned out of
office by weary, war-sick voters who decided they preferred the Labour
Party to manage their crippled economy and transform their society.
"Though [the British people] are grateful to Churchill for winning the
war," Pamela Churchill wrote to Averell Harriman, "they don't mean
to be sentimental about it."

Radicalized by the war, the people of Britain expected—and
demanded—that the enormous sacrifices they had made over the past
six years be repaid by significant social and economic postwar reforms.
Churchill continued to be bewildered by such demands. As he cam-

paigned for reelection, "he scoffs at those foolish people who want to rebuild the world," Lord Moran noted, "but beneath this bluster he is, I believe, less certain about things. He has a feeling that he is back in the thirties, alone in the world, speaking a foreign tongue." Physically and emotionally exhausted, Churchill told Moran shortly before what he called "this damned election" that "I have no message for [the people] now." He added wistfully: "I feel very lonely without a war." Nonetheless, he was convinced he would win. The Conservatives' landslide defeat—"a complete debacle," said John Colville—was a shock not only to the prime minister and his countrymen but to the rest of the world as well. It was, declared the *New York Times,* "one of the most stunning election surprises in the history of democracy."

Churchill was devastated by the loss. Pug Ismay, who saw him shortly after the results were announced, said he appeared "mortally wounded." Stricken by the suddenness of his downfall, he told Ismay: "I have no automobile, no place to live." In a matter of hours, his entire life had been turned upside down. "The whole focus of power, action and news," Mary Churchill noted, "had been transferred (with lightning speed, as it always is) to the new Prime Minister"—Clement Attlee. At 10 Downing Street, "the Map Room was deserted, the Private Office empty, there were no official telegrams."

A few days after he was turned out of office, Churchill spent a final weekend at Chequers, the scene of so many lively, historic wartime gatherings. He and Clementine invited just a few people to join them—their children, several of Churchill's closest advisers, and Winant. He and Churchill had had their difficulties over the last four years, especially in the war's final months, when the U.S. government increasingly flexed its muscle as the alliance's dominant partner. But all that was ancient history now, and the Churchills made clear they still regarded the ambassador as family.

During that somber weekend, Winant and the others did everything they could to cheer up the disconsolate former prime minister. "It was not so much the loss of power that he minded, but the sudden loss of a job to do," Sarah Churchill later remarked. "Six years geared to the utmost mental as well as physical exertion, and suddenly nothing." Above all, he missed the red dispatch boxes, filled with urgent papers, that arrived several times a day from Downing Street. According to Sarah, "they had become so much a part of his life."

The night before they left Chequers, Winant, Sarah, and the other guests signed the mansion's guestbook. For Churchill, it had always been an important ritual. Once, when Eisenhower left Chequers without signing the book, the prime minister's butler hurried after him, solemnly noting, "Sir, you have forgotten the book." The tone of the servant's voice made clear "he found it difficult to forgive my oversight," Eisenhower wrote. That final night, the last to sign was Churchill. He inscribed his name, then added one word under his signature: "Finis."

21.

"I SHALL ALWAYS
FEEL THAT I AM
A LONDONER"

B<small>Y THE AUTUMN OF 1945, THE COLOR, VIBRANCY, AND BUSTLE THAT</small> characterized wartime London had receded into the mists of memory. Londoners could now cross Piccadilly without risking life and limb, hotel rooms were plentiful, and European exiles had largely disappeared from the restaurants of Soho. The French and Belgians had left the year before, after the liberation of their countries. The Dutch, Norwegians, and Czechoslovaks followed suit in the spring, while the unhappy Poles resigned themselves to lives of permanent exile—in England and elsewhere.

The Americans, meanwhile, had vacated most of the buildings they had occupied around Grosvenor Square. Also closing their doors were Rainbow Corner and other GI clubs. On October 15, the final London edition of *Stars and Stripes* appeared, with the banner headline— "GOODBYE, ENGLAND"—emblazoned across the front page. In an accompanying story, Clement Attlee wished good luck to the departing Americans. "Now, with the immense tasks of war brought to a glorious conclusion," the prime minister said, "we look forward to continuing an ever-growing friendship with the United States in the achievements of peace."

In reality, however, that friendship was already unraveling. Eight days after the surrender of Japan, Harry Truman, FDR's successor, canceled Lend-Lease food shipments to Britain without any warning to the British government. In Washington, the British mission coordinating the dispatch of food supplies from the United States learned of the decision only when one of its ships was refused permission to sail. For battered, impoverished Britain, Truman's action could hardly have come at a worse time.

In the fall of 1945, British food supplies sank to their lowest level in six years. Instead of ending when the war was over, food rationing in the country became considerably more stringent. The ration for bacon was cut 25 percent just a few days after victory over Japan was declared, and the queues for bread, potatoes, and other vegetables often stretched a block or more. (Bread and potatoes would be rationed, too, within a short time.) A returning British soldier expressed shock at the conditions he found in London: "It is hard to realize that I am in the capital of a victorious nation. There is no thought of triumph. The chief thought among Londoners is food."

Also in short supply were clothes and housing. Even the king felt the clothing pinch, exclaiming to Attlee: "We must all have new clothes—my family is down to the lowest ebb." But, with stringent clothes rationing still in place, the monarch's plea went unanswered. Meanwhile, the loss of more than 40 percent of the country's housing stock left millions of Britons without permanent homes. Temporary housing—wooden and corrugated iron structures erected on bomb sites—had transformed some areas of London and other British cities into shantytowns.

Having lost a quarter of its wealth and two thirds of its export trade, the country, after six years of war, was virtually bankrupt. Its people had very little to look forward to. With the conflict over and the danger gone, the community spirit that marked the war years had vanished. Why, Britons asked, must they continue to scrimp, save, and sacrifice? There were bitter complaints about shortages and rationing and considerable fear about what the future might hold.

As it turned out, such fears were abundantly justified. The new Labour government began laying the groundwork for the welfare state envisaged by the 1942 Beveridge Report, but it lacked the resources to properly fund the state's new benefits. For the next several years, most of the goods that Britain produced would be for export, to resuscitate its economy and generate the revenue that the country so desperately needed. Rationing of food and clothing would continue into the 1950s, and the housing shortage would grow even more severe. Many British cities would remain dingy and dilapidated for years.

By contrast, the United States and its economy experienced virtually no trouble in making the transition from war to peace. It had ended the war with the lowest casualty rate of any major combatant country and no serious damage within its boundaries. Unlike Britain, whose industry had been devoted almost entirely to wartime production, the United States had continued to churn out a variety of consumer goods throughout the conflict. As a result, it was in the enviable postwar position not only of continuing to provide those goods to its own people but also to supply the world's export markets, including many that had formerly relied on Britain for exports.

For most Americans, the strains of war faded away almost as soon as peace was declared. "The American people are in the pleasant predicament of having to live 50 per cent better than they have ever lived before," said Fred Vinson, director of the Office of War Mobilization and Reconversion in Washington. New cars began appearing in dealers' showrooms, gasoline was plentiful once more, and refrigerators, washing machines, and other big-ticket consumer items became widely available. The pent-up demand for such goods, combined with the massive personal savings accumulated by Americans during the war, helped create an economic boom that lasted for almost a generation.

Donald Worby, a GI just returned from Europe, discovered how good the war had been for some of his countrymen when he picked up a loaf of bread one day at a bakery in his hometown. Worby, who had spent considerable time in England and admired its people for their stoicism in the face of hardship, overheard one customer tell another how sorry she was that the war was over. If it had lasted just a little longer, she explained, she and her husband could have earned enough money to pay off the loans on four buildings they had bought with their earlier wartime savings. The other woman, who had lost a son in the war, picked up a cream pie from the counter and hurled it into the budding landlady's face. Taking a wad of bills from his pocket, Worby insisted on paying for the pie.

Shocked by America's sudden termination of Lend-Lease, the British could not understand how their closest wartime ally, flush with economic prosperity, could turn its back so abruptly on them and their woes. One woman, expressing a view shared by many of her countrymen, declared of the Americans: "I think they're behaving disgustingly." Having put their faith in a 1944 verbal commitment by Roosevelt that Lend-Lease would continue for a while after Germany's defeat, British leaders had clung to the belief that America would help ease their country's difficult postwar economic recovery. Truman, however, knew nothing of his predecessor's promises, which were never written down, nor was he aware of the magnitude of Britain's financial plight. What he did know was that most members of Congress, who had grudgingly approved the Lend-Lease program as a wartime measure only, wanted it ended as quickly as possible. "We'd given our allies everything they asked for and more," said one congressman, "and now people were sick and tired of it, and didn't want to hear any more about it." A few months before his death, Roosevelt had predicted the resurgence of such an insular mood. "Anybody who thinks that isolationism is dead in this country is crazy," he told Robert Sherwood. "As soon as this war is over, it may well be stronger than ever."

Eventually, after long and acrimonious negotiations, the United States agreed to help bail Britain out of its financial crisis with a $3.5 billion loan, to be paid off over fifty years, and generous repayment terms for the Lend-Lease aid already provided. Of the $21 billion in Lend-Lease debts owed the United States, the British were asked to give back only $650 million. But the bailout came with a steep—and, in Britain's view, deeply unfair—price: British endorsement of a 1944 plan hammered out at Bretton Woods, New Hampshire, creating a new international economic order that would make the dollar the world's leading currency, eliminate Britain's imperial preference system, and greatly benefit U.S. trade in general.

The British were indignant that the United States would demand interest payments for a new loan, no matter how lenient the terms, and otherwise take advantage of the extremely perilous economic situation in which the country now found itself. "It is aggravating to find that the reward for losing a quarter of our national wealth in the common cause is to pay tribute for half a century to those who have been enriched by the war," *The Economist* declared.* In a vitriolic debate in the House of Commons, MPs blasted the loan's provisions as a sellout of the British empire and an "economic Munich." Some 100 members voted against accepting the bailout on such terms and 169 members, including Winston Churchill, abstained.

Despite his own previous clashes with the British over economic and trade policy, among other issues, Harry Hopkins agreed with the

---

* Britain made its final repayment on the loan in December 2006, sixty years after it was first agreed to.

Attlee government that America's loan terms were onerous and mis-guided. "The American people must realize the plain and simple truth that the British live by trade," Hopkins jotted down in a series of private notes. "We are probably powerful enough, if we want to use that power, to seriously injure that trade, but I do not believe it is to our self interest to do it. Why should we deliberately set about to make a weak Great Britain in the next hundred years? . . . We cannot afford to indulge in a deliberate program on either side which is going to force our two peoples further and further apart."

Furthermore, Hopkins wrote in his notes, America had a moral debt of its own to Britain. "I believe that the British have saved our skins twice—once in 1914 and again in 1940. They, with the French, took the brunt of the attack in the First World War, and the Germans came within a hair's breadth of licking them both before we got into it. This time, it was Britain alone that held the fort, and they held that fort for us just as much for themselves, because we would not have had a chance to have licked Hitler had Britain fallen."

GIL WINANT AND his subordinates at the American embassy in London were as appalled as Hopkins by the abrupt cutoff of Lend-Lease and by the continued U.S. determination to link British aid to concessions in commercial and trade policy. Having tried without success to arrange a gradual end to Lend-Lease that was as orderly and pain-free as possible, Winant warned the Truman administration that its unilateral action "would work great hardship on the British people." Wallace Carroll fumed: "Did any nation ever before sacrifice so heedlessly a colossal investment in that priceless commodity—good will?"

If Roosevelt had been alive, said Ernest Penrose, Winant's economic adviser, the ambassador "would have made one of the direct and vigorous appeals to him which in the preceding four years he had reserved for matters of the greatest urgency." But Winant did not know the new president, and, according to his secretary, the Truman administration was "alien to him." Nonetheless, he made an effort to reach out to Truman, sending him a cable shortly after he became president, saying: "I want to do everything in my power to assist you."

Truman and his lieutenants, however, showed little interest in Winant and his views and scant appreciation for what he had done to forge the Anglo-American alliance and keep it together. All that was in the past. The future, they believed, was the Cold War now developing between the West and Soviet Union. In their view, Winant's dream of international social and economic justice was passé. What was needed now was "not idealism but realism, not persuasion but coercion, not softness but hardness."

At that point, Winant's own future seemed as bleak as the outlook for Britain. Late in the war, he had lobbied to become the first secretary-general of the United Nations, and Roosevelt assured him he would do everything in his power to help him get the job. But FDR's death helped end that dream, as did the decision to put the United Nations headquarters in New York, making it politically impossible for an American to head the organization. Yet, even in the face of such impossible odds, Winant kept hoping that, somehow, he would get the post. "His nerves during those months were all on edge," a subordinate recalled. When he was finally informed he would not be given the job, he told an assistant: "I've lost the last thing I've really wanted." He remained ambassador to Britain for nine months after the war, dealing with such mundane postwar details as arranging to send GI war brides across the Atlantic. Depressed and exhausted, he exclaimed to his secretary, "I have no life!"

One of Winant's only sources of comfort was Sarah Churchill, but, even there, happiness eluded him. The end of the war had brought their relationship to a crisis point. She filed for divorce from Vic Oliver, and Winant, who told her he also planned to get a divorce, wanted her to marry him. But having married at the age of twenty, she was unwilling to give up her newly regained independence.

Like Winant, Sarah and her family had gone through an exceedingly difficult emotional time once the war was over. Both her parents had considerable trouble adjusting to life away from Downing Street and the end of wartime's adrenaline rush. "I cannot explain how it is," Clementine wrote to her daughter Mary, "but in our misery we seem, instead of clinging to each other, to be always having scenes. I'm sure it's all my fault, but I'm finding life more than I can bear. He is so unhappy & that makes him very difficult." As she had done so often in the past, Sarah played peacemaker between her mother and father, trying to cheer each of them up and repair the rift between them. Sarah, her mother wrote during the war, "has been and is a pillar of strength. . . . Everybody loves her. She has taken so much trouble with everybody to smooth out any little crossnesses and difficulties which might have arisen. . . . She looks after everybody."

Soon after Churchill was turned out of office, he took Sarah with him on a painting holiday to Italy's Lake Como. "I do not know that I ever loved him more than in the months that followed [his defeat]," she later wrote. "I burst into pent-up tears when I heard I was to accompany him to Lake Como." Shortly after they arrived, Sarah wrote to Clementine: "I wish you were here with us. . . . We never see a lovely sight that he doesn't say, 'I wish your mother were here.' " She added: "I really think he is settling down—he said last night—'I've had a happy day'! I haven't heard that for I don't know how long!" As Churchill made clear in his own letter to Clementine, one reason for his happiness was the presence of his favorite daughter: "Sarah has been a joy. She is so thoughtful, tactful, amusing, and gay. The stay here would have been wrecked without her." Father and daughter were closer than ever before, thanks in large part to Sarah's stints as unofficial aide to Churchill at Tehran and Yalta. He was the most important man in her life, and she loved being with him. Yet, determined to hold on to her independence, she was wary as ever of falling too much under his spell.

Sarah had always felt whipsawed between the men she loved. "You've no idea how tough it is, having a famous husband and a famous father," she once exclaimed to a friend. Knowing that Churchill had never forgiven Vic Oliver for snatching Sarah away from him, she worried how he would react if her relationship with Winant became public. Feeling imprisoned in a "cage of affection," Sarah told Winant she planned to resume her acting career. She deeply cared for him but saw no future with him.

ED MURROW'S PERSONAL and professional life was also in considerable flux. In the fall of 1944, his wife had resigned from the British-American Liaison Board, pleading "mental and physical exhaustion." Janet had had enough of Murrow's increasingly open affair with Pamela Churchill and decided she needed to get away to think things over. She returned to the United States to see her parents, both of whom were ailing, and to reassess her marriage. As soon as she left, Murrow began bombarding her with a series of pining letters. "For many things I owe you much," he wrote her on her birthday, September 18. "For the way you wear your hats. . . . For your kindness to friends. . . . For your willingness to risk the loss of dough and position for a principle. . . . More and more you are the important part of my life." In another letter, he observed: "I am lonesome as can be. . . . Saw Clemmie [Churchill] in the Lobby, who asked for you. . . . How long is it since we went walking together or just loafed? . . . If we have any sense, the best years of our lives should be ahead of us." In yet another, he acknowledged: "Maybe I had begun to take your love and kindness and tolerance too much for granted."

Yet, for all his tender missives to Janet, Murrow continued to see Pamela, who, while still carrying on her affair with Frederick Anderson, had greatly stepped up the pressure on Murrow to divorce Janet and marry her. In a letter to Harriman late in the war, she noted that she and Murrow had had a serious quarrel over her relationship with Anderson. The night after the row, she wrote, "Fred took me to dine at Ciro's . . . and we danced away til midnight." Notwithstanding Pamela's fickleness, Murrow, according to several friends, was indeed thinking of divorcing Janet and marrying her.

Before making a final decision, however, he returned to the United States in early 1945 for a month's vacation with Janet at a Texas dude ranch. "We didn't talk about Pamela at all," Janet recalled. "We were very happy to be together." During that time, she became pregnant. For years, both she and Murrow had longed to have a child, and the birth of their son, Casey, in November 1945 brought an end to his involvement with Churchill's daughter-in-law, even though, as he later told a friend, "I've never been so in love with anybody in my life." According to Pamela, Murrow sent her the following terse telegram breaking off the affair: "Casey Wins."

Four months after Casey was born, the Murrows, after nine years in England, prepared to move back home. Murrow had accepted an offer from Bill Paley to become vice president of news and public affairs at CBS. He didn't really want the job, telling Janet he hated the idea of being cooped up in an executive suite. In recent trips to the United States, he had also felt uncomfortable with the stark contrast between American living standards and those in England and the rest of Europe. "We live in the light, in relative comfort and complete security," he broadcast to his fellow Americans shortly before the end of the war. "We are the only nation engaged in this war which has raised its standard of living since the war began. We are not tired, as all Europe is tired."

He was concerned, too, by what he viewed as the arrogance of the United States, its seeming reluctance to work closely with Britain and other less powerful countries after the war. "This is a great nation," he told his listeners. "I have seen its power thrown round the world. But we must *live* with the world. We cannot dominate it." Yet, for all his doubts and concerns about going back to the United States, it was still home. He needed, he felt, to return to his roots.

Nonetheless, leaving London proved to be an extraordinarily wrenching experience. In the British capital, he had come of professional age, learning his craft with the help of his BBC colleagues, to whom he was considerably closer, both personally and professionally, than to the CBS staffers in New York. Indeed, midway through the war, Brendan Bracken, at Churchill's behest, had asked him to become deputy director of the BBC, in charge of all its programming—news and entertainment—worldwide. It was a remarkable offer but one that Murrow, after considerable thought, reluctantly declined. He was worried, among other things, that as an American, he would be put in "an awkward position" in the event of "a real conflict of views" between the United States and Britain after the war. Still, he was greatly moved by the honor paid him. "Can you imagine an American broadcasting company asking an Englishman to take charge of it?" he asked Felix Frankfurter.*

Shortly before leaving London in March 1946, Murrow bade farewell to the British people in a broadcast over the BBC. As a young man, he said, he had visited Britain three times—and had come away with decidedly unfavorable impressions. "Your country was a sort of a museum piece," he observed, "pleasant but small. You seemed slow, indifferent and *exceedingly* complacent. . . . I thought your streets narrow and mean, your tailors over-advertised, your climate unbearable, your class consciousness offensive. You couldn't cook. Your young men seemed without vigor or purpose. I admired your history, doubted your future, and suspected that the historians had merely agreed upon a myth." Yet, he acknowledged, "always there remained in the back of [my] youthful and undisciplined mind, the suspicion that I might be wrong."

His wartime experience in Britain, Murrow said, showed him just how wrong he was. Faced with the greatest crisis in their history, Britons proved their true mettle, fighting back with all their might

---

* When Asa Briggs's magisterial three-volume history of the BBC was published in the 1960s, Murrow's photo, along with those of prominent BBC figures, was featured on the cover of the volume featuring the war years. He was the only non-BBC broadcaster to be included.

while remaining faithful to the principles of freedom and democracy. "The government was given dictatorial power, but it was used with restraint. . . . There was still law in the land. Representative government, equality before the law, all survived. There was no retreat from the principles for which your ancestors fought. . . . [Your example] will, I think, inspire and lift men's hearts long after the names of most of the great sea and land engagements have been forgotten." With strong emphasis, Murrow added: "I have been privileged to see an entire people give the reply to tyranny that their history demanded of them. . . . You have lived a life, not an apology."

In the days following his broadcast, letters from all over Britain poured in to the CBS office. "It is men like you," one woman wrote, "who keep alive in our hearts the tiny flame of hope that some day, nations may grow to understand one another and learn to live in friendship and peace. Thank you, dear Ed Murrow." A British naval officer wrote: "Please tell your people when you get home that we may not always be easy to understand but we do want to be good and loyal friends if you let us." Echoing that view, another letter writer implored Murrow: "When you get home, make your farewell to us known to your own folk. . . . Tell them that we want, for friendship's sake and for the world's sake, the close continuing comradeship of our American Allies. You, sir, with your unmatched gift and power, can make our common cause live on. You can keep us close together and can keep alive an understanding which was good enough to win a war and surely good enough to cherish in peace."

Two weeks later, Murrow made his final CBS broadcast to listeners back home. For several hours beforehand, he moodily tramped the snowy streets of London, feeling, he told his British friends, like a deserter. At the end of the program, he signed off: "Now, for the last time, this is Edward R. Murrow in London." When he was done, BBC engineers clipped the wires of the big desktop microphone he had used for the past nine years. Attached to it was a plaque prepared by the BBC news staff and engraved with these words:

THIS MICROPHONE, TAKEN FROM STUDIO B4 OF BROAD-CASTING HOUSE, LONDON, IS PRESENTED TO EDWARD R. MURROW WHO USED IT THERE WITH SUCH DISTINCTION FOR SO MANY BROADCASTS TO CBS NEW YORK DURING THE WAR YEARS 1939 TO 1945

Murrow, who prided himself on his unemotionalism, could not hold back his tears. Years later, he told Malcolm Muggeridge in a BBC television interview that of all the prizes and honors he had received over the course of his career, the microphone given him by the BBC was "the only trophy I have ever kept" and the one "I value above anything I have."

A MONTH AFTER Murrow's departure, Gil Winant also took his leave from Britain. Truman finally had given him an appointment as America's representative to the Economic and Social Council, a United Nations agency aimed at promoting international economic and social cooperation and development. It was not the job he wanted, but it did give him an opportunity to work to revive war-shattered countries in Europe and elsewhere. In March 1946, he resigned as ambassador, and Averell Harriman was named to take his place.

As heartfelt as Britain's farewell to Murrow had been, the outpouring of love and gratitude for Winant was nothing short of astonishing. Despite the disheartening outlook for their country, the British people had not lost sight of the fact that, thanks in no small part to the U.S. ambassador, the Anglo-American alliance had held together to win the war. Such a wartime bond had never existed before—and, in all likelihood, would never be duplicated again. Winant was showered with tokens of Britain's esteem and thanks, including honorary degrees from Oxford and from Cambridge, which, in its citation, described him as a "close friend, trusted and beloved." Echoing that feeling, Prime Minister Clement Attlee declared that no ambassador to Britain had ever "commanded to such an extent the love of the people of this country."

About Winant, the *New Statesman* noted: "Almost everyone in this country knows his name and respects him as a great American and as one of the best friends this country has ever had." The ambassador was, the *Daily Express* remarked, "the personification of the finest part of America's character." The *Daily Herald* recalled how Winant "came to us in 1941 when we were in dire peril. He lived with us, suffered with us, and worked with us. His faith in us contributed immensely to our morale, and his work as a diplomat succeeded, during a vital period, in obtaining enormous reinforcements to our fast-diminishing resources. . . . He was with us, up to the neck, in our fight." The British magazine *Punch,* known for its satiric barbs, went against type and ran a cartoon entitled "A Friend Indeed." It showed a Cockney flower seller handing a bouquet to Winant and saying, "Goodbye, sir. You've helped us in bad times and we shan't forget you."

After hearing of Winant's departure, an Oxford law professor told him: "I do not think that it is possible for you to appreciate the great place that you have made for yourself in Anglo-American history." John Martin, Winston Churchill's former chief private secretary, wrote to the ambassador: "Those of us who served at No. 10 had a special opportunity of knowing what a friend in need you were to our country and how much that wonderful teamwork between the two nations is owed to you." The "rather hard-boiled" manager of the Savoy Hotel remarked to an American reporter: "When he goes, we will lose the best American we've ever had here in London." In a note to Winant, Herbert Agar, who had replaced Wallace Carroll as Office of War Information head in the British capital, declared: "My driver and all the English secretaries and charwomen have come to me asking that I tell you how personally bereft they feel at your leaving. . . . They think it is fine that the important people have told you how deeply they feel about you, but they, the little people, want to tell you too. I hope you do realize how widespread this feeling is. As for me, there is no way of expressing what I feel. The years of working for you have been the most satisfying years of my life."

The "important people," meanwhile, revealed their sense of loss at a series of farewell dinners that began with a gala function at London's Mansion House at which both Attlee and the leader of the Opposition, Winston Churchill, spoke—"a unique honor," in the words of the *Daily Telegraph*. Reporters covering that event and the others that followed were struck by the depth of feeling that speaker after speaker expressed for the U.S. envoy. "Official British reserve has seldom been so strongly forgotten as when the British Government said goodbye to Mr. Winant," one British journalist wrote. According to the *New York Times*, the paeans to Winant were "infinitely more than a collection of polite phrases on a state occasion. In the deep emotion of these farewells one could sense that for Britons, Mr. Winant had been a very great ambassador."

"In adversity, we find our real friends—and such was John Gilbert Winant," said the lord mayor of London. Lord Derby remarked: "In a long life, I do not remember any man who has ever rendered such signal service to his own country and ours." Sir Archibald Clark Kerr, about to assume new diplomatic duties as British ambassador to Washington, said about Winant: "I propose to take him as my model." Churchill, never one to hide his feelings, spoke with greater emotion than usual when he declared: "I would say without a moment of hesitation there was none who ever had a more momentous mission than Mr. Winant. There was none who came closer to the heart of Britain. There was none who, while upholding in the strictest manner the interests and rights of his own country, made us feel he was a true, faithful and unyielding friend." Turning to Winant, the former prime minister said: "He is a friend of Britain. He is more: he is a friend of justice, freedom, and truth. He has been an inspiration."

No one, however, showed more sadness over Winant's departure than Anthony Eden. In a choked voice, the former foreign secretary told an overflow crowd at a dinner at Lancaster House: "Neither you nor I nor the historian of the future will be able to estimate at its true value the contribution which Mr. Winant made to Allied unity and to Allied victory." Tears glinting in his eyes, Eden raised his glass to the man he counted as one of his closest friends. "There is no man with whom I would rather have worked in such an ordeal, in so searching and testing a time, as John Gilbert Winant. No fairer, straighter man ever walked the earth."

In his quiet response, Winant said that the five years he spent in London were "hard years and grim years, but I would wish to have spent them nowhere else.... It's not easy for me to say goodbye. I have never thought of myself as a foreigner in this land. We've shared so much together. We have had our common ideals and hopes and reverses, and our victories have been yours and ours together. I shall always feel that I am a Londoner." Gazing around at the crowd before him, he ended with several lines from a Rudyard Kipling poem:

> *I have eaten your bread and salt,*
> *I have drunk your water and wine,*
> *The deaths ye have died I have watched beside,*
> *The lives ye lent me were mine.*

As the ambassador sat down that evening, Anthony Eden was hardly the only one in the room struggling to hold back his tears.

22.

"WE ALL LOST A
FRIEND IN 'IM"

LESS THAN TWO MONTHS AFTER RETURNING HOME, GIL WINANT stood on the dais of the House of Representatives chamber, looking out at the political and military elite of Washington. Before him sat congressmen and senators, as well as members of the Supreme Court, Joint Chiefs of Staff, and cabinet. President Truman was seated in the front row, directly below Winant; Eleanor Roosevelt was behind Truman; and General Eisenhower, now the Army chief of staff, sat nearby. They were all there to pay formal tribute to Franklin D. Roosevelt, who had died sixteen months earlier. The event's organizers had asked Winant to deliver the only address. "I am so glad you are going to make this speech," Mrs. Roosevelt wrote him before the tribute. "No one could do it better."

What Winant said that day about Roosevelt could also have been said of him. "He dared to hope," the former ambassador observed of his boss and friend. "There was never a time in the dark years of the Depression, or the black years of the war, when he lost hope. He dared to hope for peace and believe in peace and to act for peace. . . . Believer in men, he thought of this republic of ours as part of that greater republic of mankind on which alone a true peace can be rested."

But there was no true peace in the world and, for Gil Winant, as for many others, very little hope. As Ed Murrow noted, "Seldom if ever has a war ended leaving the victors with such a sense of uncertainty and fear, with such a realization that the future is obscure." The Grand Alliance had fallen apart, and the Cold War had begun, with

Germany joining Eastern Europe as the conflict's main political battlegrounds. Mired in a dispute over reparations from Germany, the Soviets and their former Western allies did not, as originally planned, set up a democratic postwar government in the country and then withdraw. Instead, they set out to make permanent what were meant to be temporary zones of occupation. As Winant had feared, the division of Germany ultimately resulted in the creation of "something like independent states, each of which [was] a watertight compartment," with free movement cut off between the Soviet zone and those controlled by America, Britain, and France.

Before the end of the war, Winant and the other chief delegates of the European Advisory Commission—Britain's William Strang and the Soviet Union's Feodor Gusev—had hoped to hammer out a comprehensive, long-range policy for the development of postwar Germany. Their efforts, however, were thwarted by the governments of the United States and Soviet Union. "None of the Allies seemed to have a clear idea of the kind of Europe which should result from Germany's defeat," wrote historian Daniel J. Nelson, "and none of them had anything resembling a master plan for a new Europe."

Yet, despite the difficulties they faced (akin to "running a race hampered by both a millstone and leg irons," observed one historian), the EAC representatives could justly claim credit for some real, if limited, accomplishments. High on the list were the agreements they drew up for the division of Germany and Berlin, which, after being put into effect, helped prevent a chaotic and potentially violent East-West struggle for territory and influence in Germany at the end of the war. Indeed, although repeatedly challenged by the Soviets, the agreements remained in force until the collapse of Communism in Eastern Europe in the late 1980s.

As Strang observed in his memoirs, "Never before . . . had agreements of such volume or importance been reached with the Soviet government." An official British history, meanwhile, called the European Advisory Commission "the most successful inter-Allied organization in working with the Russians." Another study of the war described the agreements concluded by the commission as "significant achievements of wartime diplomacy . . . as important as any agreements reached at Yalta or Potsdam [a Big Three conference held in July 1945]."

The delegates' successes, restricted though they were, revealed the importance of quiet, behind-the-scenes diplomacy and negotiation, on which Winant had placed such a high value. Despite the difficulties they faced, he, Strang, and Gusev developed close personal relationships with one another during the EAC's eighteen-month tenure. "In our informal meetings, we gained each other's confidence," Strang recalled. "Step by step, we thrashed out our differences, patiently [and], it sometimes seemed, interminably." Yet, having demonstrated that the Allies could indeed work together, the three commission members were prevented by their governments from capitalizing on that cooperation and expanding their mandate.

After the war, Winant's frustration over the U.S. government's nonsupport of the EAC was exacerbated by claims from Harry Hopkins and other ex-officials of the Roosevelt administration that the EAC—not Washington or Moscow—was largely to blame for the failure to devise long-term solutions for the postwar governance of Germany. "The machinery of the EAC moved so slowly," Hopkins complained, failing to note that disarray and foot-dragging within the administration were among the key reasons for that slowness.

In the immediate aftermath of the war, Winant was also disturbed by what he believed was America's shirking of its duty to lead the way in reviving the wrecked economies of war-ravaged nations. The U.N.'s Economic and Social Council, on which he served, had no authority to force member states to take action in mending the wounds of the conflict, and, as a result, turned out to be little more than a debating society.

Depressed by his powerlessness on the world scene, the former ambassador was plagued, too, by personal difficulties. For many years, he had been deeply in debt, in large part because of his lifelong habit of giving financial aid to others. He had borrowed a great deal of money from friends and had taken out thousands of dollars in loans on his life insurance policies, only to lose the policies when he could not keep up his payments. To help pay off the huge sums he owed, Winant had signed a contract with Houghton Mifflin to write several books, including three volumes of a memoir. But writing, like speaking, proved to be extremely difficult for him. Caught up as he had been in the excitement and pressure of dealing with major world problems, he found it hard to adjust to the solitary, lower-key life of a writer. "He was much too restless a soul" to be satisfied with such an existence, noted Bernard Bellush, Winant's biographer.

Still not recovered from the physical and emotional strains of the war, Winant was also bone-tired. "I have never seen a more exhausted man in my life," a friend and former business partner of Winant's said shortly after the war. "He had aged tremendously." Mary Lee Settle would later describe the war-caused enervation that she, Winant, and others experienced as a "deep brutal exhaustion that had seeped into our souls, our bodies, our relationships with each other, a kind of fatal disease of exhaustion." Eric Sevareid, who was only thirty-two when the war ended, noted that he had "a curious feeling of age, as though I had lived through a lifetime, not merely through my youth."

Late in 1946, Winant returned to London to work on his first book, a memoir of the early years of his ambassadorship, and to try again to persuade Sarah Churchill, who had obtained her divorce a year earlier, to continue her relationship with him, although he himself was still married. When Winston Churchill learned of Sarah's divorce, he had called her to him and whispered in her ear: "Free!" She did not answer him, because she knew she was not: she was still emotionally involved with Winant. "Men can be free—perhaps—but women never," she later wrote to her father. Quoting Lord Byron—"Love is of man's life a part. Tis a woman's whole existence"—Sarah added: "Well, it is men who wish, and demand that it should be so!"

Sarah wrestled with her dilemma: to keep her independence and hurt Winant or remain involved with him and feel trapped. In that same letter, she asked her father: "Have you ever felt imprisoned? Have you ever felt a cage of circumstance, even affection, hemming you in? Or have you always been, no matter how bitter the moment, free?" She finally resolved the issue by taking an acting job in a movie shot in Italy. "For the moment," she wrote Churchill, "I am more or less free— but then again only at someone else's expense. . . . It seems I must always hurt the person who loves me."

Refusing to accept the end of the affair, Winant stayed on in London through the spring of 1947, sharing with its residents the hardships of the harshest winter in Britain since 1881. Temperatures plummeted to below zero, and a series of blizzards buried the country in a deep blanket of snow. A severe shortage of coal resulted in a draconian cutback in electricity. Schools and offices lost their heat; streetlights were turned off; shop windows were dark; pipes froze; and factories closed down temporarily, crippling British industry, so critical to the nation's economic recovery.

In February, Winant was among the guests at the wedding of Mary Churchill to Christopher Soames, a military attaché at the British embassy in Paris. The ceremony took place at St. Margaret's Church in Westminster, which was unheated and unlighted, except for four candles on the altar. The Dorchester Hotel ballroom, where the reception was held, was lit partly by candles and partly by electricity run by a small emergency generator.

That same month, Herbert Agar and his wife, Barbie, took Winant to see a play in the West End. On the way to the theater, they walked past the empty husks of the Shaftesbury and other theaters that had been bombed in the Blitz, looking eerily like Roman ruins, with their auditoriums and stages open to the sky. As he walked out of the theater lobby after the play, Winant was immediately surrounded by playgoers who recognized him. Men took off their hats, and women beamed. "Good evening, Mr. Winant," several said. He chatted with the crowd for a few minutes before going on his way.

The king of England, meanwhile, demonstrated the country's high esteem for the former ambassador in a more formal way. On New Year's Day 1947, George VI awarded Winant an honorary Order of Merit, arguably the most coveted and exclusive of all British honors and the only one that Churchill would accept for his wartime service. When the king presented the award to Winant at a Buckingham Palace ceremony, the American murmured his thanks and slipped the box containing the decoration into his pocket. Bemused, the British monarch asked: "Don't you want to look at it?" Removing the box from his pocket, Winant handed it to the king, who opened it to show him its contents. "You deserved it more than anyone," the queen told him.

Yet the honor, significant as it was, did little to assuage his growing loneliness and depression. Shortly afterward, he invited John Colville to dinner at his rented house in Mayfair. "The difference from former days," Churchill's ex–private secretary recalled, "was that on this occasion, Winant, who had been wont to listen and to supply an occasional thoughtful comment, wanted to talk." He talked through dinner and late into the night over brandy and cigars—about his days as New Hampshire governor, about the ILO, about the troubles in his marriage. Finally, at 4 A.M., Colville announced that he really must go. "Don't leave me," Winant pleaded. "*Please* don't leave me." Later, Colville would write: "Perhaps I should not have done so. I realized he was lonely and that something strange was happening under the surface; but I was very tired and I imagined we were both a little drunk."

A few months later, with Sarah now in Rome, Winant returned to New Hampshire. He finally finished the first volume of his memoirs, which provided him some relief. He also was greatly heartened when George Marshall, now Truman's secretary of state, outlined what came to be known as the Marshall Plan, a far-reaching program to jumpstart the economic recovery of Britain and the rest of Europe. Belatedly, the Truman administration had realized it must take urgent steps to assist Europe if total economic collapse and the spread of Communism were to be warded off. "It is now obvious that we grossly underestimated the destruction to the European economy by the war," said undersecretary of state Will Clayton after a fact-finding tour across the Continent. "Millions of people in cities are slowly starving." After a drought and disastrous harvest in 1946, the countries of Europe were, in the words of the writer Theodore H. White, "as close to destitution as a modern civilization can get."

In the spring of 1947, Truman sent Averell Harriman to Europe to organize and oversee distribution of Marshall Plan aid. Winant, who desperately wanted to have a role in the program, was ignored by the administration. In a speech at an international forum sponsored by the *New York Herald Tribune* in October, he challenged the audience with the question: "Are you doing as much today for peace as you did for this country and civilization in the days of war?" He added: "I know I'm not."

On November 2, Winant paid a surprise visit to Abbie Rollins Caverly, the daughter of an old friend, who had served as his assistant at the ILO in Geneva in the late 1930s. Caverly had just given birth to her first child, and Winant, who had given her away at her wedding, traveled from Concord to her home in Vermont "to make sure I was all right," she recalled. "I think he felt responsible for me in his own way." During the brief visit, she added, Winant seemed "tired and lonely . . . obviously dispirited."

Returning to Concord, Winant made a call to the Reverend Philip "Tubby" Clayton, an old friend from London, who was in the United States to encourage American young people to come to the British capital to help restore its bombed-out buildings and aid its residents. Winant had met Clayton, the vicar of All Hallows Church, near the

Tower of London, during the war and had agreed to help raise funds and recruit young Americans for his new project. On the phone, Winant told Clayton that he urgently needed to speak to him. Clayton, however, had a speech to deliver that night and said he would get together with his friend as soon as he could.

Winant, whose wife was in New York, spent much of the following day in his bedroom in Concord. Early in the evening, his housekeeper, who had been with him in Britain, brought him his dinner on a tray. When she returned a couple of hours later, the tray was untouched.

At about nine o'clock, the fifty-eight-year-old Winant rose from his bed and walked down the hall to the former bedroom of his son John, with its panoramic view of his beloved Bow Hills. Years before, he had commented about this sylvan setting, to which he had come at the age of fourteen and never really left: "To the tiny valley I owe the sense of peace and to the rolling hills a sense of time." But for John Gilbert Winant, that sense of peace was no longer to be found. Kneeling on the floor, he took a pistol from the pocket of his dressing gown. He steadied his left elbow on a chair, pointed the gun to his head, and fired. Hearing the thud of his body, his housekeeper and secretary rushed upstairs. The former U.S. ambassador to Britain died half an hour later.

In a front-page story on Winant's suicide, the *New York Times* noted that his death "has affected the people of Britain to an extent that few of his countrymen will understand. There was grief for his passing, not only in the elegant Victorian surroundings of the Connaught Hotel, where he used to dine, but in cab ranks, pubs, and fish and chip shops. . . . Tonight at the Bull and Bush in Willesden, a scrubby suburb, a little man told a reporter, 'I reckon we all lost a friend in 'im. He understood people like us, 'e did.' "

The palpable sense of loss was a remarkable tribute to a man who, in the words of the *Daily Express,* "walked with Britain at her greatest" and helped her survive. "What he said, the English trusted and believed," declared the *New York Herald Tribune.* "He did more than people will ever know to maintain the solidarity of the two great democracies in their hour of desperate need. The loss to the nation, as to his friends, is beyond measuring." About Winant's death, the *Manchester Guardian* reflected: "It is a terrible thing to consider about our postwar world that John Gilbert Winant could no longer bear to live in it."

Like most of Winant's friends, the historian Allan Nevins struggled to understand the reasons for his suicide. In an essay that took the form of an open letter to Winant, Nevins wrote: "Was it that, like Hamlet, you found the times were hopelessly out of joint—that, as one of the best idealists and most truly humane men of your age, you were laboring in an environment that could offer you nothing but hopelessly cruel frustrations?"

The former ambassador was buried at the Blossom Hill Cemetery in Concord, after a simple funeral service at which the St. Paul's School choir sang "The Strife Is O'er." His grave was heaped with flowers, including five dozen roses from Winston and Clementine Churchill and a large bouquet from Eleanor Roosevelt, who called Winant "as truly a war casualty as any of our other soldiers." In her newspaper column, Mrs. Roosevelt wrote: "My husband and I both admired him and what was more important, we trusted him completely. . . . He helped us win the war. My heart weeps for the loss of a friend and for the loss of the possibilities for service which still lay before him."

Three weeks after Winant's funeral, some five hundred people attended an unpublicized memorial service at St. Paul's Cathedral in London, at which Prime Minister Attlee read the lesson: "The souls of the righteous are in the hand of God, and there shall be no torment touch them." Winston, Clementine, and Sarah Churchill were there, as were Ernest Bevin and a shaken Anthony Eden, who told reporters, "I have lost one of my closest friends." Also at the service was twenty-two-year-old Rivington Winant, the former ambassador's younger son, who was studying at Oxford. As soon as the news of Winant's death broke, Eden retrieved Rivington from Oxford and brought him to stay with him at his country house. "He couldn't have been kinder to me," Rivington Winant said many years later. "He was really wonderful."

According to Walter Thompson, Churchill's bodyguard, Winant's "self-destruction was something Winston could not understand. He never got over it." By several accounts, Sarah Churchill was even more shattered by Winant's suicide. She had talked to him on the phone shortly before his death; afterward, she blamed herself for his depression, telling friends that she brought nothing but unhappiness to those who loved her. In the years to come, she would be relatively successful in her acting career, winning a leading role in the movie *Royal Wedding* with Fred Astaire, appearing several times on Broadway, and becoming the mistress of ceremonies of the American television series *Hallmark*

Hall of Fame, which also featured her in several of its productions. In her personal life, however, she never recovered her emotional bearings. Married twice more, she led a flamboyant life, complete with heavy drinking and wild parties, that caused considerable embarrassment for her parents. In September 1982, Sarah Churchill died in London at the age of sixty-seven.

FOR ED MURROW, the news of Gil Winant's death came as a terrible shock. He sat in a daze when he heard about it, shaking his head and exclaiming over and over, "What a waste! What a waste!" He and Janet, who were in London to visit friends and attend the wedding of Princess Elizabeth to Prince Philip of Greece, went to their old friend's memorial service at St. Paul's, held the day before the nuptials.

Unlike Winant, Murrow had profited greatly from his wartime triumph. He and his band of reporters had returned to the United States as the "class act" of American journalism—"golden boys!" the publisher Michael Bessie called them. As vice president of news for CBS, Murrow presided over a worldwide organization of correspondents, newscasters, commentators, writers, editors, and producers. He also was the star of the network's showcase radio news program *Edward R. Murrow and the News,* and, later, in the television era, of *See It Now* and *Person to Person.* He had it all, it seemed—fame, stellar reputation, large salary, lavish expense account, a luxurious apartment on Park Avenue, and a country house in upstate New York.

But, despite the trappings of success, he never felt at home in New York, finding it difficult to shift from the austerity of wartime Britain to the affluence of postwar America. Even though Murrow himself was now wealthy, he was ill at ease with the frenetic pace, prosperity, and materialism of his own booming country. More than that, he keenly missed London and its people and often talked of the "grim and glorious years" he had spent there. He frequently returned to the British capital, bringing the Churchills and other friends' food parcels and additional still scarce consumer items. He continued to order his suits from Savile Row and use British figures of speech in his conversation; one CBS colleague said he always thought of Murrow as "Sir Edward." The broadcaster told his friends he had "left all of his youth and much of his heart in England."

Like Winant, Murrow was greatly disheartened by the lack of freedom and justice in the postwar world as well by as the souring of the peace and rise of international tension. He was equally distressed by the rise of McCarthyism, which he denounced in his history-making *See It Now* broadcast in 1954, and by what was happening within his own industry—specifically, by what he considered as the decline of broadcast journalistic standards. Murrow would have liked CBS News to model itself after the BBC, whose primary objective was to serve the public interest. CBS, however, was a commercial network, not a quasi-public enterprise, and the chief aims of its chairman, Bill Paley, were profits and ratings. The news division, which had made CBS the number one network in the country during the war, was pushed into the background. Entertainment was Paley's main focus, and "news was his hobby," as Don Hewitt, the executive producer of the CBS news magazine program *60 Minutes,* put it. "He collected Murrows and Sevareids the way he collected Picassos and Manets and Degas."

Jack Gould, a television critic for the *New York Times,* once described Murrow as "an individual in a world beset by organization. . . . His office was called the Tobruk of journalism. . . . It was the fortress which defended electronic journalism in its dark hour and left a glowing heritage for a craft and a country."

The conflict between Paley and Murrow grew increasingly sharp until, in 1961, Paley and CBS made clear they had no place for Murrow anymore. At the invitation of the new president, John F. Kennedy, he left to become head of the U.S. Information Agency, the postwar successor to the Office of War Information. Four years later, he died of lung cancer at the age of fifty-seven.

Shortly before his death, Queen Elizabeth II made Murrow an honorary Knight of the British Empire. The night he died, the BBC interrupted its scheduled programming for a half-hour special report on Murrow and his achievements. According to Prime Minister Harold Wilson, who appeared on the program, the awarding of the KBE to the American was merely the formal recognition of a widely recognized reality: Murrow had been an "honorary Briton" since he first arrived in London in 1937.

UNLIKE HIS TWO wartime compatriots, Averell Harriman had little trouble adjusting to life after the war. As he had hoped, the conflict transformed him from a playboy businessman, caught in the shadow of his dominating father, to a major figure in international diplomacy. Parlaying his wartime service in London and Moscow into a distinguished forty-year government career, Harriman held significant positions in the Truman, Kennedy, and Lyndon Johnson administrations. He was, the *New York Times* observed, America's "super diplomat," the country's "plenipotentiary supreme."

Ironically, he was not happy with the first postwar diplomatic post to which he was appointed: ambassador to the Court of St. James. It was a job that, during the war, he would have been thrilled to be offered, but in 1946, Britain, impoverished and fast losing its imperial clout, was no longer a center of power and action. To his subordinates at the embassy, Harriman seemed "aloof, distant and not altogether engaged." Shortly after arriving in London, he moved into the official ambassador's residence in Prince's Gate, the mansion formerly owned by J. P. Morgan that Winant had spurned.

Harriman also renewed his affair with Pamela Churchill, who welcomed his attentions after the humiliation of being jilted by Murrow. Their relationship, however, was now considerably more problematic than it had been in the early 1940s. The freewheeling, feverish atmosphere of wartime London, where, in Harrison Salisbury's words, "sex hung in the air like a fog," had vanished. Harriman was also much more of a public figure as ambassador than he had been as Lend-Lease administrator, and he was worried that a scandal might erupt, threatening his diplomatic and political ambitions. To forestall that, he persuaded his wife to join him in London. Before she arrived, however, Truman summoned Harriman to Washington to become secretary of commerce, just six months after he had arrived in London.

As he had done with Churchill and Roosevelt, Harriman worked hard to cultivate Truman. In 1947, the president sent him to Europe with the rank of ambassador, to disburse billions of dollars in Marshall Plan aid. By most accounts, he acquitted himself well. Plodding and stiff, he had never been considered, even by his closest friends, as intellectual or even particularly bright. Lord Beaverbrook would later tell John F. Kennedy: "Never has anyone gone so far with so little." But he was ferociously hardworking, blunt, tough, determined, and acquainted with virtually every leader in postwar Europe—qualities that stood him in good stead for the rest of his government career. In 1948, Truman named Harriman as his national security adviser. According to Robert Sherwood, he "was the closest thing to a Harry Hopkins that Truman ever had"—a remark that must have given Harriman considerable pleasure.

By the late 1940s, the former Union Pacific chairman, together with such longtime friends and associates as Dean Acheson, John McCloy, George Kennan, and Robert Lovett, were widely regarded as the architects of America's overarching role in the postwar world. Known as the Wise Men, Harriman and the others were determined to create a Pax Americana throughout the globe, a vision of their country's future that, in the words of the Wise Men's biographers, Walter Isaacson and Evan Thomas, demanded the "reshaping of America's traditional role in the world and a restructuring of the global balance of power."

In a move that many of his friends believed to be breathtakingly wrongheaded, Harriman ran for the Democratic presidential nomination in 1952 and again in 1956. With no previous experience as an elected official, the wooden, imperious candidate had almost no appeal to the average voter; unsurprisingly, he lost both times, to Adlai Stevenson. In 1954, Harriman did win the governorship of New York by a small margin but was defeated by Nelson Rockefeller in his re-election bid.

Harriman was sixty-eight when Kennedy was elected president, but he was determined not to let age stand in his way of becoming a White House insider once again. "Everybody has his weaknesses, and Averell's is the desire to be near power," Arthur Schlesinger Jr., a friend of Harriman's, wrote in his diary. Harriman told another friend: "I am confident that before things end up, I will be in the inner circle. I started as a private with Roosevelt and worked to the top. And then I had to start as a private all over again with Truman and work to the top. That is what I intend to do again."

And that, indeed, is what he did. Initially skeptical of Harriman, Kennedy ended up appointing the aging diplomat as his chief international troubleshooter, later naming him undersecretary of state. At the age of seventy, Harriman negotiated the Geneva Accords ending a civil war in Laos and, two years later, led the American team that hammered out a limited test ban treaty with the Soviet Union. During Lyndon Johnson's presidency, the seventy-six-year-old Harriman traveled to Paris in 1965 to inaugurate talks with the North Vietnamese to try to end the Vietnam War—an effort that proved unsuccessful.

When he was seventy-nine, Harriman, by then a widower, encountered his wartime mistress at a dinner party at the home of *Washington*

Post owner Katharine Graham. In the years since the war, Pamela Churchill had had affairs with a number of rich and powerful men, including Elie de Rothschild and Fiat heir Gianni Agnelli, before marrying the American theatrical producer Leland Hayward, who died in 1971. Once again, Harriman and Pamela renewed their relationship, and a few months later, they were married. When Pamela told eighty-six-year-old Clementine Churchill of her impending nuptials, Clementine exclaimed with delight, "My dear, it's an old flame rekindled!"

Harriman died in 1986 at the age of ninety-four. His indefatigable wife went on to become a doyenne of the Democratic Party and U.S. ambassador to France. She was still serving as ambassador when she died of a cerebral hemorrhage in 1997, after a swim at the Ritz Hotel in Paris.

MORE THAN SIX DECADES after the end of World War II, Edward R. Murrow and Averell Harriman remain well-known figures in the United States. Widely regarded as the founding father and patron saint of broadcast news, Murrow has been the subject of several books and movies. A leading broadcasters' organization—the Radio and Television News Directors Association—presents the Edward R. Murrow Award each year for excellence in broadcast journalism. A number of schools throughout the country, including the school of communications at his alma mater, Washington State University, bear his name. As for Harriman, the Council on Foreign Relations in New York has the W. Averell Harriman program in European studies, and Columbia University houses the Harriman Institute for Russian, Eurasian, and Eastern European Studies.

John Gilbert Winant, while virtually forgotten in the United States, has been memorialized, too, albeit in a far different fashion than either Murrow or Harriman. The principal tribute to him was the brainchild of Father Tubby Clayton, the Anglican priest to whom Winant spoke the day before he died. Clayton was reportedly stricken with guilt by Winant's suicide, believing he might have prevented it if he had seen his friend the night he called.

After Winant's death, Clayton gave an impassioned speech to the students of St. Paul's School, urging them to come to London and work in the East End the following summer in honor of Winant, still a revered figure at the school. Several did, becoming members of the first group of young Americans dubbed the Winant Volunteers. Every year since then, dozens of high school and college students in the United States have spent their summers working with poverty-stricken communities in British cities. Since 1957, young Britons have returned the favor, coming to work with the underprivileged in America's towns and cities. The program is now called the Winant-Clayton Volunteers.

For some Winant-Clayton alumni, the experience turned out to be a life-changing event. "It helped me grow up and see the world for what it really was," recalled the Reverend J. Parker Jameson, who, as a recent graduate from Harvard, worked with disadvantaged youths in Liverpool in the summer of 1975. "It knocked out of me the idea that America was the center of the world. I learned that the globe is a much bigger place and that there's a whole world of hurt out there that needs to be taken care of. We need to work together to deal with it." Once the summer was over, Jameson stayed on in Liverpool for another year. When he returned to the United States, he decided to become an Episcopal priest, influenced in large part by his Winant-Clayton experience.

THE VIEW OF America that Parker Jameson gained that summer in Liverpool was not widely shared in his homeland, especially in the immediate postwar years. Having emerged from World War II as the mightiest country in the world, the United States was serenely convinced of its own omnipotence. Initially, it had little interest in close collaboration or partnership with its former Western allies, whose empires and global influence were fast disintegrating. Indeed, within months after the war, the United States had begun to displace Britain, France, and the other European colonial powers as the main economic and military force in Southeast Asia, the Pacific region, the Mediterranean, and the Middle East.

At the end of the conflict, the United States had briefly envisioned the Soviet Union as its main partner in dealing with postwar international problems. The onset of the Cold War, however, put an end to that notion, as well as to Roosevelt's plan for a speedy American withdrawal from European affairs. Having spent much of the war pacifying the Soviets, the U.S. government now launched a campaign to contain them. To do so, Washington realized it must not only maintain but increase America's wartime involvement with Europe, despite its long-held determination to stay out of Continental entanglements. Two years after the Marshall Plan was launched, the United States, Canada, and ten European countries established the North Atlantic Treaty Organization (NATO), a military alliance promising a collective defense by all member countries in the event of an armed attack on any one member. For the first time in its history, the United States had agreed to become a permanent force in keeping peace in Europe.

As they adjusted to their new role, American policymakers developed a new appreciation of their old wartime partner, Britain. "No other country has the same qualifications for being our principal ally and partner as the U.K.," a State Department paper noted. "The British, and with them the rest of the Commonwealth, particularly the older dominions, are our most reliable and useful allies, with whom a special relationship should exist."

That "special relationship" was never to be the close-knit, equal partnership that Britain had sought during and after the war. The United States always made clear who the dominant partner was, as during the Suez crisis in 1956, when American leaders put economic pressure on Britain to force a halt to an invasion of Egypt by British, French, and Israeli troops.

Yet, for all the recurrent strains and tensions, the United States and Britain had much more in common with each other than with any other ally, and their postwar connections turned out to be remarkably close, especially when compared to America's ties with the rest of the world. Such intimacy was heightened by the web of personal acquaintances and friendships that bound Britons and Americans together during the war. Having helped to smooth over problems during the conflict, those close-knit, informal relationships worked to promote cooperation after it. Speaking of the British, Robert Reich, a former Rhodes Scholar and labor secretary under President Bill Clinton, observed: "Here was a people whom Americans could trust: friends and confidants in an unfriendly and confusing world. . . . There is little doubt that American officials often sought the counsel of their British counterparts, and obtained the sort of frank and confidential advice that one can only get from an old and trusted friend whose judgment is deeply valued."

For many Americans and Britons who experienced their countries' wartime alliance firsthand, the legacy was deep and lasting. "The

Americans' coming was an education and gave me a broader outlook on life. They gave me an insight into democracy," said a woman from Liverpool. A Birmingham man, who'd been a schoolboy during the war, observed: "Whatever happens to the 'special relationship' at the national level, we worked out our own special relationships all those years ago. . . . [The Americans] were never merely 'them,' and they rapidly became 'us.' I for one will never lose the sense of good comradeship, generosity and basic solidarity we developed then."

In Schenectady, New York, a former American sailor observed: "I think I understand the people of the U.K. as well as I do the people of the U.S. In other words, I could hang my hat on either side of the Atlantic and say 'I'm home again.'" Ernie Pyle expressed much the same sentiment shortly before he was killed in the Pacific late in the war. "I have loved London ever since first seeing it in the Blitz," the columnist wrote. "It has become sort of my overseas home." *New York Times* correspondent Drew Middleton once remarked: "The years in London were the happiest of my life. . . . One can ask no more than to live in a place he knows and loves, among people he understands, respects and likes." Even the dyspeptic novelist and playwright William Saroyan, who despised virtually everything about his Army experience during the war, had nothing but good to say about London and its people. "It embarrasses me to say that I am in love with this city, for it seems such a false thing for anyone to say, but I am in love with London, and I will never stop being in love with it," declares the protagonist of Saroyan's wartime novel, *The Adventures of Wesley Jackson.*

To a number of Americans who spent time in wartime Britain, the country and its capital seemed to resemble Brigadoon—a magical place where courage, resolution, sacrifice, and a sense of unity and common purpose triumphed, if only for a few short years. Robert Arbib eloquently made that point in his memoir of the months he spent in Britain, which he wrote shortly before the end of the war. "Every Englishman you meet apologizes," he observed. "They all say, 'Too bad you are seeing England in wartime. Too bad you cannot see England at her best.'" But Arbib forcefully disagreed with that view. "Damn it," he wrote, "this is England at her best. Right here and now!"

True, the streets were dirty, the shopfronts needed paint, and the trains ran late. True, also, that food and hot water were scarce, the beer was weak, the grass in the parks was shaggy, and the lights were out. "But, to some of us, who remember other things," Arbib wrote, "who knew a country wholly united behind one purpose, a country where danger made all men friends, where sacrifice came not only to the soldier or catastrophe came only to the poor, where everyone shared in the work, where terror and trouble could not subjugate humour and wit, where gallantry and heroism was the man standing next to you at 'The Rose and Crown,' and where democracy was the duke on the bicycle and the farmer in the car—this was a nation at its best, this was an experience to be shared with pride, this was a time of greatness, and Britain a wonderland indeed."

Shortly before leaving London in October 1940, CBS correspondent Eric Sevareid expressed a similar sense of kinship with a city and a nation he had grown to admire and love. In his last broadcast, the twenty-seven-year-old Sevareid compared his departure from London to his flight from Paris just days before its fall to the Germans four months earlier: "Paris died like a beautiful woman, in a coma, without struggle, without knowing or even asking why. One left Paris with a feeling almost of relief. London one leaves with regret. Of all the great cities of Europe, London alone behaves with pride, and battered but stubborn dignity."

Throughout his paean to the British capital and its residents, Sevareid fought to keep his voice steady. At the end, he lost the struggle. His voice choked with emotion, he concluded: "Someone wrote the other day, 'When this is all over, in years to come, men will speak of this war and say, 'I was a soldier,' 'I was a sailor,' or 'I was a pilot.' Others will say with equal pride, 'I was a citizen of London.'"

ACKNOWLEDGMENTS

My FIRST EXPRESSION OF THANKS MUST GO TO THE LATE EDWARD R. Murrow, for without him, I would not have written this book or, for that matter, the two that preceded it. All three have dealt, in various ways, with Britain during World II. It's a subject that has fascinated me ever since my husband, Stan Cloud, and I started our research for *The Murrow Boys*, a book we wrote more than a decade ago about Murrow and the correspondents he hired to create CBS News. The eight years that Ed Murrow spent in Britain, most of them during the war, were the most satisfying of his life. His brilliant reporting about the country and its people not only won him international fame but made him a key player in the shaping and sustaining of America's wartime alliance with Britain.

So when I decided to write a book about the alliance and the men who helped forge it and keep it alive, it was only natural that I would choose Murrow as one of the book's three main characters. The dozens of interviews that Stan and I did with Murrow's widow, Janet; the surviving Murrow Boys; and many others who worked closely with him have added greatly to this latest effort. So has my additional research in the Edward R. Murrow and Janet Brewster Murrow papers at Mount Holyoke College—a collection that includes a new cache of the Murrows' letters and diaries, given to the college by their son, Casey. I'd like to thank Patricia Albright, Mount Holyoke's archives librarian, for her generous assistance.

Thanks, too, to the staff of the Library of Congress Manuscript Division, which houses the papers of Averell and Pamela Harriman. I owe a special debt of gratitude to Dr. John E. Haynes, the library's expert on twentieth-century politics and government, for providing me access to Pamela Harriman's papers, now in the process of being opened to researchers, which shed new light on her relationships with Harriman and Murrow. Of particular interest are the transcripts of a series of lengthy, candid, and provocative interviews she gave to her biographer, Christopher Ogden. I'm grateful to Chris and to the late Rudy Abramson, Harriman's biographer, for their shrewd and perceptive comments to me about both Harrimans.

Researching the life of John Gilbert Winant, the book's third main character, was a particular pleasure and challenge. This shy former ambassador and New Hampshire governor is a largely unknown figure in the United States today; a major aim of the book is to show how important his work was to the success of the Anglo-American partnership. The couple of weeks I spent at the Franklin D. Roosevelt Library archives, doing research in Winant's papers, were immensely fruitful, in no small part because of the encyclopedic knowledge and unstinting help of Bob Clark, the library's chief archivist, and his staff.

I also appreciated the kindness and generosity of William Gardner, New Hampshire's secretary of state, who took considerable time out of his packed schedule to track down sources who knew Winant or possessed information about him. Bill Gardner, who knows more about New Hampshire history than anyone I've ever met, spent a day in the fall of 2008 introducing me to a wide variety of sources and showing me around the state capital of Concord, while offering me his own valuable insights into Winant and his complex personality. Through Bill, I met Dean Dexter, a former New Hampshire state legislator and fellow Winant devotee, who provided me with a recording of a revealing interview he did with Abbie Rollins Caverly, a onetime Winant assistant. To Bill, Dean, Bert Whittemore, and others in New Hampshire who helped me get to know Winant better, I offer my thanks. I am similarly grateful to Rivington Winant for sharing with me his memories of his father and for the gracious hospitality he and his wife, Joan, showed me in Manhattan and Oyster Bay, New York.

Thanks also to Edwina Sandys, Ru Rauch, John Mather, Phyllis Bennett, Ray Belles, Larry DeWitt, Nancy Altman, Susanne Belovari, Paul Medlicott, Kirstin Downey, Rev. W. Jameson Parker, and Pat and Cassie Furgurson.

Working on this book has been a thoroughly enjoyable experience, thanks in large part to having Susanna Porter as my editor. Susanna's enthusiasm for the book, her support and encouragement throughout its writing, and her skilled and perceptive editing have made for a wonderfully satisfying collaboration. Gail Ross, my longtime agent and friend, is uncanny in her ability to pair her authors with the right editors; with this book, she has shown again why she's one of the best in the business.

My deepest thanks and appreciation go to my daughter, Carly, and my husband, Stan, who's the best editor and writer I know. I owe him more than I can say.

NOTES

INTRODUCTION

xiii "convinced us": Letter from unidentified sender, John Gilbert Winant scrap-book, in possession of Rivington Winant.

xiv "We were": Alex Danchev and Daniel Todman, eds., *War Diaries, 1939–1945: Field Marshal Lord Alanbrooke* (London: Weidenfeld & Nicolson, 2001), p. 248.

"There were many": John G. Winant, *A Letter from Grosvenor Square: An Account of a Stewardship* (Boston: Houghton Mifflin, 1947), p. 3.

"There was one man": *Times* (London), April 24, 1946.

"conveyed to the entire": Wallace Carroll letter to *Washington Post*, undated, Winant papers, FDRL.

xv "two prima donnas": Robert E. Sherwood, *Roosevelt and Hopkins: An Intimate History* (New York: Harper and Brothers, 1948), p. 236.

xvi "The British approached": Carlo D'Este, *Eisenhower: A Soldier's Life* (New York: Henry Holt, 2002), p. 337.

xvii "It was not Mr. Winant": "British Mourn Winant," *New York Times*, Nov. 5, 1947.

"Blacked out": Donald L. Miller, *Masters of the Air: America's Bomber Boys Who Fought the Air War Against Nazi Germany* (New York: Simon & Schuster, 2006), p. 137.

xviii "This is an American-made": Peter Clarke, *The Last Thousand Days of the British Empire: Churchill, Roosevelt, and the Birth of the Pax Americana* (New York: Bloomsbury, 2008), p. 103.

"they needed to know": Norman Longmate, *The G.I.'s: The Americans in Britain, 1942–1945* (New York: Scribner, 1975), p. 376.

"to concentrate on the things": *Star*, Feb. 3, 1941.

xix "must learn to live together": Bernard Bellush, *He Walked Alone: A Biography of John Gilbert Winant* (The Hague: Mouton, 1968), p. 216.

CHAPTER I: "THERE'S NO PLACE I'D RATHER BE THAN IN ENGLAND"

3 "I am glad": *Sunday Times*, March 2, 1941, Winant papers, FDRL.

4 "wars were bad": James Reston, *Deadline: A Memoir* (New York: Random House, 1991), p. 68.

"Isn't it wonderful": Michael R. Beschloss, *Kennedy and Roosevelt: The Uneasy Alliance* (New York: W. W. Norton, 1980), p. 177.

"England is gone": Bellush, p. 155.

4 "I'm for appeasement": Reston, p. 73.

"devote my efforts": Beschloss, p. 230.

"one of the toughest": "Winant Esteemed by British Chiefs," *New York Times*, Feb. 7, 1941.

5 "I'm very glad": *Times* (London), March 3, 1941, Winant papers, FDRL.

"significant incident": Ibid.

"not only extreme": John Keegan, "Churchill's Strategy," in Robert Blake and William Roger Louis, eds., *Churchill* (New York: W. W. Norton, 1993), p. 331.

"very distressing": John Colville, *The Fringes of Power: 10 Downing Street Diaries, 1939–1945* (New York: W. W. Norton, 1985), p. 358.

6 "even now England": Joseph P. Lash, *Roosevelt and Churchill, 1939–1941: The Partnership That Saved the West* (New York: W. W. Norton, 1976), p. 292.

"The expert politician": Ibid., p. 143.

"If Britain is to survive": Warren F. Kimball, *"The Most Unsordid Act": Lend Lease, 1939–1941* (Baltimore: Johns Hopkins University Press, 1969), p. 70.

7 "This rather": Colville, *Fringes of Power*, p. 223.

"I thought": Herbert Agar, *The Darkest Year: Britain Alone, June 1940–June 1941* (Garden City, N.Y.: Doubleday, 1973), p. 143.

"We have so far": Lash, *Roosevelt and Churchill*, p. 251.

"if we wished": Martin Gilbert, *Winston S. Churchill*, Vol. 6, *Finest Hour, 1939–1941* (Boston: Houghton Mifflin, 1983), p. 745.

8 "We seek": Christopher Hitchens, *Blood, Class and Nostalgia: Anglo-American Ironies* (New York: Farrar, Straus & Giroux, 1990), p. 202.

"When you sit": David Reynolds, *The Creation of the Anglo-American Alliance, 1937–1941* (Chapel Hill: University of North Carolina Press, 1982), p. 25.

"far more": Agar, p. 153.

9 "likable and attractive": Joseph P. Lash, *Eleanor and Franklin* (New York: W. W. Norton, 1971), p. 200.

"an untried": John Gunther, *Roosevelt in Retrospect* (New York: Harper & Brothers, 1950), p. 242.

"the life of the party": Lash, *Eleanor and Franklin*, p. 221.

"I have always": Beschloss, p. 200.

"there is a strong": Ibid.

10 "always sucking": Reston, p. 70.

"a drunken sot": Jon Meacham, *Franklin and Winston: An Intimate Portrait of an Epic Friendship* (New York: Random House, 2003), p. 51.

"supposed Churchill": David Dimbleby and David Reynolds, *An Ocean Apart: The Relationship Between Britain and America in the Twentieth Century* (New York: Random House, 1988), p. 136.

"We have not had": David Reynolds, *In Command of History: Churchill Fighting and Writing the Second World War* (London: Penguin/Allen Lane, 2004), p. 200.

"hunched in an attitude": Andrew Roberts, *"The Holy Fox": The Life of Lord Halifax* (London: Phoenix, 1997), p. 256.

"those bloody Yankees": Meacham, p. 54.

"I am not in a hurry": Gilbert, *Finest Hour*, p. 672.

11 "the most unsordid": Warren F. Kimball, *Forged in War: Roosevelt, Churchill and the Second World War* (New York: William Morrow, 1997), p. 74.

11 **"Remember, Mr. President"**: Ibid, p. 976.
12 **"The percentage"**: David Reynolds, *Rich Relations: The American Occupation of Britain, 1942–1945* (London: Phoenix, 2000), p. 41.
    "Utopian John": Bellush, p. 118.
    "extremely unhappy": Eileen Mason interview, Bellush papers, FDRL.
    "always told him": Ernest Hopkin interview, Bellush papers, FDRL.
    "came to mean": "He Multiplied the Jobs," *New York Herald Tribune*, Sept. 25, 1932, Winant papers, FDRL.
13 **"Our function"**: Alex Shoumatoff, "A Private School Affair," *Vanity Fair*, January 2006.
    "an incredibly": T. S. Matthews, *Name and Address: An Autobiography* (New York: Simon & Schuster, 1960), p. 156.
    "Like most": Ibid, p. 155.
    "all right": Janet Murrow to parents, April 24, 1943, Murrow papers, Mount Holyoke.
14 **"It was one"**: Dean Dexter interview with Abbie Rollins Caverly.
15 **"People in the audience"**: Author interview with Bert Whittemore.
    "It's too bad": Charles Murphy, "A Boy Who Meddled in Politics," *American*, April 1933, Winant papers, FDRL.
    "begin by feeling": "A New Kind of Envoy to a New Kind of Britain," *New York Times*, Feb. 16, 1941.
16 **"Railroads"**: *New York Times*, Sept. 16, 1934, Winant papers, FDRL.
    "put through": *New York Herald Tribune*, Nov. 5, 1947.
    "I don't understand Winant": "He Multiplied the Jobs," *New York Herald Tribune*, Sept. 25, 1932, Winant papers, FDRL.
    "every public policy": Larry DeWitt, "John G. Winant," Special Study #6, Social Security Historian's Office, Social Security Administration, May 1999.
17 **"carried the Christian injunction "**: Lawrence F. Whittemore speech to New Hampshire House and Senate, July 25, 1951.
    "Whenever people want": Robert Bingham interview, Bellush papers, FDRL.
    "revered and loved": Author interview with William Gardner.
    "loved to pick off": Gunther, p. 57.
18 **"transfusion of new"**: Undated newspaper clipping, Winant papers, FDRL.
    "Winant Moves": *Boston Evening Transcript*, Sept. 27, 1934, Winant papers, FDRL.
    "has caught": Charles Murphy, "A Boy Who Meddled in Politics," *American*, April 1933, Winant papers, FDRL.
    "You personally": Unsigned letter to Winant, July 12, 1934, Winant papers, FDRL.
    "would trade": Undated clipping, Winant papers, FDRL.
19 **"No, no"**: Frances Perkins interview, Bellush papers, FDRL.
    "Most Americans": "The Manager Abroad," *Time*, Dec. 1, 1947.
    "Since the war": Jean Edward Smith, *FDR* (New York: Random House, 2007), p. 22.
    "Americans dipped in": Kimball, *"The Most Unsordid Act,"* p. 1.
    "Of the hell broth": David Reynolds, *Rich Relations*, p. 8.
20 **"men rush"**: *New York Times*, Feb. 14, 1937.

20   **"He had no"**: Robert Bass interview, Bellush papers, FDRL.
21   **"He was, beyond"**: Larry DeWitt, "John G. Winant," Special Study #6, Social Security Historian's Office, Social Security Administration, May 1999.
22   **"shoddy politics"**: Bellush, p. 131.
      "at least one man": Allan B. MacMurphy to Winant, Oct. 16, 1936, Winant papers, FDRL.
      "More than any other": William L. Shirer, *Berlin Diary: The Journal of a Foreign Correspondent, 1939–1941* (New York: Alfred A. Knopf, 1941), p. 505.
      "They will take": *New York Times,* Feb. 7, 1941.
      "gave me the feeling": *Times* (London), April 24, 1946.
23   **"There is no"**: *News Chronicle,* Feb. 7, 1941, Winant papers, FDRL.
      "He is an American": *Manchester Guardian,* Feb. 7, 1941, Winant papers, FDRL.
24   **"There is something"**: "A Man of Strength and Straightness," *Times* (London), Feb. 8, 1941, Winant papers, FDRL.
      "One has often": "Mr. Winant Knows the Plain People," *Star,* Feb. 7, 1941, Winant papers, FDRL.
      "this stocky figure": Winant, *A Letter from Grosvenor Square,* p. 26.
25   **"Mr. Winant"**: *Washington Post,* March 18, 1941, Winant papers, FDRL.
      "lord of language": *Sunday Times* (London), March 23, 1941, Winant papers, FDRL.
      "Every word": Ibid.
      "rather like": "The Voice of New England," *Star,* March 19, 1941, Winant papers, FDRL.
      "not an orator": "Lincoln Comes to Town," *Daily Herald,* March 19, 1941, Winant papers, FDRL.
26   **"gone into action"**: John G. Winant, *Our Greatest Harvest: Selected Speeches of John G. Winant, 1941–1946* (London: Hodder & Stoughton, 1950), p. 7.
      "language of simple grandeur": "Mr. Winant's Success," *Evening Standard,* March 19, 1941, Winant papers, FDRL.
      "U.S. ENVOY": *Daily Mirror,* March 19, 1941, Winant papers, FDRL.
      "Nearly everyone": *Star,* March 19, 1941, Winant papers, FDRL.
      "an extraordinary triumph": *Sunday Times* (London), March 23, 1941, Winant papers, FDRL.

CHAPTER 2: "YOU ARE THE BEST REPORTER IN ALL OF EUROPE"

27   **"the most magnificent"**: Reginald Colby, *Mayfair: A Town Within London* (London: Country Life, 1966), p. 50.
      "An ambassador from": David McCullough, *John Adams* (New York: Simon & Schuster, 2001), p. 337.
      "They hate us": Ibid., p. 348.
      "studied civility": Henry Steele Commager, ed., *Britain Through American Eyes* (New York: McGraw-Hill, 1974), p. 23.
28   **"I shall never"**: Ibid., p. 26.
      "Some years hence": Geoffrey Williamson, *Star-Spangled Square: The Saga of "Little America" in London* (London: Geoffrey Bles, 1956), p. 47.
      "These people": Nathaniel Hawthorne, *The Complete Writings of Nathaniel Hawthorne,* Vol. 11 (Boston: Houghton Mifflin, 1900), p. xx.

28 "The only sure": Commager, p. 432.

29 "He cannot dance": McCullough, p. 349.

"coming so slowly": *Daily Herald*, March 4, 1941, Winant papers, FDRL.

"EXCELLENT IMPRESSION": *Washington Evening Star*, March 3, 1941, Winant papers, FDRL.

"In the first": *News Chronicle*, March 4, 1941, Winant papers, FDRL.

"His political views": William Stoneman, "Excellent Impression Made by Winant in London," *Washington Evening Star*, March 3, 1941, Winant papers, FDRL.

30 "has more influence": A. M. Sperber, *Murrow: His Life and Times* (New York: Freundlich, 1986), p. 131.

"You are the best": Nelson Poynter to Murrow, June 21, 1940, Murrow papers, Mount Holyoke.

31 "You are the No. 1": Sperber, p. 188.

"a catalytic agent": Robert E. Sherwood, *Roosevelt and Hopkins: An Intimate History* (New York: Harper & Brothers, 1948), p. 236.

"treated as tin gods": R. Franklin Smith, *Edward R. Murrow: The War Years* (Kalamazoo: New Issues Press, 1978), p. 95.

32 "Good to see you": Alexander Kendrick, *Prime Time: The Life of Edward R. Murrow* (Boston: Little, Brown, 1969), p. 231.

"I still have": Sperber, p. 122.

"Ed seemed": Joseph Persico, *Edward R. Murrow: An American Original* (New York: Dell, 1988), p. 138.

33 "the British somehow": R. Franklin Smith, p. 101.

"Ed had enormous": Sperber, p. 189.

"both rather inward-looking": Ibid.

"expected individuals": R. Franklin Smith, p. 145.

"I hope that life": Murrow to Charles Siepmann, May 6, 1940, Murrow papers, Mount Holyoke.

"If the light": Murrow to William Boutwell, July 22, 1941, Murrow papers, Mount Holyoke.

"He was concerned": Sperber, p. 172.

34 "a young American": Persico, *Edward R. Murrow*, p. 123.

"there was a satisfaction": Ben Robertson, *I Saw England* (New York: Alfred A. Knopf, 1941), p. 97.

"the most richly": Sperber, p. 53.

35 "If the rest": Ibid., p. 120.

36 "They have made": Persico, *Edward R. Murrow*, p. 150.

"Assuming that the BBC": Lynne Olson, *Troublesome Young Men: The Rebels Who Brought Churchill to Power and Helped Save England* (New York: Farrar, Straus & Giroux, 2007), p. 119.

"conspiracy of silence": Sperber, p. 131.

37 "these people": Persico, *Edward R. Murrow*, p. 150.

"They had a quick way": Ibid., p. 119.

"It's a beautiful house": Janet Murrow diary, July 13, 1941, Murrow papers, Mount Holyoke.

39 "an agreeable, comfortable": Asa Briggs, *The History of Broadcasting in the United Kingdom*, Vol. 3, *The War of Words* (Oxford: Oxford University Press, 1970), p. 22.

39   "sad and discreet": Ibid.
"I want our programs": R. Franklin Smith, p. 8.
"Ed's true": Ibid., p. 50.
"Well, brothers": Sperber, p. 138.

40   "one of the major neutrals": Tom Hickman, *What Did You Do in the War, Auntie?* (London: BBC Books, 1995), p. 30.
"The BBC": Ibid., p. 205.
"We were giving": Sperber, p. 181.
"Everyone regarded": R. Franklin Smith, p. 51.

41   "As far as I": Lynne Olson and Stanley Cloud, *A Question of Honor: The Kosciuszko Squadron: Forgotten Heroes of World War II* (New York: Alfred A. Knopf, 2003), p. 93.
"Everyone is going": Ibid., p. 94.
"We decided": Janet Murrow to parents, May 13, 1940, Murrow papers, Mount Holyoke.
"It just isn't": Janet Murrow to parents, June 11, 1940, Murrow papers, Mount Holyoke.

42   "a man of": "Quentin Reynolds Is Dead at 62," *New York Times,* March 18, 1965.
"Never before": Janet Murrow to parents, June 23, 1940, Murrow papers, Mount Holyoke.
"vultures and jackals": Harry Watt, *Don't Look at the Camera* (London: Paul Elek, 1974), p. 134.
"Here lie": Stanley Cloud and Lynne Olson, *The Murrow Boys: Pioneers on the Front Lines of Broadcast Journalism* (Boston: Houghton Mifflin, 1996), p. 88.

43   "London is burning": Sperber, p. 167.
"as continually alive": Charles Ritchie, *The Siren Years: A Canadian Diplomat Abroad, 1937–1945* (Toronto: Macmillan, 1974), p. 65.

44   "You can't do this": Eric Sevareid notes on Blitz, Sevareid papers, LC.
"Like everyone else": Robertson, p. 129.
"the same luxury": Ernie Pyle, *Ernie Pyle in England* (New York: McBride, 1941), pp. 22–23.

45   "messenger from hell": Sperber, p. 172.
"shaken to the core": R. Franklin Smith, p. 38.
"Words are such puny": Murrow broadcast, Sept. 14, 1940, National Archives.
"He made everything": R. Franklin Smith, p. 94.
"spoken word": Ibid., p. 84.

46   "looking like broken": Sperber, p. 173.
"cold, choking fog": Murrow broadcast, Dec. 2, 1940, National Archives.
"They're working": Persico, *Edward R. Murrow,* p. 174.
"the little people": Murrow broadcast, Aug. 18, 1940, National Archives.
"unsung heroes": Ibid.
"Do you think": Persico, *Edward R. Murrow,* p. 178.
"This is what": R. Franklin Smith, p. 100.

47   "Are you": Briggs, p. 295.
"I've seen some": Sperber, p. 169.
"Everyone was red-eyed": Robertson, p. 126.

47   "**You walk through**": Quentin Reynolds, *A London Diary* (New York: Random House, 1941), p. 65.
"**The city**": Robertson, p. 131.
"**It was like**": Ibid., pp. 182–83.

48   "**stiff dowagers**": Eric Sevareid, *Not So Wild a Dream* (New York: Atheneum, 1976), p. 176.
"**American stranger**": Ibid.
"**showed the world**": Ibid., p. 166.
"**They are extremely**": Philip Seib, *Broadcasts from the Blitz: How Edward R. Murrow Helped Lead America into War* (Washington: Potomac Books, 2006), p. 65.

49   "**bellowed out**": Watt, p. 141.
"**I am a neutral**": Nicholas Cull, *Selling War: The British Propaganda Campaign Against American "Neutrality" in World War II* (New York: Oxford University Press, 1995), p. 103.
"**a belief**": Watt, p. 142.
"**It must have been**": Ibid.

50   "**a good child**": Cloud and Olson, p. 58.
"**He made no pretense**": R. Franklin Smith, p. 117.
"**I have no desire**": Seib, p. 109.
"**except where**": Ibid., p. 127.
"**a thousand years**": Ibid., p. 108.

51   "**He wanted**": R. Franklin Smith, p. 109.
"**Perhaps you can**": Murrow broadcast, Sept. 30, 1940, NA.
"**Murrow and his colleagues**": R. Franklin Smith, p. 107.
"**Every shelter**": Janet Murrow to parents, Oct. 22, 1940, Murrow papers, Mount Holyoke.
"**disembodied**": Angus Calder, *The People's War: Britain, 1939–1945* (New York: Pantheon, 1969), p. 173.
"**He looked like**": Persico, *Edward R. Murrow,* p. 178.

52   "**Sometimes he seemed**": Ibid., p. 184.
"**He internalizes**": "This Is Murrow," *Time,* Sept. 30, 1957.
"**the windows**": R. Franklin Smith, p. 101.
"**You will have no**": Kendrick, p. 225.

CHAPTER 3: THE OPPORTUNITY OF A LIFETIME

54   "**malefactors of great wealth**": Christopher Ogden, *Life of the Party: The Biography of Pamela Digby Churchill Hayward Harriman* (Boston: Little, Brown, 1994), p. 112.
"**was no good**": Rudy Abramson, *Spanning the Century: The Life of W. Averell Harriman* (New York: William Morrow, 1992), p. 271.
"**He was good-looking**": Walter Isaacson and Evan Thomas, *The Wise Men: Six Friends and the World They Made* (New York: Touchstone, 1986), p. 121.

55   "**Confidentially, Franklin**": Ibid., p. 188.
"**Are we willing**": Harriman speech transcript, Feb. 14, 1941, Harriman papers, LC.

55 **"recommend everything"**: W. Averell Harriman and Elie Abel, *Special Envoy to Churchill and Stalin, 1941–1946* (New York: Random House, 1975), p. 19.
"**was a bit foggy**": Harriman memo, March 18, 1941, Harriman papers, LC.
"**as soon as**": Abramson, p. 277.

56 **"Mr. President"**: Roosevelt press conference transcript, Feb. 18, 1941, Harriman papers, LC.
"**a never-ending**": Abramson, p. 65.
"**had no fun**": Sally Bedell Smith, *Reflected Glory: The Life of Pamela Churchill Harriman* (New York: Simon & Schuster, 1996), p. 79.
"**needed reinforcement**": Abramson, p. 16.

57 **"He went into"**: Isaacson and Thomas, p. 42.
"**trying to match**": Abramson, p. 137.

58 **"Averell's a power"**: E. J. Kahn, "Profiles: Plenipotentiary—1," *New Yorker,* May 3, 1952.
"**Averell was regarded**": Abramson, p. 127.
"**Intellectually, I could reason**": Harriman and Abel, p. 6.

59 **"Anyone who says"**: Abramson, p. 273.
"**There is a sense**": Harriman to Harry Hopkins, June 6, 1940, Harriman papers, LC.

60 **"spent more"**: Henry H. Adams, *Harry Hopkins: A Biography* (New York: Putnam's, 1977), p. 22.
"**was bound**": Sherwood, p. 159.
"**Harry never had**": Ibid., p. 29.

61 **"a tongue"**: Ibid., p. 80.
"**he would snarl**": Adams, p. 52.

62 **"He was pleased"**: Sherwood, p. 6.
"**with all the vigor**": Adams, p. 152.
"**was always willing**": "Ave and the Magic Mountain," *Time,* Nov. 14, 1955.

63 **"I suppose Churchill"**: Sherwood, p. 232.
"**the personal representative**": Ibid., p. 247.

64 **"that extraordinary man"**: Winston S. Churchill, *The Grand Alliance* (Boston: Houghton Mifflin, 1950), pp. 20–21.
"**Churchill is the gov't**": Sherwood, p. 243
"**It seemed to me**": Meacham, p. 84.
"**I suppose you wish**": Adams, p. 207.

65 **"a completely changed man"**: Sherwood, p. 268.
"**This island needs**": Ibid., p. 260.
"**Let me carry**": Adams, p. 199.
"**might have something**": Abramson, p. 276.
"**Here in Washington**": James MacGregor Burns, *Roosevelt: The Soldier of Freedom* (New York: Harcourt Brace Jovanovich, 1970), p. 51.

66 **"so orderly"**: Reston, p. 98.
"**a pleasant place**": Ibid., p. 101.
"**leafy, dreaming**": Sevareid, p. 193.
"**a town**": David Brinkley, *Washington Goes to War* (New York: Alfred A. Knopf, 1988), p. xiv.
"**It is difficult**": Sherwood, p. 161.

67 **"The production program"**: Vincent Sheean to Murrow, Dec. 26, 1940, Murrow papers, Mount Holyoke.
"**repel raids**": D'Este, p. 259.
"**We are so short**": Harriman memo, March 11, 1941, Harriman papers, LC.
68 "**We can't take**": Ibid.
"**was very much disturbed**": James Leutze, ed., *The London Journal of General Raymond E. Lee, 1940–1941* (Boston: Little, Brown, 1971), p. 175.
"**Without an understanding**": Harriman memo, March 11, 1941, Harriman papers, LC.
"**as a sort**": Dimbleby and Reynolds, p. 145.
69 "**I left feeling**": Harriman memo, March 11, 1941, Harriman papers, LC.
"**He has talked to me**": Harriman to Marie Harriman, March 30, 1941, Harriman papers, LC.
"**Nothing will**": Harriman and Abel, p. 22.
"**became little short**": John Colville, *Footprints in Time: Memories* (London: Century, 1985), p. 154.
"**made four pertinent**": Ibid.
70 "**Quite early**": Winant, *A Letter from Grosvenor Square,* p. 68.
"**We had an**": Ibid., p. 67.
"**complete confidence**": Harriman to FDR, April 10, 1941, Harriman papers, LC.
"**one of the world's worst**": Theodore Achilles interview, Bellush papers, FDRL.
71 "**You might like**": Murrow to Chet Williams, May 15, 1941, Janet Murrow papers, Mount Holyoke.
"**Each of the ministers**": Harriman and Abel, p. 23.
"**I am accepted**": Harriman to Union Pacific president, May 30, 1941, Harriman papers, LC.
"**I am with**": Harriman to Marie Harriman, May 6, 1941, Harriman papers, LC.
"**I was very excited**": Harriman to Herbert Feis, undated, Harriman papers, LC.
72 "**a somewhat**": Robert Meiklejohn to Mr. Wooley, May 21, 1941, Harriman papers, LC.
"**that gilded refuge**": Sally Bedell Smith, *Reflected Glory,* p. 77.
"**a modern wartime Babylon**": Robert Rhodes James, ed., *Chips: The Diaries of Sir Henry Channon* (London: Phoenix, 1997), p. 272.
"**a fortress**": Leutze, ed., p. 61.
"**I've never seen**": Ibid.
"**I never felt easy**": Robertson, p. 137.
73 "**My mail**": Harriman to Marie Harriman, March 30, 1941, Harriman papers, LC.
"**wear the aspect**": Gilbert, *Finest Hour,* p. 972.
"**As far as I**": Ibid., p. 1040.
74 "**How the English**": Ritchie, p. 100.

CHAPTER 4: "HE SEEMS TO GET CONFIDENCE IN HAVING US AROUND"

75 "**that ghastly, tired**": Philip Ziegler, *London at War, 1939–1945* (New York: Alfred A. Knopf, 1995), p. 177.

76 **"I'm really scared"**: Sperber, p. 192.

"It's the office": Janet Murrow diary, April 16, 1941, Murrow papers, Mount Holyoke.

"many of our": Ibid.

77 **"Now that I"**: Theodore Achilles interview, Bellush papers, FDRL.

"based in human terms": Ibid.

78 **"I see no"**: Janet Murrow to mother, April 18, 1941, Murrow papers, Mount Holyoke.

"His personality": Virginia Cowles interview, Bellush papers, FDRL.

"typified to the British": Sir Arthur Salter interview, Bellush papers, FDRL.

79 **"He seems"**: Harriman to FDR, April 10, 1941, Harriman papers, LC.

"devastation such": Colville, *The Fringes of Power,* p. 373.

80 **"The news"**: Winant to FDR, April 10, 1941, Winant/State Department files, National Archives.

"He reviews": Harriman to FDR, April 11, 1941, Harriman papers, LC.

"I am sorry": Walter Thompson, *Assignment: Churchill* (New York: Farrar, Straus & Young, 1955), p. 216.

"They had been": Harriman to FDR, April 11, 1941, Harriman papers, LC.

"seemed to underline": Winant, *A Letter from Grosvenor Square,* p. 48.

81 **"They have such"**: Harriman to FDR, April 11, 1941, Harriman papers, LC.

"all this pain": Clementine Churchill to Harriman, April 15, 1941, Harriman papers, LC.

"The stench": Calder, p. 185.

82 **"It is the spirit"**: Harriman to president of Union Pacific, May 30, 1941, Harriman papers, LC.

"The women are": Harriman to Marie Harriman, April 17, 1941, Harriman papers, LC.

"What the women": Agar, p. 202.

83 **"magnificent body"**: Norman Longmate, *The Home Front: An Anthology of Personal Experience, 1938–1945* (London: Chatto & Windus, 1981), p. 75.

"living in a nightmare": Sherwood, p. 276.

84 **"There is no question"**: Leutze, ed., p. 243.

"You won't find": Vincent Sheean, *Between the Thunder and the Sun* (New York: Random House, 1943), p. 296.

"is worried": Harold Nicolson, *The War Years, 1939–1945* (New York: Atheneum, 1967), p. 164.

85 **"The fatigue"**: Winant, *A Letter from Grosvenor Square,* p. 39.

"All that the country": Nicolson, p. 162.

"Serious injury": Sherwood, p. 275.

"a disaster": Winston S. Churchill, *The Grand Alliance,* p. 190.

"Evacuation going": Lash, *Roosevelt and Churchill,* p. 301.

86 **"discouragement and disheartenment"**: Ibid., p. 312.

"I feel": Gilbert, *Finest Hour,* p. 1083.

"Mr. President": Ibid., p. 1078.

87 **"The whole thing"**: Leutze, ed., p. 244.

"The situation is": Lash, *Roosevelt and Churchill,* p. 298.

"We cannot allow": Ibid., p. 304.

88   "**The President is waiting**": William Bullitt to Harriman, April 29, 1941, Harriman papers, LC.
      "**I told Hopkins**": Lash, *Roosevelt and Churchill*, p. 321.
      "**I think**": Adams, p. 223.
      "**I do know**": Ibid., p. 224.

89   "**I cautioned him**": Doris Kearns Goodwin, *No Ordinary Time: Franklin and Eleanor Roosevelt: The Home Front in World War II* (New York: Simon & Schuster, 1994), p. 24.
      "**How much**": Jean Edward Smith, p. 492.
      "**The truth was**": Frances Perkins Oral History, Columbia University.
      "**The people as a whole**": Sperber, p. 131
      "**Why don't you**": Belle Roosevelt, speech at Hobart and Smith College, June 1945, Winant papers, FDRL.

90   "**World opinion**": Lash, *Roosevelt and Churchill*, p. 329.
      "**how he had to fight**": Ibid., p. 342.
      "**shocking to see**": Leutze, ed., p. 287.

91   "**There is still too much**": Ibid., p. 275.
      "**It is impossible**": Harriman to William Bullitt, May 21, 1941, Harriman papers, LC.
      "**using warships**": Harriman to Marie Harriman, May 6, 1941, Harriman papers, LC.
      "**England's strength**": Harriman to FDR, April 10, 1941, Harriman papers, LC.
      "**greatly encouraged**": Gilbert, *Finest Hour,* p. 1036.

92   "**two men**": Colville, *Footprints in Time,* p. 152.
      "**What America requires**": Ibid.

94   "**As an American**": Winant, *A Letter from Grosvenor Square,* p. 40.
      "**We have all slept**": "Winant Indicates He Backs Convoys," *New York Times,* May 15, 1941, Winant papers, FDRL.
      "**We have made**": Ibid.

CHAPTER 5: MEMBERS OF THE FAMILY

95   "**simply been**": Mary Soames, *Clementine Churchill: The Biography of a Marriage* (Boston: Houghton Mifflin, 2002), p. 343.

96   "**had less schedule**": Thompson, p. 127.
      "**loved an audience**": Roy Jenkins, *Churchill: A Biography* (New York: Farrar, Straus & Giroux, 2001), p. 639.
      "**as much for**": Colville, *Footprints in Time,* p. 153.

97   "**I want to thank you**": Mary Churchill to Harriman, May 13, 1941, Harriman papers, LC.

98   "**what a wonderful**": Harriman memo, May 5–9, 1943, Harriman papers, LC.
      "**the most important**": Sally Bedell Smith, *Reflected Glory,* p. 86.
      "**was a hick from America**": Pamela Harriman interview with Christopher Ogden, Pamela Harriman papers, LC.
      "**absolutely marvelous looking**": Abramson, p. 312.

99   "**I would get trapped**": Pamela Harriman interview with Christopher Ogden, Pamela Harriman papers, LC.

99   "as cold and calculated": Sally Bedell Smith, *Reflected Glory,* p. 76.
"could be quite": Mary Soames, "Father Always Came First, Second and Third," *Finest Hour,* Autumn 2002.
"One of the most": Colville, *The Fringes of Power,* p. 177.
"There was a diffused": Ziegler, p. 169.

100   "The normal barriers": Sally Bedell Smith, *In All His Glory: The Life of William S. Paley* (New York: Simon & Schuster, 1990), p. 217.
"It was a liberation": Olson and Cloud, p. 178.
"London was a Garden": Mary Welsh Hemingway, *How It Was* (New York: Ballantine, 1976), p. 105.
"Here I am": Pamela Harriman interview with Christopher Ogden, Pamela Harriman papers, LC

101   "Last night": Harriman to Marie Harriman, April 17, 1941, Harriman papers, LC.
"intercepted glances": Sally Bedell Smith, *Reflected Glory,* p. 87.
"microbe": Soames, p. 351.
"Some thought him evil": Drew Middleton, *Where Has Last July Gone?* (New York: Quadrangle, 1973), p. 68.

102   "took particular pleasure": Ogden, p. 154.
"She passed everything": Ibid., p. 123.
"It was very": Pamela Harriman interview with Christopher Ogden, Pamela Harriman papers, LC.

103   "got a big": Ibid., p. 127.
"fearing stories": Arthur M. Schlesinger Jr., *Journals, 1952–2000* (New York: Penguin, 2007), p. 343.
"could have gone": Pamela Harriman interview with Christopher Ogden, Pamela Harriman papers, LC.
"We do not": Sarah Churchill, *A Thread in the Tapestry* (London: Deutsch, 1967), p. 29.
"You know": Pamela Harriman interview with Christopher Ogden, Pamela Harriman papers, LC.

104   "feel as if": Felix Frankfurter interview, Bellush papers, FDRL.
"A man of quiet": Mary Soames, *Clementine Churchill: The Biography of a Marriage* (Boston: Houghton Mifflin, 2002), p. 390.
"gentle, dreamy": Colville, *The Fringes of Power,* p. 773.
"When Winant enters": "A New Kind of Envoy to a New Kind of Britain," *New York Times,* Feb. 16, 1941.
"There was something": Ethel M. Johnson, "The Mr. Winant I Knew," *South Atlantic Quarterly,* January 1949, Eleanor Roosevelt Correspondence, FDRL.
"quite lost": James, ed., p. 297.
"one of the most charming": Nicolson, p. 186.
"the superb": Ibid, p. 198.
"Other men": Lord Moran, *Churchill at War, 1940–45* (New York: Carroll & Graf, 2002), p. 151.
"There was Winant": Ibid., p. 152.

105   "one of those great": Danchev and Todman, eds., p. 474.
"Winant gives me": Theodore Achilles interview, Winant papers, FDRL.
"The P.M.": Moran, p. 152.

105 "liked bounders": Jenkins, p. 188.

"one more rich": Ogden, p. 119.

"understood intuitively": Soames, p. 390.

"most charming and entertaining": Meacham, p. 94.

"charming, vivacious": Janet Murrow to parents, Dec. 7, 1940, Murrow papers, Mount Holyoke.

"very attractive": Eleanor Roosevelt, *This I Remember* (New York: Harper, 1949), p. 267.

106 "One feels": Ibid.

"when she married": Sally Bedell Smith, *Reflected Glory,* p. 67.

"total egotist": John Pearson, *The Private Lives of Winston Churchill* (New York: Touchstone, 1991), p. 216.

"In his heart": Pamela Harriman interview with Christopher Ogden, Pamela Harriman papers, LC.

"I am easily satisfied": Soames, p. 103.

"for not turning": Mary Soames, "Father Always Came First, Second and Third," *Finest Hour,* Autumn 2002.

107 "never did anything": Soames, p. 266.

"A weekend here": Kathleen Harriman to Mary Fisk, undated, Harriman papers, LC.

"taking a back seat": Kathleen Harriman to Mary Fisk, June 1941, Harriman papers, LC.

108 "This sounds": Clementine Churchill to Winant, April 2, 1941, Winant papers, FDRL.

"Do not let": Soames, p. 96.

109 "She dropped on him": Ibid., p. 261.

"one of the loneliest": Dean Dexter interview with Abbie Rollins Caverly.

110 "As children": Soames, p. 268.

"A wife first": Pearson, p. 126.

"it took me": Soames, p. 266.

111 "a mixture of tenderness": Ibid., p. 267.

"an authoritarian figure": Sarah Churchill, *Keep on Dancing* (New York: Coward, McCann & Geoghegan, 1981), p. 67.

"Although her children": Soames, p. 267.

"All those": Pearson, p. 221.

"escape from": Ibid., p. 233.

"If I really": Sarah Churchill, *A Thread in the Tapestry,* pp. 31–32.

112 "I walked out": Ibid., p. 51.

"gave a good performance": Colville, *The Fringes of Power,* pp. 200–201.

"common as dirt": Pearson, p. 265.

"addressed me": Sarah Churchill, *Keep on Dancing,* p. 67.

113 "a magical creature": Edwina Sandys, "A Tribute to Sarah Churchill," *Daily Mail,* Sept. 25, 1982.

"More than anybody": Lynda Lee Potter, *Daily Mail,* Sept. 25, 1982.

"Sarah is a terribly": Kathleen Harriman to Mary Fisk, July 7, 1941, Harriman papers, LC.

"the iron curtain": Danchev and Todman, eds., p. 474.

CHAPTER 6: "MR. HARRIMAN ENJOYS MY COMPLETE CONFIDENCE"

114 **"This is worse"**: "Winant Returns; Silent on Mission," *New York Times,* May 31, 1941.

"There is no doubt,": Anne O'Hare McCormick, "The Usual Intermission for Peace Feelers," *New York Times,* June 7, 1941, Winant papers, FDRL.

"a high Washington authority": *Daily Mail,* June 2, 1941, Winant papers, FDRL.

115 **"almost a Chinese wall"**: Harriman memo to FDR, April 10, 1941, Harriman papers, LC.

"We are advertising": Burns, p. 119.

"We are deceiving": William Whitney to Harriman, Aug. 25, 1941, Harriman papers, LC.

116 **"The delivery of needed"**: Adams, p. 226.

"almost like a call": Lash, *Roosevelt and Churchill,* p. 326.

"taken as a solemn": Sherwood, p. 298.

"paralyzed between": Dean Acheson, *Present at the Creation: My Years in the State Department* (New York: W. W. Norton, 1969), p. 3.

"straining every nerve": Leutze, ed., p. 388.

"Winant asked me": Nina Davis Howland, "Ambassador John Gilbert Winant: Friend of Embattled Britain, 1941–1946," Ph.D. dissertation, University of Maryland, 1983, p. 108.

"We must not": *Daily Telegraph,* June 19, 1941, Winant papers, FDRL.

"If Munich": Longmate, *The G.I.'s,* p. 12.

117 **"an excellent mandate"**: Harriman and Abel, p. 19.

"Laddie was not": Nelson W. Aldrich Jr., *Tommy Hitchcock: An American Hero* (New York: Fleet Street, 1984), p. 208.

"we are working": Harriman to FDR, May 7, 1941, Harriman papers, LC.

"interfere in anything": Leutze, ed., p. 359.

118 **"Mr. Harriman enjoys"**: Harriman and Abel, p. 63.

"I don't think": Kathleen Harriman to Mary Fisk, June 1941, Harriman papers, LC.

"I have made": Ogden, p. 130.

119 **"I found him absolutely"**: Pearson, p. 303.

"He has definitely": Ogden, p. 131.

"a sense of complacency": Harriman to Churchill, July 1, 1941, Harriman papers, LC.

" 'Mr. Harriman is a go-getter' ": Howard Bird to Harriman, July 1, 1941, Harriman papers, LC.

"the moral foes": Olson and Cloud, p. 218.

120 **"probably never"**: Thompson, p. 224.

"He had firmly": Lash, *Roosevelt and Churchill,* p. 391.

121 **"to keep those two"**: Sherwood, p. 236.

"At last": Goodwin, p. 265.

"Does he like me": Lash, *Roosevelt and Churchill,* p. 391.

"Papa completely forgot": Meacham, p. 109.

121 **"dominating every"**: Elliott Roosevelt, *As He Saw It* (New York: Duell, Sloan & Pearce, 1946), p. 28.

"easy intimacy": Sherwood, p. 363.

122 **"take care of him"**: Thompson, p. 238.

"had broken the ice": Eleanor Roosevelt, p. 226.

"I formed": Meacham, p. 108.

"I would rather": Jean Edward Smith, p. 502.

"You've got to": Elliott Roosevelt, p. 29.

"he would look": Lash, *Roosevelt and Churchill*, p. 402.

"The President": Gilbert, *Finest Hour*, p. 1177.

123 **"The flood is raging"**: Leutze, ed., p. 383.

"I don't know": Sherwood, p. 373.

125 **"give and give"**: Isaacson and Thomas, p. 212.

"suspicion that has existed": Harriman and Abel, p. 92.

"No one will deny": Lord Ismay, *The Memoirs of Lord Ismay* (New York: Viking, 1960), p. 231.

CHAPTER 7: "I WANT TO BE IN IT WITH YOU—FROM THE START"

126 **"died that England"**: "All Britain Honors Independence Day," *New York Times,* July 5, 1941, Winant papers, FDRL.

"very much the golden boy": Alex Kershaw, *The Few: The American "Knights of the Air" Who Risked Everything to Fight in the Battle of Britain* (New York: Da Capo, 2006), p. 60.

"I want to be": Ibid., p. 58.

127 **"They were"**: Capt. John R. McCrary and Capt. David Scherman, *First of the Many: A Journal of Action with the Men of the Eighth Air Force* (London: Robson, 1944), p. 210.

"It was unbelievable": Kershaw, p. 66.

"He had no": *New York Times,* July 5, 1941, Winant papers, FDRL.

128 **"Our homes"**: Mrs. Anthony Billingham, *America's First Two Years: The Story of American Volunteers in Britain, 1939–1941* (London: John Murray, 1942), pp. 59–60.

"might lead": Kershaw, p. 55.

129 **"The Germans"**: "Americans 'Capture' Headquarters of a British Brigade in War Games," *New York Times,* July 22, 1940.

"jeopardizing U.S. neutrality": Watt, p. 157.

130 **"to play opposite"**: James Saxon Childers, *War Eagles: The Story of the Eagle Squadron* (New York: D. Appleton–Century, 1943), p. 17.

"I felt": Kershaw, p. 62.

"an overwhelming fury": James A. Goodson, *Tumult in the Clouds* (New York: St. Martin's, 1993), p. 25.

"typical Americans": Kershaw, p. 83.

131 **"the war could not"**: Philip D. Caine, *Eagles of the RAF* (Washington: National Defense University Press, 1991), p. 30.

"These people": Kershaw, pp. 160–61.

"They were always": Caine, p. 105.

131   "It just seemed": Ibid., p. 217.

132   "Once again": Kershaw, p. 214.
"a mad bunch": Ibid., p. 205.
"Their exploits": Caine, p. 148.
"Look, these people": Kershaw, p. 216.
"They were": Caine, p 218.
"To fight": Kershaw, p. 62.

133   "What's he doing?": Caine, p. 105.
"They were saboteurs": Kershaw, p. 204.

134   "politely told him": Watt, p. 155.
"four weeks": Ibid.
"Far from": Bosley Crowther, "Eagle Squadron," *New York Times*, July 3, 1942.

135   "You know": Childers, p. 15.

136   "a rather scruffy-looking": "Winant Lauds R.A.F. at Eagle Luncheon," *New York Times*, Nov. 20, 1941.
"truck drivers": Robertson, p. 71.
"laughed and joked": Ibid., p. 72.

137   "contact with life": Winant to Dr. Brister, July 1, 1943, Winant papers, FDRL.
"as gallant": Winant to unidentified recipient, Nov. 1, 1946, Winant papers, FDRL.

CHAPTER 8: "PEARL HARBOR ATTACKED?"

138   "Leaving this country": Murrow to Winant, Nov. 10, 1941, Winant papers, FDRL.
"I am convinced": Murrow to Chet Williams, May 15, 1941, Murrow papers, Mount Holyoke.
"baby the Japs along": Adams, p. 255.

139   "had done practically nothing": Danchev and Todman, eds., p. 205.

140   "In this looming crisis": Burns, p. 148.
"Nothing is more": Lash, *Roosevelt and Churchill*, p. 427.
"If some time": Murrow to Winant, Nov. 10, 1941, Winant papers, FDRL.
"Everywhere I go": Sperber, p. 188.

141   "Edward R. Murrow": Paley, p. 143.
"a period": Gunther, p. 300.
"He walked": Persico, *Edward R. Murrow,* p. 196.
"spending most": Murrow to Harold Laski, Dec. 6, 1941, Murrow papers, Mount Holyoke.

142   "It is difficult": R. Franklin Smith, p. 81.
"Almost every eminent": Paley, p. 143.
"stunned by the whole": Sperber, p. 204.
"along the banks": Kendrick, p. 238.
"You burned": Cloud and Olson, p. 143.
"You . . . who gather": FDR telegram to William Paley, Dec. 2, 1941, President's Personal File, FDRL.

143   "This means war": Adams, p. 257.
"Do you think": Winant, *A Letter from Grosvenor Square,* p. 197.

144   "The Japanese have": Harriman and Abel, p. 113.

144   "We shall declare": Winant, *A Letter from Grosvenor Square*, p. 199.
      "Mr. President": Winston S. Churchill, *The Grand Alliance*, p. 538.
      "exaltation": David Reynolds, *In Command of History*, p. 264.
      "sort of danced": Howland, p. 149.
      "They did not wail": Winston S. Churchill, *The Grand Alliance*, p. 538.
145   "We still": Seib, p. 156.
      "He was living": Frances Perkins Oral History, Columbia University.
      "You're not fit": Gunther, p. 324.
146   "Destroyed on the ground": Burns, p. 165.
      "the idea seemed": Sperber, p. 207.
      "What did you": Cloud and Olson, p. 145.

CHAPTER 9:   CREATING THE ALLIANCE

147   "He was like a child": Moran, p. 10.
      "The Winston I knew": Ibid., p. 8.
148   "one of the most beautiful": Sir John Martin, *Downing Street: The War Years*
      (London: Bloomsbury, 1991), p. 69.
      "with its myriad": Gerald Pawle, *The War and Colonel Warden* (New York: Alfred A. Knopf, 1963), p. 138.
      "We're here": Goodwin, p. 305.
      "Olympian calm": Martin Gilbert, *Winston S. Churchill*, Vol. 7, *Road to Victory 1941–1945* (Boston: Houghton Mifflin, 1986), p. 43.
      "a pair": Meacham, p. 5.
      "Being with them": Ibid.
      "was always full": Ibid., p. 157.
      "You could almost": Moran, p. 21.
149   "Sir Walter Raleigh": Winston S. Churchill, *The Grand Alliance*, p. 558.
      "cast off": Sherwood, p. 437.
      "the most complete": Dimbleby and Reynolds, p. 152.
150   "The United States": David Reynolds, *The Creation of the Anglo-American Alliance*, p. 11.
      "I have never": Mark Perry, *Partners in Command: George Marshall and Dwight Eisenhower in War and Peace* (New York: Penguin, 2007), p. 54.
      "were filled": Brinkley, p. 91.
151   "I have never": Alex Danchev, "Very Special Relationship: Field Marshal Sir John Dill and General George Marshall," Marshall Foundation essay, 1984.
      "I could see": Danchev and Todman, eds., p. 216.
      "As is usual": Sir Frederick Morgan, *Overture to Overlord* (Garden City, N.Y.: Doubleday, 1950), p. 25.
152   "One might think": Danchev and Todman, eds., p. 275.
      "We had sustained": Sir Frederick Morgan, p. 26.
      "For Marshall": Stanley Weintraub, *15 Stars: Eisenhower, MacArthur, Marshall: Three Generals Who Saved the American Century* (New York: Free Press, 2007), p. 33.
      "too much": Perry, p. 50.
153   "Not even the president": D'Este, p. 259.
      "a big man": Danchev and Todman, eds., p. 247.

153   **"By almost"**: Arthur Bryant, *The Turn of the Tide* (Garden City, N.Y.: Double-
         day, 1957), p. 6.

154   **"I found"**: Danchev and Todman, eds., p. 249.
         "Rather over-filled": Ibid., p. 246.
         "In many respects": Ibid., p. 249.
         "although he may be": Sherwood, p. 523.

155   **"In my whole experience"**: Calder, p. 265.
         "We seem to lose": Gilbert, *Road to Victory,* p. 68.
         "the greatest disaster": Sherwood, p. 501.
         "Defeat is one thing": Winston S. Churchill, *The Hinge of Fate* (Boston:
         Houghton Mifflin, 1950), p. 383.

156   **"You . . . hear"**: Mollie Panter-Downes, *London War Notes, 1939–1945* (New
         York: Farrar, Straus & Giroux, 1971), p. 205.
         "During my period": Thompson, p. 263.
         "at a very low ebb": Soames, p. 415.
         "the massacre": Sherwood, p. 498.
         "The losses": Bryant, *The Turn of the Tide,* p. 296.
         "Terrible": Moran, p. 38.

157   **"We simply"**: Nicolson, p. 196.
         "malicious delight": Juliet Gardiner, *"Overpaid, Oversexed, and Over Here": The
         American GI in World War II Britain* (New York: Canopy, 1992), p. 32.
         "Americans ought really": Ibid., p. 33.
         "has caused": Ritchie, pp. 127–28.
         "Broadly speaking": David Reynolds, *Rich Relations,* p. 38.

158   **"The seeds"**: Rick Atkinson, *An Army at Dawn: The War in North Africa,
         1942–1943* (New York: Henry Holt, 2002), p. 478.
         "Probably not one": Longmate, *The G.I.'s,* p. 2.
         "I met so many": David Reynolds, *Rich Relations,* p. 36.
         "mixture of slaves": Longmate, *The G.I.'s,* p. 27.
         "Are you": Robert S. Arbib, *Here We Are Together: The Notebook of an American
         Soldier in Britain* (London: Right Book Club, 1947), p. 79
         "I hope": *Times* (London), July 22, 1941, Winant papers, FDRL.

159   **"wanted the people"**: Wallace Carroll, *Persuade or Perish* (Boston: Houghton
         Mifflin, 1948), p. 134.
         "We set out": Ibid., p. 135.
         "British newspapers": *New York Times,* April 21, 1943.

160   **"I would like"**: Janet Murrow to parents, Feb. 28, 1943, Murrow papers, Mount
         Holyoke.
         "a surprising new": Joseph P. Lash, *From the Diaries of Felix Frankfurter* (New
         York: W. W. Norton, 1975), p. 159.
         "an oppressor people": Ibid., p. 147.
         "their factual knowledge": David Reynolds, *Rich Relations,* p. 34.
         "intense": Nicolson, p. 226.

161   **"It would be"**: Murrow to Harry Hopkins, undated, Hopkins papers, FDRL.
         "We might understand": R. Franklin Smith, p. 60.
         "a cram course": Sperber, p. 190.
         "Later on": Ibid.

162   "vigorous criticisms": Ibid.
        "Frankness and honesty": R. Franklin Smith, p. 60.

CHAPTER 10: "AN ENGLISHMAN SPOKE IN GROSVENOR SQUARE"

163   "An Englishman": David Reynolds, *Rich Relations*, p. 114.
        "an air of near-frantic": Kay Summersby Morgan, *Past Forgetting: My Love Affair with Dwight D. Eisenhower* (New York: Simon & Schuster, 1975), p. 45.
164   "the sight": *New York Times Magazine*, Nov. 1, 1942.
        "a miniature Fifth Avenue": Mrs. Robert Henrey, *The Incredible City* (London: J. M. Dent & Sons, 1944), p. 39.
        "a millionaires' club": *Daily Telegraph*, July 6, 1942, Winant papers, FDRL.
        "There was not a tailor": Henrey, *The Incredible City*, p. 40.
165   "Gentlemen": David Reynolds, *Rich Relations*, p. 95.
        "There is no question": D'Este, p. 37.
        "He feared nothing": Ibid., p. 91.
        "Makes me feel": Kay Summersby Morgan, p. 44.
        "Despite the fact": Ibid., p. 36.
166   "I don't think": Ibid.
        "After all": Harry Butcher, *My Three Years with Eisenhower* (New York: Simon & Schuster, 1946), p. 6.
        "From the outset": Ismay, p. 258.
        "was having": Butcher, p. 6.
167   "see eye to eye": Ibid., p. 36.
        "another of": Dwight D. Eisenhower interview, Bellush papers, FDRL.
        "was a big job": *New York Herald Tribune*, July 14, 1942, Winant papers, FDRL.
168   "exerted an uncanny": Wallace Carroll, letter to *Washington Post*, undated, Winant papers, FDRL.
        "Every informant": *New York Herald Tribune*, July 14, 1942, Winant papers, FDRL.
        "Many of us": Acheson, p. 38.
        "to see whether": *New York Herald Tribune*, July 14, 1942, Winant papers, FDRL.
169   "Averell substantively": Abramson, p. 303.
        "a moth": William Standley, *Admiral Ambassador to Russia* (Chicago: Regnery, 1955), p. 213.
        "Every now and then": Abramson, p. 340.
170   "I think": Harriman interview with Elie Abel, Harriman papers, LC.
        "He's not a good": Kathleen Harriman to Mary Fisk, Nov. 21, 1941, Harriman papers, LC.
        "Winant was very": Harriman interview with Elie Abel, Harriman papers, LC.
171   "Roosevelt always saw": Gunther, p. 51.
        "saw each other": Howland, p. 272.
        "a political disgrace": Reston, p. 112.
        "there were very": Eileen Mason interview, Bellush papers, FDRL.

171 **"You are doing"**: FDR to Winant, Oct. 31, 1942, President's Secretary's File, FDRL.

172 **"I have given"**: Leutze, ed., p. 353.
"be careful": Abramson, p. 304.
"I had known": Eleanor Roosevelt, p. 263.
"a feeling of inadequacy": Ibid.

173 **"a country"**: Ibid., p. 190.
"gave little thought": Ibid., p. 266.
"He took it": Jacob Beam interview, Bellush papers, FDRL.
"He carried": Theodore Achilles interview, Bellush papers, FDRL.
"If you break down": David Gray to Winant, Nov. 24, 1942, Winant/State Department papers, National Archives.
"caring much": Anthony Eden, *The Reckoning* (Boston: Houghton Mifflin, 1965), p. 295.

174 **"one of the best"**: Winant, *A Letter from Grosvenor Square,* p. 64.
"I lack the spunk": Olson, *Troublesome Young Men,* p. 99.
"I have never": Winant, *A Letter from Grosvenor Square,* p. 67.

175 **"At this very moment"**: Sarah Churchill, *Keep on Dancing,* p. 111.
"love affair": Ibid., p. 159.

CHAPTER 11: "HE'LL NEVER LET US DOWN"

176 **"He had an unusual"**: T. T. Scott interview, Bellush papers, FDRL.

177 **"He understood them"**: Arthur Jenkins, "John Winant: An Englishman's Estimate," *Christian Science Monitor,* Sept. 9, 1944, Winant papers, FDRL.
"If you went": Carroll, p. 134.
"was every bit": Juliet Gardiner, *Wartime Britain, 1939–1945* (London: Headline, 2004), p. 430.
"more of work": Calder, p. 443.

178 **"Everything save"**: Jose Harris, "Great Britain: The People's War?," in David Reynolds, Warren F. Kimball, and A. O. Chubarian, eds., *Allies at War: The Soviet, American and British Experience, 1939–1945* (New York: St. Martin's, 1994), p. 238.
"drawn so tight": Calder, pp. 323–24.
"hated, with the free": Sevareid, p. 480.
"what they were going": Ziegler, p. 262.

179 **"These British Isles"**: Eleanor Roosevelt, p. 274.
"What are the": Kendrick, p. 222.
"There must be": Sperber, p. 184.
"We would talk": Sevareid, pp. 173–74.

180 **"With Winston"**: Moran, p. 139.
"old, benevolent Tory squire": Paul Addison, "Churchill and Social Reform," in Robert Blake and William Roger Louis, eds., *Churchill* (New York: W. W. Norton, 1993), p. 77.
"He's never been": Moran, p. 301.
"In Mr. Churchill": Olson, *Troublesome Young Men,* p. 264.

181 **"This is *your*"**: Olson and Cloud, p. 392.

181   "to buy this heavy": Panter-Downes, p. 253.
"an awful windbag": Paul Addison, "Churchill and Social Reform," in Blake and Louis, eds., p. 72.

182   "When the war": *New York Times,* Feb. 7, 1941.
"without the maladjustment": Shirer, p. 505.
"There is a deep": Winant, *Our Greatest Harvest,* p. 22.
"to concentrate": *The Star,* Feb. 3, 1941.
"requires not only skill": Bellush, p. 183.

183   "You who suffered": Winant, *Our Greatest Harvest,* p. 56.
"We think, sir": *Daily Express,* June 8, 1942.

184   "WINANT TALKS": Ibid.
"a new, greater": *Daily Herald,* June 8, 1942, Winant papers, FDRL.
"one of the great": *Manchester Guardian,* June 8, 1942, Winant papers, FDRL.

CHAPTER 12:   "ARE WE FIGHTING NAZIS OR SLEEPING WITH THEM?"

185   "blackest day": Sherwood, p. 648.

186   "Only by an intellectual": Mark Stoler, "The United States: the Global Strategy," in David Reynolds et al., eds., *Allies at War,* p. 67.
"I swear to fight": Antony Beevor and Artemis Cooper, *Paris After the Liberation, 1944–1949* (New York: Doubleday, 1994), p. 13.

187   "regardless of how": Sherwood, p. 629.
"I consider": Atkinson, p. 27.
"where no major": Dwight D. Eisenhower, *Crusade in Europe* (Garden City, N.Y.: Doubleday, 1948), p. 72.
"highly trained personnel": Ismay, p. 120.
"We were still": Dwight D. Eisenhower, p. 77.

188   "this bizarre": Burns, p. 285.
"I was regaled": Dwight D. Eisenhower, p. 89.
"wonderful charm": Bryant, *The Turn of the Tide,* p. 431.

189   "had only the vaguest": Ibid.
"completely sincere": Atkinson, p. 59.
"a comparable understanding": Perry, p. 191.
"This was the": Carroll, p. 12.
"belonged to a single": Dwight D. Eisenhower, p. 76.

190   "did not understand": Sir Frederick Morgan, p. 17.
"the attitude": Dwight D. Eisenhower, p. 76.
"apparently regarding it": Ibid., p. 90.
"The British are really": Butcher, p. 239.
"It is very noticeable": David Irving, *The War Between the Generals: Inside the Allied High Command* (New York: Congdon & Lattes, 1981), p. 55.
"invade a neutral country": Dwight D. Eisenhower, p. 88.
"a three-star bundle": Kay Summersby Morgan, p. 47.
"He had aged": Perry, p. 125.

191   "men wandered": Atkinson, p. 144.
"We can only": Joseph Persico, *Roosevelt's Secret War: FDR and World War II Espionage* (New York: Random House, 2001), p. 210.

191 **"with brass bands"**: Atkinson, p. 141.
"**officers as well**": Ibid., p. 144.
"**As far**": Ibid.

192 **"had no effect whatsoever"**: Dwight D. Eisenhower, p. 104.
"**not even remotely**": Sherwood, p. 652.

193 **"In both our nations"**: Merle Miller, *Ike the Soldier: As They Knew Him* (New York: Putnam's, 1987), p. 426.
"**America had spoken**": Carroll, pp. 50–51.
"**a callow**": Atkinson, p. 159.
"**we did not**": Ibid., p. 198.
"**We have perpetuated**": Cloud and Olson, p. 161.

194 **"We must not overlook"**: François Kersaudy, *Churchill and De Gaulle* (New York: Atheneum, 1982), p. 224.
"**are convinced**": Panter-Downes, p. 252.
"**honeymoon is over**": Carroll, p. 53.
"**Much as I hate**": Dwight D. Eisenhower, p. 105.
"**Since 1776**": Winston Churchill, *The Hinge of Fate*, p. 638.

195 **"something that afflicts"**: Burns, p. 297.
"**only a temporary**": Sherwood, p. 653.
"**What the hell**": Milton S. Eisenhower, *The President Is Calling* (Garden City, N.Y.: Doubleday, 1974), p. 137.
"**there is nothing**": Kendrick, p. 254.
"**This is a matter**": Ibid.

196 **"He never raised"**: Sperber, p. 223.
"**You are endangering**": Paul White to Murrow, Jan. 27, 1943, Murrow papers, Mount Holyoke.
"**definitely dangerous**": Telegram to Murrow, Nov. 16, 1942, Murrow papers, Mount Holyoke.
"**I believe**": Murrow to unidentified, Nov. 18, 1942, Murrow papers, Mount Holyoke.
"**Developments in North Africa**": Murrow to Ted Church, Jan. 22, 1943, Murrow papers, Mount Holyoke.
"**The British fear**": Murrow to Ed Dakin, Jan. 6, 1943, Murrow papers, Mount Holyoke.

197 **"Darlan was there"**: Nicolson, p. 263.
"**No matter what**": Gunther, p. 331.
"**Giraud was**": Dwight D. Eisenhower, p. 129.

198 **"North Africa"**: Atkinson, p. 164.
"**The German army**": Ibid., p. 261.
"**The proud and cocky**": Butcher, p. 268.
"**So far as soldiering**": Atkinson, p. 471.
"**downright embarrassing**": Ibid., p. 477.

199 **"Eisenhower as a general"**: Danchev and Todman, eds., p. 351.
"**The best way**": Atkinson, p. 246.
"**we were pushing**": Danchev and Todman, eds., p. 365.
"**soft, green**": Atkinson, p. 377.
"**How he hates**": Irving, p. 15.

200 "niggling and insulting": Perry, p. 174.
"It is better": Ibid.
"In his current": Butcher, p. 274.
"One of the constant": Merle Miller, p. 459.
"as an American": Atkinson, p. 467.
"without even": Ibid.
"Ike is more": Ibid.
"damned near": Irving, p. 63.
"God, I wish": Atkinson, p. 523.
"His blood": Ibid., p. 461.

201 "The American army": Ibid., p. 415.
"acting in a minor": Ibid., p. 481.
"a marked fall": Ibid., p. 482.
"one continent": Winston S. Churchill, *The Hinge of Fate*, p. 780.
"a place to be lousy": Atkinson, p. 538.

202 "Alan Brooke": Perry, p. 110.
"the British will have": Burns, p. 315.
"the dripping": Atkinson, p. 270.
"One thing": Merle Miller, p. 454.

203 "They swarmed": Atkinson, p. 289.
"Our ideas": Bryant, *The Turn of the Tide*, p. 459.

204 "no soldier": Atkinson, p. 533.
"Before he left": Ibid.
"One of the fascinations": Ibid.
"Goddamn it": Ibid., p. 466.
"Eisenhower was probably": Merle Miller, p. 372.
"Where he shone": Danchev and Todman, eds., p. 351.

CHAPTER 13: THE FORGOTTEN ALLIES

206 "To cross over to England": Erik Hazelhoff, *Soldier of Orange* (London: Sphere, 1982), p. 42.
"all those insane": Eve Curie, *Journey Among Warriors* (Garden City, N.Y.: Doubleday, 1943), p. 481.
"swimming in": Ritchie, p. 59.

207 "ministers got reports": A. J. Liebling, *The Road Back to Paris* (Garden City, N.Y.: Doubleday, 1944), p. 148.
"No matter": Erik Hazelhoff, *In Pursuit of Life* (Phoenix Mill, U.K.: Sutton, 2003), p. 110.
"the glamor boys of England": Olson and Cloud, p. 169.

208 "As for the women": Ibid., p. 178.
"The Occupation had descended": Hazelhoff, *Soldier of Orange*, p. 38.
"It would drive": BBC listening survey of Czechoslovakia, Sept. 1941, BBC Archives.

209 "It's impossible": Tangye Lean, *Voices in the Darkness: The Story of the European Radio War* (London: Secker & Warburg, 1943), p. 149.
"almost drunk": Henrey, *The Incredible City*, p. 2.

209   "If Poland had": Olson and Cloud, p. 5.

210   "the finest": Christopher M. Andrew, *Her Majesty's Secret Service: The Making of the British Intelligence Community* (New York: Viking, 1986), p. 448.

211   "The Poles had": Douglas Dodds-Parker, *Setting Europe Ablaze* (Windlesham, Surrey: Springwood, 1983), p. 40.

212   "If you live trapped": Anthony Read and David Fisher, *Colonel X: The Secret Life of a Master of Spies* (London: Hodder & Stoughton, 1984), p. 278.
      "We arrived in London": William Casey, *The Secret War Against Hitler* (New York: Berkley, 1989), p. 37.

213   "How well I remember": Ibid., pp. 24–25.
      "The truth is": Nelson D. Lankford, *OSS Against the Reich: The World War II Diaries of Col. David K. E. Bruce* (Kent, Ohio: Kent State University Press, 1991), p. 125.
      "inestimable value": Dwight D. Eisenhower, p. 262.

214   "Britain does not solicit": Olson and Cloud, p. 96.
      "We shall conquer": Ibid., p. 90.

215   "You are alone": Kersaudy, p. 83.
      "leader of all Frenchmen": Ibid.
      "The United Nations": FDR national radio broadcast, Feb. 23, 1942, FDRL.

216   "Winston, we forgot Zog!": Meacham, p. 164.
      "talked idealism": Arthur M. Schlesinger Jr., "FDR's Internationalism," in Cornelis van Minnen and John F. Sears, eds., *FDR and His Contemporaries: Foreign Perceptions of an American President* (New York: St. Martin's, 1992), p. 15.

217   "have any territorial": Valentin Berezhkov, "Stalin and FDR," in ibid., p. 50.
      "He allowed": Lord Chandos, *The Memoirs of Lord Chandos* (New York: New American Library, 1963), pp. 296–97.
      "can't live together": Ibid., p. 297.
      "I poured water": Eden, p. 432.
      "Roosevelt was familiar": Ibid., p. 433.
      "a kind of benevolent": Olson and Cloud, p. 241.
      "There is a great fear": Murrow to Ed Dakin, Jan. 6, 1943, Murrow papers, Mount Holyoke.

218   "What would": Carroll, p. 72.
      "has produced violent": Kersaudy, p. 225.
      "positively goes out": Moran, pp. 97–98.
      "in a hideously difficult position": Ismay, p. 356.

219   "Coming to": Jean Lacouture, *De Gaulle: The Rebel, 1890–1944* (New York: W. W. Norton, 1990), p. 265.
      "I am no man's subordinate": Ibid., p. 267.
      "You think": Kersaudy, p. 138.
      "You may be right": Ibid., p. 210.

220   "is almost": De Gaulle to Pamela Churchill, undated, Pamela Harriman papers, LC.
      "France had failed": Claude Fohlen, "De Gaulle and FDR," in van Minnen and Sears, eds., p. 42.
      "He takes himself": Lacouture, p. 335.
      "convinced": Carroll, p. 103.

220 "Roosevelt meant": Jean Edward Smith, p. 567.
"talked about": Gunther, p. 54.
221 "Between Giraud": Nicolson, p. 294.
"has been": Kersaudy, p. 288.
222 "Every time": Lacouture, p. 521.
"this vain": Kersaudy, p. 275.
"we would not only": Ibid., p. 279.
"in terms of orders": Dwight D. Eisenhower, p. 137.
"It seemed": Carroll, p. 308.
223 "were being played": R. Harris Smith, *OSS: The Secret History of America's First Central Intelligence Agency* (Berkeley: University of California Press, 1972), p. 31.
"at all times": Carroll, p. 106.
"a diplomat": Charles de Gaulle, *The Complete War Memoirs of Charles de Gaulle* (New York: Carroll & Graf, 1998), p. 220.
"splendid ambassador": Ibid., p. 310.
"Who is it": Carroll, p. 107.
224 "I do not think": Ibid., p. 108.
"was in the dog kennel": Howland, p. 268.
"I am reaching": Kersaudy, p. 291.
225 "Whether you wish": Olson and Cloud, pp. 220–21.
"could afford": Edward Raczynski, *In Allied London* (London: Weidenfeld & Nicolson, 1963), p. 155.
"The increasing gravity": Olson and Cloud, p. 233.
226 "go[ing] to the peace conference": Ibid., p. 250.
"found it convenient": Max Hastings, *Armageddon: The Battle for Germany, 1944–1945* (New York: Alfred A. Knopf, 2004), p. 508.

CHAPTER 14: "A CAUL OF PRIVILEGE"

227 "a human head": Hemingway, p. 109.
"I don't suppose": Calder, p. 321.
"Many a time": Maureen Waller, *London 1945: Life in the Debris of War* (London: Griffin, 2006), p. 163.
228 "The whole island": Hemingway, p. 108.
"It is difficult": Theodora FitzGibbon, *With Love: An Autobiography, 1938–1946* (London: Pan, 1983), p. 170.
"every day was": Longmate, *The Home Front*, p. 160.
"It's a case": Janet Murrow to parents, May 16, 1943, Murrow papers, Mount Holyoke.
"I think it would": Edwin R. Hale and John Frayn Turner, *The Yanks Are Coming* (New York: Hippocrene, 1983), p. 56.
229 "No war": David Reynolds et al., eds., *Allies at War,* p. xvi.
"There was money": Sevareid, p. 214.
"an equality of sacrifice": Goodwin, p. 339.
230 "Aside from": Tania Long, "Home—After London," *New York Times,* Oct. 3, 1943.
231 Most parts": Frances Perkins Oral History, Columbia University.

231   **"The American people"**: Sherwood, p. 547.

"It really would": Robert Dallek, *Franklin D. Roosevelt and American Foreign Policy, 1932–1945* (New York: Oxford University Press, 1979), p. 440.

"The very men": Goodwin, p. 357.

"seemed to be no": Sevareid, p. 193.

232   **"less realization"**: Brinkley, p. 106.

"influential people": Ibid., p. 142.

"where manners": Mary Lee Settle, *All the Brave Promises: Memories of Aircraft Woman 2nd Class 214639* (Columbia: University of South Carolina Press, 1995), p. 3.

"makes one": Janet Murrow to parents, undated, Murrow papers, Mount Holyoke.

233   **"It was all"**: Harriman to Harry Hopkins, March 7, 1942, Harriman papers, LC.

"bought a beautiful": Kathleen Harriman to Marie Harriman, Feb. 3, 1942, Harriman papers, LC.

"It's such fun": Kathleen Harriman to Marie Harriman, undated, Harriman papers, LC.

"London was one": Arbib, p. 85.

234   **"the fastest company"**: Harrison Salisbury, *A Journey for Our Times: A Memoir* (New York: Harper & Row, 1983), p. 179.

"with a feeling": Nelson D. Lankford, *The Last American Aristocrat: The Biography of David K. E. Bruce* (Boston: Little, Brown, 1996), p. 64.

"an abounding self-esteem": Ibid., p. 63.

235   **"one of the few"**: E. J. Kahn Jr., "Profiles: Man of Means—I," *New Yorker,* Aug. 11, 1951.

"the most elaborate": Ibid.

"life had never been": Sally Bedell Smith, *In All His Glory,* p. 225.

236   **"The guy had guts"**: Jan Herman, *A Talent for Trouble: William Wyler* (New York: Putnam's, 1995), p. 255.

"propaganda worth": Ibid., p. 235.

"I was a warmonger": Ibid., p. 234.

237   **"only scratched"**: Ibid., p. 237.

"an escape *into* reality": Ibid., p. 278.

"unreal, a stage": Mary Lee Settle, "London—1944," *The Virginia Quarterly Review,* Autumn 1987.

"We were young": Settle, *All the Brave Promises,* p. 1.

"It was my first": Ibid., p. 19.

238   **"caul of privilege"**: Mary Lee Settle, *Learning to Fly: A Writer's Memoir* (New York: W. W. Norton, 2007), p. 99.

"I had had the experience": Mary Lee Settle, "London—1944," *The Virginia Quarterly Review,* Autumn 1987.

"as if I were bone china": Settle, *Learning to Fly,* p. 97.

239   **"We were really"**: Abramson, p. 316.

"It was a terrible war": Pamela Harriman interview with Christopher Ogden, Pamela Harriman papers, LC.

"They were caught out": Sally Bedell Smith, *Reflected Glory,* p. 100.

"beneath their own roof": Abramson, p. 316.

239 **"He used terrible"**: Sally Bedell Smith, *Reflected Glory,* p. 106.
"that might do": Pamela Harriman interview with Christopher Ogden, Pamela Harriman papers, LC.

240 **"Keep your affairs"**: Ogden, p. 146.
"Ave couldn't": Sally Bedell Smith, *Reflected Glory,* p. 108.
"My son": Pamela Churchill to FDR, July 1942, Pamela Harriman papers, LC.
"Unless you were": Ogden, p. 173.

241 **"could escape from"**: Sally Bedell Smith, *Reflected Glory,* p. 122.
"The information": Ibid., p. 145.
"don't want": Sevareid notes, undated 1944, Sevareid papers, LC.
"The war's just": William Bradford Huie, *The Americanization of Emily* (New York: Signet, 1959), p. 37.
"The Air Force": Kay Summersby Morgan, p. 33.
"It was the mood": Sally Bedell Smith, *Reflected Glory,* p. 115.

242 **"Well, I have"**: D'Este, p. 489.
"The war was": Kay Summersby Morgan, p. 76.
"We did not have": Irving, p. 14.
"In my life": Pamela Harriman interview with Christopher Ogden, Pamela Harriman papers, LC.

243 **"would question"**: Sally Bedell Smith, *Reflected Glory,* p. 113.
"I think of you": Sir Charles Portal to Pamela Churchill, undated, Pamela Harriman papers, LC.
"A lot of people": Pamela Harriman interview with Christopher Ogden, Pamela Harriman papers, LC.
"follow[ed] the Rooseveltian": Abramson, p. 345.
"A large number": Harriman and Abel, p. 220.

244 **"I am sure"**: Ibid., p. 219.
"That was a dark day": Pamela Harriman interview with Christopher Ogden, Pamela Harriman papers, LC.
"All through": Ibid.
"I cried on Ed's shoulder": Ibid.

245 **"I think she decided"**: Sally Bedell Smith, *Reflected Glory,* p. 119.
"Ed was knocked off": Persico, *Edward R. Murrow,* p. 217.
"his privacy": "Edward R. Murrow," *Scribner's,* December 1938.
"Ed very curt": Persico, *Edward R. Murrow,* p. 138.
"They didn't want": Author interview with Janet Murrow.
"I hate seeing": Janet Murrow diary, Feb. 16, 1940, Murrow papers, Mount Holyoke.
"Gloomy, gloomy": Janet Murrow diary, Feb. 17, 1941, Murrow papers, Mount Holyoke.
"a lovely, suave": Persico, *Edward R. Murrow,* p. 186.

246 **"I long for him"**: Janet Murrow diary, July 26, 1941, Murrow papers, Mount Holyoke.
"I know they used": Sally Bedell Smith, *Reflected Glory,* p. 119.
"Ed was very much": Pamela Harriman interview with Christopher Ogden, Pamela Harriman papers, LC.
"Averell was everything": Ibid.
" a stooge": Harriman interview with Elie Abel, Harriman papers, LC.

246 "You're spoiled": Pamela Harriman interview with Christopher Ogden, Pamela Harriman papers, LC.

247 "He was totally different": Ibid.
"He loved Janet": Sperber, p. 244.

CHAPTER 15: "A CHASE PILOT—FIRST, LAST, AND ALWAYS"

248 "in my pantheon": Andrew Turnbull, ed., *The Letters of F. Scott Fitzgerald* (New York: Scribner, 1963), p. 49.
"firing the American imagination": "Hitchcock Killed in Crash in Britain," *New York Times*, April 20, 1944.

249 "There was a sort": Sarah Ballard, "Polo Player Tommy Hitchcock Led a Life of Action from Beginning to End," *Sports Illustrated*, Nov. 3, 1986.
"Most U.S. citizens": "Centaur," *Time*, May 1, 1944.
"Sometimes he did things": Aldrich, p. 132.
"He didn't have": *Sports Illustrated*, Nov. 3, 1986.
"There was no player": Ibid.

250 "Tommy Barban was": F. Scott Fitzgerald, *Tender Is the Night* (London: Wordsworth, 1994), p. 167.

251 "Polo is exciting": *New York Times*, April 20, 1944.
"he was a chase": Aldrich, p. 125.
"How can you": Ibid., p. 132.
"knew more people": Ibid., p. 266.
"There is one thing": Donald L. Miller, p. 5.

253 "We just closed": Ibid., p. 42.

254 "the important thing": Salisbury, p. 197.
"pawns": Donald L. Miller, p. 106.
"It looked": Ibid., p. 48.

255 "high-octane outfit": Salisbury, p. 195.

256 "one of the great": Andy Rooney, *My War* (New York: Times Books, 1995), p. 136.
"We thought": Donald L. Miller, p. 64.
"You're driving": McCrary and Scherman, pp. 38–39.
"suicide missions": Donald L. Miller, p. 24.

257 "so large": Ibid., p. 69.
"grossly exaggerated": Ibid, p. 120.

258 "To fly": Salisbury, p. 196.
"There are apparently": Donald L. Miller, p. 93.
"bomber bases": Ibid., p. 127.
"With deeper": Ibid., p. 124.

259 "My personal message": Irving, p. 72.
"In those days": McCrary and Scherman, pp. 227–28.
"Since I have been": Winant to FDR, Jan. 12, 1942, President's Secretary's File, FDRL.

260 "the cleanest": McCrary and Scherman, p. 228.
"the plane the Bomber Mafia": Donald L. Miller, p. 253.
"would produce": Aldrich, p. 275.
"Sired by the English": William R. Emerson, 1962 Harmon Memorial Lecture, U.S. Air Force Academy.

261 "Look, Uncle Tommy": Aldrich, p. 278.
"pushed the very daylights": Theodore Achilles interview, Bellush papers, FDRL.
"The word *channels*": Aldrich, p. 278.

262 "His hands": James Parton, *"Air Force Spoken Here": General Ira Eaker and the Command of the Air* (Bethesda, Md.: Adler & Adler, 1986), p. 279.
"took on almost": Donald L. Miller, p. 183.

263 "It began to look": Parton, p. 277.
"to find an easy way": Ibid. p. 186.

264 "the Eighth Air Force's": Aldrich, p. 284.
"literally wiped": Donald L. Miller, p. 200.
"a catastrophic blow": Ibid., p. 201.
"the greatest concentration": Ibid., p. 16.

265 "deep sense": *Daily Express*, Oct. 12, 1943, Winant papers, FDRL.

266 "It was up to me": Donald L. Miller, p. 252.
"over Germany": Paul A. Ludwig, *Mustang: Development of the P-51 Long-Range Escort Fighter* (Hersham, Surrey: Classic Publications, 2003), p. 1.
"the Air Force's": Donald L. Miller, p. 254.
"The story of the P-51": Ludwig, p. 2.
"one of the most": Donald L. Miller, p. 253.

267 "regardless of cost": Ibid., p. 265.
"God, [the crews]": Ibid, p. 266.

268 "Colonel": Ibid., p. 279.
"Alcohol was": Ibid.
"The war of attrition": Ibid., p. 276.
"The first time": Ibid., p. 267.
"to our inability": Ibid., pp. 291–92.
"If you see": Ibid., p. 259.

269 "Tommy Hitchcock was": Aldrich, p. 283.
"the tenacity": McCrary and Scherman, p. 228.
"Life in London": Aldrich, p. 276.
"Fighting in a Mustang": McCrary and Scherman, p. 231.

270 "The amount": Aldrich, p. 292.
"I suddenly had": Ibid., p. 294.
"Tommy Hitchcock had": Ibid, p. 296.

271 "has been going": Ibid., p. 298.
"just diving": Ibid.
"brought to a close": "Hitchcock Killed in Crash in Britain," *New York Times*, April 20, 1944.
"spent every minute": Winant letter to Margaret Hitchcock, April 23, 1944, Winant papers, FDRL.

CHAPTER 16: "CROSSING THE OCEAN DOESN'T AUTOMATICALLY MAKE YOU A HERO"

272 *Dear old England's:* Juliet Gardiner, *"Overpaid, Oversexed, and Over Here,"* p. 339.
"There is not": Irving, p. 8.

272   "the greatest": Dwight D. Eisenhower, p. 49.

"It was as if": Mrs. Robert Henrey, *The Siege of London* (London: J. M. Dent & Sons, 1946), p. 45.

274   "captured—lock": Ziegler, p. 215.

"an Englishman stood": Ernie Pyle, *Brave Men* (New York: Grosset & Dunlap, 1944), p. 316.

"Everybody had to salute": Ibid., p. 317.

"show proper respect": Longmate, *The G.I.'s*, p. 113.

"bawdy, rowdy ant hill": Arbib, p. 85.

"one of the most sensational": Donald L. Miller, p. 216.

"The conviviality": Hale and Turner, p. 152.

275   "were jammed": Donald L. Miller, p. 217.

"I think that": Irving, p. 8.

"the reaction": Theodore Achilles interview, Bellush papers, FDRL.

"Every American soldier": Dwight D. Eisenhower, p. 57.

276   "The British will": Longmate, *The G.I.'s*, p. 23.

"a remarkable personal": Interview with Anthony Eden, Bellush papers, FDRL.

"No one else": Alfred D. Chandler, ed., *The Papers of Dwight David Eisenhower: The War Years*, Vol. 1 (Baltimore: Johns Hopkins University Press, 1970), pp. 650–51.

277   "The war": Arbib, p. 19.

"compensation was minimal": David Reynolds, *Rich Relations*, p. 122.

278   "autocratic and undemocratic methods": Ibid., p. 126.

"our United States allies": *Daily Express*, Dec. 15, 1943, Winant papers, FDRL.

"They hadn't wanted": Gardiner, *"Overpaid, Oversexed, and Over Here,"* p. 32.

"for us": Ibid.

"as if they owned": Margaret Mead, "A GI View of Britain," *New York Times Magazine*, March 19, 1944.

"We never saw": Ibid., p. 54.

279   "these men are fighters": Ibid.

"The general reaction": Longmate, *The G.I.'s*, p. 96.

"I like it fine": Hale and Turner, p. 24.

280   "In they slouched": Nicolson, p. 275.

281   "if an American soldier": Butcher, p. 14.

"This is a wonderful": David Reynolds, *Rich Relations*, p. 159.

"bewildered, hurt": Janet Murrow to parents, April 24, 1943, Murrow papers, Mount Holyoke.

282   "The men in these": David Reynolds, *Rich Relations*, p. 160.

"The British women": Butcher, p. 34.

"All right": Settle, *All the Brave Promises*, p. 90

283   "deliberately discourages": David Reynolds, *Rich Relations*, p. 187.

The greatest danger": Ibid., p. 161.

"American soldiers": Ibid., p. 148.

"thousands of mothers": Ibid., p. 149.

"Differences between": Dwight D. Eisenhower, p. 59.

"the listlessness": Max Hastings, p. 193.

284   "no simple": Roosevelt to Winant, Sept. 10, 1942, President's Secretary's File, FDRL.

284   "They could have": Dimbleby and Reynolds, p. 164.
"The Yanks": Donald L. Miller, p. 138.
"Wherever you go": Hale and Turner, p. 40.
"Some of these brothers": Ibid.
"In the darkness": Ibid., p. 26.

285   "wild, promiscuous": Longmate, *The G.I.'s*, p. 157.
"There was a hard core": Ibid.
"As good": Ibid., p. 91.
"The arrival": Ibid.
"was like stepping": Ibid., p. 242.

286   "To most English people": David Reynolds, *Rich Relations*, 218.
"Get out": Dimbleby and Reynolds, p. 163.
"I have personally": Longmate, *The G.I.'s*, 129.
"discrimination as regards": David Reynolds, *Rich Relations*, p. 224.
"It was desirable": Ibid., p. 226.
"The American policy": Longmate, *The G.I.'s*, p. 122.

287   "The general consensus": David Reynolds, *Rich Relations*, epigraph.
"I don't mind": Ibid., p. 303.
"The opinion": Ibid., p. 304.
"It savoured": Graham Smith, *When Jim Crow Met John Bull: Black American Soldiers in World War II Britain* (New York: St. Martin's, 1988), p. 61.
"For British people": Ibid., p. 118.
"they were in England": Ibid.
"The Negro British": David Reynolds, *Rich Relations*, p. 306.

288   "The colored troops": Graham Smith, p. 102.
"abuses": Persico, *Edward R. Murrow*, p. 199.
"Sure, man": Ibid., p. 200.
"Let's do it!": Ibid.

289   "America's polite": Graham Smith, p. 127.

290   "not think of": David Reynolds, *Rich Relations*, p. 353.
"an increasingly kindly": Ibid., p. 199.
"firmness and good sense": LaRue Brown, "John G. Winant," *Nation*, Nov. 15, 1947.
"Mr. Winant, please!": *Stars and Stripes*, July 22, 1943.
"this caring": Bernard Bellush, "After 50 Years, a GI Heeds the Call of London," *Forward*, January 2001.
"no airs": *Boston Globe*, Nov. 5, 1947.

291   "You hadn't been": Arbib, p. 141.
"ate at their": Ibid., p. 144.
"By 1943": Longmate, *The G.I.'s*, p. 157.

292   "They adopted me": "Dick Winters' Reflections," www.wildbillguarnere.com.

CHAPTER 17: "YOU WILL FIND US LINING UP WITH THE RUSSIANS"

293   "In the last": Colville, *Footprints in Time*, p. 141.
"Increasingly": Dimbleby and Reynolds, p. 166.
"For many years": Sevareid, p. 484.

294   "political reasons": Sherwood, p. 669.

295   **"Harry is sure"**: Moran, p. 131.

"glittering, impersonal": Arthur Schlesinger Jr., "The Supreme Partnership," *Atlantic*, October 1984.

"was really incapable": Goodwin, p. 306.

"a gentleman": Meacham, p. 315.

"my whole system": David Reynolds, *In Command of History*, p. 414.

"Anything like a serious": Gilbert, *Road to Victory*, p. 89.

"real friendship": Geoffrey Ward, *Closest Companion: The Unknown Story of the Intimate Friendship Between Franklin Roosevelt and Margaret Suckley* (Boston: Houghton Mifflin, 1995), p. 162.

"manner was easy": Ibid.

"*adores* the President": Ibid., p. 230.

"Roosevelt envied": Max Hastings, p. 5.

296   **"was prone to jealousy"**: Meacham, p. 327.

"They had nothing": Schlesinger, p. 575.

"Each used": David K. Adams, "Churchill and FDR: A Marriage of Convenience," in van Minnen and Sears, eds., p. 32.

"We've got to": Elliott Roosevelt, pp. 24–25.

297   **"dropped in a remark"**: Kimball, *Forged in War*, p. 193.

"One thing": Kathleen Burk, *Old World, New World: Great Britain and America from the Beginning* (New York: Atlantic Monthly Press, 2008), p. 504.

"If he had been British": Matthews, p. 245.

"not become": Dimbleby and Reynolds, p. 158.

298   **"I do not want"**: Clarke, p. 166.

"Roosevelt's picture": Justus D. Doenecke and Mark A. Stoler, *Debating Franklin D. Roosevelt's Foreign Policies, 1933–1945* (Lanham, Md.: Rowman & Littlefield, 2005), p. 9.

"British bankers": Elliott Roosevelt, p. 24.

"Roosevelt's dislike": Hitchens, p. 255.

299   **"it is similarly true"**: Burk, p. 383.

"friction and misunderstanding": Howland, p. 143.

300   **"It must be remembered"**: Clarke, p. 25.

"we should have accepted": Ibid.

"I am inclined": Danchev and Todman, eds., p. 466.

"In newspaper": Brinkley, p. 232.

301   **"I began to feel"**: Danchev and Todman, eds., p. 535.

"inability to finish": Olson and Cloud, p. 288.

"I am slowly": Danchev and Todman, eds., p. 459.

"too exhausted": Arthur Bryant, *Triumph in the West* (Garden City, N.Y.: Doubleday, 1959), p. 8.

302   **"full of disease"**: Ward, p. 250.

"I have had no information": Winant to FDR, Sept. 24, 1943, Map Room Files, FDRL.

"these things would": Winant to Hopkins, Oct. 16, 1943, Hopkins Files, FDRL.

"I know exactly": Hopkins to Winant, Oct. 25, 1943, Hopkins Files, FDRL.

303   **"Large families"**: Burns, p. 405.

"talk Mr. Stalin": Olson and Cloud, p. 292.

303   "entered his nature": Frances Perkins Oral History, Columbia University.
       "I do not think": Charles E. Bohlen, *Witness to History, 1929–1969* (New York:
       W. W. Norton, 1973), p. 211.
       "A deeper knowledge": Ibid, p. 210.

304   "You will find": Moran, p. 160.
       "endeavouring to improve": Danchev and Todman, eds., p. 485.
       "how to conduct": Abramson, p. 367.
       "Stalin has got": Moran, p. 163.
       "the impression": Olson and Cloud, p. 292.
       "not only backed": Bohlen, p. 146.
       "should have come": Ibid.
       "always enjoyed": Harriman and Abel, p. 191.
       "Winston is cranky": Olson and Cloud, p. 292.

305   "a basic error": Bohlen, p. 146.
       "childish exercise": Discussion with Winston Churchill, Coudert Institute,
       Palm Beach, Florida, March 28, 2008.
       "immediate gains": Olson and Cloud, p. 295.
       "didn't care": Ibid., p. 306.

306   "The United States": Valentin Berezhkov, "Stalin and FDR," in van Minnen
       and Sears, eds., p. 47.
       "cannot leave": Moran, p. 279.
       "become friends": Olson and Cloud, p. 298.
       "People who have": Kendrick, p. 258.
       "People seem to want": Murrow to Alfred Cohn, Dec. 29. 1943, Murrow pa-
       pers, Mount Holyoke.

307   "vague and ill defined": Kimball, *Forged in War*, p. 242.
       "fraught with danger": Doenecke and Stoler, p. 62.

308   "to postpone": Ibid., p. 73.
       "summarily turned down": Olson and Cloud, p. 247.
       "rather touchy": David Reynolds, *The Creation of the Anglo-American Alliance*,
       pp. 253–54.
       "is accused": Winant to FDR, Feb. 4, 1943, President's Secretary's File, FDRL.

310   "acutely embarrassed": Howland, p. 318.
       "I have been worrying": Ibid., p. 326.

CHAPTER 18: "WOULD THE DAMN THING WORK?"

311   "as full of traffic": Arbib, p. 202.
       "mostly something": Panter-Downs, p. 324.
       "living on": Ibid., p. 322.

312   "staying close": Arbib, p. 205.
       "as a farmer": Settle, "London 1944," *The Virginia Quarterly Review*, August
       1987.
       "making D-Day possible": Weintraub, p. 217.
       "incessant clashes": Sir Frederick Morgan, p. 41.
       "there was never": Ibid., p. 49.

313   "All entered": Ibid., p. 80.
       "For Christ's sake": Ibid., p. 72.

313 **"That way"**: Kay Summersby Morgan, p. 172.

"**developed a relationship**": Longmate, *The G.I.'s*, p. 290.

"**loved and respected**": Ibid., p. 116.

314 "**deliberately thought**": Sir John Wheeler-Bennett, *Special Relationships: America in Peace and War* (London: Macmillan, 1975), pp. 178–79.

"**regarded Ike**": Longmate, *The G.I.'s*, p. 116.

"**It was the greatest**": D'Este, p. 495.

"**a disaster**": Sir Frederick Morgan, p. 279.

"**By God**": Irving, p. 81.

315 "**we went into France**": David Reynolds, *Rich Relations*, p. 357.

"**more like**": Ibid., p. 365.

"**regard the war**": Ibid.

"**torn to shreds**": Danchev and Todman, eds., p. 551.

"**He was as nervous**": Kay Summersby Morgan, p. 182.

"**In this particular venture**": Irving, p. 94.

316 "**I decided that**": Pyle, *Brave Men*, p. 317.

"**if *Dog News***": Ibid., p. 318.

"**Everything that happened**": Sally Bedell Smith, *In All His Glory*, p. 216.

317 "**I believe**": Caroline Moorehead, *Gellhorn: A Twentieth-Century Life* (New York: Henry Holt, 2003), p. 209.

"**To me**": Carlos Baker, *Ernest Hemingway: A Life Story* (New York: Scribner, 1967), pp. 392–93.

"**They want to stay**": Hemingway, p. 133.

318 "**By God**": Cloud and Olson, p. 158.

"**Last night**": Edward Bliss Jr., *In Search of Light: The Broadcasts of Edward R. Murrow, 1938–1961* (New York: Alfred A. Knopf, 1967), p. 76.

319 "**one of the finest**": L. M. Hastings to Murrow, Dec. 4, 1943, Murrow papers.

"**magnificent**": Arthur Christensen to Murrow, Dec. 4, 1943, Murrow papers, Mount Holyoke.

"**Ed was cynical**": Pamela Harriman interview with Christopher Ogden, Pamela Harriman papers, LC.

"**the most faithful**": Kendrick, p. 262.

"**My dear Ed**": Brendan Bracken to Murrow, Dec. 21, 1943, Murrow papers, Mount Holyoke.

"**I think this was**": R. Franklin Smith, p. 45.

"**It was a drug**": Ibid., p. 47.

"**a thing about speed**": Ibid.

"**Three or four times**": Persico, *Edward R. Murrow*, p. 221.

"**In order to write**": Murrow to Remsen Bird, Jan. 31, 1944, Murrow papers, Mount Holyoke.

320 "**fatigue and frustration**": Persico, *Edward R. Murrow*, p. 222.

"**I tried to convince him**": Paley, p. 152.

"**No longer**": Arbib, pp. 206–7.

321 "**We stood**": Longmate, *The G.I.'s*, p. 298.

"**Good luck**": Hale and Turner, p. 161.

"**My heart ached**": Longmate, *The G.I.'s*, p. 310.

"**It was so drab**": Gardiner, "*Overpaid, Oversexed, and Over Here*," p. 211.

321 "like a giant factory": Bliss, p. 81.

"In perfect": Gardiner, *"Overpaid, Oversexed, and Over Here,"* p. 180.

"The sky looked": Longmate, *The G.I.'s,* p. 307.

"Ladies and gentlemen": Gardiner, *Wartime Britain,* p. 544.

322 "The church": Janet Murrow to parents, June 11, 1944, Murrow papers, Mount Holyoke.

"our sons": Burns, p. 476.

"Except for the planes": Pamela Churchill to Averell Harriman, June 8, 1944, Pamela Harriman papers, LC.

"Walking along": Kendrick, p. 269.

"There was a kind": William Saroyan, *The Adventures of Wesley Jackson* (New York: Harcourt, Brace, 1946), p. 258.

"One could sense": Panter-Downes, p. 328.

323 "If I had had": Cloud and Olson, p. 204.

324 "In the old days": Henrey, *The Siege of London,* p. 72.

"The man going home": Winston S. Churchill, *Triumph and Tragedy* (Boston: Houghton Mifflin, 1953), p. 39.

"as impersonal": Calder, p. 560.

"We now live": Ziegler, p. 292.

325 "Most of the people": David Reynolds, *Rich Relations,* p. 402.

"I'm afraid": Irving, p. 180.

"in worried tones": Dwight D. Eisenhower, p. 260.

"We have had": Ziegler, p. 299.

326 "The nation's deep": Panter-Downes, p. 350.

"Like everyone else": Wheeler-Bennett, *Special Relationships,* p. 189.

"very old": Danchev and Todman, eds., p. 544.

"how tired": Janet Murrow to parents, June 22, 1944, Murrow papers, Mount Holyoke.

"Look . . . the first time": Sperber, p. 243.

"London is deserted": Gardiner, *Wartime Britain,* p. 556.

327 "Winston never talks": Moran, pp. 185–86.

328 "Winston hated": Danchev and Todman, eds., p. 473.

"being mis-employed": Meacham, p. 294.

"I wanted you": Winant to FDR, July 3, 1944, Map Room files, FDRL.

329 "There is one name": Kersaudy, p. 354.

"We are the French": Ibid., p. 334.

"the sixty-day": Ibid., p. 332.

330 "It seems to me": Ibid., p. 331.

"feel that the French": Ibid., p. 333.

"An open clash": Dwight D. Eisenhower, p. 248.

"All circles": Irving, p. 135.

331 "a state of": Beevor and Cooper, p. 28.

"treason at the height": Lacouture, p. 524.

"It's pandemonium": Beevor and Cooper, pp. 28–29.

"girls' school": Kersaudy, p. 346.

"it was a fatal mistake": Ibid., p. 351.

"The Prime Minister": Ibid., p. 352.

332 "in the initial stages": Dwight D. Eisenhower, p. 248.
"The brigadiers": Malcolm Muggeridge, *Chronicles of Wasted Time,* Vol. 2, *The Infernal Grove* (London: Collins, 1973), p. 212.
"flogging a dead horse": Jean Edward Smith, p. 614.
"FDR . . . believes": Kersaudy, p. 361.
"He's a nut": Ibid.

333 "As a cordial": Ibid., p. 370.
"FDR's pique": Jean Edward Smith, p. 616.
"a sleepy, empty": Henrey, *The Siege of London,* p. 91.
"Where every man": Sevareid, p. 477.
"the Paris": Donald L. Miller, p. 137.

334 "in guilty splendour": Wheeler-Bennett, *Special Relationships,* p. 186.
"familiar, well-fed": Kendrick, p. 273.
"Perhaps the world": Sally Bedell Smith, *Reflected Glory,* p. 124.

CHAPTER 19: CRISIS IN THE ALLIANCE

335 "in the interests": Olson and Cloud, p. 333.
"The time has come": Harriman to Hopkins, Sept. 10, 1944, Hopkins papers, FDRL.

336 "put in the humiliating": Sherwood, p. 756.
"He wanted to operate": Abramson, p. 367.
"I cannot say": Bohlen, p. 127.

337 "They are tough": Isaacson and Thomas, p. 232.
"knew the Russians": Salisbury, p. 242.
"my views on policy": Isaacson and Thomas, p. 227.
"I used him": Ibid., p. 229.
"A great deal": Salisbury, p. 242.
"the touchstone": Isaacson and Thomas, p. 223.
"We intend": Olson and Cloud, p. 333.

338 "turned on his heel": Discussion with Winston Churchill, Coudert Institute, Palm Beach, Florida, March 28, 2008.
"rivalry for control": Bellush, p. 203.
"there will be plenty": Moran, p. 220.

339 "You can't do this!": Robert M. Hathaway, *Ambiguous Partnership: Britain and America, 1944–1947* (New York: Columbia University Press, 1981), p. 64.
"In Christ's name": Ibid.
"I dislike": Sherwood, p. 819.
"placed his prestige": Howland, p. 374.
"decided disadvantage": Ibid.
"We hear": Danchev and Todman, eds., p. 575.

340 "The only times": Meacham, p. 339.
"a national slap": D'Este, p. 599.

341 "Montgomery is a third-rate": Irving, p. 268.
"There was arrogance": Ibid., p. 392.
"Ike is bound": Ibid., p. 190.

342 "in a powerful": D'Este, p. 672.
"Between our front": Max Hastings, p. 196.

343 "He lacked": D'Este, p. 602.
"the savior": Dwight D. Eisenhower, p. 356.
"MONTGOMERY STOPS": Sevareid, p. 485.

344 "so irritated": Irving, p. 375.
"It did more": Clarke, p. 155.
"terrible": D'Este, p. 676.
"it remains impossible": Max Hastings, "How They Won," *New York Review of Books,* Nov. 22, 2007.
"behavior at moments": Merle Miller, p. 587.
"Something very like": Max Hastings, p. 222.
"pure blackmail": Colville, *The Fringes of Power,* p. 528.

345 "one might make": Hathaway, p. 83.
"Please take": FDR to Winant, Nov. 24, 1944, Map Room files, FDRL.
"that even a declaration": Colville, *The Fringes of Power,* p. 528.
"You would not send": Hitchens, p. 233.

346 "I have loyally": Clarke, p. 113.
"really irritated": Colville, *The Fringes of Power,* p. 536.
"European questions": Olson and Cloud, p. 363.
"What makes": Clarke, p. 147.
"We do not mind": Hathaway, p. 103.

347 "there is good reason": Ibid, p. 104.
"He just doesn't": Sherwood, p. 820.
"Physically": Doenecke and Stoler, p. 86.
"talking to": Clarke, p. 218.
"The P.M.'s box": Colville, *The Fringes of Power,* p. 530.

348 "I don't feel": Danchev and Todman, eds., p. 649.
"was tired": Geoffrey Best, *Churchill: A Study in Greatness* (Oxford: Oxford University Press, 2001), p. 260.
"I must say": Olson and Cloud, p. 365.
"It was two to one": Hathaway, p. 123.
"That the President": Ibid.
"Let him wait": Andrew Roberts, *Masters and Commanders,* p. 554.

349 "We went into the war": Cecil King, *With Malice Toward None: A War Diary* (London: Sidgwick & Jackson, 1970), p. 298.
"fought like a tiger": Olson and Cloud, p. 365.
"coming from America": Ibid., p. 366.

350 "We could never": Ibid.
"might reach": Bellush, p. 205.
"of the greatest urgency": Thomas M. Campbell and George C. Herring, eds., *The Diaries of Edward R. Stettinius Jr., 1943–1946* (New York: New Viewpoints, 1975), p. 227.

351 "I think our attitude": Bellush, p. 207.
"clearly wanted": Olson and Cloud, p. 383.
"Looks as if": Harriman notes, undated, Pamela Harriman papers, LC.
"the Soviet Government": Isaacson and Thomas, p. 247.

352 "There is no doubt": Olson and Cloud, p. 384.
"feeling of bitter resentment": Ibid., p. 386.
"minimize the general": Ibid., p. 387.

353 **"Berlin has lost"**: Max Hastings, p. 421.
"**Churchill's anger**": Ibid., p. 423.

CHAPTER 20: "FINIS"

354 **"Men and boys"**: Bliss, p. 91.
355 **"two rows"**: Ibid, p. 94.
356 **"What he had seen"**: R. Franklin Smith, p. 89.
"**I pray you**": Murrow broadcast, April 15, 1945, National Archives.
"**One shoe**": Kendrick, p. 279.
"**I'm Roosevelt's man**": Jacob Beam interview, Bellush papers, FDRL.
357 **"Thank God for you"**: Howland, p. 28.
"**I always think**": Ibid.
"**could make**": Robert H. Ferrell, *Choosing Truman: The Democratic Convention of 1944* (Columbia: University of Missouri Press, 1994), p. 13.
"**weeping, reminiscing**": Thompson, p. 303.
"**This country**": Hathaway, pp. 130–31.
"**quiet as**": Longmate, *The G.I.'s*, p. 317.
"**stood in the streets**": Panter-Downes, p. 368.
358 **"being stopped"**: Longmate, *The G.I.'s*, p. 317.
"**I don't think**": Ziegler, p. 310.
"**was the greatest American**": Clarke, p. 259.
"**an immense effect**": Jenkins, p. 783.
"**how greatly**": Ibid.
"**It is difficult**": Max Hastings, p. 512.
"**I think that it would**": Meacham, p. 351.
359 **"With this signing"**: Cloud and Olson, p. 237.
"**taken over**": Panter-Downes, p. 374.
360 **"Their minds"**: Bliss, p. 97.
"**almost with a start**": Kendrick, p. 280.
"**When the whole**": Henry Chancellor, *Colditz: The Untold Story of World War II's Great Escapes* (New York: William Morrow, 2001), p. 362.
"**That your anxiety**": Bellush, p. 213.
361 **"On the continent"**: Olson and Cloud, p. 392.
"**poisonous politics**": Ibid., p. 393.
"**By the time**": D'Este, p. 807.
362 **"There had been applause"**: LaRue Brown, "John G. Winant," *Nation,* Nov. 15, 1947.
"**Ike made a *wonderful***": Danchev and Todman, eds., p. 697.
"**was worried about Winston**": Moran, p. 302.
"**Though [the British people]**": Pamela Churchill to Averell Harriman, July 27, 1945, Pamela Harriman papers, LC.
363 **"he scoffs"**: Moran, p. 308.
"**this damned election**": Ibid., p. 310.
"**a complete debacle**": Pawle, p. 501.
"**one of the most stunning**": Hathaway, p. 176.
"**mortally wounded**": Campbell and Herring, eds., p. 413.
"**The whole focus**": Soames, p. 425.

363   "It was not so much": Sarah Churchill, *A Thread in the Tapestry*, p. 86.
364   "Sir, you have": Dwight D. Eisenhower, p. 242.

CHAPTER 21: "I SHALL ALWAYS FEEL THAT I AM A LONDONER"

365   "GOODBYE, ENGLAND": Longmate, *The G.I.'s*, p. 325.
366   "It is hard": Waller, p. 205.
       "We must all": Ibid., p. 241.
367   "The American people": Hathaway, p. 23.
       Donald Worby: Dimbleby and Reynolds, p. 175.
       "I think they're behaving": Waller, p. 347.
368   "We'd given": Dimbleby and Reynolds, p. 177.
       "Anybody who thinks": Sherwood, p. 827.
       "It is aggravating": Dimbleby and Reynolds, p. 180.
       "economic Munich": Ibid.
369   "The American people": Sherwood, p. 922.
       "I believe": Ibid., p. 921.
       "would work great hardship": Howland, p. 448.
       "Did any nation": Carroll, p. 142.
       "would have made": Penrose, p. 206.
       "alien to him": Howland, p. 442.
       "I want to do": Ibid.
370   "not idealism": Arnold A. Rogow, "Private Illness and Public Policy: The Cases of James Forrestal and John Winant," *American Journal of Psychiatry*, Feb. 8, 1969.
       "His nerves": Maurine Mulliner interview, Bellush papers, FDRL.
       "I've lost": Grace Hogarth interview, Bellush papers, FDRL.
       "I have no life!": Bellush, p. 215.
       "I cannot explain": Soames, p. 429.
       "has been and is": Ibid., p. 380.
371   "I do not know": Sarah Churchill, *A Thread in the Tapestry*, p. 88.
       "I wish": Ibid., p. 91.
       "Sarah has been": Soames, p. 433.
       "You've no idea": Pearson, p. 338.
       "cage of affection": Sarah Churchill, *Keep on Dancing*, p. 159.
       "mental and physical": Sally Bedell Smith, *Reflected Glory*, p. 124.
       "For many things": Murrow to Janet Murrow, Sept. 18, 1944, Murrow papers, Mount Holyoke.
372   "I am lonesome": Murrow to Janet Murrow, Sept. 29, 1944, Murrow papers, Mount Holyoke.
       "Maybe I had begun": Murrow to Janet Murrow, Oct. 28, 1944, Murrow papers, Mount Holyoke.
       "Fred took me": Pamela Churchill to Averell Harriman, March 8, 1944, Pamela Harriman papers, Mount Holyoke.
       "We didn't talk": Sally Bedell Smith, *Reflected Glory*, p. 125.
       "I've never been": Ibid., p. 125.
       "Casey Wins": Ogden, p. 181.
       "We live in the light": Kendrick, p. 275.

372   **"This is a great nation"**: Sperber, p. 257.

373   **"an awkward position"**: Lash, *From the Diaries of Felix Frankfurter*, p. 256.
       "Your country": Bliss, pp. 3–4.

374   **"It is men"**: Emilie Adams to Murrow, Feb. 24, 1946, Murrow papers, Mount Holyoke.
       "Please tell": Unidentified to Murrow, Feb. 24, 1946, Murrow papers, Mount Holyoke.
       "When you get home": W. E. C. McIlroy to Murrow, Feb. 24, 1946, Murrow papers, Mount Holyoke.
       "Now, for the last time": Persico, *Edward R. Murrow*, p. 242.
       "THIS MICROPHONE": Ibid.

375   **"the only trophy"**: R. Franklin Smith, p. 75.
       "close friend": Unidentified clipping, Nov. 29, 1945, Winant papers, FDRL.
       "commanded to such": *Manchester Guardian*, undated, Winant papers, FDRL.
       "Almost everyone": *New Statesman*, March 30, 1946, Winant papers, FDRL.
       "the personification": *Daily Express*, March 25, 1946, Winant papers, FDRL.
       "came to us": *Daily Herald*, April 27, 1946, Winant papers, FDRL.

376   **"Goodbye, sir"**: *Punch*, May 8, 1946, Winant papers, FDRL.
       "I do not think": Arthur L. Goodhart to Winant, April 15, 1946, Winant papers, FDRL.
       "Those of us": John Martin to Winant, Jan. 1, 1947, Winant papers, FDRL.
       "rather hard-boiled": Barbara Wace to Winant, April 22, 1946, Winant papers, FDRL.
       "My driver": Herbert Agar to Winant, May 2, 1946, Winant papers, FDRL.
       "a unique honor": *Daily Telegraph*, April 26, 1946, Winant papers, FDRL.
       "Official British reserve": *Concord Daily Monitor*, Jan. 18, 1947, Winant papers, FDRL.
       "infinitely more": *New York Times*, April 24, 1946, Winant papers, FDRL.
       "In adversity": *Daily Telegraph*, April 26, 1946, Winant papers, FDRL.
       "In a long life": *Daily Telegraph*, May 21, 1946, Winant papers, FDRL.

377   **"I propose"**: Ibid.
       "I would say": *Daily Telegraph*, April 26, 1946, Winant papers, FDRL.
       "Neither you": *News Chronicle*, May 1, 1946, Winant papers, FDRL.
       "No fairer": *Daily Express*, May 1, 1946, Winant papers, FDRL.
       "hard years": Unidentified clipping, May 1, 1941, Winant papers, FDRL.

CHAPTER 22: "WE ALL LOST A FRIEND IN 'IM"

378   **"I am so glad"**: Eleanor Roosevelt to Winant, June 25, 1946, Winant papers, FDRL.
       "He dared to hope": Text of Winant speech, Winant papers, FDRL.
       "Seldom if ever": Sperber, p. 256.

379   **"something like independent"**: Howland, p. 400.
       "None of the Allies": Daniel J. Nelson, *Wartime Origins of the Berlin Dilemma* (Tuscaloosa: University of Alabama Press, 1976), p. 163.
       "running a race": Howland, p. 414.
       "Never before": Ibid., p. 412.
       "the most successful": Ibid.

379 "significant achievements": Ibid., p. 311.
380 "In our informal": Nelson, p. 23.
"The machinery": Sherwood, p. 843.
"He was much too restless": Bellush, p. 226.
381 "I have never seen": Arthur Coyle interview, Bellush papers, FDRL.
"deep brutal exhaustion": Mary Lee Settle, "London—1944," *The Virginia Quarterly Review,* Autumn 1987.
"a curious feeling": Sevareid, p. 510.
"Free!": Sarah Churchill, *Keep On Dancing,* p. 159.
382 "Don't you want": Bellush, p. 228.
"The difference": Colville, *Footprints in Time,* p. 156.
383 "It is now obvious": Dimbleby and Reynolds, p. 188.
"as close to destitution": Abramson, p. 413.
"Are you doing": Louis Fischer, "The Essence of Gandhism," *Nation,* Dec. 6, 1947.
"to make sure": Dean Dexter interview with Abbie Rollins Caverly.
384 "To the tiny valley": *New York Herald Tribune,* Nov. 5, 1947, Winant papers, FDRL.
"has affected": "British Mourn Winant," *New York Times,* Nov. 5, 1947.
"walked with Britain": *Daily Express,* undated, Winant papers, FDRL.
"What he said": *New York Herald Tribune,* Nov. 5, 1947, Winant papers, FDRL.
"It is a terrible": *Manchester Guardian,* Nov. 5, 1947.
385 "Was it that": Bellush, p. viii.
"as truly": Eleanor Roosevelt, "My Day" column, undated, Winant papers, FDRL.
"I have lost": *New York Times,* Nov. 5, 1947.
"He couldn't": Author interview with Rivington Winant.
"self-destruction": Thompson, p. 217.
386 "What a waste!": Sperber, p. 298.
"golden boys": Cloud and Olson, p. 244.
"grim and glorious years": R. Franklin Smith, p. 80.
"left all of his": Ibid., p. 75.
387 "news was his hobby": Interview with Don Hewitt.
"an individual": Jack Gould, "Edward R. Murrow: 1908–1965," *New York Times,* May 2, 1965.
"honorary Briton": "Britain Mourns a Friend," *New York Times,* April 28, 1965.
388 "super diplomat": "Ex-Gov. Averell Harriman, Adviser to 4 Presidents, Dies," *New York Times,* July 27, 1986.
"aloof, distant": Abramson, p. 409.
"sex hung": Cloud and Olson, p. 197.
"Never has anyone": Isaacson and Thomas, p. 603.
"was the closest thing": E. J. Kahn, "Profiles: Plenipotentiary—1," *New Yorker,* May 3, 1952.
389 "reshaping of America's": Isaacson and Thomas, p. 407.
"Everybody has his": Schlesinger, p. 249.
"I am confident": *New York Times,* July 27, 1986.
390 "My dear": Pamela Harriman interview with Christopher Ogden, Pamela Harriman papers, LC.

391 **"It helped me"**: Interview with Rev. J. Parker Jameson.

392 **"No other country"**: Burk, p. 578.
"Here was a people": Hitchens, p. 302.
"The Americans' coming": Longmate, *The G.I.'s*, p. 375.

393 **"Whatever happens"**: Ibid., p. 376.
"I think I understand": Ibid.
"I have loved London": Pyle, *Brave Men*, p. 315.
"The years in London": Middleton, p. 186.
"It embarrasses me": Saroyan, p. 238.
"Every Englishman": Arbib, pp. 210–11.

394 **"Paris died"**: Sevareid broadcast, Oct. 4, 1940, NA.

BIBLIOGRAPHY

ARCHIVAL MATERIAL

BBC WRITTEN ARCHIVES, READING, U.K.
BBC Wartime Broadcasts Papers

FRANKLIN D. ROOSEVELT PRESIDENTIAL LIBRARY, HYDE PARK, NEW YORK
Bernard Bellush Papers
Harry Hopkins Papers
Eleanor Roosevelt Papers
Franklin D. Roosevelt Papers
John Gilbert Winant Papers

LIBRARY OF CONGRESS, WASHINGTON, D.C.
Pamela Harriman Papers
W. Averell Harriman Papers
Kermit and Belle Roosevelt Papers
Eric Sevareid Papers

MOUNT HOLYOKE COLLEGE ARCHIVES AND SPECIAL COLLECTIONS, SOUTH HADLEY, MASSACHUSETTS
Edward R. Murrow and Janet Brewster Murrow Papers

U.S. NATIONAL ARCHIVES, COLLEGE PARK, MARYLAND
CBS Wartime Broadcasts
John Gilbert Winant/State Department Papers

PUBLISHED SOURCES

Abramson, Rudy. *Spanning the Century: The Life of W. Averell Harriman.* New York: William Morrow, 1992.

Acheson, Dean. *Present at the Creation: My Years in the State Department.* New York: W. W. Norton, 1969.

Adams, Henry H. *Harry Hopkins: A Biography.* New York: Putnam's, 1977.

Agar, Herbert. *The Darkest Year: Britain Alone, June 1940–June 1941.* Garden City, N.Y.: Doubleday, 1973.

Aldrich, Nelson W., Jr. *Tommy Hitchcock: An American Hero.* New York: Fleet Street, 1984.

Andrew, Christopher M. *Her Majesty's Secret Service: The Making of the British Intelligence Community.* New York: Viking, 1986.

Andrew, Christopher M., and David Dilks, eds. *The Missing Dimension: Governments and Intelligence Communities in the Twentieth Century.* London: Macmillan, 1984.

Arbib, Robert S. *Here We Are Together: The Notebook of an American Soldier in Britain.* London: Right Book Club, 1947.

Atkinson, Rick. *An Army at Dawn: The War in North Africa, 1942–1943.* New York: Henry Holt, 2002.

Baker, Carlos. *Ernest Hemingway: A Life Story.* New York: Scribner, 1967.

Beevor, Antony, and Artemis Cooper. *Paris After the Liberation, 1944–1949.* New York: Doubleday, 1994.

Bell, P. M. H. *A Certain Eventuality: Britain and the Fall of France.* Farnborough, U.K.: Saxon House, 1974.

Bellush, Bernard. *He Walked Alone: A Biography of John Gilbert Winant.* The Hague: Mouton, 1968.

Bernstein, Matthew. *Walter Wanger, Hollywood Independent.* Berkeley: University of California Press, 1994.

Beschloss, Michael R. *Kennedy and Roosevelt: The Uneasy Alliance.* New York: W. W. Norton, 1980.

Best, Geoffrey. *Churchill: A Study in Greatness.* Oxford: Oxford University Press, 2001.

Billingham, Mrs. Anthony. *America's First Two Years: The Story of American Volunteers in Britain, 1939–1941.* London: John Murray, 1942.

Blake, Robert, and William Roger Louis, eds. *Churchill.* New York: W. W. Norton, 1993.

Bliss, Edward, Jr. *In Search of Light: The Broadcasts of Edward R. Murrow, 1938–1961.* New York: Alfred A. Knopf, 1967.

Bohlen, Charles E. *Witness to History, 1929–1969.* New York: W. W. Norton, 1973.

Briggs, Asa. *The History of Broadcasting in the United Kingdom,* Vol. 3, *The War of Words.* London: Oxford University Press, 1970.

Brinkley, David. *Washington Goes to War.* New York: Alfred A. Knopf, 1988.

Brown, Anthony Cave. *"C": The Secret Life of Sir Stewart Graham Menzies.* New York: Macmillan, 1987.

Bryant, Arthur. *Triumph in the West.* Garden City, N.Y.: Doubleday, 1959.

———. *The Turn of the Tide.* Garden City, N.Y.: Doubleday, 1957.

Burk, Kathleen. *Old World, New World: Great Britain and America from the Beginning.* New York: Atlantic Monthly Press, 2008.

Burns, James MacGregor. *Roosevelt: The Soldier of Freedom.* New York: Harcourt Brace Jovanovich, 1970.

Butcher, Harry. *My Three Years with Eisenhower.* New York: Simon & Schuster, 1946.

Caine, Philip D. *Eagles of the RAF.* Washington: National Defense University Press, 1991.

Calder, Angus. *The People's War: Britain, 1939–1945.* New York: Pantheon, 1969.

Campbell, Thomas M., and George C. Herring, eds. *The Diaries of Edward R. Stettinius Jr., 1943–1946.* New York: New Viewpoints, 1975.

Carroll, Wallace. *Persuade or Perish.* Boston: Houghton Mifflin, 1948.

Casey, William. *The Secret War Against Hitler.* New York: Berkley, 1989.

Chadwin, Mark Lincoln. *The Warhawks: American Interventionists Before Pearl Harbor.* Chapel Hill: University of North Carolina Press, 1968.

Chancellor, Henry. *Colditz: The Untold Story of World War II's Great Escapes.* New York: William Morrow, 2001.

Chandler, Alfred D., ed. *The Papers of Dwight David Eisenhower: The War Years,* Vol. 1. Baltimore: Johns Hopkins University Press, 1970.

Chandos, Lord. *The Memoirs of Lord Chandos.* New York: New American Library, 1963.

Childers, James Saxon. *War Eagles: The Story of the Eagle Squadron.* New York: D. Appleton–Century, 1943.

Chisholm, Anne, and Michael Davie. *Lord Beaverbrook: A Life.* New York: Alfred A. Knopf, 1993.

Churchill, Sarah. *The Empty Spaces: The Poems of Sarah Churchill.* New York: Dodd, Mead, 1967.

———. *Keep on Dancing.* New York: Coward, McCann & Geoghegan, 1981.

———. *A Thread in the Tapestry.* London: Deutsch, 1967.

Churchill, Winston S. *The Grand Alliance.* Boston: Houghton Mifflin, 1950.

———. *The Hinge of Fate.* Boston: Houghton Mifflin, 1950.

———. *Triumph and Tragedy.* Boston: Houghton Mifflin, 1953.

Clapper, Olive Ewing. *Washington Tapestry.* New York: McGraw-Hill, 1946.

Clarke, Peter. *The Last Thousand Days of the British Empire: Churchill, Roosevelt, and the Birth of the Pax Americana.* New York: Bloomsbury, 2008.

Cloud, Stanley, and Lynne Olson. *The Murrow Boys: Pioneers on the Front Lines of Broadcast Journalism.* Boston: Houghton Mifflin, 1996.

Colby, Reginald. *Mayfair: A Town Within London.* London: Country Life, 1966.

Colville, John. *Footprints in Time: Memories.* London: Century, 1985.

———. *The Fringes of Power: 10 Downing Street Diaries, 1939–1945.* New York: W. W. Norton, 1985.

Commager, Henry Steele, ed. *Britain Through American Eyes.* New York: McGraw-Hill, 1974.

Cray, Ed. *General of the Army: George C. Marshall.* New York: W. W. Norton, 1990.

Cull, Nicholas. *Selling War: The British Propaganda Campaign Against American "Neutrality" in World War II.* New York: Oxford University Press, 1995.

Curie, Eve. *Journey Among Warriors.* Garden City, N.Y.: Doubleday, 1943.

Dallek, Robert. *Franklin D. Roosevelt and American Foreign Policy, 1932–1945.* New York: Oxford University Press, 1979.

Danchev, Alex. *Establishing the Anglo-American Alliance: The Second World War Diaries of Brigadier Vivian Dykes.* London: Brassey's, 1990.

Danchev, Alex, and Daniel Todman, eds. *War Diaries, 1939–1945: Field Marshal Lord Alanbrooke.* London: Weidenfeld & Nicolson, 2001.

De Gaulle, Charles. *The Complete War Memoirs of Charles de Gaulle.* New York: Carroll & Graf, 1998.

D'Este, Carlo. *Eisenhower: A Soldier's Life.* New York: Henry Holt, 2002.

Dimbleby, David, and David Reynolds. *An Ocean Apart: The Relationship Between Britain and America in the Twentieth Century.* New York: Random House, 1988.

Dodds-Parker, Douglas. *Setting Europe Ablaze.* Windlesham, Surrey: Springwood, 1983.

Doenecke, Justus D., and Mark A. Stoler. *Debating Franklin D. Roosevelt's Foreign Policies, 1933–1945.* Lanham, Md.: Rowman & Littlefield, 2005.

Eden, Anthony. *The Reckoning.* Boston: Houghton Mifflin, 1965.

Eisenhower, Dwight D. *Crusade in Europe.* Garden City, N.Y.: Doubleday, 1948.

Eisenhower, Milton S. *The President Is Calling.* Garden City, N.Y.: Doubleday, 1974.

Ferrell, Robert H. *Choosing Truman: The Democratic Convention of 1944.* Columbia: University of Missouri Press, 1994.

Fitzgerald, F. Scott. *Tender Is the Night.* London: Wordsworth, 1994.

FitzGibbon, Theodora. *With Love: An Autobiography, 1938–1946.* London: Pan, 1983.

Foot, M. R. D., and J. M. Langley. *MI9: Escape and Evasion, 1939–1945.* Boston: Little, Brown, 1980.

Fussell, Paul. *Wartime: Understanding and Behavior in the Second World War.* New York: Oxford University Press, 1989.

Gaddis, John Lewis. *The United States and the Origins of the Cold War, 1941–1947.* New York: Columbia University Press, 2000.

Ganier-Raymond, Philippe. *The Tangled Web.* London: Barker, 1968.

Gardiner, Juliet. *"Overpaid, Oversexed, and Over Here": The American GI in World War II Britain.* New York: Canopy Books, 1992.

———. *Wartime Britain, 1939–1945.* London: Headline, 2004.

Garlinski, Jozef. *The Enigma War.* New York: Scribner, 1960.

Gilbert, Martin. *Winston S. Churchill,* Vol. 6, *Finest Hour, 1939–1941.* Boston: Houghton Mifflin, 1983.

———. *Winston S. Churchill,* Vol. 7, *Road to Victory, 1941–1945.* Boston: Houghton Mifflin, 1986.

Goodson, James A. *Tumult in the Clouds.* New York: St. Martin's, 1993.

Goodwin, Doris Kearns. *No Ordinary Time: Franklin and Eleanor Roosevelt: The Home Front in World War II.* New York: Simon & Schuster, 1994.

Gunther, John. *Roosevelt in Retrospect.* New York: Harper & Brothers, 1950.

Hale, Edwin R., and John Frayn Turner. *The Yanks Are Coming.* New York: Hippocrene, 1983.

Harriman, W. Averell, and Elie Abel. *Special Envoy to Churchill and Stalin, 1941–1946.* New York: Random House, 1975.

Hastings, Max. *Armageddon: The Battle for Germany, 1944–1945.* New York: Alfred A. Knopf, 2004.

Hastings, Selina. *Nancy Mitford: A Biography.* London: Hamilton, 1985.

Hathaway, Robert M. *Ambiguous Partnership: Britain and America, 1944–1947.* New York: Columbia University Press, 1981.

Hawthorne, Nathaniel. *The Compete Writings of Nathaniel Hawthorne,* Vol. 11. Boston: Houghton Mifflin, 1900.

Hazelhoff, Erik. *In Pursuit of Life.* Phoenix Mill, U.K.: Sutton, 2003.

———. *Soldier of Orange.* London: Sphere, 1982.

Hemingway, Mary Welsh. *How It Was.* New York: Ballantine, 1976.

Henrey, Mrs. Robert. *The Incredible City.* London: J. M. Dent & Sons, 1944.

———. *London.* London: J. M. Dent & Sons, 1948.

———. *The Siege of London.* London: J. M. Dent & Sons, 1946.

Herman, Jan. *A Talent for Trouble: William Wyler.* New York: Putnam's, 1995.

Hersh, Seymour M. *The Dark Side of Camelot.* Boston: Little, Brown, 1997.

Hickman, Tom. *What Did You Do in the War, Auntie?* London: BBC Books, 1995.

Hitchens, Christopher. *Blood, Class and Nostalgia: Anglo-American Ironies.* New York: Farrar, Straus & Giroux, 1990.

Hodgson, Godfrey. *The Colonel: The Life and Wars of Henry Stimson, 1867–1950.* New York: Alfred A. Knopf, 1990.

Howarth, Patrick. *Intelligence Chief Extraordinary: The Ninth Duke of Portland.* London: Bodley Head, 1986.

Howland, Nina Davis. "Ambassador John Gilbert Winant: Friend of Embattled Britain, 1941–1946." Ph.D. dissertation, University of Maryland, 1983.

Huie, William Bradford. *The Americanization of Emily.* New York: Signet, 1959.

Irving, David. *The War Between the Generals: Inside the Allied High Command.* New York: Congdon & Lattes, 1981.

Isaacson, Walter, and Evan Thomas. *The Wise Men: Six Friends and the World They Made.* New York: Touchstone, 1986.

Ismay, Lord. *The Memoirs of Lord Ismay.* New York: Viking, 1960.

Jackson, Julian. *France: The Dark Years, 1940–1944.* Oxford: Oxford University Press, 2001.

James, Robert Rhodes, ed. *Chips: The Diaries of Sir Henry Channon.* London: Phoenix, 1997.

Jenkins, Roy. *Churchill: A Biography.* New York: Farrar, Straus & Giroux, 2001.

Jones, R. V. *Reflections on Intelligence.* London: Heinemann, 1989.

Kahn, E. J., Jr. *The World of Swope.* New York: Simon & Schuster, 1965.

Kendrick, Alexander. *Prime Time: The Life of Edward R. Murrow.* Boston: Little, Brown, 1969.

Kersaudy, François. *Churchill and De Gaulle.* New York: Atheneum, 1982.

Kershaw, Alex. *The Few: The American "Knights of the Air" Who Risked Everything to Fight in the Battle of Britain.* New York: Da Capo, 2006.

Kimball, Warren F. *Churchill and Roosevelt: The Complete Correspondence,* Vols. 1–3. Princeton: Princeton University Press, 1984.

———. *Forged in War: Roosevelt, Churchill and the Second World War.* New York: William Morrow, 1997.

———. *"The Most Unsordid Act": Lend Lease, 1939–1941.* Baltimore: Johns Hopkins University Press, 1969.

King, Cecil. *With Malice Toward None: A War Diary.* London: Sidgwick & Jackson, 1970.

Klemmer, Harvey. *They'll Never Quit.* New York: W. Funk, 1941.

Kozaczuk, Wladyslaw. *Enigma.* Frederick, Md.: University Publications of America, 1984.

Lacouture, Jean. *De Gaulle: The Rebel, 1890–1944.* New York: W. W. Norton, 1990.

Lankford, Nelson D. *The Last American Aristocrat: The Biography of David K. E. Bruce.* Boston: Little, Brown, 1996.

———. *OSS Against the Reich: The World War II Diaries of Col. David K. E. Bruce.* Kent, Ohio: Kent State University Press, 1991.

Lash, Joseph P. *Eleanor and Franklin.* New York: W. W. Norton, 1971.

———. *From the Diaries of Felix Frankfurter.* New York: W. W. Norton, 1975.

———. *Roosevelt and Churchill, 1939–1941: The Partnership That Saved the West.* New York: W. W. Norton, 1976.

———. *A World of Love: Eleanor Roosevelt and Her Friends, 1943–1962.* Garden City, N.Y.: Doubleday, 1984.

Lean, Tangye. *Voices in the Darkness: The Story of the European Radio War.* London: Secker & Warburg, 1943.

Lee, Lawrence, and Barry Gifford. *Saroyan: A Biography.* New York: Harper & Row, 1984.

Leutze, James, ed. *The London Journal of General Raymond E. Lee, 1940–1941.* Boston: Little, Brown, 1971.

Liebling, A. J. *The Road Back to Paris.* Garden City, N.Y.: Doubleday, 1944.

Lockhart, Robert Bruce. *Comes the Reckoning.* London: Putnam, 1947.

Loeffler, Jane C. *The Architecture of Diplomacy: Building America's Embassies.* New York: Princeton Architectural Press, 1998.

Loewenheim, Francis L., Harold D. Langley, and Manfred Jonas, eds. *Roosevelt and Churchill: Their Secret Wartime Correspondence.* New York: Saturday Review Press, 1975.

Long, Breckinridge. *The War Diary of Breckinridge Long.* Lincoln: University of Nebraska Press, 1966.

Longmate, Norman. *The G.I.'s: The Americans in Britain, 1942–1945.* New York: Scribner, 1975.

———. *The Home Front: An Anthology of Personal Experience, 1938–1945.* London: Chatto & Windus, 1981.

Ludwig, Paul A. *Mustang: Development of the P-51 Long-Range Escort Fighter.* Hersham, Surrey: Classic Publications, 2003.

Martin, Sir John. *Downing Street: The War Years.* London: Bloomsbury, 1991.

Matthews, T. S. *Name and Address: An Autobiography.* New York: Simon & Schuster, 1960.

McCrary, Capt. John R., and Capt. David Scherman. *First of the Many: A Journal of Action with the Men of the Eighth Air Force.* London: Robson, 1944.

McCullough, David. *John Adams.* New York: Simon & Schuster, 2001.

Meacham, Jon. *Franklin and Winston: An Intimate Portrait of an Epic Friendship.* New York: Random House, 2003.

Merry, Robert W. *Taking On the World: Joseph and Stewart Alsop—Guardians of the American Century.* New York: Viking, 1996.

Middleton, Drew. *Where Has Last July Gone?* New York: Quadrangle, 1973.

Miller, Donald L. *Masters of the Air: America's Bomber Boys Who Fought the Air War Against Nazi Germany.* New York: Simon & Schuster, 2006.

Miller, Merle. *Ike the Soldier: As They Knew Him.* New York: Putnam's, 1987.

Moorehead, Caroline. *Gellhorn: A Twentieth-Century Life.* New York: Henry Holt, 2003.

Moran, Lord. *Churchill at War, 1940–45.* New York: Carroll & Graf, 2002.

Morgan, Sir Frederick. *Overture to Overlord.* Garden City, N.Y.: Doubleday, 1950.

Morgan, Kay Summersby. *Past Forgetting: My Love Affair with Dwight D. Eisenhower.* New York: Simon & Schuster, 1975.

Mortimer, Gavin. *The Longest Night: The Bombing of London on May 10, 1941.* New York: Berkley, 2005.

Muggeridge, Malcolm. *Chronicles of Wasted Time.* Vol. 2, *The Infernal Grove.* London: Collins, 1973.

Nelson, Daniel J. *Wartime Origins of the Berlin Dilemma.* Tuscaloosa: University of Alabama Press, 1976.

Nicolson, Harold. *The War Years, 1939–1945.* New York: Atheneum, 1967.

Ogden, Christopher. *Life of the Party: The Biography of Pamela Digby Churchill Hayward Harriman.* Boston: Little, Brown, 1994.

Olson, Lynne. *Troublesome Young Men: The Rebels Who Brought Churchill to Power and Helped Save England.* New York: Farrar, Straus & Giroux, 2007.

Olson, Lynne, and Stanley Cloud. *A Question of Honor: The Kosciuszko Squadron: Forgotten Heroes of World War II.* New York: Alfred A. Knopf, 2003.

Paley, William S. *As It Happened: A Memoir.* Garden City, N.Y.: Doubleday, 1979.

Panter-Downes, Mollie. *London War Notes, 1939–1945.* New York: Farrar, Straus & Giroux, 1971.

Parton, James. *"Air Force Spoken Here": General Ira Eaker and the Command of the Air.* Bethesda, Md.: Adler & Adler, 1986.

Pawle, Gerald. *The War and Colonel Warden.* New York: Alfred A. Knopf, 1963.

Pearson, John. *The Private Lives of Winston Churchill.* New York: Touchstone, 1991.

Penrose, Ernest. *Economic Planning for the Peace.* Princeton: Princeton University Press, 1953.

Perry, Mark. *Partners in Command: George Marshall and Dwight Eisenhower in War and Peace.* New York: Penguin, 2007.

Persico, Joseph. *Edward R. Murrow: An American Original.* New York: Dell, 1988.

———. *Roosevelt's Secret War: FDR and World War II Espionage.* New York: Random House, 2001.

Peszke, Michael Alfred. *The Polish Underground Army, the Western Allies, and the Failure of Strategic Unity in World War II.* Jefferson, N.C.: McFarland, 2005.

Powell, Anthony. *The Military Philosophers.* Boston: Little, Brown, 1969.

Pyle, Ernie. *Brave Men.* New York: Grosset & Dunlap, 1944.

———. *Ernie Pyle in England.* New York: McBride, 1941.

Raczynski, Edward. *In Allied London.* London: Weidenfeld & Nicolson, 1963.

Read, Anthony, and David Fisher. *Colonel X: The Secret Life of a Master of Spies.* London: Hodder & Stoughton, 1984.

Reston, James. *Deadline: A Memoir.* New York: Random House, 1991.

Reynolds, David. *The Creation of the Anglo-American Alliance, 1937–1941.* Chapel Hill: University of North Carolina Press, 1982.

———. *In Command of History: Churchill Fighting and Writing the Second World War.* London: Penguin/Allen Lane, 2004.

———. *Rich Relations: The American Occupation of Britain, 1942–1945.* London: Phoenix, 2000.

Reynolds, David, Warren F. Kimball, and A. O. Chubarian, eds. *Allies at War: The Soviet, American and British Experience, 1939–1945.* New York: St. Martin's, 1994.

Reynolds, Quentin. *By Quentin Reynolds.* New York: McGraw-Hill, 1963.

———. *A London Diary.* New York: Random House, 1941.

Ritchie, Charles. *The Siren Years: A Canadian Diplomat Abroad, 1937–1945.* Toronto: Macmillan, 1974.

Roberts, Andrew. *"The Holy Fox": The Life of Lord Halifax.* London: Phoenix, 1997.

———. *Masters and Commanders: How Four Titans Won the War in the West, 1941–1945.* New York: Harper, 2009.

Robertson, Ben. *I Saw England.* New York: Alfred A. Knopf, 1941.

Rooney, Andy. *My War.* New York: Times Books, 1995.

Roosevelt, Eleanor. *This I Remember.* New York: Harper, 1949.

Roosevelt, Elliott. *As He Saw It.* New York: Duell, Sloan & Pearce, 1946.

Salisbury, Harrison. *A Journey for Our Times: A Memoir*. New York: Harper & Row, 1983.

Sansom, William. *The Blitz: Westminster at War*. Oxford: Oxford University Press, 1947.

Saroyan, William. *The Adventures of Wesley Jackson*. New York: Harcourt, Brace, 1946.

Schellenberg, Walter. *The Schellenberg Memoirs*. London: Deutsch, 1956.

Schlesinger, Arthur M., Jr. *Journals, 1952–2000*. New York: Penguin, 2007.

Seib, Philip. *Broadcasts from the Blitz: How Edward R. Murrow Helped Lead America into War*. Washington: Potomac Books, 2006.

Settle, Mary Lee. *All the Brave Promises: Memories of Aircraft Woman 2nd Class 214639*. Columbia: University of South Carolina Press, 1995.

———. *Learning to Fly: A Writer's Memoir*. New York: W. W. Norton, 2007.

Sevareid, Eric. *Not So Wild a Dream*. New York: Atheneum, 1976.

Sheean, Vincent. *Between the Thunder and the Sun*. New York: Random House, 1943.

Sherwood, Robert E. *Roosevelt and Hopkins: An Intimate History*. New York: Harper & Brothers, 1948.

Shirer, William L. *Berlin Diary: The Journal of a Foreign Correspondent, 1939–1941*. New York: Alfred A. Knopf, 1941.

Shnayerson, Michael. *Irwin Shaw: A Biography*. New York: Putnam, 1989.

Sinclair, Andrew, ed. *The War Decade: An Anthology of the 1940s*. London: Hamilton, 1989.

Smith, Graham. *When Jim Crow Met John Bull: Black American Soldiers in World War II Britain*. New York: St. Martin's, 1988.

Smith, Jean Edward. *FDR*. New York: Random House, 2007.

Smith, R. Franklin. *Edward R. Murrow: The War Years*. Kalamazoo: New Issues Press, 1978.

Smith, R. Harris. *OSS: The Secret History of America's First Central Intelligence Agency*. New York: Dell, 1973.

Smith, Sally Bedell. *In All His Glory: The Life of William S. Paley*. New York: Simon & Schuster, 1990.

———. *Reflected Glory: The Life of Pamela Churchill Harriman*. New York: Simon & Schuster, 1996.

Soames, Mary. *Clementine Churchill: The Biography of a Marriage*. Boston: Houghton Mifflin, 2002.

Sorel, Nancy Caldwell. *The Women Who Wrote the War*. New York: Arcade, 1999.

Sperber, A. M. *Murrow: His Life and Times*. New York: Freundlich, 1986.

Stacks, John. *Scotty: James B. Reston and the Rise and Fall of American Journalism*. New York: Little, Brown, 2003.

Stafford, David. *Churchill and the Secret Service*. Woodstock, N.Y.: Overlook Press, 1998.

———. *The Silent Game: The Real World of Imaginary Spies*. Athens: University of Georgia Press, 1991.

Standley, William. *Admiral Ambassador to Russia*. Chicago: Regnery, 1955.

Thompson, Walter. *Assignment: Churchill*. New York: Farrar, Straus & Young, 1955.

Turnbull, Andrew, ed. *The Letters of F. Scott Fitzgerald*. New York: Scribner, 1963.

Van Minnen, Cornelis, and John F. Sears, eds. *FDR and His Contemporaries: Foreign Perceptions of an American President*. New York: St. Martin's, 1992.

Waller, Maureen. *London 1945: Life in the Debris of War*. London: Griffin, 2006.

Ward, Geoffrey. *Closest Companion: The Unknown Story of the Intimate Friendship Between Franklin Roosevelt and Margaret Suckley.* Boston: Houghton Mifflin, 1995.

Watt, Harry. *Don't Look at the Camera.* London: Paul Elek, 1974.

Weintraub, Stanley. *15 Stars: Eisenhower, MacArthur, Marshall: Three Generals Who Saved the American Century.* New York: Free Press, 2007.

Whalen, Richard J. *The Founding Father: The Story of Joseph P. Kennedy.* New York: New American Library, 1964.

Wheeler-Bennett, Sir John. *King George VI: His Life and Reign.* New York: St. Martin's, 1958.

———. *Special Relationships: America in Peace and War.* London: Macmillan, 1975.

Williamson, Geoffrey. *Star-Spangled Square: The Saga of "Little America" in London.* London: Geoffrey Bles, 1956.

Winant, John G. *A Letter from Grosvenor Square: An Account of a Stewardship.* Boston: Houghton Mifflin, 1947.

———. *Our Greatest Harvest: Selected Speeches of John G. Winant, 1941–1946.* London: Hodder & Stoughton, 1950.

Ziegler, Philip. *London at War, 1939–1945.* New York: Alfred A. Knopf, 1995.

PHOTO: © STANLEY CLOUD

LYNNE OLSON, a former Moscow correspondent for the
Associated Press and White House correspondent for the
Baltimore *Sun,* is the author of *Troublesome Young Men*
and *Freedom's Daughters* and co-author, with her husband,
Stanley Cloud, of *A Question of Honor* and *The Murrow
Boys.* She lives in Washington, D.C.

www.lynneolson.com

LYNNE OLSON is available for select readings and lectures. To inquire about a possible appearance, please contact
the Random House Speakers Bureau at 212-572-2013 or
rhspeakers@randomhouse.com.